The Heart of Rock & Soul
According to Dave Marsh

PAPA'S GOT A BRAND NEW BAG, James Brown
"The only way this song could be more bonerattling would be if James Brown himself leaped from your speakers, grabbed you by the shoulders and danced you around the room, all the while screaming straight into your face."

LOUIE LOUIE, The Kingsmen "Rumors circulated that the Kingsmen muffled the vocal because the song was really obscene. . . . the closer-to-correct conclusion is 'unintelligible at any speed.' "

ALL ALONG THE WATCHTOWER, Jimi Hendrix "By the time he's finished, Jimi accomplishes the unique feat of making you forget all about Bob Dylan's original version."

LIVE TO TELL, Madonna "If there weren't such massive prejudice against Madonna's overconfident displays of her sexuality, 'Live to Tell' would be ranked among the greatest pop songs written in the past decade."

LEAD ME ON, Bobby Bland "If you hear this song in the middle of the night and listen carefully to Bland's repetitions of the title phrase, you'll unavoidably start thinking about all the things they imply. Prepare to meet the dawn."

(I CAN'T GET NO) SATISFACTION, The Rolling Stones "Treatises have been written about these lyrics, most of which miss their humor. . . . If Bob Dylan and Otis Redding had ever written a song together, this is what they would have had to compete with."

1001 SONGS THAT
MADE A DIFFERENCE

THE HEART
OF
ROCK & SOUL

The 1001
Greatest Singles
Ever Made

DAVE MARSH

A PLUME BOOK

NEW AMERICAN LIBRARY

A DIVISION OF PENGUIN BOOKS USA INC., NEW YORK
PUBLISHED IN CANADA BY
PENGUIN BOOKS CANADA LIMITED, MARKHAM, ONTARIO

The author gratefully acknowledges the following permissions:
"Don't Give Up" by Peter Gabriel © 1986 CLIOFINE LTD. administered
in USA & Canada by HIDDEN PUN MUSIC, INC. (BMI) International
copyright secured. All rights reserved. Used by permission.
"Give Him a Great Big Kiss" by George Martin © 1964 Trio Music Co.,
Inc., Tender Tunes Music Co., Inc., Elwin Music, Inc. All rights reserved.
Used by permission.
"I Can't Live Without My Radio" written by James Smith & Rick Rubin
© 1985 Def Jam Music Inc. All rights reserved. Used by permission.
"I'm All Alone" written by James Sheppard © 1962 Longitude Music Co.
All rights reserved. Used by permission.
"That is Rock & Roll" by Jerry Leiber and Mike Stoller © 1959 (renewed)
Jerry Leiber Music, Mike Stoller Music, Chappell and Co. All rights
reserved. Used by permission.

SIGNET, SIGNET CLASSIC, MENTOR, ONYX, PLUME, MERIDIAN
and NAL BOOKS are published *in the United States* by
New American Library, a division of Penguin Books USA Inc.,
1633 Broadway, New York, New York 10019,
in Canada by Penguin Books Canada Limited,
2801 John Street, Markham, Ontario L3R 1B4

LIBRARY OF CONGRESS CATALOGING-IN-PUBLICATION DATA
Marsh, Dave.
The heart of rock & soul : the 1001 greatest singles ever made /
Dave Marsh.
p.   cm.
ISBN 0-452-26305-0
1. Rock music—Discography.   2. Sound recordings—Reviews.
I. Title.   II. Title: Heart of rock and soul.
ML156.4R6M37   1989
016.78242166'026'6—dc20   89-8813
                                                       CIP   MN

First Printing, October, 1989
2 3 4 5 6 7 8 9
PRINTED IN THE UNITED STATES OF AMERICA

For Sandy Choron

"You're really more than I deserve /
From my heart I mean these words."

Acknowledgments

This is a book about dialogues: among records and people, over many years and in diverse places, and for that matter, in one guy's head, alone late at night or early in the morning.

But never really alone. Across the years, ideas and rebuttals echo from almost every voice with whom I've argued and complained and rhapsodized about rock and soul music over the twenty years since I began writing.

More than any single person, the voice on the other side of that argument has belonged to Greil Marcus, my friend since 1970, my foil throughout these pages. But right along with him were Jon Landau, with whom I've been coming to grips for nearly as long; Lee Ballinger, my partner in *Rock & Roll Confidential*; and several other colleagues, sometimes in direct conversation, sometimes just because I learn so much from what they write. I'm thinking especially of Simon Frith, Steve Perry, Doug Simmons, David Hinckley, the late Rick Whitesell, J. D. Considine, and Vince Aletti, though there's half a dozen others who also fit the bill. I thank them one and all for putting up with so many strange and rancorous ideas over the years.

Not only fellow critics endure them. So have such friends as Karen Hall, Sheldon Bull, Barbara Hall, Frank Joyce, Bob Rolontz, Greg Drew, and Steve Leeds. Tony Heilbut generously shared with me some of his vast knowledge of gospel. David Landau, guitarist and tape cutter extraordinaire, read some of the early material and gave me more than a few worthwhile ideas in return. Steve Propes generously filled in some missing info, including the solution to the "Wipe Out" mystery. Jim Dunning actually persuaded me he was right about "My Girl," and can therefore never again say that I've never admitted he won an argument. Howell Begle of the Rhythm and Blues Foundation provides daily reminders of the enduring value of this music, and why it's worth fighting for; I hope some of his embattled and nurturing spirit is here.

Michael Goodwin, an old friend with whom I'd been too long out of touch, generously shared a venerable story that may be the best of all. Ben Eicher made his case for which records ought to be in and out with an unending and unyielding series of letters and tapes and phone calls, to more effect than he may suspect. Daniel Wolff responded just as generously at the other end, offering all kinds of useful comments and suggestions. It's certainly not his fault that this book is so long.

I'd also like to thank June Barsalona, who said, "*Only* a thousand?"

Barbara Carr provided much inspiration. Sasha and Kristen Carr have grown up to be two of the people I most enjoy talking (not to say arguing) about music with. So is Sandy Choron and I'm really sorry about that one Dion record.

Gary Luke believed in the idea at a moment when my own faith was shaky and he's guided it with care and consideration ever since. Such an editor is too much to expect and awfully difficult to appreciate sufficiently. I hope these few words do enough to suggest the parameters of my gratitude.

I'd also like to thank Jonathan Riley at Penguin in England, who turned his annoyance with my excessive Americanisms to useful purpose, and Wendy Goldwyn, who first gave this book a home.

Innumerable musicians, songwriters, producers, and singers deserve my thanks—in a way, this is a book of acknowledgments to musicmakers known and unknown. But I'd like to single out one of the greatest, Doc Pomus, a friend whose stories and ideas never fail to reach very close to the heart of rock and soul, probably because he's established many of my favorite corners within it. As I walk my own lonely avenue, the magic moments of his tunes and words brighten the dark.

INTRODUCTION

If Loving You Is Wrong,
I Don't Want to Be Right

"Each of us—me and my closest friends—hopes to make a *record*. There are records I love that are not good songs but are great records. Bert Berns and Jerry Ragavoy and Phil Spector and the Beatles made *records*. Records that stay records. . . . People were making significant-sounding records from the beginning of rock and roll. Elvis's records, all the Motown records. Motown made those records the way they made the '55 Chevrolet. It's still beautiful and it still drives."

> —Jackson Browne,
> in Bill Flanagan's
> *Written in My Soul*

"Why don't you write a book about the 1001 greatest albums?" somebody asked me before I'd barely begun. "Because nobody goes around humming albums," I answered without a pause. Nevertheless, having learned the hard way that even the obvious must not be taken for granted:

Singles are the essence of rock and roll. They occupy the center of all the pop music that came after it. They're the stuff of our everyday conversations and debates about music, the totems that trigger our memories. Everybody who listens with half an ear must know this. But nobody writes as if it were true. After 1970, when Charlie Gillett published his singles-based *The Sound of the City: The Rise of Rock & Roll*, the first serious history of the music that descended from rhythm and blues, the story has always been told in terms of albums, and virtually albums only. There are many source books discussing the fine points of the greatest rock-era albums; this is the first that tries to define a similar group of singles.

The distinction isn't mechanical. True, most singles eventually appear on albums. True, if the record industry had its way, there wouldn't be any singles. True, the 45 rpm vinyl disc is deader than the 33⅓ rpm vinyl LP. True, albums are pop music's most effective vehicle for expressing complexity of style and personality.

But you get a truer picture of contemporary pop history and meaning by standing those arguments on their heads. If most singles are contained within albums, the singles are also the tracks that most often provide the definitive moments on those LPs. Almost nobody of much importance in rock and soul makes suites of music; however a record is made to be heard, it's inevitably recorded track-by-track, individual songs crafted one at a time. Even performers like Randy Newman and Prince, who've created many albums of interlinked thematic material, still dole out their music one number at a time; two decades after *Sgt. Pepper's*, a performer like Frank Zappa who creates compositions that extend over an entire side of an LP stands out as a creative anomaly.

Finally, even though albums have become the record industry's greatest profit center, the music business learns each day (to its unending frustration) that there is no way to realize those profits without creating hit singles.

In fact, what we now call "singles" were just records before the post-war technology boom that delivered two new formats to supplement and eventually supplant the 10–inch 78 rpm discs that had been the industry standard since speeds were standardized in the twenties. New magnetic tape technology offered higher fidelity recording at the source, which meant that records could afford to revolve more slowly, and new manufacturing techniques made available smaller grooves, into which more information could be packed. RCA took the first step by coming up with a "microgroove" seven-inch, 45 rpm disc. CBS, the industry's other major high-tech corporation, responded by developing the 12–inch LP disc that spun at 33⅓ rpm, with the avowed goal (according to Peter Goldmark, the company's research and development chief) of accommodating an entire symphonic movement on one side so that listening wouldn't be disrupted. LPs became known as "albums" because they replaced album-like folders of the several 78s that a symphony or other extended piece would take up. 45s became "singles" in contrast.

Although it soon became obvious that LPs were a more convenient way to listen to music for extended periods of time, 45s survived a drawn-out combat between CBS and RCA, not only because RCA worked so assiduously to promote its technology (even giving away 45 rpm players and adapters that allowed narrow LP and 78 spindles to play the new discs with their wider centers) but because the 45 was oriented to the hit: It gave the consumers a single song and performance, with nothing they presumably *didn't* want, a convenience of a different kind. RCA wasn't being hidebound; it developed the 45 in the context of the driving force of the pop business from the start: the hit song, now fixed on tape and vinyl as a hit performance.

Additionally, offering just one tune/performance per disc was a big help in making sure that radio programmers weren't distracted from the labels' promotional choices. At some point, an unknown genius came up with the double-A sided promo single, a 45 with the same "plug" song on both sides, omitting whatever presumably superfluous tidbit or oddity was contained on the flip. (CBS briefly tried marketing one-sided 45s in the early eighties, primarily to cut costs.) But such ploys only existed in the first place because of radio and the market's hit record orientation, which evolved after a number of U.S. radio programmers discovered in the early fifties that a small number of songs played in not-quite-random sequence would earn more listener loyalty than a more broadly based musical selection. Such stations began to survey local and regional record retailers to find out which records sold best. Since such Top 40 radio stations played songs one at a time, not in groups by the same artist or from the same record company, singles were what they surveyed, which reinforced the tendency. (This is a mere sketch of an extraordinarily complicated process, the best account of which can be found in Ken Barnes' "Top 40 Radio: A Fragment of the Imagination," in *Facing the Music*, edited by Simon Frith.)

The earliest rock albums were issued to cash in on singles success and even now, most albums (including many of the most successful and creative in history) remain singles separated by varying amounts of filler, though nobody likes to admit it. For a couple of years in the mid-seventies, rock groups like Pink Floyd and Led Zeppelin sold millions of albums without issuing singles, but even that was mainly a matter of stubbornness born of a desire to preserve mystique. According to "progressive rock" protocol singles were unhip, supposedly because they were blatant appeals to commercialism, more likely because their shelf life is short (about three months compared to more than a decade for an LP like Floyd's *Dark Side of the Moon*) and profit margin narrow to nonexistent. So Zeppelin, for instance, refused to allow "Stairway to Heaven" to be released as a single, even though broadcasters and fans treated it as one. Such attitudes were born in the late sixties, the same time that rock criticism was born, and burgeoned in the early to mid-seventies, when writing about rock established itself as a permanent part of the landscape of pop culture coverage and commentary.

But before and since then, the concept of a hit record has implied a hit single, if not a whole string of them. It was big news in 1988 when Metallica's . . . *And Justice for All* hit the *Billboard* Top Ten without a single, because there hadn't been such a hit in so long. Metallica wasn't kicking off a trend, either; there's no other recent example of a multimillion selling album without some semblance of a hit single. (Paul Simon's 1987 *Graceland* was regarded as a commercial phenomenon because it sold several million copies without a big single but "You Can Call Me Al" reached number 23 in *Billboard* and two others at least charted.)

In most cases, record production, promotion, and marketing is entirely determined by the search for and exploitation of potential hit singles. And despite various hoary adages, the record labels aren't just looking for a hit song. In the pre-rock era, writing and performing were separate categories within the music-making industries, and because most pre-World War II sales took the form of sheet music, the songwriter became the most important figure in Tin Pan Alley. But after World War II, as recording studio technology played a more and more instrumental role in crafting sounds for mass consumption, the writer-performer became the true star. Elvis Presley was the great exception among the big stars of the fifties and sixties because he never wrote a song. For some years, his reputation suffered because of his lack of composing ability, but that opinion had to be overturned as closer observation revealed that his revamping of songs such as "Blue Suede Shoes," "Mystery Train," "Blue Moon of Kentucky," and arguably even European and Broadway themes like "It's Now or Never," "Are You Lonesome To-night," and "Blue Moon" constituted a form of writing.

The record industry and music critics continue to be heavily biased in favor of writers. Since the Beatles, it has been all but impossible for nonwriting performers to be taken seriously—as though only through songwriting can a singer or musician have a central hand in shaping his or her music, a concept that has been outmoded at least since the invention of overdubbing and possibly since the development of good studio microphones, to which critic Henry Pleasants attributes the rise of Bing Crosby and the pop crooners who followed him.

Nevertheless, the songwriter bias persists, even showing up in the inequitable way that performers and writers are paid. (In both England and America, songwriters make more, partly because a portion of their royalty income is guaranteed by statute, even if their "composition" takes the form of a 37th generation declension of a Bo Diddley riff.) One consequence has been a critical underestimation (to be charitable) of performers who don't write in favor of those who do, regardless of the relative merits of their actual records: Does anybody really think that the gallons of ink expended on Lou Reed and the ounces used for Sam & Dave accurately reflect the proportional quality of their work? (I don't mean that Reed is without merit, just that the discrepancy is too extreme to be supportable.)

A basic, though unspoken, motivation for rock critics and historians following the progressive rock (i.e., non-R&B) model in recent years is that there, writing, performing, and producing tend to merge as roles occupied, in whole or substantial part, by single individuals. Since so much criticism revolves around implications of intention, it's extraordinarily useful to have writer and performer (and perhaps producer as well) wrapped up in one person.

But that approach doesn't streamline the facts; it steamrollers them. Unromantic as it may be to say so, most great recordings aren't just the work of individuals, no matter how they're credited. Making music is most often the product of intense collaborations, in which powerful personalities play leadership roles but can't hog all the action. James Brown, the archetypal domineering record creator, relied heavily on synching his skills with those of a series of extremely accomplished bands. Bob Dylan, rock's first arty loner, indisputably made his greatest records working with bands. David Bowie, the prototype of the progressive rock Genius, might one day see his recording quality graphed precisely on the basis of how well the strengths and weaknesses of collaborators like Tony Visconti, Nile Rodgers, and Brian Eno match his own inclinations. Anti-romantic as it may be to say so, the poetic individual creating in solitude has virtually no place in rock and roll; not only the most but the best of it has always been created through a combat among wills, which can mean anything from the near-psychotherapeutic production approach of Bruce Springsteen and company to Dionne Warwicke's exasperated advice to Burt Bacharach and Hal David: "Don't make me over!" Some of the most beautiful records ever made (though you'd be hard-pressed to find it out in previous histories) are the sound of willful young men learning to unify themselves in three- or four- or five-part harmony: That is the special glory of doo-wop and restoring that music to its central place in the early chapters of the story provides one of the great lost truths of rock and soul.

A single is more than just a successfully recorded composition, though. All great records don't make great singles. Miles Davis's *In a Silent Way* (music whose sense and beauty are as heavily reliant upon recording studio techniques as most rock and soul) could never be distilled into a single. Singles are brief (two to six minutes, with the majority well under four) recorded performances, almost always based around simple patterns (sometimes melodic, sometimes purely rhythmic), constructed to leap out at the ear from the radio or the dance floor. Yes, this description is largely determined by the exaggerated emphasis the American music industry places upon Top 40 radio airplay as its central marketing vehicle. But radio isn't necessarily hit driven because it wants to be. Within our society, there's an essential cultural need (or anyway, desire) for a unitary, memorable musical motif. At some point, though I doubt it, this desire may have been consciously manufactured by shrewd entrepreneurs or some other stratum of cultural manipulators, but it hardly seems eradicable today. There may have been societies in which people preferred long compositions evolving into one coherent theme as the soundtrack for their daily lives (as distinct from just their Saturday nights), and such societies may exist again. But that's not the case in any of the urban, industrial societies in which rock and roll is created and consumed.

The record industry hates singles because the damn little things can usually be sold only as LP loss leaders. But it can't get rid of them because something happens to album sales when a hit single is involved—they explode. And, in my view, not only because radio is pounding them into everybody's brain. The function of airplay is to build word of mouth, the real *sine qua non* of commercial musical success, and radio just happens to be an uncommonly effective means to that end. (In Europe, its role is much smaller but there are still hits and they're still the kind of singles I'm talking about here.) But if a record bores the audience, no amount of airplay will make it a real hit—that's why stars as huge as Elton John find themselves periodically experiencing commercial burn out.

Sometimes what makes hits stand out is just that so much concentrated energy becomes focused on them. What makes them of lasting interest is determined by many other things, but with some of them, the dialogue they create just never burns out. In writing this book, I thought settling on "I Heard It Through the Grapevine" by Marvin Gaye was an unexceptional, certainly an uncontroversial place to start. But one of my friends, perhaps the biggest Marvin Gaye fan I've ever known, acted dejected, saying he'd far prefer "What's Going On" and a couple of the non-Marvin records that had been on my short list; a second argued that Marvin's "Grapevine" wasn't a very good record at all, that in fact, Gladys Knight's version was far better; a third, who happens to be a songwriter, told me that he didn't even think "Grapevine" was a good song. The result was three useful, provocative conversations about the nature of singles and of pop music, and of Marvin Gaye's music. For me, it was a confirmation that, twenty years down the line, Marvin's "Grapevine" was still alive (as were the comments of a half dozen friends, none of them even semi-professional raisins, who told me how glad they were I'd picked it).

That's why singles form the most complete historical imprint of rock and soul music. Albums really do provide a better platform for expressing complexity and detail; in those respects, there's no way two to six minutes of music can compete with thirty to fifty. But singles can do things that albums can't. They can distill an essence, seize a moment, sum up a movement, galvanize an audience. Imagine *Thriller* without "Billie Jean" and "Beat It," or *Highway 61 Revisited* without "Like a Rolling Stone." And singles do this all the time, if only by annoying us sufficiently to take one hand off the wheel and punch a button for another station.

Singles also have an endearing ability to get out of their own way: Imagine trying to extend "Pappa-Oom-Mow-Mow" for an entire album (and one thing you'll have imagined is a central dilemma of some of today's best recordmakers). Entire genres of pop—R&B, dance music and country, most obviously—have never been oriented to anything but singles. One reason I'm writing all this is that the albums-only orientation of rock historians and critics has effectively marginalized such styles, even though within them exists what I believe to be the most creative and compelling body of work in all popular music.

What's really marginal is the progressive rock that has produced great albums and few if any hit singles, while dominating critical discussion. Such music is pushed to the fringe by many things, largely by the weight of its own pretensions, the presumption that art and culture move in a ladder-like process of "progress" in the first place, rather than the one step up, one step back, a few to the side circularity of real life. In fact, if that kind of romantic development is your concept of progress, you're better off listening to classical (or anyway, "serious") music. Progressive rock sounds desiccated to me because it's so thoroughly divorced from the taproot of rock and roll: rhythm and blues.

Somewhere deep within these pages I grew reckless and ventured a definition of rock and roll: "Having studied it long and deeply, my conviction is that rock and roll is not mostly anything other than black-rooted popular (mainly vocal) music made in the late twentieth century, and therefore I lose all trust in the critical intelligence of those who try to confine it more narrowly." But that's only half the story. Rock may be as various as that claim, but that only means you can't write any aspect of it off simply because you hate it. Groups as hapless as the Grateful Dead and Emerson Lake & Palmer and Edie Brickell & New Bohemians are part of the rock and soul continuum. There's no denying it; believe me, I've tried hard enough.

I don't care anymore. Let all of it in. Rock's outer boundaries may amount to listening to power saws cut Fender guitars in half. OK. What matters is the center, the heart, the place (or places) where the good stuff resides. The question is how you locate it. You may think it can be done by referring to the determined intentions of post-modern punk-funk noisemakers. I think you find it out by listening as deeply as you can to the music, searching for connections—emotional, musical, lyrical, threads of theme and circumstance. You build such a picture brick by brick, glance by glance. "You listen to the music," producer Chuck Plotkin once told me about how he made records. "The music speaks to you. If you listen to it, it speaks to you."

Since I don't believe that the meaning of any kind of art can be determined in isolation (that is, by reference to the thing itself alone), all kinds of factors come into play for me that would prove utterly disruptive for a critic more wedded to a system. I care about influence and about sources, about how things fit together with the world in which they were invented, with the world that they helped to invent, with the world that others invented partly because of them. As much as anything else, pop music fascinates me because it continues to spawn so many public and private discussions.

I don't just mean the conversations that you and I have with our friends. One of the things that I hope this book demonstrates is how often and how clearly singles speak to one another, in a continual crosstalk of style and content, shape and substance. In the grinding rhythms of "You Got the Look," you can hear Prince practically telephoning Sly Stone and James Brown, getting on the cosmic horn to Elvis and Jimi, making his case for doing it his way, honoring in his own fashion the brilliance of the way they did theirs. Juxtaposing "You Can't Always Get What You Want" and "Kick Out the Jams," you can feel the tug of forces that made 1969 such a bitterly momentous year. It's not just a matter of influence, though, but of something much less concrete and more spiritual. Listen to Nolan Strong on "The Wind," and hear the wimp-perfection of mid-eighties Michael Jackson and you'll feel as spooked and confirmed as I do.

So we listen to the music and it speaks to us and that's how we participate, not as equals but with an indispensable role to play. Therefore, what I'd ask of any reader of this book is this: Consider every record here that you've never heard (or maybe never liked) as a tree fallen in a forest. Are you near enough to hear it before the echoes die out? Was anyone?

There's nothing reasonable about that request. But in the end, it's the only way I can describe the essential criterion for a record being included in *The Heart of Rock & Soul*. I listened and the music spoke to me and if I had something to contribute to the discussion, I wrote it down. And sometimes the music spoke back and we went at each other like that, all night long. You may not know this experience from listening to records. You might know it from what happens when you read books, or watch movies, or look at paintings. But you know the feeling. I hope. Because it's beyond my capacities to explain it to you.

As with many things for which I have no words of my own, there is a record that expresses what I'm talking about. Cold on the page, without the *baion* bass and strings and the crying in the singer's voice, it may tell only a part of the story. But I'll put what it says here anyway, in hope that that fragment is enough. It's a record by the Drifters, written by Doc Pomus and Mort Shuman, produced by Jerry Leiber and Mike Stoller, sung by Ben E. King:

> And then it happened
> It took me by surprise
> I knew that you felt it, too
> By the look in your eyes

This Magic Moment

From time to time, I've found rock criticism's emphasis on album artists and "progressive rock" annoying and frustrating. To the extent that my own writing has succumbed to such premises, it's left me feeling out of synch with myself. Trying to swim against its eddies would leave anyone feeling battered and gasping. It makes perfect sense to me that the work of Otis Redding and Smokey Robinson is as compelling, as intelligent, as well-planned, and finally as creatively ambitious as anything James Taylor or Bryan Ferry ever dreamed. But to try to make the case piecemeal generates more blank stares and grumbles of incomprehension than sympathetic understanding.

Having now told the whole history of rock and soul through singles, my exasperation gives way to gratitude. There remains a tremendous amount to be said about even many of the most familiar hits, just as there remain many significant singles yet to be discovered and discussed. Large as it is, this book isn't inclusive; no one-man survey of such a vast field could hope to be. Looking back a few weeks after finishing the manuscript, I tremble at my own weak grasp of latter-day funk, fret about what I've left out. Friends ask after their favorite records and if they're not here, even I wonder why. And I fall back on perhaps the oddest fact of all, the first thing I learned from making the list of records I wanted to write about: A thousand's a small number.

So, while *The Heart of Rock & Soul* may look like a guidebook to the greatest singles ever made (and for some tastes may even be one), in *my* heart it's a guidebook of a different kind—it's an attempt to jump start a stalled dialogue, a discussion that offers a possible, necessary alternative to the familiar din.

An alternative. Not the only possible one. The one I know how to argue for.

A good part of what I've hoped to accomplish here is a reopening of questions elsewhere considered settled or taken for granted: what rock and roll music is, where it came from, who makes it, what it says, what what it says means. Other perspectives aren't just possible; they're essential. These records are, in a way, just the ones that served my purpose, though to serve my purpose a record had to be pretty damn great. So maybe the whole thing is finally no more than an argument in favor of a vision (or maybe just a viewpoint). But then again, having stayed up late and risen early to ponder the psychology of "Live to Tell" and the provenance and progeny of "Louie Louie," vision and viewpoint are a pretty big deal to me.

In the rock and roll universe described in other histories, the story of rock and roll is disjointed: It was born out of rhythm and blues and country and western, reached a mid-fifties peak, then rapidly withered, only to be unexpectedly revived by the British Invasion which enjoyed brief glory before being superseded by a psychedelic era, which was displaced by an episode of singer/songwriter "soft rock," which was followed by a confused proliferation of styles without a center, unto this day.

In that Big Bang universe, black-based rhythm and blues is placed in a separate category, at first traveling alongside white rock, but ceasing to parallel its development after the sixties glories of Motown and Sly and the Family Stone and Stax/Volt and James Brown, and though soul gives rise to a variegated series of styles—funk, disco, rap, hip-hop, house, retro-nuevo, *et seq.*—it never quite intersects with its "white" offspring again.

In the Rock and Soul universe, the story of rock and roll is continuous. The line extends back beyond the first records discussed here—which come from 1952 for reasons more intuitive than planned—and its sources aren't just R&B and C&W (in proportions more like 80/20 than 50/50). Understood as it developed through singles, rock and roll early on expropriated and never abandoned all sorts of other elements: the pop harmony singing of groups like the Four Preps and Four Aces; the *bel canto* crooning of Frank Sinatra and his acolytes; the tape deck novelties of Les Paul, Dickie Goodman, and Spike Jones; the high lonesome yearnings of bluegrass; the song shapes of Tin Pan Alley (and I don't mean the Brill Building); and most of all, the emotive and musical maelstrom of gospel harmonizing and shouting.

Including these influences results in anything but minor alterations in the landscape; what you now see is the Big Bang world after a force ten hurricane. Gospel, especially, comes to the fore: The debt of every church-trained soul singer (which is every soul singer) is obvious, but "Twist and Shout" is also unimaginable without what rock and soul

took from the church. What descends from those roots is nearly everything worthwhile that we have today.*

The first crucial divergence between these parallel universes comes
when the line extends forward past the time when, in the Big Bang
world, rock and roll stars like Elvis Presley, Chuck Berry, Buddy Holly,
and Little Richard disappeared. In the Rock and Soul universe, they
also go off the map but not forever. Buddy leaves permanently, but
the others return for stays of varying length, which suggests something
richer than a series of interruptive miracles at work. What's true of
individuals is also true of styles. The urban harmony groups—doo-
woppers—who created the music's sweet and tender side also find themselves temporarily offstage and then, when needed, returning for a brief
but significant cameo, during what I've called the early sixties doo-wop
revival.

So while rock looked "dead" to the Big Bang world, in the Rock
and Soul universe it enjoyed one of its most vital phases. We're talking
about a time that witnessed, in addition to the doo-wop revival, the
rise of girl groups and Motown, the first discotheque craze, and early
inklings of Chicago and Memphis soul. Elvis and Chuck Berry returned
to prominence, and Roy Orbison and James Brown developed as artists
whose creations and mystique rival the fifties names.

For the rest of the sixties, the two universes once more converge,
though from the Rock and Soul vantage point, the relative importance
of any individual or group, style or recording may be wildly at variance
with the way things sound from out there in the land of the Bang.
Nevertheless, the sixties are indisputably the most creative period of
rock and roll in both versions of the story—just under half of the records
here are from that decade. That's a deceptive statistic, though. About
twenty percent of the entries come from the pre-Beatles period (1959–
1963) when, in the Big Bang world, there was no rock and roll. Fur-

---

*There are no gospel singles in *The Heart of Rock & Soul* quite simply because I could find
no way of contextualizing them without trivializing them. To verify my claims, I'd suggest
listening to the following: "Packing Up" and "Surely God Is Able," by the Ward Singers,
as well as their other early-fifties Savoy recordings featuring Marion Williams; "How I Got
Over," "Didn't It Rain," and the other Apollo label classics by Mahalia Jackson; "That's
Enough," "Ninety Nine and a Half," and "You Better Run" by Dorothy Love Coates and
the Gospel Harmonettes; Professor Alex Bradford's "Too Close to Heaven"; "How Jesus
Died," by the Pilgrim Travelers; "Touch the Hem of His Garment" and "The Last Mile of
the Way" by the Soul Stirrers featuring Sam Cooke as well as all that the group recorded
with its first leader, Rebert H. Harris; the Specialty recordings of the Swan Silvertones
featuring Claude Jeter and Paul Owens; the Peacock recordings of Julius Cheeks and the
Sensational Nightingales. But this barely skims the surface of the gospel/soul/rock interface.
Not only these performers but many others had distinct and direct influence on rock and
soul. For the best history and interpretation of the music, read Anthony Heilbut's *The Gospel
Sound* (Limelight Editions) and pick up the contemporary and historical albums on his
SpiritFeel label.

thermore, the British Invasion that "wiped out" American rock in the Big Bang is substantially less devastating in Rock and Soul. Rock's early styles withered and died but the reasons were more complex than simply the arrival of the English acts. Rather than being extinguished, most early styles were transformed. The source and substance of that transformation is directly linked to the social and political events that transformed the rest of American and British culture in the sixties. Acknowledging such powerful forces at work, rock and soul's creative explosion seems far less miraculous, though not any less impressive.

According to the Rock and Soul version of the story, black and white forms of pop continued to coexist and influence each other on into the seventies and eighties. Also, the flow between black and white music is always two way. Though, of course, the leakage from the black side is a flood, the trickle back the other way can't be denied: Without Frank Zappa, how would George Clinton have understood himself? Without George Michael and Boy George, could the late eighties revival of black male crooning have occurred?

As we come closer to the present, the discrepancy between the two worlds reaches its greatest intensity, though here a large part of the fault lies with the observer. I have a taste for rap and hip-hop but not much for funk, perhaps because my tolerance for even the comic-baroque is excessively limited. But undeniably, by the seventies the social fragmentation of the period had caught up (you say punk, he says disco, let's call the whole thing off). As we near the nineties, there is barely a sense of dialogue within genres, let alone among them. People are still shouting at one another, but in such strained and hopeless voices that it's hard to hear them. But then, it is *always* harder to hear what's going on at the present, or at any rate to trust what you're hearing. Part of the measure of a record's importance ought to be its staying power and so I don't much trust any selection (let alone its placement) after about 1983.

Part of my motivation for writing this book was the chance to work through this chronology. And though I knew essential parts of the Big Bang theory were false, only the research told me how far off it was. One example: It struck me as odd that I knew so many fifties doo-wop records by heart, even though I was too young to have experienced them first hand, and I didn't grow up around any unregenerate doo-woppers. It was only while looking into the background of "There's A Moon Out Tonight" by the Capris that I realized that doo-wop had had two periods of mass appeal. And of course, what that meant was that the rock and roll most often damned as trivial and ridiculed as juvenile nonsense, the one most reliant on nonsense syllables, had itself showed transgenerational appeal from almost the very beginning. More than the other R&B styles revived by the British Invasion, this proved the enduring merit of early rock for me.

Another motivation, though, was that I'd become increasingly fed up with two of the other central myths of rock criticism: that rock and roll music is essentially youth-oriented, and most of all, that the message of the music is (to borrow a slogan off the radio), all rebellion, all the time. Though they strike my colleagues as self-evident, I think they're counterproductive stereotypes.

In part, I reject these conclusions out of personal experience. Chuck Berry, original articulator of the Teen Dream, is old enough to be my father—and my particular father (a year younger than Chuck) hated rock and roll as passionately as only someone who'd accidentally spawned the likes of me could. My mother, on the other hand, loved Elvis and watched *American Bandstand* every day. So generational warfare has never struck me as the dividing line between those who get it and those who don't.

Furthermore, rock and soul-based music has been more sustaining, not less, as I've aged. That there are parts of rock that appeal most readily to teens is undeniable, as is the fact that some of the best of it quite consciously aimed itself at that audience from the start. But I did *not* die before I got old and neither did the music, and that's something to be proud of. And it is *not* better to burn out than fade away, no matter what album rock partisan Neil Young may tell you. "Stand By Me" comes far closer to the truth.

By writing off R&B and soul music, most of which has always seen itself as adult music, rock critics exempt themselves from having to deal with this idea, except as it emerges from the tongues of aging white rockers like Chrissie Hynde and Bruce Springsteen. It may be true that young people were the first people to realize that rock and soul had a serious message to convey, but that message has little or nothing to do with youth per se.

If the story rock and soul records tell was just about rebellion, the music would have long ago expired like the fad outsiders originally presumed it to be. In fact, every great account of rebellion in rock and soul history is balanced by an act of reconciliation, often out of the same mouths: I give you the Rolling Stones of "Satisfaction" and "Happy," or if you prefer, Little Richard's "Rip It Up" and "I Don't Know What You Got (But It's Got Me)," to choose a pair of particularly apposite examples. (Chosen in part because, much as I love "Twist and Shout," "Let It Be" just never meant much to me.)

If rebellion—against musical limitations and broadcasting restrictions, emotional repression and the color line, middlebrow good taste and bohemian snobbery, working-class defeatism and folk-radical false optimism—gave birth to rock and roll, what kept the music alive was its resilient ability to reconcile its own contradictions, to find some stratum of peace and ease amidst the clamor.

Album rockers like the Rolling Stones sank their knives deep into the heart of such questions and came up with nothing more than the cheap ironies of camp. "I know it's only rock 'n' roll, but I like it," sang Mick Jagger at thirty-two, desperately trying to explain himself to Bianca and her Studio 54 cronies. As though that cleared anything up.

Bohemian obsessions with youth and pleasure (the myth of "fun," a concept even more poorly and inaccurately defined than rock and roll) aren't the only explanations of the power of rock and soul. Most writers imply that when rock isn't rebelling, it's engaged in some form of personal or social capitulation—selling out its own best interests. But the real sell-out is limiting rock's import to statements of rebellion. The yearning to belong, to fit in, to *start* making sense, has all along been a part of the music's tradition. It's what's at work in records like "Reach Out I'll Be There," "Jump," "Party Lights," "Stand By Me," "Be My Baby," "Born to Run," "Everyday People," and "The Great Pretender," the whole host of great singles in which the objects of rock rebellion begin to work themselves out. Which also makes sense, since that's the only way of reaching the next stage of rebellion, as generations of avant-gardists have learned. Listen closely to records like those and you can hear dozens of singers bringing it all back home and not only for the purpose of further agitation.

Most of the artists and records mentioned in the list above never appear in histories of album rock. So banishing the nonrebellious from rock and soul means omitting from the dialogue some of the greatest and most compelling voices, it means portraying rock as a white boy's club, which isn't surprising since rock-as-rebellion is a story compiled almost exclusively by white men.

Restoring voices of reconciliation to their equally central place in rock and soul history was my principal motivation in writing this book. Partly, that just meant responding to a personal desire to write about the music to which I most often listen for pleasure. But it also meant acknowledging the inadequacy of some of my own previous portrayals of rock history—most notably in *The Rolling Stone Record Guide*, which probably bears a large share of responsibility for fostering and codifying the ideas and attitudes I work to dismantle in these pages. It was the limitations of that book that in large part steered me away from organizing this one around artists—I wanted to grapple with the particularity of all these records, and to the extent that I could, with the people who made and heard them.

The strongest point that the accumulated results make must certainly be that rock and soul is the creation, above all, of black Americans. That was in the plan, and if I do not dwell on it at this point, it's because I so often do at many others.

But in writing any book, you learn things that you hadn't expected. What I found out this time wasn't just that women had played such a significant role, but what excluding or downplaying their contribution means in terms of describing rock and soul's emotional content accurately. Avoiding the music women have made means avoiding, above all, sentimentality, or at least the kind of open, potentially weepy emotion associated with sentimentality. Rock and soul stars aren't just tough, though again the picture is often painted as if it's just that one-dimensional, which makes it little wonder that even artists like Smokey Robinson and Sam Cooke are so often portrayed only in pentimento. And for that matter, the conventional historical portrait of female performers as nothing but so many producers' puppets accounts for the omission of singers as powerful or just plain tough as Darlene Love and the Shangri-Las, not to mention the consistent undervaluation of Madonna.

So what I really learned is this: Some rock is tough; some isn't. Some of it runs on the pure adrenaline of fun; some of it's steeped in plain misery. Some of it speaks directly to the young, but then, some of it's more grown-up than almost anybody cares to face. Some of it rebels or overturns all our expectations; some of it soothes or tries to reorder all our experiences.

What I learned most of all was that rock and soul is as complex and self-contradictory as any living thing. And that it is alive and still growing. The job is to learn how to hear it, on its own terms. From across the obscure but not hard to locate universe you're about to enter, these thousand and one records—and many more—call out, like a prayer.

Author's Note

This is a book, not a list, I reminded myself a couple dozen times a day as I created new essays and reordered the text. This is a plea for the result to be read in the same spirit.

The organizational principle of *The Heart of Rock & Soul* was originally that it would present itself from best to . . . well, less best. Yet before the Top Ten was finished, I'd learned that it wasn't going to be nearly that simple. All sorts of other factors came into play: the need to cover certain stylistic bases, a desire not to crowd too many entries by the same artist too closely together, the necessity of making what *did* originate as a list into a book that flowed along its own path, and, best and most important of all, the discovery, in the heat of listening and writing, that a record I'd underestimated really belonged much higher in the scheme or, more sadly but still significantly, that a record that had given me tremendous pleasure over the years didn't quite hold up. I've frequently pushed and pulled records "out of place" in order to accommodate such demands.

Like Joe Turner's "one-eyed cat peepin' in a seafood store," I found more delights available than I could possibly consume. There are perhaps another two thousand records I could justify including and there are at least several dozen that I regret not being able to fit in. (I'm already sick of people asking what Number One is but it would thrill me no end to have someone inquire about Number 1,002.)

The information in the headings is the most complete I could find; I'd be happy to hear from anyone who can improve it. My most indispensable reference works were Joel Whitburn's remarkable compilations and breakdowns of the *Billboard* charts: *Top Pop Singles 1955–1986* belongs on every reference bookshelf, but closer to my heart are *Top R&B Singles 1942–1988* and the astonishing *Pop Memories 1890–1954*, which are themselves an education in American popular music history.

Also extraordinarily helpful were Big Al Pavlow's *The R&B Book*; Fred Bronson's *The Billboard Book of Number One Hits; Behind the Hits* by Bob Shannon and John Javna; *Million Selling Records from the 1900s to the 1980s: An Illustrated Directory* by Joseph Murrells; Phil Hardy and Dave Laing's *Encyclopedia of Rock*; Dick Jacobs' *Who Wrote That Song*; and three books on specific genres: *The Sound of Philadelphia* by Tony Cummings, *Girl Groups: The Story of a Sound* by Alan Betrock, and *The Motown Story* by Don Waller. I'm extremely grateful to all of them for providing such firm factual foundations.

The errors, of course, are entirely original creations.

Rock steady baby
Let's call this song exactly what it is
Just move your hips from side to side
Set yourself down in your car and take a ride
                              —Aretha Franklin

1 I HEARD IT THROUGH THE GRAPEVINE, Marvin Gaye

Produced by Norman Whitfield; written by Norman Whitfield and Barrett Strong
Tamla 54176   1968   *Billboard:* #1 (7 weeks)

"I Heard It Through the Grapevine" isn't a plea to save a love affair; it's Marvin Gaye's essay on salvaging the human spirit. The record distills four hundred years of paranoia and talking drum gossip into three minutes and fifteen seconds of anguished soul-searching. The proof's as readily accessible as your next unexpected encounter on the radio with the fretful, self-absorbed vocal that makes the record a lost continent of music and emotion.

How does something so familiar remain surprising for twenty years? To begin with, Gaye plays out the singing with his characteristic amalgam of power and elegance, sophistication and instinct: now hoarse, now soaring, sometimes spitting out imprecations with frightening clarity, sometimes almost chanting in pure street slang, sometimes pleading at the edge of incoherence, twisting, shortening, and elongating syllables to capture emotions words can't define. And Gaye does this not just in a line or two or three but continuously. As a result, a record that's of absolutely stereotypical length creates a world that seems to last forever.

"Grapevine" is also a triumph for producer Norman Whitfield. The music begins with an obsessively reiterated electric piano figure. Its churchy chords are followed with a plain backbeat off the drum kit and a rattlesnake tambourine, then a chopping guitar and soaring strings. So Whitfield creates a masterpiece before Gaye ever strangles a note. That ultrapercussive beat on the tambourine is the sound of the rumor reaching home; the rest of the record is about the consequences.

The welter of voices—horns, female choruses, echo, bass-drum breakdowns over string arpeggios—serves as a community of gossip, with the singer isolated but engulfed within it. Though he rails against the facts, he knows they have him trapped. What makes "Grapevine" 's most anguished lines—"Losin' you would end my life, you see / Because you mean that much to me"—so harrowing is that they come from the mouth of a man raised to believe in the literal fires of hell who now worships love. For Gaye, being cheated out of his lover is a sign of heavenly condemnation. So he lets his voice make a gospel leap for that first "you," then immediately brings it back into control, as if he's still struggling with how much she *does* mean to him.

The lyric as Gaye sings it is also an internal dialogue. In the first half of the record, as the singer grabs at the truth, it seems less likely that he's actually staging a confrontation than that he's imagining one, weighing the story he's heard against seemingly meaningless events that now assume the status of clues. By the middle verses, the shame and humiliation have overwhelmed him, and all that's left is "you coulda told me yo'self," a claim on the past that's meaningful only because of what isn't being delivered in the present. *Then*, we find out that his lover's not only left him, but that she sneaked off with "the other guy [she] loved before." From this moment through to the end, a good forty-five seconds (which is an epoch in the time scale of a three-minute single), Gaye accepts the truth and enters into mourning.

Even if that's how Whitfield and Strong conceived the lyric, it is the measure of the importance of records over songs that Gaye is the only singer who really gets to its heart. Gladys Knight, who had a hit with "Grapevine" in 1967, gave a journeyman rendition in which neither gossip nor grief seemed so significant. And the extended rock band workout Creedence Clearwater Revival gave the song in 1970, after Gaye's interpretation was already famous (and therefore seemed inevitable), is just overwrought; partly because it never catches a groove but mostly because it takes too seriously the implied voodoo rhythms, as if Detroit were New Orleans. Nevertheless, John Fogerty understood that "I Heard It Through the Grapevine" was a work of art. And there's no shame in not improving on it. Neither could anybody else.

2 JOHNNY B. GOODE, Chuck Berry
Produced by Leonard Chess; written by Chuck Berry
Chess 1691   1958   *Billboard:* #8

Buried deep in the collective unconscious of rock and roll there's a simple figure drawn from real life: One man, one guitar, singing the blues. But he's not any man. He's black, Southern, poor, and (this is the part that's easiest to miss) dreaming. In many ways, his story is terrible and terrifying. We're speaking after all of someone like Robert Johnson, by all the evidence every bit as sensitive and perceptive as, say, F. Scott Fitzgerald, but rather than pursuing lissome Zeldas through Alabama mansions, enduring the pitiless reality of sharecropping, segregation, the threat of lynching, and all but inescapable twentieth century serfdom in Mississippi.

Chuck Berry's genius lay in his ability to shape those gruesome facts into a story about joy and freedom. Not that he didn't have to make concessions to the reality he was subverting. He says in his autobiography that he wanted to sing "There lived a colored boy named Johnny B. Goode," rather than the "country boy" we now have, but "I thought it would seem biased to white fans." Especially, no doubt, those white listeners who programmed the radio stations that would determine whether the record became a hit or was not heard at all.

Already a star, Chuck Berry was on intimate terms with the pop game and the limits it imposed on famous men with black skin. Standing at the edge of the rules, Berry shot himself right past one crucial dilemma of American culture into the center of another. By changing "colored" to "country," he found that, instead of speaking for himself alone, he'd created a character who also symbolized the likes of Elvis Presley, another kid whose momma promised that "someday your name will be in lights." Horrible as the source of the compromise may have been, its effect was to treble the song's force. For ultimately, if you could identify with either Presley or Berry, there was a chance you could identify with both. The result is history—and not just pop music history.

But that isn't all. "Chuck Berry's gotta be the greatest thing that came along / He made the guitar beats and wrote the all-time greatest songs," the Beach Boys once sang. They knew this better than most since Brian Wilson not only converted "Sweet Little Sixteen" into "Surfin' U.S.A.," a tale oft-told because it wound up in court, but modernized "Johnny B. Goode," right down to the guitar intro, into that much less ambiguous anthem, "Fun Fun Fun."

You can't copyright guitar licks and maybe that's good, because if you could, Chuck might have hoarded them as he does his Cadillacs. Without The Chuck Berry Riff, we'd lose not just the Beach Boys, but essential elements of the Beatles, the Rolling Stones, Bob Dylan, Bob Seger, and Bruce Springsteen—to mention only the most obvious examples. In a way, what was at the center of the first wave of the British Invasion could be described as a Chuck Berry revival.

In those days, you weren't a rock guitarist if you didn't know the riveting lick that kicks off "Johnny B. Goode." Cut without echo or reverb, a basic progression that still demanded a suppleness that immediately separated the worthy from the merely aspiring, this—more than any other—is what people mean when they talk about "The Chuck Berry Riff." Throughout the record, that machine-gun burst of notes never leaves center stage, even after Chuck sprays out those indelible opening lines, each multisyllabic phrase all one word, a voice in imitation of a guitar:

> DeepdowninLouisiana'crossfromNewOrleans,
> waybackupinthewoodsamongtheevergreens.

Rattled off in just six seconds, it's the most exciting way that Berry could have found to sing the song, and he slows down only long enough to set the scene. When he hits the chorus, the guitar returns, splitting each phrase, propelling Chuck Berry toward fame, ecstasy, any old place he chooses that's gotta be better than here and now.

In the bridge, the riff—which by now seems to have its own life, separate from the guitar and whoever plays it—collaborates with Johnny Johnson's chugging piano to form the kind of solo conceived by guys who had to think on their feet in barrooms night after night, already beat from their day jobs but *hoping*. It's that hope that "Johnny B. Goode" drives home just like a-ringin' a bell.

3 PAPA'S GOT A BRAND NEW BAG, James Brown
Written and produced by James Brown
King 45-5999   1965   *Billboard:* #8

The only way "Papa's Got a Brand New Bag" could be more bone-rattling would be if James Brown himself leaped from your speakers, grabbed you tight by the shoulders and danced you around the room, all the while screaming straight into your face. This record doesn't have an introduction; it's just suddenly, immediately *there* in a burst of brass and Brown's shriek.

Skirting the edges of intelligibility, his voice quavering and shaking like a man with cosmic palsy, Brown declared a new order of rhythm and himself its avatar. Or at least, that's the only way in which his expostulations about digging the new breed thing and his recital of every dance craze of the previous five years fit together with the percussive frenzy of drums, bass, razor-edge guitar, and blaring horns. The result is a beat chopped up into an infinity of bright, hard shards.

Each pierces the formula that was beginning to dominate soul music as it was pulled, like any other pop genre, toward more blandness than was good for it. Brown had helped perfect that formula, but with "Papa's Got a Brand New Bag," he declared his refusal to live within its restrictions.

With the possible exception of Little Richard, no one has ever made a rock or rhythm and blues record this extreme. At a time when Motown had made comparatively ornate records seem the wave of the future, Brown posited the most radical alternative: a record so totally immersed in rhythm that you barely noticed ornamentation at all. No record before "Papa's Got a Brand New Bag" sounded anything like it. No record since—certainly no dance record—has been unmarked by it. James Brown is entitled to every bit of his vanity, because in 1965, he invented the rhythmic future in which we live today.

4 REACH OUT I'LL BE THERE, The Four Tops
Produced by Brian Holland and Lamont Dozier; written by Brian Holland, Lamont Dozier, and Eddie Holland
Motown 1098   1966   *Billboard:* #1 (2 weeks)

The shibboleth is that pop music—from jazz to soul to punk—is better off as a purely expressive vehicle in which feeling overwhelms thinking. But that's a dangerously sentimental delusion. The fact is, working in a strictly defined, even formulaic context, Holland-Dozier-Holland and Levi Stubbs came up with a record that is a match for anything in the history of rock and roll. It was in part the restrictions of Motown and Top 40 pop which made it possible, by establishing the tension that the producers and performers worked against.

"Reach Out" is perhaps the truest single of all: Motown has released "Reach Out" dozens of times, on every medium from singles to CDs, but not one of the remasterings comes close to the sheer sonic crunch of the seven-inch 45. (Not just the Motown "map label" original; even reissued singles will put away any LP track or even the digitalized CD.)

Unfortunately, in the squinched-up versions most often available, most of the things that make this the greatest Holland-Dozier-Holland record are missing. The sheer size of the sound, its physical impact; the wild echo that makes the countermelody carried by the flute exotic and eerie; equalization that polarizes voice and drums; the producers' use of what must have been about half of the Detroit Symphony as an adjunct rhythm section; whatever the hell it is that establishes the clip-clop rhythm in the intro.

Even Stubbs fans understand why his style can be too declamatory, but here he's undeniable, a man lost in a welter of misery, his shouts emerging from an abyss. The music is dizzying, the drums collide against every phrase he sings, but Levi soldiers onward, riding out a maelstrom.

There are only a couple of hints of spontaneity in what Stubbs does, and even those may be part of the plan: a "hah!" at the end of the first verse seems just a nervous tic, until it's reiterated more forcefully at the end of the second. But like a great preacher who can make merely reading the gospel a creative act, Stubbs masterfully interacts with his text—one of the great things about the single is hearing him start to sing a (probably, or at least possibly, unplanned) "Don't worry!" just before the needle lifts off.

5 YOU'VE LOST THAT LOVIN' FEELIN', The Righteous Brothers
Produced by Phil Spector; written by Barry Mann, Cynthia Weill, and Phil Spector
Philles 124   1964   Billboard: #1 (2 weeks)

The radio on my boyhood dresser was an old tabletop model with tubes. The top was cracked and at high volume, the busted brown plastic made it screech. My father got it when my great-aunt died but it looked the kind of thing you'd pick up at a junkyard. It was the greatest treasure he ever gave me.

One night, just before Christmas 1964, a strange noise began to emerge from the ancient box. A doleful male voice sang notes so draggy that it seemed someone down at the station must have slowed the turntable with his finger. Annoyed, I switched the radio off.

And right back on again. Already warm, the unreliable old tubes responded immediately, for once. In those brief seconds the record had transformed itself. A wall of sound—drums, tambourines, pianos, full female chorus, maracas, who knew what else—was carrying an uncountable number of male voices into the pits of hell.

At first, they seemed content to ride the melody together, so much so that by the end of the first verse they reminded me of Little Anthony and the Imperials, although nothing Anthony and the boys had ever done was half this weird. The second verse began lugubriously again, strings swirling up out of the mix, as the harmonies built back up. I was hooked.

Then came the bridge. Now the voices were distinctly a pair, one mordantly growling, the other so high it was almost falsetto. No longer did they work in tandem. Now, even though they were ostensibly singing alternate lines to the same lover, they were also battling between themselves. The lower voice sang four sharp "Don'ts," and then—I never did figure out another way to describe it—they just started to wig out. "Baby!" sang one. "Baby!" responded the other. "Baby!" "Baby!" Then "I'm beggin' you please . . . I need your love" and finally "Bring it on back," they screamed at one another, relentlessly, as if trapped in a nightmare of what would happen if they didn't or couldn't.

"Bring back that lovin' feelin', whoah, that lovin' feelin'," they sang and the rhythm broke back down again. As they faded away, it felt shattered and pieced back together.

The deejay told me that this was the Righteous Brothers, who I already knew from TV's *Shindig*. They were a Mutt and Jeff act. Somber-voiced Bill Medley stood way over six feet, dark and halfways handsome; tenor Bobby Hatfield was blond, five five or so and greaser cute. They were good but there was nothing in "Little Latin Lupe Lu" that suggested they had anything like "Lovin' Feelin' " in them.

Naturally, I bought the record, surprised at its red and yellow Philles label: Producer/impresario Phil Spector made girl group records with the Crystals and the Ronettes. But then again, finding "Lovin' Feelin' " among them made a kind of sense, for a couple of Spector's girl group hits approached this single's orchestrated grandiosity.

About Spector I knew only that he'd once told a TV interviewer that he was the first teen genius millionaire, or something equally astute and captivating, and that he'd been responsible for the *T.A.M.I. Show*, the only decent representation of rock and roll music ever to appear at a drive-in.

So I sat and stared at the label and being in another line of work at the time—eighth grade—came to no unnecessary conclusions. I loved the record (wore out one copy, picked up another used), harbored a half-secret devotion to the Righteous Brothers no matter what they did well into adulthood, moved on to other things but still turned "Lovin' Feelin' " way up whenever it came across the radio.

In the spring of 1987, staying at a hotel in downtown Chicago, I strapped on headphones and went for a run. There was a parade on Michigan Avenue, and I dodged in and out among the crowd until I got down by the lake, where there was almost nobody. I'd been on the road a couple of weeks, and felt homesick, a little afraid, frightfully lonely.

The tape I listened to was composed of random favorites, deliberately jumbled so I couldn't remember what came next. Somewhere over by the lake, "Lovin' Feelin' " came on. I jammed the volume all the way up and the clash of those voices came through again. When they started begging and pleading—"Baby, baby, I'd get down on my knees for you," sang Medley, "If you would only love me like you used to do," responded Hatfield—tears sprang from my eyes. In the center of the continent, at the heart of a population of six million, I was suddenly, unmistakably, nerve-tinglingly abandoned and alone.

God knows what passersby thought. But with the title—"You've lost that lovin' feelin' "—echoing in my ears I understood at last: We worship the thing we fear.

6 (I CAN'T GET NO) SATISFACTION, The Rolling Stones
Produced by Andrew Loog Oldham; written by Mick Jagger and Keith Richards
London 9766   1965   *Billboard:* #1 (4 weeks)

After "Johnny B. Goode," "Satisfaction" has the greatest guitar riff in rock and roll history. But it's not really like any other guitar. I've always thought that its hornlike quality was Keith's way of overcompensating for the Stones' lack of the horn section so crucial to the soul bands the group emulated. (Check out Otis Redding's arrangement of "Satisfaction" and you'll hear what I mean.) Blurting out those unforgettable chords for the first time, Keith's axe is as big and bold as anything the Memphis Horns had to offer. And that, before anybody else gets a lick in, makes "Satisfaction" a great record.

It's *this* great, though, because everybody else does get their licks in. Charlie Watts and Bill Wyman have never meshed more perfectly, and "Satisfaction" was Mick Jagger's first inimitable performance: sullen, slurred, mocking every bit of the lyric's existential soul man jive. Treatises have been written about these words, most of which entirely miss their humor (that stuff about cigarette commercials still cracks me up), and the overanalysis has given the record a warhorse quality. But the music is undeniable. If Bob Dylan and Otis Redding had ever written a song together, this is what they would have had to compete with.

7 LIKE A ROLLING STONE, Bob Dylan
Produced by Tom Wilson; written by Bob Dylan
Columbia 43346   1965   *Billboard:* #2

The pistol shot that opens "Like a Rolling Stone" is really a drum but it could hardly be more appropriate if it were the real thing. At the instant this record reached the Top 40, the rock and roll world exploded.

Dylan is celebrated for his lyrics, especially *these* lyrics, but his greatest contribution to pop was his voice, which redefined the whole idea of singing. "Like A Rolling Stone" is the summation of that new definition. Nasal and nasty, raw as barbed wire, Dylan's voice recasts Muddy Waters's electric blues as a medium for expressing both aesthetic outrage and a lust that's as much intellectual as it is carnal. The beat is sodden with anger, and the biting accents contributed by Mike Bloomfield's guitar and Frank Owens' piano are acid-etched. Yet for all its sour strength, there is more compassion and bittersweet comedy in "Like a Rolling Stone" than shows up on paper—something you have to hear to really understand, because it's Dylan's singing, not the unmitigated assault of his words, that establishes the song's emotional range.

Well, that and Al Kooper's nervous two-finger organ playing. (Nervous because Kooper apparently had never before played the instrument, simply showed up for the session and angled his way into the empty organ chair because he recognized the chance to enter history.) Together, the singing and the organ keep "Like A Rolling Stone" from being just another icy hipster bitch session at the level of "Positively Fourth Street" (or worse—say, "Masters of War").

This was more-or-less Dylan's last session with New York producer and engineer Tom Wilson. They'd worked together since 1964, on *Another Side of Bob Dylan*, where Dylan wrote his first rock songs but chickened out when it came time to arrange them that way, and *Bringing It All Back Home*, where his electric explorations were tentative, if not halfhearted. This time, everything gelled and the result was riotous rock and roll, as tough as the Rolling Stones and Beatles sides that inspired it.

If it's music, more than language, that sustains "Like a Rolling Stone," that doesn't mean that the words aren't continually stunning. Dylan's language is more than just colloquial, it's an *absolute* expression of the vernacular. He's not just dropping g's, he's even recasting the subjunctive into a vulgar tongue: "People'd call, say 'Beware doll . . .' " Even now, it still seems strange that the record is so long because in real life, diatribes are never allowed to last this long: Somebody interrupts.

Like a lot of other Dylan songs, "Like a Rolling Stone" is often misunderstood as advice or instruction, but it's really both a contemporary myth that actually has the nerve to begin "Once upon a time . . . ," and the narration of a tragedy. Despite the sharp-tongued surface, when Dylan sings "When you ain't got nothin', you got nothin' to lose," he comes as close to expressing heartbreak as he ever would. That's why he almost strangles on that next-to-last "Hey, to be on your own."

But even that's a deceptive interpretation, or at least an incomplete one. When Dylan sang a radically altered version of "Like a Rolling Stone" on his 1974 "comeback" tour, a lot of people noticed that he seemed to be singing to himself. Listening to the original, you've got to ask why it took so long to figure that out.

8 RESPECT, Aretha Franklin
Produced by Jerry Wexler; written by Otis Redding
Atlantic 2403   1967   *Billboard:* #1 (2 weeks)

Aretha's "Respect" is the Motown style in reverse. It sounds worked out down to the finest detail but in fact the arrangement fell together spontaneously at a late 1966 session. Producer Wexler brought together Franklin, her sister Carolyn, and a white band from Muscle Shoals, Alabama, that made some of the best hard soul hits of the day. Aretha was merely fiddling with Otis Redding's song—already an R&B hit—when she and Carolyn began pulling threads of tempo and phrasing together in a way that suggested putting them on tape.

But even though that's how it happened, don't discount the arduous excavation of vision it took to create this Everest of southern soul. The most obvious example of the work involved is the bridge. Redding's original lacked one, so Franklin and Wexler lifted the part whole from Sam and Dave's "When Something Is Wrong With My Baby."

Redding's version of "Respect" is extraordinary because it seizes a key idea of the civil rights movement and applies it to everyman's sex life. But the song meant much more as a woman's vehicle—particularly since the woman was Aretha Franklin, a legend since she was a fourteen-year-old singing in her father's Detroit Baptist church and just then declaring her artistic freedom as the finest, deepest individual musical performer of the late sixties and early seventies. She may have set out to sing "Respect" on a lark, but by the time the tape was rolling, she was all business, and Aretha when she's concentrating is as good as it gets.

As she did on all her early Atlantic hits, Aretha brought to "Respect" everything she'd learned in church and from family friends like Mahalia Jackson, Sam Cooke, and the Ward Singers. But if Franklin were only another gospel singer turning to secular themes, "Respect" wouldn't be a masterpiece and she wouldn't have more entries in this book than any other artist.

Partly because she'd just recorded for six years at Columbia Records, partly because she was the product not only of the church but of big city life up north, with its panoply of pop and ethnic cultures, Aretha approached "Respect" as a pop singer, and particularly, as a *modern* pop singer who's most at home in the recording studio. For all her vocal ability, Aretha has never been better than a journeyman gospel singer because she's never been that comfortable with pure improvisation. Though she knew personally the greatest of all recorded gospel vocalists—Jackson and the Wards' Marion Williams, the Soul Stirrers' R. H. Harris and Cooke—her principal stylistic mentor was clearly Clara Ward, a ragged voice upstaged in her own live performances by Williams and Frances Steadman but unsurpassed with the tape rolling in the studio, where calculation paid off better than freewheeling.

Franklin's inspiration on "Respect" is to use gospel chords from her own piano as a base for both the band's arrangement and for her own feints toward improvisation. She knows exactly where the song is headed and propels it there with single-minded intensity. There's not a "Hey baby" or a "Mis-tuh!" that's accidental. Had Aretha not been trained in church, she'd never have known what to do here; had this really been her first pop session, she'd never have known how.

9 TUTTI FRUTTI, Little Richard
Produced by Bumps Blackwell and Art Rupe; written by Dorothy LaBostrie, Richard Penniman, and Joe Lubin
Specialty 561   1956   *Billboard:* #17

In his heyday, Richard—at least on record—was far more commanding than any of his imitators or his own current persona can afford to acknowledge. "Tutti Frutti," which was Richard's first hit, *did* start out with scatalogical lyrics, but that makes it all the more significant that Richard found a way to pull back enough to make the record (barely) eligible for airplay. So the young Richard wasn't just a piano-pumping crazy. His records featured an intensely swinging rhythm band and the music was anything *but* an amateurish hash, no matter what critics committed to the noble savage theory believe. Neither is it accurate to describe Richard's singing style as some outer-space affectation. Intensely personal as his shouting and singing were, they also paid tribute to the gospel women from whom he snitched at least as many licks as the Beatles ever stole from him. That doesn't mean that Richard was nothing more than a secular gospel singer, just that the particulars of his inventiveness were firmly grounded: "Tutti Frutti" 's recurrent "woo" is as much pure Marion Williams as Paul McCartney's shriek in "I'm Down" is pure Little Richard. This may be a species of rebellion, but it's way too controlled for anarchy.

One of rock's more cosmic questions is how you spell the opening shout. I've always preferred "Awopbopaloobopalopbamboom," but you're welcome to your own interpretation.

10 NOWHERE TO RUN, Martha and the Vandellas
Produced by Brian Holland and Lamont Dozier; written by Brian Holland, Lamont Dozier, and Eddie Holland
Gordy 7036   1965   *Billboard: #8*

Holland-Dozier-Holland's greatest triumph? Extracting legendary music from a singer as distinctive as Levi Stubbs is one thing; pulling it out of a singer as moderately gifted as Martha Reeves is another. And "Nowhere to Run" is one of the definitive Motown 45s: huge drums and popping bass propel a riffing horn section, while the frantic lead vocal recites straight pop verses with a gospel bridge. HDH's deployment of echo and EQ enables the record to begin at the height of excitement and sustain it all the way through.

Some elements of this arrangement—the baritone sax undertow, particularly—have almost the same feel as the lighter records being made in New Orleans in the mid-sixties. But what adds weight and power to "Nowhere to Run" 's shrieking paranoia—what makes it Motown—is the rhythm section. Bassist James Jamerson is justly celebrated today as one of the two or three most creative players on that instrument ever, and there's as much to be said for drummer Benny Benjamin, another of the remarkably distinctive session players Motown never credited. On "Nowhere to Run," Benjamin simply explodes all over his tom-toms. Thanks to them, this relentlessly rhythmic record ranks with the most fearsome of all time.

11 LOUIE LOUIE, The Kingsmen
Produced by Ken Chase and Jerry Dennon; written by Richard Berry
Wand 143   1963   *Billboard: #2*

Really stupid, really great. Not really dirty, but so what?

"Louie Louie" is the most profound and sublime expression of rock and roll's ability to create something from nothing. Built up from a Morse code beat and a "duh duh duh" refrain, with scratchy lead vocal, tacky electric piano, relentless rhythm guitar, and drums that sound like the guy who's playing 'em isn't sure what comes next, "Louie

Louie" scales the heights of trash rock to challenge the credentials of all latter-day rockers: If you don't love it, you've missed the point of the whole thing.

Naturally, this Parthenon of Pop didn't spring from the head of the Muse. A Muse would probably have slain it on sight, or passed away herself from the shock of something so crude and fine. "Louie Louie" was born in much more prosaic circumstances, as the B side of "You Are My Sunshine," an R&B version of the Jimmie Davis country standard recorded by Richard Berry and the Pharoahs and released on Flip Records in 1956. Berry was a veteran Los Angeles session singer who'd sung lead on the Robins' "Riot in Cell Block #9," the first big hit for producers Jerry Leiber and Mike Stoller. The Pharoahs were Berry's cohorts of the day, Flip his patron of the moment.

"You Are My Sunshine" made only a small buzz but when L.A. deejay Hunter Hancock flipped it to play "Louie," the disc still sold a respectable 130,000 copies. Its notoriety was great enough to earn Berry a rocker's reputation and afterward, he toured with more rugged blues acts like Bobby Bland and Junior Parker for the next couple of years. "I was there to attract white audiences," he said.

"Louie Louie" had variegated parentage. Berry had been working with a Latin band, Ricky Rillera and the Rhythm Rockers, every Saturday night in 1955. The Rhythm Rockers were a twelve-piece orchestra that did a tune called "El Loco Cha Cha," a local hit by Rene Touzet. Berry borrowed "El Loco" 's "duh duh duh" opening riff. Around the same time, Chuck Berry, to whom Richard Berry is related only spiritually, had released "Havana Moon," the story of a guy trying to get back to his home in Cuba. So Richard Berry decided to tell the story of a guy yearning to get back to his home and his girl in Jamaica. He must also have been aware of "One for My Baby (And One More for the Road)," a song written as a dialogue with a bartender named Joe, which had been a hit for Lena Horne in 1945. Berry named his bartender Louie, which was rather odd, for neither the protagonist nor his girl were named at all. Where he derived the idea of singing in Jamaican patois, who knows? Harry Belafonte's "Jamaica Farewell" didn't kick off the calypso craze until October 1956 and "Louie Louie" was cut in April.

In those days, there was no rock criticism and the coterie of those who suspected that rhythm and blues might have lasting value included almost no one who didn't know Ahmet Ertegun personally. Unsold copies of local hits were destroyed or sold for pennies to be recycled in "bargain bins" for a quarter or a dime. In 1960, aspiring star Rockin' Robin Roberts found a copy of "Louie Louie" in a Seattle bargain bin.

Roberts understood the genius of "Louie Louie" and adopted it as a sort of theme in his various bands. In 1961, he cut it for a local label, Etiquette, backed by the Wailers (who had an instrumental hit with "Tall Cool One" in 1959). History, bitch that she is, has denied Roberts the immortality he deserves for recognizing the song's gutter magnificence, and for being the first to interject the squawl "Let's give it to 'em, right now!" But his version was nonetheless picked up by bands all around the Northwest and "Louie Louie" became a regional standard, in the repertoire of every halfways talented area group. (The Sonics cut a particularly ferocious version as well as a nasty take on Berry's follow-up rewrite of the "Louie" riff, "Have Love, Will Travel.")

By 1963, Portland, Oregon's rival bands, Paul Revere and the Raiders and the Kingsmen, both featured "Louie" and their audiences constantly demanded it. On a Friday in May, the Kingsmen finally gave in and did an all-"Louie Louie" set; the song went on for forty-five minutes, becoming the first "Louie" marathon. The band was bored but the crowd went wild. Next day, the Kingsmen went into the studio with local disc jockey Ken Chase and cut their version. On Sunday, the Raiders followed them to cut theirs.

Both groups based their records on Roberts's version; they'd probably never so much as heard of the Pharoahs. The Raiders basically just replicated the Seattle rendition, with one brilliant addition at the top, when Revere yowled "Grab your woman! It's 'Louie Louie' time." The Kingsmen's version was quite a bit different, mostly (it turns out) because singer Jack Ely learned the song by listening a couple of times to a jukebox 45, and he got the beat wrong. Thus the Kingsmen play 1-2-3, 1-2, 1-2-3, 1-2, rather than the more orthodox 1-2-3-4, 1-2, 1-2-3-4, 1-2 of all the earlier versions. (In the process they helped invent reggae; just listen to Toots and the Maytals' early seventies "Louie" on their album Funky Kingston.)

What Ely remembered right and even improved upon, though, was Roberts's shout just before the guitar break: "Give it to 'em, right now!" He went for it so avidly you'd have thought he'd spotted the jugular of a lifelong enemy, and, at the same time, so crudely that, at that instant, Ely sounds like Donald Duck on helium. And it's that faintly ridiculous air that makes the Kingsmen's record the classic that it is, especially since it's followed by a guitar solo that's just as wacky.

Teenage Portland took both of the new records of its favorite song to heart but deejays held the Kingsmen's a little nearer. After a Boston R&B jock also started airing it, the Kingsmen's disc was picked up for national distribution by the New York-based Wand label. (The Raiders eventually wound up with a Columbia Records contract and a sizable regional hit on the West Coast.)

Now Ely's vocal was so garbled—he didn't know the words well, and the mike was suspended too far above his head for him to sing into it properly—that it approached total unintelligibility. As airplay increased, rumors circulated that the Kingsmen muffled the vocal because the song was really obscene. The details are too unlikely to be worth reciting completely, but as I recall they centered on interpreting "Me think of girl constantly" as "Me fuck that girl all kinds of ways," and "I smell the rose in her hair" as "I stick mah bone in her there." Or something like that. Allegedly, these "true" lyrics could only be heard at some other speed—33 or 78 or 16. (Don't bother.)

The rumors caused a moral panic in Indiana when the governor banned "Louie" from the state's airwaves. Soon, the FCC and FBI were investigating, grilling both Richard Berry and Jack Ely (who'd been bounced from the Kingsmen). The Feds eventually came to a closer-to-correct conclusion: "unintelligible at any speed."

At this stage, "Louie Louie" had already passed into legend, becoming the greatest example of rock's function as a secret language for its audience. Whatever Ely sang that Saturday afternoon, what his audience believed it heard was far more important and powerful. The record stayed at the top of the charts for four months, and returned for another brief run in the spring of 1966.

In the wake of the rumors, "Louie Louie" became *the* party band staple of the sixties. More than three hundred versions were recorded, and in 1966 the Sandpipers took it back to the charts with a folk-rock Muzak version with the lyrics translated into Spanish. In 1978, John Belushi's version from the soundtrack of *Animal House* brought "Louie" into circulation again. At last, in the early and mid-eighties a couple of California radio stations, KALX in Berkeley and KFJC in Los Altos Hills, staged "Louie Louie" marathons lasting several days each, featuring all sorts of oddball renditions by famous musicians and local losers. In the late eighties, a Philadelphia disc jockey, John DelBella, began organizing "Louie" parades with proceeds going to victims of leukemia—the "Louie" disease.

In 1985, the Washington state legislature voted down a resolution to make "Louie" the state song, but in the hearts and minds of true rock and rollers, it has already achieved far greater stature. In versions made by everybody from the Beach Boys to Barry White to the punks down the block, "Louie Louie" is a true national anthem. Nobody has ever come close to topping the Kingsmen's version and nobody ever will. If you don't believe me . . .

"Let's give it to 'em. Right now!"

12 MYSTERY TRAIN, Elvis Presley
Produced by Sam Phillips; written by Junior Parker
Sun 223   1955   Did not make pop charts

What's scary about the young Elvis is his assurance, the complete ease with which he swings into action. Here, singing a song in which R&B singer Junior Parker reworked the folk images from country songs like the Carter Family's "Worried Man Blues," Elvis rides an urgent Scotty Moore guitar lick and propulsive Bill Black bass line with complete confidence: He *owns* the song and nothing within it is unknowable to him or could ever betray him. Which is pretty weird because he's singing about something close to a death ship, a "long black train got my baby and gone," which may also be looking to snatch *him*. By the end, he's persuaded himself—and you, too—that it's bringing her back.

The recording itself is a masterpiece, the sound virtually liquid as it hits the ear, the legendary Sun echo fine-tuned like a Ferrari. Junior Parker's version, a minor R&B hit in 1953, is spooky because it details what fate can do to a man. Elvis makes you want to defy all omens, hie to the graveyard and dance fearlessly at midnight.

13 SHAKE, RATTLE AND ROLL, Big Joe Turner
Produced by Ahmet Ertegun and Jerry Wexler; written by
Charles Calhoun [Jesse Stone]
Atlantic 1026   1954   Did not make pop charts

14 WHOLE LOTTA SHAKIN' GOIN' ON, Jerry Lee Lewis
Produced by Sam Phillips; written by Dave Williams and
Sunny David [Roy Hall]
Sun 267   1957   *Billboard:* #3

Winner and first runner-up in the Lewd and Lascivious category, "Shake, Rattle and Roll" and "Whole Lotta Shakin' " are the two strongest arguments for the idea that prudes really did have something to fear from rock and roll. Both Big Joe and Jerry Lee leer and drool with an indelicacy that would be comic if it weren't so intense. If there's a way to impute more pure, dripping lust into the word "shake," no one has ever found it, even though Lewis and Turner doubtless inspired many a search.

Aside from that, the records are opposites. Turner's never made the pop charts, although its wonderful, witty lyric was bowdlerized and turned into a multimillion seller by Bill Haley later the same year; Lewis got a Number One R&B hit to go with his pop success, even though R&B shouter Big Maybelle (perhaps the closest thing to a distaff equivalent of Turner) had flopped with the same song in 1955. There's a kind of double whammy here because "Whole Lotta Shakin' " began its life as a collaboration between a black man, Williams, and a white one, Hall. (Jerry Lee apparently worked from Hall's country version, even more obscure than Big Maybelle's.)

The contrast is greatest when it comes to the piano playing. Forty-three-year-old Turner, who'd been making records since the late thirties when he came East from Kansas City as part of the boogie-woogie boom, got his most famous hit with an arrangement driven by lovely triplets that wouldn't have been out of place on his first sides. Lewis, like the twenty-two-year-old hothead he was, simply guns it from the first notes, playing a cross between honky-tonk and blues shuffle at an impossible tempo, which he has the audacity to speed up after the first verse. Turner is commanding because he remains dignified even while exorcising his lust. Lewis is in charge because he's tough and arrogant enough to back up every claim his romp over the keyboards makes.

In a way, this only restates the obvious: Big Joe Turner was a blues shouter who had rhythm and blues hits in the rock and roll era. Jerry Lee Lewis was a rock and roller. Still, their finest records live on, side by side.

15 (SITTIN' ON) THE DOCK OF THE BAY, Otis Redding

Produced by Steve Cropper; written by Otis Redding and Steve Cropper
Volt 157   1968   *Billboard:* #1 (4 weeks)

Recorded on December 7, 1967, three days before he died, "Dock of the Bay" was Otis Redding's only major pop hit. If you're planning to write your own epitaph, you'll have a hard time topping this one.

Otis wrote the song in California, in the days after his triumphant appearance at the Monterey Pop Festival in the summer of 1967. He'd been listening to the Beatles' *Sgt. Pepper's Lonely Hearts Club Band*, and intended the song—or perhaps some cycle of songs into which "Dock of the Bay" fit, we'll never know—as a response to the white rock scene's artistic expansionism. Yet there's nothing bombastic about the record; to the contrary, it's quietly meditative, a pure mood piece.

But that's not all it is. Otis may have pretended to make nothing much more than a simple pop song, a meditation on how far he'd come from Georgia clay using road weariness as its metaphor. What he really did, though, was create a record that's as abstract as anything that the Beatles ever did. "(Sittin' On) The Dock of the Bay" is a contemplation of the ideas of time and space, their interaction and how passing through either, let alone both, affects a man's life.

Though Otis's singing is gentle and accepting, it's also strong and sure of itself. You can tell he has thought deeply about the meaning of these things, though you can also see that it's never occurred to him that they belonged in his music. At least, not openly. Now liberated, he speaks of what matters to him, of home and loneliness, of time that speeds by and can never be recaptured, and of repetition without end or meaning. Finally, to speak of things for which there are no words, he simply whistles the melody.

The tenderness Otis applies to his singing here is akin to the way a father's huge, calloused hands hold a tiny baby for the first time. Had Redding sustained such a fine balance of musicianship, intellect, and emotion for an entire album, he would have unquestionably made one of the greatest LPs of all time. But what we have is not a fragment. "(Sittin' On) The Dock of the Bay" is as whole, as fully realized and mature, as any record ever made.

16 EVERYDAY PEOPLE, Sly and the Family Stone
Written and produced by Sly Stone
Epic 10407 1968   *Billboard:* #1 (4 weeks)

After two hundred takes failed to get an acceptable "White Rabbit" from a pre-Jefferson Airplane group featuring Grace Slick, disc jockey/ record producer Sylvester Stewart vowed to forget that acid-rock shit. So he renamed himself Sly Stone and formed his own band to play "the first fusion of psychedelia and rhythm and blues." In the Family Stone, men and women, black and white, played and sang as equals and each member's voice matched his or her instrument (i.e., bassist Larry Graham both played and sang bass, while Cynthia Robinson had the same brassy range and timbre as her trumpet). More startling, in Sly's songs rock and soul—that is, black and white post-Presley pop—intermingled till you couldn't find where one began and the other left off.

The nursery rhyme simplicity and seductive tunefulness of "Everyday People," their third single and first Number One hit, make it almost too sweet to be true, and its fusion of rock and soul elements reflects an integrated symmetry that's still breathtaking.

"Everyday People" proposes something even more radical than "different strokes for different folks" (a phrase it placed in the permanent American vernacular). The song argues that the healing power of music even encompasses curing rifts among races and classes. That was a corny/naive idea even in 1968, yet the record remains convincing because it so delightedly practices everything it preaches. You could spend a lifetime fathoming what gives Sly the courage to declare (at a time when the unity of the civil rights movement was disintegrating into a dagger's length truce), "We got to live together!"

Even if the record's final boast, "I *AM* everyday people" means only that the "we" who had to live together were the antagonistic sides of Sly's own personality, these are words to live by.

17 ONLY THE LONELY, Roy Orbison
Produced by Fred Foster; written by Roy Orbison and Joe Melson
Monument 421   1960   *Billboard: #2*

Roy Orbison came into RCA's Nashville studio for his second session accompanied by two sidekicks. As he rehearsed his new song at the microphone, the friends whispered alongside him. Engineer Bob Porter and producer Fred Foster said it was impossible to record him that way. Well, said Roy, you'd better, because that's the sound of my next record.

What they were singing, of course, was "Dum, dum, dum, dum-dee-doo-wah; ooo, yay, yay, yay, yeah; oh, oh, oh, oo-wah; only the lonely." These nonsense syllables aren't sung or hummed or crooned; they're whispered into our hearts.

Like the rest of Orbison's hits, "Only the Lonely" has tremendous dynamics (made possible by Orbison's near-operatic range) and a lyric that renders everyday heartbreak so universal that it acquires a tinge of the cosmic. What's most remarkable, though, is that at the end, Orbison shrugs off all the agony and asks only for the chance to lose his loneliness to love once again. This transcendental dismissal of the worst life has to offer should by itself earn Orbison a place in the pantheon of rock legends. If Phil Spector is pop music's truest romantic and John Fogerty its greatest fatalist, Roy Orbison stands as its ultimate stoic. Maybe he wore those shades all the time to disguise the fact that he never blinked no matter what you threw at him.

18 (YOU MAKE FEEL LIKE) A NATURAL WOMAN, Aretha Franklin

Produced by Jerry Wexler; written by Gerry Goffin, Carole King, and Jerry Wexler
Atlantic 2441   1967   *Billboard:* #8

"A Natural Woman" is probably the greatest record ever made about female sexuality. Imagine:

A woman sits at her windowsill on a rainy morning. She feels pretty good about herself, and that's something new. Her guy is the reason. Why? Well, you can only tell between the lines, from the metaphors she uses—she'd never say it out loud—but the most sensible guess is that she's finally found someone with whom she can achieve orgasm. So she sings her song of ecstasy.

And if that's *not* it, you better have a pretty damn plausible alternative explanation for these lines: "Oh baby, what you done to me / You made me feel so good inside / And I just wanna be / Close to you, you make feel so alive."

"A Natural Woman" inverts "Respect," but in no way is it about being dependent. It's about the near-delirious experience of being fully equal, which is as close to a definition of good sex as I'd care to venture. In these days of feminist vigilance, endorsing a song in which a woman declares her devotion to a man by thanking him for helping to fulfill her "nature" is risky stuff. But that's not all that's going on here—this music is also about as beautiful and moving as you can imagine, strings skidding against drums, horns rising to announce passion that's so fully carnal that it's practically radioactive.

19 DO YOU LOVE ME, The Contours

Written and produced by Berry Gordy Jr.
Gordy 7005   1962   *Billboard:* #3

Next time somebody tells you Motown's too slick, slap this on the box and accept their apology gracefully. Benny Benjamin's drums are the lead instrument, and he's every bit as biting as anyone else's lead guitar. The drums overwhelm even Billy Gordon's hoarse lead vocal, which sounds like Frogman Henry after a shot of pure adrenaline. Breaking the beat down and putting it back together again, Benjamin dominates a record that has everything, from the best spoken introduction ever

("You broke my heart because I couldn't dance . . . ,") to an artful false ending (it fakes me out every time).*

Berry Gordy's business genius sometimes makes him seem like nothing more than the Henry Ford of pop music. In fact, he was a superb musician, songwriter, arranger, and producer—closer to Thomas Edison than Ford. Presuming he plays piano here (as he often did in Motown's early days), every one of those skills is put to use on "Do You Love Me" and the result is not only classic rock and roll but a tribute to his stature as the greatest backstage talent in rock history.

20 BE MY BABY, The Ronettes
Produced by Phil Spector; written by Phil Spector, Ellie Greenwich, and Jeff Barry
Philles 116   1963   *Billboard:* #2

21 DA DOO RON RON, The Crystals
Produced by Phil Spector; written by Phil Spector, Ellie Greenwich, and Jeff Barry
Philles 112   1963   *Billboard:* #3

22 CHRISTMAS (BABY PLEASE COME HOME), Darlene Love
Produced by Phil Spector; written by Phil Spector, Ellie Greenwich, and Jeff Barry
Philles 119   1963   Did not make pop charts

To hear folks talk, Phil Spector made music out of a solitary vision. But the evidence of his greatest hits insists that he was heavily dependent on a variety of assistance. Which makes sense: Record making is fundamentally collaborative.

Spector associates like engineer Larry Levine, arranger Jack Nitzsche, and husband-wife songwriters Jeff Barry and Ellie Greenwich

*The glory of "Do You Love Me," it must be noted, has now been bowdlerized and traduced by contemporary hit radio stations, which play an edited version made for the soundtrack of *Dirty Dancing*, that omits, among other things, the fake ending. That's an abomination, of course, because the song's so short to begin with, only 2:49, and because omitting anything from such a seamless disc disrupts the greatness of the whole. Future generations may grow up thinking that there *is* no other version of "Do You Love Me," which would be tragic and infuriating.

were simply indispensable to his teen-art concoctions. Besides them, every Spector track featured a dozen or more musicians. The constant standouts were drummer Hal Blaine, one of the most inventive and prolific in rock history, and saxophonist Steve Douglas. Finally, there were vast differences among Spector's complement of singers. An important part of Spector's genius stemmed from his ability to recruit, organize, and provide leadership within such a musical community.

Darlene Love (who also recorded for Spector with the Crystals and Bob B. Soxx and the Blue Jeans) ranks just beneath Aretha Franklin among female rock singers, and "Christmas" is her greatest record, though it was never a hit. (The track probably achieved its greatest notice in the mid-eighties, when it was used over the opening credits of Joe Dante's film, *Gremlins*.) Spector's Wall of Sound, with its continuously thundering horns and strings, never seemed more massive than it does here. But all that only punctuates Love's hysterical blend of loneliness and lust. In the end, when the mix brings up the piano and the chorus to challenge her, the best the Wall's entire weight can achieve is a draw.

The Crystals' official lead singer La La Brooks was much closer to the anonymous end of the Spector spectrum, and on "Da Doo Ron Ron," the result is a much more balanced record. Basing the song in nonsense syllables can't disguise what it really is: teen desire incarnate. The battering Blaine gives his drum kit (if anything *he's* the star of this show), the droning background "ooo," the sassy handclaps, and Steve Douglas's raging hormonal sax riff add up to more of the same. When Blaine hits his tom-toms after each line of the chorus, the effect is like moving up into overdrive—the song smoothly surges forward.

"Be My Baby" is another story. Ronnie Spector's Brooklyn accent renders her pitch always uncertain, her intonation cracks on "had" in the song's second line, and emotionally, she seems more dutiful than inspired. It doesn't matter. Phil Spector was in love with her (they eventually married), and he built a rock and roll cathedral around what little her voice had to offer. Blaine's intro is one of rock's grand statements, setting a tone of importance that Ronnie's entrance immediately cuts down to size. At the chorus, the Ronettes rise behind Ronnie, tripling her strength, and they stay with her, crooning open-throated vowels. Then there's the bridge, with its ranks of cellos, a mountainous mock-symphony that lasts for the rest of the record. Against all odds, Spector made an initially shaky proposition into what may be his greatest monument.

23 HOLD ON I'M COMIN', Sam and Dave
Written and produced by Isaac Hayes and David Porter
Stax 189   1966   *Billboard:* #21

Al Jackson plays as if Sam and Dave had just persuaded him that you could be arrested for not popping the one hard enough. Sam and Dave sing as if they said it because they believed it.

And if you know a greater statement of sexual urgency, keep it to yourself because it probably really *is* illegal.

24 BORN TO RUN, Bruce Springsteen
Produced by Bruce Springsteen and Mike Appel; written by Bruce Springsteen
Columbia 10209   1975   *Billboard:* #23

Springsteen once said that after he'd come up with this maelstrom, he walked around for the next few days wondering where he'd stolen it from. Which makes sense because "Born to Run" has the audible ambition of recapitulating the first twenty-some years of rock and roll's public history, fusing a seven-layer Duane Eddy guitar lick with Dylanesque lyrics, Roy Orbison vocal histrionics, Spectorian production effects, Stones-style rhythm section, King Curtis sax break, and subterranean references to half-forgotten one-shot hits from "Little Star" to "Mountain of Love." Critic Greil Marcus once described it as "a '57 Chevy running on melted-down Crystals records," and only the part about the car was metaphor.

Celebrated as Springsteen is for his lyrics, it's the music that makes "Born to Run." The lyrics are still remarkable, sketching a philosophy of determined outward rebellion, a desire to move, a sense of goals and purpose that skirt the edges of the larger-than-life. But this hopeful abandon is tempered by an equally powerful melancholy; the future seems so bright largely because the present's so dismal. Truth to tell, Springsteen seems most vibrant when depicting the kids cruising the Jersey strip: "The girls comb their hair in rearview mirrors and the boys try to look so hard . . . Kids are huddled on the beach in a mist."

From bar to bar, this old crate may need a tune-up, and its predetermined destination isn't necessarily where you want to live. But once in a while, you at least ought to spend the night and see the sights.

25 WHAT'S GOING ON, Marvin Gaye
Produced by Marvin Gaye; written by Al Cleveland,
Marvin Gaye, and Renaldo Benson
Tamla 54201   1967   *Billboard:* #2

"What's Going On" wasn't the same kind of breakthrough as "Papa's Got a Brand New Bag" or Sly and the Family Stone's "Dance to the Music." But it did establish a new kind of adult black pop by bathing Gaye's voice in an almost weightless atmosphere of post-psychedelic rhythm and harmony. "What's Going On" is the matrix from which was created the spectrum of ambitious black pop of the seventies: everything from the blaxploitation soundtracks of Curtis Mayfield to Giorgio Moroder's pop-disco. Not bad for a record whose backing vocalists include a pair of pro football players.

But neither its influence nor its role in breaking the grip of the Motown machine is what makes "What's Going On" great. It's great because it's every bit as gorgeous as it is ambitious. After making it, "I felt like I'd finally learned how to sing," Gaye told biographer David Ritz. Gaye taught himself to "relax, just relax," which resulted in a vocal that moves through a dreamscape in which facts and wishes are equally terrible. The song is most famous for attacking war and poverty but it's also an affirmation of love. And that's why, for all its references to long hair and Vietnam, "What's Going On" will never sound dated.

At its best "What's Going On" amalgamates soul and Latin jazz, but at times it's so laid-back that it approaches Hollywood schmaltz. What saves it then is the unmistakable Motown underpinning that comes from James Jamerson's liquid bass and what might be castanets but could just as easily be fingers popping. All the label's session stalwarts are there and they never played better, maybe because they'd never been so stringently challenged. You don't make music like this unless you're surrounded by loved ones.

26 WHO'LL STOP THE RAIN, Creedence Clearwater Revival
Written and produced by John Fogerty
Fantasy 637   1970   *Billboard:* #2

The mourning in John Fogerty's voice and the elegant guitar figure on which it rides make it seem that he's expressing some specific, tangible grief or grievance. But what's it about? Woodstock, where it poured as Creedence played? Vietnam, with America mired in mud?

The clues in other Creedence songs lead to a different conclusion: Fogerty is rock and roll's version of an Old Testament prophet, preaching pessimism rather than damnation. "Long as I remember," he begins, with an intonation that implies he forgets nothing, clear back to the beginning. Alternately furious and heartsick, he spins a tale that includes political events, rock concerts seen from both sides of the stage, and private attempts to make sense of his life and the world.

With his band, particularly drummer Doug Clifford, working at peak efficiency, Fogerty magisterially draws upon a broad knowledge of American music: The lyrics, the beat, the guitar line, the melody allude to folk songs, country tunes, old R&B hits, Stones-style rock and roll. Yet what draws you back is the grain of his voice, the things it contains and expresses but cannot speak. And this voice is as far from the assurance of Elvis or Aretha as you can get. Fogerty seems confident of only two things: his doubts and his powerlessness. Hooking his audience as firmly as he's hooked himself, Fogerty makes his worries ours. The final chords ring out anthemically without resolving anything at all.

The idea that rock and roll is lighthearted good time music stops here, at the gateway to its heart of darkness.

27 MY GIRL, The Temptations
Written and produced by Smokey Robinson and Ronald White
Gordy 7038   1965   *Billboard:* #1 (1 week)

Sometimes it's at least as much the song as the singer, and "My Girl," one of the most memorable melodies of the rock era, is a fine example. But even here, the meaning of the music is just as much in the atmospheric production, which has the same ozone-intoxicated feeling as the air just after a summer thunder shower, and in the exquisite playing, particularly the bass and guitar. David Ruffin sings as if Smokey Robinson derived his great metaphors through a direct pipeline to the singer's soul, but the moment that makes the record is the soaring bridge, strings and guitar shimmering against the Tempts' repeated "Hey hey hey," out of which Ruffin comes with a swooping yet understated "Ooooh yeah." It's done offhandedly, which is just what gives the lyric's saccharine romanticism credibility.

28 JUMP, Van Halen
Produced by Ted Templeman; written by Edward Van Halen, Alex Van Halen, Michael Anthony, and David Lee Roth
Warner Bros. 29384   1984   *Billboard:* #1 (five weeks)

Edward Van Halen has expanded heavy metal's vocabulary so much that his band's partisans claim the group no longer plays metal at all, even though its persistent vulgarity argues otherwise. But "Jump" really did take them someplace else. The song's riff, stated on synthesizer and accentuated with guitar licks, is a direct descendant of the Who's "Won't Get Fooled Again," but with a sweeter, more cogently stated melody. This is heavy metal *in excelsis.*

What takes "Jump" over the top is its scenario. Singer David Lee Roth portrays his usual swaggering stud, leaning up against a jukebox in a barroom. Soon he spies a girl he wants. But, for once, he's visited by self-doubt. In the tension between guitar and synthesizer, raspy vocal and sad chords can be felt all the anxiety and desire that grips any kid— any*body*—caught in such a scene.

The tension reaches a climax with the false ending just after Van Halen's brash guitar solo. For a minute, it seems that maybe Roth's barroom bravado has failed. For a heartbeat, it's all over—everything. Which makes the sudden eruption of those decisive, exultant shouts of "Jump!" all the more rewarding. In the heyday of the fey, Van Halen reply: "Sweet dreams are made of *this*, motherfucker."

29 TICKET TO RIDE, The Beatles
Produced by George Martin; written by John Lennon and Paul McCartney
Capitol 5407   1965   *Billboard:* #1 (1 week)

"Ticket to Ride" began its life on the pop charts at Number One and it did so on merit. They say this was one of John's personal favorites, probably because it has his most soulful vocal ever. But "Ticket to Ride" is intricate and interesting all the way through, with Paul playing mean lead guitar and Ringo dispelling all doubt about his prowess as a drummer: The groove comes straight out of his pure backbeat. The Beatles were such a prolific album act that it's sometimes hard to abstract their later singles; here, they ride their roots as a bar band in Liverpool and Hamburg to a new kind of glory.

30 THERE GOES MY BABY, The Drifters
Produced by Jerry Leiber and Mike Stoller; written by
Benjamin Nelson, Lover Patterson, and George Treadwell
Atlantic 2025   1959   *Billboard:* #2

In the best scene of *American Hot Wax*, Floyd Mutrux's 1978 film
biography of disc jockey Alan Freed, Tim McIntire's Freed, sitting in
the studio doing his show, gets a disturbing phone call from his father
back in Ohio. When it's over Freed hangs his head in his hands. The
engineer reminds him from the other room that it's time for another
record. Freed says nothing, just reaches over and cues one up. As it
begins playing, he speaks over its intro.

"This is Alan Freed and I love you," he says in a voice husky and
mysterious. "You know what—it's raining in Akron, Ohio . . . but it's
a beautiful night in New York City. These are the Drifters, and 'There
Goes My Baby.' " He reaches over and turns the record up as loud as
it'll go. Suddenly, swirling strings deliver Ben E. King's nasal voice
crying, "There goes my baby, movin' on down the line." It's a moment
meant to convince you that Freed loves the music not because it's made
him rich and famous but because it satisfies something within him. And
it succeeds.

Not only Freed but "There Goes My Baby" deserves to be en-
shrined, for the moment when those strings entered, rhythm and blues
took an irrevocable step toward soul music.

This next step in the evolution of record-making made it even more
decisively a producer's music, concocted in the studio without much
reference to what happened on stage or in doo-wop hallways with
perfect echoes. "We were trying to create some kind of collage," Jerry
Leiber once said. "We were experimenting because the things that were
planned for the date were falling apart . . . Stanley [Applebaum, the
arranger] wrote something that sounded like some Caucasian take-off
and we had this Latin beat going on this out-of-tune tympani and the
Drifters were singing something in another key but the total effect—
there was something magnificent about it." After it became a hit, he
said, "I'd be listening to the radio sometimes and hear it and I was
convinced it sounded like two stations playing one thing."

Leiber is too modest. For what the arrangement really brought
forward, by forcing King (in his debut as the Drifters' lead voice) to
sing in a key well above his natural range and underpinning the result
with so much pseudo-Tchaikovsky, was an air of abject hopelessness—
the same kind of frustrated defeat that Alan Freed might have felt after

talking to his father. The magnificence, I suppose, comes because we've now had thirty years to understand that the song sounds the same on either end of the wire.

31 WHEN A MAN LOVES A WOMAN, Percy Sledge
Produced by Quin Ivy and Marlin Greene; written by C. Lewis and A. Wright
Atlantic 2326   1966   *Billboard:* #1 (2 weeks)

Compared to something like "Reach Out I'll Be There," "When A Man Loves a Woman" is barely a record at all. It's just a guy singing his song, sparely accompanied by a rhythm section: organ, bass, guitar, lightly struck drums, a faint vocal chorus. Percy Sledge works himself into such an ecstasy of passion that, until a full horn section jumps in at the last moment, it's easy to forget that there's anybody on earth except him, his girl, and you.

A generation of lovers has treated this number as the ultimate slow dance but it was never that simple. Not only does the singer describe himself "trying to hold on to your heartless love," but the song ends with Sledge trying to find a new girl after being played "for a fool." But then, it figures his audience would miss the point. Loving eyes can never see.

32 A CHANGE IS GONNA COME, Sam Cooke
Produced by Hugo and Luigi; written by Sam Cooke
RCA 8486   1965   *Billboard:* #31

Sam Cooke's greatest records are the gospel sides he made with the Soul Stirrers. Here's the exception that proves the rule: a lush orchestral arrangement in which Cooke smoothly preaches a sermon on humanity. There are those who would argue that the single is inferior to the album track because it omits the most militant verse (about being refused admission to a movie theatre). But in 1965, much less twenty years later, what Cooke was singing about was clear enough, especially when he talks about his "brother" who knocks him to his knees. This was Cooke's final hit, and it is the one record I know that comes closest to the spirit of Dr. Martin Luther King Jr.'s self-eulogy "I've Been to the Mountaintop."

33 THAT'LL BE THE DAY, Buddy Holly and the Crickets
Produced by Norman Petty; written by Jerry Allison, Buddy Holly, and Norman Petty
Brunswick 55009   1957   *Billboard:* #1 (1 week)

The first modern rock band: self-contained for both playing and singing, wrote its own songs and featured the basic two guitars-bass-drums lineup. There are all sorts of reference points for what they get up to here, country and Mexican accents bouncing off rhythm and blues beats, with a lyric tag picked up from John Wayne in *The Searchers*. But the hottest parts are that mean guitar, firing off dangerous staccato bursts, and Holly's vocal, which abandons all sense of propriety for effects that range from hiccups to unworldly "woo" 's. This is the one where they prove they really were the Beatles' granddaddies.

34 STAY, Maurice Williams and the Zodiacs
Produced by Al Silver; written by Maurice Williams
Herald 552   1960   *Billboard:* #1 (1 week)

A combination of English language and Caribbean beat so powerfully off-center that it practically constitutes the first reggae record, an impression that's abetted by the rather primitive recording. "Stay" is sheer thrills: Williams bumping his yearning against the percussion (drums and wood blocks), the Zodiacs' chanted backing, and the slithering piano chords. The break was crucial in establishing that durable rock and roll convention and gospel bootleg: the falsetto.

35 I'VE BEEN LOVING YOU TOO LONG, Otis Redding
Produced by Steve Cropper; written by Otis Redding and Jerry Butler
Stax 126   1965   *Billboard:* #21

It's hard to say what Jerry Butler and Otis Redding had in mind when they sat down one night in a Buffalo hotel room and wrote this song. Clearly, they were weary of the road; it shows in the melancholy mood. Maybe they missed their wives or maybe one of them had just broken up with someone. Maybe they were trying to find a way to get over with a girl down the hall.

We can only guess. But everybody knows what they came up with:

the ultimate slow dance, a nonpareil seduction song, an actual *standard*, a song that will be covered as long as men and women want an excuse to clutch each other tight in public.

But then, Otis sort of messed that up, because his version is inimitable. Phrasing as though each line is coming to him only the instant before he sings it, quavering notes as if in the grip of an undeniably exquisite passion that must be consummated—now!—Otis tears the song up without showing a second's strain. Aretha may have been able to cop "Respect," but neither she nor anyone else would ever touch him on this one.

36 SINCE I DON'T HAVE YOU, The Skyliners

Produced by Joe Rock; written by Joe Rock, Lennie Martin, Jimmy Beaumont, Janet Vogel, Joseph Verscharen, Walter Lester, and John Taylor [The Skyliners]
Calico 103   1959   *Billboard:* #12

Jimmy Beaumont was a white kid from Pittsburgh with an uncanny vocal similarity to R&B smoothies like Little Willie John and Lenny Welch. Beaumont probably didn't want much beyond avoiding life in a steel mill but he did a lot to change the idea that you had to be black to sing with soul. Manager/producer Joe Rock surrounded him with a fully orchestrated arrangement complete with oboes and plucked violins. The Skyliners stand well back and just let it happen, until near the end when Beaumont hits some spectacular high notes and Janet Vogel's wordless oohs outleap him to close out the record on a totally ethereal note.

37 BERNADETTE, The Four Tops

Produced by Brian Holland and Lamont Dozier; written by Brian Holland, Lamont Dozier, and Eddie Holland
Motown 1104   1967   *Billboard:* #4

Phil Spector called "Bernadette" "a black man singing Bob Dylan," and indeed, when Levi Stubbs sings "They *pre*-tend to be my *friend*," his cadence is as unmistakably Dylanesque as anything that ever came from the mouths of the Byrds or Manfred Mann.

As the final leg of Holland-Dozier-Holland's great Four Tops trilogy, "Bernadette" is wreathed in the same dark, foreboding atmosphere as "Reach Out I'll Be There" and "Standing in the Shadows of

Love." Levi Stubbs struggles his way out of a similar sea of contrasting melodies, pushed and prodded by the bass, provoked into near panic by sharp, keening flute and organ. All the while, he fights to tell one of the most scarifying tales in the history of rock and romance.

Bernadette is not only Levi's lover, she's a mystical symbol of what men spend their lives battling to discover. Stubbs sings from within a tumultuous emotional whirlpool, boasting of Bernadette's charms and bitterly mocking other men's attempts to win her. Telling this part of the story, Stubbs becomes virtually paranoiac, claiming not only that everyone else is looking for what this charmed couple has found (and that most of them never will locate it), but that every friend he has really only wants to steal her away: "They'd give the world and all they own / For just one moment we have known."

The source of his paranoia comes clear soon enough. He's not a healthy Love Man (like Otis Redding) but a desperate Love Addict. And Bernadette is not his lover but a definition of self, their relationship not nurturing but perpetually inflammatory. Even his praise for Bernadette smacks of a junkie's self-justification. And so, when his voice breaks close to a sob as he implores his beloved to "keep on lovin' me," Stubbs speaks as nothing more than a guy craving a fix. Other men just want Bernadette; Stubbs needs her "to live."

Engulfed and trapped by the power of his own passions, needing what even Bernadette cannot ultimately provide (the very peace of mind he claims to have found yet sings as if he would never recognize if it showed up), Levi Stubbs becomes a symbol of every guy who tried to find outside himself what can only grow internally. If the potency of his embroilment at first seems seductive, what echoes is the final line, the truth he can't keep from expressing: "And Bernadette, you mean more to me / Than a woman was ever meant to mean." The man reaching out just two hits before has now succumbed to the dark side of what lurks in the shadows of love.

38 SHE LOVES YOU, The Beatles
Produced by George Martin; written by John Lennon and Paul McCartney
Swan 4152   1964   *Billboard:* #1 (2 weeks)

The Beatles arrived full-fledged. You could argue that they grew more sophisticated as the years went by, but not that they got a whole lot "better" because rock and roll doesn't get better than this. (You need the single or the CD to prove it, though. It sounds awful in LP stereo.)

"She Loves You" is the Beatles song with the "Yeah, yeah, yeah" chorus that nonbelievers made fun of when they first hit the States. Of course, any rock fan would understand that the exuberance of "yeah, yeah, yeah" is the whole essence of the form. As millions took it to heart, it was "She Loves You" more than any other record which established the Beatles as the soul of pop culture.

Yet the record isn't without darker nuances. What Lennon sings boils down to a warning to his friend: You'd better appreciate this woman's love, because if you don't, *I will*. As for art, this is the first Beatles song that Bob Dylan could have sung; it's tricky, bluesy, and well-written enough for *Blonde on Blonde*.

Yeah, yeah, yeah, *yeah*.

39 OH PRETTY WOMAN, Roy Orbison with the Candymen
Produced by Fred Foster; written by Roy Orbison and William Dees
Monument 851   1964   *Billboard:* #1 (3 weeks)

For those fully familiar with Roy's physical and spiritual persona, the image of the guy as a trolling stud—"Guess I'll go on home, it's late / There'll be tomorrow night . . ."—is more than faintly ludicrous, far better suited to David Lee Roth's latter-day macho routine (when Van Halen had a hit with the song in 1982).

But that doesn't mean that "Pretty Woman" isn't fully congruent with the rest of Orbison's work. For one thing, he imagines that the pretty woman may be in exactly the same condition he's in in almost every one of his great songs: "lonely, just like me." For another, there's a recurring motif in his lyrics in which Roy looks (and usually, *sounds*) like he's losing the girl but in fact, he's winning her ("Running Scared") or, as in "Falling," realizing that he's actually gotten his hands on the goods by accident. And that's exactly what happens at the end of "Pretty Woman." It's just that it happens without the Big O's usual completely abject presentation of his own humiliation; he's practically laughing at himself by the end, when she turns and comes back to him.

A greater mystery is *why*. I mean, he hasn't even *met* the girl, only *seen* her this once, his first outward reaction on seeing her is a lewd "Mercy!" and his second a tigerish growl, and she's supposed to buy "I need you / I'll treat you right"?

Nah. She came back for the same reason you did. That bass line's irresistible.

40 I CAN SEE FOR MILES, The Who
Produced by Kit Lambert; written by Pete Townshend
Decca 32206   1967   *Billboard: #9*

The glory of the Who was its creation of a sound that was fundamentally physical—so loud it hurt, so big it was scary, as thick as it was sharp. At best, the quartet performed like a single rough beast, grabbing its quarry by the throat and not stopping until blood ran.

"I Can See for Miles" *is* the Who's best: thunderous Keith Moon drums, a Townshend guitar line that starts out like an earthquake and finishes like a razor. The record develops in surges of pure energy, drums and guitar crashing and slashing in a duel to the break, where they simply strip whatever rational sense the song makes to shreds, as if to say: If it doesn't hurt, it doesn't count.

41 WHAT'D I SAY, Ray Charles
Produced by Ahmet Ertegun and Jerry Wexler; written by Ray Charles
Atlantic 2031   1959   *Billboard: #6*

The feel comes from gospel but the resulting witty, elegant essay on rhythm and sex and why they're inseparable is purely pagan. Indeed, if there really is such a thing as the Platonic Ideal, somewhere on Olympus sits an image of Groove which consists of Ray's piano part and his grunt-and-groan exchanges with the Raelettes. This is it: everything nonessential stripped away, as a generation of drag racers knows better than anyone else.

42 LONELY TEARDROPS, Jackie Wilson
Arranged and conducted by Dick Jacobs and Milton DeLugg; written by Berry Gordy Jr. and Tyrone Carlo [Billy Davis]
Brunswick 55105   1958   *Billboard: #7*

A parable of show business: About 1955, Berry Gordy Jr. went bankrupt running a Detroit record store that reflected his taste (jazz) at the expense of the popular lust (rhythm and blues). As a result, he had to go to work in an auto factory. As a way out, Gordy got together after work with Billy Davis and abandoned art for mammon by writing pop songs. Davis adopted the pseudonym Tyrone Carlo, but was up-front enough about what he was doing to contact his cousin, Jackie Wilson, who'd recently left Billy Ward and the Dominoes. They immediately came up with "Reet Petite," a song only Wilson, as agile vocally as he was physically, could have sung properly.

The team stayed together for a series of hits, of which "Lonely Teardrops" is the most splendid. It is the one Wilson arrangement of the fifties sufficiently spare to get every detail right: the Latin rhythm buoyed by pizzicato strings, the female chorus chanting "Say you will," the tambourine backbeat, Wilson's own spectacular vocal flourishes (never knew "home" had four syllables, didja?).

As a result of "Lonely Teardrops," which he probably thought was hackwork, Berry Gordy became both an artist and the richest black man in American history. Twenty years later, Jackie Wilson, who made many hits, some art, but not much money, collapsed onstage while singing the line "My heart is crying . . ." from "Lonely Teardrops." He never recovered.

43 ONE FINE DAY, The Chiffons
Produced by Bright Tunes Productions [The Tokens]; written by Gerry Goffin and Carole King
Laurie 3179   1963   *Billboard:* #5

Girl group records were supposed to be ready-made to a formula but not this much. Carole King cut the track with Little Eva, then gave it to the Tokens when they came looking for a sequel to "He's So Fine," and they just erased Eva and inserted the Chiffons. It was a great trade because, good as she was, Eva could never have matched the bright and tremulous lead vocal, which is perfectly suited to one of the ultimate female fantasies: Girl imagines guy will return to her because what he *really* wants is to settle down. Ha—except that when she sings "Oooh," you want her as bad as you wished she really wanted you.

44 UPTIGHT (EVERYTHING'S ALRIGHT), Little Stevie Wonder
Produced by Hank Cosby, William Stevenson, and Clarence Paul; written by Hank Cosby, Stevie Judkins [Wonder], and Sylvia Moy
Tamla 54124   1965   *Billboard:* #3

One of the greatest music videos I've ever seen was a Disney cartoon featuring Donald Duck in a jealous rage because Daisy was being wooed by some mallard Lothario. Set to "Uptight," the video winds up with

Donald in a total spitting frenzy as Daisy and her new beau enter a tunnel of love. What makes it so exciting isn't Donald's lunacy but the wildness of Stevie's music, the pure surge of magical Motown mechanics: cutting guitar, rolling bass, and thundering drums augmented by braying brass. Stevie, all of fifteen years old, sputters almost as incoherently as Donald. It took me about fifteen years to figure out that he was singing "Got empty pockets, you see, I'm a poor man's son," because he sings the whole line as if it was one word. And he pushes that hard for almost the whole song; there are other lines here that will *never* be translated, because he might as well be speaking in tongues that only he and that adrenalin addict playing drums could ever hope to comprehend.

On the other hand, some things require no translation. Like that nasty little Donald-like laugh—"Ah ha ha, *hah*"—Stevie cuts loose at the end. It perfectly prefigures Johnny Rotten at the beginning of "Anarchy in the U.K."

Stevie does want some things to be understood, so he slows down just enough to let his motto slide home: "She says no one is better than I / And I know, I'm just an average guy."

Like hell.

45 LITTLE RED CORVETTE, Prince
Written and produced by Prince
Warner Bros. 29746   1983   *Billboard:* #6

Prince so often portrays himself as a misfit eccentric that he makes it easy to forget that all the best things he does are steeped in thirty or forty years of tradition, encompassing Chuck Berry, Little Richard, Elvis Presley, James Brown, Bob Dylan, Marvin Gaye, John Lennon, Michael Jackson, and Sly and the Family Stone just for starters. He works a kind of rarefied musical mathematics, using those predecessors as theorems and integers for himself to manipulate. The eccentric genius part is that Prince has developed a formula that only he can make work so absolutely but that all the rest of dance-rock must reckon with constantly.

"Little Red Corvette" taps into the side of that equation which stems from Berry, Richard, Dylan, and Lennon, conveyed with a brand of lustful glee that's all Prince. He's celebrated for his musical innovations, but here, the music—especially the wash of organ that runs throughout—is just a skeleton on which to hang wild sexual metaphors sung with snake-oil charm.

The metaphors are cars and (Trojan) horses, romantic fidelity as code for sexual staying power. By themselves, the lyrics are bluntly sexist. (Tempered only by the fact that Prince, as rock's greatest narcissist since Little Richard, may be singing to himself anyhow.) But Prince also saves himself by creating a mood that's less raging than insistent. You could even call it wistful. And that's where the music comes in, particularly the heartrending guitar solo that bursts from the bridge.

As a graph of sexual excitement, "Little Red Corvette" can't be beaten; certainly nobody has ever brought anything half so explicit so close to the top of the charts. It's one long build to the explosive coda which ends with long wails from both Prince and his guitar as the drums pound the message home. If this doesn't meet your definition of orgasmic, pity your partner.

46 THE TRACKS OF MY TEARS, The Miracles
Produced by Smokey Robinson; written by Smokey Robinson, Warren Moore, and Marvin Tarplin
Tamla 54118   1965   *Billboard:* #16

Though he was black and indubitably one of the enduring performers of his era, Smokey Robinson wasn't really a soul singer. His singing was informed by doo-wop and R&B, but there was little gospel in it; he always remained smoother, more controlled, an unruffled ballad singer, Motown's answer to Bing Crosby.

Robinson's talents as songwriter, arranger, and producer far surpass his vocal ability anyway. Typically, it's the things that set up the singing that make his records memorable. With its crying lead and doo-wopping vocal background, "The Tracks of My Tears" is a throwback to the days of R&B smoothies like Clyde McPhatter. What brings it up to date are the details: huge drums, a lovely guitar line by cowriter Marv Tarplin, sharp horns, hi-fi dynamics. The lyrics might be flimsy if their rhyme scheme weren't so intricate. "My smile is my makeup I wear since my breakup with you" is tremendous not for what it says but because it *sings*. If you're going to be the coolest crooner around, it helps to know how to craft such material. Only one guy did.

47 BLUEBERRY HILL, Fats Domino
Produced by Dave Bartholomew; written by Al Lewis,
Larry Stock, and Vincent Rose
Imperial 5407   1956   *Billboard: #2*

"Blueberry Hill" may be a standard but it's hard to believe that any
other performer could have found in it the excuse for sly lasciviousness
that Fats did. And it's surely true that nobody else could have made
that sly lasciviousness seem so harmless as this jaunty Creole pianist,
who owned an accent so thick that Mick Jagger once said he perceived
it as a vow to be misunderstood. Don't discount the band, either: the
very sonority of Dave Bartholomew's arrangements let Fats get over
on Top 40 radio with sexually subversive sentiments whose appeal hasn't
yet been topped.

48 LIVE TO TELL, Madonna
Produced by Madonna, Patrick Leonard, Stephen Bray; written
by Madonna and Pat Leonard
Sire 28717   1986   *Billboard: #1 (1 week)*

If there weren't such massive prejudice against Madonna's overconfident displays of her sexuality, "Live to Tell" would be ranked among
the greatest pop songs written in the past decade, a penetrating psychological portrait of what psychoanalyst Alice Miller calls *The Drama
of the Gifted Child*, and a great reworking of one of the major undis-
cussed themes in contemporary pop music: spiritual abandonment, lack
of nurture, and their consequences.

The archetype of such songs is "The Great Pretender" but Madonna's lyric blows past it in the first three lines ("I have a tale to tell
/ Sometimes it gets so hard / To hide it well"), and moves on to portray
the entire complex of deceit and self-betrayal inherent in such a mental
climate. Far more powerful in its claustrophobia than *At Close Range*,
the Sean Penn/Christopher Walken film it served as a theme, "Live to
Tell" uses Pat Leonard's brilliant keyboard and synthesizer work, a
funk guitar, and a mixture of synthesized and real drumming to create
an atmosphere so soaked in the torture and dread surrounding all kinds
of child abuse that by the time you reach the bridge, you might be
reliving your worst waking nightmare.

Madonna releases the tension with a gorgeous bridge that represents
some kind of internal dialogue within the song's already internalized
structure. Far beyond such travesties as "Dear Mr. Jesus" or even a

sensitive outsider's look at child abuse like "Luka," "Live to Tell" penetrates to the very heart of a basic human mystery: How parents can so readily brutalize their own. And while it certainly doesn't solve the riddle, it does what art is supposed to do—achieves a kind of resolution within the boundaries of that mystery and then moves on.

Madonna has earned her right to party.

49 NEED YOUR LOVE SO BAD, Little Willie John
Produced by Henry Glover; written by Little Willie John
King 4841   1956   Did not make pop chart

We all know by now that success doesn't insure happiness. But how can anyone sound so abject as Little Willie John does here, on the follow-up to his biggest hit, "Fever"? Don't tell me it's just that Peggy Lee ripped him off with a version about one hundredth as good (and still pretty decent), or even that she got paid a lot, while he got paid hardly at all.

No, this man's malaise is more profound by far. He sings as if in certain knowledge of his own ultimate fate—dead before he hit forty, coughing his lungs out in a Washington State Penitentiary where he was doing time for homicide.

Oh, he just says that he's despondent because he's without a lover. But we've heard that song and dance before. Little Willie John is talking about the nether reaches of human misery, in a voice absolutely creaking in agony. Part of it might have to do with the fact that he's illiterate— "Write it on a paper so it can be read to me," he cries matter-of-factly— but mostly it's just that night is coming on, and he's going to have to get through it by himself again. If he can.

50 HEAT WAVE, Martha and the Vandellas
Produced by Brian Holland and Lamont Dozier; written by
Brian Holland, Lamont Dozier, and Eddie Holland
Gordy 7022   1963   Billboard: #4

"Heat Wave" revolves around a very basic question: "Has high blood pressure got a hold on me or is this the way love's supposed to be?" By the end, Martha knows that there is no answer: "Can't explain it, don't understand it, ain't never felt like this before." But her description of the symptoms and Holland-Dozier-Holland's use of the Motown house band as an enactment of the fever defined this particular contagion for a generation. Personally, I'd be willing to endure hospitalization for a few weeks just to feel the way that baritone sax sounds.

51 BACK IN THE U.S.A., Chuck Berry
Produced by Leonard Chess; written by Chuck Berry
Chess 1729   1959   *Billboard: #37*

Before getting all heated up about Chuck's wonderful celebration of America, it would be wise to remember that this is a record by a man who'd be sent to prison on a trumped up Mann Act charge less than a year after it hit the charts. Thus, "Back in the U.S.A." 's hooting chorus—"Un-un-huh, woo yeah"—isn't joyous so much as sardonic. The most delicious moment comes when Chuck sings "lookin' *hard* for a drive-in, searchin' for a corner cafe / Where hamburgers sizzle on an open grill night and day." He stresses "hard" because it was so tough to find one that would serve a black man. Maybe that's why, after a scintillating opening guitar run, Chuck basically turns the song over to pianist Johnny Johnson and drummer Fred Below.

On the other hand, I've been traveling for better than twenty years, and I've never returned from overseas (or even Canada) without the first two verses of "Back in the U.S.A." echoing in my head. There may be a whole generation of American travelers who share similar experiences and not because we entirely miss the point. The irony of the performance is that Berry never lets you be sure that he's coming to grips with the contradictory mess we've made of things. In the end, thanks to Johnson, Below, and that vocal, though, this is a great record even if it's about nothing more than feeling homesick.

52 CHAIN OF FOOLS, Aretha Franklin
Produced by Jerry Wexler; written by Don Covay
Atlantic 2464   1967   *Billboard: #2*

Aretha at the end of her rope. Growling guitar and bass, drums that shake the house, and backing vocals like a nagging conscience don't distract her; they just concentrate her wrath. With its imprecations and dire warnings, its catalog of intolerable sins, this is probably the closest Aretha's ever come to the kind of preaching which made her father, C.L., a gospel-circuit legend. When Franklin sings "Chainchainchain-chain," until the words lose their literal sense and become just sounds—

she might as well be singing "Janejanejanejane"—she's created a Top 40 equivalent of talking in tongues.

53 SINCE I LOST MY BABY, The Temptations
Produced by Smokey Robinson; written by Warren Moore and Smokey Robinson
Gordy 7043   1965   *Billboard:* #17

A neglected Motown masterwork. Smokey Robinson's lyric conveys everything, including the weather. But if only Smokey could have forged such forlorn wordplay ("But fun is a bore / And with money I'm poor") into a pop song, only David Ruffin could have rendered those lines with so much gritty conviction. The effortless way that Ruffin swings from the last line of the bridge ("I really really care") back to the far different rhythm of the verse by slipping in a quick "Ooh," is something no other soul singer could have pulled off so smoothly while still sounding so tough.

"Since I Lost My Baby" is perhaps Smokey Robinson's greatest production, certainly his most massive. The constant reiteration of the melody by the strings, the vibrant bass, the timing of the Temptations' backing vocals, and the brilliant commentary from the piano all lend a sense of groove, drama, and majesty.

54 HIT THE ROAD JACK, Ray Charles
Produced by Sid Feller; written by Percy Mayfield
ABC-Paramount 10244   1961   *Billboard:* #1 (1 week)

"Some people will think it's funny. Others are gonna think it's real," Percy Mayfield told Ray Charles when he brought him this high-spirited modernization of "What'd I Say." On the evidence, Ray had it both ways. "Oh woman, oh woman, don't treat me so mean, you're the meanest old woman I've ever seen," he chants, but he's smiling when he sings it, caught up in the glory of the groove, playing off the gritty (unfortunately uncredited) female responses, just enjoying the hell out of every gutted-out "Whaat'd you say!"

55 THE LOCO-MOTION, Little Eva
Produced by Gerry Goffin; written by Carole King and Gerry Goffin
Dimension 1000   1962   Billboard: #1 (1 week)

Not a song. A sound. Made by one overexcited teenager, some hand-claps, a baritone sax drone—there's a triangle in there, and probably a piano, somebody (for all I know, Eva double-tracked, but maybe it's Carole King herself) chanting "Come on baby." The details (including Eva's status as Goffin and King's babysitter) are as inconsequential as the lyrics. What matters is the wholeness of the thing, the unity of the little sounds that add up to one big sound that won't let you sit still.

56 GET OFF OF MY CLOUD, The Rolling Stones
Produced by Andrew Loog Oldham; written by Mick Jagger and Keith Richards
London 9792   1965   Billboard: #1 (2 weeks)

This "Satisfaction" sequel is basically just a knockoff. So what makes it great? The most explosive drumming Charlie Watts (or damn near anybody else) has ever done; a lyric that's twice as funny and just as true as its model; production so dense you could fall into it and never resurface—or want to.

57 DANCE TO THE MUSIC, Sly and the Family Stone
Written and produced by Sly Stone
Epic 10256   1968   Billboard: #8

I first heard "Dance to the Music" in a high school lunch line when a friend thrust a pocket-size transistor at my ear. "You won't believe *this*," he said. Who could've? Except for "Papa's Got a Brand New Bag," no great single has broken so many rules and reestablished them in its own image. Sly found a funky equivalent of the white rock artiness of the Who and the Yardbirds without losing a shred of R&B's danceability.

The lyric simply describes what's happening in the song, starting from scratch and adding one instrument at a time to build up a powerhouse of psychedelic R&B, replete with call-and-response vocals, briefly interjected solos, interspersed cries of surprised glee, and a beat that bulldozes everything in its path. It's all so joyous that it's easy to miss the "message" declared by horn players Cynthia Robinson and Jerry Martini: "All the squares go home!"

"Dance to the Music" arrived at the instant when black and white pop achieved their greatest closeness and began to move apart again, after more than a decade of frequently harmonious intersection. Since then, from Kool and the Gang to Prince, Sly and "Dance to the Music" have never been far away, and as the nineties open, their influence on pop dance music is as strong as anyone's—even James Brown's.

58 HE'S SO FINE, The Chiffons
Produced by Bright Tunes Productions [The Tokens]; written by Ronnie Mack
Laurie 3152   1963   *Billboard:* #1 (4 weeks)

Beyond "doo-lang, doo-lang," there's a special yearning in the lead vocal that stands in contrast to the rhumbalike rhythm established by the Drifters'-like *baion* bass. The lyric is purely vernacular, and pretty witty ("Sooner or later . . . hope it's not later") but phrased so flowingly that some phrases ("But then again if he's that shy, he can't shy away forever") sound like unknown single words written in a separate tongue.

59 THEN HE KISSED ME, The Crystals
Produced by Phil Spector; written by Phil Spector, Ellie Greenwich, and Jeff Barry
Philles 115   1963   *Billboard:* #6

As a kid, the way people moved in movies like *West Side Story* struck me as weird. The real teenagers who strolled the blocks near my house moved so much more fluidly and elegantly. The tableaus they set up were finer poses and better thought-out. Where Jerome Robbins made you understand something about the possibilities of human muscles, those kids back in the neighborhood made you understand everything about passion and hope.

"Then He Kissed Me" captures what they looked like in its opening lines, sung at a stately cadence:

Well, he walked up to me and he asked me if I wanted to dance
He looked kinda nice and so I said I might take a chance.

Hearing the Crystals sing those words, you can feel not only the size of the event, but exactly how he moved, slinking his way across the floor, stopping, turning, proposing as elegantly as any cadet, and envision just how she responded, with a mixture of delicacy and suppressed eagerness, each holding back smiles of relief, both hearts jangling like the busy castanets and triangles in the record's background.

Phil Spector sets the song as if it were a jewel, with the gorgeous melody established on guitar and carried away with tympani and strings and an orchestral bridge that tangibly evokes that first dance. It's no wonder that neither Brian Wilson nor Bruce Springsteen could resist covering the song, and it's no wonder that they could never match the original.

Never, because no man could make a mere kiss so meaningful. When she sings, "He kissed me in a way that I've never been kissed before / He kissed me in a way that I wanna be kissed for evermore," what you want to know, first time through, is *how*. But after a while, you realize that the real question may be *where*. There's a taboo being broken here, and it's far more meaningful than the line crossed by the Crystals' overrated "He Hit Me (And It Felt Like a Kiss)." As in Aretha Franklin's "A Natural Woman," the real dimensions of female sexuality remain unspoken, but they're hidden only if you refuse to pay attention.

And that's probably why they had to get married in the last verse.

60 ROLL OVER BEETHOVEN, Chuck Berry
Produced by Leonard Chess; written by Chuck Berry
Chess 1626   1956   *Billboard:* #29

Maximum rock and roll militance from its opening, a guitar burst played as impossibly fast as Jerry Lee Lewis's piano on "Whole Lotta Shakin'." Though this was only his second single, Chuck already displays tremendous arrogance, asserting that his music is not only the equal of Beethoven's and Tchaikovsky's, but something that would surprise and delight them. Listening to him recite the epidemiology of rockin' pneumonia and boogie-woogie flu, it's hard to find any way to imagine a cure and impossible to want one.

61 MAKING LOVE (AT THE DARK END OF THE STREET), Clarence Carter

Produced by Rick Hall; written by Chips Moman, Dan Penn, and
Clarence Carter
Atlantic 2605   1969   Did not make pop chart

In Southern soul the goal is to mingle the sexual into the spiritual so
thoroughly that they can no longer be distinguished. No one has ever
essayed the task more outrageously than Carter does in these four
minutes of preaching and thirty seconds of singing.

He begins at the beginning: With the birds and the bees, hilariously
contrasting the sexual behavior of animals with the less straightforward
procreative habits of human beings. "We like to get ourse'ves 'bout
fifty cent worth of gas. And we like to drive waaay down a country
road somewhere. Awww, and we like to make love in a *car*, children,"
says Carter, his voice rising to shout and then subsiding into one of his
patented leering chuckles: "Heh, heh, heh."

The music (orchestrated Muscle Shoals soul) swells; clown-time is
over. Carter describes the deceptive habits of folks, male and female,
who like to "slip around." Piano, horns, and drums practically sob with
the resonance of his voice as he intones the final lines of his homily. I
have heard Carter's spiel perhaps two hundred times and every time
he reaches the climax, the hair on the back of my neck begins to tickle
and goose bumps break out. It's not what he says so much as how.

"Well, I tell ya, it makes no difference if you came from the city.
And it don't matter if you came from the country," he intones, his
voice taking on even more of the preacher's rumble. "And some of
you out there within the sound of my voice may have come from the
sub-urbs. But I'd like to suggest to ya one of the best places I know
where you can make love. And that place is . . .

> At the dark end of the street
> That's where we always meet
> Hiding in the shadows where we don't belong
> Livin' in darkness, Oh Lord, to hide our wrong . . ."

The sound seems to blossom directly from his chest, an explosion of
feeling so rich that mere flesh cannot contain it. And as he booms out
the song—a single verse, no more—Carter begins again to rant: "Don't
let 'em find us! I know they gonna catch us one day. It may not be
long—it may be sooner than we think. I know they gonna find us—
somewhere at the dark end of the street."

In its brilliant transition from the absurd to the profound, in its celebration of carnality and projection of abject fear, "Making Love (At the Dark End of the Street)" demolishes the concept of the cheating song. The infidelity about which Carter is singing might be sexual, but the compulsion to make and listen to such music stems from something even more primordial. That's why it can give you the shivers if you hear it in broad daylight, let alone the dead of night.

And yet, there is nothing more absurd in all of rock and roll than that long drawn-out introduction. Carter hams it up, too, milking every line, exaggerating his Southern dialect. Maybe the most mysterious part of "Making Love" is the way that his travesty sets up the emotive power of the singing. Somehow, that ridiculous little story is indispensable to being captivated by the music.

I still can't figure out how Carter managed to get from one end of that recitation to the other without cracking up, or for that matter how Rick Hall ever had the nerve to put out such a totally bizarre recording. All that's certain is that dozens of singers have tried themselves against "Dark End of the Street," but none of them have ever touched the depths that Clarence Carter found in it while skirting as close to caricature as anybody in soul history. That might be the spookiest part of it all.

62 RAVE ON, Buddy Holly
Produced by Norman Petty; written by Sonny West, Bill Tilghman, and Norman Petty
Coral 61985   1958   *Billboard:* #37

Epiphany with hiccups and electric guitar. If you don't get it, just follow the instructions till you're dizzy, then turn it up a little higher. It worked for Bobby Vee and Bob Dylan and it won't fail you.

63 GOOD ROCKIN' TONIGHT, Elvis Presley
Produced by Sam Phillips; written by Roy Brown
Sun 210   1954   Did not make pop charts

"That's All Right, Mama," Elvis's first single, might have been a fluke. But "Good Rockin' Tonight" was more of the same, and better, establishing that all concerned—Scotty Moore, Bill Black, Sam Phillips, but especially Elvis himself—knew exactly what they were up to and, indeed, had already created a new and improved model. Thirty years later, "Good Rockin' Tonight" still sounds like what's about to happen.

Elvis wrote no songs, and none of his Sun Records material was written for him. In fact, the best of his Sun songs had already been hits for others. Of them all, only "Good Rockin' Tonight" was already great, having been done superbly in the late forties both by author Brown and by Wynonie Harris, the most famous blues shouter of the period.

If you're sufficiently familiar with Brown's style, you'll easily spot his influence. But it's still hard to believe that this is the same song, not because Elvis's version is particularly country and God knows, not because he rocks harder—try rocking harder than Wynonie Harris and you'll rupture something.

Some of the differences are in the arrangement, with Bill Black's rubbery bass and Scotty Moore's stinging guitar replacing the original, horn-based jump blues patterns. But the difference that counts is Elvis. This was only his second single, but he'd already established his weird mixture of ferocious self-confidence and complete easefulness, and he sings "Good Rockin' Tonight" as if he's inventing it. Which for all practical purposes he is. By the time he gets to the repetitions of "rock" which close out the record, Elvis has crossed over into glory.

64 I SAW HER STANDING THERE, The Beatles
Produced by George Martin; written by John Lennon and Paul McCartney
Capitol 5112   1964   *Billboard:* #14

If the Beatles had never made it in America, they would still be revered by collectors as that weird group from Liverpool who made a handful of great early sixties singles. The most famous side would be the one that opens "One, two, three, *FUH*."

What audacity, critics in an alternate universe would say. To open a record with that most taboo word in 1964! And they would go on to recount the band's brilliant primitivism, its skillful parlaying of musical building blocks derived from Motown, the Brill Building, and Roy Orbison's Nashville-Mexican harmonies, as well as (without any concept of the woodshedding in Hamburg, of course) the music's sheer sweaty drive.

Go listen to "I Saw Her Standing There" and you'll hear all this, and more. Which is exactly why the Beatles could never have been an obscure, one-shot group. They were too good, too ambitious, and anyway, that's an out-of-breath "four."

65 WHEN SOMETHING IS WRONG WITH MY BABY, Sam and Dave

Produced by Jim Stewart; written by Isaac Hayes and David Porter
Stax 210   1967   *Billboard: #42*

A landmark in the history of onomatopoeia. Sam and Dave welded themselves in sound as strongly as their song insists one must be joined with one's baby. The irony, of course, is that Sam and Dave couldn't stand one another. Nevertheless, no duo ever harmonized better than these two, and that's even more evident on this molasses-tempo ballad than on their bigger, faster hits. The vocal arrangement is pure gospel, but the solemn bass, ostinato piano, organ wash, and sonorous horn chords (which Aretha swiped for the bridge of "Respect") are the essence of the Stax/Volt sound. The result is conversational but never casual, right down to the cries of "Sure 'nuff!" and "Now!"

66 IN DREAMS, Roy Orbison

Produced by Fred Foster; written by Roy Orbison
Monument 806   1963   *Billboard: #7*

The first rock and roll dream song may well have been Elvis's "Mystery Train." But rock's most important dreamer was Roy Orbison, whose songs are suffused with fantasies in which his imagination deceives, betrays, and entices him into situations as threatening as they are compelling. In "Leah," "Dream Baby," "Blue Bayou," and several others, a dreamer awakens to find that what he's imagined true is not and is left at the end to live a life less complete than the one in his head.

It isn't surprising that there's a Freudian aspect to all this. Orbison was different than any other rock star of his period. He was relatively middle-class, college-educated and on easier terms with more kinds of music—opera and Mexican ballad singing, for instance—than any of his peers. His songs possess a psychological complexity that is commonly believed not to have existed in pop music until Dylan and the Beatles.

"In Dreams" is certainly the greatest of all Orbison's dream songs. Even David Lynch's seriocomic exploitation of it through Dean Stockwell and Dennis Hopper in *Blue Velvet* has not robbed the original of its evocative power. Actually, Stockwell's scene identifies the song's surface attraction, its almost morbid atmosphere stemming from the kitsch of the opening recitative and the overblown string arrangement.

The song's sinister side is also caught, when Hopper later grabs Kyle McLaughlin by the face and snarls the central lines into his mug, spitting the monosyllables out one by one: "In dreams . . . I *walk* with you / In dreams . . . I *talk* with you / In dreams . . . you're *mine*, ALL of the time."

But Lynch misses Orbison's deeper, more spiritual side. In the remake Roy cut for the movie, it's written out of the arrangement. The new production flattens the beat, leaving the song engulfed in its own pretensions. But in the original, the Mexican rhythm and Orbison's *ranchera* phrasing redeem the kitsch. When Orbison swings from chorus to verse, his vibrato and melisma are so fluid and graceful that he might as well be singing in Spanish rather than his more guttural native tongue. And on the climactic line "Only in dreams," he sings somewhere between *ranchera* and a cowboy yodel, the twin products of the Texas plains where he grew up.

In the realm of pop radio, this approach is positively exotic. And within its framework, Orbison creates a moody landscape suffused with imagery that's as much a metaphor for psychic disturbance as the lovelorn saga it pretends to be. In this light, "In Dreams" shows its true face and reveals its full power, even if that power threatens conventional notions of what "ought" to be contained in a pop song.

"I'll let you be in my dream if I can be in yours," Bob Dylan once sang. A generation of bright college kids thought that was an attractive offer. Had they paid more attention to Roy Orbison, they would have rethought the deal.

67 THE WIND, Nolan Strong and the Diablos
Produced by Jack and Devora Brown; written by Nolan Strong and the Diablos
Fortune 511   1954   Did not make pop charts

A guitar and bass chime the intro with *Twilight Zone* melodrama, and then the bass voice announces "Wind, wind—blow, wind." A falsetto trills wordless notes over the top. At last an unbelievably high, slightly quavering male voice begins, measuring the cadence like a man conserving heartbeats:

When the cool summer breeze sends a chill down my spine
When I long for my love's sweet caress
I know she has gone but my love lingers on
In a dream that the winds bring to me

After the second verse, the music begins to drop out until all that's left is the bass chanting "Wind, wind" underneath the corniest recitation you've ever heard. Strong speaks in a surreally wimpy voice that nevertheless possesses a certain kind of power. "Darling, when a star falls, I want you to remember," Nolan Strong declares. "And darling, when I see lovers making love, then, I long for you."

"The Wind," in other words, is a prophecy of Michael Jackson twenty years before he came along. If it had arrived in a meteorite shower, and there are times when you swear it should have, it couldn't be any spookier.

68 ON BROADWAY, The Drifters
Produced by Jerry Leiber and Mike Stoller; written by Cynthia Weill, Barry Mann, Jerry Leiber, and Mike Stoller
Atlantic 2182   1963   *Billboard:* #9

A cutting guitar that could have only been played by Leiber and Stoller's sorcererlike apprentice, Phil Spector, slices between Rudy Lewis's despairing lead and the Latin percussion underneath. But it's the way the guitar plays off against horns and strings at the bridge that persuades you that this kid really will do anything to make it—and that the search is its own reward. The facts may be otherwise, but the atmosphere here is beyond argument.

69 GLORIA, Them
Produced by Tommy Scott; written by Van Morrison
Parrot 9727   1965   *Billboard:* #71

One of the few rock songs that's actually as raunchy as its reputation—unless you think she's going up to his room for a chat. Van Morrison sings "Gloria" in a lustful croak, like a demented, horny frog, but it wouldn't mean much without the wicked guitar, reputedly played by Jimmy Page, which completes an air as exotic as it is erotic. (Appropriately, given what Morrison—and Page for that matter—were to get up to later.) The best truly dirty record ever.

70 GOOD GOLLY MISS MOLLY, Little Richard
Produced by Bumps Blackwell and Art Rupe; written by
John Marascalco and Bumps Blackwell
Specialty 624   1958   *Billboard:* #10

It doesn't get much more basic than this: a young, loud voice shouting
above piano, guitar, bass, and drums playing triplet rhythms above a
set of riffing saxophones. It doesn't get much better, either, partly
because the song's so damn wild, mostly because Richard's vocal is so
stunningly present. When he hits that awesome "wooooo" just before
the sax solo, the mike sounds like it's going to shatter. The effect is so
immediate that you want to get up and play it again and again, just to
see how long he can get away with it. So you do.

71 EVERY BREATH YOU TAKE, The Police
Produced by Hugh Padgham and the Police; written by Sting
A&M 2542   1983   *Billboard:* #1 (8 weeks)

"Every Breath You Take" belongs in that category of singles that
announce themselves as classics from the first time you hear them. In
my case, that was in heightened circumstances: driving home on a
Sunday evening, listening to a black-oriented radio station.

You didn't need to hear the singing long to know that this was no
black group (the accent is too flattened, the phrasing too free of melisma), and not having a clue to who it might be, I took a guess. Jackson
Browne, I decided, had finally come up with the grand psycho-political
metaphor, an image that pointed the barrel at Reagan, Thatcher, Mondale, Botha, D'Aubisson, Pol Pot—every traitor of the day. Though I
felt like an idiot a day later when I learned who was really singing,
once you hear the political dimension of "Every Breath You Take,"
that part of its meaning is undeniable, no matter how frequently Sting
speaks of its psychological and spiritual connotations. If he really believes in Jungian synchronicity, Sting must understand that he could
never have composed such a song without the presence of such mon-
strous public figures at the very center of current events. This is the
record that makes sense of Sting's work with Amnesty International
(even if he doesn't know it).

It's not simply as metaphor, of course, that "Every Breath You
Take" establishes itself as a permanent fixture in the pop pantheon.
The rolling bass line, Sting's cool, dry vocal, Andy Summers's precisely
plucked guitar part, and the remorseless *clop* of Stewart Copeland's

drums create an atmosphere in which that metaphor assumes a dimension just this side of terrifying. And the way the song pulls back, rejecting the heated rage that such betrayal seemingly deserves and instead serving revenge as it's meant to be consumed—with a cold, cold heart—is the most frightening facet of all.

72 STAND BY ME, Ben E. King
Produced by Jerry Leiber and Mike Stoller; written by
Ben E. King and Elmo Glick [Leiber and Stoller]
Atco 6203   1961   Billboard: #4

It's not hard to see how "Stand By Me" could reenter the Top Ten twenty-five years after it was first made. It's as timeless as a basic black dress. The theme was provided by gospel, the bass and percussion are Afro-Cuban. But the riffing cellos and soft quartet harmonies, the way the arrangement builds, adding instruments and growing more lush at each stage, is all pure Leiber-Stoller. Typically, it's also way ahead of its time, prefiguring key aspects of both Leiber-Stoller protégé Phil Spector and Motown's Holland-Dozier-Holland.

The lyric is so stark it seemed ancient when brand-new, especially with King bearing down on the poetic first lines as if the fate of the world depended upon them. What makes the performance unforgettable, though, is the way that King's intonation denies his own ritualistic protestations: "I won't cry, I won't cry," he cries, and unless he began sobbing like Johnny Ray, the contradiction couldn't be more complete. Yet holding back is King's triumph, for it's precisely by conveying the boundary between panic and restraint that "Stand By Me" achieves its unique unity of terror and reassurance.

73 PARTY LIGHTS, Claudine Clark
Written and produced by Claudine Clark
Chancellor 1113   1962   Billboard: #5

The musical highlights of Macon, Georgia, are but three but they're stupendous: Little Richard, James Brown, and Otis Redding. Then you can have "Party Lights," recorded by native Maconian Clark, for dessert.

Although Clark wrote, produced, and sang the song on her own, this is girl group music in form and spirit. Within the confines of that genre, it's extremely unusual to see a performer, much less a young unknown, granted so much responsibility. But this anomaly resolves itself when you learn that "Party Lights" began life as a quickie B side, hastily recorded to give Chancellor Records (home of Fabian, Frankie Avalon, and other vomitous muck) something to go along with the elaborately arranged (by soul veteran Jerry Ragavoy) A side, "Disappointed." Clark, a guitar and organ prodigy who left Macon to attend Philadelphia's Coombs College on a music scholarship, was being groomed as a pop diva in the Nancy Wilson/Dionne Warwick mold. "Party Lights" was a throwaway, so Chancellor not only let her do the work but keep the credit.

But "Disappointed" lived up to its name and within two weeks of its May 30 release, Chancellor was preparing to give up on promoting the record. Then a disc jockey flipped it over and his listeners flipped out. The label shifted its promotion to "Party Lights," which hit the *Billboard* Hot 100 chart for the first time (at Number 95) on June 30. For the next two months, it wended a tortuous path up the weekly listings, sometimes leaping fifteen notches, sometimes barely given a nudge. But it peaked at Number 5, making it one of the biggest surprise hits of the post-Presley, pre-Beatles era.

At least in retrospect, it's no surprise that "Party Lights" was a hit. The record opens in a thunderation of drums, with a girl group shrieking "I see the lights! I see the party lights!" Clark comes in with a voice that's like a prophesy of Aretha Franklin in its growly gospel overtones. The beat and the lyrics have their antecedents ("The Loco-Motion," "Do You Love Me," "Please Mr. Postman," "I Gotta Dance to Keep from Crying," "Having a Party") but Clark's shouting her guts out, as if all the ghosts of her hometown heroes had developed an anima for this hasty occasion. For sheer energy, "Party Lights" ranks as one of the greatest female cries of joy and frustration ever put to wax.

74 GOOD TIMES, Chic
Written and produced by Nile Rodgers and Bernard Edwards
Atlantic 3584   1979   *Billboard:* #1 (1 week)

Little Richard once threatened to call his autobiography "I Got What I Wanted But I Lost What I Had." Chic's story is quite the opposite. Guitarist Nile Rodgers and bassist Bernard Edwards began playing together in various New York-based soul and funk groups in 1970. By 1976, they'd met Tony Thompson, a like-minded drummer, and formed the Big Apple Band to play metalloid fusion-rock. But nobody in the record industry wanted to know about black guys bashing such heavy grooves. So they changed their name to Chic (Walter Murphy had already appropriated Big Apple for "A Fifth of Beethoven" anyway), added vocalists Norma Jean Thompson and Alfa Anderson and concocted a semiserious disco confection, "Dance Dance Dance (Yowsah Yowsah Yowsah)," which several labels rejected before Atlantic agreed to give it a shot. It sold a million copies in less than a month and established Chic—as the Edwards-Rodgers production team would be forever known—as one of the most creative and influential entities of the seventies.

"Good Times," which cost about five times as much to make, paid off in even greater sales success—not only for Chic but for the Sugar Hill Gang, which used the track as the basis for "Rapper's Delight," the first rap hit, and for Queen, whose "Another One Bites the Dust" completely ripped it off, right down to Edwards's imponderably liquid bass line. For a couple of years, Chic's grooves were everywhere, partly as a result of their outside productions ("Upside Down" for Diana Ross and "We Are Family" for Sister Sledge were the best) but also because rewriting Chic became almost as great a pastime of the late seventies as rewriting the Beatles was in the late sixties.

And no wonder. Edwards was one of the half-dozen most inventive electric bassists ever, the true successor of James Jamerson and Duck Dunn. Tony Thompson's drumming was as powerful as it was straight-ahead and with enough feel to land him art-rock and jazz work as well as dance sessions. Though Rodgers, separated from Edwards, could become so mechanical his work was almost brittle (listen to his production of David Bowie's *Let's Dance*), within Chic his guitar rode the bottom brilliantly. And though the focus was never really on them, the singers were among the most underrated that disco produced, lending soul to beats too often rendered heartlessly in other production schemes.

"Good Times" perfectly captures the heady, disintegrating atmosphere of New York in the late seventies, as both local and national government abandoned any hope of social equity and opened the door for the ruthless laissez-faire heyday of upper- and lower-class criminality that characterized the eighties. "Good Times! These . . . are . . . the . . . good . . . times . . . / Our . . . new . . . state . . . of . . . mind . . . ," sing Alfa Anderson and Norma Jean Thompson as if they've learned to grit their teeth by rote, while Rodgers's nasty guitar zips in and out like a premonition of the nasty crack-and-Contra era to come, and Edwards throbs underneath, imperturbable as he is implacable.

"Dance as desperation? Dance as survival? Or just useful noise?" asked critic Robert Christgau. Answer: All of the above.

75 DON'T WORRY BABY, The Beach Boys
Produced by Brian Wilson; written by Brian Wilson and Roger Christian
Capitol 5174   1964   Billboard: #24

Brian Wilson is most often celebrated for making a bunch of late sixties music nobody heard for twenty years and most weren't all that bowled over by when they did, while his best records, the Beach Boys hits of the early sixties, receive only generic critical comment—they're songs about cars, surfing, and girls, that's all. Yet Wilson was a kind of rock and roll genius not because he became a whiz at recording studio technique but because he managed to make songs about cars, surfing, girls, and the pursuit of the elusive abstraction called "fun" both personal and transcendent.

The Beach Boys early singles caught the spirit of middle-class America in the pivotal stages of post-World War II affluence. Derived in equal measure from the romantic teen fantasies of Phil Spector, from the more mocking scenarios of Chuck Berry, and from harmony groups ranging from the straight pop of the Four Freshmen to the pure R&B of Frankie Lymon and the Teenagers, those songs were not only filled with telling details—Wilson, a recluse himself, worked with lyricists who knew their stuff—but never ignored the downside of the dream. Songs like "Don't Worry Baby" set the stage for the latter-day eschatalogical ruminations of California singer/songwriters like Jackson Browne and even Randy Newman.

"Don't Worry Baby" is lush with echo and gorgeous open-throated background harmonies that set off a sweet tenor lead vocal by Wilson himself. The intro is pure Spector, as befits a song originally intended as the Ronettes' follow-up to "Be My Baby"; Hal Blaine drumbeats lead into surging harmonies, followed by a reverbless post-surf guitar slashing the meter in half.

If those are "Don't Worry Baby" 's roots, its lineage extends just as deeply into the future. Give it a country accent and you have an apotheosis of the seventies California rock epitomized by the Eagles. Similarly, Mike Love's doo-wop bass balanced by a choral backdrop drawn straight out of the Four Freshman handbook of harmonic corn sets the stage for Lindsey Buckingham's seventies arrangements for Fleetwood Mac.

With "Don't Worry Baby" Wilson casually overturns every convention of a genre he all but invented, turning melodramatic car crash numbers like "Dead Man's Curve" and "Tell Laura I Love Her" inside out. Rather than face death in order to prove his devotion or his cool, the singer is troubled because he's "shot [his] mouth off" about his car and now fears that he's going to be defeated in a drag race (and lose the car, not his life or his love). Rather than toughing it out, he confesses that he feels this foreboding *all the time*. It's a moment of male vulnerability that was probably unprecedented in rock and roll at that time, and one which laid the groundwork for every singer/songwriter confessional of the seventies. What rescues him from his own dread is his girl's reassurance, which she repeats to him in the title phrase. That's corny, too, but it's also extremely effective. Not to mention useful, and maybe even emotionally truthful.

76 54 46 (WAS MY NUMBER), Toots and the Maytals
Produced by Leslie Kong; written by Frederick [Toots] Hibbert
Beverly's (Jamaica) [no catalogue number]   1972
Did not make pop charts

If Otis Redding had been about a foot shorter and Jamaican, he'd have sounded exactly like Toots Hibbert. From the inception of reggae (which a Maytals song named) through the mid-seventies, Hibbert was the genre's greatest singer, combining licks learned from U.S. soul singers with his distinctively Jamaican dialect. In "54 46," he recounts his experiences during a two-year prison sentence for possession of marijuana that he received in 1970, when he was already one of the genre's major stars.

"54 46" is almost folkloric, opening with a Leadbelly-like evocation of a guard's cry that's neatly poised on the edge of incoherence, then quickly seguing into tight, intense call-and-response dance music. Hibbert declares himself innocent and condemns the whole self-perpetuating "justice" system with one perfectly stated, persistently reiterated fact: "54 46 was my number / Right now someone else has that number." The great parts, though, are the wordless chanting that occupies most of the song between the first verse and final chorus, and a giddy organ part that is the closest reggae has ever come to psychedelia.

77 WHITE LINES (DON'T DON'T DO IT), Grandmaster and Melle Mel

Produced by Sylvia Robinson, Melle Mel, and Joey Robinson Jr.;
written by Sylvia Robinson and Melvin Glover [Melle Mel]
Sugar Hill 465   1983   *Billboard:* #101

"White Lines" is a pure product of the recording studio, a piece of
music that couldn't conceivably have been created live because it relies
on a series of electronic effects that aren't available onstage. It could
also be described as a hip-hop novelty disc, because it's suffused with
aural and lyrical puns.

Grandmaster Flash and the Furious 5 made the first really great
rap record, "The Message," but "White Lines" beats it. Rather than
the bare-bones musical approach of their earlier records, Grandmaster
and Melle Mel build the sound back up around a jittery, obsessive bass/
drum pattern. When the bass hits its stride, heralded by the cry "Free
base!" the effect is a little like having a supersonic jet pass over your
house. Windows rattle, floors shake, children and small animals wail
and head for cover.

The topic is cocaine. "White Lines" is wholly immersed in drug
culture, its lyric steeped in an awareness of the similarities between
dope slang and music jargon. ("Free base" is the best example.) The
record covers the entire spectrum of cocaine culture, from its economics
and aesthetics to its pharmacological and sexual implications. Divining
the message is hopeless, however, because even though the verses condemn the drug world (including trenchant lines about the disparity in
the court system's treatment of street kid users and businessman dealers), in the end the singer admits that he gets high himself and that
what *really* bothers him is that the shit's so damn expensive. So, the
double negative in the subtitle says it straight.

However dubious its admonitory value, though, "White Lines"
illuminates its subject. The jagged, nervous beat and the chopped up
vocals are symptomatic, as are the musical devices. At high volume,
which is the way this music makes best sense, the tangible power residing
here becomes almost as oppressive, certainly as unavoidable, as the
drug plague itself. When you're lost in the swirl of its sound, eager to
go back for more, it's easier to understand the appeal of substances
more perniciously narcotic.

78 WOOLY BULLY, Sam the Sham and the Pharoahs

Produced by Stan Kesler; written by Sam Samudio
MGM 13322   1965   *Billboard:* #2

"Wooly Bully" towers over the mass of overrated mid-sixties garage rock not because it doesn't fulfill all the requirements of the genre, from cheesy organ riffs to exaggerated lyric silliness, but because it satisfies them entirely. For all its indecipherability, "Wooly Bully" 's tough groove and riffing sax are pure Tex-Mex rhythm and blues.

What is "wooly bully"? Only someone totally L7 would ask. But since you did, a good guess is that it's a phrase that sings great and gives Sam Samudio the chance to bleat and yowl like a drunken dadaist about sexual activities that would otherwise annoy the Federal Communications Commission.

79 AIN'T NO MOUNTAIN HIGH ENOUGH, Marvin Gaye and Tammi Terrell

Written and produced by Nicholas Ashford and Valerie Simpson
Tamla 54149   1967   *Billboard:* #19

Marvin Gaye was the greatest duet singer of the rock era, combining for hits with four different women. By far the greatest were made with Tammi Terrell. If Terrell hadn't died prematurely, it's interesting to wonder where their relationship might have gone after Gaye turned black pop around with *What's Going On.*

On the evidence of "Ain't No Mountain High Enough," Tammi could have held her own. Compared to this, Diana Ross's later, bigger solo hit with the song is just a sketch. Terrell fills in the tune's possibilities, pushing so hard that you almost forget that these are pretty prefab declarations of devotion. In the end, though, what gives you chills is Gaye and Terrell singing *together*—the way each audibly and simultaneously draws a breath before plunging into the first chorus, for instance.

The contributions of that other great duo, writer/producers Nicholas Ashford and Valerie Simpson, shouldn't be slighted. Making great music from ready-made materials was an essence of Motown. Conceptually predictable as a cheeseburger, "Ain't No Mountain High Enough" is just as durable, because it's perfectly done. Whatever deficiencies the *song* may have, the record escapes, because Ashford and Simpson knew the formula and because they were well aware that the job was to make a great *recording*. In many ways, it's their production, especially the way they use bells, tambourines, and strings to create an ever present trebly tension, that prods Gaye and Terrell to their heights of edgy urgency.

80 WHEN DOVES CRY, Prince
Written and produced by Prince
Warner Bros. 29286   1984   *Billboard:* #1 (5 weeks)

From the opening, with its psychedelic funk guitar, kinky rhythm and muzzeinlike vocal gargle, "When Doves Cry" ushered in a new era of soul—an eighties brand of Sly's Whole New Thing. But that's not all. If Bob Dylan could have written a song this straightforward in its eroticism, "When Doves Cry" could very well have fit in on, say, *Blood on the Tracks*. Which is only to say that this isn't any more a "black" project than any other record that tops the charts for more than a month (particularly not in a year when Top 40 was at its most alive and kicking).

"When Doves Cry" may have been the most influential single record of the eighties, establishing a new ground of rhythm and structure for contemporary hits. Not all of its influence has been to the good— the psychological mire of the lyrics is as powerful as their unforgettably carnal imagery—but as a piece of rhythm and harmony, this is not just an important record but a great one, virtually inexhaustible in its intricacies. The limit of its appeal, however, is Prince's coldness; it would be interesting to hear Dylan sing this song partly because they are the two indisputably great figures of the rock era who have maintained the most emotional distance from their own best material.

81 PIPELINE, The Chantays
Produced by Art Wenzel; written by Bob Spickard and
Brian Carman
Dot 16440   1963   *Billboard:* #4

Surf music *in excelsis*. This dual guitar extravaganza sounds like it was recorded underwater, with a bass line that's pure lethal undertow. No other instrumental sounds half as dangerous.

82 AIN'T NOTHIN' YOU CAN DO, Bobby Bland
Produced by Joe Scott; written by Joe Scott and
Deadric Malone
Duke 375   1964   *Billboard:* #20

Unbelievable as it seems today, there was a time when real blues had
a place on Top 40, not as recycled novelty music, but as the sound that
spoke to and from the heart of a significant segment of the pop community. Bobby Bland was the last great blues singer, and this was pretty
much his final shot as part of the pop mainstream. God knows, it's a
magnificent send-off. Scott sets ranks of horns riffing like a syncopated
locomotive. Bland sings the first few phrases of each verse with extreme
delicacy, then begins shouting against flourishes from the brass. It's a
marvelous, almost indescribably balanced performance. If Otis Redding
sang "I've Been Loving You Too Long" like a large and powerful man
cradling his own baby for the first time, Bland takes this song out as if
that child had grown up wayward, shouting and expostulating so hard
you could imagine he's foaming at the mouth, unable to force his
offspring back into line, unwilling to surrender.

83 DISCO INFERNO, The Trammps
Produced by Norman Harris; written by L. Green and Ron Kersey
Atlantic 3389   1977   *Billboard:* #11

Like a lot of rock and roll yobos, I felt pretty damn hostile to disco at
first. Too much of the new dance music seemed cold and mechanical;
if you weren't working out on the dance floor, it seemed a stylistic dead
end, especially after enjoying a decade of soul music that was emotionally fulfilling and danceable, too.

Those judgments weren't entirely off the mark. Disco *was* more
machine-tooled than any previous kind of pop music, its range of expression quite deliberately narrower than previous descendants of rhythm
and blues. But leaving the argument there strands you pretty damn
close to those who condemn rock and roll itself because of its failure
to conform to Western Europe's standards of harmonic development.
Culture is understood through its effect, and my problem was that I'd
just never found a comfortable place where disco could show me its
potential for transcendence. The static thump that sustained dancers
all night long seemed just static on the radio or on the turntable at
home.

But disco was nothing if not pervasive, and on Opening Day 1978 at Yankee Stadium, even George Steinbrenner paid his respects, as the *Saturday Night Fever* soundtrack blasted through the slowly filling stands during batting practice. Then Reggie Jackson stepped to the plate, and took a couple cuts. Warmed up, he began sending balls flying out of the park—to right and right center and one or two to left, each clearing the fence by yards. Reggie was *crushing* the ball as well as he would six months later against the Dodgers in the last game of the World Series, when he hit three that counted.

But those practice shots also counted, for me, because you could feel Reggie get pumped up right along with the music. The track was "Disco Inferno," of course, and Jackson made me feel the vitality of the music as a bubbling stew of drum and bass, building and building and boiling over and building again til you were wrung out and breathless. The chant of "Burnin'," the subdued Stax guitar lick, the horn riffs, and the hoarse vocal were anonymous to me then, but they were also as soulful and alive as the rest of the music I loved. For that matter, a dozen far more mechanistic years down the line, a presence remains inside the grooves created by Norman Harris, Reggie Baker, and their crew that constitutes one of the period's most important musical personalities. Afterwards, I felt about disco kind of the way I felt about Reggie himself: not exactly something I aspired to be but pretty damn awesome when it found its groove.

84 I WANT YOU BACK, The Jackson 5
Produced by The Corporation and Bobby Taylor; written by The Corporation
Motown 1157   1969   *Billboard:* #1 (1 week)

85 BILLIE JEAN, Michael Jackson
Produced by Quincy Jones; written by Michael Jackson
Epic 03509   1983   *Billboard:* #1 (7 weeks)

"I Want You Back" was the greatest debut single of any act since the fifties, and it's certainly the greatest record ever made by a singer who had yet to reach puberty. The guitars signal that this is post-Sly music, the rhythm section is ultra-Motown, and the vocal is just beyond belief, nuanced and knowing but at the same time, young and innocent.

"Billie Jean" is the story of what happens if you try to stay that way. The tale it tells is a long ellipsis; the best part is the stuff that Jackson can't bring himself to sing. The huge disco bass drum, the pulsating distant thunder of the bass guitar, and the nagging strings form a background reminiscent of an updated "I Heard It Through the Grapevine," parlaying gossip, rumor, and overreaction into a heady brew.

Michael sings it as if he's not sure whether to let go and express his full terror or to simply subside into giddy giggles. His voice quivers and shakes; at times, he's singing so hard he can hardly spit out the long conversational lines. "Billie Jean" tries to deny everything but in the end, it's trapped by history: the ghost of "I Want You Back," a ghost with lust in its soul. But it's hellishly fascinating to watch Jackson exhaust himself trying to avoid the truth.

86 COLD SWEAT (Parts I & II), James Brown
No producer credited; written by James Brown and Alfred Ellis
King 45-6110   1967   Billboard: #7

On the evidence presented here, sometime in 1967 James Brown concluded that the most oppressive factor in music was the tyranny of the chord change and so he decided to revolt by making music in which chord changes were superfluous. The result was the birth of modern funk, spread out over both the A and B sides of a 45.

"Give the drummer some" is the rallying cry, and that's all well and good but the constant activity emerges from Bernard Odum's bass, which assuredly moves the music along, popping and bopping. The result is dance music as skeletal as an X-ray and about as resistible as gravity.

87 THE MESSAGE, Grandmaster Flash and the Furious 5
Produced by Sylvia Robinson and J. Chase; written by E. Fletcher, Melvin Glover, Sylvia Robinson, and J. Chase
Sugar Hill 584   1982   Billboard: #62

"The Message" is famous as rap's greatest statement of contemporary urban despair, but half a dozen years into the hip-hop era that it ushered in, what's obvious is how much the words were abetted by the music: melody sketched by synthesizer, pulse provided by funk bass and glowering drums, comment added by scratchy rhythm guitar. It's also the only available answer to the question the song places at the center of street life, the one everybody from your kid to your mom to the pusher down the block has to answer: "Sometimes I wonder how I keep from goin' under." Apparently, dancing helps.

88 YAKETY YAK, The Coasters
Written and produced by Jerry Leiber and Mike Stoller
Atco 6116   1958   Billboard: #1 (1 week)

Parental lecture with saxophone. The genius of Leiber and Stoller was realizing that the song would be ten times funnier if it were done completely in the adult voice, without a single adolescent raspberry— just Bobby Nunn's editorializing bass vocal grumping "Don't talk back!" King Curtis is also a major contributor, with what must be the *sine qua non* of fifties tenor sax solos.

Parental Guidance: *Never* play this record for your teenage children. It is a weapon in their hands.

89 ONLY THE STRONG SURVIVE, Jerry Butler
Produced by Leon Gamble and Kenneth Huff; written by Leon Gamble, Kenneth Huff, and Jerry Butler
Mercury 72898   1969   Billboard: #4

"Only the Strong Survive" uses motherly wisdom about love as a code that signifies black power. The concept's as old as the blues—the guitar part *is* the blues—but Butler achieves new resonance because this is also the first record on which producers Gamble and Huff came into their own. They'd made hits before, but "Only the Strong Survive" established the pattern for the Philadelphia International sound: a blues-based rhythm section working against pop strings and choruses, the tidal groove pulling the focus from one element to another. Later Gamble and Huff productions grew much more elaborate, and much more daring in establishing the contrast between funk and MOR, but they were rarely graced by a singer as good as Butler, or blessed with a song this well-written.

90 LOVE IS STRANGE, Mickey and Sylvia
Produced by Bob Rolontz; written by Ethel Smith [Bo Diddley]
Groove 0175   1957   *Billboard:* #11

Mickey Baker's middle name was "Guitar," or anyway that's how they billed the tough, red-headed Kentuckian as one of the leaders of the great band featuring saxophonists Sam "The Man" Taylor and King Curtis that dominated New York's R&B recording scene in the fifties.

Sylvia—Little Sylvia, she was originally called—was a lot younger than Mickey but she convinced him to teach her guitar. It was also Sylvia's idea that she and Mickey should form a team (although he swears he couldn't convince her to make their relationship more intimate, which suggests something about the veracity of things that happened later). They hooked up musically sometime in 1955. Their manager persuaded Bob Rolontz, a former *Billboard* reporter running Groove Records, RCA's R&B label, to sign them up.

They came up with "Love is Strange" at their second session. Allegedly, they were given the song by Ethel Smith, Bo Diddley's wife. Maybe they were, but Smith didn't write it. Bo did. He didn't want to cut it himself because he was pissed off at his music publishers because they never gave him enough money, so he passed the song along. Rolontz at first thought the concept was crazy, especially because they wanted a children's chorus to sing the refrain, then insisted that the duo sing it themselves and rehearse the number with unheard-of thoroughness. When they knew what they wanted to do, instead of going in and cutting live, he began to overdub, building up the guitar parts through multitracking and repeated rerecordings. The staid RCA engineers told Rolontz he was crazy. He told them to shut up.

The result is the most polished version of the Bo Diddley beat ever pieced together. It's also simultaneously among the most erotic and the most comic records ever made—where the emphasis falls sort of depends on how you take the "How do you call your lover boy?" bit. There's no reason you can't have it both ways, though. After all, horny as he may be, Mickey sounds like one suave fella as he invites Sylvia's enticements. And earthy as Sylvia may be, she also sounds like she's about to dissolve into giggles any second.

The record was a smash, but not only love is strange. Mickey Baker, the first great rock and roll guitarist, hated the touring and the glitz and the TV shows. He loved music. So he broke up the partnership and moved to Paris for twenty-five years, from whence he occasionally toured 'round the world for the U.S. State Department, as a paragon of blues guitar. Sylvia got married and became Sylvia Robinson, had another sex-schmooze hit in the disco era with "Pillow Talk" and formed Sugar Hill Records to give her son a place to record the Sugar Hill Gang, guys he heard on weekends in Harlem and the Bronx. Who became the first recorded rappers—if you don't count Mickey and Sylvia.

91 THE HOUSE OF THE RISING SUN, The Animals
Produced by Mickie Most; blues standard, arranged by Alan Price
MGM 13264   1964   Billboard: #1 (3 weeks)

92 LA BAMBA, Ritchie Valens
Produced by Bob Keene; traditional, arranged by Ritchie Valens
Del-Fi 4110   1958   Billboard: #22

93 BLUE SUEDE SHOES, Carl Perkins
Produced by Sam Phillips; written by Carl Perkins
Sun 234   1956   Billboard: #2

94 I WANT YOU, Bob Dylan
Produced by Bob Johnston; written by Bob Dylan
Columbia 43683   1966   Billboard: #20

What is folk-rock? In commercial terms, the answer is simple: It's what happened when Bob Dylan went electric. But that's not adequate or accurate, not when the liner notes to Elvis Presley's first album refer to him in terms of "commercial folk music," and the cover depicts him in a pose reminiscent of no one so much as Josh White.

But all rock is not folk-rock, either, and no one today would argue that Elvis singing Little Richard songs really qualifies (although his "Old Shep" may be another matter). Carl Perkins's original "Blue Suede Shoes" is another story. Sun is famed for its echo, but there's no feeling of distance in this record; you can almost see Perkins's face an inch or so away from the mike, hear his guitar as if it was in the room. Perkins is restrained, keeping a lot more energy in reserve than, say, Jerry Lee Lewis or Little Richard or Buddy Holly, much less Elvis or even Carl himself on tracks like his revamped rendition of the Blind Lemon Jefferson folk-blues, "Matchbox." In the sense that we've come to understand the music, Elvis's version of "Blue Suede Shoes" (which was also a hit) is much more a rock and roll number. But Perkins isn't singing country and he sure isn't making rhythm and blues, and there's no brand of pop music that he fits into, either. Folk-rock explains "Blue Suede Shoes" better than anything.

Folk purists would reject Perkins's claim (if he'd ever made it) because he wrote his song as a commercial project, based on observation of a community in which he wasn't a participant. But what about "La Bamba," a traditional Mexican huapango, a wedding song from Vera Cruz? According to Del-Fi owner/producer Bob Keene, even though Ritchie Valens sang "La Bamba" for his friends all the time, he was reluctant to put this rock and roll arrangement on tape, because "he was afraid that recording it would demean his culture or something." Valens was probably worried because he'd tampered with the song something fierce, both lyrics and music, so much so that those latter-day folkies, Los Lobos, had to "correct" his interpretation when they had a hit with it in 1987. They did this so successfully that they dispersed all the manic energy of the Valens version—which for all we know may have been driven there by Ritchie's fear that Mexican nationalists would stomp him for demeaning their culture. Valens certainly sounds like he's got *something* dogging him as he utters those final dramatic "Bam-bam-bamba" 's.

If folk-rock really stemmed from Bob Dylan, though, then the first folk-rock hit was almost certainly the Animals' "House of the Rising Sun," a traditional blues whose arrangement bears telltale signs of having been learned from Dylan's all-acoustic first album. (Dylan learned it from Ur-folkie Dave Van Ronk, although, he remarked in that LP's liner notes, "I'd always known 'Risin' Sun' but never really knew I knew it until I heard Dave sing it." Which only shows how much Dylan had already learned from Little Richard.)

Where the Animals exceeded Dylan was in the amount of sheer dramatic power they found latent in the chords themselves. Alan Price's bold organ and Eric Burdon's howling vocal released all of it, as if they'd connected the ancient tune to a live wire. Problem was, Burdon was far too macho—brattish spawn of Newcastle coal miners that he was—to sing the song from a female perspective, as it had always been sung. So he turned the lyric around, portraying the prostitute as a male and, thus, himself as a catamite. Between that and the consequences of a heavy Geordie accent aping an Iron Range Minnesotan aping a

New Yorker aping a Mississippi sharecropper, which rendered the lyrics marvelously incoherent, the Animals set a new standard for all future folk-rock and blues-rock remakes.

Dylan's own "I Want You," on the other hand, isn't folk-rock at all. It's a pop song, and a love song at that, as well as his second-biggest hit of the sixties. What might throw a casual listener off is an image of folk music that connects that style to quasi-poetic lyrics and therefore labels all of Dylan's pre-*Nashville Skyline* music "folk." In fact, these lyrics aren't especially poetic anyway, though they *are* so obscurantist that you can play all kinds of games about what Dylan really means when he sings, "Now all your fathers they've gone down / True love, they've been without it / But all their daughters put me down / 'Cause I don't think about it." Having studied the disc in detail since I was sixteen, I can now state that this most likely means two things: 1) Dylan had found a clever rhyme; 2) he thought about it all the time, maybe even too much. However, the joyful music, with its kinky organ, rollicking piano, and the loopiest singing Dylan's ever done (as if he found the word "bad" intoxicating all by itself) indicate that he'd actually found a way of getting the proportions about right. Which is not a folk-rock virtue, either. But does make "I Want You" a great rock and roll record.

95 TRAMP, Otis Redding and Carla Thomas
Produced by Steve Cropper; written by Lowell Fulsom and Jimmy McCracklin
Stax 216   1967   *Billboard:* #26

According to legend, Carla Thomas improvised her insults. Certainly, Otis didn't stick very close to the script provided by Lowell Fulsom's year-old R&B hit in his replies. But if Otis and Carla were just toying with one another, what they came up with is a soul masterpiece that cuts to the essence of Stax and touches as close to the core of Otis Redding's vision of the world and his place in it as anything he ever did.

The musical tension is provided by the deployment of horns and bass against Al Jackson's muscular, sinuous bass and snare drum pattern. Jackson opens the song solo and in its brief (2:58) span, he is given two other quick breaks. The horns and bass play staccato riffs that surge without ever quite resolving themselves—a lot like the dialogue they support.

Thomas says Redding invited her to use whatever epithets she pleased, and her dripping contempt for his character—supposedly a country bumpkin but eventually revealed as a man of means—catches an entire era of black culture and its derisive mockery of new arrivals from the backwoods South. There was some truth to the roles that they played. Carla was, of course, the daughter of singer/disc jockey Rufus Thomas, which made her at least second generation Memphis black bourgeoisie. Otis grew up dirt poor, the son of a laborer/preacher/invalid, which made him common as mud.

Except that Otis Redding was a visionary. Part of that vision was a perverse pride in his origins. "You're country," Carla sneers. "You're straight from the Georgia woods." "That's *good*," drawls Otis, playing the boob but meaning it, too. Later, he comments, "My momma was . . . Poppa too." He refuses to take her seriously—except on one subject.

"You know what, Otis, I don't care what you say, you're still a tramp."

"*What!?*"

"That's right. You haven't even got a fat bankroll in your pocket. You *probably* haven't even got twenty-five cents."

Otis doesn't hesitate. "I got six Cadillacs, five Lincolns, four Fo'ds, six Mercurys, three T-Birds, a Mustang . . ." He doesn't even finish the list, because something more important is on his mind. "Oooo, I'm a luh-ver," he cries, stretching out the word, making of it an anthem, a way of defining himself and of telling this city fool what's really important.

And that, sure as the world, is the heart of Otis Redding's artistic vision. He may have been country, he may have played the fool, but when it came right down to it, he was an artist because he was a lover. Nobody has ever found a higher calling.

96 96 TEARS, ? and the Mysterians
Written and produced by Rudy Martinez
Cameo 428 1966 *Billboard:* #1 (1 week)

Could "96 Tears" be the first postmodern rock record? Stylistically, it unquestionably defines the genre (which didn't again become popular until the early eighties), structured as it is around an organ drone supported by ostinato bass and an amateurish singer (sporting dark glasses, unkempt long black hair, and clothing of questionable provenance) spewing lyrics that are half vision, half invective, with an almost parodistic misogyny. While it's just as easy to fit the record into earlier contexts (perhaps as an answer record to the Drifters' "I Count the Tears"), had R.E.M. or the Cure recorded it, "96 Tears" would be heralded as pure art-rock.

But "96 Tears" was recorded by a quartet of Tex-Mex migrant workers, and without art school credentials, all that Rudy Martinez gets credit for is creating a "garage band" classic. History will doubtless provide equity, since "96 Tears" will be remembered long after "post-modernist" spats recede into the mists that spawned them.

97 A FINE FINE BOY, Darlene Love
Produced by Phil Spector; written by Phil Spector, Ellie Greenwich, and Jeff Barry
Philles 117   1963   *Billboard:* #53

You call the way Love sings testifying. It's a good thing Hal Blaine and Phil Spector are here, too, because they're about the only people in pop who could find a way to keep up with her. For that matter, when she lets loose with a "Yeah" or charges back in after the sax break, *every*body gets left in the dust.

By the way, who says that rock and roll objectifies only women?

98 GIRLS JUST WANT TO HAVE FUN, Cyndi Lauper
Produced by Rick Chertoff; written by Robert Hazard
Portrait 04120   1983   *Billboard:* #2

The rock and soul singles aesthetic deals much more fairly with women than any album-oriented approach because it gives a much clearer picture of the areas in which women first played major roles: rhythm and blues, Motown, discotheque-era dance music, girl groups, and the many other byways left critically unexplored because they developed in the interregnum between the Presley/Holly/Berry fifties and the advent of the Beatles. In fact, from Ruth Brown and LaVern Baker to Darlene Love and Aretha Franklin to Carole King and Valerie Simpson to Patti Smith and Donna Summer, these sorts of termite-scale music have coughed up far more female talent than British rock in its elephantine first three decades, unless you think that Annie Lennox, Dusty Springfield, Marianne Faithful, and half of Chrissie Hynde outweigh all of the above or take the likes of Annie Haslam, Sandie Shaw, and Cilla Black seriously.

It's also true, though, that no part of rock or R&B has been dom-inated by women in the way that, for instance, gospel music and postwar jazz singing have been. There is no version of rock history that gives women an equal role, simply because they haven't had one. In fact, a frankly female point of view is such a rarity in rock (as opposed to R&B and soul, where it is still by no means common) that to this day, there are actually people who believe that Janis Joplin was great merely because she had one.

"Girls Just Want to Have Fun" doesn't exactly fly in the face of these facts. It just sort of romps all over them. Cyndi Lauper is singing words placed in her mouth by a man, but she trounces the lyrics, so much so that while the record was on the charts, writer Robert Hazard actually complained that she took too much credit for *his* song. In fact, the song's most important lyrics, in which Cyndi declares that *she* wants to be the one to walk in the sun, are lines she wrote herself, thereby transforming a rather sexist ditty (summarized by Exude's parody, "Boys Just Want to Have Sex") into protofeminism.

But then again, it's the singer, not the song. If "Girls" had been planned as an anthem, it might have proved as noxious as "I Am Woman." In fact, its irony was so subtly pitched that many feminists at first scorned it for exemplifying what it really criticized. Lauper was really arguing that girls just want to have fun, *too*—that is, to participate in pleasure on the same scale as boys, not that fun is all that girls want. But to get that, you had to be an active pop radio listener, which (for all the reasons suggested above and more) most feminist cultural in-terpreters apparently ain't.

The things that really must've thrown 'em off, though, were the giddy music (the arrangement is all noises and gadgets, through which both melody and harmonies are richly developed) and Lauper's affected airhead accent. As a result the message seeps across slowly, until you can barely remember when Cyndi and the chorus chanting "They just wanna, they just wanna" sounded like anything *but* a call to arms.

But it's a call in a very particular way: warmly personal, able to laugh and dance and emote with an intensity at once joyous and sad. At the end of each of the first two choruses, when Lauper stretches out the syllable "fun," she's not only celebrating the possibilities in-herent in that idea, she's displaying virtuosity in the way that's most meaningful. Not to say female.

99 RANK STRANGERS, The Stanley Brothers
Producer not credited; written by Albert Brumley
Starday 506   1960   Did not make pop chart

A man is forced by circumstance to leave his home and family to seek his fortune. Years later, he returns to find the places and faces that have visited him hourly in his longings and dreams are gone, simply disappeared. The scene is to him a desperate and despairing one. It's not just that a whole world he once knew no longer exists; it's that what has replaced it seems so completely alien. One of these rank strangers attempts to console him, telling him that the things he loves still exist in another dimension, but he is not to be solaced. "Everybody I met, seemed to be a rank stranger," he sings. "No mother or dad, not a friend could I see / They knew not my name, and I knew not their faces / I found they were all rank strangers to me."

Schematically, "Rank Strangers" is a folk tale, with an air of legend and miracle, the ashes and dust from which the Ur-myth of rock and country and soul wanderlust is fashioned. It's the template, as it were, from which Bobby Bare's "Detroit City," Gladys Knight's "Midnight Train to Georgia," Chuck Berry's "The Promised Land" and dozens of other songs were created. Or so it feels. It's almost impossible to believe that the Stanley Brothers debuted such a classic piece of American folklore as late as 1960.

Maybe the Stanleys' record of Brumley's great hymn has such continuing power because it was the last of its kind. After about 1960, folk music became what it is today: a marketing category, divorced from whatever reality it ever had as a description of how people in some communities went about making culture. The returning native in "Rank Strangers" represents many things—a Christian adrift in the temporal world, a sinner trying to storm the gates of heaven, "The Man Without A Country" of Edward Everett Hale's short story, the workingman become cosmopolitan in the course of traveling to ply his trade, perhaps above all, the southerner forced into Yankee territory and returning to find his homeland forever altered. But these words, this music, in my imagination at least, also represent the reaction of such forebears as Woody Guthrie and Robert Johnson to what rock and roll had made of the basic elements of American folk music.

Ralph and Carter Stanley came from the mountainous region on the border of Virginia and Tennessee where Ralph Peer first recorded country music (through the Carter Family and Jimmie Rodgers) so they would have understood this subtext very well. They began recording in the late forties, getting their first notice on the bluegrass circuit when they heard Bill Monroe's "Little Maggie" at a concert and stole into the studio and made a version that beat his record into the stores.

Soon enough, performing on their own with various supporting musicians always known as the Clinch Mountain Boys, they became bluegrass legends on their own merits, which were, in something like an order of importance, Carter Stanley's beautiful lead voice, which many consider the emotive equal of Hank Williams's; the most sonorous harmonies in the genre, highlighted by Ralph's tenor; a remarkable command of traditional material (particularly hymns); and an emphasis on guitar as a lead instrument, as opposed to the usual bluegrass banjo and mandolin. They cut more than 450 masters for a variety of labels, including reworkings of traditional songs like "Man of Constant Sorrow" and "Hills of Roan County," bluegrass hymns like "Gathering Flowers for the Master's Bouquet" and love songs like "How Mountain Girls Can Love" and "Love Me Darling Just Tonight." They were capable of making stuff as hoary as "Rock of Ages" and "Mountain Dew" absolutely thrilling.

"Rank Strangers" is the essence of all that made them great. Recorded in a small studio in Jacksonville, Florida, it opens with a stately guitar-mandolin duet, Carter's voice entering to gentle the sound and then stir it up again through the mandolin trills that respond at the end of each mournful line. The harmonies—a gaggle of voices including Ralph Stanley, mandolin player Curley Lambert, and guitarist Ralph Mayo—are as ethereal as the words. Though the approach is folky, this is a true *record*, including a sort of false ending after the second chorus, in which the guitar picks up the melody just as it's about to die out.

But "Rank Strangers" was the end of the line. It was the biggest hit the Stanleys ever had for Starday, and it was their last session for the label. The folk revival came and went, and when it was over, there was little room for music that seemed so ancient in the face of a world of aerospace and psychedelics. When Bob Dylan or former Clinch Mountain Boy Ricky Skaggs pay the Carters tribute today, they're honoring a tradition that has been scattered to the winds as surely as the Rank Stranger himself. Yet "Rank Strangers" is an irreducible part of the sound of its era, a gorgeous example of how the most elementary kinds of American music came to life in recording studios in those postwar years, an elegantly composed metaphor for the psychic stress that people not only endured but used to craft into something approaching art in those days of cultural turmoil.

100 ANARCHY IN THE U.K., The Sex Pistols
Produced by Malcolm McLaren; written by Johnny Rotten, Steve Jones, Glen Matlock, and Paul Cook
EMI (UK) 2566   1976   Did not make pop charts

What's this doing here? You could say that it represents the tip of an iceberg: the sum total of punk and postpunk music that "Anarchy" and the Sex Pistols inspired. But it might be more accurate to call it the entrance to a tunnel in a cave, leading to a buried universe.

"Anarchy in the U.K." is an unquestionably great rock and roll record, the kind of raging, burning rock and roll that is even more rarely heard than made. It inspired a major pop explosion in Britain and Europe, and a minor one in the United States. Yet for a fact, the bulk of what the Sex Pistols spawned lies outside the scope of *The Heart of Rock & Soul*, not because it's too wild and unruly—there are nine Little Richard singles in this book, not to mention "Kick Out the Jams"—but because the *musical* center of what the Sex Pistols spawned is so far removed from even the most radical rhythm and blues. Studio-crafted pop music based on a different rhythmic process needs and deserves a discussion all its own, not because it's weird, but because most postpunk discards the basic assumptions on which the finest records listed here are based.

Which may seem an odd thing to say given how many singles herein are celebrated as transformative breakthroughs. But there's a difference between a transformation and a fracture, between a breakthrough and a breakdown. The revolts of "Papa's Got a Brand New Bag" and "Dance to the Music" never severed the connective tissue that "Anarchy in the U.K." shreds from start to finish. A dozen years on, it seems clear that the Sex Pistols were not only sincere in their desire to make rock that smashed rock, but that they were absolutely equal to the task.

That doesn't mean anything as corny and melodramatic as the Death of Rock and Roll. It just means that somebody had figured out how to make artistically and commercially viable pop music based on a rhythmic process outside R&B, a feat unequalled since the advent of Elvis Presley, and that consequently, things were fundamentally different thereafter. In terms of the aesthetic of *The Heart of Rock & Soul*, that difference amounts to a true historic disjuncture. Which is a pretty damn longwinded way of saying that there are hardly any punk and postpunk records here for the same reason that there aren't many Chicago blues singles.

"Anarchy" fits, because both Johnny Rotten, the Pistols' overacclaimed singer, and Steve Jones, its underacclaimed guitarist, knew how to make unforgettable rock and roll. Rotten and Jones hold your feet to the fire, making a mockery of John Lennon screaming about mere blisters on his fingers. Rotten sings like a man picking at a scab, fingering it just where it hurts most, hurling every filthy and threatening imprecation he can think of, but it's Jones, with his relentlessly droning six-string crunch, who takes the record over the top, converts threats into promises, promises into accomplishments.

In a way, one of the most unfortunate things about the whole Sex Pistols story is the notion—assiduously spread by both Rotten and manager/impresario McLaren—that the band "couldn't play." Sid Vicious couldn't but the group that made this record, with Glen Matlock, who *did* know one string from another, on bass, understood perfectly how to make rock and roll effects in the recording studio. And that's the job. The evidence is that those effects aren't just amateurish; they're professionally calculated to do a job. And that's why and how a record whose aim was to smash history wound up an ineradicable part of it.

101 IF I COULD BUILD MY WHOLE WORLD AROUND YOU, Marvin Gaye and Tammi Terrell

Produced by Johnny Bristol and Harvey Fuqua; written by Johnny Bristol, V. Bullock, and Harvey Fuqua
Tamla 54161   1967   Billboard: #10

While I was driving to the Jersey shore one summer afternoon in 1984, the Top 40 disc jockey on New York's Z100 came to the end of his shift and announced that it was his last day on the air. He was returning to Florida and resuming life as a dentist. Before he left, he wanted to play one last song, which he dedicated to his wife and children, and to his listeners.

In the milliseconds between his speech and the beginning of the record, what went through everybody's mind was what *they'd* play in that situation. If the deejay got it wrong, he'd have undeniably fouled his own funeral.

The music began and at first I misidentified it as "Ain't No Mountain High Enough," and thought he'd blown it—great record, but out of context. But "If I Could Build My Whole World Around You" blossoms slowly; Marvin and Tammi each take a rather pedestrian chorus before their joy in one another explodes into wordless delight: "Doododoo, doodadoo."

As Marvin and Tammi burst forth with that nonsense, the deejay cashed his bet. Listening, you understood him, his priorities and his regrets, why he was leaving radio and how he felt about sending such sounds out over the air in the blind faith that someone would listen.

For me, the song came as a rather mournful gift. Whether Marvin and Tammi were lovers has never been that interesting to me. When they sing together here, however, it's as if to prove that they do love one another, that they have a relationship that is passionate, complex, and complete, whatever its sexual component. And this is meaningful, not just gossip, for on that day in the summer of 1984, the grass had barely had time to grow over Marvin's grave, while Tammi had been gone for better than a decade. What's grievous is not only that they died far too young, but that they don't rest side by side, like the lovers at the end of "Barbara Allen," as the rose grows round the briar.

So, yeah, "If I Could Build My Whole World Around You" is far too romantic; if you could answer its rhetorical question affirmatively, you'd be in trouble, because in real life people shouldn't always act out their dreams. But the contrary, which is too easily forgotten in cold type, is that the world robbed of the romantic illusions that foster dreams would not be worth living in. Of course, I don't *really* know why the deejay picked this record, but I can guess, because I know what keeps it close to my heart. It's what Tammi sings in the final verse, about what would happen if she and Marvin really could fashion an entire universe around themselves: "And there'd be something new with every tomorrow to make this world better as days go by." A corny wish, but without ones like it, life might truly be pitiful.

Johnny Rotten claimed he didn't know what he wanted but he knew how to get it; since he was denied, he failed on his own terms. The opposite is true here. Marvin and Tammi know just what they want and they're mistaken about the means: You can't reach tomorrow's something new just by snugglin' close. But wrong as they may be, they can *not* be denied, because dreams don't have to be realizable to be worth keeping, and reexperiencing, and saluting now and then.

102 I FOUGHT THE LAW, Bobby Fuller Four
Produced by Bob Keane; written by Bobby Fuller
Mustang 3014   1966   *Billboard:* #9

"I Fought the Law" 's peerless rebel rock lyric forces most every band worth its salt to take a shot at matching the sheer aggression of Fuller's only national hit, but nobody's ever come close to capturing the convulsive power of the original's successive bursts of drums, guitar, and voice.

These latter-day West Texas rockabillies clearly had studied Buddy Holly microscopically—just listen to that skittering guitar solo and Fuller's hiccuping vocal and the way they're layered with echo. But "I Fought The Law" isn't the Holly copy it's often made out to be (you need to hear Fuller's version of Sonny Curtis's "Love's Made a Fool of You" for that). Rather, it's Holly brought up-to-date.

And with an ending just as tragic and ten times more mysterious. On July 18, 1966, with "I Fought the Law" barely off the charts, Fuller's body was discovered in the front seat of his car, which was parked outside his Hollywood apartment. He was dead from swallowing gasoline, an apparent suicide, though it's hard to believe it was anything but the cosmic destiny of the guy who shared a sound with Buddy Holly and a manager with Ritchie Valens.

103 CRYING, Roy Orbison
Produced by Fred Foster; written by Roy Orbison and Joe Melson
Monument 447   1961   *Billboard: #2*

Roy claimed to have written this rock-bolero as the result of a true story, in which he encountered an old flame and refused to say how much she meant to him, then ran into her again when it was too late: "I would say that I had tears in my eyes—I'll go that far—but whether I was physically crying or just crying inside is the same thing."

Which means the only story we can trust is the one the music tells. And such music! Blaring strings, hammered tympani, a ghostly chorus, the gentle strum of a guitar, a hint of marimba, add up to a setting at once tender and bombastic.

Purely as singing, "Crying" is the greatest tour de force of Orbison's career. He uses at least three separate voices: his normal baritone for the first part of the song, a falsetto for a brief, *norteno*-inflected repetition of "Crying" (which sounds very much like a Spanish "yi yi yi") as the penultimate chorus, and then a full-bodied, quasi-operatic bellow for the final "Crying, crying ooooo-over you." The only singer in rock and roll history who could have come close to what Roy does here was Jackie Wilson, and Wilson's tour de force, his multioctave "Danny Boy," while it shows more range, doesn't build to its climax with anywhere near the same imagination. And no other singer with this much range displays anything like Orbison's complete emotional commitment—when Roy sings "from this moment I'll be crying," there's no reason to believe that the tears will ever stop.

In concert, Orbison sang the concluding notes, and the hair stood up on the back of your neck, and all around the house people rose from their chairs to applaud and cheer. He stepped back briefly, let the adulation fade a bit, then moved up to the mike and . . . sang the final verse again! And when he reached "Crrrry-ing ooooo-over you," the hair stood up on the back of your neck, and all around the house, those who'd been foolish enough to sit back down again rose from their chairs to applaud and cheer. Having proven his point, Roy moved on to his next number.

The big advantage of the record is that you can make him keep singing it all night long, without complaint. From him or you.

104 HONKY TONK, PART 1 and PART 2, Bill Doggett
Produced by Henry Glover; written by Bill Doggett, Shep Sheppard, Clifford Scott and Billy Butler
King 4950   1956   *Billboard:* #2

Veteran bandleader Doggett's uptempo strip-joint shuffle is the best rock and roll instrumental of the fifties, and one of the finest two-sided hits ever made. You go ahead and make your own choice between Part One, with Clifford Scott's roiling tenor sax burning off energy as quickly as it can be generated by Billy Butler's trilling guitar, and Part Two, in which handclaps push the beat while Scott plays a more melodic sax part against Butler's rumbling low notes, until the end, when Butler steps forward for a set of climactic runs. But for me, choosing between them would be like asking another guy to pick which of his kids he likes best. Anyhow, put together, the two versions aren't any longer than "Like A Rolling Stone," and they're damn near as hair-raising.

105 WILL YOU LOVE ME TOMORROW, The Shirelles
Produced by Luther Dixon; written by Gerry Goffin and Carole King
Scepter 1211   1960   *Billboard:* #1 (2 weeks)

If I had to make a bet on which of Gerry Goffin and Carole King's songs would last longest, the money would go down on "Will You Love Me Tomorrow," not only for its beautiful melody, which will always make good singers want to try it (although males should learn a lesson from Frankie Valli and dissuade themselves), but because its lyric defines a certain stage of female teenage sexuality, a subject difficult to put into song without pandering and almost impossible to render with this much pathos.

But if the song does last so long, the only version nearly everyone will know (or need to) will be the Shirelles's. Perhaps the most lush of all the girl group classics, the record is a masterpiece of early sixties New York studio craft. The riffing strings, the busy pizzicato that churns in the background along with a Leiber/Stoller-style *baion* beat exquisitely set up Shirley Owens's guileless lead vocal. It's the most memorable performance Owens ever gave, and the irony is that she hated King's piano / voice demo and had to be coerced into singing it by producer Luther Dixon and Scepter owner Florence Greenberg. They, at least, understood that "Will You Love Me Tomorrow" was virtually a guaranteed smash, because it cut to the heart of what Preston Sturges used to call Topic A.

The question (always a relevant one and not only 'twixt twelve and twenty) is "Should I or shouldn't I?" And if the stakes seemed for many years to be dwindling, at a time when sexually transmitted disease has reached life-threatening proportions and a gang of barbarians threatens to dismantle abortion rights, they're right back up there again. And because these are issues that affect millions already born and yet unable to defend themselves, Goffin's lyrical depiction of the singer's innocence—"Is this a lasting treasure / Or just a moment's pleasure / Can I believe the magic of your sigh?"—remains frighteningly up-to-date. And the fact that the issue is resolved, that the girl has implicitly made up her mind to say yes ("So tell me now, and I won't ask again . . .") makes the question that much more provocative.

I hope that the children of Tipper Gore and other music censors' children learn "Will You Love Me Tomorrow," just as much as I hope that they—and my own—find *both* "lasting treasure" and "a moment's pleasure." You *can* have it both ways.

106 THIS IS ENGLAND, The Clash
Produced by Jose Unidos; written by Joe Strummer and Bernie Rhodes
Epic 002230   1985   Did not make pop chart

107 (WHITE MAN) IN HAMMERSMITH PALAIS, The Clash

Produced by The Clash; written by Joe Strummer and Mick Jones
CBS 6383 (UK)   1978   Did not make pop chart

After leaving the English equivalent of prep school, Joe Strummer, a diplomat's son, spent a couple of years doing time in pub bands, playing music like Graham Parker's and Elvis Costello's. Punk slapped him upside the head like Saul on the road to Damascus, and he joined forces with Mick Jones to form the Clash, a band that bore the same relationship to the Sex Pistols that the Rolling Stones did to the Beatles.

In 1977, the Clash made some first-rate singles, played to audiences of converts in a style that suggested that the soul of everyone present was at stake, and made a first album that is unquestionably the best of its class. They weren't just punkers, though, playing a peculiarly offbeat brand of reggae that even legendary Jamaican producer Lee Perry found persuasive.

Punk held a moment, and then it died. So, for the next few years the Clash played a double game, sustaining their vision in the face of developments (including the idea of sustaining a career) that were absolutely contraindicated by punk ideology. Eventually, the band that had declared "I'm So Bored with the U.S.A." became worldwide stars, hyped in the States as "the only band that matters." And so they made *London Calling*, the *Blonde on Blonde* of its generation, and went dubwise with *Sandinista!*, a record whose topic was as many years ahead of its time as its sound. Finally, they made "Rock the Casbah," a tough punk-funk number danceable enough to become a Top 40 hit. By then, the Clash seemed bunkered down for the long haul.

Then Strummer and Jones split. The issue was careerism, all right, but it was Mick, the one who seemed the most like a prepunk pop star, who went purist, heading out for parts unknown with Big Audio Dynamite. Punk ideologue Joe Strummer was the one who held onto the Clash—playing with the only other original member, bassist Paul Simonon, but aided by a renewed alliance with the band's original manager, the mini-McLaren Bernie Rhodes.

Jones was the band's heart-on-its-sleeve, Strummer its remorseless theoretician. Together they were indomitable and sometimes ingenious. Apart, Jones drifted into a ganja cloud, while Strummer preached on without respite. Now, the Clash started sounding like the only band that mattered.

After their early singles, the Clash developed into an album act.

Even their hits were LP tracks jerked out of context. But the Strummer-Rhodes Clash had but one album in it, *Cut the Crap*, one of those records that seems titled as an admonition to itself.

Yet Joe Strummer had not struggled all that way from prep school and the pubs without learning a few things, and before the Clash was finished, he buckled down one last time and put together the things that he now knew. That special knowledge wasn't enough to fill up an album, or even a full side. But it was just exactly the right amount for a magnificent single whose spirit fit perfectly into the tradition that punk was supposed to have smashed.

If it was reminiscent of anything that the Clash had done previously, it could only have been "(White Man) In Hammersmith Palais," an impressionistic account of what happened when Jones attended an all-night reggae show at a famous West London theatre where he wound up feeling like the great liberal outsider, his home turf so thoroughly foreign to him that he felt like the only man in town who'd missed the news.

The guy who sings "This is England" knows the full story. Not only that, he's decided it's his duty to tell it—all of it or maybe just as much as he knows (or maybe just as much as he can stand to know). But where to start?

The record opens with a bass/drum breakdown, adds some electronic handclaps, and then mixes in the voices of children, unmistakably British voices. Synthesized strings ominously arise. Then enters Strummer's voice.

It was never a pretty vehicle. Now it's ravaged. He sounds out-of-breath before the first verse is complete. In it, he's standing in the midst of a riot when a woman grabs his arm. "Her voice spoke so cold, it matched the weapon in her palm," he says, Strummer tries to shake it all off—her arms, his words. This won't do; he's not getting it right, the scene won't fit even though it's true. So he says what's really on his mind:

> This is England, this knife of Sheffield steel
> This is England. This is how we feel.

And moving beyond words, he picks up his guitar and kicks into a riff that's all anger and pain and noise and blood and snot-filled distortion, every bad thing he knows how to convey, and he simply lets rip, sandblasting the whole goddamned story.

It doesn't help, but he can't stop himself. Keeps singing. Keeps telling what he says and cannot believe. "This is England," he clamors in disbelief. "Who I'm supposed to die for?" "This is England," the band replies. "I'm never gonna cry no more," he declares. But he raves on, and each word is as bitter as any tear.

This is punk rock, all right. Who is that woman, appearing in first verse and last, but Margaret Thatcher? Who are those children but the ones who'll grow up to no future? What is that sound but the noise of the disintegration that the Sex Pistols and the legions that followed them—the Clash in the first rank—called out. It's all there, the attacks on racism, colonialism, and cultural subjugation, the infatuation with violence and nihilism, the sense of futility that leads to the pure fire of unbridled rage. Most of all, there is the willingness to sacrifice all sense to poetry, a willingness that may have been the essence of punk and a quality once adamantly lacking in Joe Strummer, punk's Stakhanov. Joe had discarded none of his arrogance—that "we" is nothing if not imperious—but his dream of triumphing in collaboration with his friends dashed to bits at his feet, he had the humility to look at a mess and give it a name. "This is England, land of illegal dances / This is England—land of one thousand stances."

It was not a hit. The truth hurts.

108 GOOD LOVIN', The Young Rascals
Produced by the Rascals with Arif Mardin and Tom Dowd; written by Rudy Clark and Arthur Resnick
Atlantic 2321   1966   *Billboard:* #1 (1 week)

"Good Lovin' " all by itself is enough to dispel the idiotic notion that rock and roll is nothing more than white boys stealing from blacks. It's probably the greatest example ever of a remake surpassing the quality of an original without changing a thing about the arrangement. In this case, the (not bad, but far from inspired) original was produced by Jerry Ragovoy for the Olympics in March 1965; the Rascals took it to the top the next year, not just by mimicking its virtues but by extracting what was fascinating from the song and discarding the soul boilerplate. Felix Cavaliere shouts over Gene Cornish's gritty guitar riff and Dino Danelli's cascading drums, but the best part is his own showpiece organ break. That and the finale, which is so completely bar band that it damn near demands a round on the house.

109 FEVER, Little Willie John
Produced by Henry Glover; written by Joe Seneca
King 5108   1958   *Billboard:* #20

They say that the trade charts were so distorted in the fifties that even though Willie John's original version of this great torch song trailed Peggy Lee's (which made Number 8), it outsold hers by two to one. Which just proves that while America may be inhabited by bigots, they aren't completely insane. For Willie John's finger-popping arrangement—which Lee copied lick for lick—possesses a still unparalleled languor and sensuousness. His voice suggests both the confidence of hoarse experience and the nervous anxiety of high-pitched innocence. Lee was like an advertisement for sex; Willie John was the thing itself.

110 GREEN ONIONS, Booker T. and the MGs
Produced by Jim Stewart; written by Booker T. Jones, Steve Cropper, Lewis Steinberg, and Al Jackson
Stax 127   1962   *Billboard:* #3

What happens when the best backup band in the universe decides it's time to be noticed.

111 RUNAROUND SUE, Dion
Produced by Gene Schwartz; written by Dion DiMucci and Ernie Maresca
Laurie 3110   1961   *Billboard:* #1 (2 weeks)

112 THE WANDERER, Dion
Produced by Gene Schwartz; written by Ernie Maresca
Laurie 3115   1961   *Billboard:* #2

Dream Date?

This is roughly the point where Dion crossed over from being first-among-equals in the Belmonts (that is, a singer in a doo-wop group) and became one of the great Italian-American tenors of the post-Sinatra era (operative reference: Bobby Darin). On the wordless first verse, he scats everything but "ring-a-ding" (and that's implied), then turns in a swinging, finger-popping performance that's generically "rock and roll" as much because of historical context as musical style.

Someday, "Runaround Sue" may have a place in some feminist museum's exhibit on the horrors of male chauvinism—where it will again be paired with "The Wanderer," in which Dion, playing the Darin-like Italian-American pop singer smoothie to the hilt, boasts of doing everything for which he condemns Sue. But you know visitors are gonna flock to 'em even there.

113 LEAD ME ON, Bobby Bland
Produced by Joe Scott; written by Deadric Malone
Duke 318 1960 Did not make pop charts

The greatest 3:00 A.M. record ever made. This is Bland the crooner, the true Sinatra of the blues, singing with simple eloquence. "You know how it feels, you understand / What it is to be a stranger in this unfriendly land," he says softly, exploring the syllables as if phrasing one wrong would cause him great pain. "Lead Me On" is a flat-out blues, but Joe Scott's arrangement uses all manner of unlikely (for the period) instrumentation: flutes, strings, an ethereal female chorus.

If you really hear this song in the middle of the night, and listen carefully to Bland's gentle repetitions of the title phrase, you'll unavoidably start thinking about all the things they imply. Prepare to meet the dawn.

114 PEGGY SUE, Buddy Holly
Produced by Norman Petty; written by Buddy Holly, Jerry Allison, and Norman Petty
Coral 61885 1957 Billboard: #3

The biggest drum beats in rock and roll history. It's all that Holly can do to summon the strength to sing over them, and the guitar has to race to keep up. But then, if you're gonna write love songs about your best friend's girl, you better be fast.

115 DANCING IN THE STREET, Martha and the Vandellas

Produced by William Stevenson; written by William Stevenson
and Marvin Gaye
Gordy 7033   1964   Billboard: #2

As pure a product of its day as anything Dylan or the Beatles ever imagined. And the moment that those horns send out their signal cry, it's just as true and profound an anthem, even if it is "just" about "swingin', swayin' and records playin'." There have been hundreds, maybe thousands, of good songs written about dancing but none comes close to this one in conveying not only the physical experience but the emotional tenor of what it means to dance publicly.

Yet, "Dancing in the Street" can never be entirely removed from the moment when it was made. A moment when "Dancing in the Streets," after all, was also a reference to the tens of thousands of Americans who'd taken their energies to the pavement as part of the civil rights movement. Across the years, the spirit of that movement doubles the poignancy of Martha's cry for her hometown: "Can't forget the Motor City!"

But then again, it would be remiss not to mention that Martha only shares center-stage with the drummer (Benny Benjamin? Uriel Jones? Pistol Allen? *Marvin Gaye himself?*) who creates those unforgettably explosive fills and turnarounds. In the same way that Martha's vocal is the embodiment of what was already happening in the streets, the drums are a prophecy of the harsher reality to come.

116 UP ON THE ROOF, The Drifters

Produced by Jerry Leiber and Mike Stoller; written by
Gerry Goffin and Carole King
Atlantic 2162   1962   Billboard: #5

When the Drifters were inducted into the Rock and Roll Hall of Fame in 1988, Billy Joel made a speech about what their music had meant to him and his friends.

"I grew up in a housing development here in New York, out in Long Island . . . This was in the early sixties, when a roof was just the top of a house and a boardwalk was like a long stretch of wood. Broadway was this street in New York City where people with blue hair went to see plays. Saturday night, you went to the movies to see the movie. The last dance was somethin' you never hung around for.

"The Drifters changed all this for my gang. They gave us the word. The word was this: Don't just stay in the house and stare at the ceiling. Go up on the roof and look at the stars. And even Levittown looked good from up there.

Telling you more about "Up on the Roof" would, in a way, be like trying to give away a secret that can only be experienced anyhow. So take your marching orders from the song itself: "Let's go . . . up on the roof."

117 PLEASE SAY YOU WANT ME, The Schoolboys
Produced by Leroy Kirkland; written by D. Hayes and I. Nahan
Okeh 7076   1957   Did not make pop charts

Frankie Lymon was by far the greatest of all the kid doo-wop singers. But he didn't make the greatest kid doo-wop record. The world will little note nor long remember Leslie Martin and his four cohorts from a Harlem junior high school but their one great single is unforgettable, the most melancholy disc ever cut by an actual teenager. On its own Martin's singing can't compare with Lymon's, but swamped in echo and accompanied by a stately arrangement dominated by standup bass, his voice stands out well enough. And Martin's last note, riding out on three quick phrases from an alto sax, is guaranteed to send chills down any mortal spine.

118 THE BOYS OF SUMMER, Don Henley
Produced by Don Henley, Danny Kortchmar, Greg Ladanyi, and Mike Campbell; written by Don Henley and Mike Campbell
Geffen 29141   1984   *Billboard:* #5

How could Don Henley seem so jive as lead vocalist of the Eagles, yet so great on his own? Well, in baseball they call it addition by subtraction; get rid of the mediocrities and let the real talent shine. And certainly, nobody in his old band was as interesting a collaborator as (Tom Petty and the) Heartbreakers guitarist Mike Campbell.

It's also true that this is a different Henley, emphasizing the bluesy rather than country side of his vocal personality. And rather than trying to make Big Statements, he lets details accumulate. Seeing that Grateful Dead sticker on an El Dorado bumper would be a banal big deal by itself, but he gets the love lyric right, too, all the way down to the brand of her sunglasses.

119 SURFIN' BIRD, The Trashmen
Producer not credited; written by Steve Wahrer
Garrett 4002   1963   *Billboard:* #4

120 THE BIRD'S THE WORD, The Rivingtons
Produced by Jack Levy, Adam Ross, and Al Frazier; written by Al Frazier, Carl White, Turner Wilson Jr., and John Harris
Liberty 55553   1963   *Billboard:* #52

121 PAPA-OOM-MOW-MOW, The Rivingtons
Produced by Jack Levy, Adam Ross, and Al Frazier; written by Al Frazier, Carl White, Turner Wilson, and John Harris
Liberty 55427   1962   *Billboard:* #48

Today best known for fathering and grandfathering the Trashmen's legendary "Surfin' Bird," "Papa-oom-mow-mow" and "The Bird's the Word" are themselves two of the wildest pieces of noise anybody's ever tried to contain within wax. You can take them as jokes—the former a play on honky fear of liberated blacks as "mau maus," the latter a travesty of doo-wop's whole solemn bird group tradition, both joyously overboiling with R&B energy at its comic extreme—but you can also hear both records as explorations of the deep mysteries that roil within the main currents of rock and soul. "Funniest sound I ever heard / And I can't understand a single word," begins "Papa-oom-mow-mow" and the rest of the record concerns itself with trying to figure out what it means. Like the quest for "Do wah diddy diddy" and "wooly bully" which it prefigured (and the one for "da da" from which, according to critic Greil Marcus, it must descend), the point is in the search itself.

"The Bird's the Word," with its even more frenzied vocal gibberish, flute trills, and drum batterings, eclipses its precursor, just as the Trashmen (who the Rivingtons later successfully sued for plagiarism) went one step beyond either of these. But the key disc in the series is probably "The Bird's The Word" which may in fact be an answer record, the solution to the riddle of "papa-oom-mow-mow" 's meaning. Perhaps the guy of whom the singer in "Papa-oom-mow-mow" first asked the question, in that song's second verse—suspecting, it seems, that this noise he can't understand might in fact be the stranger's sacred name—suddenly sprouted wings and took off. Some will suspect a connection to a mere dance craze, as in Dee-Dee Sharp's "Do the Bird," which is not altogether out of the question and no more relevant to this part of the discussion than the mau mau joke. Because even if all the cawing cries that these sounds were "spreading all over the land" like an epidemic were just the Rivingtons' way of boosting their hopes of chart success, what the listener hears even today is portent, a warning that leads, in a sense, directly to the Beatles and Bob Dylan and everything since. (And these are the records to make you understand "The Times They Are A-Changin' " for the dull diatribe it really is.)

The Rivingtons' singing—inadequate as that word is to describe the sounds emitted here—definitely meets Bob Dylan's definition of rock and roll songs as exercises in breath control (try repeating "Papa oom mow mow" or "B-b-b-bird, bird, bird-bird's the word" this many times even at half tempo). And no surprise, because before they were the Rivingtons, Al Frazier, Carl White, Turner Wilson Jr. and John "Sonny" Harris had plenty of R&B experience, some as members of the Federal label's Lamplighters and Tenderfoots, all as the Sharps, who backed Duane Eddy on "Rebel-'Rouser" and Thurston Harris on his version of "Little Bitty Pretty One." But these men's immortality lies there no more than it does in their first "Papa-oom-mow-mow" follow-up: "Mama-oom-mow-mow," in which it is explicitly suggested that the men who make these noises aren't human because "They talk like men from outer space / I never heard nothing like 'em in the human race."

But you and I have. Specifically from the Trashmen, whose record goes beyond demented into an area of unabashed and unabated noise unequalled in Little Richard's wildest dreams. The Trashmen's case on the plagiarism issue lies not in the fact that they stole almost as much from "Wipe Out" (not to mention Nervous Norvus) but in the whole question of performance. If the essence of the Rivingtons is melody and lyrics (God forbid), it has hardly any essence at all. But if it's *spiritual*, then what the Trashmen did was anything but heretical, more like an affirmation of an apocalyptic vision.

Anyway, how can you put the "Surfin' Bird" experience into words? I mean, *they* couldn't—unlike the Rivingtons, these Minnesota frat boys could barely put it into music. But it's the very ineptitude of the presentation that exposes the absolute truth at its core. I mean, if you could lock Tipper Gore and Allan Bloom in a closet with any record, this would be it, right? Good for what ails *you*, too.

122 BLUE MONDAY, Fats Domino
Produced by Dave Bartholomew; written by Fats Domino and Dave Bartholomew
Imperial 5417   1957   *Billboard:* #5

"Blue Monday" is the foundation of a rock and roll tradition of songs about hatred of the working week and lust for lost weekends. The chain now includes such significant links as the Coasters' "What About Us," Gary "U.S." Bonds's "Seven Day Weekend" (the first call for the abolition of Mondays, blue or otherwise), the Vogues' "Five O'Clock World," "Friday on My Mind" by the Easybeats, "Manic Monday," the hit Prince wrote for the Bangles, and the Sex Pistols' "Holidays in the Sun" (in which the vision turns ugly from mass unemployment and begins to die).

Fats and "Blue Monday" spawned all this. You might argue for Chuck Berry's "Too Much Monkey Business" or Clyde McPhatter's "Money Honey" but their topic is different: the hatred of work. Fats is talking about something much more modern: the demand for leisure. He discards the working week and his loathing of it in the first verse; it's the weekend that the song dwells upon, and in the end, Fats's feeling for its excesses is clear and profound. "Sunday mornin' my head is bad," he sings, "But it's worth for it for the times that I've had."

And yet, he links himself with the earlier tradition, too, the tradition of blues and folk songs in which pleasure is just a respite from chasing "fun." "But I've got to get my rest," he sings when he comes to Sunday evening, " 'cause Monday is a mess." And that's how the song ends. By the time the rock singers who followed him have completed their songs, they're liberated: the *idea* of the "Seven Day Weekend" seems to set U.S. Bonds free, the whole purpose of "Manic Monday" for the Bangles is to put the weekend's pleasures in relief. None of them would have dared (or even thought to) end their songs as Fats ends his, with the cold hard thump of the band finishing off the last chord, the pleasure machine coming to a full stop.

123 HEY! BABY, Bruce Channel
Produced by Major Bill Smith; written by Margaret Cobb and Bruce Channel
Smash 1731   1962   *Billboard:* #1 (5 weeks)

As inspirations go, "Hey! Baby" is hard to beat, having served as a source of both the Beatles "Love Me Do" and Bruce Springsteen's

"Dancing in the Dark." What they heard is unmistakable: a lazy blues shuffle with a crying country-rock vocal and weeping harmonica solo (by latter-day critical fave Delbert McClinton). The production is cheesy, and the piano is as tacky as anything in the history of recorded sound (and the piano *playing* is at the same level).

Of course, they also were taken in by the record's sonic atmosphere, the very embodiment of Bobbie Ann Mason's definition of rock and roll as "happy music about sad stuff." Time and again, Channel tries to rise above his own despondency, tries to make himself sound gleeful at the prospect of asking this girl if she'd like to go with him, but he only manages to sound mournful and defeatist, as if that harmonica were the echo of his own lack of self-confidence. Maybe Channel was inspired by Roy Orbison (near the end she does "turn and walk away" as Roy's carnal objects were wont to do), but even Roy's prospects never sounded quite this dire so near their moment of consummation.

124 ROCK & ROLL LULLABY, B.J. Thomas
Produced by Steve Tyrell and Al Gorgoni; written by Barry Mann and Cynthia Weill
Scepter 12344   1972   *Billboard:* #15

My kind of rock opera—especially for its best line: "Now, I can't recall the words at all / It don't make sense to try." If only Pete Townshend and Ray Davies had taken that idea to heart!

The lyric recounts the life of the offspring of a teenage pregnancy who spells out what it's like to grow up side by side with your only parent. It's also about the ways they used rock and roll records for middle of the night solace. It's got all the earmarks of a tearjerker and maybe that's all it would be, if the reverberant guitar line weren't by Duane Eddy, if the male harmonies weren't a ringer for the Beach Boys, if Darlene Love wasn't part of the female chorus, or if Thomas, not much better than a B-level country-rock hack on every other record he made, didn't sing the song as if getting these particular facts straight was a matter of personal honor and dignity. If you want to know what rock and roll means to people, why many lives would be unlivable without it, this is a good place to start learning.

125 PROUD MARY,
Creedence Clearwater Revival
Written and produced by John Fogerty
Fantasy 619   1969   *Billboard: #2*

In other hands, this ersatz remembrance of the way things never were on riverboats might have seemed like a case of overexposure to *Life on the Mississippi*, especially given Fogerty's total immersion accent, which (in true New Orleans style, pretty rare for a California kid) transforms "work" to "woik," among other things.

Fogerty gets away with it, though, because he came up with a riff and a rhythm that roll along as mighty as the Mississippi itself. The surging flood of guitar and drums, the bass line's undertow and the liquid guitar solo justify every vocal and lyric affectation. By the end, the story seems natural and eternal, which maybe means that those studied qualities aren't *just* affectations, after all.

126 STANDING IN THE SHADOWS OF LOVE,
The Four Tops
Produced by Brian Holland and Lamont Dozier; written by
Brian Holland, Lamont Dozier, and Eddie Holland
Motown 1102   1966   *Billboard: #6*

The clip-clopping rhythm belongs to a soul horse opera, but the *mise en scene* is pure psychological thriller, a depiction of mental torment almost as agonized, if not quite as marvelously elaborated, as "Reach Out I'll Be There" itself. The Tops' worldview at a glance: "It may come today, it might come tomorrow / But it's for sure, I ain't got nothin' but sorrow."

127 AIN'T NO WAY, Aretha Franklin
Produced by Jerry Wexler; written by Carolyn Franklin
Atlantic 2486   1968   *Billboard: #16*

128 ANGEL, Aretha Franklin
Produced by Quincy Jones; written by Carolyn Franklin
Atlantic 2969   1973   *Billboard:* #20

Although she never gets credit for it, Carolyn Franklin was perhaps her sister's greatest collaborator. In addition to being her partner in tinkering with "Respect," she was the most frequent background vocalist on Aretha's records. And best of all, she wrote these two ethereal, deeply spiritual heartbreak ballads. Aretha sings each of them with rare inspiration and a kind of glorious freedom that she brings only to her finest material.

"I got a call the other day," Aretha says at the top of "Angel." "It was my sister Carolyn saying, 'Aretha, come by when you can, I've got something that I wanna say.' And when I got there, she said, you know, rather than go through a long drawn-out thing, I think the melody on the box will help me explain."

The song Carolyn played was about as intimate as anything Aretha has ever allowed herself, which I suppose means that it spoke for both of them. "Too long have I loved, so unattached within," she sang. "So much that I know, that I need somebody so." Aretha sings those words out of the deepest longing and loneliness, so ravaged by the end of the last verse, you can hardly believe she's made it through.

But then other voices enter, telling her "He'll be there, now don't you worry / Just keep lookin' and just keep cookin'." They buoy her up and carry her out of the song in a spirit of hope triumphant.

Carolyn Franklin must have been among those voices and maybe that's why they have that buoyancy. Certainly, it was she who gave the song its tragic spirit, because that's what the song has most in common with "Ain't No Way." She had the rare capacity to write songs in which a singer who gives of herself with Aretha's peculiar blend of creative commitment and emotional caution could be fully revealed. "Stop tryin' to be someone you're not," she had her sister sing midway through "Ain't No Way." "Hard, cold and cruel as a man who paid too much for what he got." But who was Aretha singing about?

Carolyn Franklin was only forty-three when she died of cancer in 1988. But her music continues to keep a lot of us—maybe including her sister—going from day to day, and, as far as I can tell, that makes it eternal.

129 YOUR PRECIOUS LOVE, Marvin Gaye and Tammi Terrell

Produced by Harvey Fuqua and Johnny Bristol; written by
Nickolas Ashford and Valerie Simpson
Tamla 54156   1967   Billboard: #5

The art of the soul duet as the art of intimate conversation. Everything goes right, from the gutty guitar that kicks it off to the finger-snaps that underline the half-spoken verses to the strings that shiver just before the full band kicks in for the first chorus. But mostly, we get a pair of people so totally in synch that it's almost impossible to imagine them singing standing up, or at least without wrapping each other in a gigantic embrace every few bars. I mean, this isn't a love song—this is the sound of love itself, the real deal, affection expressing itself with amazing openness, tenderness, and fully acknowledged wonderment.

You gotta figure that if Marvin or Tammi had found in real life what they so exultantly discover in each other here, they'd have lived not only more happily but far longer. But then, about whom is that not true?

130 DON'T BE CRUEL, Elvis Presley

Produced by Chet Atkins; written by Otis Blackwell
RCA 47-6604   1956   Billboard: #1 (11 weeks)

That easy Elvis style this time wears a great song the way some guys can just shrug into a $1,000 suit. Mostly, the King lays back and lets his supporting cast show their stuff: Bill Black with a virtual bass solo at the top, D.J. Fontana popping the backbeat, the Jordanaires crooning like rock's first barbershop harmony team, Scotty Moore sketching in some guitar here and there.

You could almost swear that Elvis wasn't doing anything except riding a perfectly constructed machine. But then he slides into a "mmmmm" that marks the transition between the first two verses, and you realize how masterful his relaxed style really is. The Big Bopper built an entire hit record around that tossed-off "mmmmm" but Elvis moves on as if it barely mattered. *That's* cool.

131 HIPPY HIPPY SHAKE, Chan Romero
Produced by Bob Keene; written by Chan Romero
Del Fi 4119   1959   Did not make pop chart

One of the loudest, most explosive records ever made, "Hippy Hippy Shake" has been covered twice, and both the 1963 version by the Swinging Blue Jeans and the 1988 one by the Georgia Satellites became far bigger hits without coming close to the sheer frenzy of Romero's hiccuping wildman vocal or the equally seething guitar break. Romero was meant to be Del Fi's successor to Ritchie Valens after the plane crash (indeed, he was even managed by Valens's mother for a time) but he possessed none of Ritchie's lyricism—the difference between "C'mon Let's Go," Valens' wildest number, and "Hippy Hippy Shake" is the difference between a threatening gesture and being punched in the gut. Except not even Sacher-Masoch himself ever got this much pleasure from being smacked around.

132 BORN IN THE U.S.A., Bruce Springsteen
Produced by Bruce Springsteen, Jon Landau, Chuck Plotkin, Steve Van Zandt; written by Bruce Springsteen
Columbia 04680   1984   Billboard: #9

133 MY GENERATION, The Who
Produced by Shel Talmy; written by Pete Townshend
Decca 31877   1966   Billboard: #74

At first, these records seemed to belong together because they bookend the history of pop guitar feedback. But to listen to them side by side is to understand that they share something bigger: An approach to questions of life, death, and futility in which that feedback plays a crucial role.

"My Generation" is fast, frantic and furious; "Born in the U.S.A." is slower, its mood more resigned and bitter than actively angry. Where "My Generation" dismisses the future, proclaiming "Hope I die before I get old," "Born in the U.S.A." confronts the future as the only possible means of coming to grips with the past: "Ten years burnin' down the road / Nowhere to run, got nowhere to go."

Musically, both records are remembered for their berserk guitars, but each is really motivated by other elements: "Generation" by John Entwistle's amazing bass work and Keith Moon's slashing drum attack;

"U.S.A." by Roy Bittan's martial synthesizer and Max Weinberg's explosive drums. Roger Daltrey's sputtered pillhead vocal is the voice of the kind of kid who'd really find himself in the kind of "hometown jam" that gives the Springsteen character his choice between 'Nam and a jail cell. And Springsteen's agonized singing speaks to the experiences that make that pillhead "hope I die before I get old": "Born down in a dead man's town / First kick I took was when I hit the ground."

Down through the years, these records argue with one another about the biggest issues of all, topics compared to which Vietnam was just another incident. "Hope I die before I get old," the Who shouts, with all the force men can muster. But the E Street Band cuts them off, as if to say: Well, when you learn what that really means, you'll hope something else. From a far-off cloud, Keith Moon, a cool rockin' daddy indeed, is surprised to find himself switching sides.

134 PROMISED LAND, Chuck Berry
Produced by Leonard Chess; written by Chuck Berry
Chess 1916   1964   *Billboard:* #41

Chuck's answer to Robert Frost's sententious sentiments in "The Road Not Taken." A young black man leaves his home in Norfolk, Virginia, and hops a bus west to seek his fortune. But by the time they reach Birmingham, the bus is shot. So our hero switches to the train and winds up in New Orleans, where friends buy him a silk suit, get him loaded and pour him on a jet. He wakes up "high over Albuquerque on a jet to the Promised Land." Arriving in Hollywood, he understands immediately, without leaving the terminal, that he has arrived not just in a place of possibility but in the Future. Of course, his first reaction is to call home and spread the word. Collect.

135 GOD SAVE THE QUEEN, The Sex Pistols
Produced by Chris Thomas and Bill Price; written by
Paul Cook, Steve Jones, Glen Matlock, and Johnny Rotten
Virgin [UK] 181   1977   Did not make pop chart

So much has been made of the juxtaposition of the Beatles' arrival in America with the assassination of JFK (a synchronicity I'd chalk up to hype), you'd think somebody would have made more of a similar co-incidence—how the two biggest pop explosions of the past twenty years coincided with the biggest nationalist spectacles in recent British and American culture.

The American explosion took place in 1984, the year of *Thriller* (video, tour and album), *Born in the U.S.A., Purple Rain*, the rise of MTV, and the greatest group of pop singles of the decade, from "Jump" and "Girls Just Want to Have Fun" to "What's Love Got to Do With It" and "Jam On It." It was also the year of the jingoist Olympics (American athletes cleaning up in the medal count without mention of the fact that their toughest competitors, the Eastern Europeans and Soviets, were sitting it out), the Statue of Liberty centennial, and a Presidential election campaign with all the trappings of a coronation.

In Britain, the explosive date was 1977, the year when the punk pot, set on the fire in '76, finally boiled over, the season when it became clear that what began with a crew of scabrous outsiders had utterly disrupted the whole discourse around pop music. 1977 was also the year of Queen Elizabeth II's Silver Jubilee, the twenty-fifth anniversary of her ascent to the throne from which she presided over the disintegration of an empire and the rise of the domestic rock and roll industry that the Sex Pistols, the Clash, and their cronies were bent on demolishing.

For America to have known the equivalent of "God Save the Queen," Prince or Bruce Springsteen or Michael Jackson or Cyndi Lauper (maybe Cyndi) would have had to stand up in the midst of the election and the centennial and the Olympics and declare at the top of their lungs and in the rudest fashion imaginable, that the entire self-congratulatory nationalist orgy was a fraud, that Ronald Reagan was an inhuman begetter of morons, that his regime fostered a fascist plague, and that the spectacles it fostered were a portent of the very end of the world.

That's what Johnny Rotten's taunting "No future / No future / No future for you" meant. More important, that's what it was taken to mean. "God Save the Queen" was banned from the airwaves not because it insulted the Queen—which it did, quite deliberately and eloquently—or because its blitzkrieg guitar portended riot, but because its every note and nuance and chord and cackle threatened worse than public violence. It threatened public exposure of what England had become, and it did so with malice aforethought.

Or so it seems; certainly, seemed then. But maybe not. The Sex Pistols made their record; it was banned but millions heard it—perhaps everyone in the U.K. with even the slightest interest in pop music knew it by heart. And nothing was fomented. The principal effect was to launch thousands of rock bands trying to achieve what the Sex Pistols achieved (though not very many would agree upon what that was, not with each other and certainly not with me).

If, as Dickens proposes in *Barnaby Rudge*, mobs are ruled most easily by idiots, maybe Johnny Rotten was too smart for his own good. Or maybe he was sold out by the cynicism of Malcolm McLaren's post-Situationist theory of discord, a theory whose survival is amazing in the face of its successive failures (in Paris in 1968, in London in 1977, periodically for eons before and ever since, if you believe some people).

So we are left with this . . . record, a great blast of noise, meaning to purify the world and instead, what? Corrupted by it, maybe. Or maybe just implacably telling the truth, upon the supposition that people will act if they just receive the proper information—or have the improper information torn away. There's an innocence to that, when you get right down to it, that ought to scare the shit out of anybody who believed punk ideology.

136 YOU LEFT THE WATER RUNNING, Maurice and Mac

Produced by Rick Hall; written by Dan Penn, Rick Hall, and Oscar Franks
Checker 1197   1968   Did not make pop charts

The soul duet tradition has now deteriorated so badly that Aretha Franklin is reduced to being paired with the likes of George Michael. (What next, Fabian?) Yet at one time, duets were one of soul's staple creative units, so much so that a record as fine as "You Left the Water Running" could be all but forgotten. Today, although no soul discography is complete without it, nobody really has much to say about it, and it was a project just to discover who wrote, produced, and released it. "Did not make pop charts" is an underestimation; it didn't make *Billboard*'s R&B charts, either (although it did make the lower reaches of the *Cash Box* R&B chart for three weeks). The title did, however, get mentioned in a Number Two record, the Box Tops' "Cry Like a Baby."

Maurice McAlister and McLaurin Green actually made two appearances in *The Heart of Rock & Soul* because they were also the Radiants, who made "Voice Your Choice" in 1962. Mac was drafted the following year, and they didn't get back together again until 1965, when they made a series of fine recordings in Chicago and Muscle Shoals as Maurice and Mac.

The arrangement—especially the great dripping guitar lick, with its antecedents as much in "Tall Cool One" as "Soul Man"—is classic Muscle Shoals, and Maurice and Mac sing and preach well enough to compete with even Sam and Dave, their obvious inspiration. The slow groove, set up by Roger Hawkins's drumming and punctuated with staccato sax and trumpet blasts, establishes so much tension that only singing that's this gritty and churchy can release it. That scratchy "Lord have mercy" before the final repetitions of the chorus is everything Mick Jagger ever dreamed of doing.

137 PRISONER OF LOVE, James Brown
Produced by James Brown; written by Leo Robin, Clarence Gaskill, and Russ Columbo
King 5739   1963   *Billboard:* #18

138 BEWILDERED, James Brown
Produced by James Brown; written by Leonard Whitcup and Teddy Powell
King 5442   1961   *Billboard:* #40

James Brown made it his business to revamp the whole history of popular music. It's impossible to properly evaluate how knowingly he did this, because his latter-day claims are as unbelievably grandiose as everyone else's contemporary expectations must have been limited. But certainly, Brown had a better than rough idea of the stakes when he set out to record songs like "Prisoner of Love," a standard that had four times appeared on the charts and twice been a million-seller (for Billy Eckstine in 1945 and for Perry Como in 1946) and "Bewildered," which had hit the charts twice (originally in 1938 by Tommy Dorsey and again ten years later for Eckstine).

Given Brown's raggedy voice, merely to have assayed such smooth crooner classics violated just about every standard of conventional pop music. But if Brown could not compete on pop's old smooth 'n' mellow terms, he knew something that no one else had previously discovered (or dared to attempt) about how to sell a song to an audience. When Sam Cooke and Little Richard sang standards, they brought to the material tremendous physical resources: the sheer beauty of each man's voice. And their gospel-derived phrasing and intonation gave each of them the ability to make stunningly original versions of standards like "Baby Face" (Richard) and "For Sentimental Reasons" (Cooke). But

James Brown not only lacked a spectacular voice; in Tin Pan Alley terms, his singing was rasping, cracked, and overwrought.

Yet both "Prisoner of Love" and "Bewildered" will probably be remembered as James Brown numbers long after the other renditions are forgotten (as if they haven't been already). For on these songs, Brown demolishes the conventional way of singing a pop ballad. "Bewildered" opens with a crackpot shriek of the title phrase; "Prisoner of Love" erupts in a swirl of strings and Brown appears as a man trying to fight his way out of a fog. Neither reading is anything but straight; James isn't camping it up or deliberately travestying the material. Instead, he respects it so deeply that he begins to inhabit it and each record becomes a somewhat eerie exercise in watching a man confront his most peculiar and particular sexual, romantic, and psychic demons.

What's most undeniable about these "interpretations"—reinventions is more like it—is how completely self-referential they are. It's not that there's no logic to what Brown's doing. It's that his logic is unprecedented because of everything it ignores, which is every "accepted" way of doing things. If Brown came to each of these songs because of an admiration for Billy Eckstine (as seems likely), he didn't let anything remotely resembling hero-worship inhibit his readings. Taken together, this pair of records represents a pinnacle of musical radicalism, and without them, the more drastic remodeling of R&B/pop conventions perpetrated by Otis Redding and Marvin Gaye would have been all but inconceivable. The influence of James Brown's rhythmic genius is often and justifiably exalted, but he was equally influential in creating a whole new species of ballad singer.

But "Prisoner of Love," in particular, is much more than just influential. It was the record that brought James Brown to the mass audience for the first time, his first record to crack the pop Top 20. That he did this with a bathetic, old-fashioned pop standard isn't necessarily surprising. What took audacity was doing it not by taking that standard and paring it to the bone (so that it would resemble something like "When A Man Loves A Woman," for instance) but by introducing it with distant tympani thunder and a riffing violin section—in other words, by concocting a letter-perfect parody of a Johnny Mathis pop disc, then accentuating the resemblance by singing the first lines at the top of his skimpy range.

"I'm just a prisoner," Brown says, over and over again. Sometimes it's a groan, sometimes a proclamation: "Don't let me be a prisoner!" For the longest time, he avoids completing the line, which makes sense, for he is trying to liberate himself from the shackles not of romance but of mortal musical logic.

139 STREET FIGHTIN' MAN, Rolling Stones
Produced by Jimmy Miller; written by Mick Jagger and Keith Richards
London 909   1968   *Billboard:* #48

Another Stones record that, like "Get Off Of My Cloud," brilliantly knocks off a bigger earlier hit. But "Street Fightin' Man," based as it is on the biting acoustic guitar pattern established in "Jumpin' Jack Flash," completely outstrips its source, possessing a sound that's bigger, tougher, denser, and a topic that's more dangerous and intelligible.

In fact, so dangerous and intelligible that I've often resisted it, insisting that "Jack Flash" was the better record, because I mistrusted my own inclination toward political rhetoric. But then, "Street Fightin' Man" isn't any more—or less—political than "Satisfaction" or "19th Nervous Breakdown," which are also songs that piss and moan about personal liberty. Like every other great record that the Stones have made, its ostensible worldview is just there as something to hang the music on, as if nobody would pay attention to the supercharged rhythms without this sort of calculated incitement.

There are many good answers to the song's overquoted question about what poor boys can do without being in rock and roll bands, but why bother detailing them? Especially since the insurrectionary kids in Brixton, London's West Indian ghetto, proved Jagger's premise false in 1981. Instead, take your cues from Charlie Watts, whose driving drumming amounts to a military attack. Or from Keith's slash-and-burn approach, which might be the closest anyone's come to a soundtrack of the Vietnam War.

So the music gives the lie to every line of the lyric. And a million Stones fans answer in unison: So what else is new?

140 LET'S GET IT ON, Marvin Gaye
Written and produced by Marvin Gaye and Ed Townsend
Tamla 54234   1973   *Billboard:* #1 (2 weeks)

After trying to change the world with "What's Going On" (and succeeding), Gaye turned his attention to matters more intimate. "Let's Get It On" has the same kind of slippery rhythmic base as "What's Going On," but its evocative power is trained on issues as profoundly personal as its predecessor's were social and political.

Which is pretty high-falutin' for a record that is, after all, mostly the skillful rap of a guy using all his powers of persuasion to get a woman into the sack. If there's something vaguely offensive about parts of it at this late date, it's that lines like "We're all sensitive people, with so much to give," are just that—lines, exploitative patter, not even polished sexual metaphor. The options Gaye presents—"If the spirit moves ya, let me groove ya"—aren't options at all, because their context is so coercive.

But then again, you—or at least I—will forgive Marvin anything because the vocal caresses he gives to each of the song's syllables acquire the stature of metaphor, because the arrangement's string, sax, percussion, and flute interplay equals the sensuality of the vocal, and because, however jive Gaye's approach, this is one of the few records around that gives sex its due, by recognizing the central importance of physical pleasure among *adults*. There aren't many pop records that convey much of this, but then, there aren't many movies, books, plays, or symphonies that do it, either.

141 MAYBE, The Chantels
Written and produced by Richard Barrett
End 1005   1958   *Billboard:* #15

Virginity personified as an unwelcome condition.

142 QUARTER TO THREE, Gary "U.S." Bonds
Produced by Frank Guida; written by Gene Barge and Gary Anderson [Bonds]
Legrand 1008   1961   *Billboard:* #1 (2 weeks)

"Quarter to Three" 's sound has the most peculiar unity. I've played it on stereo systems ranging in price from $49.95 to $10,000, and the equipment makes no difference. In other words, here's an exquisite example of cultural democracy in action, operating on the sacred principle: One band, one noise.

143 LITTLE STAR, The Elegants
No producer credited; written by Artie Vinosa and
Vito Picone
Apt 25005   1958   *Billboard:* #1 (1 week)

Dion and the Belmonts were the kings of Italian doo-wop. But the
prototypical Italian doo-wop *record* is this takeoff on Mozart's classical
nursery rhyme. Vito Picone opens and closes the record by asking and
answering Mozart's question, and the chorus restates the wish formula,
but aside from that, the approach is pure Belmonts—which is to say,
a husky baritone lead, a Latin feel to the rhythm, and vocals that simply
mouth open vowels, with an occasional "duh duh duh" from the bass.

144 IT WILL STAND, The Showmen
Produced by Allan Toussaint; written by
Norman [General] Johnson
Minit 632   1961   *Billboard:* #62

145 DRIFT AWAY, Dobie Gray
Written and produced by Mentor Williams
Decca 33057   1973   *Billboard:* #5

Across the years, you can hear some records speaking to one another.
Stranger still, a good bit of that dialogue is about rock and roll—what
it is, what it means, where it came from, why some hate it and others
have to have it.

When the Showmen traveled from Norfolk to New Orleans in 1961
to record with a band led by Allen Toussaint, rock and roll was regarded
as cold in the ground. General Johnson, the group's parched-voice lead
singer, thought otherwise—and with good reason. Despite everything
that's been written about the fallowness of the period between Buddy
Holly's plane crash and the emergence of the Beatles, the truth is that
the stars of 1961 weren't just a bunch of teen idols named Bobby. Doo-
wop records were being revived all along the East Coast, Elvis was
back, girl groups were coming up, significant new noises were emerging
from Detroit and Memphis, and the kids on the Atlantic seaboard from
Virginia to South Carolina never stopped dancing the shag to the hippest
rhythm and blues they could find.

Amidst all this, "It Will Stand" was still a boldly defiant stroke.
Asserting that rock and roll was great was one thing, but this song

actually implied that rock would last because it had *meaning*. This was far from Danny and the Juniors' declaration three years earlier that "Rock and Roll Is Here to Stay," because Danny and the boys explicitly declared that they didn't know why. Johnson's faith was deeper and his record is an anthem that will last as long as rock and roll is heard—"forever and ever" according to the disc itself. "It Will Stand" offers a prescription for what you need to rock—"heartbeats, drumbeats, finger-poppin' and stompin' feet, little dancin' that looks so neat . . ." The record follows its own formula, too.

More than that, though, "It Will Stand" is a description of an alternative history, with rock at the center of events. "It swept this whole wide land," Johnson bawls, "Sinkin' deep in the heart of man." No one had ever assayed such an intense explanation of this music's grip. Johnson's voice cracks with emotion but not because he's uncertain. No! His faith is so secure that he even offers compassion to the censors: "Forgive them for / They know not what they're doin'."

When Mentor Williams wrote "Drift Away" a decade later, everyone knew that rock would be around. In fact, Williams may have intended "Drift Away" as nothing more than an account of the frustrations of trying to make a living in the Nashville songmills. But rock and roll *was* in the doldrums and a lot of people besides pro songwriters were in need of a reminder of why and how to carry on.

Williams' best move was finding the right vehicle for his song: Dobie Gray, a journeyman writer/singer who'd had a hit in 1965 with "The In Crowd." Like Johnson, Gray sang on the raspy side of easeful, which made him perfect for "Drift Away" 's complex message in which the desire to rock out is presented as the desire to dream, the longing to bop is equated with the longing to be soothed. Updating "It Will Stand," "Drift Away" makes the music seem bigger simply by restating its finest accomplishment—the degree to which it sank into the hearts of men. Ten years after "It Will Stand," the idea that rock would be around was an idea to celebrate, not defend.

Dobie Gray and Mentor Williams took the Showmen at their word: They didn't nickname it, they claimed it. And somewhere in this unkind world, someone is making it through another day by humming to themselves: "Gimme the beat boys and free my soul / I wanna get lost in your rock and roll . . . and Drift Away."

146 IT TAKES TWO, Marvin Gaye and Kim Weston

Produced by William Stevenson and Henry Cosby; written by
William Stevenson and Sylvia Moy
Tamla 54141   1967   *Billboard:* #14

Superficially, this one's easily summarized: Pick any couplet. (My favorite's "One can take a walk in the moonlight, thinkin' that it's really nice / But two walkin' hand in hand is like addin' just a pinch of spice.") But that's not all there is to it. "It Takes Two" flies in the face of rock mythology, at least as it's been passed down by Anglophile rock criticism. Here, Marvin Gaye, probably the greatest iconoclast pop has ever known, speaks with tender care in favor of the most intimate collectivity. He has to be careful, because some of those great couplets, including the one above, are wordy as hell and fitting them to the song's basic Motown meter requires large doses of craft and hard work. But it's that sense of striving that proves the point. Special tip of the hat to the trombonist, who zips it all together.

147 FA-FA-FA-FA-FA (SAD SONG), Otis Redding

Produced by Otis Redding, Jim Stewart, and Steve Cropper;
written by Otis Redding and Steve Cropper
Volt 138   1966   *Billboard:* #29

Based partly in the greatest lie that Otis ever told ("It's a sweet melody tonight / Anybody can sing it, any old time") but also possessed of the greatest truths—but you can't put them on paper because "It's just a line, it tells a story / You got to get the message, a soul message." And even that's meaningless right here—it can't mean half as much without hearing Otis sing it, bend and crease those syllables in an impassioned, inspired, probably futile effort to put everything he knew and felt into a few bars of soul groove. Futile, even though Otis has the aid of a brilliant dialogue with the horns and the reflexively sympathetic support of the MGs (especially Duck Dunn, whose bass is the throb of this wild, sensitive man's heart).

Your turn.

148 CRAZY FOR YOU, Madonna
Produced by Jellybean Benitez; written by John Bettis and Jon Lind
Geffen 29051   1985   *Billboard:* #1 (1 week)

"Then He Kissed Me" brought up-to-date. But the difference is much more than twenty years or the fact that the setting is a smoky barroom rather than a street corner. Though LaLa Brooks may have been innocent of her own innuendos, Madonna capitalizes quite consciously on not-especially-ambiguous lines like "I'm crazy for you / Touch me once and you'll know it's true." Then again, in a single moment—a throaty, spoken "Crazy for you" just before the coda—Madonna transforms her record into an *adult* love song, even if it was brought into existence as the theme song of a teen melodrama (the high school football flick, *All the Right Moves*). And maybe that really is the difference between eras, because what Madonna is singing about is a state of frankly sexual desire inconceivable for any female pop singer of the sixties.

Though soon superseded by "Live to Tell," "Crazy for You" played an important role in Madonna's career by establishing her as a ballad singer as well as a dance hall queen. But that's just the problem in dealing with contemporary records. If Madonna's as good as I think she is, such considerations will seem altogether ephemeral by the time the turn of the century rolls around and she's taken for granted as one of the treasures of the eighties (much as the passage of time—and the quality of the music—rehabilitated the once unhip Creedence Clearwater). Writing about Madonna as an artist now feels as absurd as, oh, comparing Robert Johnson's creative sensitivity to F. Scott Fitzgerald's would have thirty or forty years ago. But just because nobody gets your point doesn't mean you're wrong. In the end, that may be the fundamental message of Madonna's entire career.

149 SOLDIER BOY, The Shirelles
Produced by Luther Dixon; Written by Luther Dixon and Florence Green
Scepter 1228   1962   *Billboard:* #1 (3 weeks)

Down at the bus stop you'd see them every morning, books clutched to their car coats, high-rise bouffants frosted in the early chill, wearing too much makeup and already, at fifteen or sixteen, a few too many pounds. I did not know their names and you can be certain they didn't know mine. These weren't girls who paid attention to guys their own age; they'd given up on scoring with the jocks or any of the inside crowd and the rest of us were, well, not worth so much as a glance. Not because they were snobs; because they feared the names that "smart kids" would call them, which began and ended in the catchall designation, "slut."

So I'll never know for certain if the scraps of conversation you'd pick up from sitting near them told the whole story, or whether it's really fair to fill in many details. But if you watched and listened, you heard stories that implied an experience no guy of my acquaintance could have boasted, a matter-of-fact knowingness about sex and men and the world at large that the college-bound among us didn't yet suspect. These girls might as well already have been women, because their lives were already laid out for them around a narrow set of alternatives: hasty postgraduation marriage and too many pregnancies too soon or else a job at Kroger's or wherever else they needed a check-out clerk, some job you might be able to get without even a diploma. Or getting knocked up and having the guy ditch her. Or getting knocked up and deciding to have a still-illegal abortion with the risk of being ruined or killed.

Living in those mid-America tank towns back then, you knew all sorts of stories like those, just like you knew the stories of their boy-friends, including the one summed up in that line that goes zipping by in "Born in the U.S.A.": "Got in a little hometown jam, so they put a rifle in my hand." Off they went, and after a while, you began to notice that not all of them came back. But mostly they did, and while it would be obscene to argue that that was worse, it would be unfair to exaggerate how much.

By the time they were juniors, maybe a little earlier, certainly before they graduated, a lot of those bouffant girls at the bus stop would have boyfriends serving somewhere overseas, most likely in Germany or a quiescent Korea, where bullets did not fly but nights were long and temptations many. Because the barriers between us were huge, I'm guessing again, but maybe they were just devoted pen pals, not doing so well in the high school social scene and so transferring their need to be needed to more distant objects. A lot of these same girls were the first to catch on to the Beatles, and the first to go really mad for one or another of the guys, the ultimate sexual unobtainables. Some of them had already figured that game out before the British Invasion, and they were the most loyal fans of local rock groups, often better ones than the style-setters at school listened to.

But sometimes, I suspect, those girls had real relationships with guys "in the service," not just paper ones, and their lonely nights must have been especially bereft because it was hard enough to land a guy, let alone worry about his existence a continent and an ocean away. Reputations are easy to come by and hard to get rid of, especially in your own mind. And so (I'm guessing again) they fretted.

I mention all this because everything I've ever read about "Soldier Boy" treats its enormous popularity as a mystery. Written on the spot in the studio and recorded in the final few minutes of a session, it strikes other critics and historians as perfunctory and tossed off, its unison harmonies and the unison instrumental break shared by organ and guitar insufficiently elaborated.

But whenever I've heard "Soldier Boy," it's made me think of those girls and their boyfriends, each of them lost and confused in a world that they not only didn't understand very well but which manifestly did not like them. And so they found each other, and so they were dragged apart, and so they wondered and pledged and pleaded: "In this whole world, you can love but one girl / Let me be that one girl / For I'll be true to you."

Somehow, in a barracks or a bedroom, those sweetly voiced lines must have helped a few million heads lay more comfortably upon their pillows. And so there's no mystery at all, really, except how so many people can stand right before our eyes and not be seen. Or heard.

150 LAND OF 1,000 DANCES, Cannibal and the Headhunters
Produced by Eddie Davis; written by Chris Kenner
Rampart 642   1965   *Billboard:* #30

151 LAND OF 1,000 DANCES, Chris Kenner
Produced by Allen Toussaint; written by Chris Kenner
Instant 3252   1963   *Billboard:* #77

152 LAND OF 1,000 DANCES, Wilson Pickett
Produced by Jerry Wexler; written by Chris Kenner
Atlantic 2348   1966   *Billboard:* #6

"Land of 1,000 Dances" is best known neither for its original version (Kenner's) nor for the version that became the biggest hit (Wilson Pickett took it Top Ten in 1966), but for an interim rendition that stalled in the middle of the chart but nevertheless remains definitive.

Cannibal and the Headhunters were a Chicano quartet from the East Los Angeles housing projects who learned "Land of 1,000 Dances" from a Rufus Thomas album. Thomas got it from veteran New Orleans eccentric Chris Kenner's original single, an obscurity which didn't so much as make *Billboard*'s rhythm and blues chart. Kenner more-or-less learned it in church.

A marvelous singer and songwriter, Kenner started recording around 1957. On most of his records ("I Like It Like That" and "Something You Got" are the best known), he drawled through a version of the already slinky New Orleans R&B beat so snakelike it seems as much Afro-Cuban as North American. His singing was dreamy, suggestive of smoky rooms late at night even when he was cutting party tunes. Yet however slack, the beat was always forceful, and all his hits revolve around dancing. Kenner's sparely written songs have a unique directness, closer to street language than lyrics. More than any of the other New Orleans stars of the fifties, he sang soul.

Kenner told New Orleans R&B historian John Broven that "Land of 1,000 Dances" was adapted from the spiritual, "Children Go Where I Send You," and that he "turned it around," which explains why the beat feels almost inside out. (Here's another example of a New Orleans record that feels a bit like a precursor to reggae. So why hasn't someone in Jamaica done for "Land" what Toots and the Maytals did for "Louie Louie"? Self-proclaimed "white Rasta" Patti Smith's arty reworking— "Land," on her 1975 album, *Horses*—doesn't really qualify.)

Kenner didn't enumerate anything like a thousand dances, but he ran through quite a few contemporary favorites, including the Pony, Twist, Mashed Potatoes, Alligator, Sweet Pea, Watusi, Fly, Hand Jive, Slop, Chicken, Bop, Fish, Slow Twist, Tango, and that New Orleans favorite (to which the beat was keyed), the Popeye. It was the era of the Twist and the discotheque and Kenner got vivid mileage from such reference points, not only in his choice of dance names but in the way he sang them ("the Chick'n'n'the Bop") and in the few sketchy verses:

> There's a little place, 'cross the track
> The name of this place, I Like It Like That
> Name of the band, the Twistolettes

The *Twistolettes*?! Now that's lyric imagination.

The circumstances of Cannibal and the Headhunters' discovery of the song have predictably gone unrecorded. (It's all their LP liner notes can do to get the story of their name straight, writer Tony Valdez claiming that Cannibal had no given name but had "been known as Cannibal for all of his life"—which would seem to mean that Cannibal *was* his first name, even though he's identified as Frankie in the photo just above. Valdez says that the other members were in a gang—er, "teenage club"—called the Headhunters, which is at least more credible.)

Kenner's version opens with the song's lyrics, and these days, that sounds pretty odd, like he left the best part of the song out. Cannibal begins with an extended wordless break: "Naaaa, naa, na-na-na." According to Ruben Guevara, the Toynbee of East L.A.'s prolific music scene, this arrangement came about because the Headhunters were performing the song live one night and Cannibal forgot the words and sang "Na-na-na" to improvise. It's a brilliant interpolation and shifts the focus of the song from a novelty *about* dancing to an injunction to get out and do it.

The Headhunters' "Land" was recorded with live atmosphere and with crazy falsetto introjections and bizarre shrieks in the background, Cannibal and the Headhunters created a funky garage-punk masterwork. It earned them a spot on the Beatles' 1965 U.S. tour, and they deserved it.

Pickett came along a few months later to cash in with his usual blunt instrument style, subordinating the "nah nah" and imagery to his own grunt 'n' groan rhetoric but still creating a record visceral enough to bring him his first Top Ten hit. But even Pickett's greater commercial success—which probably was due to Atlantic's superior distribution apparatus and Pickett's emergent star status—will apparently never erase the memory of Cannibal's original "Nah nah," a tribute to the public's long range good taste.

153 PLANET ROCK, Afrika Bambaataa and Soulsonic Force

Produced by Arthur Baker; written by Arthur Baker,
John Robie, and Soulsonic Force
Tommy Boy TB 831   1982   Did not make pop charts

"Planet Rock" is the record that established producer Arthur Baker and mixer Jellybean Benitez, who used rap vocals, disco rhythm devices, and audacious studio gimmickry to create dramatic, danceable pop. Jellybean got more immediately famous results by creatively underwriting Madonna's early career, but Baker remains the most consistently inventive producer on the current scene, either when starting from scratch or when reinventing tracks like "Girls Just Want to Have Fun" and "Dancing in the Dark" for superstar remixes.

"Planet Rock" is the *Pet Sounds* of eighties dance-pop, its mysterioso synthesizer effects continuously contrasted with the dance-as-destiny chants of former Bronx gangleader Bambaataa and his crew. "You gotta rock it, don't stop," they command and out on the floor, it never crosses anybody's mind to disobey.

154 THE GREAT PRETENDER, The Platters
Written and produced by Buck Ram
Mercury 70753   1955   *Billboard:* #1 (2 weeks)

Too sticky in its sentimentality for contemporary tastes? Not so fast. In an age of psychobabble, "The Great Pretender" touches the core of social and personal dysfunction and that's no joke—it's why Jackson Browne could get away with rewriting it, twenty years later, as a parable of everyman angst ("The Pretender," 1976). Sure, the presumption is that Tony Williams is singing about the loss of romantic love. But what the song's really about is alienation: "Too real is this feeling of make believe / Too real when I feel what my heart can't conceal."

Of course, that's not the reason that "The Great Pretender" wound up here; the record's here because of its ending, that grandiose moment in which what *has* been almost as bland and melodramatic as psychobabble is redeemed with a soaring effusion by Williams, seconded by the group, a sonority that reveals a peaceful center at the heart of all this mock turmoil.

155 TRY A LITTLE TENDERNESS, Otis Redding
Produced by Otis Redding, Jim Stewart, and Steve Cropper;
written by Reg Connelly, Harry Woods, and Jimmy Campbell
Volt 141   1966   *Billboard:* #25

"Try a Little Tenderness" was popularized in 1933 by Ted Lewis and Ruth Etting and eventually became associated with king crooner Bing Crosby. Sam Cooke cut it on his *Live at the Copa* album, which is where Redding's manager, Phil Walden, heard it. Walden was convinced that Otis should sing it and cajoled the singer about it for months. Finally, Walden got a call in the middle of the night.

"You know that damn song you've been on my ass about recording?" said Otis.

"Which one is that?" a weary Walden mumbled.

" 'Try a Little Tenderness.' "

"Yeah?"

"I cut the damn thing. It's a brand new song."

Which it was. Everything soft and sentimental about Cooke's and Crosby's readings was inverted; rather than a platitude, the song became a declamatory call to action. Otis begins by singing tentatively, as if he isn't quite sure where he wants to go. Drummer Al Jackson follows him like a metronome, keeping the beat slow and deliberate until Otis makes his move. The moment arrives when he repeats the word "never" over and over in disbelief. Otis starts preaching and Jackson picks the tempo up a hair. With "You won't forget it," they cut loose, Booker T.'s organ shrieking them on, and the horns building to a crescendo until finally Otis releases himself in sweaty surrender to the heat they've generated, the words and ideas coming so fast they seem by the end to become stuck in his throat. "Gotta, t' . . . t' . . . t' . . . , nah, nah, nah, gotta try a little tenderness," he exclaims.

Thus dies the Tin Pan Alley pop song, strangled in the throat of a man who did not love it. *Sic semper tyrannis.*

156 LAYLA, Derek and The Dominoes
Produced by The Dominoes (Executive Producer: Tom Dowd); written by Eric Clapton and Jim Gordon
Atco 6809   1972   *Billboard:* #10

Clocking in at 7:10, "Layla" is far too sprawling to shape up as a "classic" single but in the early seventies, it was precisely expansive records like "Layla," made by white rock stars with more control over their work than any black artist could afford (or was allowed) to imagine, that helped redefine the medium. Indeed, in its construction, especially its movement through radical shifts in mood, pitch, and tempo, "Layla" resembles the rap, dance, and disco twelve-inchers of the eighties far more than any of the blues its chords evoke.

But that doesn't constitute anything like an argument that "Layla" is the true ancestor of contemporary dance singles, just that in a society where everybody with ears hears (or heard) everything, it isn't all that surprising that Giorgio Moroder learned something from Clapton and company. Nor does it mean that what Moroder and other disco producers did with extended singles has any fundamental relationship to what big-time British rockers of the late sixties and early seventies did. At its most intense, "Layla" is as intense as anything in British rock, but it's still more laid-back than any dance record could ever afford to be.

I don't mean to build the case for "Layla" in totally negative terms.

But you know as well as I do that it is an intoxicating and feverishly beautiful piece of music and that anybody who ever claimed they play it too much on the radio lacks heart.

157 DROWN IN MY OWN TEARS, Ray Charles
Produced by Ahmet Ertegun and Jerry Wexler; written by Henry Glover
Atlantic 1085   1956   Did not make pop chart

The key to Ray's splendorous blues singing is his uncanny sense of time. Listen to the way he draws out every bit of sibilance from "I cried too much," or the way he sings "drown," then pauses, just long enough to let you know he's thinking about it, before delivering the "in my own tears" that leads into the bridge section, or his half-exhausted, half-exultant "Why can't you," where he floats into his upper register for the final word, and what you hear is a singer who commands his song as totally as if he'd written, produced, controlled every nuance of its creation from first impression to final fixing on the tape. Such a singer comes along roughly once a generation. The fact that he's also a great piano player and bandleader and holds his own on saxophone and behind the recording console merely means that this legend and this fact found it so easy to merge because there was so little discrepancy between them in the first place.

158 YOU TURN ME ON I'M A RADIO, Joni Mitchell
No producer credited; written by Joni Mitchell
Asylum 11010   1972   Billboard: #25

The one indisputably great single of the singer/songwriter movement, a simply magnificent unification of airy folk-pop melody and confessional language amidst the quasi-populism of Top 40 metaphors. Ordinarily, Mitchell's way is too icy and unfunky for my particular set of predispositions, but on the basis of "Radio," I've forgiven her almost everything, up to and including the pretensions of Mingus.

Sung with an ache in her throat that comes from just where you want it to—her heart—what makes the record so fine isn't just its sly, slick, and wicked put-downs of her deejay lover, but Mitchell's conviction that broadcasting her passions and discontents will work. And so it does.

At home, on your stereo, this might seem like nothing more than wish fulfillment. Driving around at night, or lying on the beach fighting off those sand flies, encountering "You Turn Me On" by surprise, it's the plain truth delivered in words of fewer syllables than you might imagine. With one of the all-time harmonica riffs, too.

159 SOLSBURY HILL, Peter Gabriel
Produced by Bob Ezrin; written by Peter Gabriel
Atco 7079   1977   *Billboard:* #68

Rock's greatest resignation speech. Highly metaphoric (unless you really think it took an eagle in flight to clue Gabriel in to the fact that it was time to quit Genesis; it was actually Bruce Springsteen at Hammersmith Odeon) but with a straightforward melody, carried on acoustic guitar and synthesizer and rhythm, "Solsbury Hill" is, however mystic its pretensions, finally one of the most nakedly emotional records anyone's created in the past twenty years. Using what he'd learned from tinkering with folk and classical forms as a member of Genesis, adding his own sense of pop and rock and roll, Gabriel also creates one of the most credible portraits of a star who hates his role.

What's perhaps just as extraordinary is that, from the lyrical opening to the monkeyshines at the end, "Solsbury Hill" encapsulates the next decade or so of Peter Gabriel's career. This is a record that makes bold promises and if its power has grown over the years (and it started out powerful enough), it's not only because it offers such strong inspiration whenever you need to summon the courage to make a tough move yourself. It's because Gabriel has lent it further resonance with every move he's made.

160 U GOT THE LOOK (LONG LOOK), Prince
Written and produced by Prince
Paisley Park 20727 (12")   1987   *Billboard:* #2

In the summer of 1987, America panicked over a health crisis. A good five years after it first began, the government and the national media decided to recognize the AIDS epidemic, partly because the disease was threatening millions of lives, partly as a device for further entrenching New Right moral revisionism.

Inevitably, pop music was caught up in the crisis. George Michael, the English teen idol, decided it was time to beef up his image with some musical muscle and a nod to serious lyric themes. He came up with "I Want Your Sex," which used an introduction lifted direct from the Prince of the *1999* period and a title meant to instigate a media controversy. Of course, the minute the Just Say No Puritans called his bluff, Michael backed down, calling his twelve-inch dance version of the song the "Monogamy Mix," and prefacing a video that looked like a promo trailer for *The Art of Sensual Massage* with an exculpatory introduction advocating abstinence. As topical songwriting, this was mere exploitation. And the music was as limp as the lyrics; it left you feeling about as priapic as a three-week-old banana.

And then there was Prince, out to reassert his claim to Royal Badness. Since *Purple Rain* transmuted him from cult hero to mass stardom, Prince had backed off from the sexual fixations (bisexuality, incest, orgies, masturbation) of his early records. His first hit of 1987, in fact, was "Sign O' the Times," a portentous recitation of urban social evils, including drug addiction and AIDS, that (despite its Sly & the Family Stone groove) was almost as hollow in its piety as "I Want Your Sex."

But Prince was not a simpleton, or at least, his simplest dreams were extraordinarily complex. "U Got the Look" joined him with Sheena Easton, a New Zealand pop chanteuse whose hits made George Michael seem as substantive as Stravinsky. But if anyone doubted Prince's genius for fusing unlikely elements in hot and nasty combinations, "U Got the Look" shed them forever. "I Want Your Sex" is a record *about* sex that makes the actual act seem of dubious value despite its immense consequences. "U Got the Look" is about sex without regard to consequences, and it captures the immensity of the act so perfectly that the natural (male) response is to look for the nearest receptacle and plug in.

On the radio, "U Got the Look" was wham-bam-thank-you-ma'am: a couple seconds of art-rock synth, an electronic reggae downbeat, disembodied voices out of *Axis Bold as Love*, a rhythm bed descended from the JBs deep in battle. Prince mouths the words as a staccato celebration of pure horniness, with responses from Easton that are less deeply sensual than viciously erotic. The result is a renewed awareness of why they call it rock and roll. The funk groove approaches heavy metal in its sheer intensity, and the lyrics never back off an inch from pure hedonism: "Your face is jammin' / Your body's heck-a-slammin' / If love is good, let's get to rammin'." Maybe they're using safe sex techniques, but it's hard to tell when they'd find time to slip a condom on him.

Back home with the twelve-inch on the turntable, the song opens up even more as it grows from just under four minutes to almost seven. The art-rock tease of the 45's intro becomes a full-blown tour of art-funk possibility, Pink Floyd jammin' on the one. Where the (45) "Single Cut" dwells on fucking, the (twelve-inch) "Long Look" grooves on pure lovemaking, made the more fascinating by the story line: He's picked her up after closing time because she looks "so tough" even with the lights full up. Now, the almost mumbled interjections ("Lock the door") make a different kind of sense; they're exploring each other for the first time, and they can't wait. And they see no reason why they have to. Safe sex? Condom or no, with or without penetration, when sex is happening at this level, there is no safety. And it's out of that sense of risqué danger that Prince makes his greatest music and gives the lie to opportunists and moralist fools alike.

161 SEARCHIN', The Coasters
Written and produced by Jerry Leiber and Mike Stoller
Atco 6087 1957 *Billboard:* #3

It's a better detective story than "Along Came Jones," "The Shadow Knows," or arguably even "Run, Red, Run," but what really makes "Searchin' " so fine isn't Leiber and Stoller's melodramatic words so much as the heavy backbeat established by drummer Jesse Saile and supplemented by a fine Los Angeles session band (itself augmented by a pianist named Mike Stoller, who happens to be the one who really makes the whole thing swing). Singing his bloodhound saga of relentless passion, Carl Gardner reaches for—and finds—more grit than he's ever previously displayed. If, like me, you find the Coasters' incessant goofing wearing, "Searchin' " is especially valuable because its appeal turns not on the allusions to Boston Blackie, the Northwest Mounties, and Sherlock Holmes (among others), but on the way Gardner and the band toy with time and intonation to create despair just as believable as the comic deflation that inexorably follows.

162 WALKING TO NEW ORLEANS, Fats Domino
Produced by Dave Bartholomew; written by Antoine Domino, Dave Bartholomew, and Robert Guidry
Imperial 5675 1960 *Billboard:* #6

Fats Domino was by far the most prolifically popular rhythm and blues singer. Between 1955 and 1964, Joel Whitburn lists no less than sixty-five Fats singles that made the *pop* charts. On the R&B charts, he was, if anything, slightly *less* prominent.

There are many reasons, not least the roots of the New Orleans blend of R&B in musical minglings far older and more middle-class than what was going on in any of the other original creative sites of rock and roll. Fats was the culmination of a hundred year tradition of Creole piano players, which is one reason that he was able to consistently hit with standards like "Blueberry Hill," "Coquette," "Margie," "Did You Ever See a Dream Walking," and even the 1911 "Put Your Arms Around Me Honey."

The beat behind these hits was rollicking and insistent but never raucous or threatening, and Fats' singing style amounted to one long, gregarious grin. Since smiling black performers have always been most welcome in even the whitest precincts of American culture, his ready reception on fifties and early sixties radio is no more surprising than his immediate disappearance from it once he could be replaced by equally cherubic white voices (even if they were British).

"Walking to New Orleans" is an anomaly within his career that demonstrates even more reasons for his success. It's the one slow, heavily orchestrated number that he and Dave Bartholomew made effective (in their hands the Tin Pan Alley songs never lost their groove). In fact, despite the gimmicky metronomic opening, the record's mood is virtually somber. The lyric drips blues, with an extremely wordy lyric that works because its syllables virtually demand to flow into one another: "I'm gonna need two pairs of shoes when I get through walking to you." Like (for instance) Louis Armstrong on latter-day pop hits such as "Wonderful World," Fats never seemed more disarming than when most mournful.

It's as easy to misunderstand Domino's clowning as it is Armstrong's, and for the same reasons. Fats is clearly walkin' because he's been driven out of somewhere else, though he refuses to glance over his shoulder even once. And though he's returning to a woman who's betrayed him in the past, he's gentle and forgiving even then, displaying a generosity of spirit and a devotion to domestic pleasure that is its own rebuke to anyone who would deny him.

163 BABY I NEED YOUR LOVING, The Four Tops
Produced by Brian Holland and Lamont Dozier; written by Brian Holland, Lamont Dozier, and Eddie Holland
Motown 1062   1964   *Billboard:* #11

One of the definitive Holland-Dozier-Holland riffs, stated with a full ensemble of brass, drums, clunky gospel piano, and the sharpest finger-pops this side of *77 Sunset Strip*.

The Tops are supper club smooth, bridging the prettiness of the melody and the agonized grit of Levi Stubbs's lead with wordless vowels that owe more to the decade they'd already spent as a night club act than to the traditions of doo-wop. This was their first chart hit, and Levi Stubbs is nothing less than magnificent, crooning the opening verse in his sweetest voice, making a terrific transition with a legato "I'm so lonely," swinging through the chorus, which is sharply punctuated with staccato responses (on "Got!") from the rest of the group. Stubbs grows progressively growlier as he delves deeper into HDH's gorgeous and intricately rhythmic wordplay. The climax comes when he shouts, "Empty nights echooo your name," a shout that turns the verb into pure onomatopoeia. The group exits as smoothly as it entered, without a hint of histrionics, but why not? They'd be back.

164 COLD LOVE, Donna Summer
Produced by Giorgio Moroder and Pete Bellotte; written by Pete Bellotte, Harold Faltermeyer, and Keith Forsey
Geffen 49634   1980   *Billboard:* #33

Putting Donna Summer's name on a series of graceful (if stiffly sung) late seventies dance hits made her Queen of Disco, but the real heroes of the day were producers Giorgio Moroder and Pete Bellotte, whose nonstop made-in-Munich dance beat defined the entire genre's highest aspirations.

By 1980, disco was fading and the dance-rock era was about to begin. Moroder, Bellotte, and Summer (whose voice was far better suited to rock than soul) positioned themselves perfectly for the trend with the most exciting album of her career, *The Wanderer*. But though dancing was becoming hip again, "disco" was déclassé and the Queen of Disco had little chance of changing her image. So none of the singles from *The Wanderer* got much airplay, not even "Cold Love," which is certainly as good a chunk of music as any of the participants ever created. (Within eighteen months, cowriter Keith Forsey became renowned for his soundtrack work, and Faltermeyer has since had a substantial production career. Summer, Moroder, and Bellotte have each had some success but never regained their disco era stature.)

"Cold Love" uses disco bass drum and some of the genre's typical synthesizer tactics but the beat's more taut, closer to rock, an impression reinforced by the guitar riff and solo (probably played by one of the L.A. session stars, Jeff Baxter or Steve Lukather). Summer's vocal stays on top of the beat, pushing the verse right up to the chorus, with its cries about "another shot of rock and roll love."

If "Cold Love" had been released two or three years later (or if it had been done by a singer whose image was less strictly defined), it would have been the smash it deserves to be, and the development of dance-rock would have been considerably accelerated, its relationship to disco more undeniable. (Blondie, the group that did have the first dance-rock hits, made records this good only in its dreams.) As it stands, you'll have to settle for "Cold Love" as one of the great lost possibilities of the past twenty years.

165 GET UP I FEEL LIKE BEING A SEX MACHINE, PART ONE, James Brown

Produced by James Brown; written by James Brown,
Bobby Byrd, and Ron Lenhoff
King 6318   1970   *Billboard*: #15

The by-god funkiest record ever cut in Nashville and also one of James's two or three most influential. Unquestionably, it's his most sampled, its bottom providing the inspiration (at minimum) for dozens of hip-hop hits, its piano lick (played by James himself) the foundation of the whole house style. Catfish Collins plays guitar like a monomaniac, a lick scratched out at the top of the neck and then repeated, over and over again, building an amazing tension against Bootsy Collins's liquid bass. This was a new group of JBs—first record for the Collins brothers, drummer Jabo Starks, and the horns—and the one that brought James back to the pinnacle of funk innovation, after some months of working formulas. (In those days, James was so prolific, funk so fertile, that style changed in significant increments every eight or ten weeks.)

Make sure to track down the original single version of the track; though divided into Part One and Part Two, it sounds brighter, the horns are sharper, James is raspier and there's no phony crowd noise, as on the remake they did for an LP a couple of months later. And about a minute in, it has what might be the greatest "Huh!" of James's career.

166 SILENCE IS GOLDEN, The Four Seasons
Produced by Bob Crewe; written by Bob Gaudio and Bob Crewe
Philips 40211   1964   Did not make pop chart

The most luminous of all Bob Crewe's sub-Spectorian productions, "Silence is Golden" was thrown away as the B side of "Rag Doll," and wound up becoming a hit in a vastly inferior version by the British group, the Tremeloes, who lacked a singer of Frankie Valli's spectacular dimensions much less an arranger as inspired as Charles Calello.

Whether Crewe or Calello was the real production genius here is a matter of dispute and conjecture. I've always leaned to Calello, partly because the arrangements—particularly the inventive percussion parts—are what make the Seasons' many hits so memorable, partly because there isn't much about the production atmosphere that conveys personality in the way that a producer like Phil Spector's hits do. But whoever it was that led the way (and songwriter/singer Bob Gaudio shouldn't be forgotten), the result is shattering. The harmonies were never more lush, the wood blocks and triangle that chase drummer Buddy Saltzman's beat create a sense of despair that's the equal of the dripping remorse in Valli's lead, and from time to time a reverberating guitar speaks as the most forceful voice of all. The production is so big that it encompasses an actual harp effortlessly.

The lyric is another of those stories of denial: "Silence is golden / But my eyes still see." The singer is miserable because the girl he loves is in a relationship with a guy he's sure is a rat—and he can't get himself to tell her about it, partly because it's none of his business, mostly because he's sure she'd never believe him. But the vocal speaks most clearly just before the last verse, when Valli sings, in transcendent falsetto, a wordless line right out of "The Lion Sleeps Tonight," certainly untranslatable in English but intelligible to anyone who's ever had to cover up the most important facts of his or her life.

167 LONELY AVENUE, Ray Charles
Produced by Ahmet Ertegun and Jerry Wexler; written by Doc Pomus
Atlantic 1108   1956   Did not make pop charts

Only two performers, songwriter Doc Pomus has said, always brought something unexpected to every one of his songs that they recorded. One was Elvis; the other was Ray Charles.

This brilliant recording must be about the grandest example of what Pomus meant. The herky-jerk stop-time pattern bears enough resemblance to gospel that Pomus probably wrote it that way and he certainly came up with the remarkably concrete lyrics, which offer a shiveringly tangible definition of desolation. But nobody could have guessed that Charles would turn the song into such an inimitable tour de force, his very breathing becoming part of the song's fundamental anxiety.

For Charles, singing really *is* a form of speech, just as his biographer David Ritz argues (even if, as Anthony Helibut alleges, Charles took his phrasing here from The Pilgrim Travelers' Jess Whitaker on "How Jesus Died"). But what a brand of speech it is, filled with nuances that stem from autonomous breathing patterns—here, he gasps in order to render his anxiety that much more plausible—and using a post-verbal vocabulary to encompass moans, shouts, and cackles that are beyond the ken of any but the most adept gospel singers and rarely turned to such thrilling purpose even by them.

168 (YOUR LOVE KEEPS LIFTING ME) HIGHER AND HIGHER, Jackie Wilson

Produced by Carl Davis; written by C. Smith, G. Jackson, and R. Miner
Brunswick 55336   1967   *Billboard:* #6

After he lost Berry Gordy as his chief songwriter, Jackie Wilson wandered in the wilderness for the better part of a decade. Though he had hits, Brunswick continually saddled him with blaring, overbearing "swing" arrangements of unmemorable songs. And so, after awhile, Wilson's records simply stopped making the charts. From "Baby Workout" in 1963 through late 1966, Wilson cracked the pop Top 40 only once. Without any concept of long-term career development and with pop in a continual process of radical transformation, Wilson should have washed up on the discard pile alongside so many other fine R&B singers from the fifties and pre-Motown sixties.

But in 1966, Wilson finally found a sympathetic producer, Carl Davis, a veteran of the Chicago scene, and together they proved that Jackie was just as capable as ever, first with "Whispers," which made it to Number 11, then, in 1967, all the way back to the Top Ten with "Higher and Higher."

The arrangement is sort of Stax-lite, an airier version of the Memphis groove. Wilson begins by singing quite precisely and carefully but when he is met and challenged by a female chorus, you can feel him start to push. Toward the end of the first chorus, he leaps for a keen falsetto "keeeeeep on," and when he makes it, he's all the way home.

After that, he takes the song at a quickened pace and with a smooth rhythmic assurance that shows his total command of what swing really means. When Wilson radiantly sings "Now, with my lovin' arms around you, I can stand up and face the world," he might be singing to the music that envelops him, banishing from his mouth the taste of so many seasons of schlock. He finishes by snapping off sassy phrases and toying with words like a prisoner who's just been liberated.

169 GIMME SOME LOVIN', The Spencer Davis Group

Produced by Chris Blackwell and Jimmy Miller; written by Steve Winwood
United Artists 50108   1966   Billboard: #7

Stevie Winwood was sort of the British Stevie Wonder, only he was all of seventeen when he burst forth with this roaring stomper. *What* he sang (the words are largely untrackable by Yankee ears) was far less important than *how*: like a tenor Ray Charles, with a throaty energy level as high as the Beatles'. That the song's instrumental center was his own organ playing only made the good news better. That he wrote the song himself (the band's first two British singles were written by Anglo-Jamaican Jackie Edwards) was the surest portent of how much he had to offer.

170 DOUBLE SHOT (OF MY BABY'S LOVE), Swingin' Medallions

Producer not credited; written by Don Smith and Cyril E. Vetter
Smash 2033   1966   Billboard: #17

The only frat-rock hit that sounds like it might have been recorded at Animal House. Crude, but then all hangover remedies are.

171 THINK, Aretha Franklin
Produced by Jerry Wexler, Tom Dowd, and Arif Mardin; written by Aretha Franklin and Ted White
Atlantic 2518   1968   *Billboard:* #6

Anarchic rockers could learn a lot from Franklin's strategy here, where she transforms a lyric about thought into a sermon on the subject of freedom, including condemnations of such phony forms of liberation as philandering and hustling. Her gospel shrieks and call-and-response forays are matched by the effortless groove of her piano, while Roger Hawkins plays as if to live up to producer Wexler's assessment of him as "the greatest drummer in the world."

172 DON'T LOOK BACK, The Temptations
Produced by Smokey Robinson; written by Smokey Robinson and Ronald White
Gordy 7047   1965   *Billboard:* #83

The lyric says the problem is a woman's, but David Ruffin's mournfully astringent singing of Smokey's elegant lyric makes it seem doubtful that anybody could feel worse. The Temptations offer harmonies as sharp as their choreography. And you get the Motown philosophy in a nutshell: "The past is behind you / Let nothing remind you."

173 LONDON CALLING, The Clash
Produced by Guy Stevens; Written by Joe Strummer and Mick Jones
Epic 50851   1979   *Did not make pop chart*

Joe Strummer reports from the war for the end of the world, mocking yuppie-era complacency as he beats his breast and exposes an anxiety as deep as the groaning bass line. At the dawn of the age of Thatcher and with Reaganism just over the horizon, Strummer captures the real big chill with caws and the most implacable music of the Clash's career—choppy guitars and ravaged vocals, stuff that sounds like it has looked the future in the face without flinching and understood that humanity is finished. Yet there's not a breath of misanthropy in it, nor even a touch of cynicism. Instead, there's humor and furious energy and a desire to leave a mark that even the coming Ice Age/Sunburst/Nuclear Accident cannot erase.

174 KEEP YOUR HANDS OFF MY BABY, Little Eva
Produced by Gerry Goffin; written by Gerry Goffin and Carole King
Dimension 1003   1962   *Billboard:* #12

175 DONNA, Ritchie Valens
Produced by Bob Kean; written by Ritchie Valens
Del-Fi 4110   1958   *Billboard:* #2

How teenagers talk, Lessons One and Two.

Ritchie Valens had a girlfriend; Donna was her name. Her old man hated Ritchie and forbade Donna from seeing him, because Ritchie was Mexican-American. So Valens wrote Donna a song, a heartbroken ballad that became his biggest hit. Whether love and the Top Two conquered bigotry will never be known because Valens died in a plane crash before the results were in.

Little Eva, having graduated from being the Goffin-King family's babysitter thanks to "The Loco-Motion," got herself a beau, on whose merits she bragged continually. Listening to Eva threaten her girlfriends with what might happen if they messed with her guy, Gerry Goffin (according to her) essentially transcribed her raps: "I don't mind when you lend my clothes, my jewelry and such / But honey, let's get something straight—there's one thing you don't touch." A bouncy Latinate rhythm and sugary Cookies harmonies converted her phrases into a follow-up hit, more slinky and less boisterous than "The Loco-Motion."

What's really going on here is sex role reversal. Goffin is the lyricist, King the melodist. Valens's song is the one whose song starts with a whimper ("I had a girl / Donna was her name . . ."), Little Eva's with a bang ("We've been friends for oh so long, I let you share what's mine / But when you mess with the boy I love, it's time to draw the line"). Well, actually what I love best is the whole groove of "Keep Your Hands," its rhythm amalgamated from handclaps, saxes, bass, and piano. With this beat pushing her, Little Eva doesn't just make Ritchie Valens sound like a wimp. She makes Aerosmith-meets-Run-D.M.C. seem like a folky idyll.

176 PEOPLE GET READY, Impressions
Produced by Johnny Pate; written by Curtis Mayfield
ABC-Paramount 10622   1965   *Billboard:* #14

What a terrific bundle of contradictions. A gospel arrangement in a
quartet style that was even then archaic, right down to its bluesy guitar
figure, married to a lush string setting that would sound excessive ten
years later. What lets the record work is the sweetness, soulfulness,
and endearing innocence of the singing. The lyric ranks with "A Change
is Gonna Come" as an expression of the interlinked concerns of the
civil rights movement, the black church, and the R&B record industry.
And even "A Change Is Gonna Come" didn't expropriate the imagery
of black spirituals with quite such slick precision.

177 TWIST AND SHOUT, The Beatles
Produced by George Martin; written by Phil Medley and
Bert Russell [Bert Berns]
Tollie 9001   1964   *Billboard:* #2

Even more than "Money," this is the music that must have made the
Beatles heroes in Hamburg and Liverpool: A beginning-to-end raveup that makes the Isley Brothers seem absolutely tame, Lennon shouting the lead vocal from a throat that sounds like it's been made hoarse
by a night of forty-five-minute sets and hard drinking during the breaks.
Yet the record's not just force; there's a lightness in the harmonies
(especially that last "Ahhhh") and in the guitar parts that bespeaks the
complete empathy of men who've not only grown up together but
continue to live their lives in such intimate association that there's never
a second thought in even their most complex activities. You can call
this groove or soul or you can simply sit back and let it dazzle you.

178 FINGERTIPS, PART 2, Little Stevie Wonder
Produced by Berry Gordy Jr.; written by Henry Cosby and
Clarence Paul
Tamla 54080   1963   *Billboard:* #1 (3 weeks)

A sound as huge and chromatic as that gigantic harp that he used in
those days, and like the harp, what at first seems like a gimmick turns
out to be dead serious. For that matter, the size of that huge mouth
harp equates with the size of Stevie's voice, made all the more amazing

because it came (at the time) from such a fragile-seeming blind black kid. That harp, and the blasts of pure R&B he made with it, were like a prophecy of the bull Stevie became in adulthood. In his way as precociously sexual as Michael Jackson, Stevie was perhaps able to hold on longer and with less fundamental psychic damage because even here, his knowingness is tempered by sly humor, the kind of thing that lets him whip out the melody of "Mary Had a Little Lamb" in the midst of all this Showtime at the Apollo frenzy.

Recorded live at Chicago's Regal Theatre, what pass for its lyrics improvised right there, "Fingertips" probably has the truest false ending in history, so baad it even fakes out the band, or at least the stand-in bassist (who thought Stevie's show was over and was coming back out to play with the *next* act, Mary Wells). But if somebody really didn't know "what key! what key!" everybody still plays like they've been practicing for this moment all their lives.

179 THE ADVENTURES OF GRANDMASTER FLASH ON THE WHEELS OF STEEL,
Grandmaster Flash and the Furious 5
Produced by Sylvia and Joey Robinson Jr.; writer not credited
Sugar Hill 577 (12″)   1981   Did not make pop chart

One of the most overused statements of the sixties was the one from Plato, or some ancient Greek, that claimed "When the mode of the music changes, the walls of the city shake." Well, that doesn't describe the Grateful Dead very well in my book, but play this first masterpiece of hip-hop at the crushing volume at which it was intended to be heard and shit will start shakin' you never imagined had any wobble in it. And hardly anybody outside the New York City area has ever even heard the damn thing.

The problem is legal and conceptual. There's no writer's credit for "The Adventures of Grandmaster Flash on the Wheels of Steel" because copyright law doesn't provide credit for the art of aural montage. "Adventures" cuts, splices, spins, and shatters sounds reproduced from other records: The label credits offer "special thanks" to "CHIC ('Good Times'), BLONDIE ('Rapture'), QUEEN ('Another One Bites the Dust'), SUGARHILL GANG ('8th Wonder'), FURIOUS FIVE ('Birthday Party'), SPOONIE GEE ('Monster Jam')," an act of magnanimity that didn't prevent lawsuits, threatened and filed.

The art of Grandmaster Flash consisted of cutting together excerpts from those records to create an incredible collage of urban dance beat that twists, turns, and comments upon itself underpinned by the bass and piano of Chic and the guitar and feedback of Queen. In the hands of Grandmaster Flash, and the hip-hop deejays who followed him, playing a record ceased to be a passive experience and became an occasion for actual musical creation. A concept, of course, that befuddles copyright law's presumption that those who buy "intellectual property" don't quite own it.

Flash did more than simply splice together one record with another; Dickie Goodman had been doing that sort of thing for twenty years when Flash started deejaying in the Bronx in 1976. In clubs, Flash could cut sounds together, on the beat, on the spot, without ever losing the dance rhythm that made his whole act relevant and viable. Beyond that, he used the turntable as an aggressive instrument, rubbing the needle back and forth in the grooves to repeat breaks and comments, or simply using the noise of needle and record being pushed around by hand to enhance his sound.

All this within the context of strict dance time, a feat that grows more impressive the longer you listen—scratching's not just a gimmick, it's an art form like playing percussion, because it actively and deliberately changes meaning as well as meter. For instance, in "Rapture," Debbie Harry sang the phrase "Flash is bad" with chic disdain for sartorial ostentation. On "Adventures," Grandmaster uses the same phrase to celebrate himself, completely subverting Harry's meaning (in part because in costume and demeanor, Flash is as uncool as Harry's worst dream). This shifting of texts and sources, making meaning from the everyday sounds of one's life, is the essence of hip-hop as a modern musical art. And "The Adventures of Grandmaster Flash on the Wheels of Steel" ranks as the *Birth of a Nation* of the form.

180 SWEET LITTLE SIXTEEN, Chuck Berry
Produced by Leonard Chess; written by Chuck Berry
Chess 1683   1958   *Billboard:* #2

Chuck Berry may have been a full-fledged adult by the time his teen anthems hit the charts, but he derived a good bit of his credibility the old-fashioned way: through the most finely articulated obsession with the passions of young girls since Lewis Carroll's. When he sings "all the cats wanna dance with Sweet Little Sixteen," he means to include himself, and he doesn't just mean dance.

Berry says he wrote "Sweet Little Sixteen" after a Denver concert where he spotted a girl wearing a "big flowery yellow dress." "She never saw one act fully—she was running around the arena getting autographs a mile a minute, her wallet waving high in her hand and she didn't seem to care about who was on—she only cared about when they came off, so she could get her autographs," Berry recalled in his autobiography. "I was writing as I was looking at this kid, and . . . I got several lines of 'Sweet Little Sixteen' that night—that particular night—after I came offstage."

If Chuck Berry had been perceived for what he was—a black adult male with extremely normal passions and, judging from his book, an extremely uncommon penchant for acting them out—the innuendos of "Sweet Little Sixteen" would have overwhelmed the feigned innocence of its American Bandstand references, and the record never could have become his biggest hit of the fifties. As it was, its implications probably didn't help during the trial at which he was railroaded into prison on a Mann Act charge.

But if "Sweet Little Sixteen" is the first portrait of a groupie in action, it also would have become a legendary rock and roll record without a breath of lechery, thanks to pianist Johnny Johnson and drummer Fred Below rocking at the top of their form.

181 KANSAS CITY, Wilbert Harrison
Produced by Bobby Robinson; written by Jerry Leiber and Mike Stoller
Fury 1023   1959   Billboard: #1 (2 weeks)

The story of "Kansas City," the hit record, can't be told without telling the story of "Kansas City," the blues standard, and not just because the composition predates the recording by a good seven years. "Kansas City" is one of the greatest of all blues songs of which we know the author, and yet, without Wilbert Harrison's distinctive performance it would most likely have been lost to history. Released on Federal 12110 in 1952, Little Willie Littlefield's original version of the song, then titled "K.C. Loving," never made the rhythm and blues charts, which is no surprise: It's good journeyman jump blues, nothing more.

The *song* is another story. Jerry Leiber and Mike Stoller, the greatest songwriting team of the 1950s, created it as the result of a disagreement. Leiber had come up with the words, and wanted a basic twelve-bar blues shuffle to accompany them. Stoller insisted on composing something more distinctive, although what he came up with was sufficiently generic that it had at least one significant year-old precedent. But Leiber and Stoller's gift wasn't for transforming the blues; it was for giving the classic shape unique wit and verbal coloration.

Leiber and Stoller knew nothing about Kansas City other than what their Joe Turner records told them. Each had been born on the East Coast and transplanted to Los Angeles as a kid. Leiber was a budding Hollywood sharpie who turned to lyric writing because it seemed like a good way to get into show business. Stoller's musical talent appeared early in his life; he studied composition and piano and turned to writing pop songs only after Leiber's lyrics convinced him it might be possible to create something like the blues songs he loved on records by singers like Turner.

Leiber and Stoller were aspiring "white Negroes." In New York, Leiber belonged to a Harlem social club; in L.A., he lived in a Mexican-American neighborhood and joined a Pachuco social club. By 1950, when he and Stoller attended City College in Los Angeles, they considered themselves "into a black life-style," which meant that they were bohemians who dated black girls and listened to black music. In 1952, when "K.C. Loving" was written, Leiber and Stoller were each nineteen years old. They'd been writing for a couple of years, and had garnered a bit of success in the West Coast R&B market. All of Leiber's lyrics, and most of Stoller's music, convincingly affected "black life-style."

Wilbert Harrison needed to affect nothing along those lines. He was born black in Charlotte, North Carolina in 1929. By the time he was seventeen, he'd enlisted in the Navy, where he served until 1950. Harrison found himself discharged in Miami, where he became interested in music, especially Caribbean calypso. Harrison cut his first record, "This Woman of Mine," for Miami record distributor Henry Stone in 1951, but he was best known for winning the local Rockin' House Amateur Show six straight times with a rendition of "Mule Train," a pop hit (for Frankie Laine) with country and western roots.

Recording for several small labels, Harrison's unorthodox amalgam of influences—gospel, blues, C&W, and calypso—lent him an unusually distinct style. Yet he never came close to a hit and in 1956 he packed it in and moved back to Charlotte.

For the next two years, Harrison made no records. Then Bobby Robinson, the Harlem record store owner who owned a succession of blues labels (Red Robin, Whirlin' Disc, Everlast, Enjoy, Fury) scouted him up and brought him to New York, apparently to cut some gospel records. Harrison had been doing "K.C. Loving" (which he'd renamed) since he'd heard Littlefield's recording, and they decided to give it a try at the end of the session. In less than half an hour, in spare time from a session that cost less than $40 in the first place, Harrison, Robinson, and a trio featuring guitarist Jimmy Spruill cut one of the outstanding Number Ones of the rock and roll era.

To the extent that Harrison deviated from Littlefield's arrangement he did so by reverting to his first record, "This Woman of Mine," which had the same basic beat and a strong melodic resemblance to the song Leiber and Stoller "wrote" (in this light, "assembled" might be more accurate) a year later. But either because his own style had matured or because Robinson and the New York band pushed him to greater clarity, "Kansas City" struck such a solid shuffle groove that it was unforgettable. And however derivative the rest may be, Harrison's cry of "Mercy" perfectly set up Spruill's guitar break, which is as red-hot as anything that ever topped the charts.

It might be tempting to write here of white interlopers defrauding black culture. But the legitimacy of Leiber and Stoller's "Kansas City" is no more in doubt than the legitimacy of Wilbert Harrison pilfering ideas for phrasing from hillbilly singers and accents from calypsonians. What's certain is that their convergence resulted in rock and roll unforgettable and that it's this very effect of disparate elements flying forcefully together in unlikely patterns that makes those the only terms upon which such music can be properly evaluated. While it's a shame that when everyone from Little Richard and the Beatles to Herb Alpert and Ann-Margret covered the number only Leiber and Stoller got paid, that's a problem for lawyers and politicians to work out. In the critical history of rock and roll, Wilbert Harrison's place of honor is permanent and assured, as (it should go without saying) is Leiber and Stoller's.

182 GARDEN PARTY, Rick Nelson
Written and produced by Rick Nelson
Decca 32980   1972   Billboard: #6

There are fools in this world who think that Ricky Nelson was just the first teen idol, and rank him on a scale that features David Cassidy and Bobby Sherman and George Michael and other midget talents of yesteryear and today.

"Garden Party" is about why Rick Nelson decided he didn't have to tolerate fools and simply went about being who he was. Its lyric revolves around a mistake: playing a rock and roll revival show at Madison Square Garden in 1971. Best remembered for its final line, a put-down of the very idea of such events—"If memories were all I sang, I'd rather drive a truck"—the record ought to be recalled for half a dozen other reasons: the gentle country bluesiness of Rick's vocal, the pretty steel guitar, simple shuffle rhythm, and lovely backing vocals, the generosity with which he looks upon the other old rockers going through their paces (especially Chuck Berry), his amazement that Bob Dylan and John Lennon would come along to see *him*, the courage it took to write a great song about fucking up and getting booed.

And if it's a lyric catchphrase you need, try "You can't please everyone, so you better please yourself." Then you might understand that Rick Nelson was no teen idol but one of the first and best country-rockers, and that "Garden Party" isn't a novelty but one of the finest hits of the singer/songwriter era.

183 GREAT BALLS OF FIRE, Jerry Lee Lewis
Produced by Sam Phillips; written by Hammer and Blackwell
Sun 281   1957   *Billboard: #2*

We've reached the point where the outtake dialogue in which Jerry Lee rants against the Pentecostal sacrilege of "Great Balls of Fire" (and Sam Phillips badgers him into not just singing but allowing himself to be possessed by the damnable thing) is more widely remarked upon by critics than the record that resulted. And that ain't fair, because "Great Balls of Fire" transcends everything doctrinaire and theoretical. It just sorta IS, an incomparable fragment of whoop and glissando, leering vocal and pounding rhythm. The solo and the way Jerry Lee slides out of it is as wild as anything Little Richard ever did and the way Lewis almost slips into an insane laugh at the top of the last verse tells you everything necessary about who Jerry Lee is and what his problems are. As for preaching, after this one, Jerry Lee could truly say, "Eat your heart out, Jimmy Swaggart."

184 HEARTS OF STONE, The Jewels
No producer credited; written by Eddy Ray and Rudy Jackson
R and B 1301   1954   Did not make pop chart

One of the first Number One records of 1955, the year that most chart scholars give as the dawn of rock and roll's dominance, was "Hearts of Stone" by the Fontane Sisters, a trio from New Jersey who had been regulars on Perry Como's radio and TV broadcasts for a decade. Since the Fontanes recorded for Dot, the Tennessee cover records specialist, it surprises no one to learn that the Fontanes were actually keeping a black group, Otis Williams and the Charms, out of the top spot. The Charms record peaked at Number 15.

But it wasn't quite that simple. On the West Coast, the Charms' reputation wasn't much different from the Fontanes', and for the same reason. Their hit (released on DeLuxe, a subsidiary of Cincinnati kingpin Syd Nathan's King-Federal empire) squeezed out the true original version of the song, by another R&B group, the Los Angeles-based Jewels.

Because the Charms were a black act, they got away with swiping the song. Few histories ever mention that their record was itself a cover. And that's sad because the Jewels' "Hearts of Stone" may be the finest example ever recorded of the raucous side of L.A. group harmony, which owed as much to the Southwestern roadhouse jump bands of Wynonie Harris and Roy Brown as the Northeastern variety did to bel canto.

The Charms' record offers nothing unpredictable; it's one of the first examples of rock and roll as sheer formula, although the song itself is so winning that both Memphis guitarist Bill Justis and John Fogerty, in his guise as the Blue Ridge Rangers, later took it back to the Top 40. The Jewels' record starts out with the same formula and demolishes it, though since it exists on no prominent doo-wop reissue compilation nor even as a widely distributed reissue single, it's hard to find that out.

From the first few bars, it might not be all that clear what the big deal's about. The Jewels' harmonies seem little more than a shakier version of the Charms', the backing only moderately more swinging. But as the music carries on, the backing vocals—"Doo wah dah do, doo wah, doo wah dah do"—become almost maniacal in their insistence, and then a raw tenor sax begins to bark and the drums pick up the power without altering the pace. Finally, near the end, the lead singer's repeated "No" careens off into a vector of its own, while the chorus has lost itself completely, its "doo wah dah do" coming closer and closer to the sound of a barbaric horde about to unleash itself into some altogether unmanageable dimension. When a wild tenor voice sets up on the edge of falsetto way in the back, then leaps suddenly forward at the very end, you know you've just encountered one of the true lost classics of rock and soul.

185 SWEET HOME ALABAMA, Lynyrd Skynyrd
Produced by Al Kooper; written by Edward King,
Gary Rossington, and Ronnie Van Zant
MCA 4025   1974   *Billboard:* #8

Love for the South and the perils of populism have always gone hand
in hand and here's the ultimate example, which began with Ronnie
Van Zant sitting in the back of his group's tour bus, writing a pissed-
off response to Neil Young's "Southern Man," an attack on white
Southern voters for playing into Richard Nixon's hands.

The result is half heartland hymn, with some marvelously evocative
singing about the geographical, familial, and musical beauty of Van
Zant's native territory, one quarter summation of the Southerner's
colonized alienation from events in the North, and one quarter meat-
head populist diatribe against smart guys and outsiders which winds up
trying to excuse the unforgivable (in this case, George Wallace).

By the time Skynyrd gets to the last verse and start singing about
their pals at Muscle Shoals, you'd have excused them for just about
anything even back when the issues are fresh. Now that the band is
gone in a plane crash and equally ugly creatures have appeared at the
very center of American politics, what you hear is one of the last great
bluesy numbers to reach the Top Ten.

186 ONE MORE HEARTACHE, Marvin Gaye
Produced by Smokey Robinson; written by Smokey Robinson,
Ronald White, Warren Moore, Bobby Rogers, and Marvin Tarplin
Tamla 54129   1966   *Billboard:* #29

"One More Heartache" echoes now as Gaye's greatest unrecognized
performance, with a chiming guitar line, organ drone, frantic vocal
chorus, glowering sax, lethal bass and drum groove, and lyrics and
atmosphere that serve as a prophecy of both "I Heard It Through the
Grapevine" and the end of his own life:

> One more heartache, it could turn me right around
> First you build my hopes up high, and then you let me down
> Like the house you build from toothpicks stacked up on a
>   kitchen table
> One last toothpick tore it down, the foundation was not able

The poetry is no doubt Smokey Robinson's but what makes those
long, almost unwieldy lines take your breath away is the way Marvin

finds himself engulfed by the material, the poignancy of his *total* grasp of every nuance of this story. You wanna think this is just a love song, that's fine with him. But listen deeper and you'll know better. It's a spiritual suicide note from a man who, in a merely halfway sane world, would have had everything to live for and known it.

187 LET'S GO CRAZY, Prince
Written and produced by Prince
Warner Brothers 29216   1984   *Billboard:* #1 (2 weeks)

The most concentrated dose of rock and roll Prince has ever delivered, making it an almost atomic package. The funk's still there but in the 4/4 avalanche, who cares? If the Rolling Stones had made a track this strong in the past fifteen years, I'd still be a fan. As it is, this seems like the right place to transfer allegiance: The subject is always Topic A and when Prince cuts loose like this, even his religious dementia just adds to the frenzy.

188 DEDICATED TO THE ONE I LOVE, The "5" Royales
Produced by Ralph Bass; written by Lowman Pauling and Ralph Bass
King 5453   1958   *Billboard:* #81

189 DEDICATED TO THE ONE I LOVE, The Shirelles
Produced by Luther Dixon; written by Lowman Pauling and Ralph Bass
Scepter 1203   1959   *Billboard:* #3

"Dedicated to the One I Love" may be the key record in the development of contemporary black vocal group harmony, the clearest single example of what happened as the sounds of Southern Negroes migrated to the industrialized North. The "5" Royales version reflects tough, Southern R&B in the waning days of its power. Although the disc's signature moment comes at the top, with Johnny Tanner's ragged a cappella cry, "This is dedicated to the one I-ay-I love!" the record's center is Lowman Pauling's stinging guitar lick, and the solo that he builds from it.

That's not to say that the record is crude. In fact, the Royales were perhaps the most sophisticated of all the R&B groups, and their arrangement of "Dedicated" is no exception. In this version, the song was an adult's statement of devotion despite physical separation, and Tanner sings it in a style closer to jump band vocalists like Wynonie Harris and Roy Brown than to any street corner doo-wopper.

Luther Dixon picked "Dedicated to the One I Love" for his first production with what became the first great girl group. The Shirelles were four high school kids from Passaic, New Jersey: Shirley Owens, Beverly Lee, Doris Kenner, and Mickey Harris. In early 1958, they scored a minor hit on Decca (originally, Tiara) with "I Met Him on a Sunday." When Decca, one of the industry "majors" and thus still oriented to blues-less white pop, couldn't provide a follow-up hit, their manager, Florence Greenberg started Scepter as a vehicle for the girls and a main chance for herself.

Luther Dixon's career began in the Four Buddies, a first-rate R&B quartet. By the time he hooked up with these girls, he'd had a good deal of experience as a songwriter and publisher, contributing smooth crooner ballads to the likes of Pat Boone and Perry Como. Even after the Shirelles started to click, Dixon was the most in-demand demo singer in New York. Dixon's importance on the New York pop scene was great enough that Greenberg had to give him substantial incentives to work with the Shirelles: He obtained both a piece of the action (in the form of song publishing rights and an ownership position in Scepter) and the right to produce the group to his own specifications.

"Dedicated to the One I Love" became Dixon's first production with the girls. His arrangement smoothed over much of the original grit. The guitar lick disappeared, replaced by a wordless soprano obligato, and the female chorus that had been a minor accoutrement was brought front and center. Tanner's stop-time vocal effects were replaced by straight vocal group harmonizing.

The result was as stunning in its own right as the original. At the time, female black harmony groups were all but unknown; besides "I Met Him on a Sunday," only the Chantels' "Maybe" had ever made much of a commercial or creative impression. Kenner's initial "This is dedicated to the one I love" was less melismatic but more plaintive than Tanner's, and the girls' harmonies conveyed not the story of two mature lovers trying to cope with a pragmatic dislocation but the story of two teenagers separated by social convention rather than great distance. (The boy and girl in this song might well be living next door to one another.) There's a kind of knowing innocence in the Shirelles' version of "Dedicated to the One I Love" that would thereafter become part of the common stock of rock and roll but was nowhere to be found before it. No adult singer could have given the song this implied subtext.

"Dedicated to the One I Love" brought the Shirelles back to the pop charts but not for long; the record peaked at Number 83 and dropped off the pop chart after only four weeks. But it gave Dixon a sense of direction and he focused all the group's subsequent releases around the same idea, edging into the Top 40 in September 1960 with "Tonight's the Night" and hitting the jackpot at the end of the year with "Will You Still Love Me Tomorrow," in which the subtext—female teenage sexual activity—became as overt as contemporary radio could cope with. That record went all the way to Number One, and it had a lot to do with initiating both the doo-wop revival and the dawning of the great age of the girl groups.

"Will You Still Love Me Tomorrow" was so massive, in fact, that it dragged "Dedicated to the One I Love" back to the charts. In late February 1961, "Dedicated" cracked the *Billboard* Top Ten. ("Will You Still Love Me Tomorrow" was still there, too.) It eventually reached the Top Three, and its own drawing power was so great that the "5" Royales's reissued original was pulled onto the pop charts for the first time.

For the past quarter century, "Dedicated to the One I Love" has been almost continually revived: The Mamas and Papas steam-cleaned the harmonies and took it to Number Two in 1967, and it's charted twice more since then. But in the context of today's more sexually open society, the *song's* innocence isn't really anything more than an opportunity to play nostalgic games with its contextual incongruity. These *records*, however, are stamped with the sense of daring and innovation with which they were made.

190 19TH NERVOUS BREAKDOWN, The Rolling Stones

Produced by Andrew Loog Oldham; written by Mick Jagger and Keith Richards
London 9823   1966   *Billboard: #2*

The Stones at this point—post-scruffy blues band and pre-psychedelic aristocracy—had a look and sound as lethal and streamlined as a Ferrari at full speed, with an engine (powered by Watts and Wyman) at least that efficient. Keith's guitar intro is worth the price of admission, and he keeps it up straight through to the end, where he, or Brian Jones (or somebody) comes up with the quirky, quavering riff on which Texas acid-punk hero Roky Erickson built a whole career.

Meanwhile the pithy social satire and meanspirited misogyny of the lyrics are redeemed by Jagger's self-deprecating performance (Could all this snivelling be directed at *himself*?). The lyric everybody talks about is the one about "our first trip" but the one that's unforgettable is "Nothin' I do don't seem to work / It only seems to make matters worse," a double negative so profound it would work as a review of Altamont.

191 NINETY-NINE AND A HALF WON'T DO, Wilson Pickett
Produced by Jim Stewart and Steve Cropper; written by Wilson Pickett and Steve Cropper
Atlantic 2334   1966   *Billboard:* #53

Featuring a bass line that should have been dreamed up by Stephen King, not Duck Dunn. The Memphis Horns provide lethal undertow, Steve Cropper slashes slices off the beat, and Al Jackson nails down the groove with lip-smacking precision. Pickett growls and shrieks as if they're doing it all just to please him. Eddie Van Halen *wishes* he had something this dangerous to play.

192 WHY DO FOOLS FALL IN LOVE, Frankie Lymon and the Teenagers
Produced by George Goldner; written by Frankie Lymon
Gee 1002   1956   *Billboard:* #6

Further fuel in the singer-not-the-song debate. "Why Do Fools Fall in Love" has made the *Billboard* Hot 100 six times, and the Beach Boys came close in 1964, when their version got some airplay as the flip side of "Fun Fun Fun." But Frankie Lymon's is the only memorable rendition, a scorching example of what one precocious teenager can accomplish without much ammunition except a huge voice and unwavering ambition.

Lymon's singing seems virtually unprecedented, until you realize that he's using tricks learned from the likes of Dinah Washington and Ruth Brown, just given whatever veneer of maleness a thirteen-year-old possesses. However derivative, and even given Richard Barrett and/or George Goldner's shimmering setting, it's Frankie, through the sheer yearning of his vocal, who makes the record unforgettable, forces it by an act of will to transcend the schlock of the song. Every other attempt to give the song life—from Gale Storm's 1956 attempt to steal the black kid's thunder to Diana Ross's predictably narcissistic 1981 revival—

goes to show that "Why Do Fools" isn't a great song, just a first-rate marketing vehicle. That does nothing to demean Lymon's achievement; in fact it may enhance it, since he was the only performer who figured out a way to make this particular piece of product into a commodity closely resembling art.

193 WHITE CHRISTMAS, The Drifters
Produced by Ahmet Ertegun and Jerry Wexler; written by Irving Berlin
Atlantic 1048   1955   *Billboard:* #80

It's worth wondering what Irving Berlin made of Clyde McPhatter's rendition of his most beloved song. Did he disapprove of rock and roll so completely that he resented the way the Drifters transformed the (already glorious) original Bing Crosby arrangement? Or did he understand that the way Clyde McPhatter toys with the melody enriches it, that his expansion of the word "I'm" is a truly epic commentary on the meaning of the season and that the unmistakable irony of a black group singing *this* lyric all brought his song renewed life, artistic as well as commercial?

194 MY TRUE STORY, The Jive Five
Produced by Les Cahan and Joe Rene; written by Eugene Pitt
Beltone 1006   1961   *Billboard:* #3

Had he come along at another moment in pop music history, Eugene Pitt might have been a superstar rather than just the auteur behind a few splendid throwaway hits. A thrilling doo-wop lead singer who definitely had the tools to sing soul (borne out by his magnificent early eighties version of Steely Dan's "Hey Nineteen"), he was also a skillful songwriter. Stylistically, Pitt's singing is unquestionably a link between fifties R&B styles and soul balladry. But the insular New York doo-wop scene gave him no outlet for creative growth.

Pitt grew up in Brooklyn's squalid Bedford-Stuyvesant. His first group, the Genies, had a national R&B hit with "Who's That Knocking" in 1959. Two of the other Genies went on to become Don and Juan ("What's Your Name") while Pitt gathered together others from the neighborhood and formed the Jive Five. They perfected their harmonies on subway platforms and eventually found their way to Beltone's Les Cahan, a veteran recording studio owner.

"My True Story" was the group's first record. Pitt says that he wrote the lyric based on a true experience—thus the *Dragnet* reference in the final verse ("Names have been changed, dear, to protect you and I"). But what really makes the disc is his crying lead vocal, which lends the narrative a weight its predictable triangulation would otherwise miss.

195 TODAY I MET THE BOY I'M GONNA MARRY, Darlene Love
Produced by Phil Spector; written by Phil Spector, Ellie Greenwich, and Tony Powers
Philles 111 1963   *Billboard:* #39

Alone in her room in the early autumn evening, a young woman pushes aside her homework and tells herself what sounds like the truth about the magic she believes she's found. Now that rock and roll has been taken over by those of us who *didn't* get married straight out of high school, it's hard to remember how plausible the little lies she tells herself must have sounded. But Phil Spector understood. You can tell by the glockenspiel, which tinkles away against that gorgeous melody like it's sprinkling fairy dust.

196 THANK YOU (FALETTINME BE MICE ELF AGIN), Sly and the Family Stone
Written and produced by Sly Stone
Epic 10555 1970   *Billboard:* #1 (2 weeks)

Like a lot of the best minds of his generation, Sly Stone dreamed of integration. His dream was broader than most. He imagined the merger of black and white and men and women and soul and rock and rich and poor and famous and humble. And as the sixties came crashing to a close, he saw that dream replaced by a terrible vision of separation, in which each person stood isolated and apart, fumbling in darkness to reach a single other person outside themselves.

Sly felt these forces himself. He developed the symptoms of a bleeding ulcer. He confronted demands from black nationalists that he exert his leadership of the world's most popular pop-funk in their direction. He confronted demands from record executives and management that he milk the cash cow his band had become. He confronted hostilities among the family and friends he'd drawn together in the Family Stone. He was threatened with a confrontation with an assassin's bullet, and in the wake of the murders of Martin Luther King and Malcolm X, such threats were all too believable. His own body confronted him with the demand for the cocaine that had become his insulation against the divisions and the decay.

Always inward gazing, Sly focused so deeply upon himself now that often enough, he failed to notice the outside world at all and missed shows where ten or twenty thousand or more had gathered to hear him. Always sardonic, he began to write music so bleak and sarcastic that it virtually spat in the eye of his early effusions about brotherhood and solidarity.

And yet the gathering forces of superstardom would not be denied. As long as Sly provided the right beat, the crowds would dance to whatever he had to say. This was the new contract between the performer and his audience. Neither had to listen to the other; they just had to act in the right rituals and all requirements were satisfied. And if everybody hated everybody else, well, that was just how things were.

As a musical genius, Sly Stone had no trouble meeting the demands of the time. (It would take years for the dope to eat the talent.) But when the dream died, the challenge went with it. He sat down to write a song and poison spilled out. Set it to one of the grungiest guitar-bass riffs he'd ever devised, a slinky, sinister beat, then picked up the tempo just a hair. Got more specific as the verses progressed, drew more blood from the shards of his own hopes and career, mocked his own songs. *"Thank u falettin' me be mice elf agin."*

No one caught on. The record went straight to Number One. No one heard him. He went back in the studio and tinkered. Slowed it down; forced the listener to hear the blood trickle out, drop by drop. Called it "Thank U for Talkin' to Me, Africa." It was no hit single, but the album (which he called *There's A Riot Goin' On*, a neat reference to the Robins' "Riot in Cell Block #9," except that Sly's title track clocked in at 0:00) made it. As hip dance music, not a cleansing burst of outrage. He gave up. Cranked out a few more records. Sniffed a lot more coke. Burned out. Staged a dozen comebacks, none meaning any more than his last few hits. What difference did it make?

Answer's in the grooves.

197 DOMINO, Van Morrison
Written and produced by Van Morrison
Warner Bros. 7434   1970   *Billboard: #9*

Twenty years ago, "Domino" may have seemed like an acolyte's tribute to a master, but over time, Van Morrison's credentials have come to seem every bit as substantial as Fats Domino's. So what we have today is a mannerist pastiche, using all the key elements of the Domino style to create a song as indubitably Morrisonian as anything he ever did. The brilliant brass flourishes, precisely mumbled vocalese, the entire atmosphere of brightness and exuberance are the Fats-based part. The virtually literary air of mystery, evocation of spiritual connections as a form of psychic radio, powerhouse drive, and generally philosophical air are the things Van uniquely contributed.

198 BAD MOON RISING, Creedence Clearwater Revival
Written and produced by John Fogerty
Fantasy 622   1969   *Billboard: #2*

The record that wouldn't go out of my head on Election Night 1980 and for nearly a week thereafter: "Don't go out tonight / It's bound to take your life."

Well, that was an overreaction, maybe even a predictable one, because Fogerty wrote the song about Nixon and most of us survived that, too. On the other hand, you can wake up on any random morning and feel like that bad moon's on the rise and that the jangle of the guitar isn't simply evoking old rockabilly singles, just vibrating at the same damnable frequency as your nerves. And when that happens, every single syllable John Fogerty moans is not just the truth, but the whole truth and the only truth there ever will be.

You wouldn't want to be too damn sure which of these interpretations is more political and which more personal, either.

199 LOOKING FOR THE PERFECT BEAT, Afrika Bambaataa and Soul Sonic Force

Written and produced by Arthur Baker and John Robie
Tommy Boy 823   1982   *Billboard:* #48

Like all the great hip-hop hits, "Looking for the Perfect Beat" is as much blustering sound collage as it is a "song" in the conventional sense. Music like this couldn't have existed before the early eighties, because "Looking for the Perfect Beat" is the pure product of contemporary microchip technology, built upon rapping voices overlaying electronic noises that sound like the ones on computer games, heavy doses of mixing console effects and turntable scratching atop a synthetic rhythm bed. The result is more than just danceable; it's a fascinating form of pop music cubism that never abandons the hope of achieving a mass audience. An obscure label like Tommy Boy's ability to get a record this radical halfway up the pop charts during one of the most conservative periods in the rock era is ample testimony to just how successful Baker and Company's search was.

200 GIVE HIM A GREAT BIG KISS, The Shangri-Las

Written and produced by Shadow Morton
Red Bird 018   1964   *Billboard:* #18

Of all the producer-hustler types who wanted to be Phil Spector, Shadow Morton made the best records. Of course, he made them with only one group, not the half-dozen that Spector and acolytes like Bob Crewe managed to work with. But they were magnificent.

And so was the group. Led by Mary Ann Ganser, a straight-haired blonde, accompanied by her twin, Marge, and sisters Mary and Betty Weiss, who wore brunette beehives, the Shangri-Las were a greaser's wet dream. And they looked and acted and sang as if they knew it. Compared to these girls, the Supremes, the Crystals, the Shirelles, the Ronettes, and the Vandellas were just a bunch of sorority sisters. Mary Ann and her cohorts looked like the kind of tough, wise kids who wound up pregnant in eleventh grade, then found out their boyfriends had been drafted and ended up waitressing at the Big Boy while Mom sat home with the brat, cursing the day *she'd* gotten knocked up. (If this sounds like "Soldier Boy" as farce, it should.)

In a book about the greatest lyrics in rock history, the Shangri-Las might be the preeminent performers of all time. Their songs were mainly written by Morton, with an occasional assist from Jeff Barry and Ellie Greenwich, or Red Bird co-owner Jerry Leiber. Their plots invariably revolved around some kind of teen trauma; the storied "Leader of the Pack," their biggest hit, only skims the surface of the true tortures of which they sang. In "I Can Never Go Home Anymore," a girl and her Mom fall out of touch because the kid's sick of being hassled; Mom dies without ever finding out that her daughter really loved her. In "Sophisticated Boom Boom," a wallflower is stuck in a dance crowded with squares. The boyfriend in "Long Live Our Love" is sent to the 'Nam itself and though she promises to wait, you gotta have your doubts that it'll do any good. Finally, there's the dark and stormy night of "Give Us Your Blessings," where the failure of her parents to approve of a teenage marriage leads not only to elopement but a dual highway fatality, possibly because the kids had tears in their eyes.

Over the top as they were, these songs had as much credibility as Leiber and Stoller's arch playlets for the Coasters. The language was utterly vernacular and Ganser's New York accent could render anything from a sigh to a snarl sexy and threatening.

The *typical* guy who caught the Shangri-Las interest was impossibly romantic, the kind of semi-delinquent about whom they sing in "Remember (Walking in the Sand)," or in the early, descriptive parts of "Leader of the Pack." Their passion for him reaches its apex in "Give Him a Great Big Kiss," which is miles funnier and smarter than "Leader of the Pack," and one of the greatest pieces of teen dialogue ever recorded, not to mention possessed of a great beat.

The song is one long celebration of the Great Greaser Adonis: "Big bulky sweaters, to match his eyes," sings Ganser as the other girls chant "mo'." "Dirty fingernails—oh boy! what a prize / Tight khaki pants, high button shoes / He's always lookin' like he's got the blues."

But the best bits come when the music virtually ceases except for basic drumbeats and a riffing trumpet, while the other girls interrogate Mary Ann. As well as prophesying the Michael Jackson of 1988 ("I hear he's bad." "He's good bad, but he's not evil"), the dialogue provides the song its climax. "Is he a good dancer?" they demand to know. "Whaddya mean is he a good dancuh?" snaps Mary Ann (as though there's a chance in hell she'd go out with a guy who wasn't, or admit it if she did). "Well, *how does he dance?*" "Close," she answers in a voice so sultry it might make Dusty Springfield feel faint, "very, very close."

Yo.

201 I NEVER LOVED A MAN (THE WAY I LOVE YOU), Aretha Franklin

Produced by Jerry Wexler; written by Ronny Shannon
Atlantic 2386   1967   *Billboard:* #9

Aretha's story, or at least the part of it that matters most, starts right here, in a quick session in a strange town, backed by white musicians country enough to fit together churchy organ chords with Stax saxophones, and savvy enough to follow her lead vocal to the end of the earth.

Aretha isn't singing; she's practically praying, her every breath suffused with the spirit of what she's trying to convey, and no matter how secular the subject, that's what it's all about. In the spaces between those breaths, there are those of us who would still swear you can hear the earth move a little bit, altering its shape to fit the surprise. And yet, Aretha had greater miracles than that to work. By her next record, she was finished forever with being a public victim, the role she plays so exquisitely here.

202 FUNKYTOWN, Lipps Inc.

Written and produced by Steven Greenberg
Casablanca 2233   1980   *Billboard:* #1 (4 weeks)

Sweet, soulful early (pre-Prince) Minneapolis dance-pop. Steven Greenberg ran a solo show—with female vocal assistance—and in fact, "Funkytown" is one of the earlier examples of the kind of one-man-band approach made possible by digitalized synthesizers, drum machines, and studio equipment—a style of which Prince has made himself the peerless Lancelot. Everything on "Funkytown" is not just electrified but electronic, right down to the way the voices are processed. Nevertheless, the same musical standards that applied during earlier rock eras still adhere: booming bass and big, splashy drums, with cutting guitar echoed later on in the track by (synthesized) strings, all establishing an infectiously repetitious dance-floor groove. But even clubfooted listeners succumb to "Funkytown" 's pure playfulness. And, because it helped open an era, the record can't be dismissed as a mere lighthearted novelty. However light it may be, this track isn't less filling, just loaded up on brand-new spirits.

203 LESS THAN ZERO, Elvis Costello
Produced by Nick Lowe; written by Elvis Costello
Stiff BUY-11 (UK only)   1977   Did not make pop charts

"Less Than Zero" represents the exact point at which it became un-avoidably obvious that punk had changed the terms of a big part of pop discourse. Costello's record doesn't sound anything like "punk"; its music is orderly, its thoughts sequential, the singing owes more to singer/songwriters than the New York Dolls or Iggy and the Stooges. But "Zero" 's brutal sarcasm, the way the drums forced the rhythm, the hints of garage-rock in the organ, all suggested a familiarity with the Clash, the Sex Pistols, what they'd been saying, and a need to respond. So Costello created his own picture of youth and England and what they were becoming.

A couple are making out on the couch at the home of one of their parents (it isn't clear which, only that they have no place of their own to go, and are worried that the old folks will arrive home too soon). The lights are off but the TV is on. On the tube, an interviewer is talking with Oswald Mosley, leader of Britain's fascist movement in the thirties, and Mosley's sister. Mosley is enjoying something of a revival and he has been brought to the screen to further falsify history—his own, the world's, perhaps even the singer's. But the singer is only dimly aware that Mosley's being on TV helps explain his own unem-ployment and lack of housing, partially because he's too wrapped up in his lovemaking, partially because creating unawareness is Mosley's purpose. (And those cries of "Hey, red!" in the chorus—who's shouting them, and to what end?)

This isn't something I made up. This is what Elvis Costello is singing about. It is something no one would have ever thought to sing before 1977, and it is a way of thinking that no one who takes pop music seriously can avoid ten years later.

204 THAT IS ROCK & ROLL, The Coasters
Written and produced by Jerry Leiber and Mike Stoller
Atco 6141   1959   Did not make pop chart

When I began researching *The Heart of Rock & Soul*, I took it for granted that the Coasters would be one of its constant presences. But after listening for a few months, the scary fact came home: No way.

It's certainly not that Jerry Leiber and Mike Stoller weren't great songwriters and among the best record producers who ever lived. Leiber and Stoller *are* one of the continuing presences here. But over the years, their most celebrated recordings, with the Coasters, have dated considerably, which says a lot about the ways context and timing shape meaning.

In the mid-fifties, when the Coasters had their hits, they played to a broad audience (black and white, Northern and Southern, located East and West) in an era when very little music of any kind—let alone black-based music—found such a wide listenership. What let them get so far were the sonic playlets Leiber and Stoller constructed, steeped in the everyday realities of radio drama, early TV shows, the movies, and urban street life. Beyond the fact that Leiber and Stoller used the best R&B studio musicians on two coasts, the Coasters themselves were fine singers, and both lead singer Carl Gardner and bass voice Bobby Nunn were superb musical dramatists. Nobody's ever matched their ability to portray the deadbeat "Shopping for Clothes," the high school layabout "Charlie Brown," the legion of pop culture private eyes in "Along Came Jones" and "Searchin'," or the sheer uptown strangeness of "Little Egypt," "Young Blood," and "Idol with the Golden Head."

That's a given. But you can't quite hear it that simply anymore. We now live in a climate in which covert race-baiting runs the country, from the streets of New York and Los Angeles to our political campaigns. Whites have fled the cities and today, caricatures of urban life imply Amos 'n' Andy stereotypes. In the noise of media bigotry, the subtleties and universality of all but the very greatest Coasters' characterizations are easily overwhelmed.

Of course, that's not anything that Leiber and Stoller put in their records; they were not only rock's first great record producers (by which I mean the first to master studio gimmickry so well that all that apparatus became an inherent part of their musicality), they never forgot that they were engaged in making essentially *black* records, and so they told stories relevant not only to white teens but to black adults. Listen to something like "What About Us?" today, and you'll be amazed that it's still so radical, its lyric concerns still so applicable (even though it's not, unfortunately, one of their best records). Certainly, none of what gives me pause could be heard by early Coasters' fans. It's not what I heard when I was a kid. But it's there now, poisoned by the atmosphere.

"That Is Rock & Roll" presents no such problem because, it seems to me, it's not the Coasters' story so much as it is Jerry Leiber and Mike Stoller's. "That ain't no freight train that you hear, coming down the railroad tracks / That's a country-born piano man, playing in-between the cracks," they sing, and in my mind's eye, what I see is Stoller playing piano like his life depended on it in *Jailhouse Rock*, even if the country-side where he was born was the Bronx, U.S.A.

Furthermore, there's a brilliant music intelligence at work here, starting with the arrangement itself, which uses as a major source of the beat a banjo (African origin, played Dixieland style, still associated with white country musicians in the popular mind), in the archetypal (*not* formulaic) sax solo, and in the interplay between Gardner and Nunn, which is not quite call-and-response but displays beautifully calculated interaction that's one of the hallmarks of great rock and roll from beginning to end.

Ordinarily, I'd be wary of the idea that Leiber and Stoller wrote "That Is Rock & Roll" as a defense of their love for rock and roll and R&B. But the intent of the last lines is unmistakable; it's perhaps the first great rock criticism, certainly a better summary of what the music's about than any critic has ever come up with:

> You say that music's for the birds
> And you can't understand the words
> Well, honey, if you did, you'd really blow your lid
> 'Cause, baby, that is rock & roll

205 WAY BACK HOME, Junior Walker and the All Stars

Produced by Johnny Bristol; written by Wilton Felder,
Johnny Bristol, and Gladys Knight
Soul 35090   1971   *Billboard:* #52

In 1972, a group of left-wing crazies called the Symbionese Liberation Army (SLA) kidnapped Patricia Hearst, heir to some significant segment of a famous publishing fortune, and held her not only for ransom but as a sex slave and potential convert to their cause, the exact nature of which has never been fully explored. I watched the case with fascination as it unraveled over the next couple of years, ending in bank robberies, wild shootouts, and Hearst's capture and conviction for participating in an SLA bank robbery, without learning many more specifics about what the kidnappers believed. Lots of people shared my fascination but my reason was pretty peculiar: The SLA's theme song, or anyhow their favorite record, was Junior Walker's "Way Back Home."

I loved the record, too. Walker sings it out of the sink of bad memory, in the voice of a country man who's traveled South to North in his lifetime and misses what he's lost, even as he has to acknowledge the brutality that made him leave, not to mention the impossibility of recovering the life he led. It's the one Motown record that most clearly acknowledged that the music, and the people who made it, came from somewhere, that they had a history and could not escape from it even in the complete immersion in the moment that makes their music so great.

I don't know if any of that is what made the SLA adopt "Way Back Home." Chances are, they never got past the opening lines: "Well, there's good and bad things about the South, boy / And some leave a bitter taste in my mouth / Like a black man livin' across the track / White man on the other side holdin' him back." It's hard to imagine that a group so cold and brutal could have grasped the rest, about the honeysuckle growin' on the backyard fence, the games of hide 'n' seek, the ice cream cups, the skinny-dipping in the creek.

But then again, why should Junior Walker feel so forgiving, so nostalgic that, even as he admits that even if he did go back, things wouldn't be the same, he also declares his desire to be buried "way back home." The answer's in the bitter trills of his sax, which tells a story about the meaning of home, of the South, of four hundred cruel years of slavery that drove men and women out of their minds. And still can, and still does. There are things buried there that cannot be known in Berkeley or Detroit.

206 ALL ALONG THE WATCHTOWER, Jimi Hendrix
Produced by Jimi Hendrix; written by Bob Dylan
Reprise 0767   1968   *Billboard:* #20

207 MR. TAMBOURINE MAN, The Byrds
Produced by Terry Melcher; written by Bob Dylan
Columbia 43271   1965   *Billboard:* #1 (1 week)

208 SOONER OR LATER (ONE OF US MUST KNOW), Bob Dylan
Produced by Bob Johnston; written by Bob Dylan
Columbia 43541   1966   Did not make pop charts

Bob Dylan's rank as rock and roll's poet-prince is undeniable, but as a certifiable Great Songwriter, he's radically different from any who came before. Great interpretations of Dylan songs by other people are few and far between. Lots of performers have done his songs, of course, and a few have had hits with them, but the words of an old CBS Records ad still speak the truth: Nobody sings Dylan like Dylan.

Reduced to paper "One of Us Must Know" doesn't look like much more than a nasty-tongued burst of arch hipster superiority. Who else but its composer could make this lyric, or the sketchy blues melody, seem worthwhile? It has to be The Band (or the Hawks, as they were then known—though without Levon Helm, who initially refused to become a sideman for a folksinger). Though they aren't credited, its almost impossible to believe that the cathedral organ chords could be played by somebody other than Garth Hudson or that the mathematically inspired guitar licks might be wrung out by someone besides Robbie Robertson. This is the Band's first essay at the signature sound that made "The Weight" and "Chest Fever" instant classics.

It's hard to fathom how Dylan could release a single this good as the follow-up to the biggest hits of his career ("Like a Rolling Stone" and "Positively 4th Street") and have it flop so badly. Especially when such overrated ephemera as "Can You *Please* Crawl Out Your Window" at least hit the Hot 100 and the godawful "Rainy Day Women #12 and 35" made Top Ten. You figure it out—maybe program directors were tired of having to justify his still-weird singing style to the recalcitrant part of their audience. Maybe the single was released too far in advance of *Blonde on Blonde.* Maybe history was asleep at the switch.

Anyway, even if nobody sings Dylan like Dylan, the Byrds at least came close. Their folkie vocals are too sweet to convey the lyric's pungency as well as Dylan's own wracked version—here, the song might as well really be a dopester reverie, rather than its author's more universally troubled vision. (Dylan has properly disavowed the drug connection but he's also lately tried to reduce the song to its trivial source of inspiration, a huge tambourine carried into the sessions by guitarist Bruce Langhorne. Which only proves that he's the worst judge of his own creations, no big surprise.)

On the other hand, the vocals don't need to be much, because they're set against the greatest electric twelve-string guitar riff ever created. Jim (later Roger) McGuinn got his start backing up pop-folkies like Judy Collins and he played a lot of Greenwich Village banjo to boot. But you'd never know it here, where playing alongside the great Los Angeles session group led by drummer Hal Blaine, he plays hot enough to make the likes of James Burton and Mickey Baker drool. That guitar lick has the guts the vocals lack and it stiffens up whatever's saccharine in the lyric. Maybe this actually is what the Beatles would have sounded like if they'd done a Dylan song.

"All Along the Watchtower" is unquestionably pure Jimi Hendrix, and by the time he's finished, Jimi accomplishes the unique feat of making you forget all about Dylan's original version. (By the eighties, Dylan was interpolating parts of the Hendrix arrangement into his own show.) Hendrix understands Dylan as a contemporary successor to country bluesmen like Robert Johnson (which is close to the mark of Dylan's own ambition) and his interpretation of "Watchtower" implies a world of hoodoo and juke joints, obliterating the lyric's pretensions and boiling it down to the crucial stuff. Like, "There are many here among us who feel that life is but a joke."

"Watchtower" is such an odd, abstract lyric that hardly anyone but a coequal genius could have held on long enough to spot the song hidden within it. It's a tribute to Hendrix that he not only found it, but had the nerve to expand on it, with a gorgeous psychedelic guitar solo and a fearsome instrumental yowl as the song ends on the word "howl."

209 IN THE MIDNIGHT HOUR, Wilson Pickett
Produced by Jerry Wexler and Jim Stewart; written by Steve Cropper and Wilson Pickett
Atlantic 2289   1965   Billboard: #21

Wilson Pickett at his most basic is the most emotionally direct of all soul singers, but direct is a mild description of a singer who, at his best, was pure fist-in-the-face. The good stuff here also includes a bass groove that sways and swaggers, Al Jackson's percolating drumming (based on producer Jerry Wexler's middle-aged imitation of the latest teen dance beat, the Jerk) and a horn line that defines Stax.

210 STOP HER ON SIGHT (S.O.S.), Edwin Starr
Produced by Eddie Wingate; written by A. Hamilton, R. Morris and C. Hatcher
Ric-Tic 109   1966   Billboard: #48

Edwin Starr's first hits may have been released on this minor-league Motor City label, but their every inflection established that Motown was embedded in the grooves of his destiny. "Agent Double-O Soul" preceded "S.O.S." to the charts, but it's this one that's got the goods, one of the greatest non-Motown Motown discs ever cut, with the same booting backbeat, the same thunderous baritone sax riffs and a vocal as tough and assured as any of the early Marvin Gaye's.

211 LITTLE DARLIN', The Diamonds
Produced by David Carroll; written by Maurice Williams
Mercury 71060   1957   *Billboard:* #2

Before he formed the Zodiacs and fashioned "Stay," Maurice Williams led a group called the Gladiolas. In early 1957, he wrote "Little Darlin'," an assemblage of teen love song clichés, doo-wop style, which the Gladiolas recorded and Nashville-based Excello Records released. The Gladiolas' "Little Darlin' " was a hit, making Number 11 on *Billboard*'s Rhythm and Blues chart, but an unexceptional one.

Radio stations were still reluctant to play records by black acts, even though by 1957 it was clear that R&B was the dominant trend in American music. As a result, companies like Chicago's Mercury Records developed white groups and singers who revamped black hits in a "more acceptable" style, one that fit in with the standards on "Your Hit Parade" and didn't do so much to disrupt the "How Much Is That Doggie in the Window" format many programmers (if not their audiences) felt more comfortable with. Throughout the fifties, it was still possible to sell huge amounts of records by playing to institutionalized bigotry through such fakery.

The Diamonds were such a group. Ten of their sixteen chart records were R&B covers. But even among white cover acts, the Diamonds—who consisted of a pair of Canadians, Dave Somerville and Mike Douglas, and a pair of Californians, John Felton and Evan Fisher—were something special. They were hyped as college-educated and their re-arrangements travestied R&B, which they viewed with dripping sophomoric contempt.

But "Little Darlin' " is so brutal that it transcends satire and achieves true rock and roll greatness. Every touch that's meant to be mocking and cruel *works*. From the exaggerated doo-wopping "ooh aah" to the off-time cowbell, from the absurd bass recitation to the harp glissando, this record's as unmistakably exciting as it is insincere.

It's impossible to travesty rock and roll at this level because when the thrill's the thing, who gives a fuck about intentions? After all if you just look at its surface, "Little Darlin' " could never be any sillier than "Barbara Ann" or "Get a Job" or even "Peppermint Twist," so all the Diamonds achieved was a greater shamelessness, and in rock, that's a merit. Their "Little Darlin' " is compulsively listenable because it's outright *weird*, a quality that very much fits into a music founded on the likes of "Tutti Frutti." I don't think I've ever played it once without wanting to play it twice.

Squares never do get it. When they wanted to show their superiority to rock and roll on their concert albums, both Joan Baez and Peter, Paul and Mary chose "Little Darlin' " as the target of their mockery. Of course, they didn't do the Gladiolas' version. They parodied the Diamonds' parody, a fitting tribute to the relative aesthetic suss of all concerned.

212 THE PAYOFF MIX (Mastermix OF G.L.O.B.E. AND Whiz Kid's PLAY THAT BEAT MR. D.J.), Double Dee and Steinski

Produced by Double Dee and Steinski; written by Miller and McGuire
Tommy Boy TB 867   1985   Did not make pop chart

In late 1983, Tommy Boy Records became dissatisfied with the amount of club and radio airplay being received by "Play That Beat Mr. D.J." by G.L.O.B.E. and Whiz Kid. So the label sponsored a contest for club deejays and aspiring mixers: Come up with a "mastermix" (that is, a remix of the original record using whatever electronic and studio effects were necessary to extend and improve it) and you'd win a small cash prize and have your mix distributed on the monthly anthology LP distributed by Disco-Net.

The contest caught the eye of a New York advertising jingle producer, Steve Stein, who sometimes deejayed on weekends at Brooklyn clubs, and his friend, Douglas DiFranco, an engineer with whom he hung out in Manhattan discos. Double Dee and Steinski came up with a mastermix that took the record's lyrics at their word, playing the song's basic beat against sound bites clipped from old and new hit records, movie soundtracks and more obscure sources, as well as electronified studio effects. In their version, G.L.O.B.E. and Whiz Kid sang and commented upon fragments of Culture Club's "I'll Tumble 4 Ya," Little Richard's "Tutti Frutti," Humphrey Bogart's dialogue from *Casablanca*, the Supremes' "Stop! In the Name of Love," and Chic's "Good Times," among others.

It was brilliant work and because DiFranco worked so precisely that you never heard a splice, many presumed that "The Payoff Mix" was an early and audacious example of "sampling," the process by which sounds are digitally transferred from an old source to a new tape (and in the process, may have their pitch, timbre, and tempo altered). In fact, the team worked with completely analog sources, which meant countless hours of studio time and dozens, if not hundreds of splices.

On the dance scene, where novelty reigns, "The Payoff Mix" acquired megacult status. Tommy Boy was forced to issue a tape version to radio stations, and the "Payoff" edition of the Disco-Net anthology began selling for as much as $75 to deejays and collectors. Encouraged and enthused, Stein and DiFranco released a second mix on their own label, which they called "The James Brown Mix." Filtering in most of what was on "The Payoff Mix" plus several Brown records, Clint Eastwood's best lines from *Dirty Harry*, the introduction from Brown's *Live at the Apollo* set, old dance lesson discs, "Dance to the Music," and Bugs Bunny chatter, the new record soon gained a cachet equal to the original remake.

Spotting a winner, Tommy Boy decided to release the two mixes, plus one additional mix, as a twelve-inch EP. "Lesson 3 (History of Hip-Hop Mix)" included material from Otis Redding and JFK, lines from the trash-cult film *Mars Needs Women*, an homage to Dickie Goodman (the pioneer of cut 'n' splice rock and roll), "Heeere's Johnny," a quick squib from "Jam on Revenge," Lauren Bacall's "Pucker up and blow," the Fat Boys' human beat box routine, and Groucho Marx. Like the other two, it ended with a prissy voice inquiring: "And say, children, what does it all mean?"

For Tommy Boy and Double Dee and Steinski, it immediately meant a raft of legal action as the "owners" of the sound bites began demanding compensation. The fact that the "owners" were generally unrelated to the people who'd actually done the labor constituting the "work" was, in terms of copyright law, completely beside the point. Since some of those owners were as mighty as Warner Brothers (which within two years would wind up distributing and thereby controlling most of Tommy Boy's product), there was no choice but to withdraw the mastermix.

Nothing could keep Double Dee and Steinski's accomplishments away from radio and club deejays, and even five years later, "The Payoff Mix" and its brethren were still regularly heard around the East Coast hip-hop scene. Sampling and cut 'n' splice techniques improved, with at least one major international hit, "Pump Up the Volume" by M/A/R/R/S, engendering similar litigiousness. DiFranco continued engineering without stepping into much controversy but Steinski found himself in and out of hot water over the next few years as he continued to practice this rarified form of guerilla music criticism, in which his editing and interpolations answered his own question—"Tell me, children, what does it all mean?"—perfectly well.

213 DUKE OF EARL, Gene Chandler
Produced by Bill Sheppard; written by Bernice Williams, Eugene Dixon [Chandler], and Earl Edwards
Vee-Jay 416   1962   Billboard: #1 (3 weeks)

What the hell is this song about? To promote "Duke of Earl," Gene Chandler appeared in top hat, white gloves, cloak and cane, with a monocle screwed in his left eye. Which suggests that it was largely about a misunderstanding of the nature of the European aristocracy by residents of southside Chicago.

If only such blissful ignorance ruled our nation! Imagine a government that didn't give a shit about the specific protocols attending to hereditary flunkydom but instead devoted its energies to consistently producing background noises as absurdly sublime as this record's "Dook, dook, dook" and "Baw baw, duh duh." Then, truly, there would be a pax Americana worth savoring and all could sing, with gusto: "Nothing can stop me now . . . so yay, yay, yay, yeah."

214 WALK LIKE A MAN, The Four Seasons
Produced by Bob Crewe; written by Bob Gaudio and Bob Crewe
Vee-Jay 485   1963   Billboard: #1 (3 weeks)

It wasn't just Frankie Valli's voice—stunning in both its natural tenor and falsetto ranges—that made the Four Seasons' hits something special. There was also the quality of the songs, the harmonies, and the persistently inventive use of percussion. "Walk Like a Man" opens with drums that sound like they're being played by God (Buddy Salzman is a better bet), announcing itself so forcefully that the record's already a guaranteed smash before Valli ever opens his mouth. Nasty-romantic and well-produced, it's like an early prophesy of a certain side of Prince, even if the opening couplet will forever bar him from singing it.

215 ROCKIN' ROLL BABY, The Stylistics
Produced by Thom Bell; written by Thom Bell and Linda Creed
Avco 4625   1973   Billboard: #14

With reedy falsetto his only register, Russell Thompkins would sound like a complete wimp if he weren't so soulful. Thompkins outdoes himself on this chugging blues-rock number, Bell and Creed's fairytale of a baby "born in a theatre in Bluefield, West Virginia," who spends his early days following the folks on one-nighters but ends up living in Beverly Hills. The happy ending is credible because the rhythm is so infectious you'd believe just about anything it told you. With its riffing horns and single-string guitar, the closest Philly soul ever came to gut-bucket blues, "Rockin' Roll Baby" would be valuable if all it did was provide a rare example of historical self-consciousness in black pop. But it's also as cute as it is soulful, a virtually unprecedented combination.

216 LET HER DANCE, The Bobby Fuller 4
Produced by Bob Keane; written by Bobby Fuller
Mustang 3014   1966   Billboard: #9

"La Bamba" refried as a frantic attack on infidelity. Like a lot of Tex-Mex dishes, it tastes just as good—arguably, a bit better—reheated. And in this particular case, seasoned hotter than hell with delirious group vocals and guitars that sound like the Beatles on some exotic San Antonio brand of helium.

217 SMOKE GETS IN YOUR EYES, The Platters
Produced by Buck Ram; written by Otto Harbach and Jerome Kern
Mercury 71383   1958   Billboard: #1 (3 weeks)

218 ONLY YOU (AND YOU ALONE), The Platters
Produced by Buck Ram; written by Buck Ram and Ande Rand
Mercury 70633   1955   Billboard: #5

The Platters were so influential that today, Tony Williams's lush lead vocals seem almost as conventional and corny as Johnny Mathis's. But when the Platters released "Smoke Gets in Your Eyes," Jerome Kern's widow threatened to sue.

She was dissuaded by three factors: Oscar Hammerstein publicly thanked Buck Ram and the group for reviving a dead song (it was written in 1933 for the Broadway show, Roberta and Paul Whiteman made it a Number One the next year); it turned out that song publisher

Max Dreyfus had *solicited* the Platters version; and Dreyfus told her lawyer that the new recording could earn the Kern estate royalties on over a million copies.

The Platters began as a conventional black harmony group, recording for Federal in 1953–1954 after Buck Ram, the veteran lawyer/songwriter/producer/manager who'd just scored with the Penguins' "Earth Angel," put them together. (Legend has it that he discovered the four male members—Williams, baritone Alex Hodge, second tenor David Lynch, and bass Herbert Reed—working as parking lot attendants.) The group cut nineteen sides for Federal, including three backing Williams' sister, Linda Hayes. Nothing clicked, even though toward the end of the period the group added a woman, Zola Taylor, sister of the Coasters' Cornell Gunter. (Around the same time, Paul Robi replaced Reed.)

"Only You" was the Platters' final pre-Mercury release (Federal 12444) in a version radically different than the hit. Much slower, with the arrangement centered on piano, it featured a Williams lead with virtually none of the hiccuping drama that became his specialty, and ornate group backing, including whistling that resembles bird trills. Yet the Federal "Only You" is a key to understanding why the Platters' records were groundbreaking. Here, Williams sounds constricted. On the Mercury version, recorded only a few months later, he sounds loose, far freer in his phrasing and emotional attitude. The R&B-oriented arrangement of the Federal version makes the song's pledge of eternal love into a burden; the pop-oriented Mercury version makes the same vow seem liberating.

Disc jockeys didn't find Mercury's revamped "Only You" easy to grasp, even though the arrangement had been simplified to feature Williams against a simple crooning background, accompanied by light guitar, piano, bass, and drums. The vocal was also pitched far higher, reaching the stratosphere on the final notes. Yet "Only You" had been on release for three months before Seattle disc jockey Bob Salter made it a hit on his program. It spread from there, making the Platters the first black group of the R&B era to hit the pop charts with a song that was neither a jump tune or some kind of novelty.

By the time of "Smoke Gets in Your Eyes" three years later, the Platters had established themselves as one of the most successful and important black groups. They'd scored three Number Ones (with "Twilight Time," "The Great Pretender," and "My Prayer") and charted more than a dozen others, most written, all arranged and produced, by Ram.

"Smoke Gets in Your Eyes," perhaps the greatest performance of Williams's career, shows how far their music had developed. Set in a pool of echo, with an arrangement that uses ornate piano chords, swirling strings, and eventually even a touch of tympani, Ram plays Williams's vocal theatrics for all they're worth, and the song winds up as one long crescendo, a Broadway bolero. Yet Williams' over-the-top modulations of the piss-elegant lyric ("Now, laughing friends deride / Tears I cannot hide") finally do it justice, bringing to the deeply self-serious expressions of true love a sense of conviction so complete that its protestations finally strike you as almost modest. When Williams confesses that it *hasn't* all worked out, then rises to his final, tympani-buttressed high note, he imparts to a piece of Tin Pan Alley trivia a genuine feeling of tragedy. This is what the gospel-steeped stylists of R&B brought to pop songs that none of their emotionally restrained predecessors (white or black) could ever dream of matching.

219 FUN FUN FUN, Beach Boys
Produced by Brian Wilson; written by Brian Wilson and Mike Love
Capitol 5518   1964   *Billboard:* #4

A song about a chimera. Try asking a couple people to define "fun" sometime, and you'll see what I mean. The Beach Boys apparently meant something somewhere between fucking and fucking around, I'm not really sure which.

I do know that at the end of *American Graffiti*, when Richard Dreyfuss looks down from an airplane and sees a blonde speeding away in a Thunderbird convertible, "Fun Fun Fun" has to be the song that's on the radio. And she is enjoying it immensely.

Furthermore, "Fun Fun Fun" makes it evident that there is at least one person besides Chuck Berry (be it Beach Boy Carl Wilson or session stand-in Tommy Tedesco) who knows how to play that "Johnny B. Goode" lick to perfection.

220 PRESSURE DROP, Toots and the Maytals
Produced by Leslie Kong; written by Toots Hibbert
Trojan 7709 (UK)   1970   Did not make pop charts

The metaphor is atmospheric: When that hurricane is ready to hit, the barometer plummets. Once this one makes the turntable, though, it's too late to prepare because the groove thunders down from the top and all that happens as they go along is that Toots whips himself further and further into a frenzy of marginal coherence. Meaning that I don't know what the hell he's singing about (some of it might have to do with sex or love), but it sure does sound *important*.

221 MAYBELLENE, Chuck Berry
Produced by Leonard Chess; written by Chuck Berry
Chess 1604   1955   *Billboard: #5*

They say that Chuck based "Maybellene" on a country song called "Ida Red," and indeed he may have taken something from "Ida"'s melody and tempo. But "Ida Red" is old as the hills (Okeh Records labeled it "traditional" when Roy Acuff cut it in 1939), and "Maybellene" is utterly modern, not only because it's a frustrated love song that's as much about the highway as it is about girls but because it presumes that the girl might have the bigger car.
Inspirational Verse:

> Rainwater runnin' all under my hood
> I knew it was doin' my motor good

Understand the essence of those lines and you'll have a much better grip on handling the vagaries of life.

222 FOR YOUR PRECIOUS LOVE, Jerry Butler with the Impressions
Producer not credited; written by Arthur Brooks and Jerry Butler
Vee-Jay 280   1958   *Billboard: #11*

Too measured to be gospel, this is a sermon nevertheless. Its subject is the true holiness of matrimony, the text drawn not from the Bible but from the very rivets of a man's life.

223 I GOT YOU (I FEEL GOOD), James Brown
Written and produced by James Brown
King 6015   1965   *Billboard: #3*

The follow-up to "Papa's Got a Brand New Bag" matches its predecessor by opening with a full-throated, cord-rupturing scream and, if it can't sustain quite that level of intensity, that may well be one of the reasons the record became Brown's biggest ever on the pop charts.

Certainly, there's nothing conventional about the music, a thunderous melange of powerhouse horn riffs, jet-propelled drum bursts, and skittering guitar. And James sings the song as if God had called him to earth for the primary purpose of personifying sexual ecstasy.

224 ROCK STEADY, Aretha Franklin
Produced by Jerry Wexler, Tom Dowd, and Arif Mardin; written by Aretha Franklin
Atlantic 2838 1971 *Billboard: #9*

As a genre, funk seems indisputably male and ineluctably hostile to great voices, designed as it is to shift musical priorities away from melody toward the beat. So what's "Rock Steady"—a miracle?

Not that much more miraculous than Aretha's other great records and certainly well within the range of the explicable. Given her uncanny ability to galvanize great musicians, maybe it shouldn't even surprise us that she gets some of the best performances of their careers from this augmented group of New York R&B session men. Drummer Bernard Purdie has never rocked quite this tough, and bassist Chuck Rainey and guitarist Cornell Dupree couldn't find themselves in a tighter groove if they'd been welded to one another. Donny Hathaway's organ mutates the spirit of James Brown while Dr. John and Robert Popwell busy themselves with the percussion that fragments the riffs and sustains the busy rhythmic flow, adding a tinge of the Caribbean.

Perhaps the most impressive aspect of the record, though, is Aretha's singing. She cries out like a woman backed to the wall, shouting for the truth and nothing less: "Let's call this song exactly what it is!" Sometimes she seems exhausted, but then she crops up a few bars later, refreshed and indomitable amid the turbulence of the beat, riding that bass line to glory. As much as "I Never Loved a Man" or "A Natural Woman" or "Chain of Fools," "Rock Steady" feels like the product of a woman spinning out a secret autobiography despite herself.

225 YOU CAN'T ALWAYS GET WHAT YOU WANT, The Rolling Stones
Produced by Jimmy Miller; written by Mick Jagger and Keith Richards
London 910 1969 *Billboard: #42*

"You Can't Always Get What You Want" inverts Marx's axiom about historical repetition by having the first verse sung in the farcical castrati tones of the London Bach Choir, then reprising it with Mick Jagger. Instead of his usual slur, Jagger carefully measures every syllable to convey its full weight of tragedy; near the end, he even introduces a choral "aah" with the finest James Brown scream he's ever gotten off.

On French horn, Al Kooper once more seizes an historic occasion by playing an instrument about which he knows next to nothing. (As becomes evident later in the song, he's become an accomplished organist since "Like A Rolling Stone.") On drums, Jimmy Miller does more than fill in—he plays well enough that Charlie Watts isn't missed. The result is music fit for a moment ripe for revolution, as this one seemed to be.

"You Can't Always Get What You Want" is best known as an album track (from *Let It Bleed*), and as the hokey climax of the funeral scene in *The Big Chill*. But its spirit is best incarnated in its original life as a B side, music too majestic and strange for Top 40 but so powerful that it wipes out the ostensible hit on the flip (in this case, "Honky Tonk Woman").

226 KICK OUT THE JAMS, The MC5
Produced by Jac Holzman and Bruce Botnick; written by the MC5
Elektra 45648   1969   *Billboard:* #82

Detroit in the late sixties was flush with rebel rock. Even the city's best white R&B group, the Rationals, featured a song called "Guitar Army." Meanwhile, the biggest rebels of all hid out in Ann Arbor, the college town forty miles southwest, after the going got tough in the wake of the July 1967 insurrection that burnt much of the inner city to the ground.

Now, don't get me wrong. The Five were never frauds, because the revolution they yakked about was as much a cultural concept as it was a matter of pitched battles in the streets. They came to transform pop music, and if society happened to get in the way, well, it would just have to change, too. "Rock and roll, dope and fucking in the streets" was their political program and, judging from their response to a mere riot, if it had ever come to pass, they'd have freaked out and moved to . . . Who can guess? Cambridge? Kyoto?

The revolt did not come to pass, and because the MC5 dared to mess around with revolutionary ideas at all and then had the further temerity to show up playing crudely formed punk rock overlaid with guitar distortion and a pastiche of ideas lifted from Mao Zedong and

Sun Ra, a lot of folks got the wrong impression. And their reputation never recovered; they were labeled a hype and Ann Arbor's other weirdos, Iggy and the Stooges, became the subcult celebrities. Which is sad because both live and on record, the Five could demolish the Stooges without trying hard.

Trying hard was what they did best, though. "Kick Out the Jams" was a slogan before it was a song. The slogan meant what it said: Kick out the jams or get off the stage and get somebody up here who will. Lead singer Rob Tyner wrote the lyrics as a definition of what happened when you did it right: "The wiggling guitars, girl, the crash of the drums / If you wanna keep a-rockin' til the mornin' comes / Let me be who I am and let me kick out the jams."

It's a drag that the single contains Elektra's "Brothers and sisters" version, the intro bowdlerized from their first album's uncensored introduction, in which (as he did at every concert) singer Rob Tyner started the tune by bellowing "Kick out the jams, motherfuckers!" But since the album track has also now been censored, "Brothers and sisters" is all you've probably ever heard anyway, so you'll never know you're missing the boldest, loudest shattering of verbal taboo in pop music history. (The Sex Pistols sang nothing so directly antagonistic.) But the music breaks just as many laws, so you'll get the picture without the ultimate blow.

The reason that the "Brothers and sisters" version was created in the first place was to get the music on the radio. According to George Carlin, "motherfucker" is one of the seven words the FCC won't let you get away with broadcasting, but programmers might have been reluctant to air the record even if the government had been cool about it. Hey, let's face it, programmers were reluctant to air the rest of the record no matter what it said at the top. And no goddamn wonder. "Kick Out the Jams" is pure spew. Even if you've never heard it, it's easy to understand its impetus: Just go play any Sex Pistols track, and you'll hear the same surging churn of guitar and drum and bass, all melded together with a garbled, fuzzily recorded vocal making plain sense of the universe. "Kick Out the Jams" just about defines exciting, but (unlike similarly basic fifties rock classics) it also just about defines other things, like crude and unignorable, which are concepts that aren't enduring at Top 40, and don't get you a whole lot of points for being a cool deejay in other formats, either. So the record hit Number 82 and sank like a stone.

But the MC5 left a mark in pop hit history and that alone is a singular feat, something none of the bands that succeeded it—not the Stooges, the Pistols, the New York Dolls—came close to achieving. The Clash wound up with a hit, true, but in order to have had a record on the charts that meant something similar to "Kick Out the Jams," they'd have had to place "Complete Control" there, not "Train in Vain" or "Rock the Casbah." They didn't; the Five did. The patient died but the operation was a success. What revolution?

227 1999, Prince
Written and produced by Prince
Warner Bros. 29896   1982   *Billboard:* #12

"1999" offered an anthem to a rock generation just coming into its own. Its fatalistic hedonism is one step beyond even punk nihilism. "Two thousand, zero, zero, party over, oops out of time / So tonight I'm gonna party like it's 1999," isn't idle millenarianism but a legitimate, perhaps intelligent response to the Cold War Revivalism of the late seventies and early eighties. (And Prince's embrace of this sensibility was genuinely wholehearted; he vocally backed Reagan.) To have offered a protest song in that moment would have meant enduring (not just risking) sneers and derision, turned backs and raspberries in your face. "Whoopee! We're all gonna die," sang Country Joe and the Fish at Woodstock. But they didn't mean it. Prince did. And to prove it, he created one of the hottest dance tracks ever.

"1999" opens with a slowed-down version of broadcast speech (an idea lifted from Jimi Hendrix's *Axis: Bold As Love*), then picks up a signature synthesizer riff that's so bold and basic that it sounds as if it could have been played with two fingers, a sort of digital "Chopsticks." Prince's vocal, a melding of whispers, squeals, ejaculations, and groaning is buoyed on synth, relentless bass drum, and chicken-scratch rhythm guitar, accented by an occasional cymbal splash.

That's really all there is to it, until the end, when the guitar rises up like a James Brown missile to smite and demolish the rest of the music and a child's voice asks, imploringly, "Mommy, why does everybody have a bomb?"

Not that Prince is arguing against the bomb. What he's against is the idea that you can do anything about it. He's not even angry, just annoyed at anybody who'd knock on his door with something other than partying on his mind. As others try to run from the destruction, he shrugs it off and gets his ass back into gear on the dance floor. What's really chilling is that it's so crowded.

228 I GOT YOU BABE, Sonny and Cher
Written and produced by Sonny Bono
Atco 6359   1965   *Billboard:* #1 (3 weeks)

Given her geekiness here, at the very start of her career, it's unbelievable that Cher ever became glamorous. Almost as unbelievable as "I
Got You Babe," which holds up across a couple of decades not just
because I'm a sucker for an ocarina, but thanks to the tricks Sonny
learned at Phil Spector's heel.

Both the voices on "I Got You Babe" are young and dumb, with
barely a spark of wit. Which would be reason enough to dismiss this
damn thing, if the concept weren't so brave that one's need to hear the
doltish Sonny and the cloddish Cher run through their pledges of allegiance can become compulsive. What they're saying boils down to
this: Love redeems *everything*, no matter how ridiculous, moronic, or
grotesque. Noisy and misshapen as those declarations may be, they're
also an essence of what rock and roll brought to pop music that hadn't
been there before: a sense of democracy, fun, and possibility, a willingness to reach for effects and worry about decorum later, an understanding of where to find the sublime amidst the trivial.

229 GOODNIGHT SWEETHEART GOODNIGHT, The Spaniels
Produced by Calvin Carter; written by Calvin Carter and
James (Pookie) Hudson
Vee Jay 107   1954   *Billboard:* #24

All-Time Sign Off Song. Why? Certainly not for originality of thought,
though that doesn't necessarily rule out originality . . . or thought.
Anyway, the first couple thousand times you hear it, the secret seems
to be the sweet tenor lead; the next couple thousand, it seems like it
must be the harmonies; after that, you finally realize it's that slow,
soloing bass voice—"Duh-duh, dit, duh"—become profound. Ask me
again in a couple decades, though, and I may have come to yet another,
equally valid conclusion.

230 STAGGER LEE, Lloyd Price
Produced by Don Costa; Traditional, arranged by
Harold Logan and Lloyd Price
ABC-Paramount 9927   1958   *Billboard:* #1 (4 weeks)

When Lloyd Price and Harold Logan worked up their version of the venerable Southern folk-blues "Stack-o-lee" in early 1958, they knew they were working with public domain material. That's why, even though they took as their direct model New Orleans pianist Archibald's rendition (a regional hit on Imperial in 1950), they confidently claimed composer credit. It's hardly likely, though, that they knew that they were working on material nearly a hundred years old, that the story they had germinated from a real person, a white Memphis waterfront gambler named James "Stacker" Lee. (Greil Marcus gives the full and fascinating historical development of the song in the appendix of *Mystery Train: Images of America in Rock & Roll Music*, as well as tracing the story forward to Sly Stone. Readers of this book will presumably be able to carry the image forward at least through LL Cool J.)

Price and Logan earned their writers' credit by inventing one of the most indelible openings any rock and roll record has had: "The night was clear and the moon was yellow," Price croons, "And the leaves . . . came . . . tumbling . . . DOWN," then stomps into one of the few rock and roll arrangements that vociferously *swings*. To have added such an unforgettable element to a classic folk song is a rare achievement.

"Stack-o-lee" has hundreds of verses (Marcus claims Mac "Dr. John" Rebbenack can sing it for half an hour without repeating a verse), most of which center not on Stack-o-lee's crimes but on his punishment, first at the hands of society and finally, in personal combat against Satan. In Mississippi John Hurt's version, for instance, the judge charges the jury by saying "Let's kill him, before he kills some of us." In other words, the folk "Stack-o-lee" is a song about elemental justice.

Price made it something quite different: a song about the urban badman, a bad motherfucker not to be trifled with. In his rendition (eerily reminiscent of Frank Hutchison's 1928 version, collected on the Folkways *Anthology of American Folk Music* and repeated virtually nowhere in-between), the story is condensed to the tale of Stack's crime: Cheated by Billy Lyons in a crap game, Stack returns to the bar and shoots "that boy so bad / Til the bullet came through Billy and broke the bartender's glass."

"Stagger Lee" now becomes the model for the Black Panther and the crack dealer, all the Iceberg Slim hustlers who inhabit the culture white America fears. In the Isley Brothers early sixties version, when Stagger Lee returns to the barroom and pulls his .44, the announcement "Don't nobody move" is accompanied by a machine gun guitar solo by no less than Jimi Hendrix, who lived out a very mild-mannered version of the tale (just as Clint Eastwood's *High Plains Drifter* acts it out on the frontier, with an all-white cast). Nefarious as the stereotype has become (George Bush used Willie Horton as a Stagger Lee prototype and he told America something very like what Hurt's judge told the jury), it still cuts two ways. Marcus reports that Black Panther Bobby Seale named his son after Stagger Lee, claiming him as a positive role model for black men: "Malcolm X before he became politically conscious."

Dick Clark saw it coming. As "Stagger Lee," with its romping sax and rat-tat-tat chorus ("horrendous" to New Orleans R&B historian John Broven, a magnificent example of vocal percussion to the less purist) clambered up the charts, Clark refused to book Price on *American Bandstand*. His audience could not be exposed to a song which celebrated gambling and murder.

Since Price was meeting similar resistance from other tight-assed programmers, he returned to the studio and recast Stagger Lee as Thomas Sowell: In the censored version, Stagger Lee and Billy Lyon get into an argument, not about a dice game or a Stetson hat, but about a girl. And rather than returning to his apartment to get his .44, Stagger Lee goes home and "falls down on the floor," crying. But Billy thinks it over and returns his girl and "Stagger Lee was no more sore." Redeemed by sax and drums even more magnificent than on the original (though with a vocal and chorus inestimably more jive in form as well as content), the record was permitted to top the charts.

Diehard rock and rollers have sought the real thing and shunned the fake ever since. There's a metaphor in there, if you care to look for it.

231 MONEY CHANGES EVERYTHING, Cyndi Lauper

Produced by Rick Chertoff; written by Tom Gray
Portrait 04737   1984   *Billboard*: #27

232 MONEY, Barrett Strong
Produced by Berry Gordy; written by Berry Gordy and Janie Bradford
Anna 1111   1960   *Billboard: #23*

The world has never seen a culture so puritanical as ours about the relationship between income and creativity. One reason rock is presumed to be tawdry is that its stars are flamboyantly wealthy (as though Pavarotti lived on a leaky houseboat). In fact, how much dough you've got is clearly irrelevant to aesthetics—rockers rich and poor have made great records. That doesn't deny the central issue of class in determining what *kind* of great records, of course, or the fact that almost all of the root music upon which rock has drawn originated among the poor and working class.

But those things have never been the real issue for most folks. Rock is disrespected as much because of *who* makes money from it as how much. Blacks and hillbillies and urban ethnics who reach the Horatio Alger state are supposed to make their mythic millions through drudgery and without much pleasure. Owning a chain of dry cleaners or a small factory is acceptable. Banking big bucks for doing something that seems like fun is not only suspect but downright disreputable, especially when the fun you're having amounts to the ability to speak a secret language.

But then again, it's not only the proprietors of high culture who mistrust rock's ability to generate capital. On its bohemian flank, the suspicions stem from not only a disdain for wealth but an almost superstitious faith in the beknighted taste of the masses. That's a problem Berry Gordy, scion of a Detroit family whose history virtually defines the concept of the black bourgeoisie, never had to deal with directly, once he'd abandoned his jazz ambitions. But it's a battle Cyndi Lauper will have to fight for the rest of her career.

As Gordy's first self-released independent production (he released it on a label named for his sister, a name he later changed), "Money," which revolves around the idea of avarice as a substitute for love, has come to seem almost too paradigmatic of Motown's greed. But just as mere money lust could never begin to describe the degree to which Gordy sought to control his music and artists, such a flip description misses what's great about the record. What it's really about is surely not Strong's rather tepid vocal performance (John Lennon's version with the Beatles wastes this one, especially as a plain-spoken expression of greed, but the Beatles version, unfortunately, never made it to 45). What makes this "Money" is the bluesy piano riff that bores in from the opening seconds, abetted by tambourine, guitar, and zooming bass.

Undoubtedly Berry Gordy may even have played that piano himself, which brings up another point: If he's to be castigated for wanting all that control, at least he should be given equal credit for knowing better than any other executive in record industry history what to do with it once he got it.

By the time that Cyndi Lauper came around, hipster rock and roll had developed the kind of garrett pretensions that jazz possessed when Gordy started out in the mid-fifties. Cyndi got over by expropriating a variety of boho devices, mostly in her look and attitude, but not much of her music trucked with "vanguard" ideas, unless you count her Prince cover. Instead, she made basic pop-rock and sang it with such intensity that it had to stick.

She got "Money Changes Everything" from an arty Atlanta combo called The Brains. In their hands, the song's animus seemed to derive at least as much from Rich Bitch stereotyping as from its more explicit opposition of romantic love vs. guaranteed income. Chief brain Tom Gray was hampered by low-rent production and a rather pedestrian rhythm section, which together conveyed the idea that while he had a vague sympathy with his ex-girlfriend's decision to split with the rich guy, it wasn't the kind of choice that would ever shadow his own conscience.

Placed in Cyndi Lauper's mouth, "Money Changes Everything" grew fangs, just because she *didn't* keep her distance. "We think we know what we're doin', that don't mean a thing," Lauper sang. "It's all in the past now, money changes everything." Gone is Gray's wistful mourning, replaced with rage and contempt—including an unquantifiable measure of self-loathing. But Lauper has something that Gray could never have known: a genuine sense of triumph. She has not had; now she has and, in this world, that's a victory not to be denied. (And while it's true that such victories need questioning, Lauper does a great job of selecting exactly the right queries.) Lauper sings much of the song in a voice of ridicule, and she reserves its nastiest stings for Gray's lines about false friendship, as if to say, you've chosen not to know enough about this, so I'll fill in the blanks.

233 SUPERSTITION, Stevie Wonder
Written and produced by Stevie Wonder
Tamla 54226   1972   *Billboard:* #1 (1 week)

Stevie composed "Superstition" for Jeff Beck, when the ex-Yardbird guitar hero was set to make an album at Motown in 1971. When Beck abandoned that project (after cutting but not releasing "Superstition"), Wonder transferred the biting riff to synthesizer and cut it himself.

The difference between "Superstition" being recorded by a white guitarist and by a black singer whose music was centering ever more heavily on synthesizers and other studio keyboards begins with a contrast in musical substance. When it finally saw daylight, Beck's version of the song turned out to be nothing more than bluesy light jazz, while Wonder's record helped push soul (and all of pop) further into the modern era of studio technique by supporting the cutting synth with a brash horn line and a heavy bass drum accent.

But there's a more substantial difference. In Beck's hands, "Superstition" is nothing more than a good instrumental, but even if he'd sung it as well as Wonder (unlikely, because this is one of Stevie's toughest vocals) he would at most have been addressing himself to a hippie constituency, warning them against necromancers, astrologers, and the like. Wonder's chattering intensity meant something different because it was addressed to an audience of oppressed black Americans, for whom "Superstition" could take the form of either excessive faith or excessive despair. In this context, his exclamatory "Superstition ain't the way!" becomes an injunction to move on the facts, not just suppositions.

234 BACK ON THE CHAIN GANG, Pretenders
Produced by Chris Thomas; written by Chrissie Hynde
Sire 29840   1982   *Billboard:* #5

The Pretenders' video for "Back on the Chain Gang" is the only one I've ever seen that actually made more sense of the song than you could get just by listening to the record. Everybody knows that the lyrics refer to Pretenders' guitarist James Honeyman-Scott; "Back on the Chain Gang" is the first record the group released after his death from a drug overdose. Still, Chrissie Hynde denies that the song should be understood in this context.

Hynde's denial means, it would seem, that her grief is really none of our damn business, and that she wants to ensure that's not *all* we think the song is about. It doesn't take MTV to explain that. You just have to listen to the record, which is constructed as a rock and roll elegy, with the guitars assigned the role of chief mourners.

In the video, Hynde is walking across a stone bridge somewhere in London. It's a bright English day, blustery enough that her hair is blowing. Chrissie sings as she strolls, and midway, she pauses to look out over the Thames. From time to time, the director cuts away, to scenes of the Pretenders playing their instruments amidst the kind of rock pile that prisoners break up in the movies. The parallel between Hynde, absorbing her loss privately, and Hynde, playing her music publicly, is obviously the point. And no big deal . . . til you've seen her do it with an air of pure composure in both scenes that seems to say "Yes, this hurts but not enough to make me quit. Nothing hurts that much. I will carry on. And before I'm through, I shall find a purpose. One good enough to have kept you alive."

By now, this idea is embedded in the record, at least for me. Was it there before I saw the video? I can't know that. But before I saw the video, Honeyman-Scott seemed like just another pop star who threw his life away, though he was luckier than most, since Chrissie had written such a pretty song about it. Now, I know that Hynde herself is so annoyed at her old partner that she wrote the song as much to chastise as to honor him. That's a big improvement on what I understood about "Back on the Chain Gang," and it's the best justification for MTV's brand of visual radio I've ever come across.

235 BYE BYE LOVE, The Everly Brothers
Produced by Archie Bleyer; written by Boudleaux Bryant and Felice Bryant
Cadence 1315   1957   *Billboard:* #2

The conjunction of the Everlys' bluegrass-steeped harmonies and the Bryants' transcendent Nashville songmill compositions endures long after rock's status as music for the purely juvenile has been discarded. Which only makes sense, since those harmonies evoke a few hundred years of Scotch-Irish ballad singing. That's probably why "Bye Bye Love," the group's first hit, was rejected by thirty other acts before Don and Phil finally persuaded Cadence owner Archie Bleyer that they could do something special with it. After Don added the guitar lick that revs things up in the intro, they were home free. Or, as legend would have it, with a guarantee of $128.

The Everlys were extremely close in range and timbre, so much so that even on the choruses, it's hard to pick out individual voices. This gives the disc a power rare at a time when multitracking was little-known. As they later showed on albums like *Songs Our Daddy Taught Us*, such tutored familial resemblances could make even traditional folk songs sound contemporary.

But the most outstanding characteristic of "Bye Bye Love" is the song itself. The lyric ain't much (although the final verse puts a nice ironic twist on the concept of sexual freedom), but the melody is full of twists and turns perfectly suited to the Everlys' folkish approach, a shining example of the uses of professionalism within tradition.

236 LET'S GO GET STONED, Ray Charles
Producer not credited; written by Nickolas Ashford and Valerie Simpson
ABC-Paramount 10808   1966   *Billboard:* #31

Ray's last great blast of R&B power was also his first hit after his C&W period (his previous two singles were Buck Owens songs). The record's impact far exceeded its chart status, because many radio stations refused to air a disc that spoke in such lubricious terms of the pleasures of getting wasted, let alone one cut by a notorious (and unrepentant, even if reformed) junkie. Yet Charles, no amateur at succumbing to temptation, turned in a performance that surpassed whatever petty aggravations had moved Nickolas Ashford and Valerie Simpson to write it at the end of a hard day at the offices of Scepter Records, where they worked as staff writers cranking out potential hits for the likes of Chuck Jackson and Maxine Brown.

Indeed, at this point, "Let's Go Get Stoned" is almost as significant for launching Ashford and Simpson's career as for Ray's great interpretation. They went on, it should go without saying (but probably won't), to compose the best of the Marvin Gaye and Tammi Terrell duets and all Diana Ross's early hits, as well as to enjoy substantial performance success themselves. Pretty good for a career launched by a plea to go out for a drink.

237 PEOPLE GOT TO BE FREE, Rascals
Produced by the Rascals with Arif Mardin; written by
Felix Cavaliere and Eddie Brigati
Atlantic 2537   1968   *Billboard:* #1 (5 weeks)

Sung like a funky Italian boys choir, arranged like a cross between
Dyke and the Blazers and the Buckinghams, written from the fullest
immersion in the glorious naivete of the times. Does hearing Felix try
to preach about "the train to freedom" render "People Got to Be Free"
dated? Of course. But what a glorious date, and what a way of celebrating the part of it that's eternal: "I can't understand, it's so simple
to me / People everywhere just got to be free." Ask me my opinion,
my opinion will be: Dated but *never* out of date.

238 DEVIL WITH A BLUE DRESS ON / GOOD GOLLY MISS MOLLY, Mitch Ryder and the Detroit Wheels
Produced by Bob Crewe; written by William Stevenson and Shorty Long /
John Marascalco and Bumps Blackwell
New Voice 817   1966   *Billboard:* #4

On the basis of this record, the Detroit Wheels were one of the greatest
rock bands ever. Unfortunately for that idea, much of the music wasn't
made by the Wheels. White blues legend Mike Bloomfield steps in with
the psychedelic funk guitar (picking up where he left off on *Highway
61 Revisited*) and the organ riff that rockets the record along is played
by his Electric Flag cohort, Barry Goldberg.

The best parts of "Devil" are exactly as billed, though. The opening
percussion barrage is all Detroit Wheels' drummer Johnny Bee. And
the vocal is all Mitch Ryder, including the guttural shouts he lifted
whole from the Wilson Pickett repertoire.

The format—one faintly obscure R&B gem speeded up past recognition to match one Little Richard classic—derives directly from the
Wheels' first hit, "Jenny Take A Ride" (where the antecedents were
Chuck Willis's fifties stroll-beat rendition of the blues standard "C.C.
Rider" and Richard's "Jenny Jenny"). This time, the source material
was both more famous ("Good Golly Miss Molly" was one of Richard's
two or three most memorable hits) and more obscure (who'd ever heard
the original "Devil," done by ill-fated Detroit soulster Shorty Long as
a lubricious slow blues?). According to Ryder, the "Jenny" medley
came to vinyl directly from the Wheels' notorious Motor City stage

show, while "Devil" was concocted in the studio when follow-ups failed to match "Jenny" 's chart success. Which sheds some interesting light on producer Bob Crewe's Phil Spector pretensions.

Not so interesting or indeed curious as his Ryder solo productions, like "What Now My Love," though. But then again, it's easy to see how Crewe could perceive Mitch and the guys as fitting subjects for Ike and Tina/"River Deep" style experimentation. Despite nationalist and ethnic myths, Ryder and the Wheels were legitimate R&B stylists, their European ancestry notwithstanding. Johnny Bee and everyday guitarist Jim McCarty both started out in high school bands backing black vocalists like Gino Washington; Ryder began his career singing in black clubs, alongside such stalwarts as the Four Tops. When the group got together in 1962 or so, as Billy Lee and the Rivieras, they developed a soul-style stage show that, according to legend, actually blew the likes of the Miracles off the stage. The music they medleyed was, in this regard, as least as much "theirs" to tinker with as it would have belonged to any black come-lately. (Unless you think that *The Supremes Sing Rodgers and Hart* was an ethnic rather than aesthetic error.)

Of course, that doesn't mean that a group of black musicians would have ever come up with an interpretation of the "Devil" medley anything like this one or that such a group (let alone an integrated one) could have achieved the Wheels' notoriety. What's great here, though, is precisely the impurity of everything, from the group (whose authenticity you can hear but not see, making room for a different kind of inauthenticity) to the interpretation itself (stage show brought to the studio, R&B transformed to rock and roll). If you can't dig that, dig the energy. And if you can't dig either, see ya later, Jack.

239 NEEDLES AND PINS, The Searchers
Produced by Tony Hatch; written by Jack Nitzsche and Sonny Bono
Kapp 577   1964   *Billboard:* #13

There's something about electric twelve-string guitar that sets your blood pumping. The doubled strings scythe through chords, harvesting goosebumps of shrill excitement. The sound that became identified as classic rock and roll twelve-string originated in the Searchers' "Needles and Pins," though that's not how they arrived at it: The ringing opening was achieved with a pair of six-string guitars played in unison and recorded with a heap of echo. So it remained for the Byrds to drive the point home with "Mr. Tambourine Man." (The Searchers did use electric twelve-string on a later cover of another Jackie DeShannon hit, "When You Walk in the Room.") Be that as it may, "Needles and Pins" remains one of the most exciting records of the British Invasion.

Unlike "Mr. Tambourine Man," "Needles and Pins" doesn't emphasize the guitar sound; it's just the thrilling underpinning of a harmony arrangement. The Searchers fitted into a peculiar slot among British Invasion groups. Their harmonies owed a lot more to pop-folk groups like the Springfields than to the R&B groups from which the Beatles derived their group singing style, something that became more evident in 1965 with the Kingston Trio-like "What Have They Done to the Rain." But during 1964, at least, the Searchers made far tougher sounding records than more purely teenexploitation Merseybeat groups like Gerry and the Pacemakers or Billy J. Kramer and the Dakotas. The only other British group of the period with a similar orientation was the Hollies.

The Hollies, of course, begat Graham Nash, who formed one third of Crosby, Stills and Nash, who did so much to make folk-pop harmonies the dominant strain of Los Angeles rock in the seventies. So it's fitting that the Searchers (a band named after John Ford's finest western) found their greatest hit in the quickie concoction of a pair of Phil Spector's Hollywood sidekicks, arranger Jack Nitzsche and jack of all trades and master of some Sonny Bono.

Nitzsche and Bono produced Jackie DeShannon's original rendition of "Needles and Pins" in 1963; it charted at Number 84, on the basis of mostly West Coast airplay. DeShannon's version is good, but tame. The guitar lick is there, but it's flat, and DeShannon's singing (though it became the model for a raft of singer/songwriters) conveyed more anxiety than agitation. It became a rock and roll standard only when Tony Jackson's twisted scouse accent—which rendered the title "Needles and Pin-za"—met those twelve strings ringing out the riff. The whole show's over in a mere 2:10, but once the riff gets into your head, it endures forever.

240 RIP IT UP, Little Richard
Produced by Bumps Blackwell; written by Bumps Blackwell and John Marascalco
Specialty 579   1956   *Billboard: #17*

The greatest example of *epater le bourgeoisie* in history: "Well, it's Saturday night and I just got paid / Fool about my money, don't try to save." Even more delectably, it's a hillbilly tune sung by a bouffant Negro against a vividly sensual rhythmic backdrop. Stay uptight in the face of this music and you're just saddling yourself with misery. Give in to it, and you'll not only have a great time but a standard of exhilaration to measure the rest of your life against.

241 WHAT BECOMES OF THE BROKENHEARTED, Jimmy Ruffin

Produced by Mickey Stevenson and William Weatherspoon; written by
J. Dean, William Weatherspoon, and Paul Riser
Soul 35022   1966   *Billboard: #7*

Motown at its most mystical. Ruffin wakes up immersed in a bottomless pit of orchestration, and recounts a bad dream about his travels in "this land of broken dreams," which he *says* means lack of romantic love but which everybody who's ever heard him understands to signify something a lot more disturbing and universal.

In the end, "What Becomes of the Brokenhearted" is not much more than Stevenson and Weatherspoon doing their best to imitate Holland-Dozier-Holland's Four Tops material (most notably "Reach Out I'll Be There," right down to the supplementary melody carried by the flute). But they come pretty damn close to the spirit of those Tops hits. Ruffin is no Levi Stubbs but he conveys sufficient psychic bewilderment to make credible lines like "I walk in shadows, searching for light / Cold and alone, no comfort in sight."

242 FORTUNATE SON, Creedence Clearwater Revival

Written and produced by John Fogerty
Fantasy 634   1969   *Billboard: #3*

I always hate it when anyone writes that rock and roll *is* some finite, quantifiable, narrow thing: "Rock and roll is just fun, after all," or "In the first place, rock is supposed to be dance music." If it were just one thing, it wouldn't still be here.

On the other hand, if rock *were* just one thing, and if that one thing were pure fury (perhaps with a specific class animus), then "Fortunate Son" would be its platonic distillation. John Fogerty, who wrote the song the day he got his final discharge papers from the U.S. Army, rasps out the lyrics (which might be subtitled *The Dan Quayle Story*) in a voice filled with bile and uses his guitar as a weapon to run machine-gun stitches right through everybody who's ever abused a privilege. I don't know if that's a good definition of rock and roll, but it's a hell of a start on my idea of democracy in action.

243 JUST LIKE TOM THUMB'S BLUES [live], Bob Dylan

Produced by Bob Johnston; written by Bob Dylan
Columbia 43683   1966   Did not make pop chart

If you liked the jingly folk-rock of "I Want You" enough to run out and buy the single without waiting another couple of weeks for the album (which only turned out to be *Blonde on Blonde*), you got the surprise of your life: A B side taken from Dylan's recent European tour on which he and a rock band (which only turned out to be The Band) did things to "Just Like Tom Thumb's Blues," a song from *Highway 61 Revisited*, that it's still risky to talk about in broad daylight.

Rock critics like to make a big deal about B sides but there are only maybe a dozen really great ones in the whole history of singles. This one's rank is indisputable, though, because it offers something that wasn't legally available until the early seventies: a recorded glimpse of Dylan's onstage prowess. "Just Like Tom Thumb's Blues" came out before anybody ever thought of bootlegging rock shows, before anybody this side of Jimi Hendrix quite understood Dylan as a great rock and roll stage performer. And so this vicious, majestic music, hidden away in the most obscure place he could think of putting it, struck with amazing force.

Today, it sounds like the reapings of a whirlwind, Dylan's voice as draggy, druggy, and droogy as the surreal Mexican beatnik escapade he's recounting, Robbie Robertson carving dense mathematical figures on guitar, Garth Hudson working pure hoodoo on organ. Slurred and obtuse as Little Richard reading Ezra Pound, there's a magnificence here so great that, if you had to, you could make the case for rock and roll as a species of art using this record and nothing else.

244 TUMBLING DICE, The Rolling Stones
Produced by Jimmy Miller; written by Mick Jagger and Keith Richards
Rolling Stones 19103   1972   Billboard: #7

Mick Jagger sings "Tumbling Dice" as if he'd taken a vow of incoherence; the few phrases that do jump out at you—"fever in the funkhouse now," "you can be my partner in crime," "don't you know the deuce is still wild"—are probably red herrings, planted to make you doubt that Mick is making his lines up as he goes along. He gets away with it because the song is really about everything but the words.

Like the way that Jagger shakes the title around in his mouth in addled emulation of Otis Redding; like the guitars that sound like they're searching for a new, more primitive form of abstract expressionism; like the female chorus, which seems to have been recruited from a cheap dive in a remote province. "Tumbling Dice" is a whole and inseparable sound and as such it's wholly satisfying.

One part drives the rest home. Charlie Watts once more lays his modest claim as the real heart of the Stones with the fills at the end. "Got to roll me!" the singers plead, and Charlie lays 'em out flat in the aisles.

245 I LOVE YOU, The Volumes
Produced by Richard "Popcorn" Wylie; written by Eddie Union
Chex 1002   1962   Billboard: #22

"I Love You" 's nonsense syllables and its cliched lyrics—hearts skip crazy beats, lips are warm and sweeter than wine—summarize everything squares hate about pre-Beatles rock and roll. But the startling presence of Teenie Davis's wailing first tenor shrieking "Eeeeey-ay I love you / Eeeeey-ay need you-ooo-uh-oo," the street power of Eddie Union's lead, and the resilience with which the other guys chant their responses are exactly what makes "I Love You." If you can't get past the trashiness, that's 'cause it's trashiness that grants the Volumes their glory.

246 CALL ME (COME BACK HOME), Al Green
Produced by Willie Mitchell; written by Al Green, Willie Mitchell, and Al Jackson
Hi 2235   1973   *Billboard:* #10

After the disintegration of the musical enterprises around Stax/Volt, Memphis no more fell off the musical map than did Detroit after the departure of Motown. But Memphis sustained itself more prominently, because sweet-voiced Michigan native Al Green temporarily rejuvenated the local soul scene.

Green recorded with producer Willie Mitchell, previously best-known for a series of funky instrumentals in the mid-sixties. (1964's "20-75" set a pattern which was repeated with middling success through 1969's "30-60-90.") Mitchell headed Hi Records, a label that had once had both country and R&B rosters but was essentially down-and-out by the end of the sixties. But with the demise of Stax, Mitchell, and thus Green, fell heir to the city's great group of session musicians who stuck around, most notably the immortal drummer Al Jackson.

Jackson's work with Green may be the most understated of his brilliantly understated career. His softly insistent propulsion was perfect for Green's languid vocals and Mitchell's comparatively lush (for Memphis) settings. "Call Me" is a tour de force for all three of them.

This brand of soul music might have been created in a heat wave far different from the immediacy of Martha and the Vandellas'. Green's tetchy, half-exhausted vocal, caught between a shout and a sigh, suggests it's already gone on too long. The subtle declamations of Jackson's toms and snares let him know it's not about to end any time soon. And so they ride it out together, too weary to battle more strenuously, too committed to give up the fight altogether.

247 CRUISIN', Smokey Robinson
Produced by Smokey Robinson; written by Smokey Robinson and Marvin Tarplin
Tamla 54306   1979   *Billboard:* #4

Sometimes I feel that Smokey Robinson raised me from a pup. Surely, it was his voice that first beckoned me from the radio to a world outside my house and neighborhood that was unimaginably larger than anything I'd dreamed. And though these days he's oftimes too slick and bland for his own good, his early music—not only the records he led with the Miracles but the songs he wrote and produced for the Temptations and

Marvin Gaye and other subjects of the Motown empire—remains central to my definition of what's important in pop. And though he's defined earlier in this volume as a non-soul singer, that just shows you the limitation of taking such an elastic term and giving it a purely musical definition (not that you don't have to do just that, sometimes).

When I was a kid, Smokey's voice called to me as an exemplar of smooth cool, a surface unrippled even though heartbreak lurked just beneath. It took me years to understand why the *really* dangerous aspect of what Smokey (and the singers like him) were selling was the romantic stuff, not because it represents an inadequate dream (it may represent the only adequate one, since it posits grace and gentleness and giving and love transcending lust as the greatest of all human and sexual virtues) but because it proffers an impossible reality. So there's simply no reason to feel all that abject in the moments when you don't have those things . . . or all that triumphant in the moments when, quite temporarily, you think you do. Nevertheless the ideas the records expressed were what counted, and they were both complex and transformative.

Fifteen years after our first encounter, I was cruising through Hollywood in somebody else's Cadillac when "Cruisin' " came on the radio. I'd already heard it on a Robinson album called *Where There's Smoke*, but there it was suffocated by the songs and arrangements that surrounded it.

Tooling that massive hunk of Detroit luxury iron down Sunset Strip, caught by surprise through the mysteries of the airwaves, "Cruisin' " revealed itself as something better and finer than anything else Smokey had done in his solo career. The singing absolutely glided on a bed of strings, the rhythm popped along gently, driven by nothing more forceful than conga and tambourine and the restless tug of Marvin Tarplin's soft electric guitar. He kept the tone restful and sensuous, like an airier "Let's Get It On." The result was a call to seduction so persuasive that it nearly (nearly) overrode the ambiguities raised by his selection of a gay term as the central metaphor.

A decade later, none of that seems as consequential as the thrillingly high "Aah" to which Smokey twice drives himself during the final choruses. As with "Let's Get It On," the record can't entirely conceal a predatory male perspective. (I mean, none of this breathless "Baby, tonight belongs to us" shit would really work if you said it to somebody in a bar, or even in bed. Would it?) So there's grave danger in taking it too seriously. But even if you—or rather, I—feel a little duped and entrapped by the philosophy behind those seductive phrases, there's no point in bearing a grudge. Beauty carries its own prejudices, and this is one hell of a beautiful record.

248 HE'S A REBEL, The Crystals
Produced by Phil Spector; written by Gene Pitney
Philles 106   1962   *Billboard:* #1 (2 weeks)

249 HE'S SURE THE BOY I LOVE, The Crystals
Produced by Phil Spector; written by Barry Mann and
Cynthia Weill
Philles 109   1962   *Billboard:* #11

"I imagined a sound—a sound so strong that if the material wasn't the greatest, the sound would carry the record."

So spoke Phil Spector in 1964, as a way of explaining the unprecedented music he'd been making for the past two years. But his own description didn't really go quite far enough for the sound that he imagined—product that it was not of his efforts only but of the industry of dozens of women and men—had a potency so great that he could change seemingly crucial parts without risk of detection or any decrease in either the quality of the music or the quality of the attraction.

Although Spector was never simply an apprentice or journeyman, he wasn't much more than that before he made these two hits. After understudying with Jerry Leiber and Mike Stoller, he made a variety of independent label productions, then moved to New York City and took a job at Liberty Records, where he worked under the label's Los Angeles-based A&R chief, the producer/engineer Snuff Garrett.

Nineteen-sixty-two was still the heyday of the Brill Building, the New York office building with its music publisher-operated songwriting factories that had so much control over the pre-Beatles record industry, and Spector, who knew what he wanted but couldn't create it from scratch, haunted the offices of the best publishers in both New York and L.A. Lester Sill, one of the best music publishers in Hollywood, agreed to become his partner in a new venture, Philles Records (for Phil/Les, see?). But Spector still did outside projects, and his Liberty contract hadn't yet expired.

Still in New York, Phil went to visit another of his publishing cronies, Aaron Schroeder, who played him a new song by Schroeder protege Gene Pitney (for whom Spector had already produced "Every Breath I Take"). "He's A Rebel" clearly was a smash for somebody, and Snuff Garrett planned to make that someone Liberty's ingenue, Vikki Carr. Spector couldn't wait; this was a song he *understood.* He believed that he could not only make the song a hit, he believed he could make a greater record with it than anybody else—including his boss.

He hopped a flight to L.A. and cut the song with the stellar session lineup pieced together by saxman Steve Douglas, the band that included Hal Blaine on drums with engineer Larry Levine rolling the tape and setting the echo. The track was meant for the Crystals, with whom Philles had already scored on "There's No Other (Like My Baby)" and "Uptown." But the Crystals were teenagers, still in school, and they didn't want to leave home. So Spector winged it: He got Sill to hire the Blossoms, led by Darlene Love, who were the top girl group on the L.A. session scene. For triple scale. No royalties.

Ironically, Pitney had written "Rebel" thinking about the Crystals—the real ones, not the Hollywood stand-ins—and "Uptown." But Darlene Love, one of the two or three greatest female singers in rock history, missed not a nuance of Pitney's lustful saga. She slurs the run-on lyrics—"If they don't like him that way, they won't like me, after today" sung as one gaspless line—in a husky voice that suggests that however hard he may be on the outside, she knows just the spots where he can be made to melt. Though the sax solo and handclaps date it, Larry Knechtel's piano, Love's bold shout, and Blaine's crushing drum attack mark "He's A Rebel" as an ultramodern example of studio rock and roll, the equal of what the Motown staff and George Martin and the Beatles began to create that year, and the model for an enormous amount of what came later.

The phantom Crystals were even better than the real thing, and Spector cut "He's Sure the Boy I Love," the group's next hit, with them, too. Opening with a Love soliloquy on her dream of a perfect boyfriend, each line set off with booming sax riffs, the disc explodes into life as a percussion extravaganza with drum, bass, and sleigh bells. "He doesn't hang diamonds 'round my neck," Love cries and then "whoa, whoa," as it could never possibly make any difference, as if this guy, unemployed and without prospects or qualifications ('cept for *her*) is a prize everybody in her right mind ought to envy. If "Uptown" had been Spector's tribute to the everyday heroes of his working class origins, he made "He's Sure the Boy I Love" something better—their exalted revenge, a tribute to what money can never buy.

250 I GET AROUND, The Beach Boys
Written and produced by Brian Wilson
Capitol 5174   1964   *Billboard:* #1 (2 weeks)

Brian Wilson's last great car song shows the Beach Boys in transit from basic Four Preps harmony plus Chuck Berry licks to their more ornate—or baroque—late sixties album rock. The lyric might as well be the plot outline for *American Graffiti*. The guitar and organ merge into one sound but what really rocks is the propulsive bass. Mike Love's nasality has dated even worse than the macho lyric, but Brian's falsetto makes up for both, soaring above his pedestrian mumblings, as he boasts about being "a real cool head / Makin' real good bread." Real working class poetry, huh?

251 ALL DAY AND ALL OF THE NIGHT, The Kinks
Produced by Shel Talmy; written by Ray Davies
Reprise 0334   1964   *Billboard:* #7

"Louie Louie" 's European vacation. Louie taught his limey cousins a brand new beat and Ray Davies taught him better diction (though you'd be surprised how close to "duh duh duh, duh duh, duh duh duh" the seven words in the title sound). For years, Britrock fans have argued over whether Jimmy Page or Dave Davies played the guitar solo, but whoever it was, he's lucky the Kingsmen didn't make him pay royalties.

252 PURPLE HAZE, Jimi Hendrix
Produced by Chas Chandler; written by Jimi Hendrix
Reprise 0597   1967   *Billboard:* #65

If anybody could be described as a pure album artist, it was probably Hendrix. In that sense, "Purple Haze" could be characterized as the debut single of the Album Rock Era, the first whose purpose was serving notice that the artist was up to something that could *not* be contained within this three-minute segment. Before it was anything else, "Purple Haze" was a come-on for *Are You Experienced.*

Like a lot of breakthrough hits, "Purple Haze" 's opening serves as a proclamation: an almost-march time set of guitar chords followed by a burst of fuzztone and heavy drumming, then Hendrix shouting his acid blues. Though by now it seems rather tame purely in terms of electric guitar pyrotechnics, when it first hit the airwaves, "Purple Haze" was shocking.

Not *just* because of its sonic novelty, either. If you could find a station playing it (and locating one was part of the fun) what you heard was explicit drug references—despite the hysterics, always a rare commodity at Top 40—and some rather lewd heavy breathing. Great rock and roll needn't always be salacious, but this is both.

253 WAVELENGTH, Van Morrison
Written and produced by Van Morrison
Warner Bros. 8661   1978   *Billboard: #42*

Van Morrison's fascination with radio, both as a vehicle for the transmission of music and as a metaphor for the transmission of spiritual power, amounts to an obsession. It's familiar from the stunning "Radio! Turn it up!" chant which concludes "Caravan," the best song on his great 1970 album, *Moondance*. But it reached a state of perfected grace in this single, though (relatively speaking) it flopped on the very medium it celebrated.

Like John Lennon just across the Irish Channel, Morrison first heard rock and roll and rhythm and blues through a fog of pops and crackles on foreign stations like Radio Luxembourg. No nation in Europe had any reason to regularly program such music as part of its cultural fare, but Luxembourg rented time to any record label that cared to buy it, a kind of institutionalized payola that had kids all over the Continent and throughout the British Isles glued to their receivers during the few evening hours each week when new releases were highlighted. Luxembourg's station was far away and fifties radio receivers poor; the miasmic distortion that resulted must have struck Morrison, like Lennon, as a built-in part of those strange, foreign records, a built-in part of their mystique even if it wasn't there when you played the records themselves. These secret sounds traveled only the transnational airwaves.

So when Van sings "I hear the Voice of America calling on my wavelength," he's not referring to the U.S. propaganda channel (which was mainly aimed at "the captive nations of Eastern Europe" and hardly would have played any such trash as rock and R&B anyhow) but to the music itself and the static that accompanied it. Against swirling synthesizer riffs that evoke that late night radio distortion, he sings about the transforming power of broadly transmitted music. The moments when pop music becomes the thing of glory of which even such a bitter, whimsical, cynical, mystic can sing:

> When I'm down, you always comfort me
> When I'm lonely, child, you see about me
> You are everywhere you're s'posed to be
> And I can get your station, when I need rejuvenation

In "Wavelength," Van declares that the message of those American voices on his radio was "Come back, baby, come back." And so he did. Like millions of Irishmen before him, he moved to the States. And in 1967 or 1968, found himself living in Cambridge, Massachusetts. Hardly anybody knew who Morrison was; his last hit had been that one about the "lover in the grass" referred to in these lyrics and the music he was working on, which became the immortal *Astral Weeks*, was not inclined to incite frenzied attention.

Van stayed up late and listened to the radio. In the night, he heard a strange voice calling to him once again, in the form of a frog-voiced preacher who spun blues and R&B records and shouted jive talk into the after-midnight air on station WBCN, which devoted the rest of its programming to hippie album rock. One night, Van worked up his nerve and called the station. It was a small place; the deejay answered his own phone.

Van was stunned to discover that the disc jockey was a white man named Peter Wolf. Wolf was stunned to be called by a guy who was one of his musical heroes, the writer not only of "Brown Eyed Girl" but of "Gloria," a song his own band, the Hallucinations, regularly performed. So the guy from Belfast became friends with the kid from the Bronx and they stayed in touch for the next couple of decades.

And that is a little bit of what Van Morrison means when he sings "You never let me down, no, no."

254 I'M SO YOUNG, The Students
No producer credited; written by Prez Tyus
Note 10012   1958   Did not make pop chart

Several years ago, a friend of mine asked me to take a semifamous musician who was in town from California to shop for oldies in Greenwich Village. When we got to the shop, the clerks were swooning over a bunch of Students' 45s. They played "I'm So Young," and the semifamous musician sneered—at the callowness, the wavering pitch, the concluding threat of suicide over being denied the right to marry. In this citadel of teen harmony, we were lucky to escape with our lives.

And I can't say I blame those doo-wop freaks. "Hey," I thought but didn't say, "This is somebody's *life*—who cares if it's corny and misshapen?" But because so much of doo-wop centers around teen romance fantasies, and because very few of the groups went on to anything except Harlem obscurity, it's easier to disrespect doo-woppers than any other kind of pop musician.

I don't know anything about the Students. Until Andy McKaie assembled *The Best of Chess Vocal Groups* in 1988, I wasn't able to learn so much as Prez Tyus's first name or the fact that they came from Steubenville, Ohio. Not one pop music reference book (out of the dozens in my library) gives them so much as a line. They aren't listed in anybody else's list of great records. I'm not even sure how I know this damn thing; it's on an old KYA (San Francisco) hits album and a Chess doo-wop anthology, but I don't ever remember hearing it on the radio in Detroit. (Steve Propes tells me it came out in '58 and then got reissued during the doo-wop revival in '61, because the Dovells used its B side as the basis of "Bristol Stomp.") The Beach Boys covered it on *The Beach Boys Today* (and Brian Wilson ripped it off for "We'll Run Away" on *All Summer Long*), but even then nobody paid any particular attention. Prez Tyus sang through his nose and mispronounces "says" with a long A (maybe meaning he got the tense wrong) right off the bat. In many ways, I guess, "I'm So Young" seems like a parody of a doo-wop record—for those who deride it, that's probably what it is, right down to the suicide hint at the end.

But me, I stayed up til 4:00 A.M. trying to find out where the hell it came from and listening in a search for a way to explain it to you. At the end of it, all I know is why it captivates me: Hey, man, that's somebody's *life*. Who cares if it's corny and misshapen?

255 SUMMERTIME, Billy Stewart
Produced by Billy Davis; written by George Gershwin and Du Bose Heyward
Chess 1966   1966   *Billboard:* #10

They called Billy Stewart "Fat Boy" because he weighed around 300 pounds, and "Motormouth," because of his ability to create wild trilling effects. In a sense, he was the original human beat box, although human drill-press probably comes closer to capturing the sound's effect.

"Summertime" is an absolutely sacrilegious reading of the Gershwin standard, which is exactly why it's great. Stewart's opening trills and postverbal scatting, coupled with Maurice White's all-over-the-kit drumming, completely demolish the song's always spurious claim to have anything to do with the real tenor (much less tragedy) of black American life. Out of the wreckage, they artfully reclaim even such piss-elegant blues as an art of performance rather than composition. When Bob Dylan described rock singing as "exercises in breath control," he should have been thinking of Stewart's final, almost yodelled, multibar exploration of the syllables comprising "Summertime."

256 MAGGIE MAY, Rod Stewart
Produced by Rod Stewart; written by Rod Stewart and Martin Quittenton
Mercury 73224   1971   *Billboard:* #1 (5 weeks)

By now the virtues of "Maggie May" can barely be discerned beneath the numb perceptual gauze implanted by saturation album rock broadcasting. And perhaps, in light of Rod Stewart's shift in image from sensitive if sharp-dressing young singer/songwriter/rocker to jaded middle-aged cad, the song's portrayal of the relationship between callow youth and older woman is no longer quite credible in any event.

I'm not here to argue the point. I mean, after Britt Eklund and Alana Hamilton, it's kinda hard to argue for "Oh, Maggie, I couldn't have tried any more," much less believe that *she* made a "first class fool outta" *him.*

But however personal it may be (Lester Bangs probably had the last word on that in his essay/short story/review), "Maggie May" isn't only autobiography. And in this world of tales more trustworthy than their tellers, its virtues shouldn't be so quickly dismissed. So let's listen at least once more to Mickey Waller's drumming (which critic Greil Marcus once proposed should have been awarded a Nobel Prize—in physics), Martin Quittenton's work on acoustic guitar and mandolin, and Rod's singing on the final verse (corny as those lines may be) and that last chorus, especially the lingering sub-Sam Cooke "wooo-ooo-hoh," the one thing in the song that has credibility guaranteed to outlive its author's foibles.

257 I SECOND THAT EMOTION, The Miracles
Written and produced by Smokey Robinson and Al Cleveland
Tamla 54159   1967   Billboard: #4

Smokey Robinson says that one of the principal things he learned from Berry Gordy was the importance of writing and rewriting and finely honing his lyrics. On the basis of "I Second That Emotion" alone, he deserved a Phi Beta Kappa key. Starting with a chance remark made by cowriter Al Cleveland while they were Christmas shopping, Smokey worked a series of simple, colloquial metaphors into an internally rhyming, utterly rhythmic piece of soul poetry. The opening verse, for instance, is about as intricate as soul songwriting gets, capturing not only the surface of Smokey's emotion but its complexity:

> Maybe you want to give me kisses sweet
> But only for one night with no repeat
> And maybe you'll go away and never call
> And a taste of honey is worse than none at all

So "I Second That Emotion" begins as a sort of male answer to the Shirelles' "Will You Still Love Me Tomorrow," and while it's odd to hear a guy demanding "a lifetime of devotion," that's where the parts you can't write down come in. Not only Smokey's trembly tenor but the pitter-pat congas that suggest the tripping of his heart; Marv Tarplin's guitar that cuts those lines in half, in an even more powerful suggestion of hesitancy; and the crash of drum and tambourine that pull Smokey through almost despite himself. As a soul record, "I Second That Emotion" is unquestionably classic, but as an exercise in the exposure of male vulnerability it's even bigger and better.

258 TRUE BLUE, Madonna
Written and produced by Madonna and Stephen Bray
Sire 28591   1986   Billboard: #3

One of the trickier facets of analyzing sixties girl group records is determining what people intended as opposed to what they conveyed. The difference between "real" emotion and effective contrivance shouldn't matter, being unknowable, but it does, because anyone who's touched by the yearning innocence of the best Crystals and Chiffons and Ronettes and Shirelles records wants to believe that it's all truly felt, or at least that a lot of it could be.

Madonna reframes the issue in contemporary terms. Her biography is public. You *know* she doesn't subscribe to her own tales of romantic devotion. And yet, in "True Blue," she manages to convince you for three or four minutes that she has succumbed to the romantic rhetoric of the girl group singles she's evoking. Creating such an unwilling suspension of disbelief is a tremendous achievement, for it means that Madonna's music actively subverts the publicity machinery on which a great deal of her celebrity depends.

And it's nothing other than her music that lets her get away with it. Take away the electronics—Stephen Bray's hip-hop synthesizer keyboard and drum effects—and what you'd have wouldn't be a great girl group record, but just another girl group pastiche, the kind of disc that makes it with purist collectors and flops on the charts. Take away that postdisco dance groove, and Madonna would sound as hollow and fake as she "really" is.

But the greatness of "True Blue" is that it *does* contain all this music, and the music simply melts away empiricist objections. (The twelve-inch remix—one of the best such reworkings of a pop song extant—opens with Madonna laughing, which I interpret as a triumphant giggle, which may win me an award for credulity but still makes more sense than thinking that she's behaving with outward cynicism.) Which is not to say that "True Blue" has as *much* credibility as "Be My Baby," which it emotionally and harmonically resembles, but that its credibility is founded in its awareness of the difference between what Ronnie knew then and what Madonna and the rest of us know now.

And that every time it comes on the radio, from the first encounter until the day you predecease it, you'll turn up the volume and be glad you did.

259 HELP, The Beatles
Produced by George Martin; written by John Lennon and Paul McCartney
Capitol 5476   1965   *Billboard:* #1 (3 weeks)

In his 1970 *Rolling Stone* interview with Jann Wenner, John Lennon listed "Help" along with "Strawberry Fields Forever" as "personal" records. "They were the ones I always considered my best songs," he said. "They were the ones I really wrote from experience and not projecting myself into a situation and writing a nice story about it." He was clearly substantially prouder of the recording of "Strawberry Fields," and not only because its concept was more sophisticated. "I don't like the recording that much," he said of "Help." "We did it too fast trying to be commercial."

Lennon might have meant that the Beatles tossed off the session in question, not spending enough time working over the arrangement and production, but there's another way to take his assessment: That the record's tempo was too fast and that even though it might have sold less, those famous lyrics—"When I was younger, so much younger than today / I never needed anybody's help in any way"—really should have formed a mournful, Orbison-like ballad.

By one standard, Lennon's failure to record "Help" in the spirit in which he wrote it represents what the likes of Albert Goldman would call a sell-out of his own best intentions. And given the relationship between inchoate self-expression and the best rock and roll, it's tempting to agree, to label "Help" as a jejune beat number that might have achieved actual significance if it hadn't been reined in by show business constraints.

But the record itself reminds us that no artist ever accurately judges his own work. The Beatles' "Help" isn't a compromise; it's bursting with a vitality that Lennon's less mediated solo albums never achieve. And John certainly doesn't sound like he's trying to spit the bit; he sounds triumphant, because he's found a group of kindred spirits who are offering the very spiritual assistance and emotional support for which he's begging. Paul's echoing harmonies, Ringo's jaunty drums, the boom of George's guitar speak to the heart of Lennon's passion, and though they can't cure the wound, at least they add a note of reassurance that he's not alone with his pain. You can make some great music on that basis. And they did.

260 SLIPPIN' INTO DARKNESS, War
Produced by Jerry Goldstein; written by Harold Brown, Papa Dee Allen, B. B. Dickerson, Howard Scott, Lonnie Jordan, Lee Oskar, and Charles Miller [War]
United Artists 50867   1971   Billboard: #16

Of all the funk ensembles that Sly and the Family Stone churned up in its wake, War may have been the most interesting. The group, formed in 1960 as the Creators, amalgamated rock, soul, and Latin accents in ways that could only have come together in Los Angeles. Yet it took eight years for this unique but inevitable synthesis to be recorded, and then only under the unlikely auspices first of Deacon Jones, the great Los Angeles Rams' defensive end trying to jump start a new career, and then of ex-Animal Eric Burdon, who was cruising Hollywood in search of a backing band. Supplemented by Danish harp player Lee Oskar, War made Burdon's hits, "Spill the Wine" and "They Can't Take Away Our Music."

A year later, finally unBurdoned, War took off on its own, immediately establishing a deeper funkiness. "Slippin' Into Darkness," their second hit, features drop-dead bass and sleigh bells, lethal guitar/ harp interplay, and lyrics that evoke the dissolution of the civil rights movement into the drug-laced daze of the frustrated early seventies. "You've been slippin' into darkness / Pretty soon you're gonna pay," may have been the most accurate epigram for the period that any pop song came up with. Today, those lines seem to take in everything from the melodic deterioration of soul to the scourging dementia of the late eighties crack culture.

Stylistically, "Slippin' into Darkness," with its salsa and Afro-Cuban accents, established War as a leading exponent of progressive soul, and together with "What's Going On," "It's a Family Affair," and "Freddie's Dead," presaged the deeper funk to come.

261 IT'S LIKE THAT, Run-D.M.C.
Produced by Russell Simmons and Larry Smith; written by Larry Smith, Joseph Simmons, and Darryl McDaniels
Profile PRO-7010 (12") 1983 Did not make pop chart

In the six months or so that elapsed between Grandmaster Flash's "The Message" and "It's Like That," rap traversed a generation. "The Message" spoke to everyone with ears in the urban community. Run-D.M.C. were (at least initially) concerned more with the disenfranchisement of people like themselves, people who were, specifically, young and black. "Money is the key to end all your woes," they insisted, defining the nature and limits of their rebellion.

Spouting such thoughts might have seemed—or, for that matter, might have been—puerile, were it not for the extraordinary music. At first, all that synthesizer and electronic percussion noise just seems intrusive, added solely so they can call these chants music. But after a while you understand that the flourishes are there to buoy what the group has to say, to keep the danger of their flat statements from tugging the rappers under. If not a danceable insurrection (you need more than self-justifying expositions of your own upwardly mobile grasping for that), at least they wound up with the source of some extraordinarily insurrectionary dancing.

262 HOLD WHAT YOU'VE GOT, Joe Tex
Produced by Buddy Killen; written by Joe Tex
Dial 4001   1964   *Billboard:* #5

In 1972, around the time of "I Gotcha," his last really good record, I spent an afternoon in a Detroit motel room talking with Joe Tex and an entourage of middle-aged black men who were primarily interested in talking boxing. So we sat around watching a paunchy Tex throw shadow punches at his pals and sing the praises of Muhammad Ali.

Tex seemed generally uninterested in music or at least not very interested in *discussing* it. Doing it was another thing; he was always a fervid and funny performer and had a genuine enthusiasm for it that I always figured stemmed from his preaching roots. Tex sermonized so often and at such length that he was the first pop singer to be known as "The Rapper." In fact, a great many of his hits are rhythm and blues sermonettes. Of these, "Hold What You've Got" was both first and best.

The one time that Tex became animated about his music during that long afternoon was when we got on the subject of that record. He described growing up in south Texas, traveling around as a journeyman soul performer and finally cutting "Hold What You've Got" with Buddy Killen in Nashville. Inevitably, the record came out while Tex was on the road. "I was somewhere between Shreveport and Houston, driving home," he said, "when I heard the record on the radio. But then I looked at the dial and I said, 'This can't be.' They were playing it on a station right in the middle of the dial and all the black stations were way over to the right." He stopped the car, called home and learned that he'd scored southern soul's first crossover hit.

It would have been hard to predict that Tex had stirred a movement. There's just nothing typical about "Hold What You've Got," save perhaps its horn arrangement. It's slower, less energetic than the archetypal soul hit. Tex sings sweetly on the chorus but that's basically the only place he sings at all. The rest is essentially a brief (2:01) homily on the virtues of fidelity. But if it's more sermon than song, then it's probably the greatest sermon ever to go Top Five in *Billboard*.

263 WHO DO YOU LOVE, Bo Diddley
Producer not credited; written by Ellas McDaniel
[Bo Diddley]
Checker 842   1956   Did not make pop chart

If Bo weren't almost as much the soul of R&B good humor as Fats Domino, his brilliant pun ("Hoodoo you love") and bizarre images of sexual sorcery coupled with the most primitive beat in rock history might seem sinister. Instead, especially when compared to hoodoo heirs like Jimi Hendrix, they're just a neat goof on love song expectations and the nastiest part of the whole record is the twangy guitar breaks.

264 SHERRY, The Four Seasons
Produced by Bob Crewe; written by Bob Gaudio
Vee-Jay 456   1962   Billboard: #1 (5 weeks)

Bigger and bolder they just don't come. And that plunk-plunk rhythm's not half so plodding as it first seems; it just sets up the real action, in the drums and tambourine which dance their asses off while Frankie Valli's falsetto heads for the stratosphere. And in the Seasons' Belmonts-meet-Beach Boys (on Maurice Williams' turf) style I hear a hint of how white R&B would have developed if John Lennon and Brian Jones had never gotten hold of it—music made on a scale where ambition is far less visible but so gemlike when it shows that, inevitably, some wise guy in an art school would have had to pick it up and polish it.

265 VILLAGE OF LOVE, Nathaniel Mayer and the Fabulous Twilights
Producer not credited; written by Nathaniel Mayer and Devora Brown
Fortune 449   1962   Billboard: #22

Devora Brown, who owned Fortune Records with her husband Jack, swears that Nathaniel Mayer was a sweet-tempered and well-mannered young man. But on this forgotten masterpiece, he sounds simply crazed and demented, at least as unleashed as Little Richard. The Twilights' nasal chorus and the brittle, twangy guitar lick are equally off-center, as if lust had come into season for all of them for the first time in a very long spell. You want wild and bizarre, Mayer's "Village" is as good a vacation spot as you'll find.

266 MY TOWN, The Michael Stanley Band
Produced by the Michael Stanley Band and
Bob Clearmountain; written by Michael Stanley
EMI-America 8178   1983   *Billboard:* #39

267 SMALL TOWN, John Cougar Mellencamp
Produced by John Mellencamp and Don Gehman; written
by John Mellencamp
Riva 884202   1985   *Billboard:* #6

I guess there are people who grew up in the despised places of America, small and large, who are immune to the pull of hometown patriotism, but it's unlikely that any of them have made rock and roll anthems. And for that matter, why restrict it to the States? Remember that guy who sang about how little a poor boy could do in "sleepy London town"? Or the ones who fashioned some of their best hits out of nostalgic remembrances of sights and sounds in Liverpool?

The kind of heartland rock and roll in which guys like Mellencamp and Stanley specialize has never been any more fashionable than the kind of places where those guys grew up. Coming of age in southern Indiana and northern Ohio, Mellencamp and Stanley were undoubtedly set upon with some frequency as disloyal long-haired louts, yet each of these rockers remained steeped in the sensibilities of his environment. John Mellencamp made it big; Michael Stanley barely made it at all. No matter where they went, their hearts never left.

Ties to home can be stultifying and dangerous. But understanding that the cosmopolitan values of media capitals like New York, Los Angeles, and London aren't the only way to look at things can also be liberating. And in the end, everyone knows this. Listen to a bunch of New Yorkers doo-wopping on the block or watch the eyes of a native Californian while some Beach Boys hit is spinning.

"My Town" and "Small Town" are rough and ready, defensive about their topic and yet dramatically assertive. Mellencamp's record perfects his latter-day folk-rock (C&W instruments played Rolling Stones-style); Stanley's is the one disc where Cleveland's favorite son got all the details of his Springsteen-meets-Cheap Trick synthesis just right.

"Small Town" taps into a lot of sentimental nonsense derived from America's myth of agrarian pastoralism. But play this record for an audience reared in Brooklyn and they'll tell you that growing up there felt the same way to them, because the way Mellencamp means it, a "small town" is wherever you feel like you belong, be it a village that the interstate passes by or a block teeming with tenements.

Maybe it's just the mutuality of our Rust Belt roots, but "My Town" hits me even more powerfully. It's a lot more defensive, because there is no myth in our culture that explains why their citizens love the Midwest's dirty, disheveled slices of jampacked nowhere. Stanley sings like a man determined to create such a myth even if he has to convince himself in order to do it. It's great that his tool is what sounds like a recycled metal riff, with a sketched-in and equally dated guitar solo, because it's towns like his that made music like that rule the world for a while.

The town Stanley is singing about isn't small; it might be huge (it might be Cleveland). Its problems aren't nearly so easy to relate to as the ones Mellencamp describes, because they're about sheer anonymity, not only of the places themselves but of each of their residents individually. Mellencamp sings that a small town "is probably where they'll bury me." "This Town," though, is about lives that are already buried, though still fighting for breath. When Michael Stanley sings "This town's done its share of shovellin' " he's kicking his way out, and taking a lot of others with him, if only in their dreams.

268 STARTING ALL OVER AGAIN, Mel and Tim

Produced by Barry Beckett and Roger Hawkins; written by Phillip Mitchell
Stax 0127   1972   *Billboard:* #19

Phillip Mitchell may have written the song (and it's a good one, strong soul melody and lyrics that summarize what anybody might feel on setting out to restore a relationship nearly ruined by selfishness and immaturity), but I doubt if he came up with the great opening dialogue, in which Mel Harden explains to his cousin, Tim McPherson, why he and Barbara couldn't make their relationship work the first time through. "I thought you had settled alla that, man." "Hey man, you just don't understand. I never stopped loving her, I just wasn't able to accept the love she was willing to give."

Given that opening, the temptation to take "Starting All Over Again" straight over the top with musical and vocal histrionics must have been great. Coproducers Roger Hawkins and Barry Beckett instead rein in the whole production. The vocals are kept under control, worked around a groove that pulsates out from the firm center established by Hawkins' elegant drumming and the pulse of Duck Dunn's temporarily transplanted Memphis bass, and fitted into a tight mix that includes a tough brass section and a stirring Pete Carr guitar line. Even at the end, when the arrangement rises to a crescendo and the singing is at its most impassioned, the production insists on remaining orderly.

It's that order that makes the record, because it's emotionally faithful to the commitment Mel makes at the start. He's learned a lesson, and while he still feels his love deeply, he's now mature enough to understand that excessiveness will be its ruin. It's a lesson he might have learned from the Muscle Shoals rhythm section that Beckett and Hawkins still lead, which makes a specialty to this day of keeping an even keel while cutting the deepest groove it can find.

269 BRING THE BOYS HOME, Freda Payne
Produced by Holland-Dozier-Holland; written by Ronald Dunbar and E. Wayne [Holland-Dozier-Holland] Invictus 9075   1970   Billboard: #3

Even more than "War," "Bring the Boys Home" was the Top Ten hit that told you that the U.S. was getting out of Vietnam by public demand. Edwin Starr simply comes on generically antiwar, but Payne gets down to specifics, not only condemning the practice of dragging young men away from their women in order to kill one another, but referring to the present conflict as "senseless," a statement that would have been taboo at Top 40 just a few months earlier.

Even in 1970, Holland-Dozier-Holland only got away with saying it because the music was so extraordinary. Payne, essentially a cabaret singer, managed to make herself soulful for the only time in her career, and the anonymous male singer who accompanies her has all he can do to keep up. The arrangement, so much like classic Motown, pushes Payne to the fore but never prods her to anger. Instead, the accompaniment conspires to make Payne sound mournful and yearning in the face of dread and deadly loneliness. Which may not have brought the troops back a minute sooner but certainly brought—and still brings—the emotions of the war back every time it's heard.

270 LIES, The Knickerbockers
Produced by Jerry Fuller; written by Buddy Randall and Beau Charles
Challenge 59321   1965   *Billboard:* #20

Bears exactly the same relationship to the Beatles' "She Loves You" that "All Day and All of the Night" does to "Louie Louie." John Lennon couldn't get royalties for the seizure of his soul and style any more than the Kingsmen could, but at least this time the title and lyrics are somewhat descriptive of the Knickerbockers' creative process. Who needs *Beatlemania* when four guys from Englewood could come this close?

271 HOLD BACK THE NIGHT, The Trammps
Produced by Ronnie Baker, Norman Harris, and Earl Young; written by Ronnie Baker, Norman Harris, and Alan Felder
Buddah 507   1976   *Billboard:* #35

The marriage of the orchestral lushness of Philly dance groove and the grittiness of guitar-and-vocal soul ushers in the pop-disco age.

272 PLEASE PLEASE PLEASE, James Brown
Produced by Ralph Bass; written by James Brown and Johnny Terry
Federal 12258   1956   *Billboard:* #95

According to legend, label owner Syd Nathan described "Please Please Please" as "a piece of shit" and all but ordered A&R man Ralph Bass not to record it. Bass defied him and the greatest individual career in the history of R&B was born.

I've never quite believed that tale, primarily because, even though Nathan was a truly accomplished vulgarian and philistine, he was also knowledgeable enough about gospel quartets—having recorded many of the best—that what Brown and Johnny Terry were up to must have been obvious to him. (On the other hand, maybe that was his objection: *So* obvious that there might not be any money at the other end.)

Anyway, if anybody *did* call this song "a piece of shit," they should have been run out of the record business, because however ragged James's voice already was, his dramatic timing and instinct for a dance pulse was unprecedented. "Please Please Please" on record isn't the extravaganza it became as Brown's perpetual set-closer over the next three decades, but his growly pleadings shake and quiver in an unholy cross between sexual passion and religious ecstasy. For getting a handle on the hardest-working man in show business, it was, and is, a great place to start.

273 REET PETITE, Jackie Wilson
Produced by Dick Jacobs; written by Berry Gordy and Tyrone Carlo
Brunswick 55024   1957   *Billboard:* #62

Only Jackie Wilson could have transcended the lapsed and dated (Louis Jordan's "Reet Petite and Gone" dates to 1946) jazzster argot of Gordy's first major-league songwriting effort, *plus* the debilitating excesses of Jacobs' effort at a swingin' arrangement. Jackie gets away with it because he sings so fast that the words become poetry concrete, mere toys for his exclamatory trills and guttural exclamations. As "Rrrrrreet Petite" comes boiling off his tongue, a legend is born.

274 HAVING A PARTY, Sam Cooke
Produced by Hugo and Luigi; written by Sam Cooke
RCA 8036   1962   *Billboard:* #17

At the time he sang this enduring trifle, Sam Cooke was probably the greatest, surely the sweetest, male vocalist alive. Had he lived, he might have endured the kind of criticism that Jackie Wilson did, for here the song is juvenile (though not silly—Sam's deejay requests are too knowing for that) and the arrangement overdone (full orchestration for what's basically a jump tune?). Yet it doesn't matter all that much, because Cooke really did sing well enough and the period details really are special enough to be worth dwelling on for, oh, thirty or forty years or so.

275 IF YOU DON'T KNOW ME BY NOW, Harold Melvin and the Bluenotes
Written and produced by Kenneth Gamble and Leon Huff
Philadelphia International 3520   1972   *Billboard:* #3

When "If You Don't Know Me By Now" came out, I remember editing a review of it by British critic Simon Frith, who remarked that this was exactly what he'd been trying to communicate to his wife. As I was twenty-two and callow, I read Frith's without much comprehension—after all, Teddy Pendergrass sings that he's been married for ten years, an inconceivably long time to me then.

Fifteen years later, with kids in college and having run the usual emotional gamut, the song's logic seems impeccable, and the sympathy proferred by the strings and the group vocals lands like a cool breeze just when you most need one. Pendergrass plays the role of the Dells' Marvin Junior, his mentor, to perfection; the Blue Notes respond with a letter-perfect cop of the Stylistics. And though I can't locate that old review, it's easy to see which lines Frith must have been thinking of: "We've all got our own funny moods / I've got mine, woman, you've got yours too."

I hear you, Teddy.

276 CHAPEL OF LOVE, Dixie Cups
Produced by Jerry Leiber, Mike Stoller, Jeff Barry, and Ellie Greenwich; written by Jeff Barry, Ellie Greenwich, and Phil Spector
Red Bird 001   1964   *Billboard:* #1 (3 weeks)

How do theorists of rebel rock explain that the biggest American hit during the first wave of the British Invasion—one of only three U.S.-made Number Ones in the first six months of 1964—was a record by three teenage New Orleans girls singing the praises of that ultimate act of conformity, *marriage*?

Certainly not by denying that it's a great bit of girl group rock and roll, because that's beyond deniability, especially with that lineup of behind-the-scenes talent in the credits above—a lineup that doesn't even include the crucial figure, George Goldner (label genius behind End, Gone, and et cetera), Leiber and Stoller's partner in the early days of Red Bird and the guy who picked the Dixie Cups (then called Little Miss and the Muffets) to be Red Bird's first shot at the charts after hearing a demo submitted by their manager, veteran New Orleans R&B singer Joe Jones ("You Talk Too Much").

Actually, it is a little hard to believe that it took that much talent to produce a record so disarmingly simple. Finger snaps, light horn riffs, snazzy uptown shuffle from the drums, a touch of vibes, singing more unison than harmony—that's about it, no Wall of Sound extravaganza here. And the fact is that, while those credits aren't exactly phony, they are misleading.

Spector's there, for instance, principally because "Chapel of Love" made its initial appearance as the final track on *Introducing the Ronettes, featuring Veronica*, their Philles album. Phil was upset that Barry and Greenwich decided to redo the song with the Dixie Cups and no wonder, since the Ronettes turned in one of their better performances with it.

But Barry and Greenwich had never gotten a solid shot at record production. So far, they'd been almost exclusively a songwriting team, and they wanted a hit. Their inexperience probably accounts for Leiber and Stoller's production credit—the label owners mainly supervised (a function now termed "executive producer," which is itself frequently abused by power-mad label execs).

So let's call "Chapel of Love" Jeff Barry and Ellie Greenwich's answer to Goffin and King's "Loco-Motion." If the Dixie Cups weren't quite Little Eva, and Jeff and Ellie's own marriage didn't work out, consider that even a quarter century later, their record still makes the case for giving it up and getting hitched seem damned persuasive.

277 CAROL, Chuck Berry
Produced by Leonard Chess; written by Chuck Berry
Chess 1700   1958   *Billboard:* #18

278 LONG TALL SALLY, Little Richard
Produced by Bumps Blackwell; written by E. Johnson, Richard Penniman, and Bumps Blackwell
Specialty 572   1956   *Billboard:* #6

Ask any rock and roll musician why and how they got started, from that day to this, and the answer comes back the same: Where the Girls Are. (Which is pretty strange in the case of Little Richard, but what isn't?)

In the fifties, rock singles had to play games with sex. For Chuck Berry, it would have been bad enough if people had understood that the guy who recorded "Carol" was close to thirty, let alone that the song (according to his *Autobiography*) was based on a teenager to whom he'd become sufficiently attracted to move her from New York City to Berry Park, his home outside St. Louis. Yet "Carol" feels less like drooling dirty old man exploitation than do latter-day rock songs like the Knack's "My Sharona." Instead, it comes across as a story—the tale of a night around the jukebox down at the local club (not quite a malt shop, not yet a true roadhouse, maybe a place like the Berry Park of Chuck's dreams), where the singer—a wallflower because he can't dance a step—watches his girl being wooed by fresher young fellows. As usual, getting there is half the fun, but this time, finding out you have the cutest girl in the place is all agony. This time, all you can do is stand there and plea: "Don't let 'em steal your heart away / I'm goin' to learn to dance if it takes me all night and day."

"Carol" does reveal a certain distance between singer and subject: "Don't let 'em steal your heart away" may be the line Berry repeats, but "Don't the music intrigue when they get a crowd" is the one he means. It's as if that section of the song came from another singer altogether, from the mouth of the very guy who's about to swipe the girl. So Chuck has it both ways.

If Little Richard's authorized biography could be believed (and why not, people believe the shit Albert Goldman writes), he improvised "Long Tall Sally" 's key phrases, after the unknown E. Johnson had an influential disc jockey bring its first verse to producer Bumps Blackwell. Bootlegged versions of three of the first six takes from the session held in New Orleans in January 1956 contradict that tale; Richard sings the lyric straight through from the very first take.

What changes is his confidence and with that, the degree to which the singing becomes the assaultive masterpiece recorded in Hollywood about a week later. In New Orleans, Richard's trying to cut a blues about a man cheating on his wife with the bizarre "bald head Sally" (apparently not the drag queen of a million midnight speculations) and though the end of the first take, and the whole run-through on the second are fairly uptempo, they essentially conform to the standard R&B framework.

The record we now have smashes the frame, the painting, the whole picture. No longer a blues, "Long Tall Sally" is pure rock and roll, and Richard charges recklessly through it, shouting and jumping from the first note, rocketing at a pace exceeded in the fifties only by Jerry Lee Lewis on "Whole Lotta Shakin'," spewing out the lyrics as if the very thought of this guy caught with his pants down in a back alley fills him with the greatest titillated delight.

And if we're to believe Richard's own testimony, which was that his sexual proclivities ran heavily to voyeurism, it probably did. Maybe it took him a week to get in touch with this aspect of the song, or maybe it took him that long to get up the nerve to sing what he really felt. In any event, when the whole story is finally told, "Long Tall Sally," like "Carol," reveals a subtext that has everything to do with the inner life of its creator.

Whether that's what these records "mean" is another question. Certainly, their original audiences were mostly too young and too unsophisticated (not to mention preconditioned) to imagine such things. Instead, early rock fans heard records like these as a kind of code, parts of which were decipherable (sometimes correctly, sometimes not), much of which was simply mysterious. Cracking that code was half the battle and all the fun—that's what the Beatles' and Rolling Stones' versions of these songs are about.

279 TIGHTEN UP, Archie Bell and the Drells
Produced by Skippy Lee Frazier; written by Archie Bell and Billy Butler
Atlantic 2478   1968   *Billboard:* #1 (2 weeks)

"Hi, everybody. I'm Archie Bell of the Drells, of Houston, Texas. We don't only sing, we dance just as good as we want," declares Archie at the top and the band picks up a ratcheting guitar, rolling bass, and rumbling drum concoction that suggests that they want to dance like a family of funky Fred Astaires. But "Tighten Up" isn't just one of the all-time soul grooves; it's undoubtedly the only record ever to hit Number One while its lead vocalist was recovering from a wound received in Vietnam. Indeed, Bell may have been the only rock or soul hitmaker who served in 'Nam. (Al Green, Jimi Hendrix, and John Fogerty, among—very few—others, were Vietnam era vets but never saw combat.)

Vietnam served as both the inspiration of the Drells' biggest hit and the ruination of their pop career. Bell had already been drafted and was on his way overseas when roommate Billy Butler did a little dance in his living room, trying to cheer him up. What's that? asked Archie. "The Tighten-Up," replied Butler. To fit the step, they went in and improvised rap and lyrics over a new version of a track they'd cut as a demo back in 1964. (The band, which is featured as much as Archie, and far more than the other Drells, is probably the TSU Toronados, which was Houston's "Number One Soul Band" according to the group's manager, deejay Skipper Lee Frazier.)

By the time Archie got to the West German military hospital where he was sent to recover from his leg wound, "Tighten Up" had been a Texas hit, leased to Atlantic for national distribution and, after a four month interregnum while the label tried to promote the B side, "Dog Eat Dog," rocketed up the national soul and pop charts. Archie later claimed none of his Army buddies believed that was his voice on the radio. (Maybe because he also claimed that USC tailback Ricky Bell was his brother—which also happened to be true.)

Back home, meantime, fake versions of the Drells proliferated (among them a nine piece all-white combo). Bell petitioned the Army for leave to go home and straighten things out but he was only able to pull down a series of fifteen-day passes, just enough to give the Drells a chance to hike to New York, where they recorded a pair of successful follow-ups, "I Can't Stop Dancing" and "There's Gonna Be a Showdown," under the guidance of Atlantic's new hotshot producers Kenny Gamble and Leon Huff.

"Tighten Up" hit the *Billboard* charts at the end of March 1968; Bell served another thirteen months and by the time he got home and put the real Drells back on the road, the momentum was gone, whatever small chance the group had had of lasting fame become just another bright prospect that disintegrated in the bowels of the war. Gamble and Huff did bring them back for some disco-era discs, a couple of which actually managed to work the Philly International formulas well enough for middling R&B chart success.

280 IT'S THE SAME OLD SONG, The Four Tops
Produced by Brian Holland and Lamont Dozier; written by Brian Holland, Lamont Dozier, and Eddie Holland
Motown 1081   1965   *Billboard:* #5

Freudian playground that it was, Motown habitually but without open acknowledgment released singles whose titles commented on the artists' circumstances. Thus, Diana Ross left the Supremes to the tune of "Someday We'll Be Together," while David Ruffin's first single after leaving the Temptations (a move of which the Motown organization did not approve) was "My Whole World Ended (The Moment You Left Me)."

The most cynical of all these juxtapositions was "The Same Old Song," the immediate follow-up to the Four Tops' first big hit, "I Can't Help Myself (Sugar Pie Honey Bunch)." Those titles amount to nothing less than a confession, for the former is nothing less than a remake of the latter—same melody, same beat, damn near the same sax solo. Motown pundits have made mock of the similarity for years.

Which may leave me as a majority of one here, because I've always thought that Holland-Dozier-Holland were just being honest. There's an eminent justification for it, too: "The Same Old Song" is a better record. If it's the same sax solo, it's bigger and brighter here; if the melody hardly varies, the bass line is bolder, the drums kick just a hair harder, and there's nothing quite as thrilling on "I Can't Help Myself" as "The Same Old Song" 's vibes part. It's probably a toss-up between the two lead vocals (and one reason these records were bigger hits than previous Tops efforts was the greater degree to which Levi was now featured). The lyrics are a big improvement over the cloying "Sugar pie, honey bunch / You know that I love you" (even if they do begin "You're sweet as a honey bee").

Or maybe it's just like the song says: "I keep hearing the part that used to touch our heart."

281 DANCING IN THE DARK, Bruce Springsteen
Produced by Bruce Springsteen, Jon Landau, Chuck Plotkin, and Steve Van Zandt; written by Bruce Springsteen
Columbia 04463   1984   *Billboard:* #2

A sort of locked room mystery: A guy who's been bottled up too long finally succumbs to a seizure of rage and turns on himself, dissecting with eloquent contempt everything from his hairstyle to his house-keeping habits. As rock star plaints go, this has it over all the rest, because it's frank about the real problem: He's bored. And because the whiner provides his own solution, with the hottest rhythm track he's ever created, thanks to drummer Max Weinberg and a heap of electronics.

282 PAPA DON'T PREACH, Madonna
Produced by Madonna and Stephen Bray; written by Brian Elliot and Madonna
Sire 28660   1986   *Billboard:* #1 (2 weeks)

Madonna came out of the Detroit suburbs with a chip on her shoulder, determined to irritate everybody's preconceptions. Success in that sphere presented no problem, but sustaining interest beyond outrage, never becoming predictable, insisting on a certain quality even while making the most blatantly exploitative media moves were the feats that made her the most interesting new pop star of the eighties.

"Papa Don't Preach" was her masterstroke. It's a great record with a perfectly realized late eighties dance groove and enough melodic coloration to get it over with nondancers, on which she sings with amazing intensity and just the right mixture of knowing rasp and innocent pleas. Given Madonna's reputation as "a porn queen in heat," according to both the quasi-governmental censorship group, the PMRC (Parents Music Resource Center) and (sotto voce) *Rolling Stone*, the controversy was guaranteed when she chose to sing about a knocked-up teenager. What measured Madonna's power, what pushed her here to the threshold where exploitation and artistry join, was her insistence on making from that tabloid setup a record that mattered.

" 'Papa Don't Preach' is a message song that everyone is going to take the wrong way," Madonna predicted in a prerelease (but postrecording) interview, knowing full well that her prophecy was already self-fulfilled. A dance/message record is rare enough; this one opens with Beatlesque riffing cellos. Songwriter Brian Elliott may have thought he was writing an antiabortion song; certainly, he displayed no qualms about playing off the sentiments of hard dancing right-to-lifers. And certainly, it was as a statement in favor of kids keeping their babies that "Papa Don't Preach" was heard, at least by adults. The PMRC's ex-officio bluenose Tipper Gore praised Madonna for "foster[ing] discussion between teens and their family"; feminist attorney Gloria Allred demanded that Madonna "make a public statement noting that kids have other choices, including abortion." For the first time, Madonna looked like a good Catholic girl.

Kids took the record in all sorts of other ways. Listening less superficially, they heard "baby" as an ambiguous term that referred less clearly to the singer's fetus than to her boyfriend, especially since the song is addressed to her father, who's always hated him. (How much of this subtext is in Elliott's original lyric and how much Madonna added, with words and inflections, is tough to gauge. On the record sleeve, she's credited with "additional lyrics.") All that's really sure is that Madonna herself is not the baby—she says so in the fourth line.

Heard this way, what "Papa Don't Preach" suggests is a less straightforward dialogue than ideology would allow Mrs. Gore or Ms. Allred to grasp. The singer has screwed up her courage to tell her father the facts and ask his advice—advice she would hardly need if "I've made up my mind / I'm keepin' my baby" referred to her unborn child. What she's trying to do is set a limit to their talk, to make it clear from the outset that even if it costs her her precious relationship with her father, she's keeping this guy.

In the "Papa Don't Preach" video, Danny Aiello plays the bewildered and hostile father and an anonymous updated John Travolta type plays The Baby, further staking out this version of the song's iconography. But Madonna never forecloses the other reading; the middle verse recounts what her friends have said about how getting married and raising a family will keep her from living it up. Whether she marries The Baby or not, if she keeps the kid, she'll be tied down.

So abortion remains an issue—but just one of several in a record that's a lot more complex in every dimension, from the musical to the moral, than its surface suggests. And it's when Madonna reaches that middle verse that you can feel her voice constrict, as if to indicate the terrible anxiety she feels. It's also there that she begs, "What I need right now is some good advice" in a voice that suggests the heartbreak and pain it took just to get this far. In the history of rock and soul, few performers have had the guts to envision such a scene. So far, Madonna's the only one who's pulled it off.

283 THE STROLL, The Diamonds
Produced by David Carroll; written by Clyde Otis and Nancy Lee
Mercury 71242   1957   *Billboard:* #4

One of the great lost arts of the fifties is the line dance, a bizarre adolescent ritual in which couples formed two queues, males to the left, females to the right, and then sashayed down the aisle formed in the middle to the slow, sensual beat of records like Chuck Willis's "Betty and Dupree." You needn't have visited New Guinea to understand the line dance—the most famous variant of which was The Stroll—as a mating ritual. And though the Stroll itself was over as a craze before the fifties died, the line dance persisted at least into the mid-sixties; I can remember doing it to "Dancing in the Street."

The Stroll was something special, though, maybe the greatest pre-Twist rock and roll dance style, and an important fixture in the heyday of Dick Clark's American Bandstand. Chuck Willis made his considerable career as King of the Stroll. But the definitive Stroll anthem was done by the Diamonds, the Canadian chicken-rock quartet who also contributed "Little Darlin' " and a half-dozen worse examples of R&B cover song exploitation. (Judging from Clyde Otis's writing credit, "The Stroll" was probably a cover, too, but I haven't yet tracked down the original, and it'll have to be pretty great to beat this one.)

The Stroll was anything but a frenzied dance; its tempo was exactly what the name proposed and it grew as formal as a square dance. Done right, the line dance could have the compelling quality of street ballet. Though the Diamonds clearly had no idea of its elegance, that hardly matters because their record is dominated by an absolutely lethal saxophone, which sounds like it was played by God adopting his King

Curtis persona. That horn catches every nuance of the Stroll, from its formal purity right down to its function as an understated mating game.

284 I DON'T KNOW WHAT YOU GOT, BUT IT'S GOT ME, Little Richard
Produced by J.W. Alexander; written by Horace Hall and Don Covay
Vee-Jay 698   1965   *Billboard:* #92

Little Richard always boasted that he not only invented contemporary rock and roll but everything that came after it. Here's the strongest argument in his favor: pure deep soul in the style of Joe Tex, a raspy preachment on love with Richard actually cooperating rather than competing with the band. Had it not been hurled straight into a British Invasion fueled in significant part by the energy of his fifties hits, producer J.W. Alexander might well have gotten away with the ambitious scheme of deploying Little Richard as the new Sam Cooke.

On the other hand, when he begins to preach, Richard can't help but gabble in ways that a smoothie like Cooke would never have allowed. Richard's accent grows more Southern, his stresses fall in greater and greater disorder, the words erupt in disorienting sequence and then he simply begins to holler rapid-fire, reverses direction, and starts to sing again. And it's then that you feel the links he's forged, not just to Cooke and Tex but to James Brown, Otis Redding and, just visible over the horizon, Sly Stone and Prince.

285 FREDDIE'S DEAD, Curtis Mayfield
Written and produced by Curtis Mayfield
Curtom 1975   1972   *Billboard:* #4

Of all the artists who transmuted soul music during the early seventies, Curtis Mayfield was the most veteran—he'd been with the Impressions from 1958 to 1970. Mayfield brought continuity to the new soul in other ways, as well. Though his post-Impressions songs revolved around rhythmic complexity and a solo voice, he continued to use the string washes often featured on his group harmony hits. Even Mayfield's socially conscious depictions of urban black street life, with their moralistic comments on Vietnam, greed, and especially their opposition to the thriving drug culture, connected directly to themes Mayfield had explored in his earlier songs.

Mayfield's sound centered on his (often wah-wah enhanced) guitar, backed by grunting bass and busy drumming, and colored by strings, synthesizer, and a persistent, piercing flute. (On "Freddie's Dead," there's also some nasty trumpet.) Together, these instruments created a bed of light funk that buoyed his vocal sermonettes.

Super Fly, the soundtrack to a 1972 blaxploitation flick about a dope dealer with a heart of gold, contained "Freddie's Dead" and "Superfly," Mayfield's only Top Ten pop hits, and the overall score is his best, certainly his most characteristic work. Both film and soundtrack did amazingly big crossover business and though the film has dated badly, the soundtrack retains an exciting vitality and relevance.

That's partly because "Freddie's Dead" is an instrumental on the soundtrack, but on the album contains Mayfield's most pungently realistic lyrical attack on the drug culture. Onscreen, the scene in which a sleazy pusher called Freddie finds himself cruelly betrayed and gunned down plays sympathetically. But Mayfield, though he makes a pro forma acknowledgment of the pusher's humanity, starts out by writing Freddie off. Guitars thunder ominously and the beat is remorseless while Mayfield groans wordless Smokey-like phrases, then cries, "Freddie's dead! That's what I said / Let the man with the plan say he'd see him home / But his hope was a rope, and he should have known."

That's called assigning blame, and Mayfield does it with the guileless self-assurance of a preaching true believer. Since what he's railing against now dominates our culture, especially black culture, in ways far nastier than could have been imagined in 1972, "Freddie's Dead" today has the impact of a rock shoved up your nose.

286 WILD WEEKEND, The Rockin' Rebels
Produced by Phil Todaro; written by Phil Todaro and Tom Shannon
Swan 4125   1962   *Billboard:* #8

Surf music from the St. Lawrence Seaway, starring nobody in particular (just a bunch of bozos from Buffalo) but featuring a sax-guitar duel that's the equal of any drag race Brian Wilson—or you, or me, or even Chuck Berry—ever dreamed of. Although "Wild Weekend" was originally cut as a deejay's theme song, the right place to hear it isn't on the radio but off a jukebox in a sweaty bar, just as the sun's about to come up on an August Sunday morning. Preferably close enough to smell an ocean.

287 I'M NOT A JUVENILE DELINQUENT, Frankie Lymon and the Teenagers

Produced by George Goldner; written by Morris Levy [Frankie Lymon]
Gee 1026   1956   Did not make pop chart

Frankie Lymon's chubby-cheeked smile radiated such innocence that "I'm Not a Juvenile Delinquent" has always been taken at face value, as one of those weird apologies that early rock and roll was periodically forced to make. Rather than everyday pop culture defensiveness or basic teen exploitation, "Juvenile Delinquent" emerges as an outright lie, for "juvenile delinquency" barely begins to describe the web from which Frankie Lymon's rock and roll emerged.

"I'm Not a Juvenile Delinquent" certainly was not written by Morris Levy. Levy did not write songs, though his name exists on many copyrights. He was the proprietor of Birdland, Roulette Records, Adam VIII music publishing, and the Strawberries Records retail chain, among other enterprises, who after thirty years as "godfather" of the record industry finally was convicted of conspiracy to commit extortion and sentenced to a ten year prison term in 1988.

Levy most likely got his name on "Juvenile Delinquent" because producer/label owner George Goldner was perpetually improvident, as the result of the most self-destructive gambling habit in rock history (which is really something considering the extent of Col. Tom Parker's). Goldner began releasing rock and roll on a record label called Rama; before he was done he also ran Gee, Gone, Roulette, End, Cindy, Tee-Gee, Juanita, Casino, Goldisc, and Mark-X, each eventually sold at a fraction of its value to Levy in order to raise cash to pay off his gambling debts, each new venture successful because Goldner and Levy essentially managed the great disc jockey Alan Freed and knew exactly what kind of records he needed to make his show work (and to be fair, because Goldner had a fabulous ear for rock and roll, as he proved again in the sixties, when he became Jerry Leiber and Mike Stoller's partner in Red Bird Records).

What about Frankie Lymon? He was only thirteen in 1956, a tiny little kid who was probably already working as a pimp in Harlem. Lymon had a magnificent voice, a choirboy tenor with just the right husky undertone, accompanied by an unbelievable sense of time. Sadly, the voice sustained him for only a couple of years—he cut "Why Do Fools Fall in Love" in November 1955 and by the end of 1959, the Teenagers' run as stars was finished. One reason: Frankie's voice changed and with it his thrilling style, which veered toward much more conventional crooning. Another: He'd become a junkie. By 1961, he was in drug rehabilitation. He kicked his habit for a while a couple of years later, when he got drafted into the Army, but by 1966, he was again seeking professional help for his addiction. He seemed on the road to recovery and went back "home" to Roulette, which scheduled a new record date for February 1968. To celebrate the day before the session, Frankie loaded up one last shot of smack. It was his last—he died from it. He was all of twenty-five years old, not as old as "I'm Not a Juvenile Delinquent" is today.

288 HELP ME RHONDA, The Beach Boys
Written and produced by Brian Wilson
Capitol 5395   1965   *Billboard:* #1 (2 weeks)

289 KISS ME BABY, The Beach Boys
Written and produced by Brian Wilson
Capitol 5395   1965   Did not make pop chart

My mother taught me to buy singles. Actually, she thought she was teaching me the opposite but you know kids. Albums give you so much more music, she said. Singles are too expensive.

It's advice I might have taken to heart if not for *The Beach Boys Today*. It came out in March 1965, and naturally, being a fan, my copy came home the first day it landed on the rack.

I still think it's the Beach Boys' best album. Side one was rock tunes, like "Do You Wanna Dance" and "Dance, Dance, Dance," both of which had already been hits; side two dwelled on ballads, including a remake of the Students' "I'm So Young" and a lot of Phil Spector-meets-doo-wop balladry. Each had its own musical coherence. Somebody ought to write about this stuff, I thought.

A few weeks later, "Help Me Rhonda" hit the radio, the best-sounding Beach Boys hit since "I Get Around," a fast, tight dance groove with pulsing piano bass, gorgeous open-throated harmonies, and the first lead vocal by the group's most unobtrusive member, Al Jardine. The piano break was silly but the guitar solo that picked up from it slashed apart all my reservations.

When you're a fan, the radio doesn't play even the Number One hit often enough. So side one of *The Beach Boys Today* spent a lot of time on the turntable. But it just didn't sound right. After I went all the way to K-Mart and blew another seventy-seven cents on the single, the reason was obvious: The two versions were totally different. On

Today, "Help Me Ronda" [sic] added harmonica, ukelele (!), and a tambourine. But it lost much more: in addition to the "h" in "Rhonda," the focus and tightness of its mix, its brilliant bass line, Jardine's sharp vocal.

As it turns out, the single version was a hastily done remake, put together after sometime Beach Boy collaborator Gary Usher became so confident that the song was a hit that he made noises about putting out his own version of "Rhonda" as a 45. Brian hastily assembled his group and radically improved the song by shortening it (by twenty-two seconds, which is a lot on pop radio), quickening the tempo, streamlining the arrangement, and giving the lead to Jardine, rather than himself.

The best part of owning the single, though, was flipping it over. The B side was the beautiful "Kiss Me Baby," a track that's all but thrown away on *The Beach Boys Today*. For lush romanticism, no rock song has ever exceeded it, which makes it far too lush (and far too romantic) for more squeamish intellects. I don't know a better number about breaking up. The track's wash of piano and soft percussion is so gently moving, even Mike Love's adenoids can't get in the way. Brian's falsetto absolutely soars, and whoever contributes the bass in the background singing "Whoa, baby" has mastered the modernization of doowop. I wouldn't trade this little B side for all of *Pet Sounds*.

290 YOU DON'T MISS YOUR WATER, William Bell
Produced by Chips Moman; written by William Bell
Stax 116   1962   *Billboard:* #95

Although Bell's version of "You Don't Miss Your Water" was the first I ever heard, it amazed me that he'd written it. Its cadences suggested something much older—and something much more C&W, too. (Listen to the Byrds' version on *Sweetheart of the Rodeo*, and you'll see what I mean.)

Pipesmoking and relatively intellectual, William Bell was Memphis soul's ultimate journeyman, but what's out of the ordinary is his acceptance of that second-rank status. While it wouldn't be fair to say that he courted obscurity, that's only because the evidence is too sketchy. Bell made "You Don't Miss Your Water" at producer Chips Moman's insistence; he'd already found a satisfactory niche as featured vocalist with Phineas Newborn's orchestra, the area's toniest show band. Rather than seeking the main chance, he was content to sing with Newborn and prepare for medical school. He was even ready to be drafted (as he eventually was).

It's that comparative impassivity, a form of contentment with the status quo that's alien to the usual soul story, that marks Bell's greatest song as more country than R&B. It's hard to imagine another soul star who could have sung lines like "I sit and wonder / How can this be / I never thought / You'd ever leave me," without lapsing into either total rage or paroxysms of self-reproach. (Compare Bell's original version of "Any Other Way" with the hit Chuck Jackson made of it for an even clearer example of what I mean.)

It's that very diffidence, the purposeful lack of histrionics, which makes Bell's "You Don't Miss Your Water" so much more extraordinary than any other record of the song. Because the melody is mournful, he sounds sad. But he's damned if he's *ever* going to lose control.

291 LIVING FOR THE CITY, Stevie Wonder
Written and produced by Stevie Wonder
Tamla 54242   1973   *Billboard*: #8

Stevie Wonder's seventies albums are so densely constructed that even their best singles never quite acquire a full existence as 45s. "Sir Duke" will always seem more a part of *Songs in the Key of Life*, for instance, than a moment in the spectrum of pop radio experience. There are exceptions—"Happy Birthday," "Master Blaster (Jammin')"—but not many.

On *Innervisions*, which is probably Wonder's greatest album, "Living for the City" is a seven-minute soul opera. On 45, the saga loses a full four minutes of musical and verbal dialogue and interplay. Yet the truncated version still has a strong melody and powerful lyrical message (since the excised melodrama ain't exactly *Othello*), so the single gains a little force without sacrificing any meaning.

"Living for the City" is Wonder's attempt to create a myth of black oppression that leads to pride, without evading any facts, and he pulls it off, too. Wonder, who's never more than a step or two away from fantasyland himself, bears down straight through to the end, when he sings: "This place is cruel, nowhere could be much colder," an admission of what Motown had spent a great deal of time working to deny. Yet with music this strong, singing this sweet, a groove this danceable, the message is not only palatable—it's undeniable.

292 SINCERELY, Moonglows
No producer credited; written by Harvey Fuqua and
Alan Freed
Chess 1581   1955   *Billboard:* #20

For most of its length, "Sincerely" might as well be a record by the
Mills Brothers or the Ink Spots or any of the other pop harmony quartets
who were the visible face of black vocal music prior to the rock era.
Only the "vooit-vooit" in the background and a bluesy guitar lick hint
that something a bit different might be going on. But, at the conclusion
of each verse, the arrangement swings into something more like gospel.
This oscillation between church singing and the formalities of Tin Pan
Alley-era pop is crucial to the entire ethos of doo-wop, an urban Northern idiom that was gorgeous within that structure but became a dead
end when Southern singers (Little Richard, for instance) made a
sharper, clearer break with the old ways and found a much larger
audience.

Moonglows' leader Fuqua survived, going on to become an important part of Motown, to which he introduced a post-"Sincerely"
Moonglow named Marvin Gaye. Despite that, and his later accomplishments as a producer and songwriter, "Sincerely" is Fuqua's real
monument, poised as it is on the fault between profound musical
changes.

293 OH WHAT A NIGHT, The Dells
Produced by Bobby Miller; written by Marvin Junior and
John Funches
Cadet 5649   1969   *Billboard:* #10

The idea of remaking a hit song generally stems from a perception of
how to update it and cash in on contemporary trends, while not having
to resort to the trouble and expense of coming up with new material.
When it works, the remake not only introduces a new generation to
the virtues of the song, but evokes for older listeners the pleasure they
took in the original.

In that respect, the Dells' "Oh What a Night" is the ultimate remake, for it not only updates a 1956 R&B hit so effectively that it
crossed over to the pop Top Ten, but did it with the same group (and
one whose personnel was essentially the same as on the original) and
managed it by acknowledging the nostalgia factor at the outset and
then proceeding to better all expectations.

If it's a characteristic of the very greatest records that they always sound a little better when you actually hear them than they do even in fondest memory, then the original "Oh What a Night" is by no means a great record. So the 1969 version doesn't remake the original; it remakes the memory.

The song itself helps, since its very subject is the power of memory. But the new arrangement, retaining doo-wop elements buttressed with a soul orchestration, summons far more intensity than a plain old fifties R&B combo could have done. From Chuck Barksdale's basso introduction to Marvin Junior's brilliant testifying at the end, the Dells stake their claim as the best vocal group that Chicago's thriving black music scene produced.

294 PSYCHOTIC REACTION, Count 5
Produced by Joe Hooven and Hal Winn; written by Kenn Ellner, Roy Chaney, Craig Atkinson, Sean Byrne, and John Michalski
Double Shot 104   1966   *Billboard:* #5

Refried Yardbirds, cooked up in a San José garage and served on a platter to rock critics and garage punk connoisseurs. One of rock's few comparative obscurities that actually surpasses its rep.

295 I BELIEVE TO MY SOUL, Ray Charles
Produced by Ahmet Ertegun and Jerry Wexler; written by Ray Charles
Atlantic 2043   1959   Did not make pop charts

The B side of Ray's cover of Hank Snow's country standard, "I'm Movin' On," "I Believe to My Soul" goes as far in the other direction as you could imagine: It's pure smoky back room R&B, and it was a genre classic long before Bob Dylan lifted its melody for "Ballad of a Thin Man."

Centered on a vocal full of night sweats and bad dreams, soft-spoken threats and moans of despair, tricked up with a female chorus that legend maintains is Ray himself subbing for the Raelettes, fleshed out with gospel allusions and big band flourishes, this is Ray Charles at his most complete, a live arrangement with just the right amount of studio effects.

296 MIDNIGHT TRAIN TO GEORGIA, Gladys Knight and the Pips

Produced by Tony Camillo and Gladys Knight and the Pips; written by
Jim Weatherly
Buddah 383   1973   *Billboard:* #1 (2 weeks)

Ostensibly nothing more than the obverse of the lovelorn road ballad
epitomized by Jim Webb's "By the Time I Get to Phoenix," "Midnight
Train to Georgia," in which a fed up husband determines to abandon
Hollywood and his quest for superstardom in order to return to his
roots in Georgia clay (and more amazingly, his wife agrees to come
along), is redeemed by the best vocal performance of Gladys Knight's
career, and by its setting, which in its way defines the social context of
the rock and soul era.

The demographic emphasis in rock criticism has been on the rise
of "youth culture" and its various modes of consumption. But the most
dramatic change in the United States between the end of World War
II and 1965 was not a generational shift but the massive migration off
the land into the cities. This migration (which began even before the
Great Depression but accelerated after the war) produced for many
Southerners the dislocated desire for nostalgic recollection of down
home "good old days" that has been a staple of American songwriting
since at least Stephen Foster. Rock and roll was, among other things,
the product of the merger of southern culture with the others it met in
the urban North, which is the reason that so much of it was produced
in the cities for which the migrants set out: Chicago, Detroit, Philadelphia, Los Angeles, and New York. (The special musical status of
Memphis has everything to do with its placement as the midpoint in
this path.)

So it's no great distance from the minstrel show sentiments of "My
Old Kentucky Home" to "Midnight Train"'s first verse, which declares: "He said he's goin' back to find / The world he left behind not
so long ago . . . / Said he's going back to find . . . / A simpler place
and time."

What Weatherly made of these lines it's hard to know, but Gladys
Knight alters their surface by filling her performance with telling pauses.
"L.A.," she begins, and then pauses while the orchestrated soul pumps
on, "proved too much for the man," she continues. In that break in
the action, you can feel the weariness and the inability to fathom new
customs and regulations that might drive a man back to his homeland—
even though that home is the land of lynchings and Jim Crow. And
when Knight again pauses, then draws a sharp breath, while singing

the key line of the chorus—"I'd rather live in his world . . . than live without him in mine"—she makes you feel just how fateful such a choice can be.

Nor does this reading rest solely on the fact that Knight (and presumably her husband) are black. All Southerners often felt displaced in the North and whites had almost as many good reasons to fear returning: Though the wages of black Southerners are most pitiful of all, white Southerners earn less than blacks in the North, and reduced cost of living doesn't fill the gap.

Jim Weatherly is a white man who may or may not be aware of these facts. Whatever he knew, he at least sensed something that enabled millions of Americans to relate personally to the story "Midnight Train to Georgia" told. And, no doubt, took the song even closer to their hearts because it came along in 1973, just as the bubble of economic prosperity on which the migration had been built was deflating. In the weeks and months that "Midnight Train to Georgia" lasted on the charts, the thoughts of a million transplanted Southerners, black and white, turned to the places they—or their parents—had come from. Some actually tried going back, and there are other stories to tell about what happened to them then. What Knight, with aid from Weatherly, has done is capture beautifully what moved them to the effort.

297 LET THEM TALK, Little Willie John
Produced by Henry Glover; written by Sonny Thompson
King 5274   1960   *Billboard:* #100

I don't know how many records besides "Let Them Talk" have made the very bottom rung of *Billboard*'s Hot 100 (the music industry's basic line of demarcation between pop failure and pop success) for exactly one week. But I guarantee that there haven't been any better ones.

"Let Them Talk" attacks gossips where it really hurts—Willie John *wants* the back fence predators to know how he feels. "Let them talk," he begins, "Talk don't bother *me*." And proceeds to turn in the performance that, with its grit amplified and its arrangement purified of extraneous elements (like the excessively angelic chorus) became the matrix for James Brown's entire ballad style. But not even James ever discovered anything purer than the final notes, where Willie just lets his voice soar and then hangs on for dear life.

298 WAR, Edwin Starr
Produced by Norman Whitfield; written by Norman Whitfield and Barrett Strong
Gordy 7101   1969   *Billboard:* #1 (3 weeks)

299 PAPA WAS A ROLLIN' STONE, The Temptations
Produced by Norman Whitfield; written by Norman Whitfield and Barrett Strong
Gordy 7121   1972   *Billboard:* #1 (1 week)

Norman Whitfield was so hot in these years that maybe Motown's best route to salvation during the early seventies period of soul-to-funk transition (a period that cost the label its preeminence, and from which it never fully recovered) would have been to completely turn the company over to him.

"War" is half soul, half psychedelic freak-out, with tambourines and fuzz guitars fortuitously overwhelmed by Starr, the most stentorian singer around, even at a label that also featured Levi Stubbs. The record is a tribute to the power of street level politics, but it had no responsibility for ending the war in Vietnam. Motown would never have released it if the war's end weren't already a foregone conclusion.

"Papa Was a Rolling Stone" is another matter. In a sense, it tackles a more difficult contemporary issue, the decline of the black male's role within nuclear family life. But since it does its best to skirt the issue, or at least have it both ways (Papa was a jerk, a lech, and a leech but God, we sure miss him), the record's probably more notable for its extended strings, synthesizer, wahwah guitar and orchestral harp introduction and for its rhythm bed, which pushed ideas developed in jazz by Miles Davis and in soul by Curtis Mayfield into the center of Top 40 radio. Thereby setting the table for Barry White and dozens of disco hedonists.

300 THAT'S ALRIGHT MAMA, Elvis Presley
Produced by Sam Phillips; written by Arthur Crudup
Sun 209   1954   Did not make pop charts

How well does this Rosetta stone, Presley's first single, a regional but not national hit, recorded meticulously over many hours of studio experimentation by a group of four men (Elvis, producer Phillips, guitarist

Scotty Moore, and bassist Bill Black) fit the key elements of the rock myth? Well, it wasn't spontaneous; it was as closely calculated as a fixed fight. Nor is its sound anarchic and rebellious or its tempo particularly fast. After all these years the most impressive characteristic of "That's All Right" is the way Presley projects such complete drive with so little audible effort. But the triumph isn't his alone. The sound is crystalline, the balance is exquisite, Bill Black's bass has its own everpresent assurance, and Moore's guitar—especially the solo— toughens the song up and forces it to rock. Nor is this music quite what any black bluesman or any country singer would ever have come up with. In short, "That's Alright" does the same thing now that it did then: explodes preconceptions and replaces them with something better.

301 BAD LUCK, PART 1, Harold Melvin and the Bluenotes
Produced by Kenneth Gamble and Leon Huff; written by
John Whitehead, Gene McFadden, and Victor Castarphen
Philadelphia International 3562   1975   *Billboard:* #15

Gamble and Huff go gospel, as Teddy Pendergrass preaches a sermon drawn from the newspaper he's reading while sitting on his barren bedroom floor, in the process dragging in everyone from the numbers player down the block to the President of the United States. And you thought disco was just a bunch of dumb, undifferentiated noise!

302 THIN LINE BETWEEN LOVE AND HATE, The Persuaders
Produced by the Poindexter Brothers; written by Richard Poindexter,
Robert Poindexter, and Jackie Members
Atco 6822   1971   *Billboard:* #15

The most cautionary tale in rock and soul history: "The sweetest woman in the world / Could be the meanest woman in the world. . . . She might be holding something inside / That'll really, really hurt you one day."

A slightly discordant piano introduces what at first seems nothing more than your usual soul story: A back door man returns at dawn to his long suffering wife, who's so used to his philandering ways that she doesn't even ask where he's been, just fixes breakfast.

That's the last thing he remembers until he wakes up in the hospital "in a state of shock, just that much from being dead." The singer marvels; he never saw it coming. He's hoping you'll learn.

Way better than *I, Tina*.

303 (NIGHT TIME IS) THE RIGHT TIME, Ray Charles
Produced by Ahmet Ertegun and Jerry Wexler; written by Nappy Brown, Ozzie Cadena, and L. Herman [Herman Lubinsky]
Atlantic 2010   1959   *Billboard:* #95

During its 1986–1987 season, *The Cosby Show* ended an episode by having the entire Huxtable family serenade Cliff's self-important parents with a lip-synch rendition of this Charles classic. Since the highlight of that performance was little daughter Rudy mouthing the words, and since those words are just this side of outright lewdness, I suppose "Night time is the right time" is another expression that will be absorbed into our lexicon of conventional, comfortable phrases.

If that's how today's clichés are born, listen to Ray by himself to experience life more whole. Charles and his anonymous female costar bask in the song's sensuousness; they roll the words around in their mouths and caress them with their tongues, so that you know "be with the one you love" means "the one you fuck." Furthermore, the lyric expropriates so much gospel imagery that back in the fifties, it must have seemed almost unbelievably blasphemous, which is perhaps what curtailed its chart career. (In Nappy Brown's original, the gospel overtones were there but it took the raw nerve of Ray Charles to bring them front and center.)

It's the perverse genius of the kind of TV that *Cosby* represents that it was able to bring a song whose sentiments should have been truly acceptable nowhere outside a strip joint into millions of American living rooms. And everybody loved it.

God forbid they ran into it on the radio the next day.

304 BROTHER LOUIE, Stories
Produced by Kenny Kerner and Richie Wise; written by Errol Brown and Tony Wilson
Kama Sutra 577   1973   *Billboard:* #1 (2 weeks)

Originally a British hit for Errol Brown and Tony Wilson's British group, Hot Chocolate, this updated version of the "Louie Louie" myth—in which Louie is a white guy in love with a black girl and disowned by his parents because of it—surely could never have been such a big hit if a black man (like Brown) had sung it. But even though Stories' Ian Lloyd (erstwhile member of the Left Banke of "Walk Away Renee" infamy) isn't nearly as good a singer, Stories made the better record. In the end, this disc's success says a lot about how far America has come (in order to make Number One, the Stories record had to get airplay in every section of the country) and about how appalling our attitudes still are (one reason "Brother Louie" made Number One was the shock value of hearing a song about miscegenation once an hour).

305 RESCUE ME, Fontella Bass
Produced by Billy Davis, Carl Smith, and Reynard Miner; written by Carl Smith and Reynard Miner
Checker 1120   1965   *Billboard:* #4

Best non-Aretha Aretha ever. Figures, too, because Fontella's the daughter of Martha Bass, a gospel star who got her start with the Clara Ward Singers, whose traveling preacher used to be Rev. C. L. Franklin, Aretha's father.

The difference between Aretha's Memphis-Detroit-New York-Muscle Shoals soul and Fontella's (two years early) St. Louis-meets-Windy City blend is all about the bluesy but somehow lighter Chicago studio sound. Maurice White's drumming might be the toughest he ever did, as if he anticipated Roger Hawkins as a burr under his saddle, and bassist Louis Satterfield sounds as if Duck Dunn and a pack of hell-hounds might have been on *his* trail. In any event, for this one record, at least, the Chess sessionmen proved they were the peers of their Southern brethren. Too bad they didn't get the chance to let that kind of funky interplay happen more often. But then for that, Bass would have needed not only the same roots as Aretha but the same amount of talent.

306 I'LL BE THERE, The Jackson 5
Produced by Hal Davis; written by Berry Gordy, Hal Davis, Willie Hutch, and Bob West
Motown 1171   1970   *Billboard:* #1 (5 weeks)

Michael Jackson is the only great ballad singer who came of age after first funk and then disco revolutionized soul music and began the process in which melodically centered popular songwriting all but disappeared.

But that's misleading. The Jackson 5 were very much part of soul's transformation and although he hadn't come of age, Michael was an indisputably accomplished soul balladeer by the time he was twelve years old.

What's startling about "I'll Be There" is the perfect aplomb he brings to material that ought to be both more romantic and more dramatic than he could possibly comprehend. (Certainly, Jermaine Jackson, although he's a couple years older, sounds at sea on his parts.) In a sense, Michael's composure pays tribute to his mentor, Diana Ross; the entire concept of his phrasing (even the grand moment when he shouts, "Just look over your shoulders, honey!") suggests the Ross influence, as if Michael simply figured you sang everything the way she sang "Reach Out And Touch (Somebody's Hand)." But then there's the way he oohs his way out of the choruses, a trick he might have learned from Smokey Robinson or half a dozen other mentors but twists and elongates to make completely his own. In the end, there's just no way of rationally accounting for such precocity—which shouldn't stop you, me or anybody else from taking all the pleasure it provides.

307 SERPENTINE FIRE, Earth, Wind & Fire
Produced by Maurice White; written by Maurice White, Verdine White, and Sonny Burke
Columbia 10625   1977   Billboard: #13

Perfectly self-descriptive: skittering horn lines entwine, snakelike, around vocal lines that flick in and out of the tongues of percussive blaze. Maurice White's basic approach to rhythm hasn't changed all that much since he was the Chess Records house drummer in the sixties, and these horn riffs are just Stax with icing. It's one of those times when the icing dominates the cake, though.

308 UNDER THE BOARDWALK, The Drifters
Produced by Bert Berns; written by Arthur Resnick and Kenny Young
Atlantic 2237   1964   Billboard: #4

Johnny Moore first sang with the Drifters in the mid-fifties, one of the string of moderately distinctive leads the group ran through between Clyde McPhatter and Ben E. King. Moore came up with the Drifters' two best records in that period, "Ruby Baby" and "Drip Drop," but neither was anything special. (Dion's remake of "Ruby Baby" trounces the original.)

Moore rejoined the Drifters in 1963, after they had already been disbanded and then reconstituted with first Ben E. King and then Rudy Lewis as leads. He still wasn't much more than a journeyman, but producer Bert Berns, then hitting a peak with his gimmicky but touching teen love productions (including several of Solomon Burke's hits, Betty Harris's "Cry to Me," and "A Little Bit of Soap" by the Jarmels), didn't require much more than that.

"Under the Boardwalk" is the best of all Berns's productions. The lyrics build a detailed portrait of sights and sounds at Coney Island, from the scent of hot dogs and french fries to the sound of the carousel and the action beneath the piers. The musical scenario is just as busy, with strings, castanets, a ratchet, and all manner of other percussion capturing a lazy summer's mood. The result is so aggressively ephemeral that it just might last forever.

309 THE LION SLEEPS TONIGHT (WIMOWEH), The Tokens

Produced by Hugo and Luigi; written by George Weiss, Hugo Peretti, Luigi Creatore, and Albert Stanton
RCA 7954   1961   *Billboard:* #1 (3 weeks)

In addition to the doo-wop revival, the pre-Beatle sixties featured a so-called "folk revival," which got more and better ink but produced fewer worthwhile pop hits. And I don't wanna hear about "Tom Dooley" and "Puff the Magic Dragon," let alone "Blowin' in the Wind," the most unctuous song Bob Dylan ever wrote (which considering what he's written lately, is saying a heap).

The folk movement had important antecedents in the popular-front cultural politics of the thirties and forties, and in the blacklisted nightclub pop of the Weavers, but in musical style and class orientation, it was very much a reaction against the dominance of rock and roll and R&B in the fifties. Though the folk revival produced some very worthwhile results, including the discovery and rediscovery of the greatest living rural blues singers (Skip James, Son House, Fred McDowell) and the first indications of post-McCarthy cultural activism (in the "topical" songs of Dylan, Phil Ochs, and others), folk-pop of the sort that hit the charts tailored itself to appeal primarily to white middle-class collegiates, particularly ones who found the music of contemporary blacks and working-class whites too vulgar. Ironically, while urban folk-ies upheld authenticity as the cardinal virtue, "folk" groups like Peter, Paul and Mary and the Chad Mitchell Trio were assembled and mar-keted far more self-consciously than any doo-wop group or rock band of the time.

It's fitting, therefore, that the folk revival's best hit was "The Lion Sleeps Tonight," the most musically exciting record of the genre for reasons that have everything to do with its inauthenticity and vulgarity.

The Tokens were white college kids from Brighton Beach, Brooklyn who formed a doo-wop quartet. Hank Medress had been in a group of that name since high school, when one of his bandmates was an aspiring classical pianist and pop songwriter called Neil Sedaka. The Tokens who made "Tonight I Fell in Love," a regional hit earlier in 1961, included Medress, lead singer Jay Siegal, and a pair of Brighton Beach brothers, Phil and Mitch Margo.

Jay Siegal found "The Lion Sleeps Tonight" on *The Weavers at Carnegie Hall*, a folkie icon. The Weavers called their song "Wi-moweh," after the song's chorus, but they'd learned it as "Mbube," from African pop-folk stylist Miriam Makeba, who first recorded it in 1952. Although Makeba and the Weavers presented the song as an example of African folklore, its origins aren't "folk" in the narrow sense; the tune and Zulu lyrics date to the thirties.

Siegal liked "Wimoweh" enough to persuade the Tokens to work it up, and their producers at RCA, Hugo and Luigi (of Sam Cooke and Stylistics fame), liked what they came up with. They commissioned George Weiss, a Tin Pan Alley gun-for-hire, to write lyrics, since the Weavers performed only the chorus, featuring the mysterious African word, "Wimoweh." Allegedly, Weiss had no idea what "Mbube" was about and all by himself came up with the notion of a slumbering lion outside a peaceful village. For the session, Hugo and Luigi supple-mented the Tokens with operatic soprano Anita Darien, who doubled the sax solo at the top of her range. The group, except Siegal, hated the result. "We were embarassed by it and tried to convince Hugo and Luigi not to release it," Phil Margo has said. Siegal said his mates were embarassed by the title: "We were purists then." (He presumably meant doo-wop purists, not folk purists.)

In fact, although RCA released "The Lion Sleeps Tonight" in Oc-tober 1961, it didn't hit the charts for six weeks, because the label at first plugged the other side, "Tina," a Portugese folk song. Dick Smith at WORC, in Worcester, Massachusetts flipped the disc and "Lion," with its thrilling high harmonies, doo-wop backing, rumbling drum fills, and insistently chanted "Wimoweh" shot to the top of the charts.

Folk purists looked on the Tokens' obviously commercialized rearrangement of the Weavers and Miriam Makeba disdainfully—until they learned that "Mbube" means "Lion" and the original lyric was about a lion sleeping peacefully outside a village: "Hush!, hush!" says the Zulu version, "If we're all quiet, there'll be lion meat for dinner." So in America, some ate crow, a dish so delectable that even now, it's possible to forgive the Tokens' Medress for going on to produce Tony Orlando and Dawn. It helps, though, that the group's next Number One project was even better: "He's So Fine" by the Chiffons. Arriving there via a Zulu pop song might be the finest story of the folk process at work in a modern industrial setting that there is, although I wouldn't look for Peter, Paul and Mary to tell it quite that way the next time they're sneering their way through "I dig rock and roll music."

310 I'M YOUR PUPPET, James and Bobby Purify
Produced by Papa Don Schroeder; written by Dan Penn and Spooner Oldham
Bell 648   1966   *Billboard:* #6

Although they specialized (as on "Shake a Tail Feather") in being a minor league version of Sam and Dave, with "I'm Your Puppet," the Purifys (they were cousins) came into their own by bringing to the formal mannerisms of Muscle Shoals-style deep soul the lighter, more purely pop sensibility of predecessors like Marvin and Johnny and Don and Juan. David Ruffin and Eddie Kendricks also come to mind, but the intensity is far too laid-back to really resemble the Temptations.

Cowriter Spooner Oldham gives "Puppet" its distinctive signature with his vibes work. Drummer Roger Hawkins digs a groove miles wide and just as deep and the horns settle into it and just ride. What's more all of them make it sound so easy, you can believe it's all just a matter of "Pull them little strings and I'll do anything." If the best definition of cool is that which never has to expend any energy defining itself, "I'm Your Puppet" may be the coolest soul classic ever recorded.

311 LE FREAK, Chic
Written and produced by Bernard Edwards and Nile Rodgers
Atlantic 3519   1978   *Billboard:* #1 (6 weeks)

Perhaps the mightiest of all Bernard Edwards' monumental bass lines. And that's damn near all there is to it—the string wash and the chicken-scratch guitar, the plodding bass drum and relentlessly repetitious brushstrokes on the cymbal, the anonymity of the singers and the predictable disco-is-my-life lyric are all just there to tighten the tension that leaks out exclusively from Edwards's throbbing tones.

And although it presents itself as nothing more than another *disco uber alles* anthem, take a hint from the lyric. In one context, "Le Freak" is about being liberated from "the days of stomping at the old Savoy." But in another, a "freak" is a man daring enough to practice cunnilingus. Could "chic" mean a guy brave enough to write songs about digging it?

312 FUNKY BROADWAY, Wilson Pickett
Produced by Jerry Wexler; written by Arlester (Dyke) Christian
Atlantic 2430   1967   *Billboard:* #8

313 FUNKY BROADWAY, PART 1, Dyke and the Blazers
Produced by Art Laboe and Art Barrett; written by
Arlester (Dyke) Christian
Original Sound 64   1967   *Billboard:* #65

Wilson Pickett was the personification of the bad-ass street dude. If he came along today, he'd be a rapper—with a vengeance, which is how he always sang. What he lacked in subtlety, Pickett more than made up for in vocal power. He was surrounded by great musicians in Detroit, Memphis, and Muscle Shoals, his old Falcons associates Eddie Floyd and Mack Rice frequently came up with excellent songs for him, and in Jerry Wexler, he had an insightful and sympathetic producer.

One thing that Wexler and Pickett were able to do consistently was take songs that were nothing more than isolated R&B market hits for others and cross them over into the pop market. (Ironically, they met as a result of Wexler and Solomon Burke swiping Pickett's original "If You Need Me" which had been released on a small Detroit-based label.) "Funky Broadway" epitomizes the way they worked.

The original "Funky Broadway" was made by Dyke and the Blazers, who represented the same kind of hard-as-nails image in Watts that Pickett did in Motown. As Dyke recorded it, "Funky Broadway" was a James Brown funk chant, all riff and rhythm and not much melody. Arlester "Dyke" Christian's vocal was ragged and nasal; the bass line, which establishes the beat in both versions, was noticeably faster. In the middle, the Blazers go off into a relatively extended bass and drums breakdown (it spills over from the A side of the single, "Funky Broadway, Part One," to the B side, "Funky Broadway, Part Two"). The record is completely consonant with its title—it could damn near funk you to death (and on R&B stations, it damn near did.) But in pop terms, sprawling and spacious too often registers as unfocused.

Pickett, Wexler, and the original Muscle Shoals band (which included bassists Tommy Cogbill and Junior Lowe, guitarists Chips Moman and Jimmy Johnson, Spooner Oldham on keyboards, and Roger Hawkins on drums), streamlined the song. The bass line was also carried on guitar. Rather than ruminating in funk, Hawkins stomped the backbeat. With the addition of a cutting horn riff, "Funky Broadway" became not only danceable but also a finely honed pop song. Against this backdrop, the guitar and drum fills and Pickett's vocal exhortations stood out much more sharply. Dyke and the Blazers' record seems primitive in comparison, especially since the recording itself is much duller, recorded at a lower volume and with fewer upper register peaks.

Yet, as much as anything by James Brown or Sly, Dyke's original "Funky Broadway" helped establish the conventions of that seventies marvel known as funk. The straight soul music Pickett made, fine-honed as it was, had only a few more years to grow.

314 HOT FUN IN THE SUMMERTIME, Sly and the Family Stone

Written and produced by Sly Stone
Epic 10497   1969   *Billboard:* #2

Reading most music criticism, you'd think it was against the law to tell musical jokes, but then, trying to be funny for an entire LP (or even a whole side) is a great way to begin exhibiting symptoms of elephantiasis—just ask Frank Zappa. Singles, on the other hand, are a perfect vehicle for humor, because their time limitations force you to get to the punch line economically.

"Hot Fun in the Summertime" starts out as a joke, a satire of stuff like the Cowsills' "The Rain, The Park and Other Things," phony nostalgia for an America of pastoral good times that probably never existed for anyone, and certainly never had any reality for black people. *Their* festivals were being played out in the streets as "urban riots," a biting irony that Sly did his best to exploit without explicit mention.

So Sly opened the record with piano triplets so corny they could have been composed by Booth Tarkington, added strings and plush harmonies out of the Spanky and Our Gang songbag and created a full scale sustained goof for at least a chorus. But then the Family Stone's more soulful voices come in and you get to Larry Graham's growl and the game's up as the truth shows its teeth. "Hot fun in the summertime" they sang and while enough people must have heard the litany as a version of the one that plays itself out today as "baseball, hot dogs, and Chev-ro-let" to take the record close to the top of the charts, the rest of us envisioned fire trucks, national guardsmen, rocks, rifles, and Coke bottles refilled with gasoline. Not that that was the whole story, either, since Sly's satire could never have been so convincing if summertime hadn't once been a more ordinary blast for him, too.

315 SUBSTITUTE, The Who
Produced by The Who; written by Pete Townshend
Atco 45 6409   1966   Did not make pop chart

Figures lie and liars figure. Music is the most mathematical of the arts. Pete Townshend, a great musician and an even better rock and roller, can barely balance a checkbook.

Such half-truths and fictions (I once wrote an excessively long history of the Who, but never found out anything about Townshend's apparently unremarkable mathematical aptitudes) form the substance of "Substitute," a model example of the early Who's joyous bashings. The song establishes itself with a guitar riff, but the music soon centers on John Entwistle's powerful bass and Keith Moon's wild drumming as Roger Daltrey yelps out Townshend's contradictions. The best of which comes in the penultimate verse: "Substitute! Me for him / Substitute! My Coke for gin / Substitute! You for me mum / Substitute! At least I'll get my washing done."

Back in 1966, Atco actually forced the band to rerecord the gaffe about "I look all white but my dad was black" as "I try walking forward but my feet walk back," for fear of offending programming bigots. The record flopped in the States, anyway, like almost everything that the Who did in those days. (It was so popular and influential in England that it has been rereleased with the regularity of a Christmas single.)

The Who went on to a cool career and vast popularity achieved by recording ever lengthier Townshend opuses about the distance between appearance and reality. Seen in that light, "Substitute" becomes a rehearsal for *Tommy*. But don't let that make you hate it, because looked at from *this* version of rock history, *Tommy* is simply an overblown follow-up to "Substitute."

316 HUNGRY EYES, Merle Haggard
Produced by Ken Nelson; written by Merle Haggard
Capitol 2383   1969   Did not make pop charts

The greatest of all Merle's populist hymns, and despite its lack of chart stature (it *was* a country Number One), perhaps his most pop, too, with an arrangement that features more strings than guitars. Since Merle's singing remains bluesy, the result is closer to soul than to your ordinary Bakersfield countrypolitan.

The lyrics are so evocative they approach the poetic, in the same way as Dorothea Lange's photo of the so-called "Madonna of the Depression," but what makes Merle's words especially fascinating is the way they summarize the contradictions of populism. "Mama never had the luxuries she wanted / But it wasn't 'cause my daddy didn't try," Merle sings plaintively, not once but thrice, then adds, "She only wanted things she really needed / One more reason for my momma's hungry eyes." Populism's undoing always reflects this tension: The desire for things that life in a consumer society provokes and the denial of the validity of all material desire on moral grounds. That Merle managed to make art from his own confusion will surprise no one who's heard "Okie From Muskogee" back-to-back with "Working Man Blues."

317 THERE'S NO OTHER (LIKE MY BABY), The Crystals
Produced by Phil Spector; written by L. Bates and Phil Spector
Philles 100   1961   Billboard: #20

I think the part where they're walking down the street and he promises to marry her is just as corny as you do. But the way La La Brooks sings it, there's another story being told here. It's about the importance of feeling psychically unique, especially for folks who are usually lost in the crowd. This was the first hit for the Crystals, and the first for Phil Spector at his own label, and it established a mood (elegiac in regard to teen love) and a theme (that drive to stand out somehow, no matter how the world tried to shape you). Other people made love songs as a matter of pleasure and preference; Spector's are about the crying need for romance in lives too barren to be supportable otherwise.

318 MEAN OLD WORLD, Little Walter and His Night Cats

Producer not credited; written by Walter Jacobs
Checker 764   1952   Did not make pop chart

At his best, Little Walter Jacobs played such nasty mouth harp that he might as well have been tonguing razor blades. And here, he's constantly at his best, blasting short, cutting riffs against a backdrop consisting of not much more than a walking bass line (contributed by bandmates Muddy Waters and Jimmy Rogers), and a muted shuffle flying off drummer Elgin Evans' kit, setting up a mournful vocal and the most dolorous ballad in Chicago blues. "This is a *mean* old world / 'S hard livin' by yourself," Walter begins, "Can't get the one you lovin' / Have to use somebody else."

Engulfed in his emotional quagmire, Walter sounds exhausted from the effort of trying to cope, reduced to explaining his behavior as nothing more than a tactic against his own lassitude. He's quitting, he testifies, the clash of harp against guitar suggesting his anxiety, then marches on in circles, until the whole project comes crashing to a halt that feels utterly final and nothing like a finale. Too early and too raw to be rock and roll per se, "Mean Old World" is also one of the few records of the fifties that anticipates the probing angst found in the songs of Pete Townshend and John Lennon twenty years later.

319 OH GIRL, The Chi-Lites

Written and produced by Eugene Record
Brunswick 55471   1972   *Billboard:* #1 (1 week)

The newsweeklies' idea of a pop music cover story in the early seventies was The Rise of the Singer/Songwriter. If the mass media was as good as its word, the Chi-Lites' Eugene Record would have been as big a star as James Taylor or Joni Mitchell. After all, he wrote a long string of hits (this one even uses a folkish harmonica as lead instrument) which never lacked for confessional or socio-political angst. And Record, unlike the latter-day troubadors the media chose to anoint, could actually sing the songs he wrote, in a plaintive yet effective tenor whose timbre was yet so thin that it seems in retrospect positively Tayloresque.

But Record never reached the covers of the newsstand slicks, because his records were done by a soul group, and by the seventies, group harmony—directly derived in this case from the likes of the Dells and the Impressions—had become archaic.

In "Oh Girl," Record confesses that he'd be lost without his girl . . . because he's lost the knack of looking for another. The problem with their relationship is most modern: She outearns him, and he can't stand it, wants to run away, hates the idea that he's using her and that his friends think he ought to live off her. "So I try to be hip and think like the crowd," he moans, "but even the crowd can't help me now." Strange sentiments coming from a guy who made his living defying fashion.

320 JUMPIN' JACK FLASH, The Rolling Stones
Produced by Jimmy Miller; written by Mick Jagger and Keith Richards
London 908   1968   *Billboard: #3*

It's a gas, gas, gas.

321 GEORGIA ON MY MIND, Ray Charles
Produced by Sid Feller; written by Hoagy Carmichael and Stewart Gorrell
ABC-Paramount 10135   1960   *Billboard: #1 (1 week)*

Hoagy Carmichael was the most blues-inspired writer Tin Pan Alley produced but he could never have expected that his thirties hit (it scored thrice between 1931 and 1941, first with Frankie Trombauer's group that featured Bix Beiderbecke, then as Mildred Bailey's first big record in 1932, finally in a Gene Krupa arrangement sung by Anita O'Day) would ever get a reading this deeply soulful. Who could have?

Only Tommy Brown, Ray's driver, who suggested the boss cut "Georgia" because he liked the way Ray sang it to himself as they traveled along. It's anybody's guess what Ray might have been musing about; maybe home, since he grew up just over the border in north Florida, or perhaps the stories of horror and triumph emerging as the civil rights movement gained momentum. The shadow of each lingers in his lovingly legato phrases.

Give full points to arranger Ralph Burns, too, for the delirious strings that take off as Ray gives his tortured reading of the final verse.

322 MANNISH BOY, Muddy Waters

Produced by Leonard Chess; written by Willie Dixon
Chess 1602   1955   Did not make pop chart

If there is a blues singer with an acoustic guitar hidden in the core of the Chuck Berry myth, between him and Berry is a bluesman with an electric guitar, and he's *not* anonymous. He's Muddy Waters, who learned his trade from such country-blues singers as Robert Johnson and Son House and passed it along by introducing Berry to Chess Records. A great bandleader, singer, songwriter, and guitarist, Waters almost singlehandedly figured out how to electrify rural Mississippi Delta blues. Consequently, he ranks with Louis Armstrong, Bill Monroe, Jimmy Rodgers, Hank Williams, Elvis Presley, and Robert Johnson among the master innovators of recorded American popular music. Like those men, Waters established a model upon which literally dozens of others based themselves.

Waters was never a rock and roll singer. But his relationship to the music stems from much more than being Berry's benefactor. The Bo Diddley beat is simply an extrapolation from Waters's primordial electric revampings of Johnson's slide guitar licks. "Mannish Boy," Muddy's response to Bo's "I'm a Man," proves the point. Muddy picks up Bo's basic beat, but he slows the tempo, seemingly holding it down with main strength. Bo Diddley renders "I'm a Man" (whose lyrics haven't traveled far from a couple of the country-blues standards that Waters had himself brought from Mississippi and modernized) as a fairly innocuous novelty. Coming from Waters, a mature adult figure with a voice that booms like God's, virtually the same words are far more leering and imposing. Waters isn't kidding around; he *is* a man and his sexual boasts and demands aren't fantasies, they're real.

"Mannish Boy" is certainly the most atypical and artificial song Muddy was asked to sing, something he probably did because for a few seasons in the fifties, rock and roll virtually obliterated the market for Chicago blues—hurt it almost as badly as it damaged country. "Mannish Boy" was a (mostly vain) attempt to peddle Muddy's music to a white audience—perhaps the original blues-rock crossover move. Yet no matter how cold-hearted its origins, Muddy found a way to dominate the track straight through. He did it with a field holler backed by a country-blues guitar pattern. The result is one of the great Waters sides, and something that the rock and roll tradition should be very proud to claim.

323 RUNNING SCARED, Roy Orbison
Produced by Fred Foster; written by Roy Orbison and Joe Melson
Monument 438   1961   Billboard: #1 (1 week)

Paranoid bolero with Mexican accent and strings. As in most westerns, our hero gets the girl. The difference, maybe, is that the way Roy conceived it, the woman had all the power. Not that leaving it up to her made what was going on any less a life-and-death issue.

324 THE PITTSBURGH STEALERS, The Kendalls
Produced by Brien Fisher; written by Larry Kingston and Jim Rushing
Ovation 1109   1978   Did not make pop chart

When country's "New Traditionalists"—from Ricky Skaggs to the Judds to Dwight Yoakam—appeared in the mid-eighties, they were on a mission to restore what each saw, in one way or another, as the music's lost purity. In such terms, the Kendalls were country's best-kept secret, for in their hands, the traditions of booming guitar and crystalline high mountain harmony had been safe for several years. And the Kendalls were one of country's most popular duos in the late seventies and eighties.

The concept of a father/daughter team that sings mostly cheating songs has an odd resonance until you realize that the Appalachian and Anglo-Celtic ballad traditions, whose folk tales of murder, incest, and personal and political infidelities form the foundation of commercial country music, were also family music styles, whose lyrics must have inspired equally ironic subtextual juxtapositions for generations, if not centuries. As Jeanie Kendall hits her marvelously nasal upper register, defining that musical moment when a tingle becomes a chill, you don't much care.

"The Pittsburgh Stealers" defines another contemporary country subtext that the New Traditionalists (give or take Steve Earle) wanted to obscure and avoid. That's what actually happened to C&W's mainly Southern working-class audience in the industrial North. "Found myself in Pittsburgh, workin' in a steel mill," Royce Kendall begins forlornly, as if there's something not quite right about the very idea, his perplexity harkening back to the mysteries of folk songs like "I Wish I Was A Mole in the Ground." "And I was a Southern girl whose husband did the same," Jeannie returns, snapping the story back to the everyday.

For once you can feel the generational difference between them: If she's feeling a little lost, too, she's also been liberated, given mobility and opportunity no farm or mountain miner's wife could ever even dream.

In the North, women went to work, often at jobs that earned as much or more than their husbands. But even before they had jobs, they had cars and free time the like of which was not even on the horizon back home. And so it's no accident that women became prominent actors in the C&W world for the first time in the sixties and seventies. (Kitty Wells and Patsy Cline were anomalies, albeit predictive ones.)

In this regard, "The Pittsburgh Stealers" describes a world that simply had never existed until the late fifties at the earliest. Its artistic virtues aren't minor: not only the brilliant harmonies and an arrangement more classic than any New Traditionalist record I can think of, but the greatest football metaphor in pop music history (even including Mel and Tim's "Backfield in Motion"), and a great loping bass line and guitars that sound as edgy with guilt as the words.

325 PINK HOUSES, John Cougar Mellencamp
Produced by Little Bastard and Don Gehman; written by John Cougar Mellencamp
Riva 215   1983   *Billboard:* #8

With "Pink Houses," John Mellencamp perfected his angry-young-populist-meets-the-Rolling-Stones sound and persona. For all its slash and superficial cynicism, "Pink Houses" leaped way past the defeatist smirk of self-satisfaction at the heart of "Hurts So Good" and "Jack and Diane," partly by having the nerve to open with chords ripped right out of *Beggar's Banquet* (from "Salt of the Earth," to choose the most relevant example), and partly by acknowledging that the defeated stick with the very hopes that the cynical have pushed aside for fear their hearts will break.

There's another way to measure Mellencamp's achievement. He grew up in southern Indiana, a part of the country long infested by the Ku Klux Klan. In most of the towns downstate, blacks are unknown; in all of them, they're unwelcome. Yet, in the first verse of "Pink Houses," he writes a letter-perfect description of Michael Jackson's old neighborhood up in Gary, at the northern, largely black end of the state: "He's got an interstate running through his front yard / You know he thinks he's got it so good" is exactly how things are back there. You may get that idea just from driving by, but the ability to put it across comes from somewhere else, somewhere those Klan guys have never been and fight to keep young guys like Mellencamp from going. If this accounts for how twisted his early records had to be, it also locates the rising sense of triumph that you can hear in his music.

326 POSITIVELY 4TH STREET, Bob Dylan
Produced by Bob Johnston; written by Bob Dylan
Columbia 43389   1965   *Billboard: #7*

An icy hipster bitch session, Dylan cutting loose his barbed-wire tongue at somebody luckless enough to have crossed the path of his desires. When people parody Dylan, they mostly go for the hollowed out 4:00 A.M. grouch of "4th Street"—a pure single, never released on any album until *Greatest Hits*. But no imitator has ever captured that wash of organ, those stabbing guitars—or the trickle of venom that lubricates Dylan's throat, turning what might have been merely nasty in other hands into something brilliantly poisonous.

Lyric He Lived to Regret: "I wish that for just one time you could stand inside my shoes."

327 STRANGER IN TOWN, Del Shannon
Produced by Harry Balk and Irv Machinik; written by
Del Shannon
Amy 919   1965   *Billboard: #30*

Just as rock's great fatalist is John Fogerty and its premier stoic Roy Orbison, Del Shannon is its leading paranoid. "Stranger in Town" proves it; it's one long bleat of terror, the singer and his lover pursued by some unnameable person for a reason just beyond the fringe of rational understanding. If that plot sounds sort of like David Janssen's TV series, *The Fugitive*, you've got the idea. And maybe that's why "Stranger in Town" became the theme song for Michael Mann's eighties police drama, *Crime Story*. (It's also occurred to me, and I'm sure I'm not alone, that Del's run off with an underage girl and her parents have set the cops against him.)

The song's whole structure is based on fear: the doomy recitation at the top, echoed by spare notes from the bass guitar; the way Shannon's voice rises to a shrill pitch of terror on its first encounter with the word "run," and reaches that peak again on "do to me" and "my baby," "forever," and "together"; the way the song breaks down at the end of the verses to let Shannon chant against splashy percussion some more. As for the lyrics, forget it: "Stranger in town / He's out to get me" is about as close to clinically paranoid as you can get. The clincher, though, is the wild series of falsetto "wooo"'s on which the song fades out—the sound of a man so tortured by his own thoughts that all he can do is scream his fear into the night sky.

328 TRY ME (I NEED YOU), James Brown
Produced by Andy Gibson; written by James Brown
Federal 12337   1958   *Billboard: #48*

For all his egomania, James Brown's success has a lot to do with absolute persistence. "Try Me" was the tenth follow-up to "Please Please Please." The other nine failed miserably, so badly that not one of them made any sort of *Billboard* chart and James was on the verge of being dumped by King/Federal's Syd Nathan. So there's a way in which these lyrics, in which James hoarsely begs for his lover's confidence, might be addressed to the audience which he had once held and could no longer locate.

"Try Me" made it to the top of the rhythm and blues charts and even crossed over to some pop stations, a first for Brown. Even at that, it must have been a near thing, because the song was a throwback, its group harmonies and sax solo nearer in feeling to Little Willie John and Johnny Ace than to the newer soul style. But as the world would see soon enough—"I'll Go Crazy" was only two hits away—James had innovations enough up his sleeve.

329 OOO BABY BABY, The Miracles
Produced by Smokey Robinson; written by Smokey Robinson and Warren Moore
Tamla 54113   1965   *Billboard: #16*

Smokey once told me he considered "Ooo Baby Baby" his "national anthem," because "wherever we go, it's the one song that everybody always asks for." But the record's not great just because it's a crowd-pleaser. The lyric is intricately constructed around vernacular phrases that flow into one another effortlessly, a semblance of crying that bonds grief with joy in a combination calculable only through the alchemy of Smokey's throat. Robinson's singing just about defines the soul music version of rubato, elasticizing a phrase here and double-timing one there, always hitting his marks though you could spend a lifetime figuring exactly how he does it, or just what it means when he quavers certain notes. And it'd be a worthwhile life's work, too.

330 CRYING TIME, Ray Charles
Produced by Joe Adams; written by Buck Owens
ABC-Paramount 10739   1965   *Billboard: #6*

Although Ray's *Modern Sounds in Country and Western* albums are legendary, they're not very good and, with their flatulent, excessively brassy arrangements, they sure aren't very country, not even by the relaxed standards of early sixties countrypolitan.

But "Crying Time" is another matter. Compared to the Buck Owens original, it's no more country than *The Rite of Spring*, but that hardly matters, because Ray converts the song into a deep, soulful blues and even the godawful choral background can't stop him from wrenching your guts.

331 I WONDER WHY, Dion and the Belmonts
Produced by Gene Schwartz; written by Ricardo Weeks and Melvin Anderson
Laurie 3013   1958   *Billboard: #22*

Their first hit, and the only one where any of the Belmonts ever came close to upstaging Dion. Stuttering in rock and roll has a long if ignoble history (The Who, David Bowie, and BTO are its most prominent practitioners), but no one's ever jib-jabbered with more distinction than Carlo Mastrangelo does here. Without the benefit of so much as a single real word to stumble over, he sounds like his tongue's driving rivets through the roof of his mouth. Or maybe he's just giddy from trying to sort out the romantic complications Dion details with such carefully concealed cynicism: "When you're with me, I'm sure you're always true / When I'm away, I wonder what you do / I wonder why I'm sure you're always true."

332 BIG BIRD, Eddie Floyd
Produced by Booker T. Jones; written by Booker T. Jones and Eddie Floyd
Stax 246   1968   Did not make pop chart

Floyd allegedly started writing "Big Bird" when the plane bringing him home from the Stax/Volt Revue's European tour was delayed at London's Heathrow Airport. If that's true, payback's a bitch, for this rumbling track is as close as soul music has ever come to the deteriorated blues of heavy metal. Give or take an absolutely archetypal bass, drum, and horn patterns, and occasional octave guitar runs straight out of the Motown handbook.

333 FARTHER UP THE ROAD, Bobby Bland
Produced by Joe Scott; written by Robey and Veasey
Duke 170   1957   *Billboard:* #43

A virtually perfect Texas blues that became Bland's first pop chart single. Mel Brown's signature lick provides the missing link between T-Bone Walker and Eric Clapton; Bland's deep blues vocal and Scott's arrangement, which swings as hard as it rocks, link Ray Charles's big band R&B to more modern currents in Southern soul as well as the generation of British blues singers typified by Joe Cocker (and Clapton). The lyric beautifully suggests forties and fifties prototypes without a hint of cliché. Bland made better records, but not more influential ones.

334 DO WAH DIDDY DIDDY, Manfred Mann
Produced by John Burgess; written by Jeff Barry and Ellie Greenwich
Ascot 2157   1964   *Billboard:* #1 (2 weeks)

Decades from now, long after the meaning of "Wooly Bully" has been officially parsed, scholars and pundits will still debate the meaning of "Do wah diddy diddy." Indeed whether the second diddy is necessary or even desirable may predictably form a major source of schismatic tension in twenty-first century academe.

Surviving texts show that Jeff Barry and Ellie Greenwich wrote the phrase in an attempt to find a sequel to "Da Doo Ron Ron." Not just any garbled syllables would do. "They not only have to sound right, they have to sing right," Greenwich once explained. The couple gave the song, as "Do Wah Diddy," to the Exciters, to be used as a follow-up to that group's 1962 hit, "Tell Him." Though produced by the hipster saints Leiber and Stoller, it went nowhere (well, to Number 78 in *Billboard*, which amounts to nowhere), but its philosophical import was such that its composers couldn't forget about it. Barry and Greenwich cut it themselves, under their occasional nom de studio, the Raindrops. But their version never got released because in the meantime, the guys in Manfred Mann, basically a jazz/blues act, found the Exciters record in a London bargain bin and, being beatnik philosophers themselves, understood its profundity and therefore added it to their stage act, hoping to spread the word. Their manager convinced them to record the song, and believing proselytizing a modern jazzman's sacred duty, the band did so, adding a second "Diddy" in the process, thus making them the first "Do Wah" heretics or the first to accurately render the title (since "Do wah diddy *diddy*" is what even the Exciters sang).

So what does "do wah diddy" mean? Well, if you have to ask . . .

335 I FEEL FOR YOU, Chaka Khan
Produced by Arif Mardin; written by Prince
Warner Bros. 29195   1984   *Billboard*: #3

Talk about your supersessions: written by the best new black writer of the eighties, produced by the guy who taught the Bee Gees how to boogie, rap assistance by Melle Mel, the proudest voice in Grandmaster Flash and the Furious Five, and harmonica solo by no less than Stevie Wonder. Even the decade Chaka Khan spent leading Rufus could hardly have prepared her for such an extravaganza.

Not that she mightn't have regretted it later. It's nice to attract so much attention from so many eligible fellas, but after a few months, Chaka must have found herself fed up with not being able to walk to the store without hearing a dozen trolling imitations of Melle Mel's rebounding "Chakakhanchakakhanchakakhan." Which only compounded the problem of being upstaged on your record by scratchers and rappers and a blind kid with a big harp in the first place. Although whoever came up with the idea of cutting in two sharp seconds from "Fingertips, Part Two" wins *my* eternal favor.

336 SHE THINKS I STILL CARE, George Jones
Produced by Pappy Daily; written by D. L. Lipscomb and
Dicky Lee
United Artists 424   1962   Did not make pop charts

337 DETROIT CITY, Bobby Bare
Produced by Chet Atkins; written by Danny Dill and Mel Tillis
RCA 8183   1963   *Billboard:* #16

In the beginning, rock and roll wiped out country music. Of course, country and the Nashville-based music industry that nurtured, cradled, and perhaps caged it didn't cease to exist, but country survived primarily by learning to live without hope of expansion.

Country music was developed by the music industry just before and during the Depression to appeal to rural whites, most of whom lived in the South and Southwest. After World War II, the country industry desperately needed to come to grips with the national migration from farm to factory, homestead to city streets, South to North. Like their black counterparts, those folks needed a voice which expressed their dilemmas.

Country couldn't easily provide it. Nashville was legendarily hidebound, a respecter not so much of tradition as of the reactionary nostalgia that passes for tradition among those who have a lot to lose from fundamental change. And so, when the record industry did begin to develop a new sound and style out of the cultural consequences of the postwar exodus, it came not from Nashville and country music entrepreneurs but from Memphis and a shrewd owner of a small, black-oriented record label. Sam Phillips understood—or at least, intuited—what was happening to America. So he asked for, and got, "a white singer with the Negro sound and the Negro feel." And he made, if not a billion dollars, at least a few million.

The post-rural working-class kids that Phillips recorded—Elvis, Jerry Lee Lewis, Carl Perkins, even Johnny Cash, though not so much the more sophisticated Roy Orbison and Charlie Rich—were people who came into their own in a world their parents never knew. It was a consumer society; its landscape was the city block, not a cotton or tobacco field; its quarters were temporary, not ancestral.

Rather than finding voices that told the new audience the value of these new things and celebrated the new opportunities they suggested, country records typically proclaimed that all the changes were bad and needed to be resisted. And when a country record got the tone just right, as Bobby Bare's "Detroit City" did, it could score high on the charts.

But Bare's music was as close to commercial folk as to country. His record didn't feature fiddles; it had pizzicato violins. It replaced high lonesome harmonies with a pop chorus. That's what you call countrypolitan.

What made the record was Bare's recitation describing how much he hates his job and his life in the big city. At the end, he swears he's going back home. "Detroit City" rejected the future of which people like Elvis and Jerry Lee were the cutting edge, which was especially ironic since Bare's first hit was "All American Boy," a 1958 satire of Elvis (released under the name Bill Parsons) in which he created a highly credible roman a clef about the King. Now, he sang in the mellow countrypolitan tones that Chet Atkins brought to RCA's country roster—or at least that's what Atkins did when he wasn't supervising Elvis sessions.

"Detroit City" 's most famous line is one of the great summaries of male working-class life: "By day I make the cars / By night I make the bars." Put those words in the mouth of a rockabilly singer and you'd hear a shout of defiance and triumph, akin to Little Richard's boastful "Fool about my money, don't try to save." But Bare sounds like a mean and mournful drunk; he hits the bars not even for kicks but to assuage his nostalgia. As a result, he spoke powerfully to what many transplanted southerners felt (as he did with the follow-up, "500 Miles from Home," an even bigger hit). But those were dead-end sentiments; people weren't really going back, and their lives in the North, making cars by day and hitting the bars after work, weren't really any more hateful than working the fields and only going into town on weekends, just draining in different ways.

Although most Americans have never heard of him, Bobby Bare has had a long and fruitful career. But among country stars, all that's remarkable about his story is that he actually did manage a couple of pop hits.

If you're interested in waste and tragedy, consider George Jones, the finest country voice of the post-Hank Williams generation. Like Bare, Jones had his first hit with a fifties rockabilly single. "Why Baby Why" made the country Top Ten in 1955 but never dented the pop charts. By 1962, Jones had made twenty country chart singles, including two Number Ones and six others that hit the Top Ten. To those who knew about him, he was one of the great treasures of American pop music, a blues and honky-tonk singer as powerful (if not as inventive) as Ray Charles. But his biggest pop single was "White Lightning," another quasi-rockabilly number, this one written by The Big Bopper.

Released in 1959, it was his first C&W Number One. On the pop charts, it made Number 73.

In the thirty years since "White Lightning," Jones has made the country Top Ten perhaps a dozen more times. "White Lightning" remains the biggest pop hit he's ever had.

"She Thinks I Still Care" exposes all the reasons why that has to be the case, and all the reasons why the situation is terrible. On this record fiddles are fiddles, not violins. Jones is accompanied by a chorus, because by 1962 countrypolitan touches were everywhere, but they're kept well back, and so are the drums and even the honky-tonk piano. The center of the record is his own massive, aching voice, sliding up to and around blue notes and speaking in a plain husky drawl that seems to know all the sadness one life can comprehend. Denying his enduring love, Jones is thoroughly persuasive about how badly losing it has damaged him. He might be singing about the lost possibilities of country music itself.

338 SOUL DEEP, The Box Tops
Produced by Tommy Cogbill and Chips Moman; written by Wayne Carson Thompson
Mala 12040   1969   *Billboard:* #18

Before he became the most famous—not to mention dissolute and overrated—postpunk critical darling in North America, Alex Chilton was actually among the best (albeit most spaced-out) blue-eyed soulsters in the world. "Soul Deep" is the cornerstone of his rep: sung from a ravaged throat, driven by a perfect backbeat, with a trilling flute, hotshot drums, and bursts of guitar and horns that punctuate the verses and dictate the song's pulse. Of course, that has more to do with producers Tommy Cogbill and Chips Moman than frontman Chilton, but don't tell any rock critics that and their earth won't shake.

339 GET OUTTA MY DREAMS, GET INTO MY CAR, Billy Ocean
Produced by Robert John "Mutt" Lange; written by Robert John "Mutt" Lange and Billy Ocean
Jive 9678   1988   *Billboard:* #1 (2 weeks)

Even if you're as historically attuned as I try to be, running across the latest great car song is always an unexpected pleasure. Although in this case, it had its exasperating side, since I'd vowed not once but twice that there would be no further current records added to this book. But in mid 1988 I was listening to whatever was handy at 3:00 A.M. and slapped the new Billy Ocean on the box. The moment it opened, in the roar of a hot car's ignition system, the hook sank home, as Mutt Lange's production sprang into life—a rhythmically hotter brand of the approach he uses with hard rock acts like Foreigner and AC/DC.

To me, "Get Out Of My Dreams" also sounds like a new take on car songs. As a central pop music fantasy from "Maybellene" to "Thunder Road," cars have always represented freedom, especially freedom from responsibility. But Ocean twists the story: "Get out of my dreams, get into my car," he demands, "get out of my mind, get into my life." If he's still so trapped in the old myth structure that he proposes that the girl become his "Cinderella," while he becomes her "non-stop miracle," well, once he's got her in the car, that'll change. She'll see to it. And he seems to know it. And to like the idea.

340 JIM DANDY GOT MARRIED, LaVern Baker
Produced by Ahmet Ertegun and Jerry Wexler; written by Lincoln Chase, Tyrone Carlo, Alonzo Tucker, and Al Green
Atlantic 1136   1957   *Billboard: #76*

Surrealism is probably the most misused term in rock criticism, but "Jim Dandy Got Married," a sequel overshadowed by its predecessor, is the real thing.

In "Jim Dandy," a Top 20 hit for Baker in late 1956, Jim, a love man superhero undergoes several adventures of various degrees of unlikelihood. Not only is he brave enough to climb mountains and dive into the ocean for a distressed damsel, but he's a good kisser, too.

In "Jim Dandy Got Married," his problems begin with a hasty romance: He saves Mae, falls for her, gets hitched, and heads off on his honeymoon "the very same day." After our hero "swam the ocean in a suit of steel / With a sign sayin' love is real," his loving expertise drove Mae insane. She sued for nonsupport and the judge ruled in her favor, on the grounds that "Lovin' Mae is a full-time job." *Ubu Roi* has nothing on this story. And the dadaists couldn't dance.

341 YOU NEVER CAN TELL, Chuck Berry
Produced by Leonard Chess; written by Chuck Berry
Chess 1906   1964   *Billboard: #14*

Chuck returned from doing time on his trumped-up Mann Act charge in 1964 as if his flow of hits had never been interrupted. The new batch included two of his finest, "Promised Land" and "You Never Can Tell."

"You Never Can Tell" makes an obvious break with Berry's earlier format, not so much by prominently featuring Johnny Johnson's piano as by using it with a New Orleans-style beat.

Had prison altered Chuck's gifts in any way? Nah, he was bitter and hostile before he went in. And still a poet when he came out. How else explain: "They furnished off an apartment with a two-room Roebuck sale / The coolerator was jammed with teevee dinners and ginger ale." It may not read as great as it sings, but then, neither does the rhythm of everyday life.

342 CAN I GET A WITNESS, Marvin Gaye
Produced by Brian Holland and Lamont Dozier; written by Brian Holland, Lamont Dozier, and Eddie Holland
Tamla 54087   1963   *Billboard: #22*

Guess who was the preacher in the Chapel of Love? Sermon topic this week: "Is it right to be treated so bad / When you've given everything you've had?" Deacons Holland, Dozier, and Holland have arranged for accompanists that make you dance so hard you forget to care.

343 ANY DAY NOW, Chuck Jackson
Produced by Luther Dixon; written by Burt Bacharach and Bob Hilliard
Wand 122   1962   *Billboard: #23*

Chuck Jackson remains one of the most underrated soul singers, probably because his heyday came at none of the big R&B labels (Atlantic, Stax, Motown). In fact, Jackson did most of his best work from 1962 to 1965, the precise period that rock historians most often ignore (when they aren't denying its very creative existence).

Two years younger than Elvis, Jackson joined the Del-Vikings ("Come Go With Me") after leaving the Navy, and left soon after their biggest hit to go solo. During the several years of wandering in the

R&B wilderness that followed, he recorded for a handful of labels, including Atco, without placing anything on the national charts, pop, or R&B, although he built a chitlin' circuit following. Producer Luther Dixon (the Shirelles) found Jackson singing at the Apollo Theatre, and brought him to Florence Greenberg, who put him on Wand, a label he shared with "Louie Louie."

Greenberg's operation was as small-time as they come, but it did offer Chuck the opportunity to work with Dixon and with songwriter Burt Bacharach, who contributed "Any Day Now" in 1962, when Jackson had been more than a year between hits. Bacharach had cut the track the year before, but refused to let Greenberg use it for Tommy Hunt ("Human"), a much more lightweight singer. He used good judgment. It's the contrast between Jackson's gravelly voice and Bacharach's lightly syncopated rhythm bed that gives the record its energy.

In addition to a beautiful melody, the song opens with an organ riff (repeated in the bridge) that would figure prominently over the next few years in the development of folk-rock, serving as a motif in *Blonde on Blonde* and elsewhere. The fact that such a crucial link between eras and styles has been lying around unremarked for twenty-five years suggests the hidden treasures awaiting a reevaluation of the early sixties pop scene.

344 VOICE YOUR CHOICE, The Radiants
Produced by Phil Wright; written by Gerald Sims and Maurice McAlister
Chess 1904   1964   *Billboard:* #51

Maurice McAlister was the ultimate journeyman soul singer. Journeyman because what he did was a workmanlike adaptation to the circumstances of its production: The Chicago-produced "Voice Your Choice" sounds as much like the work of Curtis Mayfield as his other great side, the Muscle Shoals-made Maurice and Mac's "You Left the Water Running," resembles Sam and Dave. Ultimate because your ordinary journeyman is lucky to hit once with a record half as good as either of those.

McAlister's groups generally featured his Maurice and Mac partner, McLarin Green, except when Green was in the Army, in 1964. As the Radiants, McAlister had recorded as a quintet and a quartet but was operating a trio (featuring Wallace Simpson—not the Duchess of Windsor, the one who made the fine gospel-soul track, "Those Precious Words"—and Leonard Caston, later to become a journeyman producer/arranger/songwriter himself) when they made "Voice Your Choice," a really scintillating Impressions knockoff, right down to its muted brass.

The origins of the title are in the late-night Top 40 gimmick, in which the deejay would pit new records against one another, two at a time, playing each a couple of times in the course of the evening. Listeners were invited to call in to "Voice Your Choice," with each night's winner moving on to the next show's challenge and the Friday victor being added to the station's everyday playlist. It's a good stunt— it still crops up in a variety of guises—but nobody ever got such mileage from it as these guys do here. The singers switch the lead from line to line, their pleas rising and falling with varying amounts of tension and raunch. It's a terrific little record, and a good reminder that becoming a journeyman is an accomplishment not entirely to be denigrated.

345 STAY IN MY CORNER, The Dells
Produced by Bobby Miller; written by Bobby Miller, Barrett Strong, and Wade Flemons
Vee-Jay 674   1965   Did not make pop charts

The most legitimate request for a loyalty oath in the twentieth century. If a kiss can be an oath.

346 YOU'RE SO FINE, The Falcons
Produced by Robert West; written by Lance Finney and Willie Schofield
Unart 2013   1959   Billboard: #17

Led now by Joe Stubbs (Levi's brother, who later fronted the Contours), this pre-Pickett version of the Falcons also featured Mack Rice ("Mustang Sally" 's originator) and Eddie Floyd ("Knock on Wood," among others). Bass vocalist Willie Schofield isn't so well known, but he was among the finest ever to play that role.

"You're So Fine" is arguably the first soul hit. Although its production isn't much more elaborate than earlier R&B harmony records, and its trilling piano, mellow sax, and gutty guitar are pure blues; Stubbs's mournful lead and a suggestion of gospel in the melody are signs of things to come from similar groups at Motown. But Stubbs owed just as much to Detroit's tradition of crying singers, which included Little Willie John, Jackie Wilson, and Johnny Ray.

347 WALK ON BY, Dionne Warwick
Written and produced by Burt Bacharach and Hal David
Scepter 1274   1964   *Billboard:* #6

348 DO I LOVE YOU?, The Ronettes
Produced by Phil Spector; written by Phil Spector,
Vinnie Poncia, and Peter Andreoli
Philles 121   1964   *Billboard:* #34

In the spring of 1964, I bought these two singles. They weren't the first records I'd ever owned, but they felt like it.

It's hard to remember why, exactly. Maybe it was just that I spent my own money on them. Whatever, the real root of the story is what they sounded like, and what those sounds represented. They were a kind of music that seemed a secret, a kind of sound that it was somehow wrong to like too much or to take as seriously as whatever British stuff was in the air at the moment. In fact, at home that night, (the memory remains distinct) when "Don't Let the Sun Catch You Crying" came on the radio, it already seemed to me that if I'd only bought a Gerry and the Pacemakers single, life would have been easier and more normal.

Maybe it would have been. Or maybe there's somebody out there who's hip enough at fourteen to like what they like and not worry about what's cool, to understand that being able to hear the voices of black women speaking to you on the most personal terms is not only nothing to be ashamed of, but something that will absolutely change and enrich your life. But I wasn't that kid.

And maybe I wasn't even that smart. Because, come to think of it, what I hear in these records (which strike me now as pretty sophisticated choices for a teenager to make at a time when the airwaves were flooded with "Love Me Do," "A World Without Love," and "My Guy") isn't even the singing. It's the prettiness of the music, the lushness of the Ronettes' strings and tympani and Dionne's strings and Latin percussion and the little trumpet introjections, and the idea that "pretty" pop songs didn't all have to be as drab and predictable as a Muzak rendition of "Autumn Leaves," the childhood memory of which is as scarring as this one is uplifting.

Of the two records, the one that stays with me best is "Walk On By." Ronnie Spector's singing just doesn't wear as well, even with Phil surrounding her with another "Be My Baby"–style cathedral of sound.

On the other hand, Dionne Warwick remains a formidable pop

singer even as we enter the 1990s, yet "Walk On By" might still be the best record she ever made. Certainly it's the closest to straight R&B, thanks to the unending scratch guitar accompaniment and the girls in the background chanting "Don't. Stop."

Listening twenty-five years later, what these records have in common seems obvious. "Do I Love You" and "Walk On By" bracket romance; the Ronettes sing about their fantasy of how great it's going to be, Warwick confesses what a misery it's been. The link is that they're both about secrets, about confessing in utterly public terms the things that you can barely stand to admit to yourself: How deeply you need to be loved, how painful it is to feel that you aren't, the grief and struggle it takes just to say these things out loud. Hearing them now, back to back, doesn't make me feel like such a dumb kid after all. At the very least, I heard what I needed and brought it back home.

349 NEW YORK'S A LONELY TOWN, The Trade Winds

Written and produced by Vinnie Poncia and Peter Andreoli
Red Bird 020   1965   *Billboard:* #32

There were two kinds of surf music, vocal and instrumental. With some memorable exceptions ("Pipeline" and "Wipe Out"), most of the instrumentals never got heard outside the West Coast, so that a record that was a formative influence for California and Pacific Northwest acts ("Church Key" by the Revels for instance) was all but unknown in the East and the Midwest.

Conversely, vocal surf records by groups like Jan and Dean and the Beach Boys snatched most of their attention in places where surfing was impossible, or at least unlikely.

Peter Andreoli and Vinnie Poncia were from Rhode Island where a few lunatics hit beaches with vicious shore breaks on New Year's Day, but surfing is not exactly your number one pastime. But surf records were big in 1965 and Red Bird's Jerry Leiber and Mike Stoller hired Andreoli and Poncia (perhaps based on their experience writing "Do I Love You" and "The Best Part of Breakin' Up" for the Ronettes) to form a studio group and make a surf hit. Which they did. Sort of.

It's almost impossible today to believe that "New York's A Lonely Town" failed to make the Top Ten, for it seems like every kid who'd ever thrilled to a Beach Boys record and cursed his parents for bringing him up east of Pasadena immediately took the Trade Winds' falsetto harmonies and Brian Wilson-imitates-Phil Spector production style to heart.

Although what really grabbed all us teenage malcontents was at least as much the singer's snowbound self-pity.

350 (I KNOW) I'M LOSING YOU, The Temptations
Produced by Norman Whitfield; written by Norman Whitfield, Eddie Holland, and Cornelius Grant
Gordy 7057   1966   *Billboard:* #8

Another one of David Ruffin's virtually solo performances. Here, he's partnered mainly with the Funk Brothers (whose leader, keyboardist Earl Van Dyke, listed "I'm Losing You" among the group's half-dozen favorite sessions), though Eddie Kendricks gets off a bluesy falsetto "Losin' you" at the end of each chorus.

The real story, though, is the conflagration in the track, horns shrieking up out of a rhythm bed in a purely paranoiac display that anticipates "I Heard It Through the Grapevine," though more spaciously, without such cloying claustrophobia. Eddie Holland's lyric goes the same route, generating a feeling that the very air is full of the murderous toxins of jealousy.

351 SIXTY MINUTE MAN, Clarence Carter
Produced by Rick Hall and Clarence Carter; written by Clarence Carter
Fame 250   1973   *Billboard:* #65

In 1973, with deep Southern soul all but withered to a stump in the wake of its pop decline, Clarence Carter blasted back for one last great gust of sexual boasting. His takeoff on the title of Billy Ward's famous fifties hit of the same title substantially improves on the original, both as a salacious promise of enduring lust (partly by grafting on the theme of "Slip Away" as a subplot but mainly due to Carter's signature sound, an unmatchably leering "Heh, heh, heh") and as music, with a great Roger Hawkins backbeat, a neat, rolling guitar line and sharp, percussive horns. Hearing it on the radio back then, "Sixty Minute Man" felt like a lost classic. And now that's just what it is.

352 PLEDGING MY LOVE, Johnny Ace
Producer not credited; written by Fred Washington and
Don Robey
Duke 136   1955   *Billboard:* #17

Because "Pledging My Love" became a hit just after Ace ended his
life on Christmas Eve, 1954 while playing Russian roulette backstage
at Houston's City Auditorium, more people know about this vibes-
driven R&B ballad than have ever heard it. That's unfortunate, for
Ace was a fine blues crooner, influenced by Charles Brown and Nat
"King" Cole, the slickest of a group of rough-and-ready stylists who
came out of Memphis in the late forties, including Bobby Bland, B. B.
King, and Little Junior Parker. "Pledging My Love" is Ace's best
record, and its ethereal moodiness makes it haunting in the best sense
as well as the worst.

353 NOBODY BUT ME, The Human Beinz
Produced by Lex D. Azevedo; written by Rudolph Isley and
O'Kelly Isley
Capitol 5990   1967   *Billboard:* #8

354 THE MONKEY TIME, Major Lance
Produced by Carl Davis; written by Curtis Mayfield
OKeh 7174   1963   *Billboard:* #8

355 SHAKE, Sam Cooke
Produced by Hugo and Luigi; written by Sam Cooke
RCA 8486   1965   *Billboard:* #7

From time to time, someone moans in my direction "Rock and roll
is mostly dance music, y'know." To which I can only respond as
Bob Dylan's God once did: "You can believe what you want, Abe,
but . . ."

Having studied it long and deeply, my conviction is that rock and
roll is not mostly *anything*, other than black-rooted popular (mainly
vocal) music made in the late twentieth century. I lose all trust in the
critical intelligence of those who try to confine it more narrowly. (The
ones to really watch out for are those who deny its musicality: "It's

just noise, man. All that other stuff doesn't count." Yeah, and Babe Ruth was just a guy with a beer belly.) Usually, the *ad hominem* "mostly dance music" line is advanced by somebody with a stake in a group so inconsequential that demanding more than a strong beat from them would be like trying to suspend Newtonian physics (could happen, not likely in these environs) or by some batch of rockabilly purists to whom Grateful Dead fans could not shake their butts on Halloween.

However, it would be fatuous (not to mention futile) to deny that dancing is one of the activities with which rock and roll most frequently concerns itself. Dancing standing up recurs in rock songs with such frequency that it's really quite amazing that nobody's ever written anything very good about it.

And I don't mean the phenomena surrounding it, I mean the thing itself. You can learn more about the theory and practice of dancing to pop music by watching *Saturday Night Fever* than by reading all of the rock history, criticism, and sociology for which trees have ever died. Not to let myself off the self-baited hook, I gotta confess I've never done the basic research even to recognize the four dance steps that the Human Beinz sing about in "Nobody But Me": Shingaling, Skate, Boogaloo, Philly. Clubfooted wallflower that I am, that's no surprise. But *somebody* ought to go back and get the facts.

"Nobody But Me," like "The Monkey Time" and "Shake," emerged from a context in which there were dances not only with names but with steps, codified ways of moving around on the floor. Generally, these dances took place with partners but the couples didn't necessarily move in tandem. The Twist, which Chubby Checker and Dick Clark pushed to Number One, was the first formal dance in which the focus was entirely on *individual* expression. (The most atomized, and boring, dance of all was the Limbo, which could only have been invented by a sadistic entertainment director at a Caribbean resort. Amnesty International is reportedly investigating several such cases even now.) By 1962, when the Isley Brothers cut the original "Nobody But Me," a record lacking any of the ferocity that makes the Human Beinz' version so great, dancing was seen as nothing less than a means to one of the great religious goals of American consumer society: self-fulfillment. "I got a thing I do, ain't nobody do it but me, babe," brag the Human Beinz and it's emblematic of the changes underfoot (so to speak) that this citation retained its value for five years across some of the most sweeping changes pop music has ever seen. Many things about "Nobody But Me" seem dated today, but that line seems as Now as the two seconds of droning feedback with which the record opens.

This new attitude metastasized so that by the summer of 1963, no less a pop philosopher than Curtis Mayfield was compelling his protege,

Major Lance, to declare: "Now you get yours, 'cause I got mine / It's Monkey Time." Nothing there that the tax evaders at Studio 54 would find objectionable. And while it's hard to imagine putting gospel call-and-response to more profane purpose, the interplay among the muted cornet, Lance's yearning voice, and the drums (could this be that master percussionist/solipsist Maurice White?) will persuade you to forgive all of them everything.

Sam Cooke helped put an end to dances with names and steps. His dance tune—his first and biggest posthumous hit—concerned the Shake, a dance that looked more like a Jell-O ad than a recognizable series of moves. Only eighteen months before, Major Lance was hectoring, "Now twist them hips, let your backbone slip." But trying to be instructive concerning the Shake reduced even the great Sam Cooke to dance-floor dadaism. "Shake it like a bowl of soup"—could even a pairing of Marcel Duchamp and Yoko Ono have deciphered that one? (Well, it'd be worth the price of admission to see 'em try.)

With its grafting of Motown horns to a rhumbalike beat, Cooke's "Shake!" could be understood simply as an imperative to move, which is how Otis Redding reads it on *Live in Europe*. Which, give or take a Hustle here and a Bump there, is mostly how people have grooved out on the floor ever since.

356 I GOTTA DANCE TO KEEP FROM CRYING, The Miracles

Produced by Brian Holland and Lamont Dozier; written by
Brian Holland, Lamont Dozier, and Eddie Holland
Tamla 54089   1963   *Billboard*: #35

Smokey Robinson wrote such great love songs that it's easy to forget that he also wrote great dance music. "I Gotta Dance to Keep from Crying" marks the place where his two styles come together: Its back-beat is as tough as "Mickey's Monkey," but Smokey sings as sad and sweet as he does on "The Love I Saw in You was Just a Mirage." And no band ever cut a deeper groove than the Motown gang does here; it's pure soul right down to the handclaps on the offbeat.

Not that Smokey neglects poetry. I mean, "Gather 'round you swingers and friends / Help me forget my hurt again"—that's what Randy Newman's spent his whole career not quite being able to say, right?

357 GOIN' BACK, The Byrds

Produced by Gary Usher; written by Gerry Goffin and Carole King
Columbia 44362   1967   *Billboard:* #89

In the context of the Summer of Love, "Goin' Back" was a brilliant anomaly. Today, it's an evocation of a spirit that was elusive even then, an expression of tender regret for an innocence that, once lost, can barely be fathomed as anything other than a phantasm.

Yet with Roger McGuinn's signature twelve-string tolling like a Pied Piper, Goffin and King's marvelous melody and the Byrds' inimitable postfolk harmonies (and a cello, among other things, lurking in the mix), "Goin' Back" may be the last great expression of what was truly indelible about the psychedelic daze. There's something more than halfway pathetic about its catchphrase: "A little bit of courage is all we lack / So catch me if you can, I'm goin' back." But "Goin' Back," with its evocations of sailboats in a pond and other childhood pleasures, its pretensions to finding wisdom only in childish pursuits, its entire attempt to deny aging and the value of adulthood, genuinely reflects what the period was all about. And for many whose musical tastes came of age in that period, it may well be what rock and roll is all about, as well. In a far more sour world, it's easy to dismiss lines like "I can recall a time when I wasn't ashamed to reach out to a friend." But maybe cynicism in the face of such faith is unwise. If someone could write such a song today, it would reflect well on the world. (Of course, if someone did write such a song today, they'd deserve to be locked up.)

To tell you the truth, I never even knew whether they were singing that "every day can be a magic carpet ride" or "every day *can't* be." What counted was the atmosphere of the music, which is so rich and complex that either reading is plausible depending on the mood in which you're listening. Which is why I don't want to know which reading is "correct," just to be given the opportunity to listen and in the process, feel out what's right this time. And that, too, is very much in the spirit of its day.

358 BACK STABBERS, The O'Jays

Produced by Kenneth Gamble and Leon Huff; written by
Leon Huff, Gene McFadden, and John Whitehead
Philadelphia International 3517. 1972   *Billboard:* #3

Like the early sixties, the first couple of years of the seventies are an
as-yet-unrecognized storehouse of musical creativity. Black music was
especially rich as disco and funk took shape, not only through the
experimentalism of Marvin Gaye, Stevie Wonder, Sly Stone, James
Brown, and Curtis Mayfield but even in the more direct and traditional
records made by the Philadelphia International factory organized behind Kenneth Gamble and Leon Huff.

The O'Jays, R&B journeymen who'd charted ten singles in the
sixties without ever cracking the pop Top 50, served as Gamble and
Huff's best vehicle during this period. (The production team had made
good records previously with the Intruders, Jerry Butler and Archie
Bell, and the Drells.) Gamble and Huff didn't change much about the
O'Jays; the beat was heavily orchestrated, but it hadn't yet reached the
steady thump-thump-thump of PI's hard disco period, and horns and
guitars color the arrangement much more freely than they later would.
The result is a perfect backdrop for the group's harmonies and Eddie
Levert's throaty gospel-based lead.

"A few of your buddies they shore look shady / Friends all alone
with a knife in their fist / Aimin' straight at your back and I don't think
they'll miss," Levert cries. In the summer that Richard Nixon's dirty
tricks brigade stole an election, one guy trying to fend off the vultures
hovering near his girlfriend as their relationship goes through a rocky
period was the perfect metaphor. As it floated off the radio between
news reports, the emotional connection between the two forms of betrayal could not have been clearer if the lovers had been named Pat
and Dick. Neither Gamble and Huff nor the O'Jays were looking for
such a metaphor. Just as clearly, the majority of their listeners never
consciously thought about the record in terms of Watergate. But in the
intoxicating swirl of the O'Jays' rhythms, you can still feel the tension
a nation experienced as its confidence in political stability momentarily
disintegrated.

359 (SWEET SWEET BABY) SINCE YOU'VE BEEN GONE, Aretha Franklin

Produced by Jerry Wexler; written by Aretha Franklin and Ted White
Atlantic 2486   1968   *Billboard:* #5

You could talk about "Since You've Been Gone" as a clinic put on by the world's greatest singer to show how to extract the maximum meaning and energy from a meaningless phrase (in this case, "Baby, baby, sweet baby"). If you look at the price of the record as tuition, that's not even a metaphor. Or you could just gape in awe at the deadly propulsion of Tommy Cogbill's bass line, which completes not just musical phrases but Aretha's very thoughts, often far better than mere words ever could.

360 IT HURTS TO BE IN LOVE, Gene Pitney

Producer not credited; written by Howard Greenfield and
Helen Miller
Musicor 1040   1964   *Billboard:* #7

I don't know which East Coast genius does the drumming here—it could be Gary Chester, Buddy Salzman, Panama Francis, or Bernard Purdie—but whoever it is, nobody east of Hal Blaine ever played with a greater balance of power and discipline. For sheer earthquake force, not even Keith Moon or John Bonham top what happens here.

But the power would go to waste without a Pitney performance that's a coequal tower of strength. Although his talent was too polished and direct for apostles of Rebel Rock (even though he wrote "He's a Rebel"), Pitney remains among the most underrated figures of the sixties. Like Roy Orbison's, his influence wasn't fully felt until the eighties, when more ornate styles of singing and arranging became fashionable, but in today's pop context, his truly visionary studio confections can finally be appreciated.

361 BLACK PEARL, Sonny Charles and the Checkmates Ltd.
Produced by Phil Spector; written by Phil Spector, Irwin Levine, and Toni Wine
A&M 1053   1969   *Billboard:* #13

"Black Pearl," not the wildly overrated "River Deep Mountain High," is Phil Spector's last great record. And leave it to Spector to use as his vehicle a multiracial lounge act, who would never make another truly memorable record, singing a song that expropriates black power rhetoric (the singer's lover must work as a servant) to celebrate transcendent romance (he vows to place her on a pedestal). Hardly anyone else would have thought of it, few would have had the nerve to try to pull it off, and only Spector could have converted the damn thing into music that's touching, even exciting.

362 TAKE TIME TO KNOW HER, Percy Sledge
Produced by Marlin Greene and Quin Ivy; written by Steve Davis
Atlantic 2490   1968   *Billboard:* #11

Not nearly so famous as "When a Man Loves a Woman," but then when it comes to romance, the plain truth has never been nearly so attractive (to anyone, including me) as a slick pack of lies. Certainly, between the two, "Take Time to Know Her" is by far the more adult perspective. God knows, it's more useful.

Here's the plot: The singer meets a girl, thinks she's wonderful, proposes, then takes her home to his mother; she says, Percy, you don't know this girl well enough, you better . . . Percy says forget it, takes his darlin' to the church. Preacher takes one look at 'em together, says, son, you better . . . "Well, it looked like everything was gonna turn out all right," Percy intones in his finest soul-wimp accent, "And then I came home a little early one night." If you grew up in the America of soap operas and true confessions magazines, you can fill in the rest.

Percy Sledge is one of about two singers in the history of rock and roll (hell, maybe Western civilization) who could get away with telling a tale this corny. The other one is Roy Orbison but Roy could never have played it straight for so many verses; he'd have succumbed to an anxiety attack the minute Mom got suspicious. Percy, in contrast, genuinely seems not to suspect what's going to happen until the very end,

even though everybody else involved in Muscle Shoals music-making—
especially the organist—catches on from the first note.

363 GIVE ME JUST A LITTLE MORE TIME, The Chairmen of the Board

Produced by Brian Holland, Lamont Dozier, and Eddie Holland; written
by Ronald Dunbar and Edythe Wayne [Holland-Dozier-Holland]
Invictus 9074   1970   *Billboard:* #3

One of Italo Calvino's final stories literally takes place in the mouths
of a couple whose relationship is on the rocks. If anybody's ever crazy
enough to film it, "Give Me Just a Little More Time" will necessarily
dominate the soundtrack, because General Johnson takes greater advantage of the cavities, declivities, and smooth surfaces of the inner
mouth than any singer since Billy Stewart. Groaning, rasping, and
trilling, Johnson sings like a man strangled by love, his passion choked
and coughed from unwilling lungs. As leader of the Showmen a decade
earlier, he'd declared that rock and roll would stand. Here, he shows
why.

364 DELIRIOUS, Prince

Written and produced by Prince
Warner Bros. 29503   1983   *Billboard:* #8

Intoxicating. And so damned self-descriptive it's virtually impossible
to know what to add. Except that nobody, but nobody, has ever made
synthesizer music that swings this hard.

365 HE WILL BREAK YOUR HEART, Jerry Butler

Produced by Calvin Carter; written by Calvin Carter,
Jerry Butler, and Curtis Mayfield
Vee Jay 354   1960   *Billboard:* #7

Teenage partners in the Impressions, Jerry Butler and Curtis Mayfield
split when Vee Jay decided to promote their first hit, "For Your Precious Love," as a Butler single, rather than co-headlining the group.
But two years later, they reunited on the road and during a drive from
Philadelphia to Atlantic City, wrote "He Will Break Your Heart."
    Butler told Vince Aletti in 1969 that he based the song on early

groupie experiences: "You go into a town; you're only gonna be there for one night; you want some company; you find a girl; you blow her mind. Now you know this girl hasn't been sittin' in that town waitin' for you to come in. She probably has another fellow and the other fellow's probably in love with her; they're probably planning to go through the whole thing, right? But you never take that into consideration on that particular night. You're lonesome, you want company; she's available or she's there and, you know . . ."

It hardly would have served Butler and Mayfield's purpose to write an overt apology. Instead, they wrote "from the standpoint of the guy that's in town all the time and that's been lovin' this girl for years and years." The resulting essay on innocence wronged has the sad-eyed lilt of a male girl group record.

Interestingly, Butler and Mayfield once again sang harmony—on the basis of the chorus, Mayfield was as entitled to a duet credit as much as, say, Dave Prater or Bobby Hatfield often were. And since Curtis also contributed the song's driving guitar part, which is the central figure in the arrangement, his claim seems especially strong. But by then, he must have been persuaded that his best move was just biding his time. And it paid off, a year later with "Gypsy Woman," followed by thirty-two other pop chart entries.

366 BRING IT ON HOME TO ME, Sam Cooke
Produced by Hugo and Luigi; written by Sam Cooke
RCA 8036　1962　　*Billboard:* #13

You want to know why the gospel music community felt ripped off when church-based stars like Cooke began exiting in the fifties? It wasn't just because the aesthetic purity of their music had been sullied. "Bring It on Home to Me" is pure gospel, even if it does have strings, a sultry sax and a country-western piano. It's gospel because of Cooke's melisma and the way he and background vocalist Lou Rawls pattern their call-and-response. But that wouldn't have been so bad, if the new wave of gospel-trained pop singers hadn't also stolen from gospel its poetry, whence stems so much of its power. From a fundamentalist Christian point of view, "Bring It On Home to Me" actively blasphemes, for Cooke declares himself a slave of love rather than a slave of God, and compounds the felony by using hymnal imagery to put the idea across.

367 WHO'S MAKING LOVE, Johnnie Taylor
Produced by Don Davis; written by Homer Banks,
Bettye Crutcher, Don Davis, and Al Jackson
Stax 0009   1968   *Billboard:* #5

In a way, "Who's Making Love" is just another cautionary cheating song, of the sort common in both R&B and C&W, in which the singer reminds us that sauce for both goose and gander can be cooked in the same bed. But the collaboration between Taylor and producer Don Davis makes it something special.

Taylor had the usual Southern soul singer's background. Born in Crawford, Arkansas, just across the Mississippi from Memphis, which is Delta blues country, he sang first in gospel quartets, eventually joining the Soul Stirrers as Sam Cooke's hand-picked replacement. It was also Cooke who brought him out of gospel into pop. Although Taylor started out as a Cooke acolyte, his mature style had little in common with his mentor's. The rasp at the edges of Sam's style was the center of Johnnie's; his Stax records were studies in raw Memphis grit.

But until he began working with Don Davis, they never got him past the boundaries of the R&B world. Davis came to Stax from Detroit and his production approach was heavily affected by the Motown-style pop-soul synthesis. Virtually every element of "Who's Makin' Love" is classic Stax but Davis adds just enough pop touches: The female chorus is pure Motown and the horns are also given some Detroit figures to cut before resolving back to their basic "These Arms of Mine" riff.

The result is just about a perfect blend of Southern and Northern soul, a record that defines a direction in which either Stax or Motown might have developed productively, if their separate forms of parochialism hadn't brought them down.

368 GOIN' OUT OF MY HEAD, Little Anthony and the Imperials
Produced by Teddy Randazzo; written by Teddy Randazzo
and Bobby Weinstein
DCP 1119   1964   *Billboard:* #6

The male Dionne Warwick, on the verge of hysteria.

369 SMOKEY JOE'S CAFE, The Robins
Written and produced by Jerry Leiber and Mike Stoller
Atco 6059   1955   *Billboard: #79*

What's unflagging about even the earliest records produced by Jerry Leiber and Mike Stoller is their musicality, the harmonies and time changes and bold arrangements, the sizzling sax riffs and biting guitar accompaniment. Even the handclaps purposefully advance the basic thrust of their best songs.

Leiber and Stoller were among the first to understand that making music for records meant making music on different terms than the stage-oriented standards of Tin Pan Alley, Broadway, and Hollywood. Even their early hits, like "Hound Dog" and "Kansas City," exhibit an awareness of these needs, and it's the essence of the records they made with the Coasters. When those records work ("Yakety Yak," "That Is Rock & Roll," and "Searchin' " are the greatest examples), their expropriation of black and teenage argot and imagery is flawlessly integrated into the songs. What might have been aural gimmickry in other hands is so finely focused that it seems organic.

"Smokey Joe's Cafe" isn't (quite) the Coasters, but it established the Leiber-Stoller playlet format and the Robins were the Coasters' literal predecessors, contributing their two most talented singers, lead Carl Gardner and comic bass Bobby Nunn, to the new group. The Robins had two similar R&B hits, "Riot in Cell Block Number Nine" (sung by "Louie Louie" composer Richard Berry), and "Framed," but "Smokey Joe's Cafe" is funnier and funkier than either.

Originally recorded for Spark Records, Leiber and Stoller's own Los Angeles-based label, "Smokey Joe's Cafe" depicts a tough-as-nails beanery with a toothsome female waitress and a lethally possessive owner. The comedy is set up by Gardner's quavering lead, accentuated by goofy guitar riffs, a single gloomy bass introjection from Nunn and a wild sax break that begins on an impossibly elongated phrase and ends in sonorous harmony with the riffing voices. By the time it's done, just singing the title phrase is worth a laugh, but without succumbing to the low "Amos 'n' Andy" comedy of "Charlie Brown."

370 THE WORLD IS A GHETTO, War
Produced by Jerry Goldstein, Lonnie Jordan, and
Howard Scott; written by Papa Dee Allen, Harold Brown,
Morris Dickerson, Lonnie Jordan, Charles Miller, Lee Oskar, and
Howard Scott
United Artists 50975   1972   Billboard: #7

Maybe War learned its style of political agitation from working with
Eric Burdon, but its sense of the world as one big, powerful prison
definitely came directly from the streets of L.A. As did its powerful
bass lines, creaking guitars, sweet 'n' smoggy vocals (War had the best
singers of any funk band), waves of percussion—everything but Lee
Oskar's pungent harmonica, a Scandinavian import. And it's the solidity
of that sense of place—Los Angeles not as an enlarged anonymous
suburb, as it is often perceived by outsiders, but as the home of millions
of black, brown, and white people, stuck together in a cauldron where
they cannot melt—that helps make the sound, the song, and the people
who crafted it internationally relevant.

371 KEEP SEARCHIN' (WE'LL FOLLOW THE SUN), Del Shannon
Produced by Harry Balk and Irving Micahnik; written by Del Shannon
Amy 915   1964   Billboard: #9

372 SWEET CHILD O'MINE, Guns 'n' Roses
Produced by Mike Clink; written by Guns 'n' Roses
Geffen 27963   1988   Billboard: #1 (2 weeks)

When Ann Arbor disc jockey Ollie McLaughlin discovered Del Shannon singing in a Battle Creek club, the singer was already twenty-one
years old, and he looked and sounded like a full-fledged adult. Yet the
themes of Shannon's best songs are central to adolescence: fantasies of
flight from nameless, shadowy pursuers whose means and motives continually slip beyond the singer's ken. "Keep Searchin' " twists the
theme, not in its plot—Del and his baby still find themselves on the
lam—but because even though the echoing handclaps, organ wash, and
Del's own keening high notes create Shannon's prototypical edgy paranoia, the song never relinquishes its promise of a sanctuary somewhere.

That search for shelter is the obverse side of rock's reach for rebellion. It's not a pure opposition, because one of the ways in which

rebellion becomes most meaningful is in its suggestion of what a place of comfort might feel like. In a sense, that hope of rest and reconciliation remains rock's greatest hidden theme.

Why isn't this impulse more often acknowledged, let alone honored? Maybe because accepting that the music contains a longing for sanctuary as powerful as its lust for action means reaching unfashionable conclusions about culture and about people.

For instance, contemporary heavy metal-style groups like Guns 'n' Roses aren't supposed to be taken seriously in the same way as singer/songwriters or heartland rockers or British pop stars. Indeed, the fundamental sexism and generalized vulgarity of such acts ought to be offputting. Boasting of their sexual conquests, their chemical intake, ostentatiously diminishing their musical sophistication, isn't just an act—these guys really are pretty fucked up. So even though Guns 'n' Roses guitarist Slash (like Edward Van Halen before him) comes up with some of the great guitar riffs, it's unimaginable that his music could be as rich in meaning as say, Tracy Chapman's.

But it is, and you don't even have to probe very deeply to hear it. Slash's melodic opening solo in "Sweet Child O'Mine" establishes the record as an elegy—an ode to lost innocence, and a spur to the quest to recover that feeling. Coming from musicians whose lives are boastfully and prolifically wasted, addressed to an audience that's equally desperate, abandoned, and isolated, "Sweet Child O'Mine" has the enormous power of the simple promises extended from one kid to another: Confidences will be kept, feelings respected, hopes and dreams preserved in privacy.

The lyrics refer with a recurrence akin to confession to what's lost to childhood: "Her hair reminds me of a warm sweet place where as a child I'd hide / And pray for the thunder and the rain to quietly pass me by." In such phrases, "Sweet Child O'Mine" speaks to a new generation of kids and housewives—the latchkey generation, the children who basically raised each other. For those who've suffered such an upbringing, those lines are as eloquent—if not as "poetic"—as anything Joni Mitchell ever wrote, and you don't have to wear tattoos to know it.

373 THERE IS SOMEONE IN THIS WORLD FOR ME, Little Willie John

Produced by Henry Glover; written by Darlynn Bonner
King 5577   1958   Did not make pop chart

With its jump blues background and single-string guitar riff, "There is Someone in This World for Me" was archaic in the rhythm and blues world of 1958 and utterly alien to that year's Top 40. (Yet not nearly as archaic and alien as the B side, a spectral version of the standard "Autumn Leaves.")

Willie John couldn't be bothered worrying about that sort of thing. He was too busy writing another significant chapter in the epic of his reign as King of Romantic Desolation. In the process, he put Phil Spector and his acolytes to shame, by using for echo no chamber more elaborate than his small but mighty chest.

374 ONE SUMMER NIGHT, The Danleers

Producer not credited; written by Danny Webb
Mercury 71322   1958   *Billboard: #7*

In a great doo-wop record, you can always feel how the weather was, the place and time. That's because, in great doo-wop records, it's always just before midnight in mid-July, the moon is always full and you're always parked in a carefully selected lonesome spot with the person you've most longed for. On "One Summer Night," Jimmy Weston's shimmering, near-falsetto lead fills in the details, physical and emotional, not as they were but as they should have been.

375 LOVE CHILD, The Supremes

Produced by Berry Gordy, Frank Wilson, Hank Cosby, Deke Richards, and R. Dean Taylor; written by Pam Sawyer, R. Dean Taylor, Frank Wilson, and Deke Richards
Motown 1135   1968   *Billboard: #1 (2 weeks)*

Diana Ross is anything but Motown's finest singer, and that's exactly why "Love Child" is her finest hour. For once, it's the very impoverishment of her voice that makes her credible, because she's singing a song that epitomizes Motown as the voice of the upwardly mobile black bourgeoisie: "No child of mine will be wearin' / The name of shame I've been bearin'."

The music, as always, rescues the histrionic excesses of the lyric. Those cries of "Tenement slum!" (perfectly cadenced doo-wop phrase that it is) would be unintentionally side-splitting except that the band—especially the drummer—makes you feel so intensely the potency of the predestination Diana is determined to deny. Among teenage virgin numbers, "Love Child" ranks somewhere below "Maybe" and "Will You Still Love Me Tomorrow." Among get-me-outta-this-ghetto hits, it's an easy Number One.

376 I'M A MAN, Bo Diddley
Produced by Leonard Chess; written by Ellas McDaniel
[Bo Diddley]
Checker 814   1955   Did not make pop chart

The essential beat personified. But you know about that. As usual with Bo, the untold half of the story lies in his manipulation and modernization of Delta blues imagery. Given the opportunity to come North and live in the city, John the Conqueroo and his cohorts functioned like an art virus, inhabiting as ghosts the music of men and women who worshipped them (the Yardbirds) or never heard of them (the Sex Pistols) or preferred to imagine they were doing something else (Steely Dan). As an influence, this makes Bo the Typhoid Mary of the genre. Or maybe the Faust.

377 SALLY GO 'ROUND THE ROSES, The Jaynetts
Produced by Abner Spector; written by Zell Sanders and Lona Spector
Tuff 369   1963   Billboard: #2

Spookiest and most exotic of all girl group discs, "Sally Go 'Round the Roses" also has one of the oddest production stories. Its slinky beat and turbulent piano—in fact, all the instrumentation except the single guitar—link it unmistakably to Phil Spector's Wall of Sound, and no doubt many, glancing at the credits, have come to the conclusion that Abner Spector was one of Phil's occasional pseudonyms.

Abner Spector wasn't even a Phil Spector relative. He came from Chicago's Tuff Records and went to New York to hook up with Zell Sanders, of J&S Records, thinking she might have a line on a girl group. Zell not only had a group, she had a song. According to legend, pianist Artie Butler (who, like Phil but not Abner Spector, had understudied with Leiber and Stoller) played everything on the record but that guitar. Butler went on to arrange most of the Shangri-Las' hits for Shadow Morton, so the story's at least plausible enough to pass along.

Zell Sanders's song operates as a metaphor, but its message is murky as week-old gossip. Superficially, Sally's friends are just warning her against going downtown, because there she'll find the "saddest thing in the whole wide world," her baby with another girl. But the mix and arrangement and the odd metaphor of the endlessly repeated chorus ("Sally, go 'round the roses / They won't tell your secret") lend the entire production an ominous air, as if some deeper tale waits to be told.

A quarter century later, after endless spins, it's no closer to being revealed.

378 YOU'RE A WONDERFUL ONE, Marvin Gaye
Produced by Brian Holland and Lamont Dozier; written by Brian Holland, Lamont Dozier, and Eddie Holland
Tamla 54093   1964   *Billboard:* #15

There are those who believe that Motown's music was a species similar to but musically distinct from rock and roll. Wonder how they explain guitarist Robert White playing "Memphis" here? That deep, biting backbeat descends from Chuck Berry just as naturally as anything the Rolling Stones ever did, and in this particular case, there isn't even much more filligree—a couple of girls in the background, a tambourine working off Benny Benjamin's powerhouse backbeat, a few brass riffs to punctuate the transition from verse to chorus.

The lyrics are another question. Gaye was probably too headstrong to be the ideal Holland-Dozier-Holland act, but from time to time, their teaming clicked with image-defining records: "How Sweet It Is (To Be Loved By You)," "Can I Get a Witness," "Baby Don't You Do It," "Little Darling I Need You." None more so than "Wonderful One," a song which might be sung by his fans to Marvin, so perfectly does it describe the intensity he brought to his music and the solace we took away. "It makes my burden a little bit lighter, makes my life a little bit brighter," he shouts and the natural response, whether you've had gospel training or not, is to stand up and testify, shout "It's true" and fall into the aisle.

379 THE BELLS, Billy Ward and the Dominoes
Produced by Ralph Bass; written by Billy Ward and
Rose Marks
Federal 12114   1953   Did not make pop chart

They call the kind of crooning lead singing that men like Clyde Mc-Phatter did in harmony groups like the Dominoes "crying," but nobody else ever took it as literally as Clyde did in this bizarre variation on the Huck Finn theme of attending your own funeral. The record consists entirely of a histrionic Clyde weeping and shrieking his way through an almost too-vivid description of a ghetto funeral. Today, the record seems more eerie because McPhatter died young in 1972, when he was only thirty-nine.

380 CRYING IN THE CHAPEL, Orioles
No producer credited; written by Artie Glenn
Jubilee 5122   1953   Did not make pop charts

The Orioles don't really do anything but a few harmony figures behind lead voice Sonny Til but this gentle, lovely spiritual ballad impressed enough teenagers to kick off a long-running craze for vocal harmony quartets named after birds, which is why rock and roll history is pop-ulated by so many Robins, Wrens, Crows, Falcons, and Flamingos.

Til never again came close to the quality of this record, because this is one case where what counts is the *song*, as evidenced by Elvis's grand 1965 remake. The concept of both song and arrangement stems from the fundamentalist churches (songwriter Darrell Glenn was white, but the interchange between black and white Pentecostals has always been great) but the connections to gospel music are tenuous, at best; any of the great gospel quartets—especially Claude Jeter's Dixie Hum-mingbirds, the bird group that inspired the Orioles—bettered both song and record half a dozen times. In fact, the Orioles harken to the pre-gospel tradition of jubilee quartets, a smoother, less testifying blend of spiritual harmony. Pop wouldn't catch up to the gospel quartets until the sixties, when the Temptations and other multilead soul groups took over Top 40 by preaching on secular themes.

381 HEARTACHES BY THE NUMBER, Ray Price
Produced by Don Law; written by Harlan Howard
Columbia 41374   1959   Did not make pop charts

It's nearly impossible to remember a time when country music this traditional—that is, this *Southern*—still had a place within the pop spectrum. Already archaic in 1959, "Heartaches" is a C&W classic: Price's booming Texas accent floating in an ocean of echo, steel guitars skidding into fiddles, a lyric that combines dripping sentimentality, songmill gimmickry, and real inspiration.

382 DAY TRIPPER, The Beatles
Produced by George Martin; written by John Lennon and Paul McCartney
Capitol 5555   1965   *Billboard:* #5

Only the Beatles could have tossed a track this hot on a B side, just as only they could have seen it reach the Top Five anyway. While "We Can Work It Out" (the A side) is a very fine McCartney ballad, I'll take Paul's playing and singing here over his singing and playing there. He never cut a deeper bass groove, just as Ringo never played funkier, and George's guitar never zoomed so sharply. Lennon's contribution is a harmony vocal that doubles the lead after the bridge (a "Twist and Shout" replica), and doubles the song's level of invective in the process. But mostly, what we're hearing here is the Beatles as a groove-oriented rock and roll band, the oldest trick in their book, now fused with their impeccable sense of studio craftsmanship. That Otis Redding chose "Day Tripper" as the Beatles song in his set is no surprise; it's the closest they ever came to making a soul record.

383 THE LONELY SURFER, Jack Nitzsche
Produced by Jimmy Bowen; written by Marty Cooper and Jack Nitzsche
Reprise 20202   1963   *Billboard:* #39

How can orchestral surf music qualify as great rock and roll? Well, the guitar is straight out of Dick Dale, and anyway, it's all part of a continuum that leads ultimately to the Who's horn voicings on *Tommy*.

384 WHAT AM I LIVING FOR, Chuck Willis
Produced by Zenas Sears; written by Chuck Willis
Atlantic 1179   1958   *Billboard: #9*

By the time "What Am I Living For" hit the charts (with "Hang Up My Rock and Roll Shoes" on the flip), Willis no longer was, having expired from an untreated stomach ailment. That's supposed to be ironic, and as an opponent of ironic inflation, it's incumbent upon me to point out that the record actually acquires its stature from a laconic melody topped by an exceedingly mellow sax and a grand vocal in Willis's prototypical dry rasp. If there's irony at work here, its genuine value is in showing us how eloquent a man can be as he nears the end of his days.

385 RUNNING ON EMPTY, Jackson Browne
Written and produced by Jackson Browne
Asylum 45460   1978   *Billboard: #11*

386 ROLL ME AWAY, Bob Seger
Produced by Jimmy Iovine; written by Bob Seger
Capitol 5235   1983   *Billboard: #27*

"Running on Empty" and "Roll Me Away" serve as generational anthems for a whole crowd of people who found the seventies and early eighties increasing both their material riches and spiritual impoverishment. They meet in the middle of mainstream (nonpunk) rock trends of the period, Browne appearing as the most fecund California singer/songwriter, Seger as the anguished embodiment of Midwestern rock. What makes the dialogue between these records more arresting is that each appeared at a moment of transition for its creator, a time when populist Seger was heading for ultraprivate concerns and the comparatively cloistered singer/songwriter Browne began to test the social limits of his personal vision.

I feel this connection strongly because it was Bob Seger who clued me in to "Running on Empty" 's finest line: "I look around for the friends that I used to turn to to pull me through / Lookin' into their eyes, I see them runnin' too." And though Waddy Wachtel's excessively wailing guitar seems more dated every year, it's hard to think of another record that speaks so forthrightly to and about a world that was disintegrating before its own eyes in a cycle of denial and repression that took the shape of rampant hedonism. "Running on Empty" is the title track of an album that winds down with a tribute to cocaine. Today, hearing the lyric that Seger's acute ear picked up so quickly, I think of a roster of Browne's friends that might include Lowell George, who overdosed and died, Warren Zevon, rehabbed and rehabbed and held together with main human strength and raw talent, and David Crosby, surviving massive cocaine addiction through a period of imprisonment but ballooned to three hundred pounds in compensation. In that crowd, "Running on Empty" was less a metaphor than a prophesy, a post-Woodstock "Dead Man's Curve."

"Everyone I know, everywhere I go / People need some reason to believe," Browne sings. And then, in the most pained voice he's ever used, he stops and shouts: "I don't know about anyone but me!" It's a cry that defines the period and Browne has spent the rest of his career trying to resolve the contradiction it expresses.

When the Selfish Seventies drew to a close, things got worse, not better. For a performer as devoted to both craft and populist insight as Bob Seger, the situation was worse than confusing. Beyond what was happening in a world run by Reagans and Thatchers and in a music scene overpopulated with art students perfectly comfortable in their contempt for the mass audience, there was a purely personal level on which it grew ever harder to walk the line between high energy Detroit rock and roll and the facts of a fortyish existence.

"Roll Me Away" speaks to all these things through the story of a cross-country motorcycle trip, rumbling from Mackinac City, the Hiawatha village where Lake Michigan converges with Lake Huron, to the Continental Divide. Along the way, Seger finds a love and lets it dissipate, turns alone into the cold winds of the Rockies and lets his frustrations and confusion congeal into one sad cry that dissolves his fate into what has happened to the whole crazy mess of a world in which he lives. He vows to keep moving, rolling away, rolling away, promises that he can straighten everything out so long as the search never ceases—so long as he never rests. And then pulls the trigger on the joke. "And as the sunset faded I spoke to the famous first starlight," Seger sings, in a perfect parody of the Saturday afternoon westerns that inspired him, "I said next time—next time—we'll get it right."

It's Roy Bittan's elegiac piano chords that tell the bitter truth. The time for roving is over. It's time to settle in, time for America to abandon its gluttonous expansionism, time for the wild boys of rock and roll to come indoors and call what they find there home. (It's what happens *after* the last scene of John Ford's *The Searchers*.)

Seger's more recent records have been bland, the lyrics glossing over issues he used to penetrate, the music too often nothing more than highly crafted country-pop. Browne has thrown himself into a virtually full-time commitment to opposing U.S. intervention in Central America; his more recent songs abandon psychological complexities for agit-prop that, no matter how highly polished, lacks the reach of his best personal material. So neither Seger nor Browne has resolved the contradiction at the heart of their best singles. But then, neither have many of the people to whom their songs most clearly speak.

387 TSOP, MFSB featuring the Three Degrees
Written and produced by Kenny Gamble and Leon Huff
Philadelphia International 3540   1974   Billboard: #1 (2 weeks)

What little controversy "TSOP" engendered when it was current concerned what the group's initials stood for. "Mother Father Sister Brother," insisted the Philadelphia International publicists, with straight faces. "Motherfuckin' son of a bitch" was the word on the street, behind a smile.

Nobody had to ask what "TSOP" stood for. It was "The Sound of Philadelphia," and when the Three Degrees show up, midway through, to chant "People all over the world!" they did nothing more than state plain fact. In 1974, this is what the world sounded like. In another six months or so, they'd convert the beat and strings into a rigid formula called disco. "TSOP" is what the ingredients sounded like in the test tube.

388 MAYBE BABY, Buddy Holly and the Crickets
Produced by Norman Petty; written by Buddy Holly and Norman Petty
Brunswick 55053   1958   Billboard: #17

The one Buddy's Mom is supposed to have written. Not quite. She came up with a couple of lines, and Buddy decided to write a song around them. But with that ringing guitar intro, those bashing drums, his vocal one of the all-time gurgles, who cares who scratched the spark?

389 I FALL TO PIECES, Patsy Cline
Produced by Owen Bradley; written by Hank Cochran
Decca 31205   1961   *Billboard: #12*

Countrypolitan—the country production approach involving the use of large string sections, uptown tempos, and big vocal choruses—might have been deliberately designed to annoy music critics by either eliminating everything beautiful in country and western or reducing it to the status of background music. If so, the effort was a complete success. But countrypolitan ruled Nashville for more than a decade. It's as easy to understand how the formula came to life (confronted with rock and roll, country had to change or die and liberating itself was too risky) as it is to understand why there have been continual rebellions against it.

The silver lining in this particular cloud is Patsy Cline. Cline had a big, chesty voice, almost like a hillbilly Kate Smith, and producer Owen Bradley swathed it in echo and ensconced it in settings filled with crooning harmonies, weeping strings, and muted steel guitars. Her records are undeniably country and the arrangements and her singing style are undeniably too cosmopolitan to fit with any earlier model of country singing.

The results of similar efforts were misshapen and bathetic when applied by just about everybody else. But Cline used the slickness of her arrangements to create an enormously sympathetic mood that's a sort of country equivalent to polished city soul. On "I Fall to Pieces," Cline's melisma is gorgeous and her instinct for just where to bear down unbeatable. Bradley's production (when you can find it in its original state—Cline's been one of Nashville's most posthumously overdubbed artists) isn't an imposition; it's the product of a thorough understanding of what his client needed to get her point across.

390 MONEY HONEY, The Drifters
Produced by Ahmet Ertegun and Jerry Wexler; written by Jesse Stone
Atlantic 1006   1953   *Did not make pop chart*

"Money Honey," the Drifters' first chart record—it went to Number One on the R&B lists—immediately established the group as part of the new rock and roll movement. This had a lot less to do with Clyde McPhatter's style, which was the same daring, quavering chatterbox tenor it had been in the Dominoes, than with the song, supplied by the unforgiveably uncelebrated Jesse Stone. Three years before Chuck Berry's "Too Much Monkey Business," six before Berry Gordy's "Money," Stone crafted a musical portrait of a guy whose troubles with everybody from the landlord to his girlfriend stem directly from lack of cash, and spelled it out in terms that were not so much black vernacular as basic American. That takes nothing away from Clyde McPhatter, who's brilliant, or for that matter, from Sam The Man Taylor's incredible sax solo. But the finest achievement of all belonged this time to the guy who crafted the concept.

391 WORD UP, Cameo
Produced by Larry Blackmon; written by Larry Blackmon and Tomi Jenkins
Atlanta Artists 884933   1986   *Billboard:* #6

Larry Blackmon ran Cameo as a run-of-the-mill funk band for the better part of a decade before locating the most profound level of his tongue and spitting out "Word Up."

Initially a twelve-piece band vaguely associated with George Clinton's ParliaFunkadelicament movement, Cameo evolved over time into leader Blackmon and whoever happened to be working with him. What Blackmon lifted from Clinton was a sense of how to make funk rock out, supported by his own brand of off-kilter humor, both qualities amply displayed in "Word Up." (The title is a black slang phrase of the mid-eighties which roughly translates as "Que pasa?") What Blackmon developed that Clinton never did was a pop craftsman's tunefulness and a sense of how to take the playfulness of post-psychedelic slop and hew it into airplay accessible fragments. If this sounds like a good description of a great singles-maker, it almost is. Problem is, Blackmon's only ever made one great single—"Word Up."

He has, however, also created a great haircut (worn today by Carl Lewis, Clarence Clemons, and Grace Jones) which, as all Brian Jones fans will understand, is almost as important. What does this all mean? Like the song says, "We don't have time for psychological romance."

392 THERE'S A MOON OUT TONIGHT, The Capris
Producer not credited; written by Al Striano, Joe Luccisano, and Al Gentile
Planet 1010   1958   *Billboard:* #3

Smooth and drippy as a vanilla ice cream cone, "There's a Moon Out Tonight" was the record that kicked off the best-kept secret in rock history, the doo-wop revival of 1960–1962. The Capris' classic took this role when it was discovered by record collector Jerry Greene, of Slim's Times Square Records, the world's greatest doo-wop shop until the mid-sixties, when the subway station where the store was located renovated it out of existence.

Greene picked up "There's A Moon Out Tonight," released on the infinitesimal Planet label in 1958, in a swap from an anonymous customer. His friends and customers heard it frequently, as he sought to find another copy, and Times Square built a demand for the disc. Finally, Greene and two friends chipped in fifty bucks each and bought the master, which they leased to Hy Weiss of Old Town. It took off from there, revealing a previously unsuspected desire for "oldies."

Schmaltzy as it is, "There's a Moon Out Tonight" reflects Greene's good taste because it's so ingeniously constructed, from the tacky piano notes at the top to the shrill falsetto at the end. But its real importance is that it provided the first visible indication that the music had both artistic continuity and a really loyal audience that did *not* outgrow its taste.

393 WESTERN MOVIES, The Olympics
Written and produced by Fred Smith and Cliff Goldsmith
Demon 1508   1958   *Billboard:* #8

Jerry Leiber and Mike Stoller moved to New York in 1958, and they took the Coasters with them. But L.A. held its own in the tragicomic soap 'n' soul sweepstakes thanks to the Olympics, a group that emerged out of L.A.'s Central High School just as Leiber, Stoller, and the Coasters were heading East.

Who knows if there was room for both groups in the same town? Lead singer Walter Ward's voice bore an amazing resemblance to Carl Gardner's, and once he and classmates Eddie Lewis, Charles Fizer, and Melvin King hooked up with producer/songwriters Fred Smith and Cliff Goldsmith, they turned out the same kind of effects-laden R&B spoofs, although unlike the Coasters, the Olympics also turned out a couple of first-rate straight dance numbers, "The Bounce" and "(Baby) Hully Gully."

But the Olympics' basic attitude is summed up in their first and biggest hit, "Western Movies," which opens with ricochet sound effects that quickly resolve into jumping, Coasters-like upbeat R&B harmony. The hapless Ward can't get a date no matter what he tries, 'cause his baby's too wrapped up in the heyday of the TV western, watching *Gunsmoke, Have Gun Will Travel, Sugarfoot*, even *Davy Crockett*. In the second verse, she bashes him in the head with a brick for interrupting the opening of *Maverick*.

In other words, she's not interested in the movies at all; forerunner of a generation, she's become the original couch potato. In the end, Ward does something unintelligible to me but it seems to win his baby's attention back. Today, the very idea of distracting somebody so far gone seems totally absurd, but remember, this record was made back when the true effects of network television were too new to be fully understood.

394 THE DARK END OF THE STREET, James Carr
Produced by Quinton Claunch and Doc Russell; written by Chips Moman and Dan Penn
Goldwax 317   1967   *Billboard: #77*

"The Dark End of the Street" is the greatest cheating song in soul history, and Carr's original performance of it probably his finest record. By now, the song has accumulated covers by everybody from the Flying Burrito Brothers to Otis Redding, yet the one with staying power (if you don't count Clarence Carter's "Making Love," which really does exist in a whole separate dimension) is still this debut rendition, with its pulsating deep soul arrangement that centers virtually all the energy on the stark lyrics, with references here and there to other soul songs (notably Jimmy Hughes' earlier Muscle Shoals cheating standard, "Steal Away"). "And when the daylight hour rolls 'round and by chance we're both downtown," Carr sings with foghorn power, as the guitar quavers in ways his voice won't allow, "If we should meet just walk on by / Oh, darling, please don't cry." There's not a singer worth anything who could resist trying to top him. And damn few good enough to compete.

395 I CAN'T EXPLAIN, The Who
Produced by Shel Talmy; written by Pete Townshend
Decca 31725   1965   *Billboard:* #93

"I Can't Explain" changed my life the first time I heard it, when I was fifteen, by giving me a sound whose power I've spent a whole lot of the rest of my life searching to renew. It was the first record I'd heard that revealed British rock with the same purifying intensity as soul and fifties rock and roll. There's no way to tell if it would mean the same thing today. But if some aspects of what makes "I Can't Explain" great have grown fuzzier with the passage of time, the central kernel of its greatness has become more obvious: Keith Moon plays lead drums the way other bands had people playing lead guitar. After two decades, the sheer audacity of that act remains amazing and inspiring.

396 SLEDGEHAMMER, Peter Gabriel
Produced by Peter Gabriel and Daniel Lanois; written by Peter Gabriel
Geffen 28718   1986   *Billboard:* #1 (1 week)

The greatest ode any man has written to the potential potency of his own penis. This much everyone can understand, whether or not they know what the hell a "fruitcage" is (let alone fathom why anybody would want to be in somebody else's).

Gabriel's even admitted it, declaring that he dedicated his life to music after seeing Otis Redding in 1966 at London's Ram Jam Club, and that he'd written "Sledgehammer" as "an attempt to recreate some of the spirit and style of . . . sixties soul. The lyrics of many of those songs were full of playful sexual innuendo and this is my contribution to that songwriting tradition."

Although he usually plays the forbiddingly visaged *artiste*, Gabriel revels here in a wicked (as in Good Bad But Not Evil) sense of humor. If he found it necessary to declare that "Sledgehammer" also concerns "the use of sex as a means of getting through a breakdown in communication," he had the good sense not to sing it that way. Instead, he phrases with the randy glee of a journeyman soul star like Johnny Taylor or Eddie Floyd cut loose on the finest double entendre—complete with an allusion to "Chauffeur Blues"—he's ever been privileged to get his tonsils 'round.

As producer, Gabriel's wisest decision was probably his simplest: He called trumpeter Wayne Jackson and asked him to organize a horn section. Jackson phoned his partner in the Memphis Horns, saxophonist Andrew Love, and with a few other down-home buddies, they flew to L.A. and gave a British pop star one of the most powerful charts they'd ever played. Resounding against synthesizer and rhythm guitar licks like tongues of famous flame, those horns sing at least as loud as Gabriel himself. Which, you gotta hand it to Gabriel, was the plan, proving that the guy fully understands that music, like sex, is best practiced not solo.

397 I WANT TO WALK YOU HOME, Fats Domino
Produced by Dave Bartholomew; written by Fats Domino
Imperial 5606   1959   *Billboard:* #8

New Orleans R&B historian John Broven has described Fats as "rock 'n' roll's safety valve . . . all he was putting down was good-times New Orleans music." But that ignores the crucial subtext of all Domino's biggest records. Behind his chubby smile lurked a leer, as if that gent so friendly and cheerful down the block secretly had his fingers up your sister's skirt. Singing nothing more lewd than "I wanna walk you home," against a standard midtempo Crescent City shuffle led by a beautifully liquid guitar figure, Fats seems all jolly innocence. But he keeps up an insistent pressure until finally you get the picture: "I saw you walkin' all alone, that's why I want to *walk you home.*" If you can catch his subtle emphasis and still think all he was looking for was a stroll, you ought to sue your parents for malpractice.

398 COULD IT BE I'M FALLING IN LOVE, The Spinners
Produced by Thom Bell; written by Melvin Steals and Mervin Steals
Atlantic 2927   1972   *Billboard:* #4

Thom Bell made the same kind of orchestrated Philly soul as his some-time associates, Kenneth Gamble and Leon Huff, but his own productions often had in abundance exactly the emotional qualities that Gamble and Huff's lacked. Where almost every Gamble-Huff production was overwhelmed in rhythm, Bell specialized in updating and modernizing traditional black group harmony sounds. His best vehicles were the Stylistics, the Delfonics, and, perhaps most prominently, the Spinners, a retread Motown group who never had much luck while trapped in the Gordy group's production machinery but became "overnight" stars when they teamed up with Bell in 1972.

"Could It Be I'm Falling in Love" uses everything in Bell's arsenal, including all five of the Spinners' voices, each distinctly deployed. A simple snare beat keeps the time, while the bass drum pounds home the groove.

What makes "Could It Be I'm Falling in Love" so much the special product of the period when soul was transforming itself into disco is lead singer Philippe Wynne, and Bell giving him space to shout and testify the way he needs to, even if that undercuts some of the producer's artfully arranged slick moves. And check the way Wynne pronounces "with" as "which," a last gasp of R&B's Southern roots amidst this most urbane setting.

399 SHAKIN' ALL OVER, The Guess Who
Producer not credited; written by Johnny Kidd
Scepter 1295   1965   *Billboard:* #22

One of the all-time trash rockers, "Shakin' All Over" ranks right up there with "Gloria" and "96 Tears" among crudely hyperactive accounts of sexual frenzy. Or it would, if anybody had ever made a record as good as the song's concept, which is to create a guitar riff that gives your spine the same shiver as sexual ecstasy. You probably wouldn't think it was possible to get that into music, so you'd probably be shocked—and stimulated—to hear (and feel) how close an electric guitar can come.

"Shakin' All Over" was originated by a pre-Beatles British band, Johnny Kidd and the Pirates, whose guitarist, Mick Green, was apparently dazzling live but never made a record as good as his rep. Green's work on Kidd's "Shakin' " is passable, but it isn't nearly as good as the ones that the Who and the MC5 used to do live. But if the Five ever recorded theirs, it was never released, and the "Shakin' " that the Who do on *Live at Leeds* is excessively psychedelicized.

That leaves the crown to the Guess Who, who popularized "Shakin' " in North America. They learned it off an import pressing of Kidd's version and probably called themselves the Guess Who in an attempt to persuade Western Hemisphere listeners that they were British. In fact, they were from Winnipeg, Manitoba, where they were called Chad Allan and the Expressions, featuring Randy Bachman on lead guitar. When "Shakin' " hit, they were stuck with being the Guess Who, a monicker that served them well for the next decade as these proud sons of the prairies went on—with a substantially different lineup, vocalist Allan being replaced by the corpulent Burton Cummings in 1966—to a whole string of pop-rock hits. After that Cummings had a mercifully brief solo career and Bachman put together the more successful Bachman-Turner Overdrive of "You Ain't Seen Nothin' Yet" fame.

BTO, in fact, played like a band in search of that truly great rendition of "Shakin' All Over." But like other pretenders and contenders, they never quite found it . . . or at least, not for long enough to commit it to tape, which is the way they measure victory in these times.

400 BRILLIANT DISGUISE, Bruce Springsteen
Produced by Bruce Springsteen, Jon Landau, and Chuck Plotkin; written by Bruce Springsteen
Columbia 07595   1987   *Billboard*: #5

Springsteen has been so often celebrated as the new Dylan or Elvis or something that his role in resuscitating the sound and feel of early sixties New York studio pop—the sound of Leiber and Stoller, Gene Pitney, Luther Dixon and Doc Pomus and Mort Shuman, not to mention Phil Spector—has been virtually overlooked. Which figures, since according to orthodox rock history, that stuff either didn't happen or didn't matter.

Which makes it all the funnier that Springsteen eased into the Top Ten with his finest pop production by gearing the whole song around a booming *baion* bass line right out of the Leiber/Stoller handbook and digging back into the Gene Pitney archives for his sense of phrasing (that "Is it meeee, baby" comes straight out of "Last Chance to Turn Around").

You could, for that matter, make a strong case that the encoded marital metaphors of "Brilliant Disguise" have clearer links to Ellie Greenwich and Jeff Barry's "You've Lost That Lovin' Feelin'," Carole King and Gerry Goffin's "Oh No Not My Baby," Burt Bacharach and Hal David's "Only Love Can Break a Heart," and perhaps most of all, Pomus and Mort Shuman's "Suspicion" than to anything by Dylan or Lennon-McCartney. But that would mean acknowledging this forbidden period of rock history not just as an "influence," but as part of the music's continuing vitality.

Springsteen is just about the only contemporary performer who *does* acknowledge the greatness of this songmill stuff as a part of rock and roll (not just ancient Tin Pan Alley) and that has a lot to do with why he's more singular than those who work ten times harder at individualism.

On the other hand, I still can't figure out what he's holding in the palm of his hand. He probably took that part from Dylan.

401 **RAG DOLL, The Four Seasons**
Produced by Bob Crewe; written by Bob Gaudio and Bob Crewe
Phillips 40211   1964   *Billboard:* #1 (2 weeks)

Leaving New York City through the Lincoln Tunnel, you drive through the neighborhood known as Hell's Kitchen. On Tenth Avenue, the kids have for many years approached stopped cars at traffic lights and wiped their windows, hoping for quarters. One afternoon in 1964, the Four Seasons' Bob Gaudio was leaving the city on his way home to New Jersey when he noticed that the kid smearing the glass was a girl.

"I saw her face—just the picture of her face and the clothes, tattered . . . with holes in her stockings, and a little cap on her head," Gaudio told Fred Bronson, author of *The Billboard Book of Number One Hits.* She finished her job and stood back as Gaudio searched his pockets for change. To his mortification, he had none. The smallest thing he had was a five.

"There was a split second where I said, 'I can't give her a five dollar bill.' But I couldn't give her nothing. So I gave her the five dollar bill. The look on her face when I was pulling away—she didn't say 'thank you,' she just stood there with the bill in her hand and I could see her in the rearview mirror, just standing in disbelief in the middle of the street with the five dollars. And that whole image stayed with me; a rag doll was what she looked like."

Gaudio went home and wrote a song about her. Only in the song, the Rag Doll became a young woman and rather than five bucks, the singer wants to offer her his love against the wishes of his family and society. Gaudio says that he and producer Bob Crewe worked for two weeks completing the writing. Then they took the Four Seasons into a New York demo studio, their ordinary headquarters being booked by others, and worked with an engineering crew they'd never met before.

The record they came up with is prototypical Four Seasons, from its crushing drum intro to the piercing glockenspiel and tambourine accoutrements, from Frankie Valli's wild falsetto to the bel canto doo-wop harmonies. As a fantasy about love in America, it's certainly the best ever contrived at a stoplight. As a record, it was one final gorgeous blast of Italian R&B at the top of the charts before the Brits took over for good. The week it fell from Number One, it was replaced by "A Hard Day's Night." It was the last Number One hit the Seasons ever had.

402 YOU HAVEN'T DONE NOTHIN', Stevie Wonder

Written and produced by Stevie Wonder
Tamla 54252   1974   *Billboard:* #1 (1 week)

How does such a wrathful, preachy rant get to pop radio, let alone rise to Number One? Wonder builds an impregnable, funky foundation from a bubbling bass and a single brushed cymbal stroke that embellishes every bar like a velvet scourge, then sets atop it a set of swinging but never blaring horns and a wahwah synthesizer riff that insinuates the melody into your bones. He integrates his vocal—and the background support of the Jackson 5, no less—into this structure as a fundamentally musical element, something that belongs as a *sound*, not just a conveyor belt for the lyric.

Which is still saying meaningful things even fifteen years later, which in the realm of current events (let alone pop music) represents impressive longevity. Stevie has never betrayed the principles of "You Haven't Done Nothin' "—not only did he push indefatigably for the Martin Luther King birthday holiday after everybody else had given up (and win the battle over the objection of a president who believed King—and probably Wonder—a communist), but though the press ridiculed him for it, it was Stevie who tried to focus "We Are the World" on the actuality of Ethiopia, rather than the fantasy of pop star nobility. Guts and genius rarely walk hand in hand. Here's the exception that proves the rule.

403 BLUE BAYOU, Roy Orbison

Produced by Fred Foster; written by Roy Orbison and Joe Melson
Monument 824   1963   *Billboard:* #29

Texas has bayous but they're over near Houston, in the southeastern portion of the state. Roy Orbison grew up about a thousand miles further west, in a town called Wink, in the flat, desolate oil-rich plains. Yet he sings so wistfully of bayous bygone and to come that it's hard to believe that he didn't grow up eating andouille and traveling in a pirogue.

But don't let the nostalgia fool you. What Roy's really singing about is the way he's feeling right now. "Oh to see my baby again, and to be with some of my friends / Maybe I'd be happy then," he croons, and what comes clear isn't how terrific someday may be, but how wrong today already is. His voice floating in off the stream of music, that mouth harp bleating like a riptide, Roy's not a guy looking over his shoulder to happier times so much as he is a man seeking any available moment of spiritual surcease.

Maybe Joe Melson was really from east Texas, but it doesn't matter. As much as any place in this world could be, "Blue Bayou" is indeed Orbison's home because its "silver moon and evening tide" exists only in his imagination. "Oh some sweet day, gonna take away, this hurting inside / I'll never be blue, my dreams come true, on blue bayou," Orbison concludes, but because you've heard him sing of waking dreams so often, you know he's really only praying.

404 THESE ARMS OF MINE, Otis Redding
Produced by Jim Stewart; written by Otis Redding
Volt 103   1962   Billboard: #85

Redding's first Memphis session, his first chart record, and he sings the opening line as if he's got all the time in the world. Crooning "Theeeese arrrms of miiine," he's out there on his own, when the MGs (with Steve Cropper chiming in on rudimentary ostinato piano for the absent Booker T. and Otis's then-boss Johnny Jenkins subbing for Cropper on guitar) burst in and one of the most sympathetic pairings of band and singer in pop history is born in full glory. The song's not much, the arrangement couldn't be simpler but Otis seizes his chance like a dog a bone, and by the time he's done, there's not a shred of meat left untouched.

405 I'M A MAN, The Yardbirds
Produced by Giorgio Gomelsky; written by Ellas McDaniel
[Bo Diddley]
Epic 9857   1965   Billboard: #17

This is the third appearance of "I'm a Man" in *The Heart of Rock & Soul*, but I'm not sure that any of these versions would recognize its brethren. Well, actually, Bo might want to file a claim against Muddy Waters's "Mannish Boy," but he must surely have looked upon the Yardbirds' droning, feedback-drenched excursion into pre-psychedelia as his most wayward child.

On the other hand, this is the record that launched a thousand noise-rock bands and made Jeff Beck a guitar legend when, after a lightning solo that ran out of notes on the neck, he began bashing strings purely for their percussive effect. But the real trick was placing this cacophony in even the lower reaches of the Top 20. You can argue in favor of myth-mongering but I'd say they got there on the basis of craft (albeit as much Mr. Diddley's as their own).

406 GET A JOB, The Silhouettes
Produced by Kae Williams; written by Earl Beal, Ray Edwards, Billy Horton, and Richard Lewis
Ember 1029 1958 *Billboard:* #1 (2 weeks)

Given rock and roll's much heralded affinity to the antinomian heresy, which contends that faith alone leads to salvation and that acts literally don't matter a damn—i.e., nothing is forbidden and everything permitted—it makes perfect sense that "Get a Job" 's cacophonous social protest should have emerged from a group that began life as a Philadelphia gospel quartet, the Gospel Tornados. Soon falling into (perhaps meaningless) perdition, they linked up with deejay Kae Williams, who released their "Yipyipyipyipyip shad-da-da-da" on his own Junior label, then licensed it to Al Silver at Ember, who sold more than a million copies in just three weeks.

With "Get a Job" 's fame in the genus of nonsense syllables, its wild sax break, and general air of subcoherence, what's most amazing is that a protest narrative as straightforward as Clyde McPhatter's "Money Honey" can be deciphered within the noise. And the record doesn't lose political relevance because of its crazed unintelligibility— it gains. The lyric (which just shows a guy getting out of bed, searching the help wanted ads, and being harassed by everybody from his girlfriend on out when he fails) would be at best agitprop without a reading that fully expressed the frustration, annoyance, and absurdity of his unemployment. God knows, the Silhouettes drive those points home.

407 LOVE TRAIN, The O'Jays
Written and produced by Kenneth Gamble and Leon Huff
Philadelphia International 3524   1973   *Billboard:* #1 (1 week)

The O'Jays were already a veteran soul trio (they first charted in 1963 with "Lonely Drifter" on Imperial) when they joined forces with then-booming Philadelphia International entrepreneurs Gamble and Huff to forge a style that was to all intents and purposes disco-gospel. It never felt more that way than it does here, where they preach their message to "People all over the world." And of course, when they shouted "All you brothers over in Africa / Tell all the folks in Egypt and Israel, too," the O'Jays had no way of knowing that by the late eighties they'd find themselves on the United Nations blacklist of performers who'd violated the cultural boycott of South Africa. Or that after they made a heartfelt, tearstained apology for letting themselves be hoodwinked (and were removed from the blacklist), the cultural boycott would be smashed by the forces of World Pop that their greatest hit putatively celebrated.

408 SCHOOL DAY, Chuck Berry
Produced by Leonard Chess; written by Chuck Berry
Chess 1653   1957   *Billboard:* #3

409 HANG UP MY ROCK AND ROLL SHOES, Chuck Willis
Produced by Zenas Sears; written by Chuck Willis
Atlantic 1179   1958   *Billboard:* #24

You think rock and roll is and always has been the authentic stuff of teen rebellion, huh? Listen here, to the real stories of two of the songs that spawned that myth.

On "School Day," drummer Fred Below's powerhouse shuffle serves as a premonition of Led Zeppelin's blues-rock while Chuck plays timeless bursts of machine-gun guitar. But the record's key is its lyric, which fully captures the energized futility of working-class public high schools with their pointless rounds preparing kids for adult lives with even less purpose. Berry gets every detail right and establishes a cornerstone of the argument that rock and roll is really youth music. But how truly teenage was this guy who was twenty-nine years old and already a husband and parent?

The irony of "Hang Up My Rock and Roll Shoes" is supposed to be that the other Chuck's declaration of faith reached the charts two weeks after his April 1958 death. But a greater irony is that this thirty-year-old R&B veteran is best-known for a testament of fidelity that had to be couched in arch-teenage terms. I don't mean the fact that the lyrics are addressed to "Mama," but the lines that vow: "Yes, I will do my homework, clean the yard everyday / Yes, I will wash the dishes, I'll do anything you say."

So the guy was thirty, and having the first big hits of his life with stroll-beat discs like this, and understanding, maybe for the first time, that what he was doing would last a while, sustain a living if not a career. And that comes through on the record, too. Because if all those pledges of allegiance to household chores are hardly credible from such a comparative graybeard, they're finally undercut by the lines that may have more truly spoken for what Willis felt: "That music got a beat that will keep you alive / The kids are rock and rollin' from eight to 85."

Of course, all that kowtowing to Mom and Dad's demands contradicts the taken-for-granted blather about rock-as-rebellion, too. But then, Willis, deejay/producer Zenas Sears, and Atlantic weren't the least bit interested in fostering adolescent insurrection. They wanted to sell some records, and they were willing to spout whatever platitudes were necessary to do it. You want rebellion? Willis died because he refused for too long to have an operation on his bleeding ulcers, a disease that represents the body rebelling against itself.

410 BABALU'S WEDDING DAY, The Eternals
Producer not credited; written by Girona, Martin, and Miranda
Hollywood 70   1959   Did not make pop chart

There's plenty of people who'll claim that you can't make a great rock and roll record about the joys of matrimony. Bullshit, buddy. This is one of the wildest, weirdest records I've ever heard, made by a group so obscure that they make folks like the Students look like talk show regulars.

The announcement that Babalu (apparently a household name in whatever universe this song is situated) is finally getting hitched sends an entire society into frantic activity. Some laugh. Some sigh. We learn that he met his fiance, Hoskie Bopalena, at a Milwaukee Braves baseball game. Then, it seems, Babalu misses the ceremony because his cheapskate friend refuses to lend him a dime to call for a ride. So he goes to work with a trained monkey, who steals all the cash and runs away as soon as work is over. That's it.

In my own view, "Babalu's Wedding Day" ranks with the wedding scene in *The Searchers* as an epitome of how such ceremonies should be conducted. That is, if I've gotten any of the details right. Amidst all the racket, it's real hard to be sure.

411 THIS MAGIC MOMENT, The Drifters
Produced by Jerry Leiber and Mike Stoller; written by Doc Pomus and Mort Shuman
Atlantic 2050   1960   *Billboard:* #16

"There was a great ballroom, the Palladium, at Fifty-third and Broadway and every Wednesday was mambo night," Mort Shuman told rhythm and blues historian Colin Escott. "You'd get two or three bands on the same bill. The place was jam-packed with people who worked in factories. Cleaning ladies. It was a great melting pot and the catalytic agent was Latin music. I was there every night it was open."

Shuman's interest in Latin rhythms transformed R&B love songs, most dramatically through the introduction of the *baion* bass but equally with the Latin accents that suffuse every one of the ballads he and Doc Pomus composed for the Drifters—"Save the Last Dance for Me," "I Count the Tears," and especially "This Magic Moment," with its swirling strings and crying Ben E. King lead.

Shuman also loved doo-wop ("tenement music") long before that music had any hip cachet. Doc Pomus, on the other hand, was probably the first white blues singer in Brooklyn in the late forties, and while his taste ranged further, the center of it never moved. In their tunes, Pomus became the guardian of the blues. He also found himself, almost by default, the lyricist, since Shuman's strengths were more musical than literary. Pomus wasn't afraid to write corny ("A Teenager in Love" is his responsibility) but he also wrote some of the era's more elegantly stated love songs. For sheer lyric felicity, "This Magic Moment" perhaps outstrips even "Save the Last Dance for Me."

Pomus subverts R&B conventions even in the opening couplet, with its distinctly nonconversational gait: "This magic moment, so different and so new / Was like any other until I met you." Such stateliness makes this one of the few R&B songs that has the kind of lyric gentility commonly found in tunes by the earlier generation of Tin Pan Alley masters.

Blessed with such fine material, Jerry Leiber and Mike Stoller framed it with the perfectionist exactitude of great musical architects, sculpting around King's weepy lead a virtual cathedral of orchestrated rhythm and harmony.

412 WAKE UP LITTLE SUSIE, The Everly Brothers
Produced by Archie Bleyer; written by Felice and Boudleaux Bryant
Cadence 1337   1957   *Billboard:* #1 (4 weeks)

Boudleaux Bryant wrote "Wake Up Little Susie" to pick up on the thrilling acoustic guitar strum that opens "Bye Bye Love," which it does in spades. But even that scythelike beat and the percussive crispness of Don and Phil's voices can't match the lyric, a tall tale about a couple who go to a drive-in and . . . fall asleep until 3:00 A.M.? The result was banishment from many radio stations (though you'll note that lack of airplay couldn't keep it from topping the charts).

Well, I'd just like to say that *I* always believed their story. Until I became the parent of teenage daughters.

413 SUSPICIOUS MINDS, Elvis Presley
Produced by Chips Moman; written by Mark James
RCA 47-9764   1969   *Billboard:* #1 (1 week)

Elvis's last Number One was also his one great modern record. Exciting in its own right as an interpretation of soul music—hillbilly Jerry Butler, more or less—"Suspicious Minds" also makes a formidable argument for Elvis-as-artist, despite all the wasted years in Hollywood. However minor and incremental, Presley's creative growth can be heard in the thoughtful reading he gives this song. Maybe he put so much into it because the lyric was halfway autobiographical, but he couldn't have communicated even that if he hadn't been completely in command of his musical faculties. So here's the final piece of evidence that what happened at Sun was no fluke.

414 HELLO MARY LOU, Ricky Nelson
Produced by Jimmie Haskell; written by Gene Pitney
Imperial 5741   1961   *Billboard:* #9

Ricky Nelson's early records generally receive most praise for the work of guitarist James Burton, an indeed ferocious talent with whom Elvis later absconded for his Vegas period band. Burton does rip off a delicious solo here, but Ricky keeps up with him all the way.

You want teen idol material, try "Travelin' Man," the A side of the 45 in question, although even that's not bad as such trifles go. "Hello Mary Lou" is another matter, though. Nelson, like "Mary Lou" co-writer Gene Pitney, has never been a hip taste. But unlike a lot of hipsters, his best records get to the core of the song's emotion, and they cut there by routes that are simple and direct. In rock and roll, those are virtues no matter what avant-gardists and tastemakers believe.

415 WHAT TIME IS IT, The Jive Five
Produced by Les Cahan and Joe Rene; written by
Bob Feldman, Richard Gottehrer, and Jerry Goldstein
Beltone 2024   1962   *Billboard:* #67

Somehow Eugene Pitt's superbly draggy lead vocal, coupled with spectral falsetto support and clocklike chimes occasionally doubled on guitar, creates something spooky from a song that's basically no more than an account of a guy who's hot for tonight's date. In other words, the kind of mystery you could pleasurably spend the rest of your days trying to fathom.

416 I CAN'T STAND THE RAIN, Ann Peebles
Produced by Willie Mitchell; written by Don Bryant and
Bernard Miller
Hi 2248   1973   *Billboard:* #38

Probably the most ravaged vocal ever to hit the Top 40, "I Can't Stand the Rain" contrasts all of Willie Mitchell's prototypical devices—sinuous bass, horn, and organ lines, Al Jackson's steady rocking drums building to a slow smoulder—with maddening repetitions, first of plucked guitar strings, then of bongos, finally of an echoing Dylanesque organ chord. Peebles, meanwhile, addresses herself to the windowpane

and her tearstained pillow in a voice as scared and hollow as the one
John Lennon used for his primal scream album.

417 SPANISH HARLEM, Ben E. King
Produced by Jerry Leiber and Mike Stoller; written by
Jerry Leiber and Phil Spector
Atco 6185   1960   *Billboard:* #10

There's nothing to it: vibes, a bass rumbling Leiber and Stoller's favorite
Caribbean rhythm, the *baion*, a chorus so much like the Drifters it
might as well be them at work, and then Ben E. King's ghostly voice,
chanting words that come almost too fast, pushed together to force the
beat and then slacking off again, setting up the complaisant atmosphere
of the bridge, with strings pushing against saxophone. You could call
it a formula. But if you'd do that, you'd also be the kind of person who
doesn't believe that love, wherever it's found, can be a miracle. And
while that's just fine, it wouldn't leave you and the people who made
this record (or the ones who treasure it) very much in common, would
it?

418 BROWN EYED GIRL, Van Morrison
Produced by Bert Berns; written by Van Morrison
Bang 545   1967   *Billboard:* #10

What's this gloomy, dark-visaged Album Rock Genius doing singing
an infectious pop melody with such effervesence? Simple. He's making
a single. Great one, too, with its lubricious imagery conveyed atop a
melody that seems the perfect breath of innocence. "Behind the stadium
with you," indeed.

419 AGENT DOUBLE-O SOUL, Edwin Starr
Produced by Eddie Wingate; written by C. Hatcher and
B. Sharpley
Ric-Tic 103   1965   *Billboard:* #21

420 SECRET AGENT MAN, Johnny Rivers
Produced by Lou Adler; written by P.F. Sloan and Steve Barri
Imperial 66159   1966   *Billboard: #3.*

Two of the few good things to come directly out of the Cold War. Or maybe it's just that, in the wake of Vietnam and Cambodia, My Lai and the Phoenix Program, being a spy is considered a lot less cool now than it was back then.

"Secret Agent Man," though it's undoubtedly Rivers's best record, was reined in by being the theme song of the television show of the same name, although "You let the wrong word slip / By kissing persuasive lips" surely betters any line Ian Fleming ever wrote. Actually, Johnny sounds, as he always did, a little doltish but the (uncredited) guitar solo generates so much torque it threatens to blast the needle off the tonearm. Together with the Hal Blaine-style drumming, "Secret Agent Man" becomes one of the last grand gasps of mid-sixties L.A. session rock.

While "Secret Agent Man" may be "swinging on the Riviera one day / Then layin' in a Bombay alley next day," Edwin Starr's "Agent Double-O Soul" never leaves the streets of the Motor City. In fact, he dwells so much on domestic differences, you've gotta figure he's really with the FBI. Although J. Edgar Hoover never would have allowed Double-O Soul his "strictly Continental suits and high collar shirts," let alone have considered his prowess at doing the Twine and the Jerk job qualifications.

When he gets down to cases, Starr suggests that he's not *that* kind of agent anyway. Tracking down "a fella who was down on rock and roll . . . he didn't have no kinda soul," Double-O Soul puts him not in prison but behind the mike, as "a deejay on a radio show."

As for that great rumbling bass line, those charging drums, the Vandellas-like background voices, the sputtering horns, and "Back in My Arms Again" piano, Detroit-based Ric-Tic was where Motown's band, the Funk Brothers, moonlighted. Berry Gordy's spies found out about their presence on Starr's first hit (all they had to do was listen), and he fined the Funk Brothers a hundred bucks apiece. In a twist Hitchcock might have appreciated, Ric-Tic owner Eddie Wingate crashed the Motown Christmas party and paid the guys back double on the spot. Then, after Starr hit again with the Funk Brothers-driven "Stop Her on Sight," which really came too close for Motown's comfort, the Goldfinger-like Gordy dealt with the matter with dispatch, buying out Wingate and his entire artist roster, making Starr's future hits his own.

421 CRAZY ARMS, Ray Price
Produced by Don Law; written by C. Seals and Ralph Mooney
Columbia 21510   1956   *Billboard:* #67

"Crazy Arms" must have sounded decades old the moment it was released, for Price spends the whole record on the edge of a pure Jimmy Rodgers yodel and the fiddles and steel guitar belong to another era, one in which Elvis and Little Richard are barely conceivable, much less standing at center stage.

On the other hand, the concept of the pop star as a person on the edge of insanity has some of its most important roots in just this kind of country record, in which the singer confesses—and genuinely seems to feel—that his behavior is a form of madness, that he has little or no control over what his body is going to do even though his mind (or at least, his conscious moral sense) urges him in a more godly (or at least sensible) direction. *You* tell *me* the difference in attitude between that posture and any random heavy metal band's.

422 THINK, The Five Royales
Producer not credited; written by Lowman Pauling
King 5053   1957   *Billboard:* #66

Few careers in rock and roll history have been longer or more distinguished than that of the Five Royales. Fewer still had so much to do with laying the music's foundations, or sustained that influence over such a long period. From 1945 through 1965, the Royales helped shape vocal group styles and guitar patterns and created landmark songs and recordings.

Formed as a gospel group around 1942 in their native Winston-Salem, North Carolina, the Royales made their first records for Apollo Records in 1948. By 1952, they'd made the transition to secular music, scoring a number of hits, including "Baby Don't Do It," "Laundromat Blues," "Crazy Crazy Crazy," and "Too Much Lovin'." A variety of factors made them distinctive, but the most noticeable were the rawness with which they secularized gospel quartet harmony, their use of two lead voices (Johnny and Eugene Tanner) and the magnificent single-string guitar playing of Lowman Pauling. Pauling also revealed himself as a first-rate songwriter, blessed with biting humor ("Monkey Hips and Rice," "Laundromat Blues") and a sense of social outrage and romantic tragedy ("The Slummer the Slum," "Baby Don't Do It").

When the group moved to King Records of Cincinnati in 1954 it really came into its own. Although, with the exception of "Think," their biggest hits were made for Apollo, the quality of the Royales' King sides is both high and amazingly consistent. For King, Pauling wrote a series of songs that were among the first rock and roll standards, tunes that have been continually reinterpreted over the ensuing decades. These included "Tell the Truth" (later covered by Ray Charles and Eric Clapton), "Dedicated to the One I Love" (a Top Ten hit and signature number for both the Shirelles and the Mamas and the Papas) and "Think," which in addition to charting for the Five Royales themselves also made the *Billboard* lists in three separate versions for James Brown. (Brown was so enamored of the Royales that in 1965 he produced a couple of singles, among the group's very last recordings.)

Listening to "Think" now, what's most striking is its prophesy of Southern soul. Johnny Tanner's crying lead would have fit on the radio any time in the sixties (even though the sax and backing harmonies wouldn't have), and Pauling's gorgeous single-string guitar is not only the equal of Albert or Freddy King, but with its mellow tone and reverb, a clear influence on Stax stalwart Steve Cropper. In a way, "Think" belongs to no particular period; it wouldn't be surprising to wake up tomorrow and find that Pauling's complaint about his lover's ingratitude had again seized the airwaves, perhaps this time in some new electronified dance mix.

423 MANY RIVERS TO CROSS, Jimmy Cliff
Written and produced by Jimmy Cliff
Island [VK] WIP 6139   1972   Did not make pop chart

Gospel music—that is, music from Christian Pentecostalists—seems to play no special role in Jamaican working-class culture, which is most prominently associated with Rastafarianism, a cult that reveres the late Emperor Haile Selassie of Ethiopia as godhead.

In any event, Jimmy Cliff is not a Rasta or a Christian. He's a Muslim. But "Many Rivers to Cross," the best song from *The Harder They Come*, soundtrack to the 1972 film, is unquestionably derived from gospel, so much so that it wouldn't be hard to imagine Sam Cooke singing it. That Cooke would have had his work cut out for him is a tribute to Cliff's gorgeous reading of a lyric that converts Ivan, the gangster dope dealer that Cliff plays in the movie, into a sympathetic figure. When sociology confronts musicality and music wins, ain't *that* good news.

424 ROCK AND ROLL, Led Zeppelin
Produced by Jimmy Page; written by Jimmy Page, Robert Plant, John Paul Jones, and John Bonham
Atlantic 2865   1972   *Billboard: #47*

For a band that often played as if it couldn't keep time with a Rolex metronome, this tribute to Robert Plant's record collection is one hell of an achievement. And so was writing this review without blowing my speakers, because there's no way to listen to "Rock and Roll" except cranked to the max. So anybody who thinks you can't get to the biggest hard-rock group of the seventies in a straight line from Chuck Berry—hell, Frankie Lymon for that matter—needs to listen up, because rather than the hippie scrap heap, Zep lifts its riffs and reasoning from "Book Of Love" and "Back in the U.S.A.," "The Stroll" and "Rumble."

425 SHE'S GOT YOU, Patsy Cline
Produced by Owen Bradley; written by Hank Cochran
Decca 31354   1962   *Billboard: #14*

The most soulful singer in country history, Patsy Cline was also the fifties pop singer who'd have been best suited to the stylistic innovations of the sixties, as proven by this beautiful midtempo ballad, a record that's no more country than it is pop or R&B—meaning, it qualifies as any of the three as well as some species all its own. Cline's legato phrasing on the verses sets up the soaring notes she releases on the bridge and the result is pure, artful ache.

426 I WISH IT WOULD RAIN, The Temptations
Produced by Norman Whitfield; written by Norman Whitfield, Barrett Strong, and Roger Penzabene
Gordy 7068   1968   *Billboard: #4*

The piano might have come from the Beatles, but the bass could only be Motown's and the singing is unquestionably the sole and exclusive province of David Ruffin, whose sandpaper smooth balladry here reaches its pinnacle of expressiveness, abetted by some nice collective trickery near the end.

427 **THE MOUNTAIN'S HIGH, Dick and DeeDee**
A Ralke-Wilder Production; written by Dick St. John
Liberty 55350   1961   *Billboard: #2*

The scary thing about all those historians of rock and roll who claim
the music was dead in the early sixties is that, maybe, when they hear
a record like "The Mountain's High," with its absolutely lethal backbeat, thrilling male and female falsettos, rhumbalike rhythm, trash-
mysterioso love lyric, and vocal gargling and gabbling, *they don't like
it.*
But then, nobody could be *that* stupid. Could they?

428 **EDGE OF SEVENTEEN (LIVE), Stevie Nicks**
Produced by Jimmy Iovine; written by Stevie Nicks
Modern 7401   1981   Did not make pop chart

The least mystical lyric Nicks ever wrote: White-winged dove and all,
it's a tale any girl standing on the verge of womanhood can recognize.
Though the male coming of age song has become one of rock's more
overwrought subgenres, any song seen clearly through the eyes of a
woman (especially a young one) remains a rarity. Here, with a crack-
erjack band that makes Fleetwood Mac sound like the Modern Folk
Quartet, Nicks creates more craftsmanlike crotch rock than Foreigner
ever dreamed. Waddy Wachtel's guitar and the dual keyboards of Roy
Bittan and Benmont Tench pound and slash like huge machines that
have learned to swing, and they push Nicks to heights where she's able
to bite straight through her own pretensions into pure rock and roll.

429 **YOUR PROMISE TO BE MINE, The Drifters**
Produced by Neshui Ertegun; written by Jimmy Oliver
Atlantic 1089   1956   Did not make pop charts

It figures that it would be Neshui, by far the more suave of the brothers
Ertegun, who came up with this letter-perfect marriage of gospel and
doo-wop, with its melismatic but remarkably controlled lead vocal by
Bubba Thrasher. The way Thrasher holds the final note evokes Jackie
Wilson's "Danny Boy," but it's probably more properly understood
the other way 'round, since Wilson must have learned a lot from the
possibilities the Drifters' fusion suggested, the more comfortably be-

cause the extraordinary results were buried on the B side of "Ruby Baby."

430 AIN'T THAT PECULIAR, Marvin Gaye
Produced by Smokey Robinson; written by Smokey Robinson, Warren Moore, Marvin Tarplin, and Bobby Rogers
Tamla 54122   1965   *Billboard:* #8

Marvin Gaye was the greatest singer Motown produced, and one of the half-dozen greatest in the history of rock and soul. Here, Gaye in his prime still finds himself outstripped by the Funk Brothers, the label's exquisite session band. The focal point, as (almost) always, is James Jamerson's melodic, restless bass line, which moves with astonishing liquidity, but the forcible backbeat of Benny Benjamin's drums, the gutty guitar work (probably by cowriter Marv Tarplin, since this was a Smokey session) and Earl Van Dyke's insistent gospel piano more than keep up. One of the definitive Motown tracks—and truth to tell, Marvin doesn't do so bad himself.

431 LITTLE SISTER, Elvis Presley
Producer not credited; written by Doc Pomus and Mort Shuman
RCA 47-7908   1961   *Billboard:* #5

Scotty Moore comes up with his greatest post-Sun guitar lick and not only converts a comparatively humdrum Pomus-Shuman teen love triangle number into the best of Elvis's early sixties hits, but (together with D.J. Fontana's heavy-footed thunderation) gives more than a few pointers toward the metallic rock to come. In other words, if the Who had been capable of rockabilly, "Little Sister" is what they would have come up with.

432 DOGGIN' AROUND, Jackie Wilson
Produced by Dick Jacobs; written by Paul Tarnopol
Brunswick 55166   1960   *Billboard:* #15

Typically in Jackie's screwed-up career, the overwrought "Night" was promoted as the A side of the single and "Doggin' Around" was relegated to an obviously very popular flip. The R&B charts reversed the priority and there, "Doggin' Around" went all the way to the top.

Wilson's vocal is pure melisma; he elongates virtually every syllable in the lyric, achieving a weird sensuality that overwhelms the fairly clumsy accompaniment. The instrumental arrangement has just one standout element, but it's enough: A tinkling honky-tonk piano that might as well be played by Floyd Cramer. The vocal chorus is too slick, of course, but that's not news. Wilson's records by this point were stew, with Jackie adding all the spice. It was enough to keep connoisseurs coming back for seconds for the next few decades.

433 SHINING STAR, Earth, Wind & Fire
Produced by Sig Shore and Charles Stepney; written by Maurice White, Philip Bailey, and Larry Dunn
Columbia 10090   1975   *Billboard:* #1 (1 week)

In many ways, the development of funk was black rock's answer to white rock's psychedelic infatuation. But while acid-rock largely proved a dead end, funk bands created some of the best album-oriented music of the seventies and laid the foundations for hip-hop and rap, the most exciting new pop styles of the eighties.

In the end, funk succumbed to almost as many excesses as psychedelia. Indeed, many of the pitfalls were the same, especially the infatuation with colorful, superficial metaphysics and the tendency to drag out musical ideas beyond the point of diminishing return. But, as pop song form disintegrated (or perhaps was abandoned) in the face of the demands and opportunities of the recording studio, funk capitalized on the breakthroughs of James Brown and Sly Stone and created a new kind of structure on which increasingly complex musical ideas could be built. George Clinton, the most acidic of all the great funkateers, worked out his multifaceted vision on a series of LPs so abrasive and brittle that even their best bits never really scored with a mass audience. Former Chess Records session drummer and Ramsey Lewis sideman Maurice White, the most eclectic of the funksters, built Earth, Wind & Fire into one of the great pop combines of the seventies, a touring and recording machine as impressively sleek and powerful (and sometimes as cold and unwieldy) as L.A. neighbors like Fleetwood Mac and the Eagles.

Naturally, White seemed more comfortable than Clinton when it came to paring down to meet the demands of a single. The African folk, soft soul, and light jazz elements of EWF's sound adapted fairly easily to Top 40 strictures, and the instrumental work of band members like bassist Verdine White and keyboardist Larry Dunn gave the music extra sheen and sophistication. But perhaps the key to "Shining Star," EWF's breakthrough hit, was vocalist Philip Bailey, whose falsetto gasps and shrieks could have fitted the Delfonics, adding a specifically pop element missing from funk since Sly's Family Stone disintegrated. In the realm of singles, it's altogether to the point that, from within the brilliant brass flourishes and deep bass grooves, such a remarkably distinctive voice should surface.

434 LOVER'S ISLAND, Blue Jays
Produced by Werly Fairburn; written by Leon Peels and Alex Manigo
Milestone 2008   1961   *Billboard:* #31

West Coast doo-wop of the highest order, recorded by a quartet of black Los Angeles teenagers under the direction of Werly Fairburn, a minor league country and western singer with the initiative (and capital) to start his own record label. Fairburn outfoxed Bumps Blackwell on this one; Blackwell passed on signing the Blue Jays (though he loved their song) just a few weeks before ol' Werly snatched them up. The key to the record, as it happened, was less the song than Leon Peels' Jesse Belvin-style lead with its trembling falsetto conveying rarified yearning for the romantic perfection the lyric fantasizes.

And what a fantasy! A dream of a place where the trees grow tall, the dusk is always golden, birds are entranced by the love that comes pouring from above, and "love never . . . never . . . never . . . grows old." As lavishly ornamented by Peels, "Lover's Island" is one of the most unbelievably pristine examples of romantic fantasy ever put on tape. It would be hard to think of a more telling comment on popular culture than that four young, underprivileged L.A. kids were able to bring so much more out of this fantasy island in three minutes than a millionaire team of Hollywood executives, writers, directors, and actors was able to do in five years.

435 HE STOPPED LOVING HER TODAY, George Jones
Produced by Billy Sherrill; written by Bobby Braddock and Curly Putnam
Epic 50867   1980   Did not make pop chart

Sung with a deep caution that might pass for wisdom, "He Stopped Loving Her Today" is not only country music's greatest obituary, its magnificently controlled vocal damn near resurrects countrypolitan slickness as well. There is probably no other idiom in which *anyone* could get away with the sheer maudlin sentimentality of Jones's recitation of the final verse. But George is so profoundly committed to the dour truth of his tale, he not only makes you accept it but draws you back again and again.

436 HAVE YOU SEEN HER, The Chi-Lites
Produced by Willie Henderson and Quinton Joseph; written by Eugene Record and Barbara Acklin
Brunswick 55462   1971   *Billboard:* #3

How canny and commanding was Eugene Record's manipulation of harmony group and funk band aesthetics? Try to think of another record that features prominent fuzz guitar and yet doesn't sound at all dated. The melody carried by the group vocals is touching, Record's recitation affecting (especially when he has to confess that he's so emotionally destitute because he took his lover for granted) and when he soars to a falsetto lead, it's like placing a cherry on top.

437 SIX DAYS ON THE ROAD, Dave Dudley
Producer not credited; written by Earl Green and Carl Montgomery
Golden Wing 3020   1963   *Billboard:* #32

Cut in a tiny little Minneapolis studio, for an even tinier label, Dave Dudley's "Six Days on the Road" had about as much impact as any hit of the early sixties—it spawned a whole genre of truck driving songs that are not only the closest contemporary equivalent of the cowboy ballads of yore but have produced some of the best country records of the past thirty years: Merle Haggard's "White Line Fever," Terry Fell's "Truck Driving Man," Red Sovine's "Phantom 309," "Girl on the Billboard" and "Looking at the World Through a Windshield," by Del

Reeves, Dick Curless's "Tombstone Every Mile," the Willis Brothers' "Give Me Forty Acres," and Dudley's own "Truck Drivin' Son of a Gun." The truck driving song's link to rock and roll, through the car song genre that extends from Chuck Berry to Prince, is also obvious and natural.

Dudley, with his booming rockabilly baritone and skeletal honky-tonk backup, captures just about every important element of the truck driving schematic—the pills, the loneliness, the horniness, the nerve-wracking life on the feathery edge of the law. He's clearly not a Southerner (in fact, he's from Spencer, Wisconsin) but there's also no denying that he's a good old boy who appreciates Elvis as much as his Georgia overdrive, as you can tell when he declares "I could have a lotta women but I'm not like-a some-a other guys" with a Presley-style slur.

438 (I'LL REMEMBER) IN THE STILL OF THE NITE, The Five Satins
Written and produced by Fred Parris
Ember 1005   1956   *Billboard:* #24

The most popular doo-wop record ever made, "In the Still of the Nite" is legendary not only because of its surging harmonies singing "shoo-doot-en-dooby-doo" but because of the circumstances of its creation. In 1955, Fred Parris was on guard duty in the middle of the freezing Korean night, thinking about home and Cole Porter's great "In the Still of the Night," when he came up with the idea for a rhythm and blues song of the same title. (He messed with the spelling to avoid confusion between the two; it didn't work.) When Parris returned to his native New Haven, Connecticut, he and some friends repaired to a church basement and cut a smash so huge that *Cashbox* reported that it was still selling heavily three years later. (Guess this makes the Satins the Pink Floyd of the fifties.)

"In the Still of the Nite" had much to do with kicking off the early sixties doo-wop revival, thanks to its inclusion on Art Laboe's first *Oldies But Goodies* album in 1959 and subsequent rerelease by Ember, with the result that the disc made the charts again in both 1960 and 1961. (Always more up-to-date, the R&B lists ignored it.)

439 NIGHT TRAIN, James Brown
Produced by James Brown; written by Oscar Washington, Lewis C. Simpkins, and Jimmy Forrest

King 5614   1962   *Billboard:* #35

440 NIGHT TRAIN, Jimmy Forrest
Producer not credited; written by Oscar Washington, Lewis C. Simpkins, and Jimmy Forrest

United 110   1952   Did not make pop chart

Rhythm and blues didn't simply sweep jazz in its wake. Veteran big band sax players, in particular, could prosper in the new small combo age, if they found the right riff. And no one ever located a better one than Jimmy Forrest, a veteran of Jay McShann's Blue Devils and the orchestras of Andy Kirk and Duke Ellington. He crafted one of the sensations of 1952 by picking up the final riff of Ellington's "Happy Go Lucky Local" and turning it into a chugging masterpiece. No one has ever described Forrest's "Night Train" better than R&B historian Big Al Pavlow: "a golden-toned tenor sax solo by Jimmy in front of a hauntingly percussive strip joint backbeat."

Forrest's riff evoked much more than strip joints, though. Its smoky atmosphere and undulating cadences were as openly sexual as any beat in the R&B repertoire. And with its call-and-response between the sputtering sax and the locomotive rhythm section, "Night Train" also evoked a time fast slipping by, the days of total American segregation, when work as a Pullman porter on the night train had about as much status as any job to which a black man might aspire.

Forrest's record never saw the light of day on the pop charts, but the song later became a substantial hit in a version by white trumpeter Buddy Morrow, which blessedly left much of the original's intensity intact. More important, "Night Train" was picked up as a staple theme of R&B combos almost from the day it was issued. The Viscounts eventually brought it back to the pop charts in 1960, as their sequel to "Harlem Nocturne."

The roots of James Brown's sound ran deep into such classic jump band honker grooves; he periodically revived late forties and early fifties dance band classics (most famously with "Prisoner of Love") and his albums are chock-full of such tunes. His "Night Train" was special even among such revampings, though. Not only did the JBs' electric bass and powerhouse percussion attack stiffen up a beat considerably accelerated from Forrest's original, but James postured himself front and center of a song that had always been an instrumental, calling off the stations at the top ("Miami, Florida!" goes the scratchy shout, perhaps deliberately evoking the destination of the trains that smoked their way through the darkness of his Georgia hometown), emitting grunts and shouts and then coming back at the very end: "Miami, Florida! Atlanta, Georgia! Raleigh, No'th Carolina. Washington, D.C.—oh, Richmond, Virginia, too. Baltimore, Maryland. Philadelphia. New York City— headed home. Boston, Massachusetts. And don't forget New Orleans, the home of the blues." Finally, he bursts out with "Night train, night train, carry me home!" repeated again and again until the unending riff fades out.

What James made of the song was something better than even Forrest's original; he'd turned it into the saga of the black man in America, his travels from South to North without ever losing sight of the "home of the blues." Which lies less in New Orleans (or Memphis or wherever you might choose) than it does in the heart and mind of a rhythm genius like James.

441 YOU DON'T KNOW LIKE I KNOW, Sam and Dave
Written and produced by Isaac Hayes and David Porter
Stax 180   1966   *Billboard: #90*

Steve Cropper plays guitar here like he's working a problem in higher math, and the Memphis Horns, especially the saxes, chime in as if they're the solution. Together, they overwhelm even Sam and Dave's nonstop preaching, and in order to do that, you have to be practicing some rare calculus indeed.

442 ROCK ME BABY, B.B. King
Produced by Jules Bihari; written by B.B. King and
Jules Bihari
Kent 393   1964   *Billboard: #34*

While "Rock Me Baby" plays virtually no role in the story of B.B. King (Charles Sawyer's excellent biography, *The Arrival of B.B. King*, mentions it only in the discography), it plays a major part in the story of rock and roll, since there could have been no British blues revival without it. "Rock Me Baby" is the epitome of what young English rock guitarists like Jeff Beck and their Anglo-American audiences loved about the blues: Its simple, syncopated sexiness provides the framework for top of the lungs shouting and extended guitar workouts. Those are the qualities that made "Rock Me Baby" King's biggest nonorchestrated pop hit, and they're certainly what drew guitar slingers like Beck and Alvin Lee of Ten Years to it. They're also what keep it sounding fresh today.

443 SHAME SHAME SHAME, Shirley (And Company)
Written and produced by Sylvia Robinson
Vibration 532   1975   *Billboard:* #12

One of the wildest one-shots of the disco period, written and produced by the Sylvia (Robinson) of Mickey and Sylvia for a studio group led by the Shirley (Goodman) of Shirley and Lee, on a theme first elucidated by the one and only Jimmy Reed. The male vocalist, Jesus Alvarez, never did anything else of note, but he damn near takes the thing away from Shirley with his falsetto squeals.

Great lyrics in the "Bird's the Word" / "Do Wah Diddy" tradition, too. Mainly, they're a plaint that the singer's partner can't (or won't) get down on the dance floor. But they reach a pinnacle of pataphysical with the final, cawing couplets: "You can't start the groove 'cause you just won't move / Got my sun roof down, got my diamond in the back / Put on your shaggy wig, woman / If you don't, *I* ain't comin' back."

444 PEPPERMINT TWIST, Joey Dee and Starlighters
Produced by Henry Glover; written by Joey Dee and Henry Glover
Roulette 4401   1962   *Billboard:* #1 (3 weeks)

The greatest Twist record—it cuts everything Chubby Checker ever did to ribbons, and though the Beatles' latter-day remake of the Isley Brothers' "Twist and Shout" beats it, the Isleys themselves didn't come close to the sheer stomping energy of Joey and his band.

Which is only fitting for the house band at the Home of the Twist, the Peppermint Lounge on Manhattan's West 45th Street, where Joey DiNicola's Jersey-bred band appeared nightly (together with a female trio from Brooklyn who soon thereafter became the Ronettes). And if their rave-ups were this hot all the time, no wonder the joint became the Studio 54 of the early sixties.

On the other hand, you've also got to wonder how much attention Joey was paying to what was going on out on the floor, since his description of the action in "Peppermint Twist"—"'Round an' roun' an' roun' an' up 'n' down / And 1–2–3, kick, 1–2–3, kick"—most certainly describes some other dance.

445 NEITHER ONE OF US (WANTS TO BE THE FIRST TO SAY GOODBYE), Gladys Knight and the Pips
Produced by Joe Porter; written by Jim Weatherly
Soul 35098   1973   *Billboard:* #2

Maudlin though it may seem, if you're ever unfortunate enough to preside over the dissolution of a relationship, especially one that had seemed enduring, this is the record you're gonna need. Weatherly's country-trained pen sketches quickly the kind of romantic befuddlement in which nobody's communicating, let alone happy, and everybody's afraid to say so. The aching husk in Knight's voice, so dry she might have been sucking lemons, proves the perfect device for breaking the ice, and her languid phrasing embodies the emotional inertia still holding such lives in thrall to one another. She doesn't even push it when she reaches the traumatic finality of the thrice-repeated "There can be no way" but she opens up and lets it soar on the final chorus, an elegant send-off for all the if-onlys left unspoken.

446 ONE OF A KIND (LOVE AFFAIR), The Spinners
Produced by Thom Bell; written by J. B. Jefferson
Atlantic 2962   1973   *Billboard:* #11

As far as I know, J.B. Jefferson never wrote another hit. But Thom Bell's seductive rhythms coax such a buoyant bed for Philippe Wynne's joyous lead vocal that the wordplay feels as intricate and invigorating as Smokey Robinson's. And just as emotionally credible.

447 EVERYBODY NEEDS SOMEBODY TO LOVE, Solomon Burke

Produced by Bert Berns; written by Bert Berns, Solomon Burke,
and Jerry Wexler
Atlantic 2241   1964   *Billboard:* #58

The porcine, gilt-fingered lay preacher testifies from the top but what
you ought to hear is writ large between the lines, especially in the
stentorian opening sermon. That is, when Burke sings "I believe that
if everybody was to sing this song, it could save the whole world," what
he really means is that if everybody sang his song, his next BMI check
would astonish nations. So he's a fraud; it's still okay, for never has a
swindle been sung so seductively. Just don't misunderstand him: When
Burke sings "I need you, you, you" that ain't love, that's recruitment.

448 AIN'T TOO PROUD TO BEG, The Temptations

Produced by Norman Whitfield; written by Norman Whitfield
and Eddie Holland
Gordy 7054   1966   *Billboard:* #13

David Ruffin on his knees, in the most abject posture a gritty-voiced
soul man has ever assumed. Where the Righteous Brothers, in "Just
Once in My Life," merely promise to grovel, David and his gang recite
in massive detail not only the depths of their love, but the steps to
which they're willing to descend to prove their need. As for myself, I
was convinced by the drums, cowbell, and piano riffs at the very start,
but even if you're harder to persuade, the contrast between Melvin
Franklin's booming bass and Eddie Kendricks' thrilling tenor leaps
oughta get to you eventually.

449 LITTLE LATIN LUPE LU, Mitch Ryder & the Detroit Wheels

Produced by Bob Crewe; written by Bill Medley
New Voice 808   1966   *Billboard:* #17

450 LITTLE LATIN LUPE LU, The Righteous Brothers
Written and produced by Bill Medley
Moonglow 215   1963   *Billboard: #49*

It's amazing to find that a garage rock classic like "Little Latin Lupe
Lu" was composed; it ought to have been discovered or maybe just
stumbled across while searching the archives of unbelievably wild human behavior.

As for who did the greatest version, unless some archeological
prototype turns up, you've gotta go with Mitch and the boys. They start
out on the wrong foot, making "Lupe" sound like not much more than
"Jenny Takes a Ride" redux, but the song picks up tremendous groove
from Johnny Bee's powerhouse bass drum and snare attack, Jimmy
McCarty's guitar achieves punk rock ecstasy during his quick solo, and
the coda is simply total atomic explosiveness. It's one of those records
that you can never quite play loud enough and it leaves your nerves
jangling for long minutes afterwards.

The Righteous Brothers, whose Bill Medley really did invent
"Lupe," make a more contained assault, voicing it in conventional
gospel-R&B rather than rockin' it up. For all of the predictable trashiness, Medley's singing is as authentically soulful as anybody who's ever
stepped to the mike, and Bobby Hatfield's Little Richard "wooo" 's at
the end are just as thrilling as the originals.

451 I DO, The Marvelows
Produced by Johnny Pate; written by Johnny Paden,
Frank Paden, Jesse Smith, Willie Stephenson, and Melvin Mason
ABC-Paramount 10629   1965   *Billboard: #37*

Melvin Mason and his buddies used to sing in southside Chicago parks,
looking to attract girls. To warm up, they sang "Do doo, do doo." And
as it turned out, that was the part that the girls liked best, the faster
the better. So Mason wrote a sketchy lyric to accompany it. And when
Marvelow Jesse Smith introduced the group to producer Johnny Pate,
then riding high with the Impressions, Pate liked it, too, and signed
them to ABC in October 1964.

Instead of bringing the group in to record with a band or against
prerecorded backings, Pate made a rough a cappella tape and embellished *that*, an almost unheard of production tactic. From the practice
number, he skillfully crafted a raucous soul shout, setting the group's
"Do-doo" and Mason's lightly rasping voice against charging horns,

their handclaps against cannonading drums. The result came off as a mixture of street corner chant, wedding vow parody, and gospel affirmation. Those who know only J. Geils' (pretty damn good) 1982 knock-off are in for a shock of pure pleasure.

452 DADDY ROLLIN' (IN YOUR ARMS), Dion
Producer not credited; written by Dion DiMucci
Laurie 3464   1968   Did not make pop chart

Dion appeared in the fifties as the very voice of Good Bad But Not Evil, rough as sharkskin, smooth as Italian knit. At his toughest, on "The Wanderer," he was a sweetheart, even if he wasn't too pretty to belong to the Fordham Baldies, the most dangerous gang in the Bronx. Back then there were lots of guys like that, lovers at heart who'd cut your throat on Saturday night. None of them could make rock and roll swing like Dion, though.

Then the hits stopped coming and Dion sank into pure evil. In 1968, he reappeared on the radio in the guise of a laid-back neo-folkie singing "Abraham, Martin and John," but his liberal piety was belied by the needle in his arm. Dion, sweet Dion, was a junkie, full-fledged shooter of smack.

Flip over "Abraham, Martin and John," and the truisms dissolve into the truth: a surging, churning, angry, anguished version of Robert Johnson's country blues. Haunted electric guitars clang and clash against one another, drums pound in from another room, uniting in a wad of noise symbolizing nothing but spelling out pain and fear.

Dion had never sung any sweeter or more powerfully than he did here, but you couldn't make out half of what he was saying because it came out through clenched teeth in yowls of grief and moans of hurt, until he released all his anguish in a moan on the chorus: "Gonna have your sweet lovin' / Daddy rollin' in your arms." He might have been singing to a woman; he might have been singing to the drug.

In the last verse, he sings as clearly as ever, as if to pin down at last the source of this primordial rhythm, this ancient symbolic virus. "You the sweetest little angel baby / Can't stand to leave you," and then he disintegrated right before your ears, singing "a-looooo-ne. A-looooo-ne." A sound beyond the blues. A sound of pure need. The sound of what happens when you just say No and that monkey spits in your face and grins.

It was the scariest music Dion ever made and in its way, the most adult. Yet for years, you knew it only if you'd happened to be attracted to the rhythms, the patriotic clichés, the sentimentality of "Abraham, Martin and John." Maybe he intended it as an antidote. Maybe he just couldn't figure out what else to do with the truest noises he'd ever made. Maybe he knew already that if you made whole albums of such sounds you didn't have long to live. Either way, it's a treasure, the kind of great lost B side critics and collectors like to talk about. Only this one delivers more than the stories promise, not just novelty but the real secrets of a great singer's life.

453 SAVE THE LAST DANCE FOR ME, The Drifters
Produced by Jerry Leiber and Mike Stoller; written by Doc Pomus and Mort Shuman
Atlantic 2071   1960   *Billboard:* #1 (3 weeks)

Doc Pomus says that he and Mort Shuman wrote many of their biggest hits soon after Shuman returned from each of his periodic Mexican vacations with some new fragment of Latin beat and melody. Pomus would then attempt to fashion a lyric that "sounded like it was translated"—lines in which the rhythm was slightly askew from American English speech patterns.

"Save the Last Dance for Me" is proof that that's not just a shaggy dog story. The way that certain lines are phrased almost forces the singer to assume Latinate phrasing. It also helps here that the guys translating Pomus and Shuman's song onto tape are Leiber and Stoller, those masters of *baion* bass, and Ben E. King, singing at the peak of his form on the last big hit of his Drifters' career.

454 I LOVE ROCK 'N' ROLL, Joan Jett & the Blackhearts
Produced by Ritchie Cordell and Kenny Laguna; written by Jake Hooker and Alan Merrill
Boardwalk 135   1982   *Billboard:* #1 (7 weeks)

An actual anthem. Well, really, just a bad-ass guitar riff and a story about a sleazy barroom pickup as told by the leather-encased heartthrob who did the picking. 'Cept this time, the point of view is female and as they head for bed, the ironies are more abundant than the fantasies.

Joan Jett played lead guitar in the Runaways, a teenage female hard rock quartet whose svengali, Kim Fowley, cultivated for them a sluttish know-nothing image. Since Fowley's production philosophy amounted to "It's all noise and who cares?" the Runaways became big in Japan, and almost nowhere else.

When they split, nobody figured they'd be hearing from the angry little brunette on lead guitar again. But Jett met up with Kenny Laguna, a Brill Building refugee who'd played and sung on all the bubble gum hits, and Ritchie Cordell, who'd written many of those hits (including "I Think We're Alone Now"). Jett was living in England performing with ex-Sex Pistols Paul Cook and Steve Jones but under Laguna's guidance she came back to the States and formed a band, which picked up on the Runaways image at least insofar as it was steeped in leather, crude 4/4, and distorted guitar.

They cut "I Love Rock 'n' Roll," and the album that went with it (which also included a remake of "Crimson and Clover," a Tommy James hit Cordell didn't write) and had it rejected by every major record label and all the significant minor ones. Finally, Laguna gave up and put the record out on his own. Favorable press attention and steady plugging at an almost underground radio level (unprecedented in the early eighties) by legendary album-rock promo man Steve Leeds brought Jett and Laguna to Neil Bogart, king of bubble gum at Buddah and Cameo/Parkway, emperor of disco at Casablanca, who was then starting a new label, Boardwalk. Bogart got the concept and more than that, he threw all his new resources behind it. That album became a hit and "I Love Rock 'n' Roll," a remake of an obscure B side by the British band, the Arrows, became one of the most phenomenal hits of the eighties.

Also one of the toughest and truest. Joan Jett, having fulfilled all her ambitions except maybe joining the starting lineup of the Baltimore Orioles, had several more hits and, in partnership with Laguna and the Blackhearts, continued to make the same uncompromising, not-nearly-as-simple as it looks music out of a raw throat and a hungry heart. So she became a postpunk icon of both the purity of rocking out and the ability of women to do the job for themselves.

455 I CAN'T TURN YOU LOOSE, Otis Redding

Produced by Otis Redding, Jim Stewart, and Steve Cropper; written by Otis Redding, Steve Cropper, and McElvoy Robinson
Volt 130   1966   Did not make pop chart

Q: As long as Otis is making music as hot as this, why would you want him to turn you loose?

A: Obviously, so you could hook up with the real stars of the show—bass player Duck Dunn and drummer Al Jackson.

456 KNOCK ON WOOD, Eddie Floyd
Produced by Jim Stewart; written by Eddie Floyd and Steve Cropper
Stax 194   1966   *Billboard:* #28

Purely as a performer, Eddie Floyd had his work cut out to reach journeyman status. But his songwriting was so good that his limitations barely mattered. "Knock on Wood" is the best of the bunch, driving Memphis funk that finds itself to this day in the repertoire of any halfways heavy soul-derived band. None of 'em are likely to beat a record on which Al Jackson plays his ass off, Steve Cropper whips through guitar changes like he's being handed crisp $100 bills at the end of every bar, and Duck Dunn accepts the maintenance of both beat and melody as his personal responsibility. Given such advantages, all Floyd has to do is not mess up—and he never does, riding their groove to glory.

457 ALL AROUND THE WORLD, Little Willie John
Produced by Henry Glover; written by Titus Turner
King 4818   1955   Did not make pop chart

That Little Willie John remains all but unknown except to aficionados of rhythm and blues is one of the great injustices of contemporary popular music. James Brown recorded a tribute album, *Thinking of Little Willie John . . . And a Few Other Nice Things* but everybody who sang R&B-based ballads in the late fifties and sixties (up to and including Elvis and Sam Cooke) owed him something. He was so influential because the emotional penetration of his music, with its continual high-pitched resonances, engulfs the listener so completely; his was soul music before anybody coined the term. Willie John was a musician's musician. His singing was breathtaking, the phrasing fearlessly original, and always blessedly free of affectation even when he slid into his slight vibrato, as he does at the end of the chorus here, quavering the word "man." He sang with the same commingling of street sense and sensitivity found in the great Chicago bluesman Little Walter. There's a roughness in his language that's belied by the caresses of his voice, just the same way that his singing is offset by a honking saxophone on "All

Around the World." Yet Willie John comes far more from the tradition that produced crooners like Nat "King" Cole and Billy Eckstine; his appropriation of the latter's "A Cottage for Sale" is one of his most unforgettable performances.

In this record's final verse and chorus (about the time he declares his woman's smiling face "a heavenly light"), Little Willie John's tremulous assurance amounts to a musical redefinition of what rock and roll "freedom" really meant. (Compare it to Little Richard's record of the same title, which is an explicit ode to rock music's orgiastic glories, and you'll see what I mean.) Though he died in prison, Willie John creates from a misunderstood lover's vale of misery a moment of release so pure that you could measure against it (as from time to time I have) all future efforts at liberation.

Little Willie John did things like this over and over again in the records he made after being discovered in 1953 by Johnny Otis, playing a Detroit rhythm and blues show which also featured Jackie Wilson and Hank Ballard. Syd Nathan of King Records was apparently reluctant to sign him, but then, Nathan was notoriously reluctant (and just plain notorious). But once he'd made the deal, Henry Glover took Willie John into the studio and put him together with a song Titus Turner had recently released on Mercury Records' Wing R&B subsidiary.

"All Around the World" belongs to a school of blues bragging with deep roots in American folklore, one that found its future in raps like LL Cool J's "I Need Love." In the song's first few lines, the singer declares himself willing to become a housefly if he can just light on his baby for a lifetime, so inspired he could dig a ditch with a toothpick and fight lions with a switch. (Nevertheless, Little Milton's 1969 revival gave the tune a more appropriate title, taking up the chorus's declaration, "Grits Ain't Groceries.")

Journeyman Turner's original is a pedestrian Lloyd Price knockoff. Willie John's is something else: guttural, legato, carried away with the twin intoxications of the love lyric and the beat, the kind of record that inaugurates an historic career.

458 SLIP AWAY, Clarence Carter
Produced by Rick Hall; written by Wilbur Terrell, William Armstrong, and Marcus Daniel
Atlantic 2508   1968   *Billboard:* #6

The Southern tradition of blind, guitar-playing singing preachers, which produced a series of brilliant performers, from Blind Willie Johnson, the finest of them all, to Reverend Gary Davis, one of the great acoustic blues rediscoveries of the fifties and sixties, reached the end of the line not long before studios like Rick Hall's Fame sprang up around the fringes of the Mississippi River delta. The greatest blind musicians of the postwar period, Ray Charles and Stevie Wonder, were both secular and primarily keyboardists (though Ray was a terrific sax player and Stevie one of the deadliest drummers around).

Clarence Carter played mean guitar and derived his entire vocal style from preachers, but he hardly qualifies as one, because his homilies are sermonettes in favor of raunch, among the most explicitly sexual expressions in all of rock and soul. Yet that only makes Carter the final link in a chain that extends to the birth of the blues, a music often carried hither and yon by blind men who had no other options except to play and sing as passionately as possible in order that more coins might fall into their cup.

Clarence Carter was born in 1936, a year after Elvis, but he sounded knowing enough at thirty-two to have learned his licks at the feet of Blind Lemon Jefferson himself. And he must have learned a few somewhere, because at the time of his first and best hit, he was courting—and winning—perhaps the best-looking (and one of the best sounding) of all the female soul singers, Candi Staton.

Carter's musical virtues begin with a stentorian voice, which he uses in a style reminiscent of B.B. King. His specialty is vigorously detailed descriptions of infidelity, embellished with his prototypically lewd "Heh, heh, heh."

"Slip Away," Carter's first hit, essays the same theme as James Carr's "Dark End of the Street" and its musical approach is typical of Carter's work. With a marvelous bass and drum groove supplied by David Hood and Roger Hawkins, the core of the Muscle Shoals rhythm section, the arrangement is colored in with sputtering horns and Carter's own mellow Fender Jaguar guitar. The result is closer to hard blues than soul, an Alabama answer to B.B. King's similar productions of the period.

"Slip Away" proposes some back door cheating, the theme to which Carter's records continually return, sometimes homiletically ("Making Love"), sometimes comically ("Backdoor Santa") but rarely so poignantly as here, where his cajoling is not so much pleading as an assertion of the right to love the one you love, no matter who you're with, a thought conveyed less in the words than in Carter's ravaged reading of them. "Now I know it's wrong, the things I ask you to do," he croaks, but he keeps right on pushing, rubbing up against that groove until you feel as sore with desire as he does.

459 DON'T IT MAKE YOU WANT TO GO HOME, Joe South

Written and produced by Joe South
Capitol 2592   1969   *Billboard:* #41

The first time I went to Atlanta, it looked something from Goethe's
Faust. Construction everwhere kicking up red Georgia clay, buildings
thrown up where highways hadn't been built yet, highways cutting
through places that looked like they'd never be developed, the continual
din and blare of jackhammers and airhorns, and at least a dozen streets,
roads, and avenues named Peachtree. Others might have seen prospects
but all I felt was confusion and restlessness, a sense of frustration that
came not from the past being shattered, but from the sheer ugliness of
its replacement. What made it all especially Faustian was the sense that
this mad construction binge had been going on since time before memory, and that it would never be finished.

That was in the early eighties but I have a hunch that outsiders
have seen Atlanta that way since about two weeks after Sherman passed
through. Rhett Butler would have understood.

Joe South definitely does—he's a homeboy. South summarizes his
feelings in the opening of "Don't It Make You Want to Go Home,"
in which a swirl of belle epoque strings gives way to a laconic, wistful
blues guitar. Suffused with nostalgia, South sits and strums, talking
hopefully about a trip back to the homeplace, his memory detailed and
precise. And then he arrives and turns away in stunned surprise:
"There's a dragstrip down by the riverside, where my grandma's cow
used to graze / Now the grass don't grow and the river don't flow, like
it did in my childhood days." He steps back and draws a quiet breath.
"Don't it make you wanna go home, now, don't it make you wanna
go home," he sings and that's it—for the rest of the song he sings
nothing else, as the music swells with strings and horns, gospel choruses
and handclaps on the offbeat. Trying to take the Beatles' advice and
"get back," he's totally trapped in the ugliness of the present, yet he
can't let go of the dream. It's not a condition you have to be from
Atlanta to understand.

460 LAWDY MISS CLAWDY, Lloyd Price
Produced by Art Rupe; written by Lloyd Price
Specialty 428   1952   Did not make pop chart

Art Rupe's version of the creation of "Lawdy Miss Clawdy" holds that Lloyd Price was "chewing up the clock" at Cosimo Matassa's J&M Studio in New Orleans, where Rupe was working during a March 1952 recording trip from L.A. He rehearsed Price for hour after expensive hour without getting anything on tape. Finally, Rupe says, he told Price to get his act together or forget it. At which point, the kid started to cry and the record man relented and heard, for the first time, "Lawdy Miss Clawdy." Understanding that he'd found at least a hit and at best a star, Rupe postponed his trip home and cut that song and several others with a band featuring Fats Domino on piano.

You'd have to trust record company owners more than I do to fully credit that yarn (for one thing, "Lawdy" was written for one of the top Crescent City deejays, Okey Dokey, on whose show Price and his five-piece band, the Blueboys, were appearing), but on the other hand, that's clearly Fats playing the legendary intro and Lloyd sure seems upset about *something*.

More than anything Fats did at this period, "Lawdy Miss Clawdy" set the pattern for the rock and roll years in New Orleans, especially through Earl Palmer's loping, midtempo shuffle beats with their busy ride cymbal and through the vocal shouted over the top of the groove. Though the beat never gets to run wild, as it soon would when unleashed through Little Richard, it would be hard to imagine Richard's actual music—not the flash stuff on top but its underpinnings—without something as raucous as "Lawdy Miss Clawdy" to pave its way.

461 RUMBLE, Link Wray & His Ray Men
Produced by Milt Grant; written by Link Wray
Cadence 1347   1958   *Billboard:* #16

The musical equivalent of football's forearm shiver: Hits you straight through the central nervous system, glazes your eyes, and drops you in your tracks. Short. Nasty. Potentially lethal. So much fun it may even be addictive—and it's one habit you'll never want to kick.

462 HOLIDAYS IN THE SUN, The Sex Pistols
Produced by Chris Thomas and Bill Price; written by
Paul Cook, Steve Jones, Johnny Rotten, and Sid Vicious
Virgin 191 (UK)   1977   Did not make pop chart

"Holidays in the Sun" is a blur, roaring and crashing in waves of fragmented noise. Within, over and under through that noise, Johnny Rotten's vocal spits and cackles. It's an assault and what's being assaulted isn't a concept of "good music" so much as the very concept of culture in a society that endures the reality of Belsen through the desensitizing apparatus of liberal moralism. "In sensurround sound in a two-inch wall" (in other words, on TV) Rotten peers over the Berlin Wall, as those on the other side peer back; he's surprised to find that what he sees not only dismantles his own presumptions about the people over there but somehow reconnects him to the history that pop culture was supposed to numb him enough to escape. And since the real text of almost all Sex Pistols songs is Rotten's utter loathing of his own physicality, it's hardly surprising that his reaction is total revulsion: He wants to go over the Berlin Wall, perhaps because the "culture" on the other side seems better able to keep its citizens numb.

Steve Jones plays guitar riffs brittle and brutal enough to suggest the things that make Rotten long to lose consciousness, sheets of guitar energy that explode any hope of personal comfort or psychological security, so much so that Rotten's barely coherent babbling at the record's end seems deliriously Dylanesque, almost comic in its agitation. Yet not taking this music, this song, this man and his moody words seriously would be the worst mistake you could make, if only because Rotten and his crew seem determined to fatigue and castigate everybody whose attention flags for even an instant.

What's going on in "Holidays in the Sun" is a lot like what Allen Ginsberg meant when he described William Burroughs's writing as a "naked lunch, where everybody sees what's at the end of every fork." For almost three and a half minutes, from the jackbooted opening beat to the last line—a sneering "Please don't be waiting for me"—Johnny Rotten rubs your face in it. Next to this, merely publicly pissing on the Queen or telling a TV interviewer to get fucked on the air was child's play.

463 BROWN EYED HANDSOME MAN, Chuck Berry
Produced by Leonard Chess; written by Chuck Berry
Chess 1635   1956   Did not make pop chart

A decade before "black is beautiful" achieved radical chic, Chuck communicated that very message with a jittery, ragged guitar line and rapid-fire vocal delivery that suggested just how much he risked merely by celebrating the facts. I've always wondered whether that home run hitter in the final verse was Jackie Robinson or Willie Mays, but what really matters is that it's the most organic connection anybody's ever made between rock and baseball, Bruce Springsteen and John Fogerty included. Here, Chuck fakes nothing—except for his substitution of "-eyed" for "-skinned," of course.

464 THINK IT OVER, Buddy Holly & the Crickets
Produced by Norman Petty; written by Buddy Holly,
Norman Petty, and Jerry Allison
Brunswick 55072   1958   Billboard: #27

465 I'M LOOKIN' FOR SOMEONE TO LOVE, Buddy Holly and the Crickets
Produced by Norman Petty; written by Buddy Holly and Norman Petty
Brunswick 55009   1957   Did not make pop chart

I used to think that the one really great novel that needed to be written about rock and roll was the story of what would have happened if Buddy Holly had lived.

Some folks think he was on a disastrous course, and it's true that "It Doesn't Matter Anymore" is the only oldie that actually deserved to have Linda Ronstadt butcher it all the way to the Top 40. But if Holly was expanding his music beyond the basic rock band vocabulary, it wasn't entirely to soften it up. Besides string arrangements of Paul Anka pop songs, toward the end of his life he worked with King Curtis and Mickey Baker and started producing Waylon Jennings, none of whom was likely to persuade him in directions inclined to cheer Norman Petty or his various mentors at the Decca records group. Some of the greatest names in rhythm and blues were experimenting with overdubbing strings in 1958, and if Leiber and Stoller never released anything as bathetic as "Raining in My Heart," there's sure lots of Drifters' hits as syrupy as "It Doesn't Matter Anymore."

What's striking is how well prepared to meet the creative challenges of the sixties Holly would have been. When he died, he was just beginning to master studio technique, but he was born a master of rock and roll: "I'm Lookin' for Someone to Love" not only has the very guitar attack that made the Beatles so distinctive, but the kind of whimsical lyricism that made Bob Dylan unique. "Drunk man, street car, foot slip, there you are," Holly sings, and it's like being thrown forward into "Subterranean Homesick Blues." And that's a track he threw away on the B side of his first single.

Holly made all his hits in less than three years, and his growth was exponential. "Think It Over" uses a Sun Records-style wash of echo and cymbal and a booming piano bass solo to create a more deliberate version of a Jerry Lee Lewis record. It's not much more than a teenage love song but the wordplay displays an intricate humor that Holly's chopped up phrasing pushes to the bounds of logic. "Are you sure that I'm *not* the one?" he asks, and the negation jumps out at you. And rather than singing "A lonely heart grows cold and old," he pauses for less than a beat, just long enough to make the afterthought apparent: "A lonely heart grows cold . . . and old." That kind of phrasing and writing and playing and recording stands out in any era.

466 TIRED OF BEING ALONE, Al Green
Produced by Willie Mitchell; written by Al Green
Hi 2194   1971   *Billboard:* #11

Fitting, isn't it, that one of the few big hits the most famous soul solipsist wrote without collaborators is a plaint against not loneliness, but the state of being alone. Green's internal focus is so deep that he's fascinating as he begs the woman he wants to worship him, squeezing out perfect, gentle falsetto notes as if muttering to himself. But if you think he'd have a chance of convincing her without that gorgeous arrangement, kicked along by perfectly timed Al Jackson drumming and Teenie Hodges's pretty little guitar figure, you're dreaming as deeply as he is.

467 (I'M A) ROAD RUNNER, Junior Walker and the All Stars

Produced by Brian Holland and Lamont Dozier; written by Brian Holland,
Lamont Dozier, and Eddie Holland
Soul 35015   1966   *Billboard:* #20

More Motown rusticism. The historic antecedent for Walker's re-
monstrances ("You can love me if you wanna but I do declare / When
I get restless, I gotta move somewhere") is certainly Robert Johnson's
"New Walking Blues," but even that immortal country bluesman never
saw the like of this blend of booming bass, tanked-up tambourine, and
gritty guitar. Much less Walker's fractured saxophone. As for whether
these are the bourgeois blues one would expect from Berry Gordy and
company, all I can tell you is that while Walker was the one genuinely
gutbucket star in Motown's heavens, he still remembers to take hold
of his toothbrush before he hits the trail.

468 SHAKE A HAND, Faye Adams

Produced by Al Silver; written by Joe Morris
Herald 416   1953   *Billboard:* #22

For a purist like historian Charlie Gillett, Faye Adams isn't a rock and
roll artist at all. She's a rhythm and blues singer who never made the
transition. "Shake A Hand," a beautiful gospel blues which managed
to cross over and make *Billboard*'s pop lists at a time when that was
all but impossible for black artists, argues otherwise, not only in its
commerciality but in its mingling of secular and gospel technique.
There's grit and soul here that few other women have ever brought to
a pop record.

469 GYPSY WOMAN, The Impressions

Producer not credited; written by Curtis Mayfield
ABC-Paramount 10241   1961   *Billboard:* #20

The Impressions' Top 20 debut, after a long layoff following their split
with Jerry Butler in the wake of a squabble over the credit on "For
Your Precious Love." "Gypsy Woman" 's most striking feature is of
course Curtis Mayfield's unusual high tenor, to all intents and purposes
a falsetto, except that he seems to have no "natural" lower register.
Little of Mayfield's gospel heritage comes through here; the accents

instead derive from the Latin-inflected R&B of the Drifters. Add some church music, though, and you've got the prototype for "People Get Ready" and all their other hits.

470 AMANDA, Waylon Jennings
Produced by Richie Albright; written by Bob McDill
RCA 11596   1979   *Billboard:* #54

Had he come along in any decade other than the seventies, Bob McDill would have become one of the most celebrated songwriters of his day. The country songs he wrote revolve around soft, folkish, measured melodies that express an uncommonly gentle sensuality. With their homespun philosophizing and domestic centeredness, McDill songs like "Amanda" and even "Good Ole Boys Like Me" own the maturity and balance that most singer/songwriters captured only in their dreams.

That McDill remains obscure has a lot to do with being a nonperformer trapped in Nashville. It also may not have helped much that his principal vehicle was Don Williams, the grave-voiced former leader of the pop-folk Pozo Seco Singers. Though Williams was all but worshipped by British rock stars like Eric Clapton and Pete Townshend (each of whom recorded McDill-Williams songs), their endorsement didn't give him and his records the pop push that the acclaim of British stars had done for blues and soul performers in the sixties. What such aging rockers liked so much in Williams, though, was really his appropriately tender readings of McDill's material.

"Amanda," an anthem for beat-up and dusty dreamers, is McDill's masterpiece, and it was a hit twice, once on the country charts for Williams in 1973, and again in 1979 for Waylon Jennings. Where Williams sounded mournful and almost senescent, Jennings gave the lyric fire and heart.

"Amanda" is sung in the voice of an aging musician, pouring out his worries in what amounts to an apologetic love letter to his wife but is also a kind of *apologia pro vita sua* with electric guitar. In the opening verse, he stands before a mirror and notices crow's feet and gray hair. He speaks cryptically, never quite finishing a thought (this may be a letter that'll never be mailed) but what he does manage to spit out makes the point:

> Well, a measure of people who don't understand
> The pleasures of life in a hillbilly band
> I got my first git-tar when I was fourteen
> Now I'm crowding forty and still wearin' jeans

Change "hillbilly" to "rock and roll" and "thirty" to "forty" (fifty?) and you've got Eric Clapton's next hit record.

But it's tough to see how Clapton would match, let alone better, Waylon's version. Williams made "Amanda" a pure country song, filled with resentment and resignation. But Jennings, pioneer of "outlaw country" that he was, lets himself go: He's pissed off, he feels cheated not only for himself but for the woman he loves. From a purist standpoint, it might not be his greatest performance. But it is the one that reminds you that Waylon Jennings began his singing career as Buddy Holly's protege. And why.

471 IT'S TOO LATE, Carole King
Produced by Lou Adler; written by Carole King and Toni Stern
Ode 66015   1971   *Billboard:* #1 (5 weeks)

There exists a tape of Alan Freed on WABC in 1959, just before the payola scandal went down. He's doing his show a couple of drinks past his prime. With an air of exasperation, he puts on a new record by a girl named Carole King. It's a simpering vocal, the female equivalent of a Fabian song, and both singer and song are close to making the rhythm and blues purist gag. Freed goes on to openly express his slurred resentment that his ABC radio bosses are making him play this crap just because the record's on the record label they own. (Freed, of course, was made a criminal and destroyed for such practices. The broadcasting executives have yet to be labelled.) The record pops and crackles. "At least they could put this crap on decent vinyl," Freed groans.

Three years later, Carole King and Gerry Goffin had written half a dozen hits, including some that Freed might have loved. Carole even got a hit for herself with "It Might as Well Rain Until September." It was still pretty fey, but it had a great melody.

Another decade went by and King's reputation grew. Toward the end of the sixties, she began making solo albums and in 1971, she scored big with *Tapestry*, one of the handful of albums that's ever sold more than ten million copies. "It's Too Late" was the record that kicked off the *Tapestry* craze. It's a long way from R&B—the melody is pure Tin Pan Alley pop, the arrangement owes something to light jazz and a whole lot more to L.A. studio craftsmanship—but it has bite, resonance, even a mature theme.

Beyond the melody, there's the lyric, an account of a very pained breakup, as it might be written in a note left on the kitchen table when somebody's slipped out for good while her partner's back was turned. King didn't write that lyric—she wrote very few songs without a collaborator, and none of them are among her best—but she expresses Toni Stern's words as perfectly as those words are matched to the emotional tenor of King's music. And perhaps because her collaborator is a woman, maybe because the date coincided with an upsurge of interest in feminism, or it could be just the way King makes the words roll over her tongue, "It's Too Late" expresses an implicit feminism: She leaves *him*, she sets the terms of her own departure, she provides not mystical wisdom but a hardheaded view of the situation's practicalities—"There'll be good times again for me and you / But we just can't stay together—doncha feel it too / Still, I'm glad for what we had and how I once loved you."

Tapestry helped kick off a singer/songwriter boom that produced some of the most pallid pop hits of the rock era. Understated as it is, "It's Too Late" is beyond all that, because the music, the lyrics, and King's singing convey such powerful emotional intensity. I bet Alan Freed would have played it gladly.

472 BABY I LOVE YOU, Aretha Franklin
Produced by Jerry Wexler; written by Ronnie Shannon
Atlantic 2427   1967   *Billboard:* #4

Fifteen years before she hitched down that Freeway of Love, Aretha put herself on the Interstate of Soul, accompanied by a slow drag rhythm section and call-and-response horns that have the same terrifying effect as watching a sixteen wheeler start to jackknife in the next lane: Once the adrenaline rush lets up, you feel relieved that it was just another close call. Though with "Baby I Love You," unlike the highway, even sane men go right out and do it again. If only because it's so hard to believe that, on this occasion, the Muscle Shoals band was so good it actually made Aretha struggle to stay in the same gear.

473 SLIPPIN' AND SLIDIN', Little Richard
Produced by Bumps Blackwell; written by
Richard Penniman, Albert Collins, Eddie Bocage, and James Smith
Specialty 572   1956   *Billboard:* #33

The B side of "Long Tall Sally" is probably the closest Richard has ever come to the musical anarchy with which he's often charged. The lyric is a batch of barely coherent nonsense, the sax break veers off in all kinds of crazy directions, the tempo would be unsustainable for much longer than the 2:03 this take lasts, and Richard spends the whole time wailing beyond all reason.

But a listen to one of the first takes of the song reveals something entirely different: A loose gaited, midtempo New Orleans piano blues that's not much more than an imitation of Professor Longhair (or perhaps local R&B journeyman Eddie Bo, one of the song's cowriters). Seeing this many names on the songwriting credits of a period superstar's hit always makes one suspicious, but if Richard took that totally conventional tune and made out of it this powerful monstrosity, he deserves more than some publishing money—maybe a Nobel Prize in alchemy.

474 I'M IN LOVE AGAIN, Fats Domino
Produced by Dave Bartholomew; written by Fats Domino and Dave Bartholomew
Imperial 5386   1956   *Billboard:* #3

Fats, the smiling personification of bottomless horniness, was rock's ultimate one-track mind. Never has anybody made sexual frustration sound more pleasant and attractive—almost like fun. Until you realize what he's really saying, the stuff in the growl of the saxophones that the jollity of the piano can't quite erase. The dead giveaway is all that mad dog imagery. Trilling "Oowee, baby, oowee" or not, this guy is hard up and itchy for action. What does this have to do with the grinning Fats seen in the movies and displayed in rock and roll myth, you might well ask. Not much, unless you're aware of why black male desire is required to wear a wary mask at all times in America.

475 NO WOMAN, NO CRY, Bob Marley and the Wailers
Produced by Chris Blackwell and Steve Smith; written by Bob Marley
Island 037   1975   Did not make pop chart

Bob Marley was more like an international rock star than any other reggae artist at least partly because he was so album-oriented. After the original Wailers disintegrated, he made few memorable singles. But "No Woman No Cry," in its live version from his historic 1974 concert at London's Lyceum, ranks with "Layla" and "Maggie May" as a relic of the album rock period whose emotional authority survives despite its status as FM radio cliche.

The melody is so delicious that you'll occasionally find it annoying you in elevators, even though the song never came close to the American Top 40. (Black pop stations play even less reggae than white ones.) The annoyance isn't just the product of Muzak's bland treatment, but also because it's Marley's performance that gives the song its resonance. Always a philosopher-king, here he dispenses gentle advice and nurture that's as wise as its pretensions demand.

476 ON THE RADIO, Donna Summer
Produced by Giorgio Moroder and Pete Bellotte; written by Giorgio Moroder and Donna Summer
Casablanca 2236   1980   *Billboard:* #5

A dedication from an old boyfriend is read over the radio and hearing it, his ex-lover all but falls apart. Crying her lungs out as Their Song plays in the background with a disco beat, wanting him back, knowing he isn't coming, avoiding the gaze of the lover with whom she's replaced him—a guy she got by listening to the radio.

Though its straight disco break dates it (and the twelve-inch version is too much of a good thing for me), "On the Radio" remains one of the great songs about the power of radio. In fact, coming from the Queen of a genre whose root environment was the late night dance club, the record reemphasizes the primacy of broadcasting as *the* means of communication in the Top 40 age.

Never a particularly flexible stylist, Summer nevertheless rode the beat on every one of her hits like a rodeo star. Here, in the first few bars she actually achieves a kind of heartfelt edginess and it carries over into the waves of dance-beat that follow.

Best of all, Summer tells a tale for every lost and lonely soul to whom Casey Kasem and his brethren ever reached out:

Yeah, it kinda made me feel proud when I heard him say,
You couldn't find the words to say it yourself
And now in my heart I know I can say what I really feel
'Cause they said it really loud, they said it in the air—on the radio

That's a message the King of Rock and Roll himself would have to salute.

477 GROOVIN', The Rascals
Produced by The Rascals; written by Felix Cavaliere and Eddie Brigati
Atlantic 2401   1967   Billboard: #1 (4 weeks)

Atlantic Records chief Jerry Wexler made some great records, and some big mistakes. He hated the Drifters' "There Goes My Baby" in 1959, calling it "a mess," until it hit Number Two. And Wexler led Atlantic's widespread prerelease criticism of the Rascals' fifth single, claiming it was too laid-back, not enough like the white soul of "Good Lovin'," with which the group had topped the charts in 1966.

But "Groovin'" not only wasn't too laid-back—it took only four weeks to reach Number One, which is about as fast as the chart can be climbed by mortals—its impact stemmed from one of the more important insights of Felix Cavaliere's career. "I discovered that most of the rhythms that our soul-rock . . . are based on, come from Afro-Cuban rhythms," he remembered years later. "So I was able to put a conga into a song and it felt very nice. I mean, to me it felt very nice but to the record company it did not feel nice at all."

Ironically, what lends "Groovin' " its great groove isn't just the conga, nice touch though it is, but Chuck Rainey's bass. (The Rascals had no bass player, so they picked up a session man whenever they needed one in the studio.) And Rainey's bass pattern is based, once again, on the Cuban *baion*, the rhythm that Mort Shuman brought back from his Mexican vacation, and used with his partner, Doc Pomus, on so many hits for the Drifters, during the "There Goes My Baby" days. More than anything else, even the greeting card romanticism of the lyrics, that's what made "Groovin' " such a great and lasting hit.

478 NIGHT MOVES, Bob Seger
Produced by Jack Richardson and Bob Seger; written by Bob Seger
Capitol 4369   1976   Billboard: #4

The story of the way it was, back when it was as it always should have been. Seger says that "Night Moves" was inspired by *American Graffiti*, but he tells much more than George Lucas seemed to know. For one thing, the kids in "Night Moves" fumble around trying to fuck without any pledges of fidelity. For another, the record's last verse tells the truth about how trivial such a crucial moment has become a quarter century down the line—but then, sixteen is more than half a lifetime away long before you hit forty.

479 RAMBLIN' MAN, The Allman Brothers Band
Produced by Johnny Sandlin and the Allman Brothers Band; written by Richard Betts
Capricorn 0027   1973   *Billboard: #2*

Definitive album rockers that they were (How definitive? You know anybody else who covered a Donovan song at such length that it occupied more than one side of an LP?), the Allmans nevertheless steeped themselves so deeply in blues verities that it was all but inevitable that they'd come up with at least one great 45.

This is it, probably the closest real blues slide guitar has come to topping the chart. Dicky Betts's liquid tone and a shuffle beat so simple and seamless you'd hardly know there were two drummers pushing it, perfectly offset Gregg Allman's vocal, which is two parts B.B. King and one part George Jones.

There are those who'd argue, I suppose, that at 4:48 "Ramblin' Man" goes on at least ninety seconds too long, but if it comes across the radio on any interstate in the nation, I guarantee you'll be sorry when it ends if only because it slows you down.

480 BABY LET'S PLAY HOUSE, Elvis Presley
Produced by Sam Phillips; written by Arthur Gunter
Sun 217   1955   Did not make pop chart

In which Elvis introduces two central rock and roll concepts: the vocal stutter and the lust for the Pink Cadillac. Other than that, it's guitarist Scotty Moore's show, and he sets a few precedents of his own.

481 DON'T STOP 'TIL YOU GET ENOUGH, Michael Jackson
Produced by Quincy Jones; written by Michael Jackson
Epic 50742   1979   *Billboard: #1 (1 week)*

For a guy reportedly unsure of his ability to succeed on his own, Michael Jackson comes on awful strong on his first true solo single (he'd had a few releases under his own name at Motown but without any say in creating the songs or arrangements). Strong enough to stagger (the record lost its bullet a couple of weeks into its chart run, generally an indicator of doom) all the way to the top of chart, kicked along by an arrangement that, even though caught up in now-dated late seventies disco conventions, builds in brilliant waves to an intoxicating series of squealed and gasped releases.

And for a wimp who's not supposed to really get the picture about sex, Michael comes on awful strong here, presenting an image that's much more mature and believable than the one he forged on his even bigger-selling eighties successes. Maybe, just starting out, he was afraid to show the utter innocence of his true self? Or has stardom always meant regression for him?

But then, for a fella who claims to only want "enough," Michael sure seems ambitious to have it all, and maybe sexual maturity just gets in the way of the totality of that desire.

482 LAWYERS IN LOVE, Jackson Browne
Produced by Jackson Browne and Greg Ladanyi; written by Jackson Browne
Asylum 69826   1983   Billboard: #13

Jackson Browne found "Lawyers in Love" totally misunderstood as a satire on those upwardly greedy types called yuppies, which only goes to show you how far gone rockin' America already was, since the record's real theme—opposition to the New Cold War—was expressed in metaphors unmistakable to those with half a clue. Commercially, the misunderstanding may have been a blessing; brutal savagings of contemporary jingoism rarely find favor with broadcasters. Artistically, it may have been catastrophic, since the song's poor reception seems to have convinced Browne that his points could only be made by abandoning metaphor for political blunt weapons.

Too bad, because "Lawyers" stands as one of Browne's two or three best pop sides—not quite as rocking as "Running on Empty," but deeper, funnier, more elaborately conceived and executed than "Somebody's Baby" or "Doctor My Eyes." Its mockery of the American lust for multinational lebensraum extends the frontier to outer space, its bass line recaps "I Think We're Alone Now," and it has the best falsetto yodels since "The Lion Sleeps Tonight." As an assessment of xenophobia and anti-Communism no one has matched the last verse, in which Browne dreams Ronald Reagan's blood fantasy. The devious

Russians "escape while we weren't watching them / As Russians will," and the U.S. gets what it wants: the whole planet, the moon, and the Soviet Empire turned into "vacationland for lawyers in love."

And intelligent people thought this record was about *lawyers*?!?

483 GO YOUR OWN WAY, Fleetwood Mac
Produced by Fleetwood Mac with Richard Dashut and Ken Caillat; written by Lindsey Buckingham
Warner Bros. 8304   1977   *Billboard:* #10

In the best-selling edition of Fleetwood Mac, the melodic focus of California pop, replete with Beach Boys-derived vocal harmonies, Spectorian production flourishes, and a folk-rock (not to say singer/songwriterish) sense of personal relevance, met the tight and moderately funky groove of the British blues groups from which the band originally descended. The exquisite songs of Christine McVie, the unalloyed chromatic daze of Stevie Nicks, and the rough-and-tumble rhythms of Mick Fleetwood and John McVie notwithstanding, their musical leader was Lindsey Buckingham.

Buckingham grew up in Northern California without seeming to be affected much by psychedelic music at all. The dead giveaway of where *he's* coming from was the inclusion of a single studio track on Fleetwood's live LP: a version of Brian Wilson's "Farmer's Daughter," a beauteous obscurity from the *Surfin' U.S.A.* LP. Although all the Macs except drummer/manager Fleetwood romantically intermingled with someone else in the band at one point or another, it was Buckingham's songs that brought this predilection into focus as the group's central theme, and it was their tempestuous songs about muddled sexual fortune that made Fleetwood Mac one of the two biggest-selling rock acts of the late seventies. (The other was the Eagles.)

More important, perhaps, it was Buckingham who had the studio savvy and production diligence to make their records far livelier models of craftsmanship than ordinary pop-rock. Although their concoctions are also truly Californian because they're so lightweight that the mere touch of the stylus practically brings them to a froth, "Go Your Own Way" with its churning guitar, heavy-footed bass drum, and Buckingham's keening lead vocal (and its subtextual status as an answer record to the songs Nicks wrote about the breakup of their relationship) is as close to the heart of rock and soul as anybody's studio elect have come in the post-Beatles period.

484 ANNA (GO TO HIM), Arthur Alexander
Produced by Noel Ball; written by Arthur Alexander
Dot 16387   1962   *Billboard:* #68

Absolutely gorgeous early soul, its gently swinging rhythm set up by drumming as tough as it is syncopated, and capped with a vocal that makes of a lover's kiss-off something like the end of the world. "All of my life, I've been searching for a girl, now / To love me like I, love you," Alexander croaks and you realize—right there—that this is where John Lennon learned to sing stuff like "In My Life."

485 STEPPIN' OUT, Paul Revere and the Raiders
Produced by Terry Melcher; written by Paul Revere and Mark Lindsay
Columbia 43375   1965   *Billboard:* #46

One of the great lost singles bands, Paul Revere and the Raiders are precisely the kind of act whose quality got lost on LP, though whether that was because "Louie Louie" roots simply didn't adapt well to twelve-inch pretensions or because they were simply in it for kicks beats me.

But what counts is that the Raiders, usually with the underrated Terry Melcher at the controls, made a whole series of first-rate singles, beginning with second-best "Louie Louie" ever and going on to the lustful "Louie" rewrite "Just Like Me," the anti-drug "Kicks," the anthemic "Hungry," and the near-soul "Good Things." And though the Raiders' tenure as house band on Dick Clark's post-*Bandstand* program, *Where the Action Is*, not only demolished their hip credentials (at least until the postmodernist principle "good bad but not evil" became more widely understood), it also was a career move obviously destined to travel a paved road to hell—or in this case, Vegas lounges, not that you or I could tell the difference.

The records got tamer as they went along, and so the wildest of all is "Just Like Me," the first conceived for an audience outside Seattle/Portland but still so close to its roots that it sounds like it was arranged, if not recorded, in somebody's garage. Jet-propelled bass and sleigh bells ride the beat while a wailing guitar buttresses Mark Lindsay's gravelly shouts. Presuming that the band played on its own records (I never heard they didn't but this was Hollywood so who knows?), guitarist Jim Valley does some things here that come close to the licks Mike Bloomfield gets off on *Highway 61 Revisited*. And some of Lindsay's phrasing and lyrics ("When I come back I heard the bad, bah-ad nooo-s") is more purely Dylanesque than anything on *Rubber Soul*. Kinda makes you wonder how closely Dylan might have been listening to his labelmates, though he never came up with anything quite as unique as the final organ break. That was up to the Blues Magoos.

486 HIDE AWAY, Freddy King
Produced by Sonny Thompson; written by Freddy King and Sonny Thompson
Federal 12401   1961   *Billboard:* #29

Because their angles of intersection are so obtuse, deciding which blues records to include in this selection of rock and R&B 45s has been one of the trickiest of all my tasks. But "Hide Away" slides in easily, and not only because of its bold, bossy tone, which suggests a marriage of Duane Eddy and Bill Doggett. You've also gotta figure that King's stiletto attack on this side became one of the biggest influences on Eric Clapton, spawning a whole style of rock and roll (albeit one that was expressed on albums, not singles). If you can imagine three minutes of blues instrumental spawning Cream's *Wheels of Fire* (which is exactly what it did), "Hide Away" will grab you as very rock and roll indeed.

487 ONE MINT JULEP, The Clovers
Produced by Ahmet Ertegun and Jerry Wexler; written by Rudolph Toombs
Atlantic 963   1952   Did not make pop chart

During its early years, Atlantic's secret weapons included great arranger/songwriters like Jesse Stone and Rudy Toombs. Stone contributed "Money Honey" to the Drifters and an uncounted (and uncredited) number of intricate, soulful arrangements. Toombs, who wrote but didn't arrange, was less prolific—he specialized in writing songs about the dire consequences of boozing, which may be a clue—but his best material is as enduring as anything from its era. "One Mint Julep" is Toombs's very best, so good that Ray Charles revived it a decade later as a blaring big band instrumental that became one of the source points of soul-jazz.

But the definitive "One Mint Julep" remains the Clovers' original, which features not only a great melody but a lyric in which "One Mint Julep" leads to a shotgun wedding and, six kids later, Buddy Bailey's lachrymose account of the dangers of mixing your drinks with your date. Charlie Gillett says that Bailey's lead vocal "sounds like a fugitive from a jump blues band," rather than a standard harmony group, and that's just what's so grand about it. The backing track, featuring a terrific Harry Van Walls piano lead and a nice rumbling acoustic bass, is something special, too.

488 HONKY TONK WOMAN, The Rolling Stones
Produced by Jimmy Miller; written by Mick Jagger and Keith Richards
London 910   1969   *Billboard:* #1 (4 weeks)

If there'd been any question about whether the Stones could keep the quality up without Brian Jones, the release of "Honky Tonk Woman" the day after his funeral settled it. The clunking cowbell was weird, Charlie Watts's downbeat an epitome of white funk, and the country-blues tang of Keith's guitar cinched the issue. Even Jagger's vocal, nicely layered with echo, rang with malicious conviction. Of course, the lyric was stupid and sexist but when you're dancing this hard, it can take a couple of years to notice. And if, by the end of this one, your ass isn't shaking, you ought to take a look around and see if Brian Jones might be nearby.

489 BETCHA BY GOLLY WOW, The Stylistics
Produced by Thom Bell; written by Thom Bell and Linda Creed
Avco 4591   1972   *Billboard:* #3

Written, orchestrated, and sung as if you could be fined in Philadelphia for not wearing your heart on your sleeve. Only singing as over-the-top as Russell Thompkins's could match lyrics as unapologetically cow-eyed as Creed's ("You're a genie in disguise / Full of wonder and surprise"), and Thompkins is utterly dependent upon Bell's unabashed devotion to milking the melody with a harp, horns, and strings. Superficially, there's nothing going on here that doesn't go on hourly over at Hallmark Cards. But "Betcha By Golly Wow" is swathed in such sweet innocence that you have to believe that these folks would have risked being this corny even if there wasn't a pile of dough at the end of their rainbow.

490 SAY MAN, Bo Diddley
Produced by Leonard Chess; written by Ellas McDaniel
[Bo Diddley]
Checker 931   1959   *Billboard: #20*

If there'd been rock critics in 1959, and one of them had written of Bo
Diddley as "Rock and Roll Future," he'd have been a prophet worth
following at least as far as the nearest race track. For thirty years later,
with the preeminence of rap and heavy metal, Bo is now the present.

How did it come to pass that the most primitive of all the creators
of fifties rock remained so influential for so long? Well, first of all, we
live in a beat-crazed age, and the Bo Diddley beat is an irreducible
statement of rock and roll. Speed it up or slow it down and the sledgehammer accent menaces just the same. And then there's the lyrics.
"Say Man" is not only a rap, but, as a variation on the dangerous game
of street insults called the dozens, it's the original dis. Not many rappers
can get away with jokes this old ("You that thing I throw peanuts at!")
but few would have the audacity to so baldly characterize the ugliness
of a pal's girlfriend to his very face. Much less the ability to insist on
their roots in South America, and mean Texas.

491 SHE'S ABOUT A MOVER, The Sir Douglas Quintet
Produced by Huey Meaux; written by Doug Sahm
Tribe 8308   1965   *Billboard: #13*

492 NIGHT-TIME, The Strangeloves
Produced by Bob Feldman, Jerry Goldstein, and
Richard Gottehrer; written by Bob Feldman, Jerry Goldstein,
Richard Gottehrer, and Bert Berns
Bang 514   1966   *Billboard: #30*

The British Invasion didn't destroy American-made popular music.
Berry Gordy and Motown more than held their own, the Beach Boys
kept pace through 1966 or so. But, as an unavoidable consequence of
rock and roll's new international stature, many of the indigenous
styles—Brill Building pop, Southern neo-rockabilly, surf music, New
Orleans R&B, the various forms of studio rock that were oriented to
singers or vocal groups rather than bands—were all but wiped out and
many others (notably, deep Southern soul) kept virtually underground.

For the marginal, the regional, and the eccentric, the British Invasion was neither a joke nor a metaphor, but a good description of how things happened.

Few cagier types exist in our species than the independent producers who fostered rock in its first decade. However much damage to ongoing trade the Beatles and their spawn might have done, the canniest among them saw in the new style simply another kind of Main Chance. And ran with it.

Resourceful barely begins to describe Huey Meaux, the self-styled "Crazy Cajun," who has served time as a barber, promotion man, independent producer, label owner, talent scout, and prison inmate. Meaux made his first record in 1959 and by '65, he'd already scored as a producer with Dale and Grace ("I'm Leaving It Up to You") and Barbara Lynn ("You'll Lose a Good Thing") as well as working with such Texas rockers as T. K. Hulin, Jimmy Donley, Joey Long and Johnny Winter, with Roy Head ("Treat Her Right"), the Hombres ("Let It All Hang Out"), and Archie Bell and the Drells ("Tighten Up") just over the horizon.

That list, encompassing neo-rockabillies, albino bluesmen, black show bands, and primitive Southern soul, very nearly summarizes the kinds of music for which the Brits made life difficult. So when Meaux found a new group from San Antonio, a batch of rowdy Tex-Mex border types whose hair was longer than the worst dreams harbored by the parents of Rolling Stones fans, he knew just what to do: Give 'em a vaguely English-sounding name and call their sound Merseybeat, no matter what it really was.

It worked and the Sir Douglas Quintet had its hit, one so good that it earned them a place in rock history even if they'd never done anything else, but maybe not so much because of Meaux's crude hustle. Merseybeat, my ass—"She's About a Mover" just juices up *norteno*'s two-step polka beat; what counts is Doug Sahm singing the hell out of it alongside Augie Meyer's ultrainsistent organ riff.

Anyway, Meaux apparently never required the Quintet to publicly perjure themselves regarding their national origin. By the time their first album came out, he'd moved on to bigger forms of hype: That debut album is called *The Best of Sir Douglas Quintet*, and while the liner notes do mention the "Merseybeat" nonsense, they spend more time implying that the group was really big stuff in Texas. (They weren't, though Doug Sahm *had* been a country and western prodigy, appearing on *Louisiana Hayride*, the Opry of the deep South, in 1952, when he was just nine, and cutting a batch of regional rock and roll records in the late fifties.) For a cynical music biz veteran like Huey Meaux, the

British Invasion was just one more obstacle between him and his next paycheck. No doubt he'd fixed worse problems.

For songmill employees up in New York City, the outlook was much bleaker. Some second-rank British groups (notably the Animals and Manfred Mann) used outside material, but the trend the Beatles spawned was toward self-contained writer/performers.

Brill Building denizens Bob Feldman, Jerry Goldstein, and Richard Gotterher decided that if the public wasn't interested in domestic acts, they'd reinvent themselves as foreigners. So they passed themselves off as three Australian brothers, Miles, Giles, and Niles Strangelove. They claimed to have taken their rhythmic ideas from aborigines and to have added Masai drums to their sound after they heard them while on an African safari. Reflecting the coming trend toward bohemian economic nonchalance, the liner notes to their first album claimed that they were independently wealthy as a result of developing "the now famous breed of long hair sheep known as the Gotterher Sheep," which were registered with the Feldman-Goldstein Company in Australia.

Their scam worked as well as Meaux's. The Strangeloves' first record, "I Want Candy," got to Number 11, with those "Masai drums" (actually, tympani with a backbeat) leading the way. Their best record, though, was the third, "Night-Time," and there was nothing Mersey-beat about it. The pounding beat, jagged guitar licks, and bottom-heavy blues piano neatly expropriated the shouted blues style of U.K. acts like the Animals, and the yowling vocals and the sociosexual nastiness of the lyrics ("I jump in the shower, try to get the world off my back / I'm gonna getcha baby, that's a natural fact") rank as one of the greatest Mick Jagger parodies ever created.

And the Strangeloves carried the fantasy all the way. Goldstein, Feldman, and Gotterher outfitted themselves with shaggy wigs and tympani, found a down-and-out English actor to help them forge British accents and hit the road, as opening act for the Beach Boys. The Beach Boys were in on the gag, but neither the public nor the British groups that the Strangeloves toured with on package shows over the next couple years ever caught on.

493 LOVE'S GONNA LIVE HERE, Buck Owens
Produced by Ken Nelson; written by Buck Owens
Capitol 5025   1963   Did not make pop chart

Buck Owens was probably the greatest country artist of the 1960s, and certainly the one most influenced by rock and soul. Along with Merle

Haggard, Owens expanded country's horizons by establishing a distinctly non-Nashville base in his hometown, Bakersfield, California, for a time the genre's first real rival to Music City as a production center.

A master of emotional indirection, in "Love's Gonna Live Here," his first country Number One, Owens uses a deceptively bright and melodic arrangement, centered on Don Rich's jangly acoustic guitar, to spin a sweet fantasy of the delights in store for him in the wake of divorce. "No more loneliness, only happiness, love's gonna live here again," he declares.

But what follows those lines is a booming, gritty guitar solo and it's impossible not to notice how conditional and willful Owens' declarations of paradise finally are. "Things are gonna be the way they were before," he sings, but of course, how they were before was lousy enough to cause the breakup in the first place. And it's not just the guitar that notices this: From the very beginning, the bass chugs along like the voice of common sense.

It's not hard to see what kept this ingenious little tune off pop radio. Despite its tricky arrangement, it stays well within the bounds of country, making no compromises. Although its beat is bluesy, there's no drummer. But it's not just the music that pop ears might find distancing. The record's whole tone—the way that Owens not only accepts his condition but his bright-eyed demeanor and his refusal to acknowledge the pain he can't conceal—subverts any attempt to reduce its emotional complexity. That doesn't mean that pop songs are just platitudes (taken at face value, which may be the way Buck hoped it would be taken, "Love's Gonna Live Here" is virtually a greeting card) but it does suggest that the twists and turns involved in a record like this one might be a little rugged for mass consumption.

494 MOUNTAIN OF LOVE, Harold Dorman
Produced by Roland Janes; written by Harold Dorman
Rita 1003　1960　　*Billboard:* #21

Harold Dorman cut sides for Sam Phillips at Sun Records in Memphis in 1955, 1956, and 1957. Although he knew the songs and the singing were good, Phillips heard nothing worth releasing. But Dorman's soft rockabilly style intrigued former Jerry Lee Lewis sideman and Sun session guitarist Roland Janes. When Janes and fellow sideman Billy Lee Riley formed Rita Records in the autumn of 1959, they called Dorman, then working as a parking lot attendant.

Although he was already thirty-three years old, Dorman's voice had mellowed and his confidence increased and before the year was out, Janes, Riley, engineer Jack Clement (another Sun alumnus), and a band that included another Lewis vet, bassist James Van Eaton, cut half a dozen sides with him.

Among them was "Mountain of Love," and though the producers heard it as a hit, they couldn't find a bigger label who agreed enough to lease the master. So they decided to make it one of Rita's first two releases, along with Van Eaton's "Beat-Nik." Finding a disc jockey in relatively nearby Macon, Georgia who liked it, they began pushing "Mountain" all through the South, getting airplay in Atlanta, Memphis, and on all-important WLAC, Nashville, where deejay John R stayed up all night, pumping 50,000 watts of black and white boogie to a nationwide audience.

Like many tiny record labels, Rita didn't have the resources to do true national distribution—if it had tried, the most likely results would have been losing the attention the record was getting because supply and promotion lines were stretched too thin, or bankrupting the entire enterprise because the network of regional independent distributors was at best slow to pay.

So Rita took the record to Bill Lowery's promotion and distribution group in Atlanta, where another pair of Sun veterans, Bill Justis and Jud Phillips (Sam's brother) had recently gone to work. Justis and Phillips thought that northern stations wouldn't play the record unless it had "a little more class." So in early 1960, strings were overdubbed and then a chorus. "To me, the fewer things you put on a record the better," Janes told Sun historian Colin Escott in 1988. "Only add them if they do something for the record. But, during that era, people were string happy and I guess the strings helped us to get play in areas where we might not have sold records [otherwise]."

As it happens, the undubbed "Mountain of Love" appears on the album that Escott's interview serves as liner notes: *Harold Dorman— Mountain of Love* (Bear Family [W. Germany] BFX 15262). So it's possible to compare the versions.

The original, undubbed "Mountain" reeks with authenticity. Peggy Dorman, Harold's wife, told Escott that her husband wrote the song thinking about a hill near his hometown, Sledge, Mississippi, a hamlet in the Delta cotton country between Clarksdale and Memphis, one of the flattest landscapes in North America. And the undubbed "Mountain of Love" is just that homespun, just that modest. The timbre of Dorman's voice seems flatter, the entire production smaller, not just in instrumentation but in force. The time still breaks down midway through, you can hear Van Eaton struggling to bring it back together, and Martin Willis's saxophone is more prominent. A purist might call all this more "authentic."

In rock and roll, though, authenticity is something that ought to be warily respected. The overdubbed "Mountain of Love" would have been inconceivable when the blues were first recorded in Memphis, back before the days of tape, when men like Don Law just tried to get the energy and spirit of roadhouse and juke joint performances into the grooves of wire or metal masters. But rock and roll as Sam Phillips, Elvis Presley, Scotty Moore, and Bill Black (among many others) invented it in the fifties was very much a product of tinkering in the recording studio with electric guitars and microphones and erasable magnetic tape on which whole layers of sounds could be added or subtracted and an *emotionally* true performance might be pieced together by carefully picking over many available options, or by listening to earlier takes many, many times.

"Mountain of Love," without the overdubs, is a quaint and touching rockabilly ballad. But with the strings and chorus, it's a powerfully evocative blues-tinged *recording* that deserved to rise even higher on the charts than it did.

But at least "Mountain of Love" entered rock history, the more so after Johnny Rivers took the song Top Ten in 1964. Harold Dorman faded back into the woodwork for another decade, working as a typewriter repairman and leather maker until Charley Pride picked up his "Mississippi Cotton Picking Delta Town" and made it a country hit. After that, a few of Dorman's other good songs had some country chart success. In 1982, Pride even got some country airplay with "Mountain of Love."

495 MAY I, Maurice Williams & the Zodiacs
Produced by Marshall Sehorn; written by Maurice Williams
Deesu 304   c.1962   Did not make pop chart

Another great falsetto turn by Williams, with a danceable track that's the essence of Carolinian "beach music," "May I" also contains the most outrageously overt proposition in the history of rhythm and blues. "May I have your love? May I be your beau?" Williams cries against a track that's nothing much more than organ, bass, and drums rapping out a generic shag beat. Then a deep baritone enters: "May I sleep with you?" he inquires, "May I bring you joy?" *Whaaat?*

I've been trying to figure for twenty years how the hell they expected to get *that* on the radio. (Maybe someday I'll listen to the record and find a way to decipher what he's singing in some other way.* They must have gotten loads of spins in the Myrtle Beach clubs, because the track was picked up and reissued on Vee-Jay and on Atlantic's great *Beach Beat, Volume Two.* But, in context, those lines are a move at least as radical as anything that the Sex Pistols ever came up with.

496 **WHAT A FOOL BELIEVES, The Doobie Bros.**
Produced by Ted Templeman; written by Kenny Loggins and Michael McDonald
Warner Bros. 8725   1979   *Billboard:* #1 (1 week)

Ted Templeman may have been the most underrated record producer of the seventies. He made some of Van Morrison's best records and gave pop sheen to the metal basics of both the Doobie Brothers and Van Halen, which isn't bad for a guy whose career began with Harper's Bizarre's unctuous rendition of Paul Simon's "59th Street Bridge Song (Feelin' Groovy)."

The Doobies were probably Templeman's quintessential project; he guided them from biker bar band to more loosely affiliated studio group without ever losing commercial or creative stride. Myriad personnel changes notwithstanding, the Doobies remained one of the more distinctive trash pop groups of the seventies, evolving increasingly sophisticated approaches to good-time groove songs.

The Doobies' most celebrated coup was probably landing former Steely Dan guitarist Jeff "Skunk" Baxter in 1974, but it was another Steely Dan alumnus, keyboardist Michael McDonald, who led their best records. As a keyboard player, McDonald was good enough; far more important, he had one of the all-time blue-eyed soul falsettos, and under Templeman's direction, he used it well on a whole series of hits, beginning with "Takin' It to the Streets" and "It Keeps You Runnin' " in 1976. These records defined the light soul sensibility of late seventies and early eighties L.A. pop.

The apotheosis of the style was "What a Fool Believes." McDonald began writing it while flying from New York to L.A. He imagined a man and a woman, former lovers, meeting unexpectedly in a restaurant. To the guy, their love affair had been the great romance of his life; to

---

* To tell the truth, I've since heard the version of "May I" by Bill Deal and the Rhondells, a blue-eyed soul remake, and *he* clearly sings "May I *speak* with you." That still doesn't mean it's *necessarily* what Maurice Williams sings, though. In the spirit of this entire enterprise, then, I've given myself permission to continue hearing the secret filth in the original version. And Williams' solicitousness doesn't disappear even with the alternate reading.

her, it was an incident and it was over. So the guy made a fool of himself by risking an emotional exposure that never came close to being reciprocated.

When he got home, McDonald worked on the melody, but only got as far as the bridge when he found himself stuck. He played as much of it as he'd completed for Templeman, who loved it but had no solution.

Meantime, Doobies bassist Tiran Porter suggested that McDonald get together with Kenny Loggins, who had only recently split from his long-running duo act with Jim Messina. McDonald invited Loggins to his house to do some collaborating, but the idea made him nervous. To calm down, he played piano for his sister Maureen.

He was playing "What a Fool Believes" when Loggins pulled into the driveway. While taking his guitar out of his trunk, Loggins heard the melody and imagined the missing bridge. He walked up and knocked on the door, introduced himself to McDonald and said, "You know that thing you were just playing. Play that again because I think I have an idea." They worked on the song for the rest of the day, then completed it over the phone a few days later. The Doobies recorded it soon thereafter and it not only went to Number One but won three Grammys.

For once, the Grammys spent its accolades where they were deserved. Carefully crafted, gorgeously sung, beautifully arranged, and pristinely recorded, "What a Fool Believes" holds up as one of the finest samples of seventies L.A. pop. Meanwhile, America took the song to heart and spent the next decade proving McDonald's point, quadrennially at the ballot box and on most of the days in between.

497 HULLY GULLY CALLIN' TIME, The Jive Five
Produced by Les Cahan and Joe Rene; written by Culver, Cafarelli, and Rene
Beltone 2019   1962   Did not make pop chart

It wasn't just Eugene Pitt's extraordinary lead vocals that made the Jive Five the last of the great doo-wop groups. Their records tended to be more sophisticated than most, even this late in the game, because Beltone Records began as a subsidiary of Joe Rene's main business, the Beltone Recording Studio. As a result, arranger Les Cahan and the group were able to afford dozens of takes, mixes, and overdubs, discovering effects economics denied to other groups.

Though nobody here had the vision that Phil Spector brought to similarly expansive productions—in fact, Beltone so poorly understood the strength of the music that "Hully Gully Callin' Time" was tossed off as the B side of the group's third single, "No No Not Again"—the sound is remarkable, way beyond the bounds of doo-wop and East Coast studio rock conventions. Indeed, even though the lyrics, beat, and sax riff are closely focused on dance craze details, the piercing organ, biting harmonica, and Pitts's wild vocal gesticulations mark "Hully Gully Callin' Time" as another precursor of the style now thought of as Dylanesque.

498 SO MUCH IN LOVE, The Tymes
Produced by Billy Jackson; written by Billy Jackson, Roy Stargis, and George Williams
Parkway 871   1963   *Billboard:* #1 (1 week)

What Johnny Mathis would have sounded like if he'd been in a rhythm and blues group. (In fact, the Tymes' second hit was a cover of Mathis's first, "Wonderful Wonderful.") The lead singer with the uncanny resemblance to Mathis is George Williams, last to join a Philadelphia quintet that had called itself the Latineers before his arrival. Tenors Albert "Caesar" Berry and George Hilliard set up the eerie falsetto background, whose "oo-weee-ooh" became a rudiment of Philly soul, and baritone Norman Burnett and bassist Donald Banks establish the funky foundation of a disc whose dominant instruments are finger-snaps and claves.

499 TRYING TO LIVE MY LIFE WITHOUT YOU, Otis Clay
Produced by Willie Mitchell; written by Eugene Williams
Hi 2226   1972   Did not make pop chart

Having done my share of railing against the idea that white rock and roll is *just* a rip-off of rhythm and blues, it would be foolish not to acknowledge one of the most outrageous examples in which it was. In 1979, the Eagles took "Trying to Live My Life Without You" Top Ten as a song they "wrote," "The Long Run," the title song of their final multiplatinum LP.

Of course, the differences are of the essence: Clay's song is a blues about reconciling himself to the loss of his lover, a task he claims is harder than kicking cigarettes and booze. The Eagles "composed" a metaphoric love song, ostensibly about the longevity of a relationship though it was hard to miss the subtext: the band's obsession with its lack of critical standing (i.e., "We'll see whose opinion is valid in the long run"). Since most rock critics aren't R&B fans, the last of the bird groups was rarely called out for this transgression, although their buddy Bob Seger's later cover of "Trying to Live My Life Without You" was said to have been inspired by his desire to make amends.

Musically, there's simply no comparison. Don Henley is a fine singer but he lacks the raw soul Otis Clay exudes, and while Henley's a decent studio drummer, nobody competes with Al Jackson at his best, and this is one of Jackson's better post-Stax performances. The Eagles have Joe Walsh's guitar on their side but one good guitar was never any match for the combined weight of the Memphis Horns. In the short term, it's true, the Eagles made more dough from this music, but in the long run, listeners will weary of their whining long before they tire of Clay's more modest, more emotionally compelling music.

500 BOOK OF RULES, The Heptones
Produced by Harry Johnson; written by Barry Llewellyn and Harry Johnson
Island [UK] WIP 6179   1976   Did not make pop chart

In reggae, the elements of style shift continuously but the foundation remains the Caribbean's firmest, most inverted beat, New Orleans R&B played inside out. In the genre's heyday, those accents were accompanied by sinuous harmonies that took language already rendered as much rhythmically as cognitively and elevated it to a form of sound-poetry.

"Book of Rules" came a little late in the day to belong to reggae's fullest flowering. But Leroy Sibbles's group had been very much a part of the great moment (thanks to the comic "Fatty Fatty," among others) and they recapture its spirit in this mid-seventies recording. The languor never reaches the lassitude latter-day reggae sustains as a banner; it simply keys into an intensity more slowly built than most. The lyrics are a straight paraphrase of the Bible, the potential of human lives interpreted in a way peculiar to Jamaicans, living as they do in a trap between the squalid beauties of a preindustrial culture and the disintegrating splendors of an imperial one. In other words, it's the kind of song Bob Dylan and the self-help oriented singer/songwriters who travel in his wake would be proud (and lucky) to write or sing: "I said, common people like you and me / We'll be builders for eternity / Each is given a bag of tools / A shapeless mask and a book of rules."

501 YOU'VE REALLY GOT A HOLD ON ME, The Miracles

Written and produced by Smokey Robinson
Tamla 54073   1962   *Billboard:* #8

A year or so after "You've Really Got a Hold on Me" left the charts, a radio station in Pontiac, Michigan played it on its Sunday night oldies show. It reached my ears as a call to action, and before it was through, my world had changed, caught up in the magic of a sound which revealed to me—don't ask just how because I never will fully grasp the mechanism—the falsity of the racism within which I'd been raised. Maybe it was just hearing the humanity in Smokey Robinson's voice, and finally putting it together with the knowledge that he was a black man.

I'd like to think the answer was that simple and direct. A lot of what grabbed me was in Smokey's voice, there's no denying it, but the ache in my heart had just as much to do with Marv Tarplin's descending guitar line and the roll of Benny Benjamin's drums. The music ensured that whatever Smokey said had to be the truth.

What it never had much to do with was the words—except for the title phrase, and that as an afterthought that justified what the music already made me feel. In later years, "I don't like you / But I love you," the song's opening lines, have come to have some use for me as an almost talismanic motto. But not then. What I heard that night in 1964, what drew me to this music, was not words. Words I understood. What I heard was something that passed beyond understanding. It was a sound, whole and complete.

"You've Really Got a Hold On Me" afforded me such a watershed experience that I'll never be able to judge its quality with any accuracy. A lot of the time, it's too powerful for me to listen to and so I play it less often than records I find less compelling. But then, did the context of my life create the compulsion or was it the other way around? Since I can't quite figure it out, yet this is the one record that *has* to be here, I've placed it dead center, hoping more than usual that you'll get hold of it and decide for yourself.

502 PRETTY LITTLE ANGEL EYES, Curtis Lee
Produced by Phil Spector; written by Curtis Lee and
Tommy Boyce
Dunes 2007   1961   *Billboard:* #7

The first really crazed record Phil Spector ever made, and still one of
the most powerful. Lee (who actually got his start by phoning the staff
of *Dig*, an L.A. teen magazine, and singing to them over the phone—
they brought him to Hollywood from his home in Yuma, Arizona)
wasn't going anywhere before he ran into Spector with his finger cymbals ringing like a cash register, and he wasn't going anywhere after
the wild sax solo, but while he and that deep bass careened along, he
was one of the greatest rock and roll singers in the world.

503 CHOICE OF COLORS, The Impressions
Written and produced by Curtis Mayfield
Curtom 1943   1969   *Billboard:* #21

504 THIS IS MY COUNTRY, The Impressions
Written and produced by Curtis Mayfield
Curtom 1934   1968   *Billboard:* #25

Somewhere around the end of 1968, Curtis Mayfield snapped. Fed up,
he stopped disguising his antiracist, black-consciousness moralism with
metaphors and went after the problem head on. From "We're a Winner" and "We're Rolling On" to "This Is My Country" and "Choice
of Colors" may seem like orderly continuity twenty years later, but at
the time, those songs (and the response to them) represented a breathtaking leap.

Mayfield was no radical. "This Is My Country" wants to seize nothing more than admission to the normal Democratic-Republican oscillation, though he does give it the brilliant flourish of incorporating a
paraphrase of Lincoln's Second Inaugural. Without abandoning the
group's sweet gospel-soul harmony format, Mayfield had found a way
to drag the central fact of American history—slavery and its consequences—onto center stage.

"Choice of Colors" goes it one better; it stakes its claim not only
on the basis of historic injustice but on the idea of inherent equality.

Again, Mayfield's thinking never left the political mainstream. His questions derive from folk wisdom, not sophisticated analysis: "How long have you hated your white teacher? / Who told you to love your black preacher? / Can you respect your brother's woman friend / And share with black folks not of kin?" But in a country where George Wallace was a serious presidential candidate, and Richard Nixon the one who got elected, putting these sentiments over constituted an appreciable feat.

505 SOUL MAN, Sam and Dave
Written and produced by Isaac Hayes and David Porter
Stax 231   1967   *Billboard:* #12

Ice-cold truth, told as much by trumpet and guitar as by the fabulous interplay of voices. In the history of braggadocio, few have been so convincing.

506 AIN'T NOTHING LIKE THE REAL THING, Marvin Gaye and Tammi Terrell
Written and produced by Nicholas Ashford and Valerie Simpson
Tamla 54163   1968   *Billboard:* #8

Lost in the mists is whether Marvin and Tammi were copping a lick from Coke, or whether Coke had an ad agency sufficiently perspicacious to pick up on a Motown hit with unmistakable tambourine percussion and bass plus splendid harmonies. Best bet is that Coke came first, which is only fair since Marvin and Tammi got to be best.

507 HEY JOE, Jimi Hendrix
Produced by Chas Chandler; written by William Roberts
Polydor [UK] 56139   1967   Did not make pop chart

"Hey Joe" and the story of its genesis probably fit the academic definition of the "folk process" better than any other rock and roll song. Although it clearly didn't exist until the mid-sixties, no one seems entirely certain who wrote it: The question isn't just who "William Roberts" might be, but whether that's even the correct pseudonym. The Leaves, who had the biggest hit with the song (it reached Number 31 in 1966) credited it to Chester Powers, which was said to be the pen name of Dino Valente, later a member of Quicksilver Messenger Service. Even if you knew where BMI sends the royalty checks, that might not prove anything, since tunes are bought and sold like stocks and bonds.

Since "Hey Joe" is tacked together from a batch of staple blues concepts—the badman, betrayed by his woman, shoots her and her boyfriend and cuts out for parts unknown—the threads of the saga reach back further than anyone can comfortably claim to trace, anyhow.

After the Leaves, the deluge. Every band in L.A. seemed to have its version of "Hey Joe," with Love coming up with the best straight-ahead recording (on its first album). Cher actually put it back on the charts in 1967. But by then, the tune was a repertoire requirement for every halfway hip high school band in the country.

Jimi Hendrix put an end to that. "Hey Joe" hadn't hit in England yet, so producer Chas Chandler and Jimi worked it up for his British debut single in January 1967. But Hendrix didn't just cover the song, he possessed it. It's slowed down, the tempo making the undercurrent of violence into the song's most tangible quality. Noel Redding's bass tugs the beat forward, Mitch Mitchell crashes all over his kit, and Hendrix uses his voice and guitar like a set of matched blades, carving up rhythm and lyrics into vicious little shreds of energy.

You can call this music psychedelic if you want to, but Jimi's "Hey Joe" comes closer to bloodlust, not exactly the kind of thing I'd personally want to find myself hallucinating.

508 DO RIGHT WOMAN—DO RIGHT MAN, Aretha Franklin

Produced by Jerry Wexler; written by Dan Penn and Chips Moman
Atlantic 2386   1967   Did not make pop chart

Aretha came to Stax Studios in Memphis looking for a hit. She and her then-husband Ted White traveled there without so much as a song, looking for what producer Jerry Wexler and the Stax staff might come up with. She struck all kinds of gold, including one of the finest ballads of her career, a song as fine as anything she's ever done and damn near as well known, even though it never made it any closer to the charts than the B side of "I Never Loved A Man," her first Atlantic single.

Aretha's impossibly fine singing—including some overdubbed call-and-response with herself—is matched by her impossibly supple piano playing, which is in turn equaled by the gorgeously philosophical lyric, which establishes once and for all that this is not only a new *way* of singing but something new that Lady Soul is singing about: "They say that it's a man's world / But you can't prove that by me / And as long as we're together, baby, show some respect for me."

I mean, is that prophecy or perfection or both?

509 KEEP A-KNOCKIN', Little Richard
Produced by Bumps Blackwell; written by Richard Penniman
Specialty 611   1957   *Billboard:* #8

In 1947, a song called "Open the Door, Richard!" swept the recording industry. Based on a wheezy old off-color routine by chitlin' circuit comic Dusty Fletcher, the music was composed by trumpeter Jack McVea, who'd been a Lionel Hampton sideman. Fletcher, McVea, Count Basie, the Charioteers, the Three Flames, and, perhaps most memorably, Louis Jordan all scored with the song. More significantly, "Richard!" became one of the first "race" records to cross over and receive across-the-board national radio attention. Count Basie's version hit Number One on *Billboard*'s pop chart and all the others got at least some pop attention, laying a small but significant foundation for the R&B stars of the fifties.

In addition to all that, "Open the door, Richard!" became the youthful bane of every unfortunate kid saddled with that name; it's no pleasure growing up with a monicker that guarantees you status as the butt of a national joke. Lord knows, little Richard Penniman's youth must already have been sufficiently plagued with undesired attention.

Payback's a bitch. Louis Jordan recorded "Keep A-Knockin' " in 1939, when it was already an old song. (James Wiggins recorded it in the late twenties.) Jordan's version is a fairly tame small-combo jump blues, whose lyric concerns sexual revenge: "I hear you been cheatin' 'round with other men / I'm busy and you can't come in."

Little Richard, who was a big Jordan fan, certainly didn't arrive at his version by studying the 1939 record. He opens with a rush of cymbal and piano and lustfully screamed vocal, adds a booting saxophone, and simply races through whoops and flourishes and repetitions of its half-remembered chorus for two minutes and twenty seconds of sustained mania. The fact that Richard actually performed this chaotic fragment in a movie (*Mr. Rock 'n' Roll* with Alan Freed) is one of the great cultural wonders of the 1950s.

510 TIME AFTER TIME, Cyndi Lauper
Produced by Rick Chertoff; written by Cyndi Lauper and
Rob Hyman
Portrait 04432   1984   *Billboard:* #1 (2 weeks)

Lying in bed, a young woman stares up at the ceiling and sees the stars beyond the grime. Unable to sleep, she dreams of changing worlds, not least or just her own. The ticking of a clock counts the score.

Cyndi Lauper perhaps wrote "Time After Time" as a parable of her own life as a misfit artiste but she scored with it by capturing the wee hours heebie-jeebies of just about any old body. The music—mainly a wash of synthesizer, a heartbeat bass drum, metronomic snare shots and a growly guitar—resonates at exactly the right frequency to put her mood across, but it's the gently desperate singing that clinches the deal. If she let that misfit metaphor slide over into a reincarnation fantasy, she'd have confirmed her bubblehead surface. Instead, she totally subverted it by making her most mystical-sounding line into a ferocious cry of fidelity. "*I* will be waiting," Cyndi shouts, and everybody in earshot wakes up.

511 OVER YOU, Roxy Music
Produced by Rhett Davies; written by Bryan Ferry and
Andy Mackay
Atco 7301   1980   *Billboard:* #80

The reader may by this point be pardoned for having noticed an antipathy here for what might have been called "art-rock," if we were not engaged in a project the purpose of which is to redefine the idea of art in rock to make it a matter of soul and vision, rather than form and intention, so that Aretha Franklin, let's say, appears more creative and imaginative than, oh, to pick a name entirely at random, David Bowie.

Compared to other rock criticism, of course, the very idea amounts to pure science fiction, the creation of an alternate universe in which Steve Cropper's guitar playing and James Jamerson's bass and the songwriting of Smokey Robinson are more important than, just to pick a few more random examples, anything ever accomplished by Robert Fripp, Greg Lake, or the combined works of Syd Barrett and Roger Waters.

Truth to tell, the sort of thing that passes itself off as art in our society is a generally specious commodity, and it's probably not much more worth railing against the blowhardism, fake poetry, and presumed sensitivity of your average art-rocker (whether a posing Brit, a post-academic New Yorker or a California psychedelic type) than it is against painters who daub muddy sketches and adorn them with chipped crockery or novelists who sententiously babble of the maunderings of a decadent Manhattan claque (or for that matter, of a Pecksniffian academic coterie). This is the world we live in today; its standards are phony, and it therefore isn't surprising that its basic unit of measurement for creativity is an exhausted artificiality, though one's ultimate fury against such entropy may be measured by how annoying it remains that the product is also so proudly pedestrian, so utterly middlebrow in its supposed assault on bourgeois standards.

Roxy Music is the exception that proves the rule, at least in part because it is not entirely an exception, having visited upon the world the naked elitism of Brian Eno and having itself a tendency to make overblown music that loses sight of groove in favor of inventions without an emotional core.

As an art student, Roxy Music leader Bryan Ferry trained with Richard Hamilton, the British painter whose metier was ironic commentary on pop culture. Hamilton's vision of pop art, a distanced comment on the mass society in which the artist lived but did not willingly participate, is very much the spirit of Roxy Music. (It's not the only available version of high art meets trash culture, however, the most prominent alternative being the more deeply immersed paintings of Peter Blake and the whatever-the-hells they are of Red Grooms, not to mention the sonic visions of John Lennon and Pete Townshend.)

So Ferry learned to manipulate the rudiments of pop without sullying his work with the taint of emotion or sentiment. Except that he had this damn band to work with which—despite the presence of such even more *echt* art-rock figures as "Over You" cowriter Phil Manzenera and synthesizer player Eddie Jobson—kept inserting passion into the mix. Ferry fought this manfully and on his late eighties solo albums finally found the complete desiccation he'd long sought.

Meantime, Roxy Music from time to time produced slices of music that were compulsively listenable, adding a dangerous groove to a fantasy Top 40 (since none of them actually reached it, in the States at least) in which such ironic distance might have actually communicated something other than the performers' feelings of inherent superiority to the genres in which they trafficked. Invariably, these pieces presented themselves as singles. Among the more memorable were "Do the Strand," an anticipatory (1973) parody of early eighties dance rock moves, and "Love is the Drug," a trenchant satire (I think) of love songs and romantic love *per se*.

Best of all, though, was "Over You," its title a multilayered pun (which was perhaps even scatalogical in some dimensions), its topic an essence of banality, but its groove quite irresistible. Ferry's singing succumbs to the seductions of the beat and actually shows some life, so that even though the lyrics are actually quite as predictable as they want to be, their juxtaposition with heavily romantic piano chords, synth riffs, and Andy Mackay's soprano sax solo lends them a lush romanticism, as if the love song overlay were genuinely felt by all concerned.

But that's not even impossible, it's unthinkable.

512 IF I WERE YOUR WOMAN, Gladys Knight and the Pips
Produced by Clay McMurray; written by Pam Sawyer, Gloria Jones, and Clay McMurray
Soul 35078   1970   *Billboard:* #9

The record on which Knight really found her calling. Her earlier attempts at making Motown rhythm records did okay on the charts, but they were pedestrian products of the company formula. "If I Were Your Woman" is an *adult* love ballad, and it gives Gladys the chance to emote boldly and copiously all over the idea of cheating with someone else's man. This is the original of the sophisticated pop-soul that made Knight, for a couple of years in the early seventies, the black Barbra Streisand.

513 BLUE MOON, The Marcels
Produced by Stu Phillips; written by Richard Rogers and Lorenz Hart
Colpix 186   1961   *Billboard:* #1 (3 weeks)

When show tune writers Richard Rodgers and Lorenz Hart spin in their graves, it means that someone, somewhere, is playing the Marcels' "Blue Moon" again. Not only did Broadway's great composer/lyricist team never suspect that they were writing a rock and roll classic (it was also a hit in an extremely spectral Elvis Presley version in 1956), the debonaire Hart never expected to have appended to his carefully wrought lines the supercharged introduction: "Bomp ba ba bomp / Ba bomp ba bomp bomp / Ba ba bomp ba ba bomp / Da dang da dangdang / Da ding-a-dong ding." You wanna know why Tin Pan Alley writers hated rock and roll? Nobody was ever meant to have *this kind* of fun with their music; to an uninitiated ear, it must have sounded like gobbledygook piled upon greatness. ("Blue Moon," it must be said, is one of the genuine treasures of the Rodgers and Hart repertoire, so good that it claims the rare distinction for a song of the thirties of becoming a standard without first appearing in a show or movie.)

It was all an accident, of course. The Marcels (two white guys and three black ones from Pittsburgh) sent Stu Phillips of Colpix a demo tape, on which they recreated old R&B hits in their own fashion. Phillips liked what he heard and brought the group to New York, although he had no support from the label bosses. He ran an unofficial session on a February evening, cutting three sides, all remakes. He suggested finishing off with "Heart and Soul," but nobody in the group knew it. One of them did know "Blue Moon" so they broke for an hour and came back with basically the very arrangement on the record, to which Phillips grafted the nonsense intro from one of the unused tunes on the demo. They did two takes; the second was the keeper.

Phillips gave a tape to the local Colpix promo man, who played it for Murray the K, who'd replaced Alan Freed as the most important deejay at New York's WINS. Murray loved it so much he played it on his show twenty-six times in one night. Colpix, which hadn't been committed to releasing anything by the Marcels, was forced to rush release the track. It came out at the end of February; within a month, it hit Number One in *Billboard*, the fastest rising chart-topping single between Elvis and the Beatles.

Which just shows what you can do if you know what "do wah diddy" means and aren't afraid to upset the experts.

514 SORRY (I RAN ALL THE WAY HOME), The Impalas

Produced by Ray Ellis; written by Harry Giosasi and Artie Zwirin
Cub 9022   1959   *Billboard: #2*

It's a striking contravention of orthodox rock history that so many of the best doo-wop records were made by integrated groups. The Impalas are one more example. Tenor Tony Carlucci and baritones Lenny Renda and Richard Wagner began rehearsing at their local candy store in Brooklyn's working-class Canarsie section, developing a distinct harmony blend. But by the end of the fifties, harmony alone couldn't get a group over; it needed a distinctive lead singer. The Canarsie kids found one in Joe "Speedo" Frazier (not to be confused with Earl

"Speedo" Carroll of the Cadillacs). Frazier was a black kid from Manhattan. They called themselves the Impalas, after Renda's father's new Chevy.

Auditioning in New York, they met Artie Zwirin, who teamed them with his song "Sorry (I Ran All the Way Home)," and persuaded disc jockey supreme Alan Freed to recommend the act to MGM's new rhythm and blues subsidiary, Cub Records. Cub assigned act and song to veteran pop arranger Ray Ellis, who'd worked with Atlantic Records acts like Clyde McPhatter ("Seven Days") and LaVern Baker ("See See Rider").

The record they made starts out like a conventional doo-wop disc, with a full choral arrangement: "Sorry, sorry, oh so sorry." Then somebody gulps "Uh-oh," and a downbeat and clanging guitar kick off something a lot wilder. Frazier's voice, layered with echo, sings counterpoint with nonsense syllables from the rest of the group, while the band just bashes away, with occasional horn and guitar interludes where the music can't seem to make up its mind whether to rock out or succumb to Top 40 conventions, a move prophetic of early sixties Jackie Wilson productions.

"Sorry" nevertheless smacks more of craft than chaos—Ellis knew what he was doing, even if the group didn't. He'd return to the Top 40, while the Impalas disappeared until the invention of the oldies circuit a few years later.

515 SEXUAL HEALING, Marvin Gaye
Written and produced by Marvin Gaye, Odell Brown, and David Ritz
Columbia 03302   1982   *Billboard:* #3

It figures that Marvin's last gasp (as well as groan and moan) would be devoted to advancing the idea that fucking is an all-purpose spiritual remedy. And in a few years, when the tears clear from our eyes, maybe the end of his life will matter less than the incredible music that he made right up to the end. Right now, "Sexual Healing" is neither true nor false as a philosophical proposition, just twice as tragic as it is danceable.

516 IT'S ALL RIGHT, The Impressions
Producer not credited; written by Curtis Mayfield
ABC-Paramount 10487   1963   *Billboard:* #4

Not just the most repetitions of a three-word slang phrase in pop music history (if you like that part, check out their "Amen"), but an absolute instruction manual for the cure of depression: "When you wake up early in the mornin' / Feelin' sad like so many of us do / Hum a little soul, make life your goal / And surely somethin's gotta come to you." From somebody who's often had it work, I'd just like to say, thanks, Curtis, Fred, and Sam.

517 SURFIN' U.S.A., The Beach Boys
Produced by Nik Venet; written by Brian Wilson and
Chuck Berry
Capitol 4932   1963   *Billboard:* #3

Had I known that it was Hal Blaine and Tommy Tedesco, not Dennis and Carl Wilson, playing on "Surfin' U.S.A." (and the Beach Boys' other big hits), my landlocked adolescence would have been considerably different. Not as different, however, as if I had discovered even a couple of years sooner that the first line of this song is "If everybody had an ocean," instead of "If everybody had a notion. . . ."

What Mike Love actually sings is self-evident, just a place to start Brian Wilson's description of what was going on after school in his town. (Well, actually, he started by lifting a beat, melody, chord structure, and arrangement from "Sweet Little Sixteen," which resulted in a lawsuit, which is how he and Chuck Berry came to "collaborate.")

But what I heard—for many, many years, so many it would be embarrassing to count them—made of "Surfin' U.S.A." and Brian Wilson and the Beach Boys something far greater. "If everybody had a notion" makes surfing an act of will and philosophy; in my imagination, those weren't just kids swimming around with fiberglass sticks, they were men walking on water. And after a quarter of a century, having lived with both ideas of the song and the scene, the truth pales against the fantasy, and I truly believe that (whether they understood Love's flat accent right or not) that's what a lot of other hopeless Beach Boys fans stuck in the dry flatlands heard, one way or another: surf music as the will to power.

518 SINCE I MET YOU BABY, Ivory Joe Hunter
Produced by Ahmet Ertegun and Jerry Wexler; written by Ivory Joe Hunter
Atlantic 1111 1956 *Billboard: #12*

"If he had never written but this one song," no less an authority than Sam Phillips once said, "Ivory Joe Hunter should go down as one of the true greats."

Hunter not only wrote many other fine songs, this wasn't even the first time he'd written this one, nor even the first time he'd had a hit with it. Its father, "I Almost Lost My Mind," had been a Number One R&B hit for Hunter in 1950. The two songs share a virtually identical melody, interchangable lyrics, and a C&W piano ballad style. The principal musical difference boils down to the Taft Jordan trumpet solo on "Mind" and Jesse Powell's sax solo and Ray Ellis's somewhat more streamlined orchestration and choral arrangement on the Atlantic side.

The other important difference: In 1950, Ivory Joe Hunter's country-accented R&B style got no pop airplay. "I Almost Lost My Mind" made the pop charts through the much more mainstream vehicle of Nat "King" Cole, also a black performer but one whose approach was Northern and Tin Pan Alley. Hunter's version of "Since I Lost My Baby," on the other hand, made the pop charts two weeks *before* it hit R&B.

What had changed in those six years wasn't Ivory Joe Hunter's style, which remained all but immutable from his first R&B Number One, "Pretty Mama Blues" in 1946, through the final performance of his life, at the Grand Ole Opry in 1974. It was the entire record and broadcasting industries, reflecting even more sweeping changes in the nation and the world.

519 EVERYBODY LOVES A WINNER, William Bell
Produced by Booker T. Jones; written by William Bell and Booker T. Jones
Stax 212 1967 *Billboard: #95*

Once more, Booker T. contributes languorous country piano chords to a fine Bell soul ballad. Together with splendid legato phrasing, an especially sonorous horn chart, and a lyric that epitomizes the not-quite-derelict condition of the journeyman soulster, "Everybody Loves a Winner" is the finest of all Bell's "You Don't Miss Your Water" follow-ups, a rare moment of overt introspection amidst the day-to-day clamor that pervaded Memphis R&B.

520 I LOVE MUSIC, The O'Jays
Written and produced by Kenny Gamble and Leon Huff
Philadelphia International 3577   1975   *Billboard: #5*

Half accelerant, half intoxicant, the Philly International groove came as close to providing a Motown/Spectorian lingua franca as anything in the disco era. Here, Eddie Levert and friends put the reason in so many words: "Music is the healing force of the world / Understood by every man, woman, boy and girl," and then a verse later, "Music makes the atmosphere so fine / 'Specially when you got a cold glass of wine." And there you have the ethos of the disco world, bifurcated by quasi-religious fervor on one side and plain old lust for kicks on the other. Or maybe not split so much as it seems to outsiders; spun into a frenzy by the force of these sounds, it's not hard to imagine men and women, boys and girls driven to a religiosity of ecstasy. Certainly, judging from Kenny Gamble's later lyrics and liner notes, that was what *he* had in mind.

521 CATHY'S CLOWN, The Everly Brothers
Produced by Dick Glasser; written by Don and Phil Everly
Warner 5151   1960   *Billboard: #1 (5 weeks)*

The Everly's first hit for Warner Brothers was also their all-time best seller, not bad for a song written about Don's high school girlfriend a good five years after the breakup. The real story, though, is the interplay between their harmonies and the drums, which add an anxious edge that makes it sound like Don faces a firing squad, not just homeroom humiliation. (Though come to think of it . . . Were you ever humiliated in homeroom?)

522 LOVE MAN, Otis Redding
Produced by Steve Cropper; written by Otis Redding
Atco 6677   1969   *Billboard: #72*

Otis's final pop chart entry isn't a macho boast but a creative act of self-definition. When he stammers " 'cau-, cau-, cau-, cause I'm a . . . love man!" that's not the result of not knowing quite what to say, it's the product of having put his finger on it at last. And with Al Jackson rocking the world at his back, he's got the strength and vision to spit it out: "I'm a love man, that's what they call me, I'm a love man." No one who's heard the rest of the story could doubt him.

523 THE WAY YOU DO THE THINGS YOU DO, The Temptations
Produced by Smokey Robinson; written by Bobby Rogers and Smokey Robinson
Gordy 7028   1964   *Billboard:* #11

"When I first heard the Temptations, I knew they reminded me of something," David Ruffin mused publicly on the night that the Temptations were inducted into the Rock and Roll Hall of Fame. "Tonight, when I saw the Soul Stirrers, I remembered what it was."

It's not hard to figure what he meant, since the Stirrers with R.H. Harris and J.J. Farley were the gospel quartet that made the mold out of which all of soul's dual-lead groups (four piece backups with an alternating fifth member out front) were stamped. In this sense, the version of the Temptations that starred Ruffin and Eddie Kendricks was the Stirrers' secular heir to an even greater extent than Stirrers' graduate Sam Cooke.

"The Way You Do the Things You Do" was the Tempts' first record with Ruffin aboard, and though it's Kendricks who takes that shattering high lead, it's still appropriate that it became their first national hit. Not that Ruffin and Kendricks were the only weapons in the group's arsenal. Smokey Robinson turned in one of his jauntiest melodies, some of his best, most extended rhymes, and drew from Marv Tarplin one of Motown's most unforgettable guitar figures, while Benny Benjamin and James Jamerson worked the backbeat as if they'd invented it. The lesser Temptations—especially the great bass, Melvin Franklin—also play prominent parts in the intricate harmony arrangement. And then there's the wild call of that saxophone, seeming to charge straight out of "Dancing in the Streets."

"You make my life so bright, you make me feel all right," cries Kendricks at the end and all around the nation, everybody said Yeaaaah!

524 YOU AND YOUR FOLKS, ME AND MY FOLKS, Funkadelic

Produced by George Clinton; written by George Clinton,
Bernie Worrell, and J. Jones
Westbound 175   1971   *Billboard:* #91

525 TEAR THE ROOF OFF THE SUCKER (GIVE UP THE FUNK), Parliament

Produced by George Clinton; written by George Clinton,
Bootsy Collins, and Jerome Brailey
Casablanca 856   1976   *Billboard:* #15

George Clinton's bumpy brand of psychedelic funk made for less cogent singles than you might expect. Clinton didn't really make disco records, and his bizarre visions often required an entire LP side to fully unfold. But from time to time he just nailed it, coming up with deep grooves in contexts that would have made sense at gunpoint or in your most delirious dreams, either of which seemed likely as the music built to its successive climaxes. (Master of excess that he was, the Clinton of the seventies never stopped at one.) If the Parliafunkadelicment Thang sometimes seemed like a scam, at its best moments Clinton's vision seemed not only inclusive but embracing. (Frankly, though, if you want to hear the best of it you need to buy the Bootsy Collins solo albums, on which the jokes *always* work and are always on everybody, including you and Bootsy.)

"You and Your Folks," one of the first Funkadelic sides after Clinton's conversion from minor R&B hustler to acid-inspired funkster, uses discordant piano and polyrhythmic percussion to set up a vision of world peace that's not without sinister undercurrents, an impression abetted by Clinton's ravaged screams, the female "Yeah, yeah, yeah" that sounds so much like "Nah, nah, nah," and the group's arm's-length involvement with the Mansonoid Process Church of the Final Judgment.

"Tear the Roof Off the Sucker," which sold a million despite its inconspicuous place on the pop charts, is the greatest hit of Parliament's mature period, if you can talk about maturity with a group whose self-descriptions include "Cosmic Slop." Opening with a section heavily influenced by Norman Whitfield's acid-soul productions for the Temptations, the band takes over to exemplify the lyrics: "You gotta feel everything goin' down, gettin' down / There's a whole lotta rhythm goin' down." Even if you didn't know that half these guys had served time in James Brown's bands, you'd guess it from the way the horns and guitars collide and cooperate. And even if you'd never heard Prince, you'd have to expect his immanence from just about every nuance here, especially the synthesizer flourishes and the quasi-mystical philosophizing (out on the dance floor, "give up the funk" meant one thing, but in the expanded, album-length version of the P-Funk message, it had connotations too unlikely to be detailed here, just as Prince's records used sex and God interchangeably). As a bridge from past to future, this stuff can hardly be beat, no matter what my reservations about taking it on its own terms.

526 IT'S TOO LATE, Chuck Willis
Produced by Zenas Sears; written by Chuck Willis
Atlantic 1098   1956   Did not make pop chart

Willis's first Atlantic hit was this slow ballad that provides the missing link between the Southwestern jump blues of Wynonie Harris and his acolytes and Marvin Gaye and soul eccentrics yet to come. The arrangement features a nice sax, a little too much vocal support by the Cookies (later, the Raelettes), and odd effects from what might as easily be music box chimes and a glockenspiel as vibes.

The essence of "It's Too Late" as a record spurring the transition from one mode of black pop to the next is none of this, however. It's the languorous mood and tone of the piece, and that came from nowhere but paying close attention to country and western music, whose subtly integrated inflections contribute much to this song's understated beauty.

527 I ONLY HAVE EYES FOR YOU, Flamingos
Produced by George Goldner; written by Harry Warren
End 1046   1959   Billboard: #11

Another resuscitation of a Tin Pan Alley standard: "I Only Have Eyes for You" emerged from the 1934 movie, *Dames*. It made Number Two that year, in a version by the now-forgotten Ben Selvin.

It's anybody's guess why the Flamingos revived it. Unlike today's bands, who can make do with a riff and a beat, vocal groups needed strong melodies and hoped for interesting lyrics, wrapping their vocal exotica around whatever met their criteria, no matter its provenance. And because the Flamingos were veterans, having first recorded in 1952 (for Al Sheridan's Chance label, after being told by another Chicago diskery, United, that they weren't "black enough"), their influences were quite broad, encompassing gospel (the core of the group was two pairs of cousins who started singing in their Pentecostal church choir), and the silken pop harmonies of the Mills Brothers and Four Freshmen as well as R&B-oriented groups. As the split between Tin Pan Alley and the Brill Building became more pronounced over the next decade, and as Southern and gospel stylings became more pronounced, fewer and fewer groups would have any idea what to do with a standard, a problem these guys never had.

But the Flamingos could hardly be described as respecting tradition. From the opening statement of the theme on a reverberant electric guitar to the acres of echo in which the background "shoo-bop-she-bops" are encased to Johnny Carter's high tenor cries, there's nothing about this record that really relates to Ben Selvin's or anybody else's. Except maybe Tommy Hunt's measured, careful lead, which harks back to the conventions of early fifties doo-wop even as the rest of the arrangement shatters them: He might as well really be blind—or deaf—to his environment. And the quiet eeriness of that disparity is a big part of what makes "I Only Have Eyes" one of rock's continuing marvels.

528 THE THRILL IS GONE, B.B. King
Produced by Bill Szymczyk; written by Arthur H. Benson and Dale Petite
BluesWay 61032   1969   *Billboard*: #15

The last great blues record? Anyway, confirmation not just of King's overwhelming stature but of his overwhelming prowess, too. The single-string guitar picking is splendid (he's done better, but not often) and the section at the end where he plays counterpoint to a bass violin is more arresting—and, Lord knows, soulful—than any of the Beatles' similar experiments. King is famous primarily as a guitarist, but his vocal on "The Thrill is Gone" is a magnificent growl of mingled rage and bereavement.

529 BEAT IT, Michael Jackson
Produced by Quincy Jones; written by Michael Jackson
Epic 03759   1983   *Billboard*: #1 (7 weeks)

530 ROCK BOX, Run-D.M.C.
Produced by Russell Simmons and Larry Smith; written by
Larry Smith, Darryl McDaniels, and Joseph Simmons
Profile 7045   1984   Did not make pop chart

531 BAD GIRLS, Donna Summer
Produced by Giorgio Moroder and Pete Bellotte; written by
Donna Summer, Bruce Sudano, Eddie Hokenson, and Joe Esposito
Casablanca 988   1979   *Billboard:* #1 (5 weeks)

By the late seventies, white rock and the various forms of black pop
descended from R&B and soul—basically, disco and funk—seemed to
have diverged completely, an impression abetted by the lack of any
really homogeneous pop radio. Top 40 programming became a lost art
in those years, swamped by "narrowcast" formats that played either
all album rock or all disco. The result was, among other things, the
development of a rock audience trained to believe that even integration
within musical forms was impossible, unfair, and most likely unnatural.

The absurdity of such thinking, while now obvious, was fostered
by a music industry that retreated to a state of segregation nearly as
absolute as what prevailed before Presley. The ultimate irony was that,
all along, musicians regularly trounced racial boundaries (though no
radio programmer and few record labels were willing to traipse so lightly
over them). The album-oriented "funk" of Rick James and George
Clinton was not much different from various forms of album "rock"
even in its most annoying excesses, just as white groups like the Doobie
Brothers regularly employed modern dance music devices in their hits.
Steely Dan and Earth, Wind and Fire were brothers under the skin.
And then there were the Rolling Stones and "Some Girls," a record
widely celebrated by white rock fans who wouldn't have given a moment's attention to a record with the same beat if it had been performed
by a black group.

By 1979, with the coming of Prince, the barriers began to audibly
disintegrate in ways that were unignorable by everybody except the
hidebound fools at the top of the broadcasting and recording businesses.
The point was not lost, at least, on Donna Summer and her producers,
Giorgio Moroder and Pete Bellotte. Summer's earlier records made
her Queen of Disco, but she was also married to Bruce Sudano, leader
of a rock group. At decade's end, with the bottom ready to drop out
of the disco phenomenon, Summer knew it was time to make her move.

"Hot Stuff" retains the basic thump-thump-thump that identifies disco but its entire attack stems from guitar that's a hell of a lot more rocking than "Some Girls," its most obvious antecedent not only in musical terms but in the Jaggeresque way that Summer projects herself as a sexual dynamo. At least some music critics picked up on the connection, which helped move the music scene toward an open-eyed acknowledgment of de facto pop music integration, no matter what the lawgivers at the local station wanted the audience to believe.

The segregationists' fate was sealed not by any given single but by an album: Prince's 1980 *Dirty Mind*, an undeniable fusion of funk, soul, and post-acid rock. His 1982 follow-up, *1999*, finally brought him to what was left of Top 40, with "1999" and "Little Red Corvette," the latter so utterly rock and roll in form and content that even MTV's avid strategists of musical apartheid had to air it.

But the real landmark was Michael Jackson's "Beat It," which mated the top pop hero of revitalized Top 40 (known now as CHR, or Contemporary Hit Radio) with Edward Van Halen, guitar king of heavy metal. While its massive chart stature was undoubtedly fueled by doses of hype and wishful thinking on the part of everybody involved from everyday listeners to broadcasters (nobody wanted to be left out of the *biggest action ever seen*), Van Halen's bludgeoning solo in fact captures an essence of heavy metal that could perhaps only be so sharply defined in contact with the more regimented rhythmic dance framework Jackson provided. "Beat It" was a genuine break toward the reintegration of rock.

On the other hand, Jackson used heavy metal only to score a coup. The pursuit of an actual metal/funk fusion interested him not at all and he's never followed up. His next album, *Victory*, with the Jacksons, contained no funk-rock and his next solo record, *Bad*, used metal only perfunctorily. By then, he'd already been surpassed by a number of hip-hop performers, most notably Run-D.M.C.

As it turned out, metal records had long been favorites of hip-hop's East Coast B-boy culture, mainly because they had heavy instrumental parts that were useful to mix with disco breaks. Run-D.M.C. were big Aerosmith fans, for instance, and by 1986, a remake of Aerosmith's "Walk This Way" (featuring that band's leaders, Steven Tyler and Joe Perry) gave them their first step into the Top 40. But well before "Walk This Way," Run-D.M.C. used metal in its singles. The first and best of them was "Rock Box," five-and-a-half nasty minutes of metal and rap reduced to their noisy basics. "Rock Box" and its successors (not only "Walk This Way" but "King of Rock" too) encouraged the main musical styles of the urban disenfranchised, heavy metal and rap, to come together in a renewed dialogue.

532 STAND!, Sly & the Family Stone
Written and produced by Sly Stone
Epic 10450   1969   *Billboard:* #22

Call to arms—and legs and feet, not forgetting the brain. You probably remember "Stand!" mostly as a rhythm record, and you're not wrong, but it's also one of Sly's best vocal harmony vehicles, and the inspirational verses outweigh the declamation that serves as title and chorus. And how's this for political complexity, John and Yoko: "Stand! Don't you know you are free / Well, at least in your mind if you want to be."

533 SOLDIERS OF LOVE, Arthur Alexander
Producer not credited; written by Cason and Moon
Dot 16357   1962   Did not make pop chart

The ships from America brought all kinds of cargo to Liverpool, most notably cotton for the mills of England but also rhythm and blues to fuel the imaginations of the country's aspiring musicians.

The cotton and other goods came as part of regulated commerce. The music arrived piggyback, after the fashion of roaches and rats, in the duffles of sailors black and white. Like any other organism removed from the ecology that spawned it, it assumed odd mutated forms. And the stuff that survived wasn't always what would have lasted back on home turf.

The specifics of "Soldiers of Love" landing in the U.K. will never be known. Perhaps it was brought there by the same sailor who arrived with "Anna," Arthur Alexander's other 1962 single, which actually made the R&B chart. Maybe somebody in Liverpool had heard "Anna" and asked some Yank navvy for more of the same. You can't know. John Lennon's dead and he might not have found the circumstances worth remembering, anyway.

But, if you love rock and soul music, you didn't have to be the best rock critic of your generation to understand that "Soldiers of Love" was a great record. The off-center Latin rhythm, Alexander's almost C&W vocal, and the remarkable consonance of lyric and melody form a sustained metaphor in which strife among lovers becomes a cry for universal peace. "Soldier of Love" was not the first or the last R&B obscurity to assume such grandiose dimensions, but it was one of the best.

For a variety of reasons, many of them self-evident, if the Beatles had not found "Soldiers of Love," it would have been lost to history.

As it was, almost nobody outside of a few soul collectors really knew the song until the late seventies, when a bootleg tape of Beatles' outtakes surfaced in the hands of a very different group of music fanatics. Since the original record was swallowed up in the British Invasion, in the truest sense, "Soldiers of Love" was rescued by the Beatles.

And as exhausted lovers everywhere sink back and listen to Arthur Alexander talk insistent sense within the record's inexorable rhythmic flow—"Use your arms to hold me tight, baby I don't wanna fight no more" in one line, with no pause for breath—we thank him and them.

534 RUNAWAY, Del Shannon
Produced by Harry Balk and Irving Micahnik; written by Del Shannon and Max Crook
Big Top 3067   1961   *Billboard:* #1 (4 weeks)

Time changes everything, as a country and western bard once said. Especially the import of song lyrics.

Del Shannon (a pseudonym Charles Westover copped from a guy who owed him money) wrote "Runaway" while playing the Hi-Lo Club in his hometown, Battle Creek, Michigan, the home of the American cereal industry, a town as full of farmers and roughnecks as you'd expect from a place on the fringes of the Detroit-Chicago industrial axis. So Del played country and soul and a lot of rock. It was a tough joint— "the kind of place where they'd smash bottles on the floor and keep right on dancing"—but Del was no kid. He'd already done a hitch in the Army (where he was featured on a radio show called "Get Up and Go").

Ann Arbor disc jockey Ollie McLaughlin came into the place one night because he'd heard about Del and his band. McLaughlin (discoverer of Barbara Lewis, the Capitols, Deon Jackson, and others) arranged a New York audition for Shannon with Harry Balk and Irving Micahnik, a couple of transplanted Motor City boys who were looking to score in rock and roll. They did one session but got nothing worth releasing; they needed a song before they could do another.

Rehearsing at the Hi-Lo before a show one night soon after, organist Max Crook hit an unplanned change on his electric organ: A minor followed by G, the oddness of the sequence enhanced by a Musitron, a clip-on electronics effect, perhaps the first one ever used by a pop band. "I never heard such a great change as that," Del said. "Play it again." On the spot, they came up with a song based around those unlikely chords. The next day, Del scribbled off some lyrics.

Shannon said he wrote the words about himself because he was forever running away from relationships. Anyway, the tenor of his lyrics certainly fit the mood of the music, with its booting sax and tinkling piano and eerie Musitron-organ break. His singing added an edgy, paranoiac touch. After working it up for another few weeks at the Hi-Lo, they took it to Balk and Micahnik. And quickly cut a smash.

In the eighties, of course, runaways aren't found in pop songs but on the sides of milk cartons. And kids don't run away to join anything as benign as the circus (doesn't that musitron somehow suggest a calliope?). And the edge of panic in the vocal might come, not from a downhearted lover walking and w-w-wondering in the rain about how he's blown it this time, but from a parent trying to figure out how and where and why "she ran away . . . and where she will stay."

So if an unknown Del Shannon put out "Runaway" today, he'd just as likely be investigated as celebrated. A cop could make quite a lot out of the fact that he'd changed his name, just for starters. Which would make what you hear in his voice not paranoia but the real thing. Fortunately, that was then, not now.

535 YOU'RE GONNA MISS ME, The Thirteenth Floor Elevators
Producer not credited; written by Roky Erickson
International Artists 107   1966   Billboard: #55

In 1972, Lenny Kaye assembled an album called *Nuggets: Original Artyfacts from the First Psychedelic Era, 1965–1968*, thus making him a hero of protopunk rock long before he was ever known for picking up a guitar in support of Patti Smith or for producing Suzanne Vega's "Luka."

The records Kaye put together may or may not have been psychedelic; today, they'd be more likely lumped together as garage rock. But it's indisputable that they were great *singles* (many of them also included in *The Heart of Rock & Soul*), and that Kaye's extensively annotated package was an important assertion of singles aesthetics at the height of the album rock epoch. From "I Had Too Much to Dream (Last Night)" by the Electric Prunes to "It's A-Happening" by the Magic Mushrooms, *Nuggets* celebrated one-shot white rock at its trashiest.

Of all the *Nuggets* Kaye put together, none was stranger than "You're Gonna Miss Me," a minor but indelible hit in the summer before the Summer of Love. Released on an ultraobscure Texas label, filled with shrieks, what sounded like atomic jug band effects, and a lunatic vocal, it's one of the most demented examples of great rock and roll in existence. (How crazed? Lead Elevator Roky Erickson eventually psychedelized himself into an institution.)

Kaye reports that the Elevators' album liner notes described "You're Gonna Miss Me" as a song about "those people who for the sake of appearances take on the superficial aspects of the quest." Yet another definitive argument in favor of buying the single.

536 WHAT KIND OF FOOL (DO YOU THINK I AM), The Tams
Produced by Joe South; written by Ray Whitley
ABC-Paramount 10502   1963   *Billboard:* #9

In stereotype, Southern soul is deep and bluesy, so intense it's virtually worth your life to encounter it. But it wasn't that way at the beginning. The Tams came out of Atlanta, five black kids who kicked around that city's local circuit from the late 1950s until 1962, when they hooked up with music publisher Bill Lowery, who became the group's manager and brought them to Rick Hall's Fame Studio in Muscle Shoals, Alabama. They hit the charts with "Untie Me," then scored big with "What Kind of Fool."

"What Kind of Fool" defies Southern gospel-blues clichés. Featuring a basso lead vocal as goofy as it is gritty and an arrangement highlighted by the light, bright tones of a flute, the record's joyous infectiousness owes more to relatively gimmicky New York pop-R&B of the Leiber-Stoller school than to what was about to occur in Memphis. Yet the rumbling drums and the graceful guitar figures very much foreshadow future Muscle Shoals productions.

537 C'MON EVERYBODY, Eddie Cochran
Written and produced by Eddie Cochran and Jerry Capehart
Liberty 55166   1958   *Billboard:* #8

Greatest party invitation of the rock and roll era.

538 THERE IS, The Dells
Produced by Bobby Miller; written by Raymond Miner and Bobby Miller
Cadet 5590   1968   *Billboard:* #20

"Man, we were stone hooligans," Chuck Barksdale, the Dells' great bass voice, once told *Hit Parader*. "We broke out car windows and threw pumpkins at buses. We were bad, man. But we were always singing."

And here's the record that proves that every word was true.

539 TEMPTATION 'BOUT TO GET ME, The Knight Brothers
Producer not credited; written by James Diggs
Checker 1107   1965   *Billboard:* #70

For once, a deep soul duet that owes nothing to Sam and Dave or Marvin and Tammi. Instead, singer/guitarist/songwriter James Diggs and his boyhood friend, Richard Dunbar, sing straight gospel, so clearly that if the lyrics placed them on the Temple Mount or in the depths of Gethsemane, you wouldn't be surprised, even though Diggs's loss of faith stems from nothing more than his girlfriend's failure to phone or write during a long trip.

That's a setup for soul cliché. Redemption appears through a glorious Chicago soul arrangement, the kind of band playing that typifies mid-sixties records by the likes of the Dells and the Impressions: booming drums, sharp bleats of cornet, deep rumblings from a baritone sax, plus some tenor saxophone blasts that make sense of the Knights' impatience. That might be Gabriel up there, getting ready to write his own ending to their woe.

540 SHOUT, PART 2, The Isley Brothers
Produced by Hugo and Luigi; written by O'Kelly Isley, Ronald Isley, and Rudolph Isley
RCA 7588   1959   *Billboard:* #47

Starts where "What'd I Say" leaves off; goes nowhere and has a great time doing it. (Part One has the "lyrics" but its ending is as truly anticlimatic as anything in Western art.)

541 BORN TO BE WILD, Steppenwolf
Produced by Gabriel Mekler; written by Mars Bonfire
Dunhill 4138   1968   *Billboard:* #2

One of the all-time cheesy organ riffs, a hopelessly dated "psychedelic" fuzz guitar, big splashy cymbal crashes, and a vocal that sounds like it's a little confused about the lyrics' translation from the original Biker. This is both the greatest motorcycle song in history (edging out "Blue's Theme" by Dave Allan and the Arrows, the anthem from Roger Corman's *The Wild Angels*) and, thanks to its evanescent rumble and the third line of its first verse, possibly the eytomological source point of "heavy metal." (You didn't really think it was William Burroughs, did you?)

542 SOUL ON FIRE, LaVern Baker
Produced by Ahmet Ertegun and Jerry Wexler; written by LaVern Baker, Jerry Wexler, and Ahmet Ertegun
Atlantic 1004   1953   Did not make pop chart

Not only male blues singers made the transition to rock and roll. LaVern Baker shot out of Detroit in the late forties as Little Miss Sharecropper, a jump band singer, and her roots in jazz balladry show clearly on this extraordinarily funky blues from her first Atlantic session. "Soul on Fire" is as tough and bopping as anything any of the guys on the circuit could claim. Baker's melismatic growls at the end show the gospel origins of her style, but her smooth confidence with the worldly lyric, her patience in allowing the song to develop and her empathy with the small combo backing her all suggest her nightclub experience. Which is probably why LaVern resented being labelled a rock and roll singer— not that she wasn't a great one.

543 PUMP UP THE VOLUME, M/A/R/R/S
Produced by Martyn Young; written by Martyn and Steve Young
Fourth and Broadway 452   1987   *Billboard:* #13

Contemporary British pop dance music, sampled within an inch of its life—sort of. Actually, the original "Pump Up the Volume," a hit in England earlier in 1987 than in the United States, used all sorts of bits electronically lifted from the dance discs produced by, among others, the *schlock meisters* Stock/Aiken/Waterman. S/A/W sued M/A/R/R/S, who just said fuck it and put the record out in the U.S. with a live band filling in the bits they'd originally lifted. The exact relationship of all this to *Mars Needs Women*, a flimsy bit of sixties cinematic detritus in which Martians invade Earth looking for girls, must mystify everybody who didn't buy Peter Wolf's first solo album. (Which Peter Wolf remains a lesson for another day, unless you're already a staunch fan of J. Geils or Michael Jonzun.)

544 I AIN'T GONNA EAT OUT MY HEART ANYMORE, The Rascals
Produced by the Rascals with Arif Mardin and Tom Dowd; written by Pam Sawyer and Laurie Burton
Atlantic 2312   1965   *Billboard:* #52

By the time they signed with Atlantic Records in 1965, the Rascals were veterans of so many R&B-based lounge and disco acts (most notably, Joey Dee and the Starliters, where the membership first coalesced) that their blue-eyed soul routine had been absorbed as completely natural. Atlantic's willingness to allow them to produce themselves (even with Mardin and Dowd's "supervision") reflects that level of experience, as does the immediate result, "I Ain't Gonna Eat Out My Heart Anymore," an amazing concoction of crazed rock and roll moves picked up from the British beat boom and the toughest, most syncopated group soul.

Eddie Brigati's exuberant vocal fights off Felix Cavaliere's slashing, Dylanesque organ to become the centerpoint of a virtuosic performance. Dino Danelli plays like a domestic Charlie Watts. Though the Rascals had an almost teen idol image, Gene Cornish's lethally distorted guitar solo and Brigati's anguished interpretation of Sawyer and Burton's lyric give "I Ain't Gonna Eat Out My Heart Anymore" a mood much more akin to deep soul than teenybop pop, reflecting a stylistic maturity utterly belied by those Lord Fauntleroy costumes.

545 I FOUND A LOVE, The Falcons
Produced by Robert West; written by Wilson Pickett, Willie Schofield, and Robert West
LuPine 1003   1962   *Billboard:* #75

Wilson Pickett's original greatest hit: Howling gospel plus guitar sets the format for pre-Motown Detroit soul.

546 DEAREST DARLING, Bo Diddley
Produced by Leonard Chess; written by Bo Diddley
Checker 896   1958   Did not make pop chart

Bo Diddley generally finds himself described as a primitive. "Dearest Darling" makes a good case for it. The beat is a shuffle in roughly the same way as an earthquake. Lafayette Leake's piano falls like rain. Bo emits his vocal in massive grunts and growls. Amidst all this, the lyrics must have been divinely inspired, like the books of the Bible, to which they continually refer.

Force of nature or not, Bo Diddley is His Own Man. "If I get to heaven, and you're not there," he declaims, "I'm gonna write your name on the heavenly stair / If you're not there by judgment day / Then I'm goin', baby, the other way." Guess that must be how primitive democracy works in a theocracy.

547 WAY OVER THERE, The Miracles
Written and produced by Berry Gordy and Smokey Robinson
Tamla 54069   1962   Billboard: #94

Although it was their eighth Tamla record to chart, "Way Over There" was the Miracles' first Tamla release. The story behind that unlikely event tells much about Motown, Berry Gordy, the Miracles, and what happened to rhythm and blues as it evolved toward soul.

As is well-known, Berry Gordy's first major professional achievement was writing a series of hits for Jackie Wilson, beginning with "Reet Petite" in 1957. Soon afterwards Gordy began producing records. His first release came that same year: "Ooh Shucks" by the Five Stars, licensed to George Goldner's New York-based Mark X label. So when he met the Miracles (then a five member group, including Smokey Robinson's wife-to-be, Claudette), Gordy quickly prepared to record them and licensed their first two singles, "Got a Job" (a reply to the Silhouettes' raucous "Get a Job"), and "I Cry," to another of Goldner's labels, End. "Got a Job" got a lot of Detroit airplay, and a little elsewhere; "I Cry" flopped. But Gordy continued to work intensely with the Miracles, as well as several other Detroit acts.

The third Miracles single, "Bad Girl," possessed a lot more chart potential and both Philadelphia's Cameo-Parkway and Chicago-based Chess bid for it; Chess won. The record had substantial R&B success and became the first Gordy production to make the national pop charts.

Berry Gordy was nearly a decade older than Smokey Robinson, but they were close from the start, as symbolized not only by their writing all these songs together but by the fact that they are credited with *producing* them together. Perhaps Gordy simply hadn't grown so stingy with credits as he later would, but more likely, Smokey's contributions were unignorable. Nevertheless, it was unmistakably a master/student relationship, with Gordy prodding Robinson to pay ever greater attention to melodic, lyric, and production detail.

Both Gordy and Robinson were true originals, but they were in no way immune to trendiness. (Otherwise, they probably would not have started so many trends later.) In 1959, the biggest group in R&B was the new version of the Drifters led by Ben E. King, and their principal stylistic innovation was the use of strings in their first hit, "There Goes My Baby," a trend reinforced by the success of the Skyliners' similarly arranged "Since I Don't Have You."

Gordy was a gambler, too, unafraid to yank a record off the market and put out a distinctly different version if he felt he'd come up with a better, or at least more commercial, concept. The most famous example is "Shop Around," the Miracles' second Tamla record, but it happened with "Way Over There," too. And not once, but twice.

Tamla catalog number 54028 was initially assigned to the Miracles' "The Feeling is So Fine," which historian Don Waller describes as similar to "Way Over There," but faster and underpinned with a baritone sax. Only four copies of "The Feeling is So Fine" are known to have survived, though, because Gordy soon pulled that song back and replaced it with "Way Over There," using the same catalog number. Then, he pulled *that* one back, too, not to change songs but to change arrangements. The initial version had no strings, while the now-familiar one uses them in a riffing, zinging pattern reminiscent of "There Goes My Baby."

"Way Over There" didn't make the 1959 charts, anyway. Maybe it simply wasn't sufficiently distinctive to become the first hit for a label based in a music industry backwater like Detroit, although that didn't stop anybody with "Shop Around" (to my ears, not nearly so good a record). Certainly, the song's Latinate beat, the use of the strings with piano and drums to form the basic rhythm, the way Smokey's crying lead soars over the "yi-yi-yi" of his group are all highly reminiscent of the Drifters, just as the lyric is unmistakably similar to Johnnie and Joe's "Over the Mountain; Across the Sea." But Smokey's vocal is uniquely his own and the lyrics, however derivative, rhyme in the flowing, ultravernacular style that made him legendary.

So it's no surprise that when the movement toward soul took a break during the doo-wop revival a couple of years later, "Way Over

There" was one of the records momentarily rescued from obscurity. By then, both Berry Gordy and Smokey Robinson were well on their way to myth and millions and so the song fits easily into the pattern of their current 1962 releases, an indication of how much they'd already done to change the face of pop.

548 OUT OF LIMITS, The Marketts
Produced by Dick Glasser; written by Michael Z. Gordon
Warner Bros. 5391   1963   *Billboard:* #3

"Out of Limits" is based on the theme song not of *The Outer Limits*, the early sixties science-fiction TV series from which it takes its name, but on the theme for the better-known *The Twilight Zone*. But its rushing guitar and organ grooves owe less to either than to Jack Nitzsche's "The Lonely Surfer," which failed to click earlier in 1963. As with all the best sub-surf instrumentals, the feel here is so aquatic that when you're finished listening to it you practically need to towel off, this time from the undertow of foggy French horn and the pared down rush of twangy guitar reverb. It ain't "Pipeline" but it'll do.

549 RUN THROUGH THE JUNGLE, Creedence Clearwater Revival
Written and produced by John Fogerty
Fantasy 641   1970   *Billboard:* #4

It's The Singer, Not the Songwriter:
Three minutes of spooky swamp rock that sounds like it might have been recorded on an active jetway, "Run Through the Jungle" is filled with gravel-voiced howls, a bass line that seems determined to knife the choogling guitar riff in its heart, and a lyric so dire you're glad when it turns out to be more vague than specific.

Fogerty so enriched his bandmates and their record label that they were able to toss such an extraordinary single off as a B side. Appearing on the flip of the innocuous "Up Around the Bend," "Run Through the Jungle" nevertheless remains one of the songs by which Fogerty and Creedence are best remembered. And that's just the problem.

Creedence Clearwater started out in the late fifties as just another Northern California high school band, formed by Fogerty, his brother Tom, and a couple of friends, Stu Cook and Doug Clifford. (They were called, among other things, the Blue Velvets and the Golliwogs.) They got a chance at recording for Fantasy, basically a jazz label, only because it happened to be in the neighborhood and the boys had found jobs in the warehouse. They got the kind of record deal you'd expect from that situation, one in which the label not only didn't have to pay much in royalties but also controlled their song publishing rights.

Somewhere along the way, out of their own avarice and some bad judgment, Creedence was convinced to invest its royalties in an offshore banking tax dodge. Several Fantasy executives also poured money into the scam. Unfortunately, the bank they chose was a Bahamian shell called the Castle Bank, which went down in one of the great financial swindles of the century, leaving Creedence short more than $3 million and with huge overdue payments to the IRS (which stepped in for its bite once the scheme crashed).

Bitter, John Fogerty sued everybody including Fantasy. For the best part of a decade, he litigated but made no music. Meantime, his songs and records continued to generate huge income for Fantasy (which took its profits and produced, among other things, the movie *One Flew Over the Cuckoo's Nest*).

Fogerty was still pissed when he finally made another record, *Centerfield*, in 1985. The final track on each side was an unmistakable slug at Fantasy owner Saul Zaentz: "Mr. Greed" and "Zanz Kant Danz." Zaentz, apparently feeling as vindictive as Fogerty, sued for libel, asking $142 million damages, then charged Fogerty with infringing on a Fantasy copyright—"Run Through the Jungle."

Centerfield's first track, and its first single, was "The Old Man Down the Road." Everybody who heard it remarked on its amazing similarity to "Run Through the Jungle." And so Fantasy sued Fogerty for royalties plus damages for plagiarizing his own song!

Amazingly enough, the case actually went to trial and in the fall of 1988, John Fogerty spent two days on the witness stand with a guitar on his lap, explaining "swamp rock" and its limitations to a jury. Pressed about the similarity between the two songs, he finally snapped, "Yeah, I did use that half-step. What do you want me to do, get an inoculation?"

Even if Fantasy did, the jury didn't. They acquitted him in early November 1988, and, having proven his skills in running through the modern jungle, John Fogerty went back to making his new record. Which he vowed would sound not approximately but *exactly* like Creedence.

550 I CAN'T LIVE WITHOUT MY RADIO, LL Cool J
Produced by Rick Rubin; written by James Smith [LL Cool J] and Rick Rubin
Def Jam 05665   1985   Did not make pop chart

Although it arrived a few weeks too soon to become part of rap's post-"Walk Way This Way" Top 40 breakthrough, "I Can't Live Without My Radio" is the anthem that shows why hip-hop culture fits squarely within the bounds of rock and soul tradition.

Because it's steeped in B-boy vernacular ("Y'know what I mean—that's where the crib's at"), rap know-nothings (somebody like Randy Newman, for example) might dis "Radio" by portraying it as nothing but the work of a braggart. But if "Royal Chief Rocker" Cool J's undeniably bragging, he's also describing what it takes to survive in his community:

> Terrorizing my neighbors with the heavy bass
> I keep the suckers in fear by the look on my face

And though the beat may be skeletal, with nothing more than a hint of a melody and the central nonpercussion instrument the scratching of Cut Creator's turntable, the music is anything but primitive. In fact, the sound is cued to every nuance of Cool J's passionate defense of his life-style and attitude, which is neither entirely antisocial ("Don't mean to offend other citizens / But I kick my volume way past ten") nor entirely without humility ("My name is Cool J, I devastate the show / But I couldn't survive without my radio"). As attitude, you can call it what you want—the blues, rock 'n' rebellion, street corner hooliganism—but it definitely fits in.

551 ANYONE WHO HAD A HEART, Dionne Warwick
Written and produced by Burt Bacharach and Hal David
Scepter 1262   1963   Billboard: #8

Although she's never gotten much critical respect, and given her bathetic eighties work may never get it, Dionne Warwick was perhaps the finest female pop-R&B singer before Aretha Franklin. Because her phrasing comes from show biz rather than the church (her gospel roots are much more concealed than those of her niece, Whitney Houston), and because the songs and settings Bacharach and David provided her were close to standards (some of them now *are* standards), Warwick seemed to be part of a spectrum that ranged, perhaps, from Lena Horne to Nancy Wilson.

That's not quite so. Bacharach and David worked with Warwick at a time when they were also working with R&B singers like Chuck Jackson. Their pop success with a black woman singing material with a pronounced beat was almost unprecedented. And if there *was* a precedent, it was Dinah Washington, who herself laid more groundwork for Aretha than most suspect. Not that Warwick's soaring high notes weren't better suited to Vegas and cabarets than to church and the chitlin' circuit. But the virtue of elegance ought not to make her an outlaw from rock aesthetics.

552 MYSTIC EYES, Them
Produced by Tommy Scott; written by Van Morrison
Parrot 9796   1965   *Billboard*: #33

Reference books generally list this overamped blues jam as an instrumental, which I suppose is a way of dealing with the fact that when Van Morrison's voice finally emerges out of the harp and guitar interplay, about halfway through, it's so overamped itself that it really functions as another instrument, all snarls and slashes and without any more literal coherence than any of the dumb instruments upon which his bandmates whack and thrash. Which is a hell of a lot better than calling it, as contemporary critics would Postmodern Blues, a way of accounting for the fact that Howlin' Wolf wouldn't have said it like that, but it is what he would have said.

553 BRIDGE OVER TROUBLED WATER, Aretha Franklin
Produced by Jerry Wexler, Tom Dowd, and Arif Mardin; written by Paul Simon
Atlantic 2796   1971   *Billboard*: #6

Gospel music is about miracles and while it would go too far to claim that Aretha Franklin is a miracle-worker, her ability to replenish the meaning of "Bridge Over Troubled Water" after it had already been reduced to cliché by Art Garfunkel's oversung rendition at the very least ranks somewhere beyond the order of the simply surprising.

Paul Simon took his inspiration for "Bridge" from the Swan Silvertones' "O Mary Don't You Weep," in which Reverend Claude Jeter rushes through a variety of interpolations, including the quasi-Biblical line, "I'll be a bridge over deep water if you trust in my name." From this, Simon fashioned one of pop's most spiritual love songs, and together with engineer Roy Halee, concocted an ornate yet somehow perfectly embellished setting. (Oversung Simon and Garfunkel's "Bridge" may be; overproduced it is not, because the orchestration and other accoutrements are so well conceived.)

Art Garfunkel sang "Bridge" as a virtual solo, and his weightless, trembly tenor removed all traces of Pentecostal testifying, lending the record an Anglican choirboy purity that explains much about why it immediately became the biggest selling record in U.K. history.

Aretha Franklin, daughter of Reverend C. L. Franklin, one of America's most famous Pentecostal preachers, came to "Bridge Over Troubled Water" as if her historic mission was to restore the song's gospel roots. She did the job audaciously; though it was recorded as a single, "Bridge Over Troubled Water" clocks in at a little longer than five and a half minutes. And Aretha takes her time getting to the verses that are the popular heart of the song, opening with about two minutes of meditative piano playing and undemonstrative call-and-response interchange with her backing singers, one of the most introspective interludes in the history of pop music (even if most radio stations edit it out).

When she hits the lyrics, though, they're damn near pulled apart by the surging release of tension. The performance never reaches the frantic, declamatory heights that can be found in the greatest Ward Singers records ("Packing Up," "Surely God Is Able"), but then, Aretha isn't a gospel singer.

554 LET IT ROCK, Chuck Berry
Produced by Leonard Chess; written by E. Anderson
[Chuck Berry]
Chess 1747   1960   *Billboard:* #64

Keith Richards's announcement, in Taylor Hackford's 1987 film bio of Berry, *Hail Hail Rock and Roll Hero*, that Chuck actually modeled many of his guitar riffs on the ideas Johnny Johnson played on piano wouldn't have been greeted as such a revelation if more people knew this great railroad blues song, the most mysteriously folkloric record Berry ever created.

The story's pure shaggy dog: A Mobile, Alabama railroad section gang goofing off by shooting craps inside a tent spread over the tracks is disrupted by an "off-schedule train." But Berry fires off a barrage of detail, either imitating the nonstop chatter of the dice players or celebrating his girl, or both. (Who knows, maybe he was remembering a real incident, which would account for his use of a pseudonym for the only time in his Chess career.)

Meantime, the music rolls on with locomotive power and precision. For once, Chuck's guitar follows. After the de rigeur "Johnny B. Goode" intro, it's Johnson's riotous piano that sets the mood and gets all the choice space. Maybe that's why the song's called "Let It Rock," a phrase that never appears in it.

555 RESPECT YOURSELF, The Staple Singers
Produced by Al Bell; written by Mack Rice and Luther Ingram
Stax 0104   1971   Billboard: #12

The Staple Singers turned from gospel to pop with either the most purely innocent or the most hypocritical intentions. Always among the folkier groups in gospel, maybe they just got sick of having stuff like "The Last Time" ripped off lick-for-lick by the Rolling Stones. And with Pop Staples the best gospel guitarist since Sister Rosetta Tharpe and elder sister Mavis able to do one of the best Arethas this side of Ms. Franklin herself, there was no reason not to give the charts a shot, which isn't something you can do while preaching Jesus directly.

But Pop vowed his clan would sing secular only so long as they could still sing songs with a spiritual message. A promise the group pretty much kept (though Mavis's solo records have wandered fairly far afield). Exactly how that made them different from Curtis Mayfield and the Impressions, I don't know, but as long as the basic Stax setup lasted, it worked out fine, though they had a hell of a lot of unholy help from such worldly types as Roger Hawkins and the gang down at Muscle Shoals.

"Respect Yourself" stands as one of the most reactionary message songs of its era. The problem with the world today, according to Mack Rice and Luther Ingram (a couple of writers generally more comfortable philosophizing about philandering) boils down to individual impoliteness: "Keep talking about the President won't stop air pollution / Put your hand over your mouth when you cough—that'll help the solution." So much for carbon monoxide.

But with the lowering horns and bass and Hawkins's vigorous runs across the toms backing up the Staples always fine harmonies, dumbness didn't make much difference. And nobody has ever accused anybody of having their head up their ass more gently (or eloquently) than the Staples do in the second verse.

556 TRAGIC, The Sheppards
Produced by Bunky Sheppard; written by Kermit Chandler and O.C. Perkins
Apex 7762   1961   Did not make pop chart

One of the unsung heroes of sixties rhythm and blues, Bunky Sheppard remains unknown long after the soul revival because his biggest national hit, the Esquires' "Get On Up," is pop-soul at its trashiest and his best records are all but unknown outside of collectors' circles even in Chicago, where he was based. Yet Sheppard was not only a first-rate producer, he had a fine ear for talent, which led him to work with singers as good as Gene Chandler and to hire the windy City's best sessionmen, including guitarists Phil Upchurch and Lefty Bates and drummers Maurice White and Al Duncan.

The Sheppards, who took their name from Bunky, remain his greatest find. Although they never had a national hit, this six-piece group (five singers in their early twenties and teenage guitarist Kermit Chandler) turned out some of the finest harmony records of the early sixties.

Although they could perform as raucously as Wilson Pickett's Falcons or the Isley Brothers, the Sheppards seemed more comfortable in a latter-day doo-wop mode, crooning smooth heartbreak ballads. "Tragic" (their biggest regional hit, and the only one that earned them so much as a guest shot on *American Bandstand*) is very much in that mode. It's clearly based on the Platters, with a heavy organ wash, fifteen-year-old Chandler's beautifully reverberating guitar lick, and a strong tenor lead by Millard Edwards. The arrangement, with Edwards beginning phrases that the band completes, sucks all the melodrama from a lyric that dwells less on the tragedy of a romantic breakup than on the opportunities it presents for almost gleeful revenge. The credit goes mostly to Sheppard, because it's the sweet-breathed musical atmosphere that makes the vengeance credible as well as palatable.

557 BEAUTY IS ONLY SKIN DEEP, The Temptations
Produced by Norman Whitfield; written by Norman Whitfield and Eddie Holland
Gordy 7055   1966   *Billboard*: #3

558 JUST MY IMAGINATION, The Temptations
Produced by Norman Whitfield; written by Norman Whitfield and Barrett Strong
Gordy 7105   1971   *Billboard*: #1 (2 weeks)

Motown's reputation as a monolith is so proverbial that perhaps only its most devoted fans understand the nuances and variations that made the company's output so startlingly different from year to year (sometimes even from A side to B side). Motown supposedly made its magic on an assembly line of interchangable parts, even though you wouldn't have to be much of a fan at all to discourse on the differences among, say, David Ruffin, Eddie Kendricks, Diana Ross, Stevie Wonder, and Smokey Robinson, or the various production and writing styles of Robinson, Holland-Dozier-Holland, Nickolas Ashford and Valerie Simpson, and Norman Whitfield and Barrett Strong.

In fact, Motown acts (except the ever-volatile Marvin Gaye) always paired off with specific producers; even the longest-lived groups working regularly only with one or two teamings. Much of the difference between the Four Tops and the Temptations, for instance, comes down to the difference in approach between Holland-Dozier-Holland, who produced all the important Four Tops singles, and Robinson, who produced the first Tempts' hits, the ones that established their identity. And the difference between Robinson's Temptations productions and Norman Whitfield's, which began with "The Girl's Alright with Me" and "Girl (Why You Wanna Make Me Blue)," and picked up full-time a couple of records later, is just as pronounced, Smokey featuring softer, more romantic harmony sounds and Whitfield digging deeper into dance beats.

With the longer-lasting Motown groups, changes in personnel also make a big difference. Though both "Beauty's Only Skin Deep" and "Just My Imagination" sported Norman Whitfield production, they're radically different productions, the former a smashing dance hit, the latter a ballad so winsome it's almost wimpy. Each has great sound and their introductions are among the most memorable in Top 40 history. But the most significant change between one and the other is the presence of David Ruffin at the center of "Beauty" and the lead of Eddie Kendricks on "Imagination."

Ruffin's gravelly gospel inflections soak up an enormous amount of energy and Whitfield keeps pouring it on, drumbeat after pounding drumbeat, until the listener—but never the music—threatens to break down from sheer sonic overload. Ruffin projects himself straight into the center of the recording and refuses to budge, even while the other Tempts are doing their faintly hilarious "Beauty's only skin deep / Yeah, yeah, yeah." Kendricks, on the other hand, occupies center stage in "Imagination" as if by happenstance; his singing, far prettier than Ruffin's, is also more subtle and introspective, the musings of a dreamer rather than the proclamations of a love man.

If you didn't know it, you'd hardly guess these great discs were the product of the same group. What connects them, in the end, is the surging energy of the band, though even there, the change from the rocket propulsion of "Beauty" to the soaring glide of "Imagination" is anything but the result of applying a rigid formula.

559 RED RED WINE, UB40
Produced by UB40 and Ray "Pablo" Falconer; written by Neil Diamond
A&M 1244   1984   *Billboard:* #1 (1 week)

Neil Diamond wrote and recorded "Red Red Wine" in 1968, as the last of his Jeff Barry and Ellie Greenwich-produced hits for Bang Records. But that's not where UB40 learned it—they knew Tony Tribe's reggae version, a mid-seventies hit on the Jamaican and U.K. club circuits.

UB40 remade "Red Red Wine" for a 1984 album, *Labour of Love*, in which they recreated ten of the reggae records that inspired them as kids growing up in an integrated working class neighborhood in Birmingham, the largest city in Britain's industrial midlands. Lead vocalist Ali and guitarist Robin Campbell are the sons of Ian Campbell, a communist-aligned folksinger of the fifties and sixties; several other members, including bassist Earl Falconer, his brother Ray, who produces, and toaster Astro are British-born West Indians. From their first album, released in 1980, UB40 played straight reggae with postpunk attitude and modern rock production values and radical, anti-Thatcher/ pro-socialist politics. (UB40 is the bureaucratic designation of the British unemployment benefits form.)

The group's first album made them British stars, and gave them international critical credibility, but it wasn't until the mid-eighties that their albums even saw U.S. release and not until "Red Red Wine" that they hit the *Billboard* charts. It tarried there for fifteen weeks, rising to Number 34. Cracking the North American Top 40 with a reggae record is a rare occurrence, but UB40's music virtually shimmers and the lugubrious Jamaican beat and brightly but softly pumping keyboard accents are perfect stuff for transmitting the aura of a hangover. Ali's yearning tenor is brilliantly offset by Astro's toasting (chanting), sometimes as counterpoint, sometimes as a mumble beneath the main vocal, sometimes placed out front.

The only other chart appearance by UB40 came in 1985, with a remake of Sonny and Cher's "I Got You Babe," featuring the Pretenders' Chrissie Hynde (who virtually discovered the band) in the Cher role. Then, in late spring 1988, a Phoenix radio station found that when its disc jockeys traveled to high schools to play records during lunch breaks (an ongoing station promotion), one of the most requested tracks was "Red Red Wine." The station's programmer decided to test the record on the air. It hit so hard that his crosstown competition followed suit, and soon, radio stations around the U.S. were playing the record. It started selling heavily enough for A&M to again promote it and delay release of the group's new single.

By September, "Red Red Wine" was Number One—only the fifth single of the rock era to top the Hot 100 after initially falling off the chart. (The others were at best forgettable: "Running Bear" by Johnny Preston, Helen Reddy's "I Am Woman," Patti Austin and James Ingram's "Baby Come to Me," and Billy Vera and the Beaters' "At This Moment.") "Red Red Wine" was also the first—and at this writing, still the only—reggae single ever to top the North American charts (although two reggae-influenced records, Johnny Nash's "I Can See Clearly Now," and Eric Clapton's remake of Bob Marley's "I Shot the Sheriff" hit Number One in the seventies).

560 JENNY TAKE A RIDE, Mitch Ryder and the Detroit Wheels
Produced by Bob Crewe; written by Enotis Johnson and
Richard Penniman/Ma Rainey
New Voice 806   1965   *Billboard:* #10

They called themselves Billy Lee and the Rivieras, leather and satin greasers from east-side Detroit's Pershing High School in the inner city, where they began playing black clubs as soon as they were old enough to drive. As they built up a local reputation, they moved their act out to the suburbs, to a dance barn called the Walled Lake Casino, which held a couple thousand kids who wanted to hear rock and R&B and the new soul stuff and wanted it hot and tight and sweaty. Out there, the kids packed themselves in so tight that there was just room at the edges for a thin stream of them to travel in concentric circles, boys clockwise, girls counterclockwise, cruising for partners for the small, dark corners. Meantime, up on the stage, the Rivieras were leaping from instrument to instrument, Billy Lee doing unpadded kneedrops until he was black and blue. This was rock and roll before it got too cool to be a show.

Dave Prince, the best of Detroit's Top 40 deejays, liked the guys and he called New York producer Bob Crewe, who saw them do a gig opening for the Dave Clark Five, who they blew off the stage. Crewe told them to come to New York; they drove out, he put them up in a roach-infested Needle Park hotel, and put that stage show on tape.

Billy Lee (now Mitch Ryder, a name he swears he found by thumbing through the phone book) loved Little Richard. Drummer Johnny Badanjek—the one they called Johnny Bee—and guitarist Jim McCarty fused Richard's "Jenny Jenny" with "C.C. Rider," an ancient blues Chuck Willis made into a stroll-era R&B hit. This unnamed medley was the highlight of their show, with McCarty's guitar winding up incredible knots of tension while Bee's killer backbeat pushed the frenzy into a bedrock groove. It was maybe the most exciting white rock and roll anybody in America produced during the British Invasion. Billy Lee and the boys carried on from there, though not far.

561 WHEN I'M GONE, Brenda Holloway
Written and produced by Smokey Robinson
Tamla 54111   1965   *Billboard:* #25

One of the toughest female vocals ever, and certainly the most swinging arrangement Smokey Robinson ever came up with. Though Holloway was a gifted writer and arranger, she never again sounded quite as good as she did in this scornful account of the consequences of her guy being stupid enough to split. The finger-pops, nimble piano, and swirling strings might almost belong to Henry Mancini, though the backbeat and bassline are pure Motown. And the lover with the Jekyll and Hyde personality is pure Smokey, as every Mary Wells fan ought to be aware.

562 PEANUT BUTTER, The Marathons
Produced by Fred Smith and Cliff Goldsmith; written by Fred Smith, Cliff Goldsmith, H.B. Barnum, and Martin J. Cooper
Arvee 5027   1961   *Billboard:* #20

Trying to pull a fast one on their tiny record label, L.A.-based Arvee, the Olympics and producers Fred Smith and Cliff Goldsmith sold a single to Argo, an affiliate of Chicago's Chess. Since the group was still under contract out West, it had to be called the Marathons, a name whose unsubtle connection to the Olympics is matched by the equally obvious musical relationship of "Peanut Butter" to the 1960 Olympics hit, "(Baby) Hully Gully." So without much litigation, Arvee wound up with the record anyway, and the group landed right back where it started.

Well, not entirely. The Hully Gully was a real dance step from the first discotheque era; the Dovells ("Hully Gully Baby") and Little Caesar and the Romans ("Hully Gully Again") also had hits based on it. The Olympics had the best one, by far, as befits a lyric with the nerve to begin, "There's a dance spreadin' 'round like an awful dis-ease . . ." But somehow, in translating the song's concern from the shuffling of feet to the wadding together of jaws ("There's a food goin' 'round that's a sticky, sticky goo . . ."), the Marathons/Olympics discovered a nonsensical lewdness entirely missing from the original. "Scarf now!" Walter Ward yells and from the gleeful way he says it, you've gotta wonder just what he might be chewing on.

563 BABY IT'S YOU, The Shirelles
Produced by Luther Dixon; written by Mack David, Burt Bacharach, and Barney Williams
Scepter 1227   1961   *Billboard:* #8

The ineffability of romance, captured in two lines: "It's not the way you smile that touched my heart / It's not the way you kiss that tears me apart." This is either the sappiest song Burt Bacharach ever had a hand in writing, or the most cosmic. It's definitely the sexiest singing Shirley ever did, and if her crying "I can't help myself" seems a little pale today, you've gotta remember that back then, Aretha hadn't shown everybody else the ropes.

564 I DO LOVE YOU, Billy Stewart
Produced by Phil Wright; written by Billy Stewart
Chess 1922   1965   *Billboard: #26*

Soul balladry can be the gentlest form of musical expression, and here, the massive Stewart caresses each soaring note, keeping even his trademark trills to a minimum as he declares his devotion in the plainest, most basic terms. Until he lets his voice go wild and leaps for a falsetto "Pleeeeze," all out of keeping with the lightly nuanced backing music—led by Leonard Caston's piano and Maurice White's drums—but perfectly in tune with the strategies of his heart.

565 GREEN RIVER, Creedence Clearwater Revival
Written and produced by John Fogerty
Fantasy 625   1969   *Billboard: #2*

John Fogerty has spoken of "Green River" as his most beloved place of reverie, and the reverential reading he gives the song remains impressive, despite the phony New Orleans mush-mouth accent. But then, as a confirmed pessimist, maybe Fogerty's idylls have to occur on fake terrain. Beyond the stinging, rolling guitar licks, the song's best moment comes when he admits even here an odor of doom: "Old Cody Junior took me over / Said you're gonna find the world is smoulderin' / If you get lost, come on home to Green River."

566 PRIVATE NUMBER, William Bell and Judy Clay
Produced by Booker T. Jones; written by William Bell and Booker T. Jones
Stax 0005   1968   *Billboard: #75*

Memphis's answer to Marvin Gaye and Tammi Terrell was not Otis Redding and Carla Thomas, whose duets were about as equal as Kissinger-Nixon diplomacy, as it was these two understated journeymen. Bell, the most country-music influenced of all the Stax singers, pairs perfectly with the hoarse voiced Clay, who must have seen her work with him as a payoff for her dreadful duets with the inept Billy Vera.

Unlike Marvin and Tammi, whose records were hot, tight, and unrelenting, "Private Number" features a gentle dialogue, buoyed at first by an almost lilting Steve Cropper guitar lick and then by a surging string arrangement that owes more to Leiber and Stoller's work with Ben E. King and the Drifters than to Motown. Against this backdrop, quite elaborate for Stax, Bell's tenor pleas and Clay's hoarse no-nonsense replies join exquisitely.

567 SH-BOOM, The Chords
Produced by Ahmet Ertegun and Jerry Wexler; written by Jimmy Keys, Carl Feaster, Claude Feaster, Floyd McRae, and William Edwards
Cat 104   1954   *Billboard:* #5

The Chords came as close as any group in the history of doo-wop to being discovered on a street corner: Joe Glaser of Associated Booking, the leading black talent agency, spotted them singing as they walked into a Bronx subway station. They'd been singing together at their homes and at P.S. 99 in the Bronx for a couple of years, basing their sound on what first tenor Jimmy Keys called "top-shelf" harmony groups: the Ravens, Orioles, Modernaires, and Four Freshmen. In other words, not just R&B vocalists but pop stylists, too.

The song Glaser heard was probably "Sh-Boom," which the group worked up collectively after Carl Feaster devised the original melody and the first few words. They calculated one of the most thrilling and intricate of all the early rock and roll harmony arrangements, and one of the clearest examples of spontaneous-sounding early rock and roll as the product of long labor even though "Sh-Boom" is such a vernacular masterpiece that it virtually seems fated to have been stumbled across on a street corner or in a subway station. Carl Feaster's scatted introduction to the final verse, in particular, seems to just bubble up out of his throat, without a second's conscious effort.

In any event, "Sh-Boom" was virtually a finished product when the Chords arrived at Atlantic Records. Ahmet Ertegun and Jerry Wexler immediately snapped the group up, because its harmony style seemed tailor-made for the new style of R&B then finding a market among white teenagers. The industry called this new music "rock and roll" but Wexler, a former short story writer who'd helped *Billboard* editor Paul Ackerman come up with the term "rhythm and blues" during his tenure as a trade paper reporter, decided that "cat music" was a better term, and that's the name Atlantic gave its rock and roll subsidiary.

Atlantic was less certain of "Sh-Boom." Instead of making it the plug side of the first Chords' single, they chose to cut a rock version of a recent Patti Page hit, "Cross Over the Bridge." The record, embellished with a magnificent sax solo by Sam "The Man" Taylor and a neat guitar figure by Mickey Baker, came out the first week in March, 1954, and soon showed strong pop and R&B airplay and sales action—for its B side. More impressively, though the record was covered by the Crew Cuts, and though the cover hit Number One, the Chords' version hit the Top 10 anyway, indicating increasing sophistication among the "cat music" audience.

"Sh-Boom" also weathered a nasty, condescending parody by Stan Freberg, the professed anti-rock and roll bigot who declared that he hoped his travesty "destroyed rhythm and blues forever." The Chords never had another hit but they're remembered and beloved today in places where fools like Freberg will never be known.

568 WHEN THE LOVELIGHT STARTS SHINING THROUGH HIS EYES, Supremes

Produced by Brian Holland and Lamont Dozier; written by Brian Holland, Lamont Dozier, and Eddie Holland
Motown 1051   1963   *Billboard:* #23

569 YOU CAN'T HURRY LOVE, The Supremes

Produced by Brian Holland and Lamont Dozier; written by Brian Holland, Lamont Dozier, and Eddie Holland
Motown 1097   1966   *Billboard:* #1 (2 weeks)

Present-day critics and historians are likely to write off the Supremes, above everything else that Motown wrought, as overproduced, too slick, and excessively reliant on Diana Ross's glitzy effervescence; in general, too pop.

Perhaps it's just that I'm a poor purist but that strikes me as a half-baked judgment even when it comes to trash like "The Happening," and an utterly ignorant assessment when it comes to records as dynamic as these. The Supremes, after all, were the pet project not just of Berry Gordy and his hirelings in the Motown choreography and costume departments but of Holland-Dozier-Holland, the label's most potent songwriting and production team. The classic HDH productions (these are two) feature gutty backbeats, powerhouse bass lines, lyrics that reek of backyard philosophy, and vocals that echo gospel shouts. As for the confectionary leadership of Diana Ross, well, you may disdain the crust but that doesn't mean that what's beneath isn't pie.

Even with Diana out front, the finger-pops and handclaps and farting baritone sax make "Lovelight" as fearsome as a Four Tops record (and indeed, that might well be Levi and the guys on the mighty grunt—"Urghhhhhh!"—in the middle of the bridge).

Despite its weedy reproduction in the mouth of Phil Collins, "You Can't Hurry Love" is an equally invigorating groove record, which Ross turns into one of the most soulful vocals of her career. Three years into her reign as the Queen of Pop, you can still feel the anxious insecurities that drove Diana into those skinny, spangled dresses. It ain't, I guess, a pretty picture of herself she paints—this song's about romance as a matter of cold calculation—but it's an open, honest reflection of her deep emotions, and that's exactly what soul's *supposed* to be all about.

570 RESPECT, Otis Redding
Produced by Steve Cropper; written by Otis Redding
Volt 128 1965 *Billboard:* #35

They were sitting around the studio that day in 1965, when Otis began to complain about the ruination touring was making of his home life. Drummer Al Jackson contradicted him, with a remark as laid-back but certain as his playing. "What are you griping about," he said. "You're on the road all the time. All you can look for is a little respect when you come home."

Otis took Jackson's remark and made it into a song. Then they got their little Memphis soul band together—Duck Dunn playing bass as liquid and fiery as lead guitar, Jackson muscling the beat like a syncopated steamroller, the Memphis Horns chorusing their hearts out, William Bell adding "Hey, hey, hey!" at the end of each verse. It might have been halfway intended as a joke but by the end of the song, they'd pushed Otis right out of the script and into his heart's desires. "Respect is what I want, respect is what I need—got-ta, got-ta have it, give it to me when I want it, give it to me when I need it." It wasn't a joke anymore.

571 REBEL-'ROUSER, Duane Eddy
Produced by Lester Sill and Lee Hazlewood; written by
Duane Eddy and Lee Hazlewood
Jamie 1104   1958   *Billboard: #6*

Although everybody—including me—thinks back on "Rebel-'Rouser" as a pure guitar exercise, there's a great sax riff going on here, too. And you could argue for the echo chamber ("a big old water tank with a speaker in one end and a mike in the other," Eddy says) as a third predominant instrumental voice.

Some of the greatest names in rock history made "Rebel-'Rouser." After Eddy, Lee Hazlewood is probably the best known of them, although that's unfortunately more for his silly duet with Nancy Sinatra on "These Boots Are Made for Walkin' " than for any of the dozen or so better discs he made as a producer. Musicians know Steve Douglas as the chief saxophone in Phil Spector's Wall of Sound (at the start, he was also Spector's contractor, rounding up all the other musicians for the dates). The coproducer was Lester Sill, the man who gave Leiber and Stoller their start, who provided the "les" in Philles and one of the storied figures of American music publishing (at last look, he was running Jobete Music for Berry Gordy). Mixed in the back somewhere, hooting like a bunch of cowboys, is a black L.A. harmony group known as the Sharps, who later changed their name to the Rivingtons and made some of the greatest vocal instrumentals of all time, and wrote the sacred phrase "papa-oom-mow-mow."

572 SHE THINKS I STILL CARE, Little Willie John
No producer credited; written by Dickey Lee
King 5667   1962   Did not make pop chart

An outrageously perfect matching of singer and song. Little Willie John trying to deny he's feeling sad is like Ralph Kramden trying to conceal his anger. But what a weird arrangement! It might have been lifted whole from the George Jones original, with its oodles of choral harmony, honky-tonk piano licks and loping rhythm. But it's the differences that count, because they spell out the contrast between C&W and R&B. Jones sounds like he can't tell the truth about his feelings because he can't imagine changing his circumstances. Willie John sounds like he's on the verge of an anxiety attack because if the true depth of his sorrow were ever admitted, the situation would feel even darker. Indeed, so lost in his misery does Willie John become that near the end, he loses the thread of the lyric altogether and begins to sing in disjointed fragments: "Oooooh, just because I spoke her name . . . ," and then, as if in afterthought, "somewhere." Nobody's ever sounded lonelier.

573 JUST LIKE REAL PEOPLE, Kendalls
Produced by Brien Fisher; written by Bob McDill
Ovation 1125   1979   Did not make pop chart

Jeannie Kendall sings solo on this country restatement of the "Let It Be" chords. The message isn't that far from the Beatles, either, since she's singing about self-acceptance, although from a much more desperate vantage point. But Kendall's not vaguely trying to cheer the world; she's getting down to cases, mainly her own. The problem is a deep feeling of inadequacy (as if Jeannie can't hear the beauty of her own voice), based not just in a lack of love but in a stoically detailed assessment of every mistake she's ever made. And in that regard, it makes sense that Royce isn't here to answer her, as you'd expect from their other duets—there are no answers to what she's saying.

In the country context, Kendall's declaration that she's "no angel in white satin" is to be expected. What's more intriguing is her desire to be "just like real people," who "settle down and have . . . a home." But is her conviction that her failure to find "much to believe in" and her "mistake or two," are unforgivable, unless she can find unconditional love within the arms of one man, the product of class self-loathing or sexist preconceptions? How about both?

574 WAKE UP EVERYBODY, Harold Melvin and the Bluenotes
Produced by Kenneth Gamble and Leon Huff; written by
Gene McFadden, John Whitehead, and Victor Castarphen
Philadelphia International 3579   1975   Billboard: #12

If uniting opposites appeals to you, then you'll love this fusion of Gamble and Huff's spit-polished and intoxicated disco narcissism and Teddy Pendergrass's gravelly post-gospel sermonizing. Pendergrass's insistence that "the world won't get no better if we just let it be" in the face of the arrangement's full-blown hedonism amounts to a doctoral thesis discrepancy. None of which implies an effective synthesis, but that doesn't mean that you don't get one. For instance, that guitar is fiddling with blues figures and Teddy's singing matter-of-factly modulates between the Temptations' David Ruffin and the Dells' Marvin Junior.

575 MILKCOW BLUES BOOGIE, Elvis Presley
Produced by Sam Phillips; written by Kokomo Arnold
Sun 215   1955   Did not make pop chart

Going on thirty-five years later, and it still works—that corny false start, Elvis mewling like some hokey country bluesman (see, he *could* have gone to Harvard), then breaking off to command, "Hold it, fellas, that don't move me. Let's get real, real gone for a change," before crashing into a jumped up, hiccuping version of the same tune. Had Sam Phillips subtitled it "History Lesson Number One," the point couldn't have been clearer. Or more irrefutable.

576 UM UM UM UM UM, Major Lance
Produced by Carl Davis; written by Curtis Mayfield
Okeh 7187   1964   *Billboard:* #5

577 THE OOGUM BOOGUM SONG, Brenton Wood
Produced by Joe Hooven and Hal Winn; written by Arthur Smith
[Brenton Wood]
Double Shot 111   1967   *Billboard:* #34

Allegedly, rock and soul records are filled with nonsense syllables. But one man's nonsense may be another's best effort at explication. Certainly, for everybody *I* know, there are times when the most sensible response to the mysteries and intricacies of sex calls for something that can only be trivialized by rendering it into words. Yet, your mouth will move, even then.

Wandering through a Chicago park at dusk one day, Major Lance saw (perhaps through the eyes of Curtis Mayfield, but nevertheless) a man sitting on a fence, head bowed and moaning: "Um, um, um, um, um." Over and over again. Curious, Major went up to him and asked him if he'd be so kind as to explain what was troubling him. "Um, um, um, um, um," replied the man, without lifting his head. Major left but the scene stayed in his mind. And, with cornets and shuffling drums, he tells us here that he understands: "Sometimes everyone must sing this song." But he does not translate. He was no fool.

What reached the Top Ten in 1964 as tragedy returned to the Top 40 three years later as farce. In Hollywood's happier clime, Brenton Wood ran across a sight that stirred him to expostulations of ecstasy: A girl walking down the street, day after day, in an array of costumes that beggar description: hip-hugger suits and high-heeled boots, cute trench coats in which she stood and posed, big earrings, long hair and things, and then one day, in nothing but a mini-skirt and her brother's big sloppy shirt. The groove of the music grabs Wood just as hard as the sight of this vision and the syllables slip so effortlessly from his lips that they assume a sense of their own, as if in another language, until by the end, after begging for mercy, Brenton chortles "Check out the boots, eh?" so many times and so fluently that it becomes "Check out the poossah, check out the pooosah," which is probably exactly what kept the record out of the Top Ten but is certainly what allows it to live on in the hearts of all mortals similarly affected by such views.

578 PRETTY FLAMINGO, Manfred Mann
Produced by John Burgess; written by Mark Barkan
United Artists 50040   1966   *Billboard: #29*

The prettiest love song of the entire British Invasion, sung by its most underrated vocalist. No, not Mann (he played keyboards) but Paul Jones, who shortly thereafter left music to become an actor (he starred in *Privilege*, which is to rock films what *The Name of the Rose* is to historical novels). Not that Manfred and the band didn't play a key role—the guitar strums that drag Jones's vocal out of him are the best indication ever of how well Britain's best Dylan imitators learned their lessons.

579 VOODOO CHILE (SLIGHT RETURN), Jimi Hendrix
Written and produced by Jimi Hendrix
Track 2095001 (UK)   1970   *Did not make pop chart*

The original "Voodoo Chile" is an overlong extravaganza of psychedelic incoherence that's my least favorite aspect of the Hendrix persona. The short one, which concludes the *Electric Ladyland* album and was rush-released as a 45 along with "Hey Joe" and "All Along the Watchtower" the week after Jimi died in 1970, focuses all that energy into something that within two more weeks became Hendrix's only Number One single in England.

In America . . . look, let's not be silly, okay? You think Bill Drake was gonna play 5:11 of elaborately constructed guitar washes and a lyric that might have spun Spiro Agnew into the grave with its implications of drug abuse and demonism? In America, "Voodoo Chile (Slight Return)" was not a single.

Too bad, too, because I could dig having it come on the oldies stations between "25 or 6 to 4" and "The First Time Ever I Saw Your Face" every once in a while, just to shock the shit out of geezers. And also because it makes me feel better about Jimi's departure from this plane every time I hear him declare, right at the start:

> Well I stand up next to a mountain
> Chop it down with the edge of my hand
> Pick up all the pieces and make an island
> Might even raise a little sand

The graffiti said that Clapton was God; "Voodoo Chile" says you can make a better case for Hendrix, and the lyrics aren't the only way it stakes its claim.

580 I NEED YOUR LOVING, Don Gardner and Dee Dee Ford

Produced by Bobby Robinson; written by Don Gardner and
Bobby Robinson
Fire 508　1962　　*Billboard: #20*

From the opening "Whoa-woo-woo-woh," Don Gardner is the personification of rhythm and blues in rut. Rather than cooling him off, Dee Dee Ford takes it as her bounden duty to fan the flames of desire. Consequently, by the time they hit the last verse, Gardner's change of "every day" to "every hour" sounds like no more than a bare statement of fact.

581 SHOTGUN, Junior Walker and the All Stars
Produced by Berry Gordy and Lawrence Horn; written by
Autry DeWitt [Junior Walker]
Soul 35008   1965   *Billboard:* #4

Junior Walker claims that he sang "Shotgun" only because the vocalist
failed to show up at the session. Maybe. In any event, the record is
utterly of a piece with the six sides he'd cut beginning in 1962 for Harvey
Fuqua's Harvey label and the earlier single, "Monkey Jump," he'd
made for Motown's Soul subsidiary.

Walker grew up in South Bend and split his youth between various
towns in northern Indiana and southern Michigan, but his musical approach is pure country. "Shotgun," the prototype for almost everything
else he's ever done, remains one of the most *primeval* rhythm records
in Motown history. Even the opening gun blast (Berry Gordy's idea)
echoes the backwoods, as do the thick pungency and staccato bursts
of his alto sax and guttural, incantatory singing. Smoking through these
three minutes of funk, Walker is as far from the polish of Motown acts
like the Supremes and Four Tops as any of their allies conceivably could
be.

582 LA LA MEANS I LOVE YOU, The Delfonics
Produced by Stan Watson; written by Thom Bell and
William Hart
Philly-Groove 150   1968   *Billboard:* #4

One of the most gorgeous examples of the Philadelphia falsetto harmony, and the source of one of rock and roll's great linguistic mysteries:
If that's what "La la" means, what about "fa fa"? Otis Redding never
told us, exactly, although Love's Arthur Lee must have had a few clues
since he borrowed so much of this record's orchestral voicing for *Forever
Changes*.

If Stan Watson really produced "La La Means I Love You," Thom
Bell must have been standing by with notebook in hand, because this
is the mold out of which came all Bell's later hits with the Stylistics and
the Spinners. More likely, Bell's minor credit here reflects dues-paying,
not his real creative contribution. Bell not only arranged but, according
to Tony Cummings's definitive *The Sound of Philadelphia*, as a result
of Philly Groove's impecunious state, he also played tympani and most
of the other orchestral sweetening. Fair enough, I guess—he built a
career out of the formula it suggested.

583 FOR THE LOVE OF MONEY, The O'Jays
Produced by Kenny Gamble and Leon Huff; written by
Kenny Gamble, Leon Huff, and Anthony Jackson
Philadelphia International 3544   1974   *Billboard: #9*

The spookiest of all the O'Jays' Philly International records, thanks
not only to Eddie Levert's ravaged vocal but the gory guitar and a bass
line that's pure bad news. The dance beat never quite disappears but
with Levert's condemnations of greed and a hollowed-out *Bitches Brew*
trumpet ringing in your ears, total surrender to this bumpy groove must
be quite a feat.

584 DON'T STOP, Fleetwood Mac
Produced by Fleetwood Mac with Richard Dashut and
Ken Caillat; written by Christine McVie
Warner Bros. 8413   1977   *Billboard: #3*

Retrospectively, what made Fleetwood Mac such a massive success in
the late seventies, when it made two consecutive albums that sold
around ten million copies each and scored ten consecutive Top 20 hits,
including six in a row that hit the Top 10, was the thoroughly individ-
ualistic nature of the group. In Fleetwood Mac, Stevie Nicks's spacey
romantic visions never needed to be reconciled to Lindsey Buckingham's more defeatist ones, because they found their sensibilities linked
by Christine McVie's realistic optimism and by the explosive English-
bred, blues-trained rhythm section. Buckingham's Californiocentric
grasp of studio technique and pop gloss nurtured everybody's songs.
Three distinctive lead singers guaranteed not only diversity but the finest
harmonies around at a time when the quality of pop vocal harmony
was on a twenty-year downslide.

Unfortunately, all these advantages too readily reduced to formula.
Nicks might have been no more the airhead than Diana Ross, but the
combined talents of Buckingham and the rhythm section didn't equal
Holland-Dozier-Holland in rescuing her from her own vagaries. (Diana,
fortunately, wrote none of her own material.) And in the end, Fleetwood Mac dedicated itself to a hedonist superficiality that holds up less
well than admirers of mass pop taste would hope. "Don't Stop," with
McVie generously sharing the lead with Buckingham, was the pinnacle
of the band's quasi-democratic spirit but its text—not even its subtext,
its overt message—was forget the past and move your ass along. For
all its chic and sheen, you tell me how that's any less insubstantial and

retrograde than the message of the same era's most vulgar disco hits.

585 SHAKE SHERRY, The Contours
Written and produced by Berry Gordy
Gordy 7012   1962   Billboard: #43

As low-down and bluesy as Motown ever got, and with the boss himself at the helm, no less. The background vocals are plain crazed, the bass voice the Motor City equivalent of "Papa-oom-mow-mow," the rhythm's built around a battered cowbell, the baritone sax lurches through the whole thing like a fart with a mind of its own, and if Billy Gordon sang any harder, he'd have needed the world's first lung transplant.

586 DAWN, The Four Seasons
Produced by Bob Crewe; written by Sandy Linzer and Bob Gaudio
Philips 40166   1964   Billboard: #4

Bob Gaudio's songs bear such a potent sense of American class restrictions and carry their resentment of it so close to the edge of hysteria that I'm not sure that a singer less histrionic than the young Frankie Valli could have gotten away with singing them. In "Dawn," after all, the guy's gotta talk his girl into going off with another guy, who's got a future while our boy has none, not because he's a slouch but because he was born without one. This is not the land of limitless opportunity that more celebrated Yankee tunesmiths celebrate.

"Dawn" is a product of Bob Crewe's period of complete infatuation with Phil Spector's Wall of Sound, which too often resulted in records so cluttered you could have called the approach The Kitchen Sink, but here, everything's judiciously applied to increase the music's throw-weight, from the organ wash to the bells and triangles and handclaps that add even more percussion to a record that could also be described as a tom-tom and snare solo with vocal distractions.

587 TO THE AISLE, 5 Satins
Producer not credited; Written by Freeman, Murphy, Brown, Baker and Killebrew
Ember 1019   1957   *Billboard:* #25

In some ways, a more fascinating record than the Satins' "In the Still of the Nite," certainly the most popular doo-wop single of all time. Fred Parris tenderly recounts the story of a romance right out of *True Love* comics, from first meeting to the proposal. The bleating, reedy sax is unmatchably corny, but it's just setting up the real payoff in the final verse, where the girl accepts a ring and "tears start flowing awhile." I guess those are supposed to be tears of joy, but it feels a lot more like a premonition of shaky times to come.

588 (WHAT'S SO FUNNY 'BOUT) PEACE, LOVE AND UNDERSTANDING, Elvis Costello
Written and produced by Nick Lowe
Columbia 1172   1978   Did not make pop chart

Nick Lowe wrote "(What's So Funny About) Peace, Love and Understanding" in the mid-seventies, while a member of the pub-rock band Brinsley Schwarz. Like all pub-rockers, Brinsley Schwarz were lapsed hippies, playing folky-funky in flannel shirts and jeans. Unlike most, Nick Lowe combined his hippie roots with an absolute faith in the corruptibility of mankind. So he sang "Peace, Love and Understanding" in the voice of a man who'd been through the Balkanization of the counterculture and simply refused to countenance the situation any longer.

After Brinsley Schwarz broke up, Lowe became a solo artist and record producer, making Elvis Costello's first three albums and the Pretenders' first single, "Stop Your Sobbing," among others. The records sounded crappy, because Lowe believed that the best way to capture pop was simply to slap things together, but they had heart and an emphasis on songs and structure and harmony rare among new wavers.

Elvis Costello transformed "Peace, Love and Understanding." Recorded during the sessions for *Armed Forces*, when hope still tempered his misanthropy, Costello eradicated Lowe's cynicism and replaced it with joyous acceptance and thinly veiled remorse. "Peace, Love and Understanding" is Costello's most openly emotive record; even on his soul reworkings, he's never left himself this uncovered. And though what he reveals is anything but peaceful—he's angry, choking on tears of rage—when Elvis sings "Each time I feel like this inside / It just makes me want to cry," you not only feel he might, but that you've cracked the code of many of his own obtuse songs as well.

"Peace, Love and Understanding" is also the hottest rock and roll his band, the Attractions, ever made. Though Lowe botched the production by muffling the band's essential presence, what comes rumbling through are cascading drum rolls from Pete Thomas, a Steve Nieve organ groove that sounds like it was developed on the field of battle, and Elvis with a guitar line as fierce as his vocal. If the group slumped into arty mechanics and Costello's writing withered in the face of its own game-playing pretensions, for this one single Elvis Costello and the Attractions were as good as any rock band in the world. Singing clichés, they redeemed them—and discovered themselves. A pretty good definition of what it's all about.

589 I CRIED A TEAR, LaVern Baker
Produced by Ahmet Ertegun and Jerry Wexler; written by Al Julia and Fred Jay
Atlantic 2007   1958   *Billboard:* #6

LaVern Baker, a skillful and sophisticated jazz vocalist (she was discovered by venerable band leader Fletcher Henderson), complained long and bitterly about being saddled with such rock and roll novelty numbers as "Tweedlee Dee" and "Jim Dandy." Those remain the records by which she's best remembered, which is fairly awful evidence of the puerile tastes of most of those who've written rock and roll history so far, especially since "I Cried A Tear," one of the great R&B torch tunes, was her biggest hit, and the only one to make the pop Top Ten, which even as late as 1958 represented an unusually potent (and therefore, unignorable) black-to-white crossover.

The stately arrangement owes a lot to Chuck Willis; the sax line, in particular, recapitulates the melody of "What Am I Living For," which preceded Baker's record to the charts by eight months, and the beat is a legato version of the stroll tunes Willis popularized. Baker's parched melisma gives the performance such a distinctly personal stamp that even if this isn't the record she'll be remembered by, it's the one she should be.

590 RUNAWAY TRAIN, Rosanne Cash
Produced by Rodney Crowell; written by John Stewart
Columbia 07988   1988   Did not make pop chart

As the eighties waned, America prepared itself for the second Singer/
Songwriter Era, emerging this time under a new guise, as many leftovers
from the first moved to Nashville. Meantime, Rosanne Cash—daughter
of a Nashville giant, wife of Rodney Crowell, the best country songwriter of the decade—sang her heart out on a rock arrangement of a
song written by one of the original singer/songwriter cult heroes, and
almost nobody in pop music got to hear her.

Cash sings softly above crashing drums—a trick so hard that most
vocalists won't even attempt it. The melody is carried on Morse code
guitars that perfectly set up the telegraphic imagery of love running off
the rails: "Blind boys and gamblers, they invented the blues / We'll
pay up in blood when this marker comes due / To try and get off now,
it's about as insane / As those who wave lanterns at runaway trains."
In the singing, you can hear echoes of Stevie Nicks; the guitar solo is
pure David Lindley; the drumming owes its heart to Mick Fleetwood.

But Cash and Crowell bring a rare sense of rhythmic and vocal
urgency to their version of California rock: It comes from the husk of
Rosanne's singing and the thrash of those drums, which evoke without
flinching a million exhausted midnight fights between lovers too familiar
with each other's moves to be taken by surprise or learn anything new,
too wrapped up in each other's lives to know how to quit.

Maybe "Runaway Train" wasn't the hit it deserved to be because
it hit too close to too many homes.

591 ALL RIGHT NOW, Free
Produced by Free; written by Paul Rodgers and Andy Fraser
A&M 1206   1970   Billboard: #4

Cock rock extraordinaire. Time was when the likes of Free vocalist
Paul Rodgers' swaggering macho was the height of uncool, not really
as Elvis-like as it thought it was. And Elvis had a way of defusing his
more studly routines, with a knowing grin that refrained from becoming
a leer. Rodgers knew no move so innocent, and anyway, Free's bludgeoning pre-heavy metal had no space for it. Which is one reason it
was always so funny to hear hard rockers mock disco's sweaty Lotharios.

"All Right Now" isn't just cock rock—it's the apotheosis of the
form, as unrelenting as a hard hat's street corner come-ons. That, in

fact, seems to be the metaphoric site of the song, with Rodgers spotting a slick chick and trying to get next to her with such sophisticated come-ons as, "Hey, what's your name, baby. Maybe we can see things the same."

Of course, she turns the table when they get back to her place, responding in high dudgeon when he dares raise the subject of love (which undoubtedly means unbridled worship of his body from penis to pectorals). Naturally, no tale of machismo is complete until the woman has somehow "victimized" the man by denying his desires.

Thereafter, Andy Fraser rips off a guitar solo that justifies the entire enterprise by itself and when it concludes, Rodgers yelps his way out with a series of "All Right Nows!" which indicate that, spurned or successful, he went back into the night in further pursuit of the only game he could imagine, a predator to the end. Soon thereafter, Rodgers concocted Bad Company in which he conducted similar experiments with identical objectives, though not such spectacular guitar parts.

592 BORN UNDER A BAD SIGN, Albert King
Produced by Jim Stewart; written by Booker T. Jones and William Bell
Stax 217 1967   Did not make pop chart

Although permanently linked to the other unrelated guitar Kings, B.B. and Freddy, Albert came closer to fitting the (or at least, my) definition of soul man than bluesman. His best records—especially this one and "Crosscut Saw"—were composed and produced by associates with pop chart credentials, and though his singing owes a great deal to B.B., it owes just as much to Bobby Bland. In fact, deemphasize guitar and replace it with a call-and-response vocal chorus and you'd have here pretty much a standard Southern soul track, like a slowed-down version of Wilson Pickett's "Ninety Nine and A Half." But it's King's unique guitar work (the best left-handed style this side of Jimi Hendrix), that makes it special. Coupled here with a song so classic it sounds like it must have been unearthed rather than written, the result is virtually timeless.

593 JUICY FRUIT, Mtume
Written and produced by James Mtume
Epic 03578   1983   *Billboard:* #45

Why is it, do you figure, that heavy metal, the music of the rude 'n' crude white working class, concerns itself so often with oral sex as applied to men by women while dance music, the sound of the black working class, so frequently takes as its (often more covert) subject oral sex as done by men to women? Could it be a matter of contrasting cultural taboos meeting a common desire to sing about doing what's just not done?

James Mtume, veteran of Miles Davis's band that he is, might not approve of the class characterization but the subject matter of this spacey, languid, somewhat giggly dance item argues otherwise. I mean, what else could the long slow build with that deep bass to a lip-smacking percussive climax mean, especially when Tawatha Agee sings that "You're the only love that gives me good 'n' plenty?" Much less, "I'll be your lollipop / You can lick me everywhere." (She's ready to return the favor but just as a means to an end.)

Dirty records from the early days of R&B are more widely celebrated, but Hank Ballard never got any of his "Annie" records this far up the charts. Of course, he also didn't come up with a riff half as exciting or danceable as the shattered-glass synth part here.

594 SOME KIND OF WONDERFUL, The Soul Brothers Six
Producer not credited; written by John Ellison
Atlantic 2406   1967   *Billboard:* #91

How does a record make the nether regions of the *Billboard* chart and then disappear, in this case after but a single week?

In the case of "Some Kind of Wonderful" (which has nothing at all in common with the Drifters' record of the same title), probably by becoming a hit on Detroit's black stations and then crossing over to Top 40 there without picking up any new cities.

That doesn't mean that "Some Kind of Wonderful" disappeared, though. In fact, within a year, almost every band with a shred of soul in Michigan was performing its four-square funk riff, though of course all of them replaced John Ellison's gritty gospel vocal shout with blasts of guitar raunch. By 1969, the riff had been polished by Norman Whitfield and became the Temptations' "I Can't Get Next to You," a Number One. That wasn't the rip-off the linkage might imply; "Some Kind of Wonderful" itself isn't much more than a particularly energized application of the basic Motown/gospel pastiche. A rawer version of "I Can't Get Next to You" (back closer to the source though he might not have known it) became Al Green's first (minor) hit in 1970. By that time, the groove had traversed the Atlantic and appeared on both Rod Stewart's first solo album, as "An Old Raincoat Won't Ever Let You Down" and on the first album he made with the Faces, as "Three Button Hand Me Down."

As for the Soul Brothers Six, who knows what became of them? They seem to have been from Philadelphia; judging from what I can hear, they may have been that town's answer to Dyke and the Blazers. Boston record collector Fred Lewis once showed me a picture of the group; with bouffant blonde hair stacked up on their heads, they looked like a black version of the Hullabaloos. "Some Kind of Wonderful" wasn't their only single—the others sometimes turn up on Japanese reissues of Atlantic soul obscurities—but it was by far their best and it certainly had the most interesting role to play.

595 MAMA HE TREATS YOUR DAUGHTER MEAN, Ruth Brown

Produced by Herb Abramson; written by Johnny Wallace
and Herbert Lance
Atlantic 986   1953   *Billboard*: #23

The first woman explicitly identified as a "rock and roll singer," Ruth Brown perfected a light yet tough vocal persona that tightened up the kind of jump blues arrangements she'd sung in a short stint with bandleader Lucky Millinder. A singer's singer, she was a star in both Detroit and Washington well before her recording stardom started, and in fact, signed with Atlantic only after a spirited bidding competition with Capitol.

Like LaVern Baker, Brown showed far more sophistication than almost any of her male contemporaries in rock and roll. The suggestive squeals she places with great calculation in the teen-oriented lyric of "Mama" can't disguise a style that's essentially meant for supper clubs and jazz orchestrations. Yet the record's cutting guitar and riffing sax are so emblematic of Atlantic's "cat music" concept of rock and roll that it fits the genre anyway.

Brown's talent remains enormous and her influence extensive. But she clearly followed her own instincts more closely when making a series of relatively uncommercial jazz albums after leaving Atlantic. So in the end, perhaps the best way to understand the great chart success of such an otherwise unlucky hitmaker is to consider the entire spectrum of talent at work, particularly at the control board. In that light, Brown's hits suggest how different Atlantic's R&B might have been if cofounder Herb Abramson hadn't been aced out early, since it was his production synthesis, far jazzier than either Ahmet Ertegun or Jerry Wexler's, that brought Brown her biggest hits. Whether Atlantic would have been as successful or as widely emulated if it had applied such cosmopolitan standards to all its efforts is one of rock's great unanswered questions.

596 LET THE FOUR WINDS BLOW, Fats Domino
Produced by Dave Bartholomew; written by
Dave Bartholomew and Fats Domino
Imperial 5764   1961   Billboard: #15

Bandleader Dave Bartholomew first recorded "Let the Four Winds Blow" in 1957, with Roy Brown, the author of "Good Rockin' To-night," and one of the most innovative and imitated (by Elvis, among others) of the late forties New Orleans jump blues singers. That first version of this song became Brown's only Top 40 hit (though his 1950 "Hard Luck Blues" probably sold at least a million back in the days of total market segregation).

For years later, in the twilight of *his* Top 40 career, Fats Domino cut "Let the Four Winds Blow" in a version that lays Brown's to waste. It's a virtually perfect New Orleans piano shuffle (whether that's Fats or James Booker at the keys) and it deserved its Top 20 status, the last Fats record that climbed anywhere near that high.

597 YOU REALLY GOT ME, The Kinks
Produced by Shel Talmy; written by Ray Davies
Reprise 0334   1964   Billboard: #7

There are two ways to think about Ray Davies's original "Louie Louie" rewrite. Many rock fans adore it, and thank Davies nightly for providing the song that not only sustained The World's Trashiest Riff but also provided Eddie Van Halen his first great throb-metal vehicle. And then there are those who would like to think of "You Really Got Me" as a vulgar aberration and adore Ray Davies for his latter-day mopery, like "David Watts" and "Waterloo Sunset." By now you know why this is the one that landed here, while the Anglo-wimpy stuff lies on the cutting room floor.

598 I'M DOWN, The Beatles
Produced by George Martin; written by John Lennon and Paul McCartney
Capitol 5476   1965   Did not make pop chart

Cut at the same session as "Yesterday," sneaked out as the B side of "Help," not issued on an LP for many years, "I'm Down" is emblematic of the Beatles' full greatness. Because in the history of rock and roll, there was probably nobody else who could have come up with a letter-perfect update of Little Richard, right down to the gospel yowls, and there was certainly no one who could have then afforded to just throw it away. Other bands would have dredged a career out of that silly little electric organ alone.

599 SOOTHE ME, Sam and Dave
Produced by Jim Stewart; written by Sam Cooke
Stax 218   1967   Billboard: #56

Sam Cooke wrote "Soothe Me" for his proteges, the Sims Twins, who had a minor hit with it on Cooke's own Sar label in 1961. Sam and Dave picked up on it as an ideal vehicle and indeed, they never sounded more churchy, even if the souls at stake fail to distinguish between the sensual and the spiritual.

600 IF IT AIN'T ONE THING . . . IT'S ANOTHER, Richard "Dimples" Fields
Written and produced by Richard "Dimples" Fields and Belinda Wilson
Boardwalk 139   1982   Billboard: #47

On the single, "If It Ain't One Thing . . ." uses Fields's sweet gospel falsetto and a groove that owes a lot to "Superfly"-era Curtis Mayfield to salve a lyric that's as detailed and pained (though not nearly as poetic) as "What's Going On." It's as if the Stylistics' Russell Thompkins had awakened from his romantic reveries and decided to take a hard look at real life. Recounting his woes, Fields gets personal (he's in the middle of a paternity fight, his girlfriend's a puzzle, he hates his job, he can't quit smoking), preachy (he complains of drugs, claims "books and movies are corrupt," rails against "shacking up" and divorce) and political (he's worried by everything from taxes to racism). But because Fields sings the hell out of the song, and because he's simply cataloging an Everyman's list of woes, even the preachy stuff goes down smooth.

The extended version on his *Mr. Look So Good!* album, however, concludes with a long pitch that turns the record into a tract, replete with grandmotherly homilies and extensive references to Bible verses. And Fields doesn't turn these preachments to the kind of advantage a gospel singer could; he's not shouting and praising, he's just haranguing.

On the radio, or listening to the 45, you never had to deal with this crap. And that's a real blessing.

601 LOVE CAN'T TURN AROUND (CLUB MIX), Farley "Jackmaster" Funk and Jesse Sanders

Produced by Brothers by Music; written by J.M. Funk and Jesse Sanders
House FU10   1986   Did not make pop charts

House has become one of the most intriguing new styles of the eighties because it builds contemporary dance-pop using techniques drawn from the blues (the bluesy piano breaks), Broadway (the haute-mannered vocals), seventies disco (the basic beats), and eighties hip-hop (the studio and synthesizer effects). In the right hands, what results isn't messy melange but a fascinating dance-rock bouillabaisse. "Love Can't Turn Around," which takes more than seven minutes to complete its "Club Mix," is a pyrotechnic paragon of house, its only drawback the corny lead vocal and love lyrics, which only come on in the last minute or so anyhow. The rest of the time, the music's cool sheen overheats, boils, and settles back down over and over again, developing enough subtleties to keep even nondancers fascinated.

602 RIDE YOUR PONY, Lee Dorsey

Produced by Allen Toussaint and Marshall Sehorn; written by Naomi Neville (Allen Toussaint)
Amy 927   1965   *Billboard:* #28

New Orleans' answer to "Dancing in the Street," an ominous rumble with Dorsey's raggedy shouts directing the dancers like traffic, baritone saxes grunting and complaining all the while that bass and guitar move along unhurriedly, and the drums loiter, linger, and then explode all over the kit and your consciousness. Provided you haven't been distracted in contemplation of exactly what kind of pony he's talking about saddling up.

603 I'LL GO CRAZY, James Brown
Written and produced by James Brown
King 6020   1966   *Billboard:* #73

After the Soul Degree Zero of "Papa's Got a Brand New Bag" and "I Got You (I Feel Good)," JB returned to relative R&B normalcy. So much so that he found himself covered by the Blues Magoos and other pedestrian forces for whom the image of madness was more a codified cultural convenience than a (not very) oblique statement of permanent human condition.

604 ALL I HAVE TO DO IS DREAM, The Everly Brothers
Produced by Archie Bleyer; written by Felice and Boudleaux Bryant
Cadence 1348   1958   *Billboard:* #1 (5 weeks)

The story goes that when Felice Bryant first met Boudleaux (she was working as an elevator operator in the Milwaukee hotel where he was playing in a jazz band), she knew him immediately. She'd dreamed his face as her future husband when she was eight years old. "All I Have to Do is Dream," then, is perhaps closer to being the Bryants' own story than any of their other hits. Like all their best, the song feels so natural and right in its beautiful hesitations and thoughtful syncopations that it might as well be fated. And what other writers could have pulled off a rhyme like "Only trouble is / Gee whiz"?

The Everly Brothers sing easy as dreamers themselves, but so soulfully that their biggest-ever ballad also topped the rhythm and blues charts for five weeks. In the background, Chet Atkins plays a tremolo part designed to make fools of those who claim he didn't know how to make great rock and roll.

605 IT'S GROWING, The Temptations
Produced by Smokey Robinson; written by Smokey Robinson and Warren Moore
Gordy 7040   1965   *Billboard:* #18

Beginning with amateurish piano notes that sound like they're being played by somebody at the end of their first day of studying rhythm and blues, and continuing with a lyric whose metaphors are almost comically profuse, "It's Growing" seems more like a sketch for a Smokey Robinson song than a great one.

But those piano notes are building blocks, and the metaphors are as rhythmically eloquent as they are literarily overextended. Anyway, it's David Ruffin and the Motown band that make Smokey's song shine; as you listen longer and deeper, "It's Growing" obeys its own injunction and enlarges itself, until by the end it has grown into a minor Motown masterwork.

606 TRENCHTOWN ROCK, The Wailers
Produced by Lee Perry; written by Bob Marley
Island   1971   Did not make pop chart

Reggae's international anthem: "One good thing about music / When it hits you feel no pain." Out of the mouths of four Trench Town (i.e., Kingston slum) postadolescents, the credibility was as instant as the dance groove. Nor were the two things separable. Any more than Bob Marley and Peter Tosh were at the time separable. Soon enough unity disintegrated and Bob went on to arguably greater, certainly far bigger things. But not truer or more powerful ones because there are none.

607 EXPRESSWAY TO YOUR HEART, The Soul Survivors
Written and produced by Kenny Gamble and Leon Huff
Crimson 1010   1967   *Billboard:* #4

What the Rascals would have sounded like if they'd grown up at the other end of the Jersey Turnpike. Actually, Philly soul historian Tony Cummings claims the Survivors wanted to be Mitch Ryder and the Detroit Wheels, but lead vocalists Charlie and Richard Ingui are a lot closer to Felix Cavaliere and Eddie Brigati here, and Gamble and Huff's arrangement far more akin to Atlantic soul than the Wheels' hot white rhythm and blues. As Huff told Cummings, "It wasn't soul, it was like soul-influenced pop." On the downside, he also told him that the song was inspired by nothing more romantic than the opening of Philly's first expressway.

608 ASK THE LONELY, The Four Tops
Written and produced by William Stevenson and Ivy Hunter
Motown 1073   1965   *Billboard*: #24

Further evidence that there is a place in the dark heart of the soul where it is always 4:00 A.M. As an artist, Levi Stubbs stayed up as late as F. Scott Fitzgerald. And it was time well spent.

609 ALMOST GROWN, Chuck Berry
Produced by Leonard Chess; written by Chuck Berry
Chess 1722   1959   *Billboard*: #32

Chuck virtually croons this teen dream, in a style derived from late forties mentors like Charles Brown, though the side-of-the-mouth humor brings him back to his original idol, Louis Jordan. These reference points are fitting because, after a wicked opening guitar downbeat, the track is basically a piano-led jump blues, shuffling drums and bass underpinning Johnnie Johnson's greatest piano parts. Understood in this context, "Almost Grown" is far more sophisticated than its adolescent topic suggests. The flowing lyrics are a form of colloquial poetry; the steady stream of seamless syllables creates the music's drive as much as anything the instruments put out. "Got my eye on a little guh-rul / Ah, she's really outta this wuh-rrr-ld," Berry sings and you can practically hear him licking his chops.

610 THE LAST TIME, The Rolling Stones
Produced by Andrew Loog Oldham; written by Mick Jagger and Keith Richards
London 9741   1965   *Billboard*: #9

Of the Rolling Stones' first two American Top Ten hits, the debut, "Time Is On My Side," directly knocked off Irma Thomas's arrangement, while the second, "The Last Time," copied a song first made famous by the Staple Singers note-for-note, inflection-for-inflection, lick-for-lick. The latter is far more original.

The differences between the Staples' and the Stones' versions are three: Pop Roebuck sings with far more gravity than the young Jagger; the guitar lick is growlier on the Staples record; and the Staples' lyrics are religious rather than romantic. The difference between the way the Stones plundered "Time Is On My Side" and the way they plundered "The Last Time" is one: Norman Meade, author of the former, got credit; Roebuck "Pop" Staples, who arranged the latter, got nothing.

Does this mean the early Stones were just rip-off artists? Hardly. Speeding up "The Last Time" may even have improved it; certainly, there's no way the Staples record would have been played on the radio, and that group soon enough secularized itself anyway. But they should have *paid* the man.

So speaking in their own avaricious terms, this may be the one truly unholy record the Stones have ever made.

611 YOU'LL LOSE A GOOD THING, Barbara Lynn
Produced by Huey P. Meaux; written by Barbara Lynn Ozen
Jamie 1220   1962   *Billboard:* #8

The most famous female blues singer from Port Arthur, Texas was Janis Joplin, but the best, by far, was a left-handed guitarist named Barbara Lynn Ozen. She made "You'll Lose a Good Thing," a smoky back room blues featuring a mellow sax and intricate New Orleans-bred backbeat, when she was just twenty years old—but you'd never guess it from her gritty threats about the inevitable inferiority of any replacement her roving-eyed lover might find. The tautly controlled rage of Lynn's performance would have been striking coming from a singer twice her age, and it's the opposite of Joplin's declamatory histrionics.

612 BLUE MOON OF KENTUCKY, Elvis Presley
Produced by Sam Phillips; written by Bill Monroe
Sun 209   1954   Did not make pop chart

High lonesome with ants in its pants.

If you don't think Elvis's expropriation of country standards like this was as audacious as his blues reworkings, you haven't grasped the barricades the Nashville establishment can throw in the way of change to this very day. With its gutbucket bass and rocketing guitar solos and that relentless rattling—probably Elvis banging on the body of his guitar "like it was the lid of a garbage can," as he once described it—"Blue Moon of Kentucky" radically recasts one of the most sacrosanct numbers in all bluegrass. And bluegrass, though actually the product of a synthesis that Bill Monroe pioneered with as much calculation as Sam Phillips did rockabilly, has such ancient roots that it is regarded in country circles as the untouchable Ur music.

No wonder Nashville had to fight him off. The moment Elvis broke through, the die was cast and in fact, the country market suffered far more in the face of white rock's onslaught than the R&B market ever did. Great country was being made in 1954, but to admit Elvis to the C&W charts was an acknowledgment that there was an essential vitality missing from all of it. Sure as the governor of Mississippi had to bar that schoolhouse door, country had to hold off the facts (and they're the same facts) as long as it could.

613 KILLER JOE, The Rocky Fellers
Produced by Bert Berns; written by Bert Russell [Berns], Bob Elgin, and Phil Medley
Scepter 1246   1963   Billboard: #16

If Michael Jackson had been a prepubescent Filipino-American recorded at the height of the discotheque era by the men who brought you "Twist and Shout," "Killer Joe" is the record he would have made. Of course, if he'd gotten his start in that era, critics and collectors would venerate his producer's name and nobody'd be able to tell you his.

614 THE SHOOP SHOOP SONG (IT'S IN HIS KISS), Betty Everett
Produced by Calvin Carter; written by Rudy Clark
Vee-Jay 585   1964   Billboard: #6

Though it's presented as a solo performance, "It's In His Kiss" (the title by which everybody remembers it), is one of the finest girl group hits, undoubtedly the best one made outside the genre's New York/ Philadelphia/Los Angeles axis. In fact, the record presents itself as a dialogue between a group of less experienced teenage girls, who can't quite figure out the rules for when a guy's protestations of love are to be believed, and Betty, who reduces the process to the simple formula in the title. "How 'bout the way he acts?" the chorus inquires and Betty impatiently replies, "No, no, that's not the way, and you're not listening to all I say." In that line, you can hear the same sneer she used in her other big hits, "Gettin' Mighty Crowded" and "You're No Good." And when she gets to the bridge, and describes how it feels when he's for real, you can hear what made her duet with Jerry Butler on the brilliantly mawkish "Let It Be Me" such a smash.

Latter-day field reports suggest that Betty's strategy may have been seriously defective, but when this record is playing, she's as inerrant as the Pope is supposed to be on faith and morals.

615 SHAKE YOU DOWN, Gregory Abbott
Written and produced by Gregory Abbott
Columbia 06191   1987   *Billboard:* #1 (1 week)

Abbott's hit was homemade but he was no street hustler with nothing more than a song and a dream. Possessor of degrees from Stanford and Boston University, he was working on Wall Street as a researcher in 1984 when some of his brokerage friends bankrolled an elaborate home recording setup.

They weren't the first to appreciate Abbott's talent. Earlier in the decade, after dropping out of the University of California's doctoral program, he moved to Los Angeles and married Freda Payne ("Band of Gold," "Bring the Boys Home") and understudied with no less than Marvin Gaye.

It's something like the sensuality of Gaye's later records ("Let's Get It On," "Sexual Healing," and the like) that motivates "Shake You Down," a slinky seduction song that uses traditional R&B harmony techniques in a contemporary rhythm ballad context. His piercing shouts and high, floating cries atop a sizzling percussion bed are far more formulaic than Gaye's, but then, few aren't. Even if "Shake You Down" proves to have been more a one-shot than a prelude to a meaningful career, its magnificence will not dim.

616 THE WEIGHT, The Band
Produced by The Band and John Simon; written by Robbie Robertson
Capitol 2269   1968   *Billboard:* #63

How important is a hit single, even in the album rock era? The Band, a group which never cracked the Top 20, serves as the most instructive example. For all Robbie Robertson's brooding self-importance—and if there have been more brooding figures in rock, for self-importance he has no equal—he's simply nothing like a household word.

Robertson undeniably participated in the making of some great music. The problem is that his role in the Band was never quite as central as critics pretend. Robertson may have been his group's chief writer (although, at least on its acclaimed debut album, he was seriously taxed for the pole position by both Richard Manuel and Rick Danko), but he was never its voice. Among the five members of the Band, Robertson was the fourth best singer (and Garth Hudson basically kept his mouth shut) and even the elliptically wise Americana of his lyrics is an interpretation of what he heard from the Band's great drummer, raconteur, and chief vocalist, Levon Helm. (Robertson certainly learned what he knew about the South from Helm, since Robbie himself grew up in the far North: Toronto, to be exact.)

Yet if one would argue just whose triumph "The Weight" is, it would be foolish to argue that it isn't a triumphant piece of rock and roll. Opening with stately guitar and drum beats that lock in with the dead certainty of a firing squad, adding elegiac honky-tonk piano chords from Manuel, crowned by Helm's singing on the verse, Danko's vocal on the bridge, and harmonies tossed around like a live grenade, "The Weight" is as fine an example of rock and roll record-making as existed in the year of its birth and it has dated not a whit. You can already feel the constriction that led to the hollow pomposity of the Band's later years (in twenty years, to the monumental pomposity of Robertson's first solo album), but it works like the constrictions of the Motown formulas, establishing a framework out of which emotion and meaning may explode.

And they do, right beyond the bounds of Robertson's acutely studied Dylanisms. The words are bizarre but the meaning that the singers bring to them has an everyday concreteness and that's the contradiction that the music fights to resolve. Populated by weirdnesses ("Carmen and the Devil walkin' side by side," Crazy Chester with his "bag . . . sinkin' low," ol' Luke who's "waitin' for the Judgment Day"), told in crazy-quilt time, never quite cohering into a story but with a chilling sense of place and time, "The Weight" is as oblique as it is masterful.

The Band came closer to a hit—"Up on Cripple Creek" got to Number 25 and they cracked the Top 40 with a live version of Marvin Gaye's "Don't Do It" which was about a tenth as good as the studio take they never officially released. But, to indulge in the sort of hyperbole Robertson likes to abuse, they never quite reached the promised land. And because the Top Ten (or even Top 20), the region that indicates mass acceptance rather than cult success or some species of hype, eluded them, the group's story feels unsettled, maybe unfinished. What that finally means, I think, is that the Band wasn't quite as good as its promise or at least, that it was never quite as important as it was good. There are greater tragedies, but that one's sad enough for me.

617 WHEN WILL I SEE YOU AGAIN, The Three Degrees
Written and produced by Kenneth Gamble and Leon Huff
Philadelphia International 3550   1974   Billboard: #2

Go-Gos and Bangles notwithstanding, "When Will I See You Again" is the last chapter in the girl group story. Which makes unsurprising sense as a matter of geography; girl groups were stylistically East Coast no matter where Darlene Love grew up. The surprise comes from the breathy singing and the pulsating light funk arrangement, the way the lead vocal moves from oh-but-of-course Diana Ross mannerisms to Oh-My-God! Ronettes references, stuff you suspected Gamble-Huff drilled out of any of their minions who might have had it in them. Then, you learn that Sheila Ferguson and her cohorts were trained by doo-wop guru Richard Barrett and order is restored to the universe. Not that the sound is any less haunting once you know where it's coming from— indeed, awareness of its origins makes "When Will I See You Again" seem a kind of ghost itself.

618 GOOD TIMES, Sam Cooke
Produced by Hugo and Luigi; written by Sam Cooke
RCA 8368   1964   Billboard: #11

The greatest version of the Cajun bon temps roulet theme turns out to come not directly from New Orleans (although Shirley and Lee didn't do a bad job at all) but from a Mississippi-born, Chicago-bred gospel singer working with a pair of New York-based Italian-American pop producers in a Hollywood studio, with a group of musicians some—but by no means all—of whose key members had landed in L.A. from the Big Easy. And *that's* what's at the heart of rock and roll.

619 **CRY LIKE A BABY, The Box Tops**
Produced by Dan Penn; written by Dan Penn and Spooner Oldham
Mala 593   1968   *Billboard: #2*

620 **CRY CRY CRY, Bobby Bland**
Produced by Joe Scott; written by Deadric Malone
Duke 327   1960   *Billboard: #71*

The vast, implacable sonorities of the records made by Bobby Bland, the most sophisticated of Southern bluesmen and the most country of all soul singers, inspired a generation of white Southerners as they tried to imitate the inimitable. That meant trying to capture not only the preternatural dignity of Bland's singing but the resonances and angularities of Joe Scott's brilliant arrangements, which were both the site of Bland's sophistication and the key to his synthesis. "Cry Cry Cry" ranks as a better example of Scott's work than of Bland's, since the real source of its ever-increasing excitement comes from the softly swinging support. Although Bland cuts loose for a quick, gospelly rant near the end, what's forever surprising here is the way the music reveals a tremendous amount of energy but keeps it contained. It's like a definition of bottled lightning.

Dan Penn and Spooner Oldham caught the bug and that's what gives "Cry Like a Baby" its majestic sweep: horns, guitars, chorus, and strings complement not only a first-rate lyric but an exceptionally tart Alex Chilton vocal. As in "Cry Cry Cry," the tears that fall here are mannered and controlled, and perhaps more explosive for all of that.

621 **I THANK YOU, Sam and Dave**
Written and produced by Isaac Hayes and David Porter
Stax 242   1968   *Billboard: #9*

The debut of the Hayes-Porter production team finds Sam and Dave put through their typical paces with a special touch, meaning what you get is a dialogue that's 90 percent Sam but accompanied by fuzztone guitar and splendidly cheesy organ. The bass and horns are eternal, as perfect things ought to be.

622 WRAP IT UP, Sam and Dave
Written and produced by Isaac Hayes and David Porter
Stax 242   1968   Did not make pop chart

After looking at the preliminary list of records to be included in this book, my friend Greil Marcus remarked (among other things) "Too many records by Sam and Dave."

Maybe there's two kinds of rock and soul fans: Those for whom there is such a thing as too many records by Sam and Dave, and those for whom that's like saying "Too much fresh air." The latter camp clearly holds my allegiance. So much so that I even favor B sides like "Wrap It Up."

The idea that a record as powerful and appealing as "Wrap It Up" could be tossed off as a flip side—the side of the single that's *not* going to be promoted—is itself fairly awesome. Recorded on the same day (January 5, 1968) as "I Thank You," the duo's historic first session with Isaac Hayes and David Porter, "Wrap It Up" has everything Stax must have been looking for, rhythm section, horns, lyric, and melody melded into a seamless dance-demanding whole.

Like every great Sam and Dave single, though, what "Wrap It Up" ultimately has going for it is their voices, the way they battle each other for space. If they really disliked each other as much as they later claimed (and every observer confirms), maybe what their sound was about wasn't unity so much as the ultimate soul cutting contest, the spectacle growing more intense each beat deeper into the song, as Sam fought off Dave's claims and Dave refused to give in. Dave was even saddled with a much inferior instrument, which somehow made his efforts seem even more poignant, like the Polish cavalry trying to hold back German tank battalions at the onset of World War II.

There are critics who would argue that a *Heart of Cinema* might have too many war movies on it, I guess. But I wouldn't be among them, especially if one of the most spectacularly gifted creative ensembles in history had specialized in them. Maybe Sam and Dave fight the same battle over and over again, but they brawl with such spirit that they can keep you listening with fascination for decades.

623 SOMETHING IN THE AIR, Thunderclap Newman

Produced by Pete Townshend; written by Speedy Keen
Track 2656   1969   *Billboard:* #37

Of all the sixties' testimonies to the necessity for immediate social revolution, "Something in the Air" is by far the most elegantly atmospheric. Pete Townshend constructed it around Andy "Thunderclap" Newman, a piano playing, train-spotting eccentric he'd idolized since art school; Speedy Keen, a drummer and former Townshend roommate who'd written the Who's "Armenia City in the Sky," one of the few rock fantasies as winningly utopian as "Something in the Air"; teenage guitarist Jimmy McCulloch, who went on to a key role in Paul McCartney's Wings but overdosed young; and Bijou Drains, a bassist with a giant beak, pipestem legs and unorthodox windmill playing style.

Few rock records so effectively combine majestic orchestration and a hard beat, and although to a degree the parts feel pasted together, the project's anticipatory innocence captures the atmosphere of imminence that suffused the late sixties, when the culture and political order could be felt wobbling every hour. Of course, we should all have known that combining "Hand out the arms and ammo" with the horn line from "The Lonely Surfer" was no model for successful insurrection. But we didn't, and even so many years on the wrong edge of that dilapidated possibility, it's often a pleasure to hear someone warn so sweetly and confidently that "The revolution's near / And you know that it's right."

Although I guess what lingers longest is what follows: "We have got to get it together / We have got to get it together now."

624 SOMETHING SO STRONG, Crowded House

Produced by Mitchell Froom; written by Neil Finn and Mitchell Froom
Capital 5695   1987   *Billboard:* #7

Every year, when half a dozen new groups come along promising Beatlesque, they presumably mean sprightly harmonies, quirky melodies, rockin' rhythms, and oddball humor. People inclined to get their hopes up must find themselves in a continual state of disillusionment; the rest of us just ignore the hype.

Crowded House, through writer/vocalist Neil Finn, actually delivers on all the above, though of course there's nothing breathtakingly original about the group. (If there were, "Beatlesque" would apply better and be irrelevant.) Both John Lennon and Paul McCartney leave solid echoes in Finn's vocals, and his lyrics have a wit and portent that's akin to early Beatles love songs, when they implied they had more to say without actually getting too specific about what it might be.

625 HUNGRY HEART, Bruce Springsteen
Produced by Bruce Springsteen, Jon Landau, Chuck Plotkin, and Steve Van Zandt; written by Bruce Springsteen
Columbia 11391   1980   *Billboard:* #5

Rock and roll natural that he undeniably is, it still took Springsteen five years after "Born to Run" to figure out the mechanics of making a good single and even then, he seemed diffident about the whole thing, as if he mistrusts fixing the kind of fun he has on stage every night in any more permanent form. A hell of an attitude for a guy who once regularly expropriated "Quarter to Three."

"Hungry Heart" erupted out of *The River* (and then, Top 40 radio) with fevered brightness, all splashy drums and keyboards, underpinned by baritone sax and topped off by soaring Flo and Eddie (i.e., post-Turtles Turtles) harmonies and a Springsteen vocal sped up to the limits of pitch control. In its own way, the production is as kitchen-sink as "Born to Run," but that doesn't make it gimmicky, exactly, just lush and elaborate, less angular and hard, more resilient and pop than his other songs of the period. Which is probably exactly why it was the most popular.

Well, that and the lyric, which begins with one of the more disruptive opening couplets of the eighties: "Got a wife and kids in Baltimore, Jack / Went out for a ride and I never came back." Springsteen has a knack for working variations on urban folklore and here's the familiar family legend of the husband and father who goes out for a pack of cigarettes and isn't seen again for twenty years, til he turns up on the doorstep with some vague sob story just like this.

Well, not *just* like this. Out of the mouth of an iconic loner like Springsteen, assertions that "Everybody wants to have a home . . . Ain't nobody like to be alone" acquire a resonance that goes beyond folklore into cultural psychodrama of unusual frankness. Not very many of rock's guitar-lugging hard boys have ever had quite enough guts to acknowledge their vulnerability and desire to be reconciled, to be brought in from the cold hard night of their own aimless rebellions.

Which is maybe another reason why this music revolves around piano and organ, which ain't exactly the instruments you carry on the trail with you.

626 BE-BOP-A-LULA, Gene Vincent
Produced by Ken Nelson; written by Gene Vincent
Capitol 3450   1956   *Billboard: #7*

After Elvis Presley hit with "Heartbreak Hotel," every record label in the business desperately sought a good-looking, spit-curled, white rock and roll singer. Capitol Records, the most upstart of the majors (founded in 1942 by a trio of Hollywood songwriters), was especially desperate, until Sheriff Tex Davis, a Norfolk, Virginia disc jockey, contacted Nashville A&R chief Ken Nelson with a three-song demo tape cut at his station, WCMS, of three songs by Gene Vincent, a young disabled Navy veteran.

Vincent had Presley-like good looks—although his crippled leg, smashed in a motorcycle accident and held together with a brace and tremendous pain, gave him a limp that did nothing to enhance his idolhood. More important, Vincent had a sulky country-blues baritone that fit the new rock and roll songs. And he had the Blue Caps, the band Davis and WCMS station manager, Ray Lamear, assembled around him, including ace guitarist Cliff Gallup. Best of all, Vincent (along with a now unknown collaborator, bought out by Davis) had written a potential hit, "Be-Bop-A-Lula," based on comic strip character Little Lulu, though it would take the comics another decade or so to create a character nearly so sensual.

When Vincent arrived for the May 4, 1956 session at Owen Bradley's Nashville studio, where Buddy Holly had cut his first sides earlier that year, producer Nelson had a session band standing by. But once the producer heard Gallup, there was no question about using the Blue Caps and indeed, the guitarist turned in a pair of concise, cutting breaks that rivaled Scotty Moore's work with Elvis. Vincent's trembling, hiccuping vocal straddled the midpoint between what Elvis had already accomplished (which Gene studied carefully after seeing Presley perform in Hank Snow's show in 1955) and what Holly was about to.

Suffused with the blues and bluegrass he'd heard while sitting on the porch of his parents' general store on the Virginia/North Carolina border, Vincent's "Be-Bop-A-Lula" was typical rockabilly. But unlike most other rockabillies, he understood also how to pull from his material its fundamental theatricality, in which he was abetted enormously by the Blue Caps' showy drumming and bass work. "Be-Bop-A-Lula" also represented a significant early step on the road toward rock-as-product (commodity it was from birth), proof that Sam Phillips wasn't the only smart record professional who could profitably manipulate the new musical synthesis in the studio, and that major labels could do so as effectively as independents.

627 RAPPER'S DELIGHT, The Sugarhill Gang
Produced by Sylvia Robinson; written by Sylvia Robinson, Big Bank Hank Jackson, Wonder Mike Wright, and Master Gee O'Brien
Sugarhill 542   1979   *Billboard:* #36

The first rap record, the one which established the genre's basic format, both musically (the track is a reiteration of the track from Chic's "Good Times") and thematically—the rap is a singsong litany of boasts, gross-outs, boasts, parental wisdom, group introductions which serve as boasts, some tangential ghetto narrative, and boasts. A decade later, "Delight" still sounds fresh, in every sense of the term.

628 MERCY MERCY ME (THE ECOLOGY), Marvin Gaye
Written and produced by Marvin Gaye
Tamla 54207   1971   *Billboard:* #4

Ironic, isn't it, that Save the Earth music became one of the ultimate white-bread genres of the seventies and eighties, a Luddite province that rejected all the musical developments of rock and soul in favor of a return to the false-faced pastoralism of nebulous "folk culture," when the greatest piece of music ever written in favor of the survival of the environment appeared on the greatest black pop album ever made. Of course, Marvin Gaye in the Top Ten is itself a concept (let alone a reality) that violates the precepts of Earth First in half-a-dozen ways.

Yet on "Mercy Mercy Me," the *echo* alone is enough to make you mourn the extinction of Marvin Gaye, a species of musical human being that's at least as endangered (by itself, among many other things) as any whale or rain forest. "Mercy Mercy Me" bows like a willow in a storm, Marvin's voice a cool breeze above supple percussion, unearthly choir, tenor sax thunderation, vibes like wind chimes, a waterfall of guitar and piano chords. Like the great outdoors, it all seems so simple it's barely worth bothering with until you begin to notice that it's made up of the finest details, exquisitely assembled, engulfing everything around it, including the observer.

629 DO YOU BELIEVE IN MAGIC, The Lovin' Spoonful

Produced by Charles Koppleman and Don Rubin; written by John Sebastian
Kama Sutra 201   1965   Billboard: #9

In the summer of 1987, when the media decided that the twentieth anniversary of the Summer of Love was a story worth covering, the Spoonful's John Sebastian was dragged out of mothballs to appear on a talk show, where one of the other guests was me. The question was why the music of that period had such special power. Sebastian insisted that it didn't; he said that the pop songs his generation created—including his own—meant nothing more to us than the swing records that his mother had listened to.

If Sebastian always thought that way—and he hinted that he had— "Do You Believe in Magic" (which centers on the protestation "Believe in the magic that can set you free," and concludes with John Sebastian himself singing "Do you believe like I believe?"), ranks as the most cynical record ever made. Or maybe not, since the story is that Sebastian wrote it after watching teenage girls at the early Lovin' Spoonful shows, when folk-rock was young and respectable collegiates of all ages believed it was restoring vitality to the pop music they'd heretofor disdained.

So "Do You Believe in Magic" is not, like "It Will Stand" or "Drift Away," a loyalty oath or even an anthem, just a description. When Carl Perkins saw the guy who was more concerned with his blue suede shoes than his girlfriend, he thought the guy was a dope but he was enough of a craftsman to recognize a theme. When Sebastian stood on the stage and observed the misty joy his band was inciting, he did the same. But it seems it never meant any more to *him* than the theme to "Welcome Back Kotter," except he probably got paid better for the TV show.

So what do we do with "Do You Believe in Magic," with its great rolling rhythm, wonderful guitar lick and Sebastian's infectious singing? I'd say, you believe the song and forget the singer. You know, claim it, not nickname it.

630 2000 MILES, The Pretenders
Produced by Christmas Thomas; written by Chrissie Hynde
Real (UK) 20   1983   Did not make pop chart

The best new Christmas single of the eighties, and of course it didn't receive a U.S. release until the Pretenders' 1987 greatest hits album. Too bad, cause this is some of the most remarkably evocative music Chrissie Hynde has ever made, a tingly ballad in which she imagines herself in the persona of a woman whose husband is off on the road at the holidays, but puts so much passion into it you know that she's really seeing herself on both sides of the tale. In the cold chill of the greed decade, though, it's her emotional distance from the holiday spirit that tears you up: "I hear people singing / It must be Christmas time," she cries. At that point, two thousand miles or two inches is quite beside the point.

631 DANCE DANCE DANCE (YOWSAH YOWSAH YOWSAH), Chic
Produced by Bernard Edwards and Nile Rodgers; written by
Bernard Edwards, Nile Rodgers, and Kenny Lehman
Atlantic 3435   1977   Billboard: #6

As industrial product, rock and soul records are subject to the same inanities as, say, automobiles and foodstuffs. Meaning that quality matters little unless somebody has figured out how to make a buck from it, and he who deviates from the expected had better find a powerful patron if he wants a reasonable shot at success.

Bernard Edwards and Nile Rodgers had little reputation when they came up with their melange of disco drumming, Edwards's uniquely fluid basswork, punchy horns, disembodied female singers, and a chant that exposed the mock liberation of disco's "dance, dance, dance" obsession, by adding "Yowsah, yowsah, yowsah," an explicit, ironic comment on the fact that within this heralded crossover, black singers and musicians were in fact conforming to a more ancient role, as happy-foot entertainers.

Chic's new synthesis hardly disrupted disco, which proved even more able than most brands of industrialized noise to deflect the potentially deflating. But the message and sound were too radical for the ears of most major record labels. For months, every record label passed on the Chic demo until finally Atlantic's Jerry Greenberg, who got his training as an R&B-oriented promo man, put up the bucks.

Whereupon "Dance Dance Dance" sold a million copies in a month, yowsahs and all, and Edwards and Rodgers became so heavily in demand as producers and arrangers that the most creative of all disco production teams all but burned itself out in less than three years.

632 HEAVEN HELP US ALL, Stevie Wonder
Produced by Ron Miller and Tom Baird; written by Ron Miller
Tamla 54200 1970 *Billboard: #9*

As close to a gospel record as anything Stevie ever recorded, and a crucial stepping-stone to the free-spirited, socially conscious music Wonder would make when he finally became able to call his own shots the next year. The choirlike support gets in the way on the choruses, as choirs are wont to do, but the brilliantly controlled phrasing of the verses radiates the kind of assurance that only Elvis Presley and Ray Charles have been able to bring to material this close to Greeting Card Verse. And the shrieking high notes to which Stevie resorts during the fadeout suggest an equal debt to Aretha Franklin. Wonder's triumph, of course, results precisely from his ability to synthesize the styles of even such giants into something uniquely personal.

633 PUSHIN' TOO HARD, The Seeds
Producer not credited; written by Sky Saxon
GNP Crescendo 372 1966 *Billboard: #36*

The Seeds were Hollywood's first psychedelic heroes, capable of earning six grand a night (according to Lenny Kaye's *Nuggets* liner notes) at a time when $500 was a fortune. Kaye claims their acid-rock orientation was largely the product of shrewd marketing by manager Tim Hudson, though Hudson certainly never intended lead singer Sky Saxon to go as far off the deep end into Tim Leary-land as he later did.

The great thing about "psychedelic" Top 40 from this period is its innocence. Like the Thirteenth Floor Elevators' "You're Gonna Miss Me," which it resembles structurally and in its use of obsessively and unsubtly repeated rhythm devices, "Pushin' Too Hard" mistakes adolescent rebelliousness and flagrant male chauvinism for New Consciousness: "All I want is to just have fun, live my life like it's just begun," Saxon declares in the first verse, seeming to declare war on parents and educators and cops and such, but in the next, he reveals that he's really chastising his girlfriend for "runnin' around all over town."

Oh well. I really only put this one in for its fantastic fuzztone and reverb guitar solo, a landmark in the history of garage-punk trash.

634 THE GYPSY CRIED, Lou Christie
Produced by Nick Cenci; written by Twyla Herbert and Lou Christie
C&C 102   1962   *Billboard:* #24

In 1957, fourteen-year-old Lou Sacco, who grew up to be Lou Christie, formed a group called the Crewnecks with his sister, Amy. They did an audition for a bogus record label in the basement of a church in their exurban Pittsburgh neighborhood and though they got no deal out of it, the occasion may have been fated anyway, for it was in that church basement that Lou Sacco met Twyla Herbert, a bohemian gypsy, psychic, and former concert pianist twice his age.

Over the next few years, Lou sang with the Classics, which included Twyla's daughter, Shirley, with his own Lugee and the Lions, and as a background vocalist with local artists like Marcy Joe. The Classics and the Lions both recorded local label singles, not that they went anywhere.

Then, one night in October 1962, Christie came racing into Herbert's home as Twyla was cooking dinner for her family, declaring he had a song idea. Dinner may not have burned, but in the next fifteen minutes, the music definitely did, and when that quarter hour was up, "The Gypsy Cried" was written right down to its falsetto "yi yi yi." Amy and Lou rehearsed it in their basement, then drove the twenty miles into Pittsburgh to record the song at Two Track Studios, coming up with a master they sold cheap to C&C, a tiny local diskery.

C&C might not have suspected it, but they'd just landed a national hit. The track wasn't much but Christie's falsetto yips were thrilling and the lyric had the spirit and some of the form of recently popular hits by stars like Del Shannon and Gene Pitney. In the song, a guy goes to a gypsy fortune-teller to find out when his girl will marry him. The gypsy just puts her face in her hands and begins to weep, warning him that the girl does not love him. By the time Christie reaches the gypsy's advice, though, he's singing at such an odd kilter that you practically need a map to make out the words: "Wash yer step uhoh shellhurt yeh yeht." The guy's reaction is even better: a careening falsetto "Oh no, no, no," as if the bad news has cut Christie loose of all his emotional moorings.

Although C&C basically condemned him to teen idolhood by licensing his masters to Roulette (it was as Roulette 4457 that "Gypsy" reached the national Top 40 in 1963), Christie managed to make several winning numbers in the same style over the next few years. The most notable was "Two Faces Have I," the immediate follow-up to "Gypsy," but there were also the widely banned "Rhapsody in the Rain," with its "suggestive" rhythmic windshield wipers, the wild, Jack Nitzsche-produced "If My Car Could Only Talk," the quasi-anthemic "Self Expression (The Kids on the Street Will Never Give In)" and "Cryin' in the Streets," and the massively successful "Lightning Strikes." Almost every one of them was the product of the Herbert-Christie collaboration, which kind of makes you wonder if that gypsy wasn't shedding crocodile tears all the way to the bank.

635 SUMMER OF '69, Bryan Adams
Produced by Bryan Adams and Bob Clearmountain; written by Bryan Adams and Jim Vallance
A&M 2739   1985   *Billboard:* #5

636 GET BACK, The Beatles
Produced by George Martin; written by John Lennon and Paul McCartney
Apple 2490   1969   *Billboard:* #1 (5 weeks)

Nostalgia is a time-proven failure as a remedy for anything that ails anybody, but that doesn't mean it doesn't have value as a pop music resource. It doesn't matter what your summer was—mine was '66, Bryan Adams says his *wasn't* '69, John Lennon pointed to '57 and "Whole Lotta Shakin'." What counts is an accumulation of experiences and sensations against which you'll perhaps measure the rest of your life. If it comes along early and intensely enough, a malcontent (or a critic or a journalist or maybe even a certain breed of pop star) may be born.

Bryan Adams looks at all this more simply: He's stalking a moment when time seemed to freeze, when simple things—good, right, and true—abounded, a moment that ought to be mythical but in many lives tangibly and persuasively presents itself as a yardstick for future and past alike. And if he didn't choose 1969 as a matter of autobiography, maybe he selected it because he's part of an entire generation that's had the mass-scale pop events of the sixties rubbed in its face for what's already almost half a lifetime (or about eight pop lifetimes, if you measure these things on the scale most pundits use).

Paul McCartney felt much the same way during the sixties themselves, but he had nastier facts to take into account, like the ongoing disintegration of the drug-based counterculture the Beatles had helped spawn. For if 1969 was the year of Woodstock, it was also the year of Altamont and the road to the Manson Family, paved by a few thousand kilowatts too intense an interpretation of the White Album. When the "Get Back" session started, maybe McCartney intended to sing only about music, proposing a return to values learned from Little Richard and Fats Domino (thanks to Billy Preston, the sound's most obvious antecedents) but "Get Back" quickly sets itself up as an admonition to hippies: Jo-Jo of the first verse (could he be kin to John Fogerty's oft-admonished Jody?) leaves home for south Arizona and California grass, the kind of venture McCartney and his brethren had saluted only a year or two before but at which they now looked askance.

With more than two decades gone by, it may be possible to be quite happily nostalgic about 1969, but maintaining that front was damn near impossible in the waning days of the sixties. And on the other hand, I think that Adams made a slightly more exciting record. So what does that prove? That the illusion of the past is more powerful than the facts about it, or that things have soured so badly that even the spectacle of hope debauched and deranged is better than none at all?

637 KHARMA CHAMELEON, Culture Club
Produced by Steve Levine; written by George O'Dowd [Boy George], Jon Moss, Roy Hay, Mikey Craig, and Phil Pickett
Epic 04221   1983   *Billboard:* #1 (3 weeks)

638 INSTANT KARMA (WE ALL SHINE ON), John Lennon
Produced by Phil Spector; written by John Lennon
Apple 18181   1970   *Billboard:* #3

In rock mythology, the big distinction is made between the sixties and the seventies, but as Lennon's record (a sixties swan song) and Boy George's demonstrate, the sixties and the eighties contrast more starkly. Both records toy with the idea of "karma" as a symbol of cosmic comeuppance for the star-struck, but while it's interesting that pop stars of such different generations, with the careers of their peers splayed out before them like so many used-up Corn Kings, return to a concept steeped in rebirth, there the resemblance ends.

Over the clunkiest track Phil Spector ever produced, Lennon does his best to level himself, not in order to obliterate his own superstardom but as a means to (at least theoretically) elevate everybody else. By "instant karma" he seems to mean immediate consequences. Having just emerged from the cocoon of the Beatles, he spoke with tremendous authority about the havoc wreaked by trying to keep your head in the valet-attended clouds. Whether he's identified a universally applicable cosmic revenge principle is harder to say.

Where Boy George and Culture Club come from, authority means nothing. In their version of pop culture, authority is powerless and it's around that conundrum that they base their song. "Lovin' would be easy if your colors were like my dreams," declares George, over the slickest soul track his group ever made. For him, consequences can be avoided by becoming a changeling who eschews anything resembling permanent allegiance. Permanence itself may be the problem: "I'm a man without conviction," George says and then without a wink, "I'm a man who doesn't know / How to sell a contradiction." But of course, that's all he's ever sold.

Boy George sings as if in toying with the idea of a love that might last, a future that might actually come to exist, he's found the greatest sorrow of his life. And the harmonica backs him up. Lennon, for all his espousals of faith, struggles to keep up with the inexorable cadences of guitar and drum. Neither, in the end, mastered fate at all.

639 IT'S MY LIFE, The Animals
Produced by Mickey Most; written by Roger Atkins and Carl D'Errico
MGM 13414   1965   *Billboard:* #23

What do the two New York hustlers who wrote this song have in common with the quintet of coal miners' sons from Newcastle, England who made it a hit? A singular emotional fury, established with Chas Chandler's ominous bass notes at the very top, and capped with Eric Burdon's teeth-clenched "Don't push me!" just before the fade.

640 HOLLYWOOD SWINGIN', Kool and the Gang
Produced by Ronald "Kool" Bell and K & G Productions; written by
Ricky West and Kool and the Gang
De-Lite 561   1974   *Billboard: #6*

A great band—one of the first full-fledged funk ensembles, ranking
among the aristocracy of black album rock—celebrates itself. The swing
reference in the title is no brag, just fact. Like most rock and soul,
Kool's is syncretic: the guitars are straight out of James Brown, the
bass line and vocal wails sound like the Family Stone. But if the horn
charts and vocal chants feel reminiscent, that's because the Gang provided the format for about a quarter of the funk that's come down the
pike since.

641 I'LL TRY SOMETHING NEW, The Miracles
Produced by Smokey Robinson and Berry Gordy; written by
Smokey Robinson
Tamla 54059   1962   *Billboard: #39*

It's probably always a mistake to presume what anybody was up to in
the past, especially when what happened seems to have been foreor-
dained. Today, for instance, it's regarded as indisputable that Berry
Gordy and his companions at Motown wanted to bring rhythm and
blues power to the Top 40 as a way of crossing over into greater personal
wealth and power.

But what if Gordy and his colleagues, including Smokey Robinson,
his best friend, just wanted to get over, any which way they could, and
transformed the Top 40 while fumbling around looking for fool's gold?
The facts don't change but history does because a lot of our suppositions
have to be altered.

And listening to "I'll Try Something New" today, you have to
wonder. The Miracles hadn't had a really big hit since "Shop Around,"
eighteen months (that is, half an eon) before. And their fortunes hadn't
been much fairer on the national R&B chart. Outside of Detroit, who'd
ever even heard of these guys?

So they were free to experiment. Not only free to do so, but im-
periled if they didn't. In that light, even the title of this tribute to the
power of romantic imagination might have spurred them to seek novelty. As producer, Berry Gordy had the first and perhaps the most
elaborately constructed of all Smokey's extended metaphor songs to

work with, but he already knew a good song wouldn't cut it alone. So they tried some Johnny Mathis moves, plunged Robinson's lead vocal deep in echo, introduced the melody with a harp and carried it forward with string flourishes. They made a pop record, and discarded R&B ambition for the moment.

Maybe that's not how it happened. But that's what it sounds like. Except that, seeing as how that's Smokey Robinson, not Johnny Mathis at the mike, the results are still touching.

642 PSYCHO, Elvis Costello
Produced by Elvis Costello; written by Leon Payne
F-Beat XX19 (UK)   1981   Did not make pop chart

Written and first recorded by the great blind country writer/performer Leon Payne ("Lost Highway," "I Love You Because"), "Psycho" is nevertheless as great a vehicle as Elvis Costello has ever found for the darkest particularities of his own vision. Recorded live at the Palomino, a Los Angeles country club, in February 1979, Costello's portrayal of a homicidal maniac is most remarkable for the complete composure and assurance with which he delivers it.

Costello was still living in the aftermath of the notorious Ohio barroom incident in which he characterized Ray Charles and James Brown as "niggers." Although that incident didn't ruin his commercial career in the States (as he'd later claim), Costello must have taken it as a sign that his flirtation with pop stardom had done some psychic damage. He retreated to whole albums of country and soul music. And came across Payne's song, on an obscure 45.

Costello conveys psychosis by entering an imperturbable calm, greatly aided by the lyric, which opens with the singer demanding fried fish from his mother, sighing exhaustedly at the crying of his baby, and in the same tired but inexpressive voice, confessing to two murders. An edge of tension rises as he enters the chorus. "You think I'm psycho, don't you, momma," he croons and then, without any pause or alteration of tone, "I didn't mean to break your cup."

This isn't a song that Costello would have written; its kitsch is too naked to satisfy his writerly aspirations. But there's no other singer who could have so fully encompassed both the singer's dissociation from his own actions and his absolute engulfment in self-pity. At the end, when he finally notices, with the rising inflection of traditional country, that the only woman he ever loved is dead, you've tapped close to the heart of a dementia more widespread than Leon Payne and a horde of textbook writers could ever guess. Costello has actually become the kind of guy whose life Bruce Springsteen took notes upon for *Nebraska*.

643 DIDN'T I (BLOW YOUR MIND THIS TIME), The Delfonics
Produced by Stan Watson and Thom Bell; written by Thom Bell and William Hart
Philly Groove 161   1970   *Billboard:* #10

One of Thom Bell's finest songs and arrangements: Gorgeous harmonies, lovely upper-register exclamations, orchestration that never strays across the fine line between the dramatic and the bombastic, a guitar that actually dares to suggest grunge amidst such pristine surroundings.

644 WE GOT MORE SOUL, Dyke and the Blazers
Produced by Art Laboe and Art Barrett; written by Arlester (Dyke) Christian
Original Sound 86   1969   *Billboard:* #35

645 SWEET SOUL MUSIC, Arthur Conley
Produced by Otis Redding; written by Otis Redding and Arthur Conley
Atco 6463   1967   *Billboard:* #2

The R&B tribute song by now is a tradition, which it wasn't when Otis Redding helped his protege, Arthur Conley, rewrite Sam Cooke's "Yeah Man" and created a litany in which Conley turned the spotlight on (consecutively) Lou Rawls, Sam and Dave, Wilson Pickett, Otis himself, and finally James Brown ("He's the king of 'em all, y'all," a heavy admission coming from Redding). It was too late to put the spotlight on Cooke, but despite the distinctively Memphis horns, Conley's singing is even closer to Sam's turn of phrase than Otis's was. Which may have had a lot to do with why Redding, who idolized Sam Cooke, took Conley under his wing in the first place.

There are those who believe that "Sweet Soul Music" is over the top, that Conley's performance is a parody of soul rather than the real stuff. To me, it seems like Otis's best outside production, and it's unquestionably a major improvement on Sam Cooke's song, which is so roughly mixed you have to suspect that it never would have seen the light of day if he'd lived. (It was released on *Shake*, his first posthumous album.)

If you want to hear soul-as-parody, consider Spyder Turner's exercise in long distance ventriloquy, a remake of "Stand By Me" that features not just invocations of soul superstars' names but Turner's actual impersonations of them: He presents Ben E. King's greatest hit as Jackie Wilson, David Ruffin, Billy Stewart, Smokey Robinson, and Chuck Jackson might sing it. Now *that's* over the top.

Dyke and the Blazers seem to exist in a parallel universe to all this. Their sound is as crude as "Yeah Man," but it's clearly deliberately designed to be sketchy, as befits a leader of funk's rebellion against soul's increasing slickness. Over slicing guitar, wicked saxes, and bottomless bass and drums, Dyke urgently grunts out a list of those who've "got more soul" (than who or what he never spells out), a lethal pantheon that includes Ray Charles, James Brown, Johnnie Taylor, Aretha Franklin, Nancy Wilson . . . Wait a minute. *Nancy Wilson*?! The supper club singer? That's so weird it's as if Arthur Conley replaced Sam and Dave with Sammy Davis Jr. No wonder Dyke had so much trouble getting folks to pay attention, even when he made music as dark and rich as this.

646 SEARCHING FOR MY LOVE, Bobby Moore & the Rhythm Aces
Produced by Rick Hall; written by Bobby Moore
Checker 1129   1966   *Billboard:* #27

One of the first pop hits to make its way out of Rick Hall's Fame Studios, "Searching for My Love" doesn't feature the redoubtable Muscle Shoals house band but Moore's own journeyman soul group. Even so, the record's light but durable groove and Moore's softly preaching style is classic Muscle Shoals, and that's something Moore, a guy who'd been kicking around the South for fifteen years as opening act for everyone from Otis Redding to Mitty Collier, deserves.

647 SAY BOSS MAN, Bo Diddley
Producer not credited; written by Ellas McDaniel
[Bo Diddley]
Checker 878   1957   Did not make pop chart

In which Bo, ninety-three days behind on the rent and saddled with nineteen hungry, shoeless children, tries to extract blood from a stone, by convincing his boss to give him his job back after a strike. Or at least, it seems like the boss must be made of stone, if he won't dance to this spectacularly slinky version of Bo's tune.

648 (I WANNA) TESTIFY, The Parliaments
Produced by George Clinton; written by D. Taylor and George Clinton
Revilot 207   1967   Billboard: #20

Before George Clinton became King of Cosmic Slop, he led the Parliaments (which begat Funkadelic, which merged into the Parliafunkadelicment Thang, which begat the Mothership) as Motor City mini-Temptations, and crafted one near-perfect example of soul-funk. "Testify" rumbles in at 2:50, at which point latter-day Clinton works are just beginning to lift off, and rather than washes of bass 'n' drums 'n' percussion 'n' synth 'n' keyboard 'n' voice 'n' what-have-you, it offers the kind of carefully sculpted bass, drum, and guitar licks that made the Tempts so powerful in their Norman Whitfield period.

Except that "Testify" predates "Psychedelic Shack" and "Cloud Nine," which probably means that the smart ears at Motown were listening, just as Clinton's own smart ears were picking up on what was happening, not only with Sly and James Brown (whose bassist, Bootsy Collins, soon enough became absorbed into George's funkadelicized milieu) but in the burgeoning land of Anglo-American acid-rock. As a result, George became the godfather of black album rock, hastening the demise of singles culture altogether. "Testify" cuts a groove so sharp, deep, and nasty you'll forgive him for it.

649 YOU MAKE ME FEEL BRAND NEW, The Stylistics

Produced by Thom Bell; written by Thom Bell and Linda Creed
Avco 4634   1974   *Billboard: #2*

The Stylistics' last Thom Bell-produced hit was also their last Top Ten single. Also, one of their best, thanks to Linda Creed's sweetest lyric, a Bell arrangement that redefines soul cool in its own image (the opening string crescendo is ridiculously overblown and he makes you feel that it's somehow appropriate to the occasion), and a Russell Thompkins lead in which every single phrase is uttered so precisely that you'd think that getting an emotional nuance wrong was a capital offense in Philadelphia.

Even if it was, everybody involved in this record would survive.

650 A SUNDAY KIND OF LOVE, The Harptones

Produced by George Goldner; written by Barbara Belle, Louis Prima, Anita Leonard, and Stan Rhodes
Bruce 101   1953   Did not make pop chart

A great song (about ten years old by the time the Harptones got hold of it) yet anything but a great production. Nevertheless, the moment that Willie Winfield's breathtaking tenor enters, with a lingering "I want a Sunday kind of love," the sketchy organ backing and crude sound quality hardly matter. This is simply one of the all-time doo-wop leads, reason enough by itself for Winfield to have earned the nickname "Sultan of Smooth." The Harptones' harmonies are also fine, but it's Winfield's voice that raises them above the merely good; this "artisan of perfect pitch" got it right emotionally, as well. He'd have been one of the outstanding pop singers in any era.

651 JAM ON IT, Newcleus

Produced by Joe Webb and Frank Fair; written by M. B. Cenac
Sunnyview 3010   1984   *Billboard: #56*

The finest novelty record of the eighties is also indicative of one of hip-hop's more lovable qualities: a sense of humor, especially about itself (which brings into focus just how self-serious most dance music—let alone rock—tends to be).

A virtually all-electronic extravaganza, "Jam On It" features a great bass line and sped-up voices that achieve a funkiness beyond the Chipmunks' wildest dreams. It's the story of an interstellar b-boy, Cosmo D from Outer Space, who comes to Earth to "rock the human race." Cosmo presents the ultimate rapper's boast, grunted over a bleating synth: He's not just the finest dancer on the planet, he's the best in the whole universe, and not only that, he comes from a planet where nearly everybody moves this good.

Meantime, the cosmic Chipmunks natter on, chanting "wikki-wikki-wikki" and "Jam oh-n it, jam *oh*-n it," then lapsing into a final verse whose wimpy precision takes rap boasting to even more ridiculous extremes. And all the while, the bass digs a groove so deep, you'd have to blast off to avoid it.

652 RIP VAN WINKLE, The Devotions
Producer not credited; written by Ray Sanchez
Roulette 4541   1964   *Billboard:* #36

With its bowling alley sound effects and Woody Woodpecker-like giggling gremlins, "Rip Van Winkle" stands as the great sixties precursor of "Jam On It." The lyric, retelling the Washington Irving fable with basso-falsetto exaggeration, is just about as outré as the Newcleus tale of dance divas from outer space, too.

653 2 + 2 = ?, Bob Seger
Produced by Bob Seger and Punch Andrews; written by Bob Seger
Capitol 6/59   1968   Did not make pop chart

Rock and roll's role as a central force in waging the war against the war in Vietnam is overrated. Although lots of antiwar activists listened to pop records, very few of those records paid much attention to the combat zone. Not many even dealt with the draft, an issue more immediately relevant in the lives of both musicians and audience.

This is more true of singles-oriented rock than its album-based counterpart, but the discrepancy isn't as great as you might think. Memorable rock records about Vietnam or even the draft are simply scarce, and records from the period are even rarer. After all, it's not that easy to write a song about foreign policy, and it was damn near impossible to get one on the radio—even if it supported the war that nobody much wanted to acknowledge was going on. Unless you count "Alice's Restaurant," there wasn't a major hit single opposing our role in Vietnam until "Bring the Boys Home." It would take more than a decade until a white rocker had that much nerve. ("Ohio" doesn't count because it's about domestic insurrection and leaves the Southeast Asian question alone.)

So it took a lot of guts for Bob Seger to release "2+2=?" as the followup to his first Top 20 hit, "Ramblin' Gamblin' Man." In the teeth of Tet and Khe Sanh, Seger raged explicitly against the basic human mathematics of the conflict and came up with the right answers: "It's the statesmen not the soldiers that are my real enemy."

"2+2=?" is a thunderous crash of a record, with phased cymbals, pounding toms and snares, and a honking guitar. Seger's finest achievement, though, was his lyric, which spelled out the inequity of what was going on in terms stark and terrorized, first describing his own hatred of war and the men who might make him fight it, then telling about a high school friend, "just an average friendly guy" who is sent to fight and winds up "buried in the mud of a foreign jungle land." And then he turns on the full fury of his Wilson Pickett voice and his overamped band:

> So you say he died for freedom
> What if he died to save your lies—
> Go ahead and call me yellow
> Two plus two is on my mind

If you wanted to know how much America had changed in a year, you could note that in 1967, Seger (as the Beach Bums, but the voice was unmistakable) had recorded a half-joking anti-draft dodger number, "Ballad of the Yellow Berets." Had he come full circle as the result of some real life encounter with his draft board? Because a friend really had stepped on a land mine? Or was he just sick of watching the carnage on the news each night?

Cynics will say he spotted a chance to cash in, but if so, it was a ridiculous long shot. Seger's singles always sold fifty to a hundred thousand copies on the basis of airplay in and around Detroit, but "2+2=?" could barely get on the radio at all. It flopped miserably until the following autumn, when the massive response to the National Mobilization against the war encouraged Capitol to once more promote it. But there still wasn't enough support and the record remains buried, an unknown, minor, but still brave casualty of the conflict.

654 POURING WATER ON A DROWNING MAN, James Carr

Produced by Quinton Claunch and Rudolph V. "Doc" Russell;
written by D. Baker and D. McCormick
Goldwax 311   1966   Billboard: #33

The damnedest cults form around musicians, and for the damnedest reasons. In the annals of deep Southern soul, James Carr never ranked with the true geniuses—compared to Otis Redding, he was inarguably minor league—though he was something more than a journeyman. His records convey tremendous feeling at a fever pitch but without the deep, restless intelligence of Redding or Aretha Franklin. With a ravaged voice whose timbre suggests Wilson Pickett and Solomon Burke, Carr sang with more power than grace, more intensity than craftsmanship. And churned out a couple of timeless records, among them "Pouring Water (On a Drowning Man)," in which he makes you feel every bit of the inundation metaphor.

These days, though, Carr may be best-known not for his fine music but for his near-catatonic mental condition, which arguably prevented his career from ever reaching the heights of the more famous singers to whom he's often compared. Fact is, his lack of national stature probably has more to do with the fact that he cut his sides for tiny Goldwax rather than Stax/Volt or Atlantic than anybody's schizophrenia.

But don't be deterred by the fact that his biggest fans often miss the point of his life and career. "I guess I missed my calling / I shoulda been a clown," James Carr rasps here. But he's wrong—with a voice like his, he must have been born to sing the blues.

655 U.S. MALE, Elvis Presley

No producer credited; written by Jerry Reed
RCA 47-9465   1968   Billboard: #28

They say that Elvis Presley's late sixties comeback—the greatest artistic resurrection in show biz history—began with his TV special at Christmastime in 1968. But for me, he'd already been all the way back for six or eight months by then. I first heard "U.S. Male" shivering in a car that March, while cutting class for a long lunch, and immediately knew that his voice had returned with a force that it hadn't had for years. More than anything else, "U.S. Male" restored to Elvis the very

Southernness that the movies denied him. And with that restoration, his mythic power was also reborn.

"Now I'm a U.S. male 'cause I was born," he began, as the Jordanaires hummed a chord behind him, "in a Miss'ssippi town on a Sunday morn. Now Miss'ssippi just happens to occupy a place, in the Southeastern portion of this here U-nited States. Now that's a matter of fact, buddy, and you know it well. So I just call myself the U.S. male." Jerry Reed's country boogie guitar jangled. "That's m-a-l-e, son. That's me." Then the tempo picked up and Elvis stunned me: He started to sing, bearing down on the hard guy lyrics, not sending them up or overplaying them but tossing them around with that astonishingly tough yet gentle assurance that he brought to his Sun records.

I'm not saying "U.S. Male" was really as good as his fifties hits, or that Elvis didn't do better on the TV show and in the records that followed the special. But what he did on "U.S. Male" cut to the heart of who he was, acknowledged who we wanted him to be, and toyed with the discrepancy.

Although "U.S. Male" wasn't a chart-topper (and chart-topping was intrinsic to full Elvishood), it remains a fascinating first step back. For even if what you remembered best about Elvis was not his musicality but his physicality, the distinguishing mark of that physicality was the half-conscious sneer that marked him as a hillbilly punk and proud of it. And not only is that exactly the character "U.S. Male" is about, by the time he's finished with that introduction—by the time he coolly pronounces, "That's me"—you can feel the sneer in a way that *no* other Elvis record delivers quite so forcefully.

656 REVOLUTION, The Beatles
Produced by George Martin; written by John Lennon and Paul McCartney
Apple 2276   1968   *Billboard:* #12

Perhaps the truest Beatles *single* of all, since they recorded it twice, changing not only the music but the message. Although it appears on the White Album as a softened up blues with Lennon announcing "You can count me in," the real gem is the 45, with its ferocious fuzztone rock and roll attack and Lennon snarling "You can count me *out*." Not a progressive sentiment but as regards those who went around carrying pictures of Chairman Mao, he was right. And Lennon self-righteous could be a wonder to behold.

657 BREAK UP TO MAKE UP, The Stylistics
Produced by Thom Bell; written by Thom Bell, Linda Creed, and Kenneth Gamble
Avco 4611   1973   *Billboard: #5*

Sometimes, Russell Thompkins phrases so carefully that he seems to be singing phonetically, like a visitor from the Planet of Falsetto Ecstasy (don't know how to get there personally but sign me up if you're going out to explore). But then, consider what Russell's trying to do here: Talk sense to his girl in the midst of a fight. In such a dialogue, you'd *better* choose each syllable with great deliberation, especially if you're going to risk criticizing her phone conversations with her girlfriends. Not that it'll do you all that much good, but you've got to try, just to get the basic point across: "Break up to make up / That's all we do / First you love me, then you hate me / That's a game for fools." And everybody plays the fool sometimes.

658 I DON'T WANT TO CRY, Chuck Jackson
Produced by Luther Dixon; written by Chuck Jackson and Luther Dixon
Wand 106   1961   *Billboard: #36*

Jackson's first national hit exemplifies the virtues of early sixties New York R&B: A terrific song, slickly arranged by Carole King with cascades of rhythmic strings, quasi-classical piano part, and a busy, Latin-accented beat, all in service of a hoarse, gritty but polished and controlled vocal performance. Producer Dixon's best idea was working out a call-and-response between Chuck and the cellos on the chorus, but the point about such records is that the inspiration was the result of genuinely collaborative efforts and the only measurement that mattered was the result in terms of airplay, sales, and maybe, just before they called it a day, an exchanged glance of mutual gratification.

659 WHY CAN'T WE BE FRIENDS, War
Produced by Jerry Goldstein, Lonnie Jordan, and Howard Scott; written by Papa Dee Allen, Harold Brown, B.B. Dickerson, Jerry Goldstein, Lonnie Jordan, Charles Miller, Lee Oskar, and Howard Scott [War]
United Artists 629   1975   *Billboard:* #6

High-spirited, socially conscious pop-funk of the sort that had by 1975 all but died out in the face of disco's singleminded onslaught. The beat—with its dolorous horns and Caribbean accents—may well be more fashionable in the late eighties than when it first popped up, and the lyrics, partly ghetto dozens playing in which everybody takes a turn, partly political cartoon, have never been more applicable than today. I mean, "I hear you're workin' for the CIA / They wouldn't have you in the Maf-eye-ay" is the Christic Institute's Conspiracy Theory expressed with more precision than Jackson Browne's ever managed.

660 AIN'T THAT A SHAME, Fats Domino
Produced by Dave Bartholomew; written by Fats Domino and Dave Bartholomew
Imperial 5348   1955   *Billboard:* #10

Fats placed a total of sixty-six songs on the pop charts alone—a bunch more made the national R&B lists, and some great stuff never escaped New Orleans (or for that matter, Imperial's vaults). "Ain't That a Shame" was his first to hit pop, and one of the most characteristic of a style that never rocked any harder than it needed to but never relented a whit, either. The piano communicates so much joy, it never drowns the sadness of the lyric in its own sweetness. Part of his not giving in, however, is Fats's insistence on this bright little rocker carrying the weight of that contradiction without ever resolving it.

661 NADINE, Chuck Berry
Produced by Leonard Chess; written by Chuck Berry
Chess 1883   1964   *Billboard:* #23

Perhaps the most modern sounding of all Chuck's records, maybe because of the droning sax that drools its libidinousness straight through every chorus. Meantime, Chuck's out there with the usual on his mind—trying to catch up to Nadine, just like with Maybellene, though by now he's so frantic that he takes the desperate step (for this notorious tight-wad) of ditching the city bus he's riding, flagging down an occupied cab, paying the occupants' tab and tossing the driver a twenty to put him in hot pursuit.

As with so many of Berry's post-prison hits, his interplay with pianist Johnny Johnson is at its most intense and the imagery ranks with his finest—not just the "coffee colored Cadillac" of yore but Chuck leaving the bus "campaign shoutin' like a Southern diplomat."

662 TOO BUSY THINKING ABOUT MY BABY, Marvin Gaye

Produced by Norman Whitfield; written by Norman Whitfield and
Janie Bradford
Tamla 54181   1969   *Billboard: #4*

Poised to make a break with conventional soul music, Marvin recorded this utterly conventional song with the air of a man wandering the hallways of his home, musing to himself. Only this was a man with the courage to put those musings on public display. Is this courage or foolishness? In a way, what making his break with convention was all about was finding the answer to that question. Thirteen years later, after "Sexual Healing," he was no closer to an answer and neither were we.

663 WANG DANG DOODLE, Koko Taylor

Written and produced by Willie Dixon
Checker 1135   1966   *Billboard: #58*

The only female hit in the history of Chicago blues owes at least as much to Buddy Guy's ringing guitar as to Koko Taylor's growls, but not as much as it owes to Willie Dixon's amazingly vivid portrayal of a hot, hard Saturday night on the South Side. In fact, the cast has enough wild names to make up a whole album for Springsteen or Dylan: Automatic Slim, Razor Totin' Jim, Butcher Knife Totin' Annie, Fast Talkin' Fannie, Boudoir Crawlin' Red, Abyssinia Ned, Pistol Pete, Fats, Washboard Sam, Shaky, Boxcar Joe, Peggy and Caroline Dime. Hell, even Brecht and Weill would be humbled by such a list.

And with that lineup, who cares that these lyrics are probably a bowdlerized version of a song far more salty in an unrecorded original in which "Fast Talkin' " translates as an activity more lewd and the scent that fills the air is more pungent than mere fish. The intensity with which Taylor anticipates the evening's events makes it obvious enough that they're planning to pitch a very specific kind of ball down to the union hall.

664 I'LL BE AROUND, The Spinners
Produced by Thom Bell; written by Thom Bell and Phil Hurtt
Atlantic 2904   1972   *Billboard:* #3

Throughout the seventies and well into the eighties, soul vocalists generally, and black harmony groups in particular, suffered from the ready-made and often relatively inflexible structures necessitated by contemporary tastes in rhythm and production. In part, what made Thom Bell so great was that his productions with the Stylistics and the Spinners found ways to circumvent the dominance of the beat and restore some space to the vocalists.

"I'll Be Around" basically takes the shape of a solo by Spinners' leader Philippe Wynne. (His vocal backups certainly aren't the Spinners, being female.) And superficially Wynne isn't given much to work with—essentially just one extended motif, without a verse-chorus structure.

But that's part of Bell's strategy. The lack of song structure frees the music to develop in increments of intensity, kicking off with a guitar and bongo groove, adding instruments as Wynne ups the emotional voltage. The result is not only kinetic and eminently danceable but expressive of the singer's gut determination not to let his lover slip away without an epic battle.

665 AIN'T GOT NO HOME, Clarence "Frogman" Henry
Produced by Paul Gayten; written by Clarence "Frogman" Henry
Argo 5259   1956   *Billboard:* #20

New Orleans had the best sense of humor of all the rock and roll capitals, and on purely musical terms, "Ain't Got No Home" may be the funniest of all New Orleans hits. Henry had a terrific voice and five years later he played "But I Do," his biggest hit, perfectly straight, but here, he's more concerned with establishing a certain type of versatility. "I sing like a girl / And I sing like a frog," Henry declares at the outset and he's not kidding a bit. Soon enough, the guy you're feeling bad for because society's given him no place to rest his head becomes a girl who lacks a lover and a song, then transmutes into a frog whose worries stem, I guess, from his lack of family just as the local swamps are drying up. In their entire careers, neither Prince or Michael Jackson has come up with anything quite *this* strange.

666 ROCKIN' ROBIN, Bobby Day
Produced by Googie Rene; written by Jimmie Thomas
Class 229   1958   *Billboard: #2*

Bobby Day, who also sang under his real name, Bobby Byrd (which would never have done here, I guess) made some of the wildest L.A. doo-wop records: the original "Little Bitty Pretty One" (Thurston Harris had the bigger hit with a black-on-black cover version), the Hollywood Flames' "Buzz Buzz Buzz," and on his own, "Over and Over" (same one that Dave Clark later hit with), "The Bluebird, the Buzzard and the Oriole" (a "Rockin' Robin" sequel) and others.

Of them all, the best is "Rockin' Robin," which picks up where "Little Bitty Pretty One" left off. The beat and "tweedlee-dee-dee / tweet tweet" harmonies are light but the drums play a killer shuffle, and there are a batch of nice touches—the super-syncopated handclaps, the trilling flute, Day's own tongue-twisting vocal, and perhaps the funniest metaphor for sexual prowess ever composed: "He outbopped the buzzard and the oriole." You don't say.

667 I'D RATHER GO BLIND, Etta James
Produced by Rick Hall; written by Ellington Jordan and Billy Foster
Cadet 5578   1967   Did not make pop chart

Etta made her excursion to Muscle Shoals during a brief intermission from heroin addiction, and turned out one of the best two-sided female soul singles of all time. The hit was "Tell Mama," but the unforgettable side was "I'd Rather Go Blind," a more languorous version of the Southern soul groove. Although she came from California by way of Chess in Chicago, Etta sang those Muscle Shoals blues like she'd been born to them. Of course, the fact that the song provides a great metaphor for her drug addiction intensifies the story, even if lyrical discretion requires replacing smack with booze. But what you're here for is just as much Jimmy Johnson's great guitar and the grand Bowlegs Miller-led horn section.

668 HURT, Elvis Presley
Produced by Felton Jarvis; written by Jimmy Crane and Al Jacobs
RCA PB 10601   1976   *Billboard: #28*

His last great bellow. If he felt the way he sounded, the wonder isn't that he had only a year left to live but that he managed to survive that long.

669 GOODNIGHT MY LOVE, Jesse Belvin
Produced by George Motola; written by George Motola and Jesse Belvin
Modern 1005   1956   *Did not make pop chart*

Jesse Belvin was the king of L.A. doo-wop. A prolific composer, a fabulous mellow balladeer, studio singer without peer, Belvin began recording with Big Jay McNeely's band while still in his teens. Although he didn't live to see thirty, he was responsible for a wide range of hits including the Penguins' "Earth Angel" (which many believe he wrote, though he lost the credit), "So Fine" by the Sheiks (later a bigger, though still minor, hit for the Fiestas), the Cliques' "The Girl in My Dreams" (a duo he formed with Eugene Church), "You Cheated" by the Shields (where he stepped in as falsetto lead with a preexisting group) and under his own name in a variety of guises for a bewildering variety of labels from the smallest one-shot indies to one of the biggest, RCA, for whom he was working at the time of his death in a February 1960 car crash. He was only twenty-eight years old.

Belvin sang just about every kind of fifties R&B but his specialty was crooning. Stylistically, "Goodnight My Love" stands midway between the smooth piano blues of Charles Brown and Nat "King" Cole and the rawer, more gospel-inflected sounds that came from Sam Cooke (upon whom Belvin was a major influence) and his successors. Though the arrangement features strings and a full female chorus, the only part that really matters is Belvin's vocal, intoning verses guaranteed to melt any dream date at her doorstep. You don't have to buy a word of it to wither a little yourself.

670 LUCILLE, Little Richard
Produced by Bumps Blackwell; written by Richard Penniman and Albert Collins
Specialty 598   1957   *Billboard:* #21

The Moral Purity types who flail at eighties rock claim to love the rock and soul of the fifties and sixties. So I'd sure like to hear one of them explain "Lucille," which represents in my view rock's apogee of Sexual Kink.

Against a sly and insinuating beat, Little Richard screams like a man with a week-old erection: "Lucille, you won't do your sister's will!" And as if that allusion to the pleasures and deflations of an incestuous menage weren't enough, he continues in a similar vein, reaching an apogee of agony when he describes the aftermath of their orgiastic trysts:

> I woke up this morning, Lucille was not in sight
> I asked my friends about 'er but all they did was cry . . .
> Lucille!

Now, some of the censors would no doubt explain that this reads too much into what is, after all, nothing more than a song about a guy trying to get his girlfriend back, and that when he cries for her to "satisfy my heart . . . You lay down with me baby and gave me such a wonderful start," Richard speaks only metaphorically. But he wasn't, even though many of their targets are.

671 DADDY'S HOME, Shep and the Limelites
Producer not credited; written by James "Shep" Sheppard
Hull 740   1961   *Billboard:* #2

672 A THOUSAND MILES AWAY, The Heartbeats
Producer not credited; written by James Sheppard and W. Miller
Hull 720   1956   *Billboard:* #53

673 I'M ALL ALONE, Shep and the Limelites
Producer not credited; written by James Sheppard
Hull 767   1962   Did not make pop chart

You think Frank Zappa or Pete Townshend or Ray Davies or Brian Wilson or the Beatles are big deals because they invented the "concept album"? Years before any of them dreamed of entering a record studio, James "Shep" Sheppard invented the concept single. Virtually every 45 his two groups, the Heartbeats and Shep and the Limelites, released over a period of six years was part of the same yarn, an ongoing saga of a boy, a girl, and the physical and emotional distance between them. By the end of the tale, they had been married and separated and the singer was sitting by himself, reviewing their whole relationship, from beginning to end.

The sequence began not with "A Thousand Miles Away" but three singles earlier, with "Crazy for You," in which Shep declared his mad devotion. "A Thousand Miles Away," the Heartbeats' finest record and a doo-wop landmark, was written after Sheppard's real-life girl-friend moved to Texas, literally a thousand miles from Queens, the New York City borough whence the Heartbeats hailed. That one was a major hit, especially on the East Coast.

The Heartbeats made five follow-ups to "A Thousand Miles Away," each extending the story. On the A side of the fourth, "After New Year's Eve," the couple is reunited and make plans for a future together. On the flip, "500 Miles to Go" (not the Bobby Bare country hit), Shep gets anxious, sends all sorts of wires and telegrams and pleads for her to marry him. But in the final Heartbeats number, "One Million Years," he's despondent; she no longer even returns his phone calls.

Aside from "A Thousand Miles Away," not one of these records so much as made *Billboard*'s R&B charts, and by 1958, the harmony group era was finished. Doo-wop went the way of the buffalo and the Heartbeats broke up. Listening to the group's records—which are among the best in the genre—it's not hard to see why. Although Sheppard was a distinctive lead, tenor Albert Crump quite gifted, and the other four above average, there is a remarkable melodic similarity among the records. Doo-wop is formula music, and like most genre arts, only its most outstanding efforts bear much repetition. The Heartbeats' problems were those of doo-wop writ large; what makes those records worth hearing is Sheppard's remarkable narrative ambition, which really was years ahead of its time.

In 1961, the first rock and roll revival began. It centered almost entirely on doo-wop, although that category was broad enough to include several styles of rhythm and blues group harmony. Centered, as doo-wop had been, in the Northeast, the revival was powerful enough to revive a number of hits, among them "A Thousand Miles Away."

Sheppard put together a new group, Shep and the Limelites, to cash in. The group was unique because it was a trio (previous R&B singing groups had almost always been quartets or quintets), with no bass voice. The result was even more emphasis on Shep's lead vocals, with an especially ethereal backing, emphasized by the use of vibes and celeste (instruments that had also been featured in the Heartbeats, though there the effect had been to spotlight Crump).

"A Thousand Miles Away" ended by promising "Daddy's coming home soon," which makes "Daddy's Home" a rather unusual example of the answer record. (Answer records, records which reply to earlier hits, are usually done by *different* artists in the *immediate* aftermath of a hit. Famous examples include Kitty Wells's "It Wasn't God Who Made Honky Tonk Angels," replying to Hank Thompson's "The Wild Side of Life," and the Miracles' "Got a Job," responding to the Silhouettes' "Get a Job.") Though even most fans didn't know it, the "A Thousand Miles Away"/"Daddy's Home" cycle was now about ten records long, and Shep perpetuated it with an additional five singles, culminating in the abject "I'm All Alone," where Shep sings bitterly against a tremulous, almost country guitar:

> But I'll keep on searching
> until I can find
> A love so true, to me not to you
> Then I won't be alone

"Daddy's Home" is the most captivating record in the sequence, opening with chimes, then Sheppard's voice singing a melodic evocation of both "A Thousand Miles Away" and "Crazy for You." The harmonies are rich, the sax line mellow and Sheppard stays up to date by interpolating the sort of gospel and pop devices (the way he sings "treasure," the way he jumps up a couple of notes for "Your best friend wrote and told me" then quickly descends again to complete the line) that were the developing basis of sixties soul. And he ends as beautifully as he began, crying "I'm not a thousand miles away."

None of the "Daddy's Home" follow-ups scored on the charts, and by 1963, Shep and the Limelites had broken up. Shep reformed the group for the Rock and Roll Revival tour of 1969. But on January 24, 1970, he was found in a car parked on the shoulder of the Long Island Expressway, bludgeoned to death. The crime has never been solved.

674 PLEASE MR. POSTMAN, The Marvelettes
Produced by Brian Holland and Robert Bateman; written by Brian Holland, Robert Bateman, William Garrett, and Georgia Dobbins
Tamla 54046   1961   *Billboard:* #1 (1 week)

Every history of Motown I've ever read claims that the Marvelettes hailed from Inkster, Michigan, "a suburb of Detroit." Well, not quite. That's where Gladys Horton and her three girlfriends went to high school, but suburb doesn't adequately describe the place. When Henry Ford built a company town outside the city limits to control the housing and lives of his workers, he called it Dearborn. When he started hiring blacks (partly to bust the UAW), the bigot-entrepreneur built them separate and of course, inferior facilities. That was Inkster. The name, I suppose, was Ford's idea of a joke.

"Please Mr. Postman" sounds less suburban than any other memorable girl group record—and more like a girl group record than any other Motown hit. The label's first Number One, it combines frothy harmonies, Horton's gritty lead, a nifty blues piano and some remarkably funky drumming by the young Marvin Gaye. The Beatles and the Carpenters hit with the song later, but it's the Marvelettes' version—with Gladys Horton's indelible "Delivah the lettah / The soonah the bettah"—that lingers in memory.

675 WELL ALL RIGHT, Buddy Holly and the Crickets
Produced by Norman Petty; written by Buddy Holly, Jerry Allison, Norman Petty, and Joe B. Mauldin
Coral 62051   1958   Did not make pop chart

If Buddy Holly had lived to see the seventies, he would have been heralded as the Father of the Singer/Songwriters. Indeed, there's nothing James Taylor has done that expresses the soft rock sensibility half so well as this quietly lovely number, issued as the B side of the rinky-dink "Heartbeat" in May 1958, soon after the plane crash.

It's just Buddy on softly strummed guitar, Joe Mauldin playing a very muted bass, and Jerry Allison keeping himself busy with brushed cymbals and a triangle. If Buddy had lived, who knows but that this spare and compelling record, given some promotion, might not have clicked as an A side. Holly clearly was preparing himself to make more mature music, and it needn't have been as sappy as "Raining in My Heart" (or for that matter, "Heartbeat"). If even one rock star of the first era had made that turn, much less done it with the ease with which Holly wrote and sang "Well All Right," how many others might have been inspired?

A clue might be taken from the Beatles, who professed a love for Buddy Holly so great that they named themselves in mock-homage to the Crickets. But it was surely not only "Rave On" and "That'll Be the Day" that they admired. "Well All Right" sounds, among other things, like a song that might have leaked out from John Lennon's pen sometime around *Rubber Soul*: "Well all right so I'm being foolish / Well all right let the people know / About the dreams and wishes you wish, at night when the lights are low." Says here that there's no way to get to "You've Got to Hide Your Love Away" (or "In My Life," or for that matter, *Plastic Ono Band* and "Imagine") without this one.

676 THE HOMECOMING, Tom T. Hall
Produced by Jerry Kennedy; written by Tom T. Hall
Mercury 72951   1969   Did not make pop chart

Musically, "The Homecoming" might be the least interesting record in this book, nothing more than a simple guitar strum and Hall's muted, conversational voice. But the story that voice is telling is perfectly crafted. A country star arrives at his father's house after long absence. He's been gone so long he isn't aware that his Dad now has a phone; he's so alienated from his former life that he managed to miss his mother's funeral.

Hall's elliptical exposition reveals a performer oscillating between boastful egotism and downplaying his life-style, a reaction intensified by his father's hostility to his profession. More skillfully written than almost any other effort at depicting the everyday—Hall even gets to the banalities about gravestones and illness that are supposed to release and in fact only intensify familial tensions. Few page writers can claim as much.

677 SMILING FACES SOMETIMES, Undisputed Truth
Produced by Norman Whitfield; written by Norman Whitfield and Barrett Strong
Gordy 7108   1971   *Billboard:* #3

Norman Whitfield's most peculiar habit was his love of recording the same song with two different acts, effectively forcing them to compete to see which version became the single and—Motown was so hot at the time—the hit. The most famous example, of course, was "I Heard It Through the Grapevine," Marvin Gaye's record sitting in the can for more than a year while Gladys Knight went Top Ten with hers. But no song ever caused Whitfield more grief than "Smiling Faces Sometimes."

In addition to Undisputed Truth, a trio (Joe Harris, Billie Rae Calvin, and Brenda Joyce Evans) that Whitfield formed in 1970 to serve as a vehicle for his material, the Temptations also recorded the song. It was the featured track on the Tempts' *Sky's the Limit* and as established stars, they naturally expected to get the first bite at a single release. But Motown decided otherwise—not surprisingly since the Temptations' version is less distinctive than Undisputed Truth's—and as a result, the Temptations refused to work with Whitfield for the next year.

Although Undisputed Truth went on to accomplish nothing, "Smiling Faces Sometimes" remains one of the best examples of the vaguely paranoid pop-funk hits that were the heart of black Top 40 in the first years of the seventies, ranking with "Back Stabbers," "Freddie's Dead," "What's Going In," and ironically, the Temptations' Whitfield-produced "Papa Was a Rolling Stone"—the song that Undisputed Truth released as its follow-up to "Smiling Faces Sometimes." It flopped at Number 63.

678 PAIN IN MY HEART, Otis Redding
Produced by Jim Stewart; written by Naomi Neville
Volt 112 1963   *Billboard:* #61

Yeah, it's true: Otis lifted "Pain in My Heart" directly from Irma Thomas's "Ruler of My Heart." The information usually not received along with that trivia tidbit, however, regards the substantial improvements made by Otis and the Stax house musicians. From Thomas's perfunctory R&B exercise, they sculpted a harrowing deep soul portrait of love in anguish. Otis's ravaged passion ebbs and flows on a cosmic tide established by the surging lines of the Memphis Horns and the vibrato-laden chords of guitarist Steve Cropper, while Al Jackson maintains the pulse with soft rimshots, and Booker T. plays a piano ostinato that hovers in the background like the ghost of good love gone bad. Where they got it isn't the point at all; it's where they took it that matters.

679 DE DOO DOO, DE DA DA DA, The Police
Produced by The Police and Nigel Gray; written by Sting
A&M 2275   1980   *Billboard: #10*

Though they didn't prove to be the Beatles of the eighties (as some people seriously predicted at the time), at their best, the Police were a machine that ran like a Porsche, with a tight, hard thrum. Here, Andy Summers' guitar bursts at the end of each line perfectly complement the best deliberately nonsensical lyrics Sting's ever written, and Stewart Copeland's drumming sets up a roadway engineered for a ride as smooth and powerful as the autobahns themselves. Sting may have conceived the song as a tirade against the misuse of communication by the Establishment or as a paean to human innocence in the face of such malicious blather but on the record, what matters is nothing but the pure, intense groove.

680 PART TIME LOVE, Little Johnny Taylor
Produced by Cliff Goldsmith; written by Clay Hammond
Galaxy 722   1963   *Billboard: #19*

681 PART TIME LOVE, Ann Peebles
Produced by Wilie Mitchell; written by Clay Hammond
Hi 2178   1970   *Billboard: #45*

I've never been sure just where the blues leave off and R&B begins, which probably leaves me in the good company of most of the people who made the music—except that I care. Somehow, most Muddy Waters and Little Walter and Howlin' Wolf and T-Bone Walker and even B.B. King records fall outside R&B for me, linking more clearly to the older tradition of blues. Wolf's wild man routines, Waters's pure energy, the shrillness of Walter's harp, the guitar pyrotechnics of Walker and King have all left large marks on the rock and roll era, but somehow, they are not *of* it. Some of their records may wind up here anyhow, because they were working in the same marketplace as anyone else, and from time to time the sensibilities synched. But the bluesmen's music was conceived for a far more insular market than anything that came along after Ray Charles, let alone James Brown.

Little Johnny Taylor's "Part Time Love" straddles that line. Its central features are a nasty, B.B.-like guitar lick and a horn line that might have been lifted right off a T-Bone record. On the other hand, Little Johnny (as distinguished from the bigger Johnnie Taylor of Stax fame) sings much more like a gospel shouter than a bluesman ("Most people say I should have been a preacher," he once said), and the lyric, rather than being composed of blues rudiments, bears the marks of songmill craftsmanship. Which only proves that it's an open border and that, in trying to distinguish what lies on either side of it, I'm as arbitrary as anybody else.

Even though she recorded in Tennessee, Peebles is a lot further from down-home—or at least, down-home as a bluesman would have understood it. Few women made Mississippi and Texas country blues in the first place, and anyway stylistically Peebles owes everything to Aretha Franklin. Producer Mitchell deemphasizes guitars in this arrangement (though Teenie Hodges gets off some fine licks), bringing forward the Memphis Horns and some nice piano work by Charles Hodges.

682 I'M A KING BEE, Slim Harpo
Produced by J.D. Miller; written by James Moore
[Slim Harpo]
Excello 2113   1957   Did not make pop chart

What's going on here isn't just the model for Mick Jagger's most nasal R&B impressions, a wicked harp riff fronting one of the all-time sexual metaphors, or even the perfection of Guitar Gable's stinging guitar comments. No, the story of "King Bee" is told in its entirety by the buzzing bass of Fats Perrodin, an effect so oddball that it could only have been concocted in a recording studio and thus qualifies on two fronts as a rock and roll landmark.

683 WHAT'S YOUR NAME, Don & Juan
Produced by Embee Productions; written by Claude Johnson
Big Top 3079   1962   Billboard: #7

Perhaps the most modern sounding of all doo-wop records, this hit from the early sixties revival period ostensibly features Roland Trone ("Don") and Claude Johnson ("Juan"), a pair of New York City apartment painters who harmonized on the job, got an audition, and came up with a great song written by Claude. In fact, both had already been

in the Genies, who'd had a local bite with "Who's That Knockin' "
during the fifties. In all probability, Trone doesn't even appear on the
record; the vocals are presumably Johnson lushly double-tracked.

The idea of double-tracking is credible here because "What's Your
Name" is anything but a street corner arrangement. There's nothing
amateurish about the mainly unison vocals and the plush strings, not
to mention the abundant use of reverb. In fact, despite the lyric's setting
"on the block," "What's Your Name" is pure recording studio music,
which is precisely what gives it continuing vitality long after "more
authentic" products of the period sound uncomfortably dated.

684 TENDER YEARS, George Jones
Produced by Shelby Singleton; written by Darrell Edwards
Mercury 71804   1961   Billboard: #76

Perhaps the greatest pledge of unrequited love ever recorded—the guy
who sings "Tender Years" could be the one that George sings *about*
in "He Stopped Loving Her Today." And in a sense, that's appropriate
because, though "Tender Years" was Jones's seventeenth record on
the country charts and his second Number One, it was the first of his
great ballads about love in the face of an ugly fate. Typically, because
Jones keeps his phrasing plain and clear, the intensity of his anguish
comes through with extraordinary, undeniable power. And whoever
played piano understands exactly the correlation between honky-tonk
and heartache.

685 BRAND NEW ME, Aretha Franklin
Produced by Jerry Wexler and Arif Mardin; written by
Kenneth Gamble, Theresa Bell, and Jerry Butler
Atlantic 2796   1971   Billboard: #6

Aretha never had a hit with an arrangement so swinging as the one
Arif Mardin gives her here; when the tempo picks up, it feels like she's
singing an old Ray Charles chart, though really the basic pulse is far
more modern.

But that's not all there is to it. Aretha's art is entirely concerned
with personal transformation and she's turned in many of her most
compelling and lasting performances singing about changes made or on
the way; "Respect," "Since You've Been Gone," "The House That
Jack Built," and "Rock Steady" are only the most obvious examples.

"Brand New Me" (issued as the flip side of "Bridge Over Troubled Water," but widely played anyway) not only talks about big changes but heralds them: "Bridge" was her first pop Top Ten hit in nearly three years and it was followed by three more, including the monumental "Rock Steady."

Indeed, Aretha had changed. If Ray Charles is one obvious antecedent of this arrangement, another is the arrangements John Hammond provided for her early Columbia sides. "Brand New Me" and the hits that followed it (up through "Until You Come Back to Me," in 1973, her last Atlantic Top Ten) carefully balanced her Southern pop-gospel shouting with the uptown pop-jazz that represented the vastly underrated best of her Columbia period. This was the maturing glory of one of the two or three greatest singers of the rock and soul era.

686 (MY FRIENDS ARE GONNA BE) STRANGERS, Merle Haggard
Produced by Fuzzy Owen; written by Liz Anderson
Tally 179   1964   Did not make pop chart

If there were such a thing as the typical Merle Haggard record (the sheer diversity of his music makes that impossible), "Strangers," with its deep blues feeling, biting guitar, and sweet-voiced reading of bitterly ironic lyrics, would probably be the one. Which only makes sense, for this is the hit—it was Top Ten on the C&W chart—that kicked off Haggard's career. The nicest touch was naming his band after it, as if they were the only friends he'd ever have or need.

687 HONEY DON'T, Carl Perkins
Produced by Sam Phillips; written by Carl Perkins
Sun 234   1956   Did not make pop chart

"Honey Don't" is now better-known as a track from *Beatles '65* than for the original version that appeared as the B side of "Blue Suede Shoes." But Sam Phillips originally picked it as the A side of the third Perkins single he released and not because he'd made a mistake: This is red-hot rockabilly with Perkins riding a heavy bed of amped-up bass and drums, accentuated by the bite of his own guitar. If his shouts and asides are tossed off with a sense of containment closer to country than R&B, that's probably the best evidence that homespun Carl, not

R&B-driven Elvis or manic-eclectic Jerry Lee, was the archetypal rockabilly.

688 REFUGEE, Tom Petty and the Heartbreakers
Produced by Jimmy Iovine and Tom Petty; written by Tom Petty and Mike Campbell
Backstreet 41169   1980   *Billboard:* #15

In the early days of rock and roll, having even one hit single tended to be pretty miraculous to all concerned, from listener to performer. If a whole string of hits popped up, most performers could barely imagine remaining musicians; they took a shot at movies or TV. And faded fast. (*That* was no surprise.)

Later generations of rockers went into the game with the hope of forging careers. They'd seen Elvis and the Beatles and the Stones (and in different ways, Jerry Lee Lewis and Fats Domino and even Chuck Berry) pull it off. Today, musicians expect to make many records if they get the opportunity to make one, and most at least harbor some hope of being taken seriously by an audience.

Which makes it difficult to assess an artist like Tom Petty. If he'd come along in the fifties, he'd be a storied rocker, a guy who ran a great band and came up with a couple of classic sides, most notably "Refugee," an anthem of resistance to life's banalities. Today, judged against a surprisingly strong crop of mid-eighties mainstream American rockers, he suffers in comparison with Springsteen and Mellencamp and some of the rest, because he hasn't been able to sustain the quality of his best records.

A fair enough assessment, but that doesn't mean you should take the good stuff for granted just because it lacks a proper retinue.

689 IT'S ONLY MAKE BELIEVE, Conway Twitty
Produced by Jim Vinneau; written by Conway Twitty and Jack Nance
MGM 12677   1958   *Billboard:* #1 (2 weeks)

Before he stuffed his shirt to become a Nashville fat cat, Conway Twitty came up with this record, one long crescendo whose title seems to be an internal pun because it's probably the greatest-ever impersonation of Elvis Presley's booming early ballad style. I mean right down to the Jordanaires.

690 WE'RE AN AMERICAN BAND, Grand Funk
Produced by Todd Rundgren; written by Don Brewer
Capitol 3660   1973   *Billboard:* #1 (1 week)

Sitting in a Baton Rouge bar late one night in 1973, the three guys in Grand Funk Railroad, at the time America's most popular and despised (by nonfans and critics) group, were lapping up the suds with the boys from Humble Pie, a voguish blues-boogie group featuring Steve Marriott (Peter Frampton had already departed). Neither group's career had long to run but they were young and full of themselves, and the future undoubtedly seemed a long way off.

The belligerence began with an argument over the relative merits of British versus American rock. Drummer Don Brewer, Grand Funk's champion, roared out of his chair and in a style of classic argumentation familiar to anyone with experience around the Michigan auto factories from which his band sprung, declaimed the virtues of Jerry Lee Lewis, Fats Domino, Little Richard, and—clinching it pretty well for a guy who couldn't play a simple shuffle to save his ass—ELVIS PRESLEY! Then he gave the assembled Brits a bleary gimlet glare and proudly announced, "We're an American band!"

In the cold light of dawn, the statement seemed truer yet, and Brewer had soon written a song quite unlike any of the heavy metal hatchet jobs in which Grand Funk had previously specialized. The group shortly got together with producer Todd Rundgren (who was working with them for two reasons—Capitol had begun selling Grand Funk records more slowly than the one every four seconds of their peak and they needed his artistic credibility). Showing he was worth his royalties, Rundgren quickly grasped the concept that Brewer had written a hit.

So eager was Capitol, in the wake of the Beatles' breakup, for some Top 40 action that the label issued a press release about "We're An American Band" before the song was even recorded, and released it before the mix was even finished.

Maybe they were wise to do so, because further polishing could only have detracted from a band that produced what Rod Stewart called "the all-time loud white noise." "We're An American Band" thundered onto the chart at Number 83 on July 28, 1973 and by the end of September it topped the lists, more than pretty good for a group whose previous best-selling single was "Closer to Home," which peaked at Number 22 three years earlier.

Actually, the biggest difference in the music probably wasn't Rundgren's production, though he certainly lent them an unaccustomed sense of song shape, or even the fact that Brewer had, for once, given them a lyric that defined their boys'-night-out sensibility, with its references to playing poker til dawn with Freddy King, living it up with a Little Rock groupie, and hotel destruction. No, the biggest change was the addition of piano player Craig Frost, who plays an insanely repetitious treble riff that runs through the chorus like the Morse code designation for Motor City high energy. It's this added coloration that hooks you by lending an undercurrent of excitement to Farner's prototypically cheesy garage rock guitar breaks and Brewer's powerful, if unfunky, drumming.

691 THAT LADY, The Isley Brothers
Produced by The Isley Brothers; written by Christopher Isley, Ernest Isley, and Marvin Isley
T-Neck 2251   1973   *Billboard: #6*

Guitarist Ernie Isley, younger nephew of the original trio, would be the best-kept secret of the Isley Brothers, if you could keep musical secrets that are this obvious (and after all, people somehow found out about James Jamerson, despite Berry Gordy's best efforts). "That Lady," a remake of a Bert Berns-produced, stamped-from-the-mill 1964 Isleys track, unites Ernie's newfangled Hendrix-fed guitar pyrotechnics with his uncles' long-established soul harmony grit. This is also the record that pushed the Isleys into their third decade of R&B innovation. Long after its basic dance accent has become passe, the wash of Ernie's wah-wah (possibly the most pleasant use ever made of the infernal device) keeps "That Lady" vibrant. Sweeter funk hath no men wrought. Nor their nephews, either.

692 (THE MAN WHO SHOT) LIBERTY VALANCE, Gene Pitney
Written and produced by Burt Bacharach and Hal David
Musicor 1020   1962   *Billboard: #4*

John Ford, America's greatest filmmaker, complained long and bitterly about the music movie studios tacked onto his great films. Rather than Dmitri Tiomkin scores, he said, he'd have preferred something simpler, like the western folk music that showed up in occasional set pieces within his sagebrush dramas.

The Man Who Shot Liberty Valance was Ford's last great picture, a mythic elegy for the western and the way of life it symbolized. Ford probably didn't like the score any better than any of the others, and the studio must have disliked Gene Pitney's vocal take on the Bacharach-David theme song even more, because they didn't use it even over the titles.

Fortunately, Musicor owner (and Pitney's mentor) Aaron Schroeder decided to release the record anyway. The result was the best rock-based movie theme song of the pre-Beatles era.

The lyric not only respects the story; it gets to the essence of the theme, which is what happens when civilization reaches the frontier and decides to stay. The music, meanwhile, updates the studio version of western folk songs, taking it even a step beyond the slick pop-country balladry of Marty Robbins.

Gene Pitney could sing anything, from swarmy Italian pop to white rhythm and blues, though he was generally best off when doing his own songs or Bacharach-David's. Here, his occasional duet work with country stars like George Jones and Melba Montgomery pays off. Connecticut kid Pitney knows just how to balance his phrasing between the claims of authenticity and dramaturgy.

693 SUN CITY, Artists United Against Apartheid

Produced by Little Steven and Arthur Baker; written by Little Steven
Manhattan 50017   1985   *Billboard:* #38

As pop culture phenomena go, the run of socially responsible benefit records in 1984 and 1985 wasn't terribly surprising; in fact it was almost predictable as a necessary corrective to the previous wave of self-indulgence and narcissism. "Do They Know It's Christmas," by the British Band-Aid collection of superstars, fit comfortably within a spectrum of sentimental English Christmas charities whose roots go back at least to Dickens's tales of Scrooge and Tiny Tim. U.S.A. for Africa's "We Are the World" at least offered a multigeneric gaggle of superstar voices and thus, music that transcended the limits of its Friars Club do-goodism. Most of the others—for a time, it seemed that every disease and disaster without a telethon would have to run a pop single at the charts—lacked either musical or any other kind of conviction.

That was the context in which Little Steven Van Zandt and Arthur Baker devised the antiapartheid project that became "Sun City." It was a context that exploded the minute that they touched it, mainly because their approach and concerns were explicitly political, both in choice of topic and in assembling the troupe to perform on it. And politics was what the charity rock movement eschewed.

Presuming that South African liberation isn't all that far away, "Sun City" 's political immediacy may fade—but the stellar lineup never will. Having Bruce Springsteen, Miles Davis, Bobby Womack, Ruben Blades, the Ramones, Pete Townshend, and Run-D.M.C. on one track isn't just an eclectic coup, it's a remarkable breakthrough in artistic unity, at least within what had been pop music's own kind of apartheid.

Yet the thing assures that "Sun City" will last is its stature as one of the most inventive hip-hop records extant, as well as a scorching example of how combustible things can really get when dance-pop and rock are brought together full-bore. So, while not ignoring the catalytic and creative role of organizer/songwriter Van Zandt, give extra credit to Baker and extend praise wherever else it's due for the creation of an actual left-wing anthem that not only can but *must* be danced to. From Woody Guthrie to Billy Bragg, no one else has pulled that one off.

694 SAVE IT FOR LATER, The English Beat
Produced by Bob Sargeant; written by The English Beat
I.R.S. 9909   1983   Did not make pop chart

The real stars of this British "two-tone" (i.e., racially integrated bands playing music that was rhythmically West Indian, otherwise rock) group's closest shot at the American charts (it made the "Bubbling Under the Hot 100" chart at Number 106 for a week) aren't the surface attractions—the song, with its witty oral sex japes, and Dave Wakeling's goofy, nervous, run-on singing—but the gently cutting twin guitar attack of Wakeling and Andy Cox, together with the honking tenor work of Saxa, the group's over-fifty horn man. The result is a record as modern as any recent Britpop but encased in a sound with deep, funky roots.

695 YOU AIN'T SEEN NOTHIN' YET, Bachman-Turner Overdrive
Written and produced by Randy Bachman
Mercury 73622   1974   Billboard: #1 (1 week)

The ultimate Who pastiche came from this band of overfed Guess Who leftovers. Yet even rolling in from the Canadian prairies, "Won't Get

Fooled Again" distilled to its trashy Top 40 essence is something to hear. Bachman managed to swipe *all* the elements that made Pete Townshend's music great, including the cowbell, the blend of electric and acoustic guitars, and, of course, the stutter that starts as a stammer and hints at obscenity. B.T.O.'s assays at improvisation may be feeble, but they're funny, especially Randy's vocal introjections: "You need education! Gotta go back to *school!*" he bellows, as if he'd just discovered some new bit of hip lingo.

On the other hand, Bachman's babble is keyed to an idea ("Any love is good love / So I took what I could get") that was hailed as an essence of hipster liberation when Stephen Stills toyed with it in "Love the One You're With," so maybe all that B.T.O. really needs or needed for credibility is a cover version as good as the one that the Isley Brothers did for Stills.

696 STORY UNTOLD, The Nutmegs
Produced by Al Silver; written by Leroy Griffin
Herald 452   1955   Did not make pop charts

One of those doo-wop records whose title seems to promise the secret of the universe and is sung as if that's exactly what the group's after. Yet superb as Leroy Griffin's voice is, what's going on here is just another doo-wop love ballad. Unless doo-wop love ballads *are* the secret of the universe. Which, during the time when you're listening to "Story Untold," seems less unlikely than it does in the cold light of day.

697 WISHIN' AND HOPIN', Dusty Springfield
Producer not credited; written by Burt Bacharach and Hal David
Philips 40207 · 1964   *Billboard:* #6

Best Dionne Warwick knockoff in history. The fact that Dionne's favorite writer/producer team provide the instrumental drama helps a lot, but not nearly so much as a similar vocal huskiness that takes this sisterly sexual encouragement beyond advice to the lovelorn into genuinely sensual realms.

698 SO FAR AWAY, The Pastels
Producer not credited; written by Big Dee Irwin and J.B. Willingham
Argo 5314   1958   Did not make pop chart

The Pastels' first record, "Been So Long," was a slightly bigger hit (it made the national rhythm and blues chart) but "So Far Away" is clearly the better one, if only for its radiantly disembodied background chant, which sounds like it's done by a heavenly quartet of Frankie Lymons, and for the abject helplessness of Big Dee Irwin's dry-throated lead. Although they wrote it in Greenland, where the group formed while stationed there by the Air Force, Irwin's so downhearted, you'd believe it if somebody told you his sweetheart had been selected for the space shuttle.

699 WE CAN WORK IT OUT, The Beatles
Produced by George Martin; written by John Lennon and Paul McCartney
Capitol 5555   1966   Billboard: #1 (3 weeks)

If the sixties had been an age of revolution rather than just revolt, the Beatles never could have scored with sentiments as thoroughly meliorist as these. But if, for all the storm and thunder, heat and lightning, the crisis must be managed, far better Paul McCartney with a sweet-tempered Dylanesque arrangement to do the negotiating than a "My Generation"-destructoid like Henry Kissinger.

700 DREAM LOVER, Bobby Darin
Produced by Ahmet Ertegun; written by Bobby Darin
Atco 6140   1959   Billboard: #2

Bobby Darin—even more than Dion—was the best-equipped of all the early Italian-American rock and roll singers to follow in the bel canto pop footsteps of Frank Sinatra. Yet his best early records have a smooth, legato blues groove that belies such influences. So Darin was a rocker by choice, if not instinct—"Splish Splash" just about defines contrived. Maybe that's why "Dream Lover," though it's a ballad, stands as his best record, not only because his wailing vocal is so soulful but because of a marvelous pizzicato string bit that carries the rhythm and an utter unity of sound and performance that marks it as one of the most thoroughly conceived of all the early Atlantic hits.

701 ONE DYIN' AND A-BURYIN', Roger Miller
Produced by Jerry Kennedy; written by Roger Miller
Smash 1994   1965   *Billboard:* #34

Not just the funniest punster in country music—one of the finest American pop songwriters of the mid-sixties, and possessed of a nice froggy voice to boot. "One Dyin' " features a somber, folkish background, and some of Miller's most cutting phrases and phrasing, making connections between the longing for freedom and the longing for death that'll wipe that smile right off your face as it sinks in like a knife with a heated blade.

702 LEADER OF THE PACK, The Shangri-Las
Produced by Shadow Morton; written by Jeff Barry, Ellie Greenwich, and Shadow Morton
Red Bird 014   1964   *Billboard:* #1 (1 week)

Far from the greatest teen drama ever recorded—its kitsch isn't all on the surface, it goes deep into the meat of the thing, and the result edges perilously close to the self-contempt of camp. And yet, who can resist Shadow Morton's fundamental violation of conventional morality—the Leader's death isn't just the result of a parent-child misunderstanding about the class requirements of proper dating decorum, it's unmistakable and unrepentantly All Dad's Fault. Inconceivable in the movies or on TV; pure rock and roll. And therefore not camp at all, but an authentic emotional parable of our time. If the Shangri-Las had recorded "Leader" three years later, it would have been understood as a Vietnam allegory. And a better one than "Waist Deep in the Big Muddy," at that.

703 WIPE OUT, The Surfaris
Produced by S. Molin; written by Pat Connelly, Jim Fuller, Ron Wilson, and Bob Berryhill
Dot 16479   1963   *Billboard: #2*

I saw the best minds of my generation laughing maniacally, drumming for hours on study hall desktops with fingers and pencils, eraser-end upward, not giving a good goddamn whether this was the first version the Surfaris recorded, much less whether it was actually composed by somebody named Merrell Funkhauser, knowing only that this beat was the craziest sound they'd ever heard and desperately needing to participate, digging into the groove.

I should add that I also saw the best minds of my generation sentenced to detention for those very same things.

704 THE HOUSE THAT JACK BUILT, Aretha Franklin
Produced by Jerry Wexler; written by Bob Lance and Fran Robins
Atlantic 2546   1968   *Billboard: #6*

One of my indelible memories of Aretha Franklin is hearing a radio report one morning in the late sixties or early seventies that she'd been found, battered and incoherent, sitting in a car in a parking lot. There wasn't any follow-up but the symptoms of wife battering were there for anyone to see. So whenever Aretha plays the romantic victim, she has special credibility with me.

In this same respect, the apologetic tone of "The House That Jack Built," one of her most countrified recordings, a grand Southern shout from start to finish, still strikes me funny; Aretha's dumped her lover and now she's kicking herself for losing that "upright man." Makes me feel terrible every time—she shouldn't blame herself, I always think. But I keep coming back for more, to listen with fascination as she convinces me, in just these few lines, of the vivid vitality of love that didn't quite work out but in which, for one shining moment, she possessed everything a person could reasonably ask.

705 TWO TRIBES, Frankie Goes to Hollywood
Produced by Trevor Horn; written by Peter Gill, Holly Johnson, and Mark O'Toole
ZTT/Island DMD 760   1984   *Billboard:* #43

British producer Trevor Horn established ZTT in 1983 as a fount of New Pop (antirock) sensibility—he'd make unapologetically hedonist dance records informed by postpunk sensibility. Frankie Goes to Hollywood, a pack of androgynes led by Holly Johnson, was developed as the label's principal vehicle. Their first record, "Relax," engendered major controversy for its admonition: "Relax . . . when you want to come," an instance of useful household advice that the BBC found worthy of banishment from its airwaves. The record quickly became a huge British hit. Thereafter, Horn and ZTT presented FGTH as an elaborate scam, akin to Malcolm McLaren's view of the Sex Pistols: The act as entrepreneurial toy. (In 1988, British courts voided Holy Johnson's contract with Horn and his wife on the grounds that they controlled all his potential activities in restraint of fair trade. In the process, Johnson seemed to establish that the FGTH material was in important respects developed by him.)

"Two Tribes," the follow-up to "Relax," meant to sensationalize international, especially European, anxiety about the potential for nuclear war, using "postmodern" language: The United States and the Soviet Union are presented as "two tribes" on the brink of battle for barbaric reasons. The record featured bombastic synth-pop, a travesty of international relations ("When two tribes go to war / Money is all that you can score"), almost comically portentous (at the beginning, the band introduce themselves—"My name's Martin, My name's Matt"—climaxing with a stentorian "Mine is The Last Voice That You Will Ever Hear—Don't Be Alarmed"). But whatever its pretensions and foibles, the music also smoked for eight urgent minutes, the fight for space among synthesizers and guitars conjuring an atmosphere that acknowledged the destruction looming over everybody's head. Trevor Horn may have been a half-assed culture theorist but he was a hell of a good record producer.

Even the Thatcherite BBC couldn't ban it (else they'd have had to ban James Bond), and "Two Tribes" sold two million copies in the U.K. In America, most radio stations simply ignored it, although MTV put the excellent video into heavy rotation. Horn never thought of an adequate follow-up, and FGTH and ZTT were both down the tubes within two years. Even so, at this writing "Two Tribes" still sounds prophetic. Fortunately.

706 DON'T DREAM IT'S OVER, Crowded House

Produced by Mitchell Froom; written by Neil Finn
Capitol 5614   1987   *Billboard: #2*

If you wanted to argue that they don't write 'em like this anymore, I'd be the last to disagree. And to tell the truth, even though it's beyond doubt that the most important part of making pop music in the rock and roll era is performance, one of the biggest reasons that records made in the sixties dominate any discussion of this music is the extraordinary number and quality of songwriters who were at work back then. (The other, just so you don't get me wrong, is the extraordinary diversity and quality of performers who recorded those tunes.) The post-"Cold Sweat" deemphasis of melody, the almost frantic drive for new beats in the wake of disco, the deterioration of white blues past heavy metal toward sheer noise, the art-rock focus on minimalism and primitivism are all contributing factors to a decline in the number of genuinely memorable songs. (Which is, collaterally, one reason why the eighties saw such an upsurge in remakes of old songs.)

Maybe that's why the rock world hasn't quite known how to deal with Neil Finn, the leader of Crowded House, the most gifted songwriter to appear in the late eighties. Finn's not a singer/songwriter, like Tracy Chapman, and the band he leads has no pretensions to avant-gardism: This isn't the Talking Heads. In a sense, he's a throwback but there's no sense of nostalgia or revivalism about what he does. Finn writes compact songs around pretty pop melodies, and sings them in an accent that's derived in equal measures from Liverpool, L.A., and his native New Zealand.

Critics have often upbraided Finn for being too explicitly influenced by the Beatles, but you can hear as much of "A Whiter Shade of Pale" (meaning, arty white soul) here. In fact, the limit of the song is not its music nearly so much as the densely impacted lyrics. Finn knows how to write words that demand to be sung, and you can feel him intoxicate himself with the sheer grace and flow of these syllables. But what's meant to be elusive he sometimes renders as not much more than murky. Nonetheless, when you hear a voice this plain and sure of itself crying from the radio, it sits you up straight and makes you realize what's been missing amidst the static.

707 I PITY THE FOOL, Bobby Bland
Produced by Joe Scott; written by Deadric Malone
Duke 332   1961   *Billboard: #46*

Covers by a thousand bad white blues imitators damn near wore the song out. But the record is such classic blues that it seems to have sprouted directly from Bland's lungs into an existence too vibrant for mediocre imitations to kill off. Joe Scott sets up a riffing brigade of sax and brass big enough to be heard over Bobby's shouts, without letting their blare overwhelm him. As Mel Brown's great guitar fill plays through the fade, you feel a lot more sympathetic toward all those amateurs: Nobody can match this stuff but any musician worth his salt has to *try.*

708 WHAT'S LOVE GOT TO DO WITH IT, Tina Turner
Produced by Terry Britten; written by Terry Britten and Graham Lyle
Capitol 5354   1984   *Billboard: #1 (3 weeks)*

Eat your heart out, Phil Spector—*this* is the best record Tina ever made. And it didn't take genius assistance, either, just a competent studio craftsman, a decent song, and a framework closer to her real life than childhood fantasies of rag dolls and puppies. Eschewing Jaggeresque microphone fellatio, Tina makes herself sexier than ever by facing up to pain and humiliation, frustration and rage—not incidentally, never denying the tug of her own gonads.

709 MARY'S LITTLE LAMB, Otis Redding
Produced by Jim Stewart; written by Otis Redding
Volt 109   1963   Did not make pop chart

Undoubtedly the greatest rock and roll record ever made from a nursery rhyme, not only because Otis manages to find a way to turn the concept into a confession of his passion for the little lamb tender and of his deep disgust at how the school authorities have done her wrong, but because he winds up shouting it out like a garage-band Little Richard while the MGs and the Memphis Horns have the time of their lives. Anybody who thinks soul isn't a form of rock and roll has yet to reckon with this one. (Naturally, it got lost on the B side of his second single, a flop.)

710 HELLO STRANGER, Barbara Lewis
Produced by Ollie McLaughlin; written by Barbara Lewis
Atlantic 2184   1963   *Billboard:* #3

711 MAKE ME YOUR BABY, Barbara Lewis
Produced by Bert Berns and Ollie McLaughlin; written by
Roger Atkins and Helen Miller
Atlantic 2300   1965   *Billboard:* #11

Until the independent R&B record companies began being absorbed into the multinational majors in the late 1960s, the process of locating and recording new talent worked on an impressively informal basis. Band leaders like Johnny Otis and Ike Turner roved North and South, functioning as much as scouts as musicians, recruiting fresh blood into their acts and then, when they hit a recording center, selling it off to the highest bidder. Elsewhere, those doing the looking included furniture and record store owners (the former sold phonographs, and in those days of slapdash distribution, sometimes the records to play on them), nightclub owners and disc jockeys like Zenas Sears in Atlanta, John Richbourg (the legendary John R) in Nashville, and Ollie McLaughlin in Detroit.

Of these, McLaughlin was one of the oddest, one of the last, and one of the best. In the first place, McLaughlin appeared on the radio not in Detroit, with its sizable black community, but forty miles southwest, in Ann Arbor, home of the University of Michigan, a city with relatively few blacks outside of the offensive and defensive lines. But McLaughlin's program on WHRB and the live shows he promoted around the state equaled the influence of even the fabled Ernie Durham at WCHB in the Motor City proper. Among others, McLaughlin discovered the Capitols ("Cool Jerk"), Deon Jackson ("Love Makes the World Go 'Round"), and Del Shannon.

Finding Shannon, the one white rocker in the bunch, led McLaughlin to leave radio and concert promotion to become a full time manager/producer. He immediately struck gold with Barbara Lewis.

Lewis and McLaughlin first linked up in 1961, cutting sides that year and the next both at Chess Studios down the road in Chicago and back in Detroit at Berry Gordy's newly opened Hitsville facility (then still for rent to outsiders). The second Chess session produced Lewis's first hit, the lovely "Hello Stranger," with its Hammond organ lead and the Dells on backing vocals. There was no particular marketing niche for Lewis—she had lacked any facility for uptempo R&B, she sang without partners so she didn't fit the girl group trend, and though ballads were her forte, her style was smoother and less gospel-inflected than any of the new Motown stars.

Lewis didn't need a trend, though, because she had a classic voice with achingly rich timbre and a marvelously legato way of phrasing love songs that conveyed the trembling prospect of utter heartbreak and/or paradisical romance with equal conviction.

"Hello Stranger" was Lewis's only Top Ten hit, and she didn't have another on the charts until the next year, when McLaughlin, having flopped with several follow-ups, took her to New York in search of some professional production help from Bert Berns, another legendary and underrated character. Whether because Berns, as a fixture on the Brill Building scene, had access to better material, or simply had better studio skills, Lewis returned to the Top 20 with two consecutive singles, both ballads, "Baby I'm Yours" and "Make Me Your Baby." Though the former wasn't quite up to the mark of "Hello Stranger," the latter was a near-perfect expression of almost everything that Lewis did well and a nice turn on the kind of nightclub R&B that Dionne Warwick had begun to popularize.

Soon after, with several further releases failing, Lewis retired with the same quiet grace with which she sang. Today, her records remain beloved of R&B ballad fans, Detroit soul afficionados, Carolina beach music partisans, and California low-riders.

712 STREETS IN AFRICA, Big Youth
Produced by Big Youth; written by War and Manley Buchanan [Big Youth]
Negusa Nagast [Jamaica—no catalog number]   1972   Did not make pop chart

A decade before U.S. street kids developed rap, Jamaicans favored "D.J.s" chanting over prerecorded instrumental tracks in a style called "toasting." Big Youth was the first great star of Jamaican deejay style, crafting a series of hits around material as unlikely as Ray Charles's "Hit the Road Jack" and getting the most out of tracks as promising as War's "The World is a Ghetto"—which became "Streets in Africa." Youth stays pretty close to the War arrangement, bringing the bass line forward, inverting the rhythmic accents to a reggae beat, and actually retaining the melody while coming as close to singing as he ever did. Not surprisingly, the idea of a worldwide ghetto has different overtones when sung by a Third World pop star than by an L.A. funk group—

there's more gloom here, and a more tangible sense of oppression, but in the cries that counterpoint the main vocal, Youth delivers a strong sense of liberation as well.

713 I CAN'T HELP MYSELF (SUGAR PIE, HONEY BUNCH), The Four Tops

Produced by Brian Holland and Lamont Dozier; written by Brian Holland, Lamont Dozier, and Eddie Holland
Motown 1076   1965   Billboard: #1 (2 weeks)

"I Can't Help Myself" rode the top of the national charts for two weeks. In Detroit, every radio station blasted it once an hour for the whole damn summer, and believe me, when you hear it that often, its title becomes "Sugar pie, honey bunch" all right. It seemed like you couldn't work that damnably corny phrase out of your ears with a Q-Tip and a crane. By the time that summer ended, I was sick of it, so much so that I transferred my allegiance to the Temptations.

Temporarily. In fact, Levi Stubbs personifies one of my ideas of what a singer ought to be: A huge presence, vibrating with spiritual energy as he puts his song across. As he is even here, on the most confectionary piece of material he ever had (well, at least until he cut "MacArthur Park" in 1971).

From time to time, the Tops' pre-Motown decade as Motor City nightclub hacks shows through all too plainly, and what you're left with are the Gordy machine's cardinal virtues of bass, drums, percussion, gospel piano, and high-level EQ. But always, in the end, Levi turns it on, redeeming even songs as insipid as this one. Of course, it's of inestimable help that, until his Moment arrives, those cardinal virtues cook steadily along. Here, the hook doesn't set until almost the end. "When I call your name / Girl, it starts to flame," he shouts, and brings me back to thinking, *Jesus*, I wish I could do that.

714 OH ME OH MY (I'M A FOOL FOR YOU BABY), Aretha Franklin

Produced by Jerry Wexler and Arif Mardin; written by Jim Doris
Atlantic 2838   1971   Billboard: #73

Both as a song and in its orchestrated jazz combo arrangement, "Oh Me Oh My" harkens back to the pop material that Franklin recorded at Columbia Records before reaching Atlantic's more sympathetic, gospel-oriented production approach in 1967. Those Columbia sessions have been far too much maligned; from "Today I Sing the Blues"— her first pop recording—onward, Aretha was an outstanding pop vocalist. And had "Oh Me Oh My" been a bigger pop hit, it might have vindicated John Hammond's perception of her as the successor of Billie Holiday. Such an ambition was clearly not entirely outside Aretha's desires.

Unfortunately or not, it didn't work out that way. Not only were Aretha's Columbia sides overwhelmed in kind and quality by the magnificence of what she achieved in Memphis, but "Oh Me Oh My" was itself overwhelmed by the A side of Atlantic 2838, the great grinding funk of "Rock Steady." The fact that Atlantic would toss off a performance as beautiful as "Oh Me Oh My" as a B side is almost as stunning as the fact that such studiously adult pop made the charts at all.

Certainly, Franklin was far more comfortable in the jazz diva role than is the overstylized likes of Anita Baker, and while her level of musical improvisation here isn't especially impressive, her casual interpolations (for instance, the guttural "sty-yi-yi-yle" in the first verse) suggest what might have been if a direction both more personal and popular hadn't presented itself. When the full orchestration kicks in, and Aretha confronts herself in full foolishness at last, she's offering an experience that's as personal (and perhaps, given her checkered love life, as confessional) as anything in her repertoire.

715 I'LL BE DOGGONE, Marvin Gaye

Produced by Smokey Robinson; written by Smokey Robinson, Warren Moore, and Marvin Tarplin
Tamla 54112   1965   *Billboard:* #8

Motown expert Don Waller says Marvin Tarplin's guitar line (it couldn't be by anybody else) makes "I'll Be Doggone" Byrds-like folk rock, and I suppose he's right, but if the Byrds or any folk-rock act had ever been supported by a groove this deep, or topped by singing this gritty, they'd have had to invent a new name for the genre. Folk-soul? Not with those strings, I guess, but it's a helluva thought, huh? Maybe the very reason that Dylan called Smokey Robinson America's greatest living poet.

716 STAYIN' ALIVE, The Bee Gees
Produced by the Bee Gees, Karl Richardson, and Albhy Galuten; written by Barry, Robin, and Maurice Gibb
RSO 885   1977   *Billboard:* #1 (4 weeks)

It's the summer of 1978 and Roger Daltrey is sitting in the back of a limousine on the way to a New York airport, ready to return home after doing a series of interviews to promote another nondescript Who album. He's finishing the last of them jabbering to the journalist about what's been on the radio lately, moaning about how much punk ripped off his band's early records and his own dislike of disco. Particularly the latter.

"Look at great huge Maurice Gibb, singing like Donald Duck on 'Stayin' Alive,' " says the exasperated, if diminutive, Cockney. "And that's a great song. Bruce Springsteen could sing that lyric."

Daltrey persuades the journalist that it might be wise to pay closer attention to the Bee Gees' biggest hit. Which is no problem, as their biggest hit utterly dominates the airwaves, even several months after it's peaked on the charts.

What he discovers, beyond the numbing banalities of the beat (whose annoying aspect has diminished over the years) is a first-rate piece of pop falsetto. Not at the Stylistics level, mind you, but still real good. And a good, class-based lyric. Not at Springsteen's level, mind you, but real good.

And something else. The journalist in question also practices as a critic, and his *bete noir* has always been lyrics. He often hears them at least a little askew, often resulting in highly entertaining but way-off-base interpretations. Interpreting "Stayin' Alive" isn't such a big problem—it's the theme song of *Saturday Night Fever* and the movie is as omnipresent as its soundtrack—but try as he might, he keeps hearing one line that *can't* be right. Over the years, he keeps meaning to find out what it really is, but never gets around to it probably because what he *thinks* he hears is so gratifying.

A decade later, sitting down to write about it, he listens a few dozen times to "Stayin' Alive," but he still hears what he hears, and so he decides to repeat it in public, in the faith that others will understand why he's held to it:

> Well it's all right, it's OK
> I'll live to see another day
> We can try to understand
> The New York *Times* don't make a man

717 WE ARE THE WORLD, U.S.A. for Africa

Produced by Quincy Jones; written by Michael Jackson and Lionel Richie
Columbia 605　1985　　*Billboard:* #1 (4 weeks)

In November 1985, British pop musician Bob Geldof, who led a second division band called the Boomtown Rats, saw a television report of famine in Ethiopia. Repulsed and fascinated, he summoned his rage and collected friends and acquaintances (among them, Boy George and Jon Moss of Culture Club, Sting, Phil Collins, Bananarama, George Michael, U2, and Duran Duran). As Band Aid, they recorded his song, "Do They Know Its Christmas," with all proceeds earmarked for aid to the starving in Africa's (perhaps, the world's) poorest nation.

In Britain, where the sentimental Christmas record links itself to a couple of centuries of sentimental tradition, "Do They Know It's Christmas" became the best-selling single of all time, moving about ten million copies. It raised about eight million pounds (close to $20 million) and created a mildly political controversy around itself for several reasons: Geldof, an Irish-born hothead, began his media campaign on behalf of Band Aid by accusing all Western European governments, particularly his own, of ignoring the starvation; Ethiopia is the only Marxist-Leninist state in Africa (although the famine was clearly the result of drought and primitive farming conditions, not recent agricultural policies); Mrs. Thatcher's British government refused to waive the sales tax on the record, thus preventing even more money from being raised.

"Do They Know It's Christmas" also became a hit in the United States, though not such a big one, peaking at Number 13 in *Billboard*. That was still enough to call it to the attention of Harry Belafonte, who wondered why Yank artists had not similarly extended themselves.

Belafonte took that thought to manager Ken Kragen, who helped him round up Quincy Jones, Lionel Richie, and Michael Jackson. Richie and Jackson, two of the three biggest black pop stars in the world would compose a song; Jones, hot off *Thriller*, would get the music arranged, cut a backing track, and produce the record; Belafonte, who hadn't had a hit since "Island in the Sun" in 1957, and Kragen would round up an all-star cast to sing on the record. They'd do the session the night of the American Music Awards broadcast, when many of the artists they wanted to feature would be readily available.

Jackson came up with the basic idea for the song; Richie worked with him to complete it. "We Are the World," the result, basked in gospel changes and California feel-good philosophy. On paper, its imagery was nothing less than an awful, self-congratulatory stew in which the problems of the starving were declared by psychobabble fiat to be no match for the power of positive thinking:

> Send them your heart so they'll know that someone cares
> And their lives will be stronger and free

Yeah, stronger and freer for the fifteen additional seconds that those lives would last without more material succor.

But that was just the song. The singing was another matter. Because the date was assembled by middle-of-the-road music-makers, the song was big and bland. Because so many of these music-makers were black, however, they had access to a variety and quality of voices that Band Aid simply couldn't command. (Although Geldof had, to his credit, recruited for Band Aid some members of Kool and the Gang who happened to be in London.) The cast for "We Are the World" was breathtaking, featuring legends—Ray Charles, Stevie Wonder, Bob Dylan, Smokey Robinson, Dionne Warwick—mingling with the hottest contemporary stars: Jackson, Richie, Bruce Springsteen, Cyndi Lauper. Within the realm of mainstream rock and soul, only heavy metal, punk, and rap were not represented but nevertheless, U.S.A. for Africa, as the group was called, featured a degree of racial interaction that made a domestic political comment of its own, if only by calling attention to the rarity of such gatherings.

If you accept its origins in MOR soul, "We Are the World" 's flaws are few. True, a few of the performers seemed anomalously selected (most notably Kragen management clients Kenny Rogers, a has-been, and Kim Carnes, a one-hit wonder); true, the unctuousness of the lyrics couldn't entirely be dispelled, even by performances as grand as those of Charles, Wonder, Springsteen, Lauper, and James Ingram; true, funk took a backseat to polish, especially when Prince failed to show up. But associate producer Tom Bahler's vocal arrangement ingeniously wrapped all those famous voices around one another and, unlike "Do They Know Its Christmas," "We Are the World" became not only a best-seller (it spent four weeks at Number One, sold in its own eight-figure quantities, generated additional megamillions, with 90 percent devoted to African relief, ten percent to the hungry and homeless in the United States) but a memorable piece of music.

Rock critics, by and large, hated it, contending that "We Are the World" sent a variety of muddled and mistaken messages. Undoubtedly, this was true as it would be of any record that advanced private philanthropy as a solution to starvation, a problem whose dimensions are inextricably political. (There was, after all, enough food *in the world*, there was simply no profitable mechanism for delivering it to the dying.) Others attacked the superstar hegemony that made "We

Are the World" such an event in the first place, noting that it excluded the most radical forms of music; for those who believed in an equation between radical noise and radical thought, that problem was insurmountable. As a result, many denied that the record would do any good at all, pointing out that even $50 million would do no more than dent the problems of drought, starvation, and agricultural insufficiency in Ethiopia, and contending that MOR music intrinsically led to politics that were at best ineffective, at worst corrupt, because they were not sufficiently oppositional.

Critic Greil Marcus went even further. "Melanie Klein posited the infant's projection of itself on the world, and its instinctive attempt to devour the world; beneath perfectly decent, thoughtless intentions, that's what's to be heard on 'We Are the World'. . . . Ethiopians may not have anything to eat, but at least these people [the stars on the record] get to eat Ethiopians."

If you believed this line of reasoning, the central impulse animating "We Are the World" was the promotion not merely of celebrity do-goodism, but the annihilation of the very concept of the starving—in Africa or anywhere—as people. In a way, Marcus and others argued, the net effect of such superstar projects was to announce that all non-stars were not quite legitimate in their humanity. It was just a new version of the old imperialist song and dance: Ethiopians and other have-nots would be fed by the beneficent gestures of their betters, people you could tell were better (and more real) because they possessed the essentials (and far more) that the starving did not.

If there weren't a significant kernel of truth to these contentions, it would be utterly ludicrous to rehearse them here. It's true that "We are the world, we are the people," in the smug tones of Lionel Richie or Paul Simon, obliterates all feelings not directly related to self-satisfaction. At those moments, the record's message has as much or more to do with how the singers feel as what the Ethiopians are experiencing.

But pop songs are always and inevitably and appropriately about what the singer is feeling. And despite Marcus, that message is not subliminal—it isn't even hidden. The topic is right out front, because among them, Richie, Jackson, Jones, and Kragen didn't have enough objectivity or guile to see things in a more broadly politicized context. This wasn't a group of people with the duplicitous media sensitivity of the CIA, but a bunch of craftsmen who happened to be rich enough to afford a certain solipsism. What's most fascinating, perhaps, is that intellectuals interested in pop music so often found it necessary to attack a record whose limits of effectiveness were all but emblazoned on the foreheads of the performers before the tape ever started to roll.

But what critics of "We Are the World" really wanted was an *oppositional* record about the famine, a record that would confirm the vision of rock as exclusively rebellious. Instead, they got something from the side of the music that's about reconciliation and, typically, were unable to grant it any validity. Consequently, such critics were immobilized by their own denial, unable to join forces with the authentic inclination to solve the world's problems that "We Are the World" tapped into, and thus left "charity rock" (which eventually extended to mega-events like Live Aid and the 1988 Human Rights Now tour for Amnesty International) even more subject to a swift, probably permanent descent into ineffective and compromised liberalism. Critics may like to pretend that that result was inherent in the process, but that just begs the question of the narrowness and inadequacy of their own response.

Or at least, of their own professional response. British critic Simon Frith later reported that, after a symposium in which Marcus and others roasted charity rock for several hours, an assemblage of rebel-rock critics and scholars was shown the video made for "We Are the World." "The mocking mood was soon stilled and, by the end, viewers were quite emotional," Frith wrote. " 'Damn it,' said someone, tears on his face, 'the bastards always get you.' "

The real question is whether it's always wrong to be gotten or whether the rebel-rock prejudice against ever being reconciled to the world around amounts, in the end, to hostility to everything alive.

718 PISS FACTORY, Patti Smith
Produced by Lenny Kaye; written by Patti Smith
Mer 601   1974   Did not make pop chart

Patti Smith is Queen of Rebel Rock. "Piss Factory," her first record, is as far from the pop homilies of "We Are the World" as *Naked Lunch* is from *The Power of Positive Thinking*.

Musically, "Piss Factory" 's real affinity isn't to punk or acid rock so much as to beat-era efforts to fuse snappy poetry readings (by the likes of Kenneth Rexroth and Lawrence Ferlinghetti) with cool jazz (by the likes of performers generally too mediocre to be recalled). Smith is backed by rockers—pianist Richard d.n.v. Sohl and guitarist Lenny Kaye—but then, she'd have to be, because not only a great deal of her imagery (James Brown and Philly deejay George Woods make an appearance in one stanza), but all of her rhythm derives from rock and R&B. Far more than on "Because the Night," where the melody simply overmatches her, Smith unites herself perfectly with this material, a blast of rage and revenge, a shaggy dog story posing as a dirty joke that winds up as an anthem to show biz ambition very much in the tradition of "On Broadway." Which kind of makes you wonder whether Patti Smith didn't become one of the greatest of all rebel rockers partly through the expedient of acknowledging—in fact, even reveling in— her own ameliorating impulses. The fact that she had no choice but to tell her story in a voice less sweet than Smokey Robinson's doesn't mean that there's such a long distance between "Piss Factory" and, say, "Got a Job."

719 ACT NATURALLY, Buck Owens
Produced by Ken Nelson; written by John Russell and Voni Morrison
Capitol 4937   1960   Did not make pop chart

720 UNDER YOUR SPELL AGAIN, Buck Owens
Produced by Ken Nelson; written by Buck Owens and Dusty Rhodes
Capitol 4245   1959   Did not make pop chart

When the Beatles chose to ennoble Buck Owens in the annals of rock and roll, they weren't choosing idly or for that matter, even just expediently, although "Act Naturally" of course provided Ringo the perfect vehicle to make mock of the group's movie career. More important, the Beatles were responding to an underlying similarity between Owens's music and theirs, for each threw at a hidebound establishment (one in London, one in Nashville) a brave and creative eclectic synthesis which respected only the broadest boundaries and closed the door to no influence whatsoever.

Or you could look beyond even that and notice that of all the country singers of the Beatles era, even Merle Haggard, it was Buck Owens whose sense of swing most evidently came from R&B. In "Act Naturally," C&W provides the accent but the groove is only a step or so away from falling into Elvis-like midtempo rock and roll. Coming from a performer who went on to vow (in a paid trade paper advertisement) to play nothing but pure country music for the rest of his career, and immediately followed up with a version of Chuck Berry's "Memphis," sung in a spirit of mock-agony that the Coasters would well recognize, "Act Naturally" isn't rock and roll mostly because of an accident of birth and nomenclature.

It was no fluke. Although the Beatles and most other pop fans would have had no way of knowing it, Owens had been even bluesier at the beginning of his career (and, on the sides he had a hand in writing, remained so). "Under Your Spell Again," his second country chartmaker, possesses the potency of pure soul, no matter how prominent the fiddle and steel guitar. The witty pathos of its internal rhymes sounds like Smokey Robinson—only Smokey didn't get this good for another couple of years. As the sad words trill joyously off Buck's tongue, there's no point worrying about genre; this is just a fine modern American pop record, unbounded by anybody's worries about convention.

721 THE MIGHTY QUINN (QUINN THE ESKIMO), Manfred Mann
Producer not credited; written by Bob Dylan
Mercury 72770   1968   *Billboard:* #10

For a long time, Manfred Mann's reputation as Bob Dylan's best interpreter was a hype, based on nothing much more than a passing remark that Dylan, a notoriously fickle put-on artist, may have intended as nothing more than a slight to Roger McGuinn and the Byrds. Mann's entire Dylan output was then a few obscure early album tracks, the best of which was probably "With God On Our Side," although the group did have a U.K. hit with "Just Like A Woman."

But Dylan's verbal largesse did offer Mann an unusual opportunity to hear one of the earliest circulated editions of The Basement Tapes (which were originally intended as nothing more than song publishers' demos, the kind used to scare up cover versions). And, his credentials on the line, Mann did have the perspicacity to discern hit potential in "The Mighty Quinn," obscurantist lyrics and all.

It's one of those songs that hit Top Ten on the basis of mystery as much as music: Mann's raucous arrangement, featuring a flute and neo-Beach Boys harmony, was certainly one of the most daring arrangements of a Dylan tune . . . except for the Wonder Who's Four Seasons-like "Don't Think Twice," probably *the* most radical reworking a Dylan tune ever received from a pop group. But the music wasn't much more than plain old good stuff, the kind that flops all over the charts a hundred times a year. What gave "Quinn" its extra kick was Mike D'Abo's reading of the lyric, utterly straight-faced even though Dylan's absurdist language all but begged for some kind of symbolic interpretation.

So "Quinn the Eskimo" was "about" Dylan's inspired viewing of Anthony Quinn in *Savage Innocents*, a fictionalized *Nanook of the North*. Or else it was "about" dope: "When Quinn the Eskimo gets here, everybody's gonna want a dose . . . jump for joy . . . run to him." "I don't know what it was about," Dylan later alleged in the liner notes to *Biograph*. "It was some kind of nursery rhyme." Much as his fans might appreciate his refusal to ruin a good thing, the same can be said for D'Abo's reading, which is so fundamentally blank that almost anything—or a harmless nothing, which helps on the radio—can be read into it. Years later, when singers from David Bowie to David Byrne worked overtime to perfect it, this absence of thought and emotion became the hallmark of rock's new wave style. Which perhaps explains why I always thought that Dylan wrote "Quinn" because he was jealous of Beckett's "Waiting for Godot."

To their credit, the guys in Manfred Mann gave such shit short shrift and simply got on with bashing out the tune, not as a statement against interpretation, but simply as the most readily available means of getting to the point.

722 SIR DUKE, Stevie Wonder
Written and produced by Stevie Wonder
Tamla 54281   1977   *Billboard:* #1 (3 weeks)

From 1963's *Tribute to Uncle Ray*, in honor of Ray Charles, to 1980's "Master Blaster (Jammin')," an homage to Bob Marley, Stevie Wonder has acknowledged his favorites and influences more avidly than any other rock or soul musician. But is "Sir Duke," its lyric and arrangement composed as an elegy for Duke Ellington (with bowing asides in the direction of Count Basie, Louis Armstrong, Glenn Miller, and Ella Fitzgerald) just a tribute from a student to a master? Or from the nonpareil of one generation to the peers among his predecessors? As the horns swing through that jumping coda, that question seems less relevant than wondering who, in the next generation, might be talented enough to be able to return the favor.

723 SKINNY LEGS AND ALL, Joe Tex
Produced by Buddy Killen; written by Joe Tex
Dial 4063   1967   *Billboard:* #10

Many years before the Sugar Hill Gang and Kurtis Blow, Atlantic released a Joe Tex album called *From the Roots Came the Rapper*. And indeed, the Joe Tex brand of soul owed as much to street corner dozens playing, storefront preaching, and for that matter stand-up comedy, as it did to the gospel shouter, pop balladeer, and harmony crooner sources from which his mates in the soul clan took their inspiration.

"Skinny Legs and All," Joe's first million-seller and his highest impact pop hit, anticipates rap right down to the sexual hostility (albeit, this version's insults are much more diplomatically—not to mention hysterically—voiced). The climactic track of his *Live 'n' Lively* LP (ostensibly recorded live although even in those days, you never knew for sure), the song features a murderous bass riff, fatback drums, mean horn flourishes and some cutting harmonica, gritty little guitar fills and the semblance of a chorus, but its real focus is Joe trying to find a mate for the lady in the front row with the undernourished gams.

In that sense, I suppose you could look at "Skinny Legs and All" as a sequel to that hoary old blues, "Big Leg Woman."

724 IT'S YOUR THING, The Isley Brothers
Written and produced by Ronald Isley, Kelly Isley, and Rudolph Isley
T-Neck 901   1969   *Billboard:* #2

The record with which the Isleys made the transition from R&B-bred harmony group to post-"Cold Sweat" funk band. Having just served an apprenticeship at Motown to avoid getting the bends, they dive in deep for the debut release on their own label, coming up with a skillful blend of bursting contemporary horns and patented raw-throated shouts, hollering the usual mix of hippie sentiment and sexual come-on (an award to anyone capable of figuring out where one begins and the other ends). If there was nothing here to make James or Sly fear for his stature at the apex of creative activity in black pop, there was also no reason for any of the million-plus who bought it to apologize for lack of taste. As if any of them would have stopped dancing long enough to feel that twinge, anyway.

725 TELL ME SOMETHING GOOD, Rufus featuring Chaka Khan
Produced by Bob Monaco and Rufus; written by
Stevie Wonder
ABC 11427   1974   *Billboard: #3*

Rufus and the indomitable Chaka's first hit—written by Stevie Wonder on the spur of the moment when he happened to stop by their session and liked what he heard enough to want to play along. What he gave them wasn't just a son-of-"Superstition" hit, it was role defining, establishing, in one fell swoop, Chaka as a demanding, tough 'n' sultry siren, and Rufus as one of the premiere black rock bands of the seventies, designations to which they've devoted the rest of their careers.

726 FRIDAY ON MY MIND, The Easybeats
Written and produced by Harry Vanda and George Young
United Artists 50106   1967   *Billboard: #16*

727 MANIC MONDAY, The Bangles
Produced by David Kahne; written by Christopher [Prince]
Columbia 05757   1986   *Billboard: #2*

728 LONELY WEEKENDS, Charlie Rich
Produced by Sam Phillips; written by Charlie Rich
Phillips International 3552   1960   *Billboard: #22*

Answer records are supposed to occur immediately, not be separated by twenty years, but listening to Prince's offering to heartthrob Susannah Hoffs, the connection with the Easybeats' "Friday on My Mind" is unmistakable. To be more precise, "Manic Monday" musically fuses "Friday," the first major Australian rock hit, with the Left Banke's wimp serenade "Pretty Ballerina." But the connection also extends to the similarities in phrasing between Hoffs and Easybeats' vocalist Stevie Wright. ("Friday" rocks harder; "Manic" has some of the best imagery Prince has ever created—even if I never could figure out whether it was the boss or the bus that's already there.) And while it's worth wondering where it would have been possible for a female group to have uttered such complaints about the hazards of working life in 1967, before it was taken for granted that as many women held jobs as men, the indisputable link is between their condemnations of the poles of the working week.

Well, not indisputable, since Charlie Rich claims, in his first national hit, that the real problem is when the job starts and life begins: "Well, I make it all right / From Monday morning to Friday night / But oh! Those lonely weekends." With its big, echoey chorus and swinging beat, "Lonely Weekends" is finally more of a pop record than a rocker, even though the sax break is pure R&B. Maybe that's why it works at right angles to the basically bohemian (i.e., antiwork) rock and roll philosophy.

729 DON'T LET ME BE MISUNDERSTOOD, The Animals
Produced by Mickie Most; written by Bennie Benjamin, Sol Marcus, and Gloria Caldwell
MGM 13311   1965   Billboard: #15

Eric Burdon was the best singer in the first wave of the British Invasion (the second wave brought Steve Winwood), but if it were just up to Burdon, "Don't Let Me Be Misunderstood" might be as draggy as Nina Simone's original. What snaps it to life is Alan Price whose "tremendous organ phrases" (as producer Mickie Most once called them) work with Hilton Valentine's seething guitar to create a language all their own. You could call it the blues and you wouldn't be far wrong.

730 I WANT TO KNOW WHAT LOVE IS, Foreigner
Produced by Alex Sadkin and Mick Jones; written by Mick Jones
Atlantic 89596   1984   Billboard: #1 (2 weeks)

The Sistine Chapel of cock rock and not only because they were smart enough to recruit the New Jersey Mass Choir and Jennifer Holliday for a taste of gospel authenticity. U2 made the same move but without nearly such mesmerizing consequences, because their song wasn't so arresting to begin with and because Lou Gramm, given the best tune of his life, can sing rings around Bono any day.

What really makes the record isn't the sheet of choral voices thrown behind Gramm at the end, or Holliday's moaning testifying. It's the psychological web in which Gramm feels himself entombed; in that respect, "I Want to Know What Love Is" is a true successor to the Four Tops' "Bernadette," even if the performance and production fall a little short of such a heady mark.

731 SEA OF LOVE, Phil Phillips
Produced by Eddie Shuler; written by George Khoury and Phil Batiste
Mercury 71465   1959   *Billboard: #2*

It helps to know that Phillips's real last name was Batiste and that he was from Lake Charles, Louisiana, because it's hard to know where he got the syrupy beat of this swamp-pop ballad until you connect it to New Orleans and the Cajun culture of the Mississippi River bayous. Phillips, a former bellhop and gospel quartet singer, allegedly wrote the song to prove his love to a hard-to-persuade girlfriend; whether it worked or not remains unrecorded but here, at least, Phillips sounds like he would have taken a deep dive if she hadn't bought his line.

732 MEMPHIS SOUL STEW, King Curtis and the Kingpins
Produced by Tom Dowd and Tommy Cogbill; written by King Curtis
Atco 6511   1967   *Billboard: #33*

Not an instrumental, because Curtis vocalizes all the way through it, describing the proper way to make music cook. The recipe's great but pulling it off requires a master chef—maybe even a Mix Master. And they don't make 'em like that any more.

733 BABY WHAT YOU WANT ME TO DO, Jimmy Reed
Produced by Calvin Carter, Jimmy Bracken, and Ewart Abner; written by Jimmy Reed
Vee-Jay 333   1960   *Billboard: #37*

Somehow the lazy beat of Reed's muted electric guitar and rack-mounted harmonica, backed by Eddie Taylor's more developed shuffle figures, created an improbably sinuous and sensual groove that persistently turned up on the pop charts between 1955 and 1965, despite the fact that no other blues singer (except maybe B.B. King) enjoyed anything close to similar success. In fact, Reed's hits may owe more to folk revivalism than to rock and roll; they certainly have more in common with the gentle strums of the Kingston Trio than the ferocious bursts of Muddy Waters and Howlin' Wolf that led to the Rolling Stones *et seq.* Except that no folkie could have come up with this plaint for the pussy-whipped, sung (of course) with his wife, the celebrated Mama Reed, harmonizing right in Jimmy's ear.

734 LOVE IS LIKE AN ITCHING IN MY HEART, The Supremes
Produced by Brian Holland and Lamont Dozier; written by Brian Holland, Lamont Dozier, and Eddie Holland
Motown 1094   1966   *Billboard:* #9

If I thought that the crew at Motown fooled around, I'd think that using Diana Ross, the most uptight singer in either rhythm and blues or girl group music, to personify female horniness was one of the greatest jokes in rock and roll history. But Holland-Dozier-Holland never fooled, and there's no mistaking the meaning of the song ("Now when you're ill, you take a pill / When you're thirsty, drink your fill," plus a baritone sax that tugs the beat along like an intravenous fix of pure hormone), so I guess this must be the Diana Ross who dated Gene Simmons of Kiss. Who *undoubtedly* knew how to scratch it.

735 DO IT AGAIN, Steely Dan
Produced by Gary Katz; written by Walter Becker and Donald Fagen
ABC 11338   1972   *Billboard:* #6

736 RIKKI DON'T LOSE THAT NUMBER, Steely Dan
Produced by Gary Katz; written by Walter Becker and Donald Fagen
ABC 11439   1974   *Billboard:* #4

If there were such a thing as anti-singles rock, Steely Dan would be its exemplar. To start with, instead of a band with a rhythm section, Steely Dan was a group consisting of two composer/performers, Walter Becker and Donald Fagen, and a record producer, Gary Katz. A rock band with no regular drummer or bass player is already pretty anomalous and it's interesting that, during the group's lifespan, much more comment was made about its neglect of touring, a far more logical outgrowth of studio precision and now a commonplace career tack.

Katz, Becker, and Fagen spurned singles not so much because their vision could only be expressed through long suites (until quite late in its career, Steely Dan's compositions tended to be quite discrete) but because singles created a mass context—immediate, hasty, casual—that not only didn't interest them very much but actively subverted many of their most precious ambitions.

As songwriters, Walter Becker and Donald Fagen were the ultimate wry, obscurantist postcollegiates. A number of their songs use their years at tiny, avant-gardish Bard College as a backdrop; almost all reflect an interest in the modish, academically centered "minimalist" allusiveness of contemporary fiction writers like Donald Barthelme and quasi-surrealist work like that of Jorge Borges and Gabriel Garcia Marquez. The group even took its name from a milk-squirting dildo used by a lesbian to bugger males in William Burroughs's hallucinatory *Naked Lunch*. Steely Dan songs were often puzzles, filled with elliptical jokes, and musical and verbal puns. After awhile, those lacking a taste for working sonic acrostics lost interest.

But the music was undeniably compelling. The production raised the concept of studio polish to a tight-assed apogee, yet the band recruited so many first-rate players and so often gave them imposing structures to work within, that the results could be breathtaking (at least until the music petered out in the arty background noise of *Gaucho* and *Aja*).

None of this has much to do with the hot 'n' nasty Top 40 context. But Becker and Fagen established their credentials with a series of hits, and until very near the end, whenever they needed to revive flagging public interest (i.e., sales), they came up with another.

Becker and Fagen formed several bands at Bard; after leaving school, they became backup musicians for Jay and the Americans. They moved to New York, tried to sell songs to publishers without success, then met Katz, who got them good jobs as "staff songwriters" with cubbyhole offices at ABC Records in Los Angeles. But their songs were far too strange for the kind of journeyman pop singers reduced to begging material from a second-rate record label. So Katz took the pair into the studio to record their ditties themselves; perhaps this was his plan all along.

They worked with a number of first-rate musicians, most notably guitarist Elliot Randall, and released their debut LP, *Can't Buy a Thrill*, in 1972. Its outstanding tracks, "Do It Again" and "Reeling in the

Years," were both hits. But neither Fagen nor Becker sang them; they used singer David Palmer instead. After Palmer departed, their next album lacked hits altogether, but with *Pretzel Logic*, Fagen's singing came into its own and actually found a Top 40 platform with "Rikki Don't Lose That Number," which became Steely's biggest hit.

In retrospect, what's especially interesting is the similarity between these two records, the way they're written and the way they're phrased, each singer biting off and elongating syllables and phrases with less regard to the lyrics than to the contours of the groove.

Were it not so purposefully unspontaneous, Steely Dan's music might even qualify as a species of "jazz-rock." But in the end, the puzzles these records present are trivial (the travelogue in "Do It Again" is, if anything, the more intriguing of the two; "Rikki," for all its literary echoes, is basically just a love song) and what keeps you coming back are solid pop basics: the beat, the hot guitar licks, some amusing word play. In this context at least, that's their salvation.

737 BOOGIE WONDERLAND, Earth, Wind and Fire with the Emotions

Produced by Maurice White and Al McKay; written by Jonathan Lind and Allee Willis
Columbia ARC 10956   1979   *Billboard:* #6

Second-rate Supremes during their Stax tenure, the Emotions became the perfect disembodied divas for late disco under the tutelage of Maurice White. He jettisoned their vestigial gospel links for slicker, shriller pop modes that pushed lead Wanda Hutchinson way higher than her natural range, a tactic that worked because White's productions always provided plenty of funk underneath.

Even so, none of the Emotions' own hits matches this collaboration with EWF, in which horns scamper beneath the hyper female voices counterpointed by Philip Bailey's dry male responses, while bass and drum build a surging groove that coils and springs so often that it threatens to shatter—prototypical late seventies disco etched on glass.

738 IF YOU NEED ME, Wilson Pickett
Produced by Wilson Pickett; written by Wilson Pickett, Robert Bateman, and Sonny Sanders
Double-L 713   1963   *Billboard: #64*

Wilson Pickett might have reached stardom two years earlier and maybe even a whole lot less angry if he hadn't had his first big solo hit stolen right out from under him by Atlantic's Jerry Wexler and Solomon Burke.

Rock and soul could be a vicious game back then, and when Wexler heard that Pickett's version of "If You Need Me" was kicking up some regional noise on Lloyd Price's fledgling Double-L label, he immediately moved to cover it with Solomon Burke. This wasn't any less shameless or cutthroat than what white acts had been doing to black performers a few years earlier, but Atlantic's stature as critical darlings has always left the story to be portrayed as a joke or some weird kind of honor for Pickett, the ultimate prize for which was his being signed to an Atlantic contract two years later.

Maybe it might be, if Burke's version (which eked its way into the pop Top Forty after going to Number 2 R&B) hadn't been a down-the-line rip-off of Pickett's or if he'd improved on Wilson's fantastic performance (he didn't). In fact, on the basis of the deep gospel-blues of "If You Need Me," with its choice guitar and horn lines and interactive chorus, you could just about argue that Pickett was one performer who arrived at Atlantic—and Stax and Muscle Shoals—with his style intact. Since that style is so hammerheaded, that's perhaps not terribly surprising. But nobody at his future home did him any favors or paid him any compliments by retarding his progress back in 1963.

739 RAMBLIN' GAMBLIN' MAN, The Bob Seger System
Produced by Punch Andrews and Bob Seger; written by Bob Seger
Capitol 2297   1968   *Billboard: #17*

Bob Seger wandered in the wilderness for a dozen years before "Night Moves," and unlike most prophets, he found recognition and honor *only* at home—in Detroit, where he made a series of singles between 1965 and 1975 that sold more than fifty thousand copies a piece (a number which, projected to the Top 20 markets, equals a million). Yet in all that time, almost nowhere else paid any attention. "Ramblin'

Gamblin' Man" represents the closest Seger came to the mountaintop in all those years, and it measures as well how far and why he fell short.

As clunky as it is funky, its soul organ clashing with a cymbal-splashing drum pattern that prefigures heavy metal, Seger's white Wilson Pickett shout crests the top of the wave of Motor City high energy. According to legend, when Jon Landau got together with the MC5 to produce their classic *Back in the U.S.A.*, "Gamblin' Man" was their model. And though they never achieved anything nearly this soulful, they did come up with a record whose equalization was just as excessive, a noise so shrill that it not only virtually cancels out the whole bottom end of the sound, but presses the midrange to the edge of extinction, too. For sheer sonic tension, it's hard to top this approach. Problem is, it gets in the way of communicating anything else, which is one reason why Seger had to make like Moses for so long.

740 LIFE'S LITTLE UPS AND DOWNS, Charlie Rich
Produced by Billy Sherrill; written by Margaret-Ann Rich
Epic 10492   1969   Did not make pop chart

Margaret-Ann Rich created "Life's Little Ups and Downs" as a thinly disguised roman a clef about being married to an alcoholic singer/piano player who almost-but-not-quite reached superstardom not once but thrice: At Sun Records, where he made "Lonely Weekends," among others, in the fifties; at Smash Records where he cut "Mohair Sam" in the early sixties; and a decade later, at Epic, where Charlie made a cycle of slickly produced country-pop discs that began with this one and culminated in 1973 with "Behind Closed Doors" and "The Most Beautiful Girl."

In "Life's Little Ups and Downs," Rich describes his failure to get a raise and keep himself out of drunken jams, then sings lines about his wife (written by his wife) that characterize their lot:

> She knows that life has its little ups and downs, like
> ponies on a merry-go-round
> And no one grabs the brass ring every time
> She don't mind, she don't mind
> She wears a gold ring on her finger, and I'm so glad that
> she's mine

Most critics have interpreted Margaret-Ann's lyric as a criticism of the American class system, but that's not really supportable. Neither Rich rails against things as they are; the song is truly country because it absolutely accepts the status quo. Its wearied lack of resistance is typical of many kinds of people, but the level of aspiration described here—a raise in pay, a new dress—isn't about unfulfilled need as much as it's about unfulfilled desire, and that's not about class so much as it's about history, the period of postwar prosperity that affected almost every stratum of Americans.

For all its passivity, the record remains worthy, because Charlie brought to it just what Margaret-Ann must have known he would: deep sensitivity and intelligence, an unshrinking acceptance of the fact that at its core, this *was* his own story. Bob Dylan once called Charlie Rich his favorite singer, and after you hear "Life's Little Ups and Downs" for the first time, he may well head for the top of your list, too.

741 CHERRY OH BABY, Eric Donaldson
Produced by Tommy Cowan and Bunny Lee; written by Eric Donaldson
Trojan   1971   Did not make pop chart

Give this much credit to the Rolling Stones: When they stole, they swiped the very best. Just as they took the greatest rhythm and blues and soul hits for their early albums, when they chose to raid the reggae pantry in the late seventies, they quickly focused on one of the genre's great songs. In Donaldson's original, "Cherry Oh Baby" uses reggae's classic stop-start format to offset a grainy vocal seasoned with just enough bluesy rasp. And where Jagger bemoaning his lovelorn fate could never be anything but absurd, Eric Donaldson manages to be completely convincing, not so much through his rendition of the words but because of the cascading yelps and yowls with which he concludes each verse.

742 OH, BOY!, Buddy Holly and the Crickets
Produced by Norman Petty; written by Sonny West, Bill Tilghman, and Norman Petty
Brunswick 55035   1957   Billboard: #10

At first, "Oh, Boy!" seems to have a lot more to do with the side of Buddy's music that spawned Paul Anka than the part that puts him in the ranks of the great early rock and rollers. Edgy and excited, he sings the opening way too fast, like a kid who's just been told he can stay up late. And the Picks' backing vocals are mixed way up, like a chorus of Eddie Haskell cousins.

But as he jitters along, the cause of Buddy's nervousness becomes more clear: He's about to get laid. Probably for the very first time. What else could account for that rising lump in his throat, his fight to keep his voice from cracking, the mounting tension as he worries whether he'll go home having achieved his goal? And then, suddenly, on the heels of a wicked scream, the guitar cuts in and takes over the tune and not even the bad conscience of those backing singers can dilute the sheer magic of the occasion.

"All my life I've been a-waitin' / Tonight there'll be no hesitatin'," Buddy exclaims, and you know he's practically home free. But thirty years down the line you also want to say, "Go, boy. But stay cool—you'll last longer."

743 STAND BY YOUR MAN, Tammy Wynette
Produced by Billy Sherrill; written by Tammy Wynette and
Billy Sherrill
Epic 10398   1968   *Billboard:* #19

"For over a year, I walked around with an idea on a little piece of paper in my pocket," said Billy Sherrill in a 1975 book about country songwriters. "After being barraged by Women's Lib and ERA, I wanted it to be a song for all the women out there who didn't agree; a song for the truly liberated woman, one who is secure enough in her identity to enjoy it. Even though to some skeptics it may hint of chauvinism, as far as I'm concerned, they can like it or lump it. Because 'Stand By Your Man' is just another way of saying 'I love you'—without reservations."

Since Sherrill is not only a reactionary in regard to feminism but musically, as the architect of much of the slickest, most bathetic crap ever to emerge from Nashville, it's a pleasure to report that, no matter what he may believe, the most famous record he ever made totally undercuts his premise. Despite a lyric that's every bit as chauvinist as Sherrill's hopes, the reservations about her love expressed in Tammy Wynette's voice are awesome. She sings out of a dry throat and an aching heart, and you can't help but feel that though she'll stand by her guy, it's mostly out of an inability to perceive any other option and that, given one, she'd boot ol' Billy in the balls and hit the highway. Or didn't you notice that the song bursts into life as soon as she admits, in a voice far more pitying than pitiable, "After all, he's just a man."

Sherrill may have thought he'd found a perfect puppet, but Tammy may have been a guerilla in disguise.

744 ONE'S ON THE WAY, Loretta Lynn
Producer not credited; written by Shel Silverstein
Decca 32900   1971   Did not make pop chart

745 THE PILL, Loretta Lynn
Producer not credited; written by Allen McHan and T.D. Bayless
MCA 40358   1975   *Billboard: #70*

The ultimate answer records to the antifeminist fantasy Billy Sherrill put in Tammy Wynette's mouth didn't arrive for several years, but when they did, they served as both better and more bitter reflections of women's everyday reality. And because they came from one of the few female country singers whose stature approached Wynette's, they had special authority (not undercut at all by the fact that both were written by men, and the better of them by a guy who makes a lot of his living as a *Playboy* cartoonist).

Not that Loretta lets the middle-class biases of feminists off the hook. In real life, Lynn had her first baby at fourteen, so she brings a special credibility to "One's on the Way" 's complaints at the excesses of Liz and Jackie and Raquel and their ilk, while her description of life on the homefront (kids run rampant through the house, the doorbell rings, her husband's bringing company for dinner but can't be persuaded to pick up bread and milk on the way home) remains amazingly unaffected by our knowledge, unignorable in the wake of *Coal Miner's Daughter*, that she really spends most of her life traveling on the C&W concert circuit.

Loretta sings about her plight in a voice so chipper that even a devoted chauvinist like Sherrill might be able to swallow her description of how much the woman standing by her man must endure. But "The Pill," the musical rewrite of "One's on the Way" that Lynn checked in with four years later, is a Declaration of Independence so frank that it amounts to a catalog of everything macho males fear about female liberation. Not only does Lynn admit that, relieved of the worry of getting pregnant, "the feelin' good comes easy now," but she declares: "This chicken's done tore up her nest and I'm ready to make a deal / And you can't afford to turn it down, 'cause now I've got the pill."

Here's hoping that when he spotted this one atop the C&W chart, Sherrill blanched as white as a Klansman's sheet.

746 HOLIDAY, Madonna
Produced by Jellybean Benitez; written by Curtis Hudson and Lisa Stevens
Sire 29478   1983   *Billboard: #16*

Released at the height of Ronald Reagan's first term, "Holiday," with its joyous Latin disco beat and Madonna's winsome yet forlorn vocal, perfectly captures the spirit of its time. In the disparity between her singing and the music, you can hear the whole story, the conflict between the boom economy at the top of society and conditions that grew progressively more desperate as you descended the ranks. The lyrics practically summarize the Reagan-Bush platform: "All across the world / In every nation / It's time for the good times / Forget about the bad times." And that may be just what the songwriters intended. Yet, in a way that can't be entirely uncalculated, Madonna manages to insert into this spectacle of bounty a spectre of dread, which amounts to doubting the reality of that bubble of ecstasy. And any doubt is powerful enough to burst the bubble, if the angle of impact is right.

747 WILD NIGHT, Van Morrison
Produced by Van Morrison and Ted Templeman; written by Van Morrison
Warner Bros. 7518   1971   *Billboard: #28*

Is this night wild because of what it holds in store—the perfection of a moment when "all the girls walk by dressed up for each other / And the boys do the boogie-woogie on the corner of the street"—or because it's already blowing up a gale while Van strolls aimlessly in the downpour and recalls, or tries to, how it once was, how he wishes it could be again, how it might be if he only knew how to get in touch with the feeling he had back when he was part of it, not just one of those people who "stare in wild wonder" without really comprehending the magnificence of all that street life?

Structurally, this is hippie soul, right down to the soprano sax solo, but unlike all those Woodstock-to-Marin funk hopefuls, Morrison has the stuff to pull it off, not only because his singing is the ideal blend of blarney and blues but because his spirit and vision demand both the brightest and the darkest images that can be found.

748 SMARTY PANTS, First Choice
Produced by Stan Watson and Staff; written by Alan Felder and Norman Harris
Philly Groove 179   1973   *Billboard:* #56

In 1973, Philadelphia broke out as America's most important record production center, with an amazing outpouring of pop and R&B chart hits including the O'Jays' "For the Love of Money," "Mighty Love" by the Spinners, MFSB's "TSOP," "You Make Me Feel Brand New" by the Stylistics, Blue Magic's "Side Show," "The Love I Lost" by Harold Melvin and the Bluenotes, and "I Wanna Know Your Name" by the Intruders. This string of successes heralded a new era for black— and eventually all—pop music. As they ushered in the new rhythms of the new disco era, these records broke up the conventions previously established in soul and R&B, especially those which made the singer and the song central. In the Philly sound, everything served the beat.

The changes centered in rhythm affected everything, perhaps especially modes of singing. That was certainly true among women, where Aretha Franklin had been the dominant influence for the better part of a decade. Aretha's records brought to the Top 40 gospel's values of ultrapersonal expression, along with a dedication to dominating the beat—the rhythm of her records was established by Franklin's internal clock, not any metronomic outside source. Most other women in black pop followed (or tried to follow) Aretha's lead.

The new dance music needed singers whose power was more straightforward, and whose phrasing was precisely metronomic, adaptable to the demands of the rest of the record. This style was more theatrical (not to say histrionic) and it benefited singers whose taste and background stemmed more from Broadway than the Church of God in Christ.

One of the first and most successful of these was First Choice's throaty contralto, Rochelle Fleming, whose mannered exclamations and midrange vocalizations might have been machine-tooled for the arrangements developed by Norman Harris and his Sigma Sound associates. Fresh out of high school, this hometown trio (Joyce Jones and Annette Guess provided the choral responses to Fleming's lead) scored three times for Philly Groove, with "Armed and Extremely Dangerous" just before "Smarty Pants," and then "The Player" about a year later.

Their records had the dense, almost orchestral Philly feel, with an unusually frank awareness of sexuality, street life, and their interconnection with the budding dance club subculture.

On the other hand, not everything had changed yet. In the final verse, Fleming reveals that, though Miss Smarty Pants has won and then dumped her man, nine months later, "Looks like the joke's on me / Dan's still on the corner / And I'm a mother to be." That's a form of retribution with which disco in its hedonist heyday utterly dispensed.

749 A LOVER'S QUESTION, Clyde McPhatter
Produced by Ahmet Ertegun and Jerry Wexler; written by Brook Benton and Jimmy Williams
Atlantic 1199   1958   *Billboard:* #6

Just say yes.

750 OLIVER'S ARMY, Elvis Costello
Produced by Nick Lowe; written by Elvis Costello
Radar ADA 31 (UK)   1979   Did not make pop chart

Before critics or his own pretensions persuaded him that he was a litterateur, Elvis Costello wrote concise pop songs with a detailed density of sophisticated political and verbal expression the equal of anyone since Bob Dylan. He hasn't come up with anything that good since swearing off the mass audience after *Armed Forces*, but this hit from that last grasp at the big brass ring (it made Number Two in England) works as a grand melodic pop song (Steve Nieve's *Blonde on Blonde* piano insists on staying in your brain from the last time you've heard it til you rise the next day), as a quirky political comment on imperialism and as a series of not-quite-opaque puns. "Have you got yourself an occupation?" asks the song's Kafkaesque narrator, and you can only wonder whether he's a military recruiter, trying to lure jobless British kids into the Army, or whether he's speaking as an international banker, offering an oligarch prosperity at the price of independence. Either way, this is a great record and it's symptomatic of the all-around breakdown of the cycle of recording artist, radio broadcaster, and record buyers that it wasn't able to hit in the States (though the *album* did become Costello's biggest seller). Unless you want to blame it on Nick Lowe's far-muddier-than-required production.

751 HOPES ON HOLD, Ruben Blades
Produced by Tommy LiPuma and Carlos Rios; written by Ruben Blades and Lou Reed
Elektra 7-69407 1988 Did not make pop chart

752 SIGN YOUR NAME, Terence Trent D'Arby
Produced by Martyn Ware and Terence Trent D'Arby; written by Terence Trent D'Arby
Columbia 38-07911 1988 Billboard: #4

One way to define the rock and soul aesthetic that separates singles from albums is to think of it as love songs with implications. Sometimes those implications reside in what's left unspoken within the lyrics ("Up on the Roof," "Dock of the Bay"), but more often, those implications are a message sent by the singer's phrasing, which reaches for something that can't quite be spelled out, or holds back from things that would be defiled by being rendered literally.

Pop music from the mid-seventies to the late eighties has been so dominated by dance beats and image-mongering that such subtleties sometimes appeared to have been wiped out. Cynics and purists, who are not breeds apart, can describe with eloquence (and some accuracy) the deterioration of quality, especially the quality of meaning, in today's pop music. But it ain't that simple, not only because snobbery still steers us too easily away from the songs that are richest in such sub-textual implications, but also because the *musical* basis today is often as vulgar and grating as the R&B-based harmony singers of the past were elegant. Whatever has been gained rhythmically, the decline in the standard of pop singing and songwriting is as incontestable as it is tragic (and, maybe, given the demise of the traditions that nurtured earlier generations, unavoidable).

But if the vocal and musical traditions spawned in the fifties and sixties had died with it, they really wouldn't be worth much except as nostalgia. So it's both reassuring and a source of wonderment (at our good fortune, if nothing else) when interesting new voices singing love songs with implications turn up here and now. Terence Trent D'Arby and Ruben Blades assert themselves so brilliantly that there can be little doubt that they belong.

Superficially, D'Arby and Blades are entirely different cases. D'Arby is an American: reared in a Pentecostal family in Florida, a product of integrated Southern high schools, he emigrated to Europe where he became the first black American expatriate pop star of any consequence since Jimi Hendrix. Blades is a Panamanian who's long resided in the United States; recognized as one of salsa's key innovators for more than a decade, he was trained as a lawyer both at home and at Harvard. D'Arby's naked ambitions are those of the pop star. Blades wears the more careful garb of the pop politician. In 1988, D'Arby was in his mid-twenties, Blades in his late thirties. That year, "Sign Your Name" became a major hit, off a multiplatinum album. "Hopes On Hold" was barely heard anywhere.

"Sign Your Name" was the deepest soul track on D'Arby's brash debut LP. D'Arby's music is classic black pop in a tradition that owes a lot to gospel and Motown, but also, like any post-disco pop music, pays close attention to current dance fashion. Still, his heart remains in his singing. "Sign your name across my heart" serves as both invitation and warning; like Roy Orbison, D'Arby knows love hurts but refuses to flinch.

Unlike Orbison (or the equally introverted peer to whom he's most often compared, Michael Jackson), D'Arby intends to do unto others. "Sign your name across my heart," as he sings it, becomes a line that cuts through every listener's defenses. The line might have been written as nothing more than a cute devotional metaphor, but in D'Arby's mouth it was transformed. And that's the job.

"Sign Your Name" came from a multiplatinum debut album by a singer to whom CBS Records devoted all its multinational muscle. "Hopes On Hold" came from *Nothing But the Truth*, the first English language album Blades ever made and one to which Warner Communications contributed few resources beyond the basic recording budget. Even with the assistance of stars and superstars (here, Lou Reed; elsewhere, Elvis Costello and Sting), it was just too damn hard to market a Latin-rock fusion (even one that struck world pop advocates as "too rock") to America's narrowing radio formats.

But for me, "Hopes on Hold" was a great song from the moment I first heard it. At the start, I just loved its slinky, modish melodicism, Carlos Rios's beautiful guitar figure, and Jason Miles's almost spooky synthesizer work. But the key to the song is Blades, a singer whose voice may be less spectacularly rangy than D'Arby's but who knows things about phrasing (in two languages) that only the best ever discover. And since "Hopes on Hold" reached me in a particularly dark hour, the tenderness in Blades's voice and the conviction in the words he wrote (and Reed gave "more of an edge") were the equivalent of a life raft.

"Every time we place our faith in other hands, we stand the chance those hands might let it fall / But second guessing, feeling starts to run away and hope's on hold." I must have heard Blades sing those lines a hundred times in the summer of 1988 and though the sentiment is almost overfamiliar (it's just that old Ray Davies refrain about the anxiety associated with "Something Better Beginning"), the fact that he'd articulated just what I was worrying about never ceased to strike me as miraculous. "Do you want to know the truth?" he asked (and I knew I was hearing Reed's blade at work, sharpening the point). "You shouldn't settle for a lie." When it's sung the way that Ruben Blades sings it, that line can cut you to the quick, and keep you alive.

Because Ruben Blades, like Terence Trent D'Arby, speaks to me in that singularly powerful way that Muddy Waters, Little Willie John, Smokey Robinson, Marvin Gaye, Van Morrison, and a few others have in the past, I know that the story has much longer to run than most suspect. There are times when that alone will let you sleep better at night.

753 BIRD DOG, The Everly Brothers
Produced by Archie Bleyer; written by Felice and Boudleaux Bryant
Cadence 1350   1958   *Billboard:* #1 (1 week)

Raised and trained for the Grand Ole Opry, the Everly Brothers never rebelled. They just added so much rhythm and blues to the mix that they outgrew the Opry and its narrow world before they ever had the chance to appear on it. Retaining their nasal harmonies, they picked up from black pop the slurring tendencies that make "Heeez a burd / Heeez a dawg . . . Heeez a burrrd dawg" one of the most sly and memorable comic routines this side of the Coasters. "Bird Dog" is probably the slightest song the Bryants ever contributed to the Everlys but it's so funny, and the reprise of the "Wake Up Little Susie" guitar licks so effervescent, that its lack of substance becomes an active advantage.

754 ALISON, Elvis Costello
Produced by Nick Lowe; written by Elvis Costello
Stiff BUY-14 (UK)   1977   Did not make pop chart

"I'm not gonna get too sentimental like those other sticky valentines," declares Elvis Costello at the start of his first great love song, but he immediately violates that pledge with a series of arguments that amount to a declaration that only his love can save Alison, a notion as sentimental as any in the history of love poetry, even if the terms of its expression are far more touching and biting than most.

But Costello's performance is uncommonly redemptive, because it lets you feel the intensity with which Costello fights his own jealousy (Alison not only "let some friend of mine take off your party dress," she went on to marry a creep) and the anguish with which he observes the mess she's made of her life. Whatever the song may be about, the *record* is focused squarely on Elvis Costello's feelings and desires— Alison's are barely an afterthought. Every nuance of this muted arrangement is designed to bring forward the singer's emotions, while "Alison," who must have her own perspective on all this, recedes step by step, until finally she's written out of the project entirely and as the music fades, we're left with Elvis musing to himself about the one fact that matters within the universe he's established: "My aim is true."

755 WITHOUT LOVE, Aretha Franklin
Produced by Jerry Wexler, Arif Mardin, and Aretha Franklin; written by Ivy Joe Hunter and Carolyn Franklin
Atlantic 3224　1974　　*Billboard*: #45

756 WITHOUT LOVE (THERE IS NOTHING), Clyde McPhatter
Produced by Ahmet Ertegun and Jerry Wexler; written by Danny Small
Atlantic 1117　1957　　*Billboard*: #19

There was nothing neutral about black vocalists bringing Pentecostal imagery and syntax into popular music. In the fifties, the controversy stirred by the process of secularizing church music came from the churches, which saw the conversion of praise songs from spiritual to sexual uses not only as blasphemous but as a theft of crucial and exclusive traditions that might endanger the very survival of church life.

On the pop side, nobody seems to have given much thought to the ways in which gospel influence changed the rhetoric of love songs. Yet some of the confusion and hysteria, if not the disdain and contempt, with which Tin Pan Alley viewed the rise of gospel-based rhythm and blues songs is understandable. Gospel's praise metaphors are extravagant. When lovers of Cole Porter and Irving Berlin heard them in their secular translations, however, what they thought they were hearing (not knowing or caring much about the tradition from which something like "Hallelujah I Love Her So" sprang) was mere hackwork.

And they weren't entirely wrong. Clyde McPhatter's "Without love, there is nothing at all," as written, is way over the top. Even a Porter or a Berlin might not have been able to get away with such a naked sentiment. Clyde McPhatter recounts the opening lines ("I awakened this morning / I was filled with despair / All my dreams turned to ashes and gold") against nothing much more than a clunky piano, a creaking churchlike atmosphere. And when he reaches the chorus—"Without love, I had nothing at all"—it's everything even this extraordinary singer can do to reach up to the words. Of course, if you change the lyric (as you easily could) to "Without God . . ." and place it in a religious context, there's no problem at all.

It was the blessing of McPhatter and Sam Cooke and Ray Charles and their brethren and successors that they were such excellent singers that they made this overreaching at least plausible and at best, the most thrilling experience of a young person's life. And it was the curse of those who heard them to believe and perhaps to seek and demand the impossible.

It also makes things twice as tough when it comes time to write the next song and you need a metaphor commensurate with those raised expectations. Twenty years down the line, this was a situation that presented itself all the time to gospel-soul singers, even ones as immensely gifted as Aretha Franklin. Remarkably, the tradition from which these metaphors were lifted is so resilient that it continues to provide a seemingly bottomless well of invention.

Aretha's "Without Love," like a story from the Old Testament, begins with a waking dream. She recounts it against a backing that updates McPhatter's accompaniment: an organ replaces the piano, there's a steady pulse from bass and drums, the chorus is closer to a choir.

The waking dream is the song, and what the dream-song says to sleepless Aretha is this: "Without love, there's nothing you can do / Without love, you're not even you." And it's here, at the juncture where psychology and religion intertwine (at the place where what's most spiritual is also most personal) that the gospel tradition is in its true glory. And so is Aretha, for given a metaphor that corresponds with both her private dilemmas and those of the church in which she was reared, she seizes it and squeezes until every last fragment of its musical emotion is extracted.

757 COME ON, LET'S GO, Ritchie Valens

Produced by Bob Keane; written by Ritchie Valens

Del-Fi 4106 1958 *Billboard:* #42

The plane stayed in the air . . .

The Big Bopper laughed it off. Scored another hit or two, then changed his name back to J.P. Richardson and became a TV game show host, halfway between Wink Martindale and Monty Hall, with an expensive collection of hairpieces, the most famous weight control problem in the United States, and two weeks a year live in Vegas, doing stand-up and a little old-time rock and roll schtick.

There, he'd occasionally run into Buddy, who quit the tour after the close call in Clear Lake, just refused to get back on the tour bus and waited out the storm in a motel room, got a ride back home and told promoter Irving Felt to stuff it. When the lawsuits were over, he and Maria Elena tried moving back to Lubbock, but it was impossible for a white man and a Puerto Rican woman to be comfortably married in west Texas. They came back to New York and in 1965, split up. Maria Elena kept their three children, and half of Buddy's increasingly lucrative catalog of copyrights.

Buddy toured with the Beatles, who spoke of him worshipfully, but after his 1964 album produced by Phil Spector, had no more hits as a performer. As a writer, he remained in demand and in 1972, wrote a show based on the old days on the rock and roll circuit, bringing a lot of his old friends—Guitar Baker, King Curtis, the Crickets, Darlene Love—back to the limelight for the first time in a few years. But Buddy wasn't in the show; he said he'd lost the desire. John Lennon said it was the best thing he'd seen since the Jerry Lee Lewis tour of Britain in the fifties. Bob Dylan said nothing, but he went three nights running. When it closed on Broadway, the show went on the road and then set up in Vegas, where it ran on the Strip as a revue for fifteen years.

Neither Buddy nor the Bopper ever saw much of Ritchie, though of course he was offered a part in Holly's revival show. He was now a 300-pound session guitarist and mostly invisible to the rock and roll world, working jingle dates and living in East L.A., where he was a legend to the few who knew the whole story and respected as the best guitar teacher in the community. Offers to make records he greeted with a shrug, though he made one nice duet LP with Carlos Santana.

The couple times Ritchie did albums under his own name, though, the results were half-hearted. He told his daughter that success was one thing, but record labels messed with your music too much. The only one of his hits that he'd agree to play at all was "C'mon Let's

Go," because it was just a guitar tune. He refused to even consider playing "La Bamba," which he regarded as a travesty of Mexican folk culture, or "Donna," because he hated his own confessions of puppy love weakness. And he never wanted anything to do with touring again.

758 BABY WORKOUT, Jackie Wilson
Producer not credited; written by Alonzo Tucker and Jackie Wilson
Brunswick 55239   1963   *Billboard:* #5

It's All Wrong But It's All Right.

Saddled with another of Brunswick's blaring, clunky essays at a swingin' dance tune, complete with a chorus that must have been recruited straight off *Sing Along with Mitch*—burdened, that is, with material that would have seemed exceptionally phony even in a fifties schlock teen flick—Wilson triumphs through sheer vocal power, opening with a scream worthy of James Brown and going on to dazzle with singing so naturally exclamatory that his ersatz setting begins to seem, if not fitting, at least somehow acceptable. And when Jackie turns himself into a siren a few bars before the end, he's clinched the deal, converting clubfooted swing into a genuine dance classic.

759 RIVERS OF BABYLON, The Melodians
Produced by Leslie Kong; written by B. Dowe and T. McNaughton
Trojan   1970   Did not make pop chart

The Melodians aren't singing about Hebrews enslaved in Babylon; their gorgeous harmonizing and light but deep rhythms instead spell out why Rastafarians, who conceive themselves exiled from a paradisical Africa to a hostile Babylon that encompasses the rest of the world, learned to sing—because the "wicked [who] carried us away captivity / Require from us a song." Singing against their wills, then, the slaves handed down a tradition in which their descendants now revel, while vowing never to let the memory of that enslavement dwindle. With songs this sinuous and compelling to carry it on, it never will.

760 BIG BOSS MAN, Jimmy Reed
Produced by Calvin Carter; written by Al Smith and
Luther Dixon
Vee-Jay 380   1961   *Billboard:* #78

Model for a hundred hits, from "Hi-Heel Sneakers" to half the early
Who's repertoire, a statement of class antagonism at least as potent as
anything from either Lennon or Lenin, twelve-bar blues attacked at an
angle as eccentric as anybody's found since Charley Patton, "Big Boss
Man" goes beyond basic into realms of crudity that would be unen-
durable if Jimmy Reed's croaking voice and scorched earth mouth harp
didn't combine so uniquely with Eddie Taylor's boogie guitar riff and
the rudimentary drumming, which arguably has been piped in from an
alternate universe, where folks bow down to backbeat as a god. By the
time you're through with this one, you may feel as if Reed and company
have transported you there, too.

761 ROCK THE BELLS, LL Cool J
Produced by Rick Rubin; written by James Smith [LL Cool J]
and Rick Rubin
Def Jam 44-05349   1985   Did not make pop chart

In-your-face heavy metal hip-hop by a black New York teenager with
more than just the nerve to dis Springsteen, Madonna, Michael, and
Prince, the girl down the block and her boyfriend. Thanks to his deejay,
the great Cut Creator, he makes it stick by effacing in his own image
the deepest, most metallic grooves he can find.

762 THE LOVE I LOST (Part One), Harold Melvin and the Bluenotes
Written and produced by Kenneth Gamble and Leon Huff
Philadelphia International 3533   1972   *Billboard:* #3

One of the great things about listening to Philadelphia International
hits on the radio (or even on 45s) was the edits. At full length, "The
Love I Lost" runs 6:24, and even with Teddy Pendergrass preaching
his brains out, that's too much—unless you're on the dance floor, when
maybe it's over too soon. In getting rid of a couple of minutes, the
single crops out Teddy's full-scale testifying, but since he was among
the ultimate one-track minds, it doesn't make a lot of difference. Unless

you're really into hearing the Blue Notes doing about a hundred rep-etitions of "Sorry I lost it." Trust me, it's more likely Memorex than live anyhow.

763 SOMETHING ABOUT YOU, The Four Tops
Produced by Brian Holland and Lamont Dozier; written by Brian Holland, Lamont Dozier, and Eddie Holland
Motown 1084   1965   *Billboard:* #19

"Dumplin'! Dumplin'!"
Yeah, that's how Levi Stubbs kicks it off. If he'd left it there to stew in its own vaudevillian juices, it would lend credence, I suppose, to the wearisomely stupid allegation that Motown records weren't es-pecially "black."

But it definitely doesn't quit there—in fact, the intensity picks up through just about every succeeding bar, and rather than buttressing the too-pop charge, Holland-Dozier-Holland and the Tops disembowel it. Crunching baritone sax riff after bombarding bass lick, with the solid snap of Pentecostal tambourine and Levi's unquenchable soul, they fire back. And yeah, the whole show's underpinned by tympani, and the ringing vibes lend it a lot of its urgency, but what did you think R&B was about—rules? No, it's about the kind of emotional expansiveness that erupts from these grooves, the pure tension between Motown formula and Levi's uncontrollable passions.

Nobody ever had the nerve to say not soulful enough.

764 JUST ONCE IN MY LIFE, The Righteous Brothers
Produced by Phil Spector; written by Gerry Goffin, Carole King, and Cynthia Weill
Philles 127   1965   *Billboard:* #1

Every record that Phil Spector made with the Righteous Brothers was a paranoiac symphony, and "Just Once in My Life," with its looming tympani and nerve-wracked strings, may be the most paranoid of all ("Lovin' Feelin' " is just the most symphonic). Bill Medley sings it virtually solo, until he's joined by Bobby Hatfield for the lines that demarcate the real spiritual thicket in which they're trapped: "I can't give you the world but I will crawl for you girl," Medley declares. "I will crawl," and then, joined by Hatfield, *"Every day,* I will crawl."

Thank God that Goffin, King, and Weill didn't write together more often.

765 ALWAYS TOGETHER, The Dells
Written and produced by Bobby Miller
Cadet 5621   1968   *Billboard:* #18

Intimacy and shouting rarely make a good blend, as dozens of us have learned the hard way. But when Marvin Junior explodes in the third line of "Always Together," he makes top of the voice growling seem as tender as sotto voce.

That's thanks not so much to Bobby Miller's extraordinary song and arrangement as to Johnny Carter's fabulous falsetto, which together with Marvin Junior's booming and Chuck Barksdale's crooning, gives the Dells a unique three-voice lead system that lends them an intensity akin to their gospel group models (R. H. Harris's Soul Stirrers and Claude Jeter's Swan Silvertones). Like gospel vocalists, when these guys sing "always," they do it in a way inclined to make you think about eternity.

766 CAN'T HELP FALLING IN LOVE, Elvis Presley
Produced by Chet Atkins; written by Hugo Peretti,
Luigi Creatore, and George Weiss
RCA 47-7968   1961   *Billboard:* #2

When Elvis first showed up at Sun Records, Sam Phillips asked him what he sang. "I sing all kinds," Elvis replied, and he meant it. Phillips says that Presley's ambition at the time was not to sing anything new but to sing exactly what the singers he liked on the radio and the jukeboxes were doing. After he left Sun and Phillips for RCA and went to Hollywood to make thirty-odd movie soundtracks, Elvis not only got to sing what he wanted, his way (which in the end bore precious little relationship to any previous pop singer), he sang a lot of material on which even his most indiscriminate hero, Dean Martin, might have gagged.

One thing that meant was the occasional reworking of a classical theme, and if this was done with any sensitivity at all, Elvis always shone. RCA staffers Hugo and Luigi (Sam Cooke's studio assistants during his days there) and George Weiss came up with "Can't Help Falling in Love" for the soundtrack of *Blue Hawaii,* Elvis's biggest-ever movie, by adapting "Plaisir d'Amour," an eighteenth century melody by Italian composer Giovanni Martini.

Out of this funklessness, Elvis fashioned one of the great ballad performances of his career, singing with such gentle insistence and delicacy of phrasing ("Shall I stay" pronounced as if the words are fragile as crystal) that the corniness of the arrangement, with the Jordanaires mixed too high in the background and a steel guitar intruding on everything, makes little or no difference.

What's most persuasive of all, perhaps, is the song's utter fatalism. Years later, when he used "Can't Help Falling in Love" to end every one of his concerts, the song was a kind of joke, or at least Elvis's ironic commentary on how people seemed to feel about *him*. But in the original rendition, the song seems less like a gag than a confession of Presley's complete surrender to the whims of forces greater than he can comprehend. "Like the river flows, surely to the sea / Darling so it goes, some things are meant to be" is not a declaration of devotion, but an acknowledgement of powerlessness. Whether true or not, this is what Elvis Presley believed and that is why he renders the song with such tremendous conviction.

767 I'M STONE IN LOVE WITH YOU, The Stylistics
Produced by Thom Bell; written by Thom Bell, Linda Creed, and Anthony Bell
Avco 4603   1972   *Billboard*: #10

Thom Bell's secret weapon was his songwriting partner, Linda Creed, a white woman from the Philadelphia suburbs whose lyrics give so many Stylistics, Spinners, and Delfonics songs the tangy romantic tilt that lets them bear comparison with the best of Smokey Robinson's. Creed's wonderful use of metaphor and slang reflected a passionate attention to detail that finally represents a vision of the world. For a few moments in the early and middle seventies, Creed's writing was as good as it got.

"I'm Stone in Love with You," with its gilded metaphors encompassing fantasies of movie stardom, Wall Street dominance, and utopian Moonscape real-estate monopoly (offsetting a bridge in which Russell Thompkins declares himself "just a man, an average man") is an epitome of Creed's style. Its smooth elegance may not express life's bohemian ironies as well as singer/songwriter smarm, but it does a far finer job of depicting the world most of us try to live in everyday.

768 DEVIL OR ANGEL, The Clovers
Produced by Ahmet Ertegun and Jerry Wexler; written by
Blanche Carter
Atlantic 1083   1956   Did not make pop chart

The Clovers' final hit (it made Number 4 on the R&B chart) was an
uncharacteristic ballad, but to these ears, its mellow tones are more
sustaining than the group's jump tunes and the pace is far livelier than
1954's molasseslike (but still brilliant) "Blue Velvet." Bobby Vee later
corrupted the song but Buddy Bailey's trembling lead vocal will remain
pure until some vinyl version of Dutch elm disease eliminates every
last copy of the disc.

769 A LOVE SO FINE, The Chiffons
Produced by Bright Tunes Productions [The Tokens]; written
by G. Kerr, S. Barnes, and The Tokens
Laurie 3195   1963   Billboard: #40

One of the true treasures of the girl group era, with characteristic joyous
bounce and drive, one of the last really booting sax riffs to hit the Top
40 and in the final verse, one of the all-time tambourine parts in pop
history. So fine that it doesn't even seem absurd to expend so much
energy and creativity upon a discourse about the definitive fineness of
the guy who just asked Barbara Pittman out. It's a good thing about
that tambourine, though, because in the last verse it virtually blots out
Pittman's assertion that they'll never break up. That's a bit of a stretch
even for a true believer like me.

770 WHAT HAVE YOU DONE FOR ME LATELY, Janet Jackson
Written and produced by James Harris III [Jimmy Jam],
Terry Lewis, and Janet Jackson
A&M 2812   1986   Billboard: #4

The Michael Jackson fable presents him as coming from a multitalented
musical family. In fact, until 1986, his many siblings distinguished themselves solely by their ability to follow. Sister Rebbie reached the Top
Ten with "Centipede," but that was really a ride on Michael's back,
since he wrote and produced. The best of his brothers, Jermaine, scored
his biggest hit, "Let's Get Serious," by linking up with Stevie Wonder.

The others generally did nothing unless and until Michael was willing to make an album with them. Four years after their 1984 swan song tour, only Marlon had released an album, and it wasn't much to shout about.

Of all Michael's nine siblings, the only one who ever accomplished much without him was his sister, Janet, next younger to him on the family ladder. In the late seventies and early eighties, Janet was a regular on TV shows like *Good Times, Diff'rent Strokes*, and *Fame*, and by the mid-eighties, she'd made a couple of albums on her own, neither of which had anything of the flavor of piggyback about them, either. She had even rebelled against her parents and siblings by marrying James DeBarge of the DeBarges, the family singing group that had replaced the Jackson 5 at Motown. The marriage lasted only six months, but it separated Janet Jackson for good from her role as just another pawn in the familial shell game.

So in 1985, after the marriage broke up, Janet headed to Minneapolis to work with producers Jimmy Jam and Terry Lewis, just then the hottest production team in R&B and former partisans of Prince's Twin Cities cabal as members of the Time. Jam and Lewis had made hits for Force M.D.s, Cherrelle, and Alexander O'Neal and Patti Austin.

Jam and Lewis had already written a set of tracks for an album they were planning to make with Sharon Bryant, late of Atlantic Starr. Bryant rejected them as too rambunctious. When the opportunity to make Janet Jackson's third album presented itself, they recycled those tapes. According to Jackson, what Jam and Lewis played for her were rough rhythm beds, atop which they then created keyboard and vocal arrangements, with input from the performer herself significant enough to earn her the first coproduction credit Jam and Lewis ever surrendered.

Certainly, Janet must have written her own lyrics, which went after men—in particular, not very well disguised stand-ins for her father and former husband—more venomously than another guy would have dared. *Control*, the resulting album, was one of the biggest-sellers of 1986–1987, producing five hit singles. Of them, it was "When I Think of You" that went to Number One but the most memorable was "What Have You Done for Me Lately," three and a half minutes of nasty sass, in which Janet projected a bad girl persona so totally convincing that a rumor went around that she was really her brother in drag. As dedicated listeners learned from *Bad*, however, Michael didn't have it in him to play such a tough role. Balanced against some of the sharpest pop-funk of the decade, his sister thrust herself into it like she was born for the job.

771 NEVER GIVE YOU UP, Jerry Butler
Produced by Kenny Gamble and Leon Huff; written by Kenny Gamble, Leon Huff, and Jerry Butler
Mercury 72798   1968   *Billboard:* #20

Abjection again, and this time with no disclaimer from Butler that he's really singing about someone else (as he says about "He Will Break Your Heart"). Indeed, he's virtually inviting his beloved to keep on humiliating him.

But hey, Jerry, you really ought to think about this: If this arrangement, one of the first full-blown Gamble and Huff production epics, replete with vibes, zooming bass, and horns flourished like ceremonial sabres, can't win her over, if the deep pleading in your voice can't get to her, *maybe she's dead.*

772 FAST CAR, Tracy Chapman
Produced by David Kershenbaum; written by Tracy Chapman
Elektra 69412   1988   *Billboard:* #1

Tracy Chapman was the Bright New Face of 1988, earning a landslide of commercial and critical acclaim, and if this were a book that ranked artists, rather than records, that would most likely be reason enough to fear including her. Such stature ought to prove itself over time.

Yet of "Fast Car" 's stature as a classic single, there can be little doubt, even for somebody like me who has more than a few reservations about the portent and meaning of the late eighties revival of the singer/songwriter style. Yet whether that movement plays out as another temporary death for harder sounds on the Top Forty—indeed, whether Tracy Chapman ever makes another interesting record again—"Fast Car" will continue to pop up on the radio from time to time. Heard not hourly but at intervals more like three to six months, this story of two lovers and their flight from reality will mark its day, sustaining itself, not wearing out quickly as even seriously intentioned novelties like "American Pie" have done.

The reasons have more to do with her writing than the way that Chapman sings—Aretha Franklin she ain't, though Joan Armatrading she's already bettered (and who cares?)—or with her elementary musical approach (to call it skeletal would imply a desire for flesh this music has never known). These lyrics tell a harrowing story that makes skilled use of both its muddled moments and its mysteries. Unlike almost any other hit single of its type (certainly far more than Suzanne Vega's "Luka," the only other late eighties hit that even vaguely resembles it), "Fast Car" leaves you longing to know more: When is all this happening? What kind of shelter are they in? How much of the story is fantasy, even within the "real" lives of the characters? What happens next?

Those are questions we expect to ask of literature, not music. But this is rock and roll, all right—somewhere on the fringe perhaps but it fits right in. You can't tell from the beat (though when the drums kick in, you feel 'em in your gut) so much as from the words again. This is a car song—the title refers to the kind of aimless driving that's fueled rocker fantasies from Chuck Berry to Bruce Springsteen, Jackie Brenston's "Rocket 88," to Prince's "Little Red Corvette."

And then, beyond that, there's the chorus. "I-ay had a feeling that I belonged," she sings, "I-ay had a feeling that I could be someone / Be someone." If that's not a rock and roll story, I'll never recognize one.

773 DON'T MESS UP A GOOD THING, Fontella Bass and Bobby McClure
Written and produced by Oliver Sain
Checker 1097   1965   *Billboard: #33*

"Don't Mess Up a Good Thing" always sounded like uptown Jimmy Reed to me; that's the same chunka-chunka guitar, even if it is augmented by horns and a steady dance pulse from drummer Maurice White. That may have been how it was planned to sound but according to rhythm and blues historian Robert Pruter, the session was going nowhere until Chess A&R man Billy Davis proposed changing the tempo to make it fit Chicago's mid-'65 dance craze, the Uncle Willie.

Chicago spawned a host of sixties dances, many of which later achieved national popularity: the Monkey, the Watusi, and the Bird all began in the Windy City, and though the Barracuda and the Twine never made it much further east than Gary as steps, Alvin Cash got hit records out of them anyway. But the Uncle Willie, which started in late 1963, really stayed home. According to Pruter, "Basically, it was a to-and-fro sideways shuffle done mostly on the balls of one's feet. The difficulty was that one could continue the to-and-fro shuffle only a short time before losing momentum."

Pruter also reports that among Chicago R&B artists, several of whom cut Uncle Willie records (Bobby Miller's "Uncle Willie Time" was the first and biggest), it was the custom to get the latest beat right by having kids come into the studio and dance during the session. Apparently, that didn't happen that day at Chess, though, leaving the door open for Billy Davis to fulfill his historic destiny by getting the singers and musicians to dance it themselves, thus providing Fontella Bass a duet hit to go with "Rescue Me."

774 (I WANNA) LOVE MY LIFE AWAY, Gene Pitney
Written and produced by Gene Pitney
Musicor 1002   1961   Billboard: #39

"Love My Life Away" ranks as the best pre-Stevie Wonder one-man recording ever to crack the rock era Top 40.

Aspiring songwriter Pitney gave his debut recording to music publisher Aaron Schroeder as a demo; Schroeder was so taken with Gene's exuberant tenor, the way he used himself as percussive vocal chorus, and the way he caps each repetition of the title phrase with a single cymbal splash, that he formed the Musicor label to release it. That's about all there is to it, and it's that very simplicity that keeps it from falling into the bathetic morass that all but inevitably sank similar productions featuring Neil Sedaka.

775 FOOLS FALL IN LOVE, The Drifters
Written and produced by Jerry Leiber and Mike Stoller
Atlantic 1123   1957   Billboard: #69

How fine a song? During research for the credits above, I happened across a reference to an Irving Berlin tune called "Fools Fall in Love," which he'd originally written for a 1940 Broadway show, Louisiana Purchase, and it took a heap of staring at the credits on the actual Drifters' record to persuade me that this song, with its great last verse payoff and lovely Tin Pan Alley-style melody, wasn't it. I'd bet money Leiber and Stoller knew Berlin's tune, and just as much that the Drifters didn't. In any event, their rendition is so high-spirited it makes you proud to be a fool yourself.

776 HEAVEN MUST HAVE SENT YOU, The Elgins
Produced by Brian Holland and Lamont Dozier; written by
Brian Holland, Lamont Dozier, and Eddie Holland
V.I.P. 25037   1966   *Billboard:* #50

777 STOP! IN THE NAME OF LOVE, The Supremes
Produced by Brian Holland and Lamont Dozier; written by
Brian Holland, Lamont Dozier, and Eddie Holland
Motown 1074   1965   *Billboard:* #1 (2 weeks)

778 YOU LOST THE SWEETEST BOY, Mary Wells
Produced by Brian Holland and Lamont Dozier; written
by Brian Holland, Lamont Dozier, and Eddie Holland
Motown 1048   1963   *Billboard:* #22

As Motown's (and arguably the world's) premier production team, Holland-Dozier-Holland have as much right to be considered artists as anybody in the history of rock and soul. Their records had an essential coherence that went way beyond the specific acts with which they worked. Yes, the unifying thread in all the Four Tops music is Levi Stubbs's indelible singing, but there is another unity at work in the classic records that the group made with HDH at the helm.

That was even more true of the Supremes, a group whose sound was as radically affected by the departure of its writing and production team as it was by the loss of Diana Ross herself. In fact, even Ross, as stylized a performer as exists in any medium, changed drastically after HDH left Motown. Mainly, what she lost was novelty, which forced her into an ever-narrowing reiteration of the same few traits, an inexorable path to the essential self-parody her career has been since (to be generous) "Touch Me in the Morning" in 1973.

The Supremes were able to establish their amazing string of five straight Number Ones (out of a total of nine under the guidance of the Holland-Dozier-Holland team) mainly because HDH kept each record fresh and distinct. Though they never broke the essential formula that kept Diana in the spotlight, they bent it all the time: "Love Is Here and Now You're Gone" is virtually a straight recitation, "The Happening" took them into a realm of pop that deserved its place at the Copa, "You Keep Me Hangin' On" had the density of the Tops' productions, "I Hear A Symphony" had the kitchen sink.

"Stop!" moves with the grace of HDH's greatest productions, propelled by James Jamerson's earthquake bass, the statutory baritone sax and ringing vibes, and an organ part that tightens the tension and suggests a gospel quality that was otherwise impossible within the limits of Ross's style.

Holland-Dozier records used gospel inflections much more proudly and directly than any of the label's other production teams (including Nickolas Ashford and Valerie Simpson, who met in a church choir). It was their records that brought forth the centrality of the fabled Motown tambourine, one of the fundamental Pentecostal instruments. You can hear the contrast between what HDH and the rest of Motown were up to in an especially striking fashion on Mary Wells's "You Lost the Sweetest Boy." There's a profound difference between this surging piano, bass, and drums rocker and the sweeter, less jumping tunes Smokey Robinson gave Wells, the label's biggest female star before Ross.

Holland-Dozier-Holland probably only got the Wells assignment because Smokey's recent discs with Wells had flopped. Robinson reclaimed the job for Mary's next release and, having been pushed, came up with the biggest hit of her career, "My Guy," Motown's first pop Number One. To my taste, "Sweetest Boy" is a far more exciting and danceable record. (Smokey was on the right track, but "My Guy" is no "My Girl.")

But the Hollands and Dozier applied themselves no matter who they were working with. The Elgins, a rare mixed quartet featuring two women and two men, never had big pop hits ("Heaven" was their biggest), but they made some excellent rhythm 'n' harmony sides, including "Darling Baby," "Put Yourself in My Place," and the wonderful "Stay in My Lonely Arms."

"Heaven Must Have Sent You" was the best of all. The roisterous piano-led track resembles the more spacious, upbeat Tops numbers of this period (in fact, their "I'll Turn to Stone" is virtually the same song) and though Saundra Edwards is no Stubbs, she's close enough to Martha Reeves to pull it off. Indeed, for pre-Aretha female soul, this is about as gritty as it gets, though the record also has an element of wistfulness that harkens to the New York-centered girl groups just then fading from the scene. The combination results in something Motown almost never displayed: a feeling of romantic innocence.

779 ('TIL) I KISSED YOU, The Everly Brothers
Produced by Archie Bleyer; written by Don Everly
Cadence 1369   1959   *Billboard:* #4

Meant to be their "Peggy Sue" knockoff, right down to hiring Jerry Allison to do those beyond-belief drum rolls—and Jerry was probably glad to have the work, the Crickets having gone down even before Buddy's plane. So while he was at it, he brought along the remainder of the group, guitarist Sonny Curtis and bassist Joe Mauldin, to fill out the track, which they do splendidly. The result is perhaps the most swinging side the Everlys ever cut and so evocative of Buddy's music that it can get a diehard fan downright upset . . . because there ought to be dozens more like it.

780 GAMES PEOPLE PLAY, Joe South
Written and produced by Joe South
Capitol 2248   1969   *Billboard:* #12

Joe South played guitar for everybody in Nashville during the sixties, up to and including Bob Dylan on *Blonde on Blonde*. He played like a country boy who'd gotten his first instrument as a Christmas present when he was eleven years old, which he was and did. His sensitivity extended to everything from rockabilly to country to blues. By the time he was in his mid-twenties, South not only had a rep as an ace Nashville session man, he'd earned his spurs as a record producer, too.

By 1968, he'd had enough of the background. He recorded "Birds of a Feather," a country hit, and then the album *Introspect*, which contained "Games People Play." And he won three Grammys, had more hits (the fine "Walk a Mile in My Shoes" and "Don't It Make You Want to Go Home" among them), and enjoyed some fleeting stardom.

South's records packed modest, bluesy songs with homespun philosophy. "Games" comes closest to fitting his worldview in a nutshell (or at least on seven inches of 45 RPM vinyl). It's a song about hypocrisy and its cost, a bitter spiritual answer record to the sweeter homilies of Otis Redding's "Dock of the Bay." The comparison is appropriate not only because South is equally concerned with the ways in which humans waste time and energy, but because the song's undercurrent—especially his most vociferously sung phrase, "And furthermore, to hell with hate!"—speaks truth into the teeth of racism. You think that wasn't a big deal coming from a Southerner in 1969? Too bad you missed George Wallace.

781 FREE NELSON MANDELA, Special AKA
Produced by Elvis Costello; written by Jerry Dammers
Chrysalis 1868   1984   Did not make pop chart

The best record by the best band to come out of Britain's early eighties ska revival, arguably the most visceral disc Elvis Costello's ever produced, and certainly the most politically daring of all the charity/political wingdings thrown in 1983–1985: They're talking about getting Nelson *out*, no strings attached, by peaceful means or otherwise, a position considerably to the left of, for instance, Amnesty International, which spurns him. While it's not as stylistically daring as "Sun City," it's also not the last we'll see of this bunch—nor even the strangest context for such a visit with them.

782 ACROSS THE STREET, Lenny O'Henry
Producer not credited; written by Bob Crewe,
Charles Calello, and Valmond Harris Jr.
Atco 6291   1964   Billboard: #98

The male "Party Lights," except soul man Lenny might be in even worse shape. Claudine Clark's mother just won't let her go over to the shindig. Lenny's *not invited*. And the action's right outside his window, where he can see his friends "dancin' and romancin' " with his girl, Lily.

We never do learn what infraction caused Lenny's banishment into this particularly cruel form of Outer Darkness. He simply explains that he's going to go over there and get her, "make her feel silly" and "love her so she'll never return."

"Across the Street" rode low on *Billboard*'s pop chart, but it was popular both in Detroit and on the Carolina beach music scene. Figure out what those two locales have in common with Four Seasons producer Bob Crewe and arranger Charles Calello and you've defined the sound.

783 CRACKIN' UP, The Gants
Produced by Dallas Smith; written by Ellas McDaniel
[Bo Diddley]
Liberty 55884   1966   Did not make pop chart

Authentic Mississippi frat boys (so much so that they named themselves after a brand of preppy sport shirts), the Gants built their rep as Beatles imitators (abetted by a local deejay who used to leak them advance pressings of the new British hits, letting the Gants do to Limeys what the Brits specialized in doing to American soul men). Yet the band remained obscure, despite the midchart success of their first single, a cover of Bo Diddley's "Roadrunner," because Mississippi State University (the very institution where Governor Ross Barnett barred the door against Negro students while cheered on by frat boys in Gant-style shirts and slacks) vowed to report them to their draft boards if they dared take a break from school to tour.

"Crackin' Up," the Gants' fourth single, might have been a response to that bad news (or an alternative way of dealing with it, since anybody in a rock band in 1966 probably had a leg up on proving he was too crazy for the military) but probably wasn't. It definitely *was* better than Bo's original, his standard chunky beat beefed up with nasty guitar licks (these guys had clearly studied the early Yardbirds) and a vocal that's as close to hoarse rebel yell as anything ever applied to R&B maneuvers.

784 HAPPY XMAS (WAR IS OVER), John Lennon and Yoko Ono
Produced by John and Yoko and Phil Spector; written by John Lennon and Yoko Ono
Apple 1842   1971   Did not make pop chart

John Lennon was always rock's most Dickensian character, and here, he emulates "A Christmas Carol" to a tee, stopping just short of pronouncing "God bless us, every one!" Well, Christmas is the season of sentimentality and if there were greater sentimentalists in rock history than Lennon (at least in one of his guises) and Phil Spector, I've never heard of them. Let's remember, then, that Dickens is remembered in part because of, not despite, his warm and open emotionalism and that "A Christmas Carol" is the best-loved of all his stories not only because it fits the season's hopes, but because, like the best records of the Beatles and Phil Spector, the love it inspires is equal to the love it creates.

785 JUST OUT OF REACH (OF MY TWO OPEN ARMS), Solomon Burke

Produced by Jerry Wexler; written by V.F. Stewart
Atlantic 2114   1961   *Billboard: #24*

Burke's first pop hit is one of the most brilliant straight takes of a country and western song that any R&B singer this side of Ray Charles has ever pulled off. Ironically, if it were done by an actual country singer, the arrangement, with its female chorus and churchy organ and mellow sax solo, would qualify as pure countrypolitan. In a soul context, though, it possesses just the right admixture of down-home and uptown, a balance King Solomon's histrionic preachings achieved too rarely.

786 BABY, I LOVE YOU, The Ronettes

Produced by Phil Spector; written by Phil Spector, Ellie Greenwich, and Jeff Barry
Philles 118   1963   *Billboard: #24*

Hal Blaine's greatest hits may be defined as the first through fourth beats of every bar. Not that they're any greater on "Baby I Love You" in particular than on any other Ronettes (or Crystals or Beach Boys or . . . you get the idea) record.

The rest of the record is one of Phil Spector's more purely confectionary creations, strings and sleigh bells pushed to the precipice of unquestionable schmaltz and Ronnie Spector's voice floating in the mix like the soul of Teen Dream incarnate. Although when you come right down to it, those repetitions of "whoa-uh-oh-ooh" are more lustful than spiritual.

787 BORDERLINE, Madonna

Written and produced by Reggie Lucas
Sire 29354   1984   *Billboard: #10*

Madonna's early successes inspired the most virulent attacks I've seen in twenty years around rock criticism and journalism. At perigee, a *Rolling Stone* feature brutally demeaned her for having the kind of sex life for which the same magazine frequently offers nudge-and-a-wink hosannas to Mick Jagger. But it wasn't just *Rolling Stone*.

And it wasn't just Madonna's obvious hedonism, either. If anything, it was only her raw sensuality that made her raw ambition palatable. So what made folks despise Madonna so powerfully?

It wasn't the music, exactly. Sure, she made dance records, but beat 'n' rhythm became hip again once disco died as a middle-class movement and the late night clubs had been returned to bohos and others who didn't need to get out of bed in the morning. At the very time Madonna found herself castigated, Donna Summer finally began to get some positive attention (several years after it mattered, sad to say).

But then again, maybe it was the music. Criticism of Madonna centered on her relationships with her boyfriends, especially boyfriends who'd played significant roles in advancing her career, men like the deejay and producer Jellybean Benitez and musician/arranger Stephen Bray. Such associations made Madonna the Queen of Latin Hip-Hop, a new kind of post-midnight princess.

Heady role for a blonde girl from Michigan. And maybe that was the trouble right there. Madonna's music tended toward the black and Latin. So did her boyfriends. It's hard not to imagine that the young white males who raged against her hardest didn't find something out of order there.

Such attacks, the debacle of her starring movie roles after *Desperately Seeking Susan*, the shambles of her marriage to Sean Penn, the derision of her music as producer-manipulated trash would have destroyed most careers. Madonna has instead prospered, and although she might see it differently, there's only one reason: The music's too damn good to be denied, no matter whose value system it disrupts. Lose yourself for a few minutes in these grooves and you'll see the point.

788 LOVE WILL TEAR US APART, Joy Division
Produced by Joy Division and Martin Hannett; written by Joy Division
Factory FAC032 [UK]   1980   Did not make pop chart

789 THE COLD HARD FACTS OF LIFE, Porter Wagoner
Producer not credited; written by Bill Anderson
RCA 9067   1967   Did not make pop chart

What in the world does a country and western murder ballad from the late sixties have in common with a British trance-rock disc from the postpunk dawn? They represent The Love Song As Suicide Note. Furthermore, each gets where it's going as the product of the singer's conviction that a perspective intoxicated with bitterness represents a coming to grips with the truth.

If each of these records proceeds from demented logic, the specifics of their linkage can be traced to the real men who sing them. Nudie-suited Wagoner sang of electroshock experiences in "The Rubber Room," while Joy Division's black-clad beatnik Ian Curtis hung himself (as the result of a failed love affair, a lousy marriage or "worsening epilepsy," depending on who you believe). In the context of these songs, the released excerpt from Curtis's suicide note could speak for both men: *"At this very moment I just wish I were dead. I just can't cope any more."*

Their approaches to this theme are of course quite distinct. Wagoner speaks concretely and kills himself abstractly. In "Cold Hard Facts of Life," he takes on the persona of a man returning home early from a business trip only to find his wife with another man. They don't see him and he returns to his car, where he notices the liquor he's just bought in anticipation of celebrating his homecoming. He drives round and round the block, polishing off the bottle, then enters the house and knifes the lovers to death. As the song ends, he anticipates his own end with a certain relish: "I guess I'll go to hell or I'll rot here in this cell / But who taught who the cold hard facts of life?"

Typical of classic country songs, "Cold Hard Facts of Life" centers completely around Wagoner's voice, the music designed purely as accompaniment. "Love Will Tear Us Apart," on the other hand, focuses on music, and Curtis's Jim Morrison-like mumble has to struggle to be heard.

It's the nature of that music that first grabs the ear: a rush of rapidly, powerfully strummed acoustic guitar, something like the intro to the Who's "Won't Get Fooled Again," dissolving into a wash of droning synthesizer and crashing drums. Curtis's voice thus becomes a test of the music's tensile strength; he's the force that would tear the sound apart, if he could only get a grip. Like Wagoner, Curtis seems compelled by an underlying mistrust of physical sexuality (represented by the music) that amounts to fear and loathing. But unlike the country singer, who must become an actor in the drama he's witnessing, Curtis merely finds himself engulfed, a hapless victim of his own passions. (A haplessness the band's philosophy extended into an overall misanthropy; that's one reason it took its name from the Nazi concentration camp term for prisoner-prostitutes.) The record's sound is not just droning but relentless and hypnotic, a cold, cruel rejoinder to the lyric's pleas for any kind of meaning, any kind of surcease.

In the end, the denial of those pleas, the remorselessly forcible way in which painful realities assert and reassert themselves, is exactly what links these unlikely companions.

790 DON'T SAY NOTHIN' BAD ABOUT MY BABY, The Cookies
Produced by Gerry Goffin; written by Gerry Goffin and Carole King
Dimension 1008   1963   *Billboard: #7*

The rolling piano-based melody identifies "Don't Say Nothin' Bad About My Baby" as classic Goffin-King, a girl group treasure enhanced by a husky, droning lead vocal, if not its excessively reedy sax solo. Goffin's glowering lyrics convey the same threat as the stuff he came up with for Little Eva's similar "Keep Your Hands Off My Baby," though without reaching such a peak of pique. A tougher song than "Chains" (which is better known only because the Beatles covered it) but it didn't do much damage to the Cookies' status as anonymous backing singers.

791 ONE MONKEY DON'T STOP NO SHOW, Joe Tex
Produced by Buddy Killen; written by Joe Tex
Dial 4011   1965   *Billboard: #65*

What's this? A sermon arguing that people in New York exhibit greater sexual fidelity than people in Texas? Even a preacher as great as Martin Luther King would have trouble making that proposition credible. But sometimes the thrill's in the hunt and listening to Joe trying to persuade you of the impossible is enough to convince you that the *right* monkey actually might do the trick.

792 SWEET DREAMS (ARE MADE OF THIS), Eurythmics
Produced by Dave Stewart; written by Annie Lennox and Dave Stewart
RCA 13533   1983   *Billboard: #1 (1 week)*

Not just the smartest synth-pop riff; the smartest synth-pop *song*, too. Although Annie Lennox doesn't seem to have intended it that way, "Sweet Dreams" is in fact a pointed critique of the commodity culture of late twentieth century capitalism, a description of its processes and its seductions. That's not why it was a hit—it was a hit because Dave Stewart found a great riff and then rode it into the ground—but it's why the record outlasted its moment on the charts.

Annie Lennox does her original antistar turn as the disembodied semiotic queen, and though the vocal obligato at the end of each verse (and throughout the bridge) foreshadows her ersatz soul moves to come, here it works, because she's still aspiring to be heard, not just delivering "wisdom" like baggage. Also, because what she's singing has real meat on its bones: "I travel the world and the seven seas / Everybody's looking for something" is a sharp summary of the process of reification that commodity culture has brought to every corner of the globe (*Billboard* headline, circa 1973: "Viet Nam: A Major Market Fades"). Ultimately, however, the long-term appeal of "Sweet Dreams" rests with Lennox's not-quite-bored, not-quite-frustrated delivery of the relentlessly repeated title phrase: "Sweet dreams are made of this / Who am I to disagree?" Here you can learn everything you need to know about the ways in which excessive devotion to mere things can sap your will and turn you into everything you've always feared and hated.

Then, of course, you're supposed to run right out and buy the record.

793 JET, Paul McCartney and Wings
Written and produced by Paul McCartney
Apple 1871　1974　*Billboard: #7*

"Jet" represents the one time that Paul McCartney has approached the drive and density of his work with the Beatles. It was recorded, along with all the *Band on the Run* album, in Lagos, Nigeria, but because McCartney worked virtually solo (with assistance only from guitarist Denny Laine and his nonmusician wife), there's not an audible shred of African influence, certainly no hint of complex polyrhythms. Instead, what you get is the kind of slick but nevertheless powerful rock he'd created on *Abbey Road*, a grand pop radio confection, no more and no less, but proof he still can if he wants to.

I don't know what the words mean either.

794 BETTE DAVIS EYES, Kim Carnes
Produced by Val Garay; written by Donna Weiss and
Jackie DeShannon
EMI-America 8077   1981   *Billboard:* #1 (9 weeks)

795 MONEY, The Flying Lizards
Produced by David Cunningham; written by Berry Gordy Jr.
and Janie Bradford
Virgin 67003   1979   *Billboard:* #50

In a way, the glory of pop music in the eighties—the reason today's studio rock and dance records are far more exciting than the studied stuff of the seventies, even though almost none are based in the immediacy of live playing—boils down to electronic percussion. Coupled with all manner of elements, from disembodied postdisco voices to atonal postpunk riffs to rich orchestrations, synthesized rhythm sounds have generated an escalating aural excitement that marks as great a change in pop as any instrumental innovation since the introduction of the electric bass.

Partly that's because cheap technology gives amateurs all the way down to the level of street kids the tools to eradicate old rules and disrupt conventions. But even in the most professional contexts, the scratchy, splashy, spacey new slaps and boings have transformed their settings (even if technobeat already shows signs of becoming the latest breed of tyrannical conventionality.)

"Money," a remake of the Barrett Strong classic, may have been the first record built around syndrums to hit the charts. The record crashes along on what sound like dog barks and battered pots and pans. Meanwhile, an atonal female voice recites the lyrics with an absence of emotion which amounts to a satire (if not a critique) of their message. But she blows it by ad libbing the obvious: "I want your money. In fact, I want so much money. Give me your money."

By itself, such obviousness deserved worse than flopping midchart. What raises these British art-rock smart-asses above the level of mundane parody is the repeated ricochet of what sounds like a synthesized monkey bashing upon an empty barrel. In fact, the sounds are exact counterpoints of the ones on the Atari video game Breakout, which only shows that just about everybody got pretty much the same noises out of the same small number of musical microchips then available.

The real breakthrough record for electronic percussion, though, was "Bette Davis Eyes," one of the most massive hits of the decade (it spent five weeks at Number One, got knocked out by the dreadful "Stars on 45", then returned for another month). Another first-rate song that had been previously recorded (by writer DeShannon, in a Hollywood country version), this remake features a brilliant keyboard synth line and a fine, hoarse vocal—Carnes is the female Rod Stewart, if you need one. But what was strikingly new about it was the same kind of tinny syndrum battering that the Flying Lizards had employed. Val Garay was no amateur, though. He coupled the racket with a heavy beat from a regular (should one say, "natural"?) drum kit and the most relentless maracas since Bo Diddley. You can still hear this record's echoes in Madonna and her imitators.

Of course, "Bette Davis Eyes" also found its way to the top because of the lyrics, all mystique and little detail, an evocation of one of the great movie icons that took the wise strategy of leaving its real meaning mysterious.

796 IT'S A MAN'S MAN'S MAN'S WORLD, James Brown

No producer credited; written by Bert Jones and James Brown
King 6035   1966   *Billboard: #8*

"It's a Man's Man's Man's World" could only have been created as the last great burble of male chauvinism before the emergence of the feminist era. The lyric dwells so heavily on achievements allegedly singularly male that it might make the heartiest chauvinist reconsider. Or it might not—certainly didn't seem to make James rethink anything, not even the degree to which the totality of his professed need for a woman might be a little on the unhealthy side.

That's one way to look at it, but you could also say that "It's a Man's Man's Man's World," with its orchestral opening immediately pared back to straight blues guitar (on the mono single mix; the stereo is too lush) argues exactly the way thousands of Ordinary Joes, getting up and going out to life-robbing jobs every day, feel about it, then and now. And that the reason the record seems archaic now is that it isn't only Ordinary Joes but also Ordinary Jills who have to do that in today's world.

In other words, the pleasure you can take in James's singing and the preposterous melodrama of the arrangement is entirely disproportionate to whatever degree of rationale you can possibly bring to the damn record. Reason enough for its inclusion here.

797 WHERE DID OUR LOVE GO, The Supremes
Produced by Brian Holland and Lamont Dozier; written by Brian Holland, Lamont Dozier, and Eddie Holland
Motown 1060   1964   *Billboard:* #1 (2 weeks)

The sexiest Diana Ross ever sounded—thanks to smoldering sax, one of Motown's funkiest piano parts, and some of the most easily parodied, hardest-to-reproduce backing vocals and handclaps in pop history. Pray you don't hear it early in the day, because that insistent melody's guaranteed to linger in your mind until you sleep.

798 WE GOTTA GET OUT OF THIS PLACE, The Animals
Produced by Mickie Most; written by Cynthia Weill and Barry Mann
MGM 13382   1965   *Billboard:* #13

"We Gotta Get Out of This Place" speaks for just about anybody ever trapped in a tank town—or for that matter, any average American high school. The source of Eric Burdon's vocal bitterness is meant to be pure class rage, but it's really just as much bohemian anger at the news that life requires effort. That's why his singing, which seems rather callow in its description of "daddy" 's arduous labors, reaches its nastiest with the thrown-away interpolation "I been workin' too." From the adolescent perspective, this is, of course, *Veritas*.

799 JENNY JENNY, Little Richard
Produced by Bumps Blackwell; written by Enotis Johnson and Richard Penniman
Specialty 606   1957   *Billboard:* #10

800 DEVIL WITH THE BLUE DRESS, Shorty Long
Produced by William Stevenson; written by Shorty Long and William Stevenson
Soul 35001   1964   Did not make pop chart

Where did Mitch Ryder learn the songs that make up those R&B medleys? According to what he told me twenty years ago, he first heard a lot of 'em from keeping the radio under his pillow tuned to John R's fabulous 50,000 watts from WLAC, Nashville. If you had a buck or so, John R would mail order all kinds of discs—especially including Little Richard sides, like "Jenny Jenny," the one where the whole show nearly breaks down when he runs out of breath, but the band keeps pumping and in a few seconds, Richard's back on his feet.

The record collector in the Wheels, was drummer Johnny Bee. But it was ace guitarist Jim McCarty who benefited from the choice of Shorty Long's "Devil with a Blue Dress," since that record, the first release on Motown's Soul subsidiary, was distinguished not only by a slow drag tempo that plumped up every nuance of its sexual innuendo but by an explosive blues guitar break.

Filthy-minded as Long could be, as auteur of "Function at the Junction" and the musical "Here Comes the Judge" and as Motortown Revue MC, the Wheels locked in on his one purely musical success. Not that filthy-minded was ever all that far from their minds, as connoisseurs of their "Sock It To Me" ("Every time you kiss me, feels like a . . ." whaaaat?!?) know well.

801 THE BOXER, Simon and Garfunkel
Produced by Paul Simon, Arthur Garfunkel, and Roy Halee; written by Paul Simon
Columbia 44785   1969   *Billboard:* #7

Despite the baldly middlebrow poesy he's inspired—let alone written—Paul Simon's melodic gift now extends over three pop music generations (and a half dozen different plundered subcultures, though that's another story), a measure of its size. As a friend of mine used to say, "He writes hits in his sleep." (He didn't offer "The Dangling Conversation" as evidence but I might.) But that's not why "The Boxer" belongs here.

Simon's talent survives even the vast wimpiness of Art Garfunkel's singing, the product of a man who never understood that "choirboy purity" becomes anachronistic around the time the hairline begins to recede. On "The Boxer," Garfunkel's piety is undercut by the excessively lilting chorus ("Li-la-li, li-la-li-li-li-li"), and engineer Roy Halee balances the harmonies with percussion, thought it takes tympani to do the trick. More than any of their other sixties collaborations, "The Boxer" remains a record, meaning its gimmicks mainly outweigh its pretensions, that the performance brings the composition to life, and that filtering in the orchestration toward the end actually works as something other than a post-Beatles pop convention. Then there's that droning thing (a bassoon? a fog horn? a synthesizer?). But that's not why "The Boxer" belongs here.

"The Boxer" belongs because it's the one example of Simon and/or Garfunkel ever using rock and roll diction and possibly even humor. So in the second verse, it's all but impossible not to hear Simon's boast about slumming as "Seeking out the poor reporters where the ragged people go / Looking for the places only they would know," and imagine that he's written a tribute to Jimmy Breslin and Murray Kempton. Hey, I'm almost forty. *I know* he wrote "poorer quarters," but if Simon can take time in the Top 40 to brag about taking "comfort" from hookers, (wonder if he fucked 'em), I can certainly get my kicks. He says so himself. "All lies in jest / Still a man hears what he wants to hear and disregards the rest." Good advice.

802 ADORABLE, The Drifters
Produced by Nesuhi Ertegun; written by Buck Ram
Atlantic 1078   1955   Did not make pop chart

When he was inducted into the Rock and Roll Hall of Fame, Atlantic's Jerry Wexler said with a wink that he believed that of all the records his company had made, it was Neshui Ertegun's that would last longest. Figuring he meant the jazz discs on which Neshui had expended most of his energy, I wrote it off as a curiously snobbish statement of infidelity to the evening's premise.

But as Atlantic has done a better job of reissuing its old rock and roll, it's become easier to see another meaning in what Wexler said. Every rock record that Neshui Ertegun touched has a deep and lasting musicality, none more so than "Adorable." A minor West Coast hit by the Colts, one of the groups Buck Ram managed, Atlantic deliberately set out to cover it—to squelch the sales of a potential hit for the tiny L.A. independent label Vita in favor of its own interests, just as major labels did to Atlantic all the time. (Such sharp practice was far more common among the supposedly righteous independents than historians liked to acknowledge.)

Neshui Ertegun became involved because the Drifters were on the West Coast and so was he. His partners, Wexler and younger brother Ahmet, phoned and asked him to fill in with the group, which they usually produced themselves. Neshui did a great job, cutting five songs in three and a half hours and getting one of the biggest two-sided hits of the Drifters' career: "Adorable," with tenor Johnny Moore on lead, went to Number One on the R&B charts (the Colts got to Number 11), while the flip side, the more gimmicky "Steamboat," fronted by bass voice Bill Pinkney, made Number Five.

Whatever the ethics of what Atlantic was up to, the musical quality is beyond dispute. Moore sings his heart out (and if he's truly copying the Colts, then they were deeply engaged in stealing Clyde McPhatter's thunder themselves), the group's responses are sharp and soulful, and the arrangement is beautifully nuanced with grunting sax, restless drums, and staccato piano. A hell of a rush job.

803 HITCH HIKE, Marvin Gaye
Produced by William Stevenson; written by Marvin Gaye, Clarence Paul, and William Stevenson
Tamla 54075   1963   *Billboard:* #30

An odyssey from town to town—his destination seems to be "that street corner, Sixth and Third," but exactly what town featuring that location (L.A.? Chicago? New York?) we never learn—as well as from one of Motown's guttiest vocals to one of its earliest Lite Soul arrangements, featuring gutbucket bass and fatback drums right alongside a trilling flute.

804 WENDY, The Beach Boys
Written and produced by Brian Wilson
Capitol R5267   1964   *Billboard:* #44

It's difficult to judge whether EPs belong in *The Heart of Rock & Soul*. Pressed and indecisive (and buttressed by Joel Whitburn, who lists EPs with singles rather than albums in his chart chronicles), I come down here in favor of what's most important—music. "Wendy," and the three songs that accompanied it on *4—By the Beach Boys* (which also included the drab car song "Little Honda"; "Don't Back Down," Brian Wilson's last really great surf song, one about eighty times more compelling than "Surf's Up"; and "Hushabye," the group's remake of Pomus and Shuman's falsetto doo-wop standard) is a landmark of the last genuinely great period of Beach Boys music, which extended from "I Get Around" and "Don't Worry Baby" through "Wild Honey" and reached a peak with the albums *All Summer Long* and *The Beach Boys Today*. All the music on *4—By the Beach Boys*, Capitol's companion piece to the more successful *4—By the Beatles*, was drawn from the former LP.

The distillation is a boon, because in the end, this *was* a singles band, only it was operating at such a high rate of productivity at the time that it was impossible to force all its airplay-worthy material out as pop singles. ("Wendy" probably would have charted higher, in fact, if it had been released as a full-fledged single and not squeezed out in the month between "When I Grow Up to Be a Man" and "Dance Dance Dance," both of which went Top Ten, even though neither's as good.)

At which point, the lay reader is entitled to ask: "What the fuck is an EP?" Simple to ask; more difficult to answer, unless you grasp the concept of a mule easily. EP stands for Extended Play, and it was developed by RCA Records when it became clear that that company's preferred format, the seven-inch 45 RPM disc, was losing the marketing war to Columbia Records' twelve-inch 33⅓ RPM LP. EPs retained the seven-inch shape (although many of them had an LP-sized spindle hole rather than the donutlike center of the true 45) but used advanced microgroove recording techniques, which allowed longer musical selections to be squeezed into the same amount of vinyl space without appreciable loss of quality, to add an additional song or two per side. The EP never acquired a creative definition of its own. Which is odd, in a way, because it seems like the perfect compromise for acts who have just a little too much to say to be squeezed onto a single and not enough to fill up an album. It's never worked out that way in practice, probably because it creates confusion when it's time to market and promote the damnable devices.

Which probably means you'll never have to try to figure out the concept of the EP again for the rest of your life, unless you become a fan of early eighties speed rock, in which case bless you and be on your way. I wouldn't even bring it up here except that:

1. "Wendy" is one of the finer obscure concoctions of the Beach Boys career and its thrilling near-falsetto lead and Ronettes-soundalike rhythm section, fired by another of those unmistakable and inimitable Hal Blaine percussion parts, fits here far better than it does in stuff like "Little Deuce Coupe" or even "Surfer Girl." Besides, Mike Love doesn't sing nearly as much of it as, say, "California Girls."

2. Brian Wilson wrote this lovelorn number upon the birth of his daughter, Wendy, which strikes me as kind of kinky and probably won't really be grappled with in the movie about him and his shrink.

3. It remains important to understand how utterly accidental, if not arbitrary, it is that we have the tradition of telling the story of rock and roll through the album medium. In another alternate universe, the whole discussion could be ordered around EPs. Not that I'd be inclined to live there.

805 MIDDLE OF THE ROAD, The Pretenders
Produced by Chris Thomas; written by Chrissie Hynde
Sire 29444   1983   Billboard: #19

A memo from former punkette Chrissie Hynde to her fans: "I'm not the kind I used to be / I've got a kid, I'm 33."

That's the meat of one of the all-time message songs, maybe the first rock record which revolves around acceptance of the idea that everybody ages. Not exactly a wholehearted acceptance but Hynde's looking to circumvent nothing—not that the bashing rhythms of the music would let her. Annoyed at the fact that her fans won't let her walk from a cab to the curb without asking for an autograph, scared shitless of nuclear warfare, humiliated by the consequences of her native land(s) owning "a big chunk of the bloody Third World" where "dead babies come with the scenery," Chrissie's at the end of her rope, unable anymore to maintain the bohemian pretense of eternal youth, but equally incapable of just shrugging it off and moving along.

Stuck with what she's got, Hynde epitomizes the dilemma of the careerist rock and roller, from Elvis Presley the day the Army cut him loose, to Pete Townshend the week he met the Sex Pistols, to Joe Strummer the moment he realized the implications of his own ideology. Unlike the others, because she's stuck her neck out the window and bellowed the truth at the world, maybe Hynde has a chance of creative survival.

Wicked temper, though.

806 DON'T PLAY THAT SONG, Aretha Franklin
Produced by Jerry Wexler, Tom Dowd, and Arif Mardin; written by Betty Nelson and Ahmet Ertegun
Atlantic 2751   1970   Billboard: #11

807 DON'T PLAY THAT SONG (YOU LIED), Ben E. King
Produced by Ahmet Ertegun and Jerry Wexler; written by Ahmet Ertegun and Betty Nelson
Atco 6222   1962   Billboard: #11

What are the odds of the same record label producing two versions of the same song (a tune cowritten by the company's founder, at that)

that top out in exactly the same spot in *Billboard*'s Hot 100 eight years apart? Even if that's sheer coincidence it's still a hell of a song that can be done so distinctively by two performers so different.

Of course, all Ben E. did was sing it against a slightly up-tempo recapitulation of "Stand By Me," while Aretha transforms it, turning in one of her most soulfully swinging early seventies groove numbers. So even if the song remains the same, the differences are what count the most. For King, the right way to convey the song's conviction of his lover as a liar is through pained restraint. True to her gospel heritage, Aretha's art requires exuberant eruptions, and I guarantee nobody's ever sounded more joyous while pointing a finger. "You lied, you lied, ooooo-ooh, you lied," she cries and the song changes its entire coloration, becomes a celebration of her release into the bright light of the truth.

808 YOU KEEP ME HANGING ON, The Supremes
Produced by Brian Holland and Lamont Dozier; written by Brian Holland, Lamont Dozier, and Eddie Holland
Motown 1101   1966   *Billboard:* #1 (2 weeks)

Worth hearing not so much for Diana Ross's ultra-airhead vocal (it does have a certain charm, if you can resist shouting "Why don't you just tell him to fuck off, then?") as for the Morse code guitar, one of the definitive Motown tambourine bits and a deep, dark drum and bass pattern. The music can't elevate Ross's minor discomfort into the realm of tragedy, but thanks to the Funk Brothers band, at least it approaches the region of melodrama.

809 THE GRAND TOUR, George Jones
Produced by Billy Sherrill; written by N. Wilson, C. Taylor, and G. Richey
Epic 11122   1974   *Did not make pop chart*

Talking with Waylon Jennings about the rebuilding of the Grand Ole Opry in the early seventies, which involved its removal to suburban Nashville to be juxtaposed with something called Opryland, I remarked, reasonably enough it seemed at the time, "What's the Hank Williams ride gonna be? A long black limousine?" Jennings looked like he was gonna choke.

A couple of years later, George Jones made the joke come true, after his own fashion. As a ride, "The Grand Tour" appears in the shape of the guide's own inconsolable broken heart. Why, that's ol' George Jones himself, and he . . . those are tears in his eyes as he leads us through, touching an object here and there and fighting off the pain each memory evokes. The part I liked best, I guess, was the closet where she left her clothes. And George? His best line was certainly, "As you leave you'll see the nursery / Oh she left me without mercy."

Go back? Probably. If we happened to be passing through. Wonder how he feels to be stuck there, though? Well, being left behind is all he ever seems to think about, so maybe he's happy. As happy as he could ever be.

810 DONNA THE PRIMA DONNA, Dion
Produced by Robert Mersey; written by Dion DiMucci and Ernie Maresca
Columbia 42852   1963   *Billboard: #6*

Dion's move from the independent Laurie Records to big-leaguer Columbia may have been a great business deal but creatively, it sent him off on the wrong track. Columbia had him repeating his old hit sound as a formula, drifting off toward pop arrangements closer to Bobby Darin's than he could afford and altogether losing his bluesy feeling. Except for his remake of "Ruby Baby" and the striking album track "I Can't Help But Wonder Where I'm Bound," Dion's years there were the creative nadir of his career. Once the most consistently imaginative performer in the whole doo-wop field, he now seemed to grind out music as much to meet the demands of his raging drug habit as anything else.

In that context, "Donna" is especially remarkable, the one Columbia disc that comes close to his earlier inventiveness. Dion's singing once more perfectly merges the intense and the relaxed, while the arrangement, with its goofy chorus and claves, handclaps and finger-snaps, perks up a lyric that almost openly satirizes his early tributes to teen temptresses. And you gotta admit that rhyming "five and ten cent store," "Zsa Zsa Gabor," and "girl next door" is a coup.

811 NOBODY KNOWS WHAT'S GOIN' ON (IN MY MIND BUT ME), Chiffons

Produced by Bright Sounds Productions [The Tokens]; written by
Brute Force
Laurie 3301   1965   Billboard: #49

The girl group record that fully captures the quality of obsession inherent in teenage love affairs. With its big buildup to an enormous
orchestrated finish, it's probably well over the top for most tastes, but
somehow, the frantically repeated "Nobody knows what's goin' on in
my mind but me," continuously escalating until it bursts forth in the
chorus chanting "No no no no no" (or in the second "verse," although
this song's structure isn't nearly that simple, "Whoa, whoa, whoa,
whoa") makes the orchestration, when it finally arrives, seem closer to
the Beatles than a misguided application of the Wall of Sound (which
is probably what it intended to be). If you've ever had a thought race
through your head without cease, "Nobody Knows What's Goin' On"
says it all.

812 CHURCH OF THE POISON MIND, Culture Club

Produced by Steve Levine; written by George O'Dowd [Boy George],
Jon Moss, Roy Hay, and Mikey Craig [Culture Club]
Epic/Virgin 04144   1983   Billboard: #10

What got lost in all the hoopla over Boy George's preferences in sex
and dress and drugs wasn't just his soulful singing but the skillfulness
of his band, which played sophisticated modern pop-soul charts as well
as any group in New York, L.A., or London. That's why "Church of
the Poison Mind," with its latter-day Philly soul bottom and scathing
harmonica break, its Stax-like horn punctuation, and Helen Terry's
wailing vocal responses, remains thrilling long after all George's secrets
(at least, all the ones anyone cared about) have been told.

   In a sense, it's hard to see what the sexual-sartorial fuss was all
about. From Little Richard and Bobby Marchan on one extreme to
Liberace and Milton Berle on the other, cross-dressing has been a
common habit among Anglo-American performers. It was George's
posture not just as a drag queen but as a fairly unapologetic homosexual
(he could be coy, but he never denied his tastes) that required strong
punishment. Just as Elton John's career fell off for several years after
his revelation of his "bisexuality," George's star crashed long before

the London cops decided to do their bit for Fleet Street with his arrest for heroin (cruelly timed for just the moment when he was going clean).

Like most of Culture Club's songs, "Church of the Poison Mind" doesn't make its meaning especially clear. Mainly, it seems to concern an especially ideal pickup (and perhaps some self-criticism on George's part for his own dirty wishes upon first viewing that fine young thing). But there's nothing overeager about hearing the title as a slap at the voyeuristic world in which we live, and at least part of the mounting, moaning tension in George's vocal as an entirely reasonable sense of trepidation at the potential consequences for himself.

813 IT'S ALL IN THE GAME, Van Morrison
Produced by Van Morrison; written by Carl Sigman and Charles Dawes
Mercury (UK) 99   1979   Did not make pop chart

Van Morrison sings as if he's inherited the entire rhythm and blues tradition and it's his job not only to nurture it but to keep it growing and expanding. That's a metaphor Charles Dawes, a Chicago banker who served as Vice President in the second Calvin Coolidge administration, might have appreciated, though Dawes might not have been so happy with what happened to the wordless tune he composed as "Melody in A Major" in 1912.

In 1951, lyricist Carl Sigman devised words for Dawes's song and Sammy Kaye, Carmen Cavallaro, Dinah Shore, and Tommy Edwards all recorded it. It was Edwards, a smooth balladeer in the Nat Cole mold, who did best with the song, getting it to Number 18 in *Billboard*. Though Edwards was a black man, there was nothing of rhythm and blues in his rendition; the arrangement was straight pop.

By 1958, Edwards was still looking for a follow-up. MGM Records offered him one last session, on which they wanted him to rerecord "It's All in the Game," so they'd have a stereo master to reissue. Edwards went them one better, rearranging the song with an R&B beat—it was still a ballad but he gave the song an emotional coloration reminiscent of the new wave of rock and roll singers. Within six weeks, the new version had eclipsed the old, going to Number One in both the U.S. and the U.K.

There "It's All in the Game" lay for two decades. Cliff Richard nudged it into the Top 30 in 1964; the Four Tops got it about as high in 1970. Neither version was especially memorable. "It's All in the Game" was just another pop tune lying fallow.

In 1979, Van Morrison made his first album for Mercury Records, after spending more than ten years with Warner Bros. Maybe that change made him feel retrospective. Maybe retrospect was just where his always ruminative muse led him that year. In any event, Morrison's Mercury debut LP, *Into the Music*, was one of his strongest and strangest, a record utterly out of sync with fashion made by a man completely in tune with his soul and his sound.

In America, no one released such eccentric music on singles any more; the sole purpose of singles was to get airplay on Top 40 radio. Nobody at Top 40 was going to play anything on *Into the Music*, and that went double for the album that followed, *Beautiful Vision*. But in England, where airplay is less important, singles are issued as a matter of course. And the one they released from *Beautiful Vision* distilled both albums with rare efficiency. The A side was "Cleaning Windows," Van's song about the day job he held as a kid, and the records he used to buy back then, and his own bemusement at how far he'd come. The B side was "It's All in the Game."

I'm not sure why Morrison coupled those songs. Maybe the record company just went ahead and did it without asking him. But there's no doubt that the two tracks function as an elegant comment on each other, as if "It's All in the Game" were the direct product of all that musing about his youth, as if "Cleaning Windows" had been written in the wake of some chance encounter with a favorite old record like Tommy Edwards's "It's All in the Game," the one that inspired him to record that song in the first place, and Van just never got around to finishing the new song for *Into the Music*.

Van's lyrics to "Cleaning Windows," I should add, suggest nothing so unhip as a teenage kid listening to sentimental R&B ballads—he talks only about listening to records by blues heroes like Muddy Waters, Blind Lemon Jefferson, Jimmy Rogers, and Sonny Terry. But truth to . tell, the song Van wrote isn't nearly as powerful as the song that he stole.

And steal it is just what he does. Tommy Edwards suggests "It's All in the Game" has potential as a rhythm and blues song. Morrison excavates all those nuances; his performance is a tour de force of blues gesticulation, filled with guttural asides and half-swallowed interpolations, the kind of thing that could only be done by a guy who'd spent a lifetime trying to figure out how to beat Ray Charles at his own game. The beat never rises above Edwards's moderate tempo, but Morrison makes it feel so much more intense that by the end, he might as well be screaming and quaking with gospel passion. Tucked away on a B side, it's one of the most emotionally revealing travels through the history of pop music, from 1912 or some point in an even more distant beyond to the moment it clutches your gut.

814 AIN'T NO STOPPIN' US NOW, McFadden & Whitehead
Written and produced by Gene McFadden, John Whitehead, and Jerry Cohen
Philadelphia International 3681   1979   *Billboard:* #13

Disco's most assertive anthem—released, naturally, just as the genre took a commercial nosedive from which it never quite recovered. What survives is a subtext far more powerful even when it was held beneath the surface: "Ain't No Stoppin' Us Now" as an anthem of black pride. Placed on the threshold of the eighties civil rights rollback, that message wasn't exactly opportunely timed, but there's so much strength and conviction in this music—especially in John Whitehead's preaching lead vocal—that nothing can deny it. And there's a lesson in that, too.

815 CAN'T GIVE HER UP (12″ Mix), Skipworth and Turner
Produced by Patrick Adams; written by Rodney Skipworth and Phil Turner
Warner Bros. 28695   1986   Did not make pop chart

One of the great lost dance records, from the Ph.D. bass intro to the vibes break to the vocal glossalia that makes "Don't Worry Be Happy" sound as soulful as the CBS Evening News. Inspirational Verse: "I love the way that she walks / It goes so good with the way that she talks."

816 WELCOME TO THE BOOMTOWN, David and David
Produced by Davitt Sigerson; written by David Baerwald and David Ricketts
A&M 2857   1986   *Billboard:* #37

Southern California songwriters spent a couple of decades trying to define the city's psychocultural uniqueness, with results as opaque as Brian Wilson's "Surf's Up," as scathing but mystifying as the Eagles'

"Hotel California," as funny but superficial as Randy Newman's "I Love L.A." But nobody ever came closer to defining the frenetic grasp for glamour and power, the sleaze within the tinsel, than this pair of out-of-town transplants. And they did it not so much with the images they purvey or the stories they tell as in a single line: "All that money makes such a succulent sound," and the way "succulent" rolls out lush and venomous from David Baerwald's mouth, a noise with a slithering life of its own. It recalls not just the cheap glory and short lives of the lowlifes who appear in the lyrics (and similar works going back to Raymond Chandler's 1940 novel, *Farewell My Lovely*) but, in its original time and place, to the addled fanaticisms of the sort of mad John Bircher industrialists who envisioned placing a second-rate actor on the pedestal of the Presidency and actually had the cruel nerve and stamina to pull it off. If this music doesn't scare you, you're not listening closely enough.

817 GOOD THING, Paul Revere and the Raiders
Produced by Terry Melcher; written by Terry Melcher, Mark Lindsay, and Paul Revere
Columbia 43907   1966   *Billboard:* #4

The closest they ever came to a soul record, with Mark Lindsay filling in the Wilson Pickett role. (Wilson would have been better off with this hard rocker than, say, "Sugar Sugar," too.) And what a great guitar sound—maybe the best argument of all for Terry Melcher as the most underrated Hollywood producer of the sixties.

818 LEAVIN' HERE, Eddie Holland
Produced by Brian Holland and Lamont Dozier; written by Brian Holland, Lamont Dozier, and Eddie Holland
Motown 1052   1964   *Billboard:* #76

819 JAMIE, Eddie Holland
Produced by William Stevenson; written by William Stevenson and Barrett Strong
Motown 1021   1962   *Billboard:* #30

Eddie Holland played a key role in the Motown story from before the beginning. His first music industry job was singing on the demos of the songs Berry Gordy wrote for Jackie Wilson. Holland's "You," a 1958 flop on Mercury, was one of Gordy's first productions, and when Gordy formed his Tamla production company, Eddie's "Merry Go Round" was the second single he leased to United Artists.

United Artists signed up Holland for the next four years, although the records he made there didn't amount to anything. They failed to contract him as a songwriter, though, so he worked with his brother, Brian, and his new partner, Lamont Dozier, from their start at Motown. Eddie's chief contribution to Holland-Dozier-Holland came in the form of lyrics, but even though he was credited only as a songwriter, he played a key role in the production process: He taught each singer how he wanted the lyrics phrased.

He had the authority because he was himself a successful Motown artist. "Jamie," a lively, lovely Jackie Wilson knockoff, was one of the label's most important hits in 1962, the year that the company really took off. In fact, the singing apes Wilson so closely that what's finally most impressive about "Jamie" is the completeness of the imperson-ation, extending to an arrangement that manages to use all the jive elements in the Brunswick catalog—syrupy strings, swingin' rhythm section, domineering brass—but applies them with taste and discretion. If Jackie himself had ever had a song and a production this good, he would have become the first human in orbit.

Eddie Holland made ten Motown singles before abandoning his artistic career, which insiders attribute to a combination of personal reticence (both he and Brian are notoriously shy) and cold calculation (Eddie went to accounting school and he understood that songwriters outlast performers, not to mention receiving legally fixed royalties for their work.)

Before he quit, though, Eddie delivered one last unforgettable num-ber to the rock and roll repertoire. A staple of up-and-coming mid-sixties bands in both London and Detroit—covered by everyone from the Who to the Rationals—"Leaving Here" was so far ahead of its time that it really deserves a cover by Chrissie Hynde or Joan Jett.

"Leaving Here" gives a hint of what a Jackie Wilson record pro-duced by HDH might have sounded like: a bursting, gospel piano-led shouter, sounding, for that matter, very much like the template for their later uptempo productions for Marvin Gaye. It also has one of the team's most imaginative story lines in which Eddie falls asleep and dreams that every girl in town is gonna split, because they've had enough of men's perfidy. He awakes to bring the message: "One day, one day, and it won't be long," he declares, "aaaaall these fine girls'll be gone." Amidst an atmosphere so roisterous, it's impossible to doubt him.

And frankly, if you'd made a record this hot and the best record label in the world couldn't take it past Number 76, you might give up, too.

820 I CAN'T GET NEXT TO YOU, Al Green
Produced by Willie Mitchell; written by Barrett Strong and Norman Whitfield
Hi 2182 1970 *Billboard:* #60

This wasn't Al Green's first hit. "Back Up Train," a so-so soul ballad, came closer to cracking the pop Top 40 in 1967, stalling at Number 41. For which Green ought to be forever grateful, for if that record had been a mite more successful, or if its follow-ups had done a shade better, he might never have gone to Memphis and met up with Willie Mitchell, and then he might have entered history as just another soul journeyman. And even though "I Can't Get Next to You," his first hit for Hi Records, did barely half as well on the charts, it established Green as one of the most inventive singers around.

"Back Up Train" respects convention in every way; though of course Green's vocal is distinctive, it's never adventurous. "I Can't Get Next to You," already a hit for the Temptations, may not have been original material, but the arrangement and singing went way beyond the original. Mitchell's production keys into Green's almost solipsistic introspection so deftly that he even presents Green responding in faint echo to his own declarations of magical prowess, a method that softens the sound without interfering at all with the funkiness of the Al Jackson-driven band. Thus, Green's hoots, whispers, grunts, and cries are given a canvas on which they can be spread in all their glory. Except for a dated guitar solo, "I Can't Get Next to You" establishes the classic pattern of Green's hits, probably the most influential rhythm ballads of the seventies.

821 FOR YOUR LOVE, The Yardbirds
Produced by Giorgio Gomelsky; written by Graham Gouldman
Epic 9790 1965 *Billboard:* #6

Eric Clapton quit the Yardbirds over the lapse in blues purism that resulted in this vaguely Oriental hit, with its guitar and vocal drones over bongos and an R&B backbeat. But maybe he should have stayed put because Clapton's own contribution to the track is as effulgent a guitar line as ever cracked the Top Ten, blossoming with blessed brevity in the bridge into something even closer to heavy metal than Cream's "Spoonful."

In the end, though, Clapton already had found his mission: the invention and sanctification of album rock, with Cream as his vehicle. For the lapsed art student, pop artifacts, even fine ones like "For Your Love," never had a chance against such "progressive" material as "Tales of Brave Ulysses" and "Pressed Rat and Warthog."

822 IT'S GONNA WORK OUT FINE, Ike and Tina Turner
Produced by Juggy Murray; written by Rose Marie McCoy and Sylvia McKinney
Sue 749   1961   Billboard: #14

Given Tina's latter-day revelations about Ike's activities as slave driver and wife-beater, the title and concept (she's trying to trap him into getting hitched) could hardly be more ironic. Her hoarse shrieks now have an entirely different meaning, as do his drawled professions of winking innocence. The arrangement is still driven along by Ike's twanging blues guitar though, which maybe makes "It's Gonna Work Out Fine" the final proof that horrible humans can make great music.

823 LIAR, LIAR, The Castaways
Producer not credited; written by Jim Donna
Soma 1433   1965   Billboard: #12

Second most famous frat-rockers to attend the University of Minnesota—the first was Bob Dylan, of course. This is probably the kind of juvenile noise that drove folky Bob out of Dinkytown and into Greenwich Village—an overamped organ, guitar, falsetto, and scream raveup that makes up in the inelegance of garage band simplicity and energy what it lacks by every other measurement. Twenty years later, Prince came out of the same town with two-finger organ riffs that surpassed this one, but it took that long to beat 'em.

824 COME AND GET THESE MEMORIES, Martha and the Vandellas
Produced by Brian Holland and Lamont Dozier; written by Brian Holland, Lamont Dozier, and Eddie Holland
Gordy 7014   1963   *Billboard: #29*

At the outset, Martha and her gang were just another girl group, their records replete with confectionary teen angst lyrics like this one's deep nostalgia for passions not six months old, set up with bouncy beat and just-corny-enough trombone solo. In three months, "Heat Wave" would introduce Martha and the girls as queens of the high school panic attack, and history would be different. As it was then, they fit in.

825 I'M WALKIN', Fats Domino
Produced by Dave Bartholomew; written by Fats Domino and Dave Bartholomew
Imperial 5428   1957   *Billboard: #4*

It wasn't until the sixties that rock and roll really became guitar-dominated music. In the fifties, it revolved around piano, drums, and most of all, saxophone, as "I'm Walkin' " more than amply shows. Its furious snare-centered shuffle beat, played in counterpoint to something that might be cymbals, might be handclaps, provides an indisputable link to classic New Orleans jazz. The center of the song then becomes not the straight-ahead rapid-fire jollity of Fats's vocal, but the pair of honking sax breaks, which elevate the proceedings from the ordinary with grit and funk.

826 SUMMERTIME BLUES, Eddie Cochran
Written and produced by Jerry Capeheart and Eddie Cochran
Liberty 55144   1958   *Billboard: #8*

Eddie Cochran undoubtedly stands as the most overrated fifties rocker, benefiting enormously from the fact that he looked the part more perfectly than anybody but Elvis, and from the circumstances of his death, which occurred not just in a traffic accident, but in a car crash while riding with Gene Vincent. In *England*, where Elvis himself never toured. Had he lived, it's hard to believe that Cochran would be regarded as one of the handful of rockabilly giants.

Mainly, he was an average singer and prolific, able songwriter who made two great teen dream singles: "C'mon Everybody" and "Summertime Blues." The latter has a great acoustic guitar riff, a nice bass voice gimmick (Eddie overdubbed in a voice he derived from Kingfish on "Amos 'n' Andy"), and terrific lyrics, probably written by his chief collaborator, Jerry Capeheart. That riff remains amazingly resilient—to have survived Blue Cheer's battering, it'd have to be—and those words define an essential rite of passage for the sons and daughters of postwar prosperity. (Not just American kids, though in the Who's version, it's weird to hear Roger Daltrey phone his Congressman.) Nevertheless Cochran remains, for me, a figure much closer to teen idolhood—image triumphing over substance—than, say, Rick Nelson.

827 TONITE TONITE, The Mello-Kings
Produced by Al Silver; written by Billy Myles
Herald 502   1957   *Billboard: #77*

Another doo-wop racial ellipsis: white group, white producer, black "musical arranger," and a sound so totally street corner that deejays and listeners all over the country were initially persuaded they must be black. Today, you can hear the straight pop harmony elements (they formed at a high school audition for *South Pacific*) more clearly as part of an irreducible blend that gave such fifties harmony discs a kick that was a hell of a lot more than sociological—not that the sociological kick didn't help the Mello-Kings transcend their drippier inclinations.

828 LODI, Creedence Clearwater Revival
Written and produced by John Fogerty
Fantasy 622   1969   *Billboard: #52*

829 WISH SOMEONE WOULD CARE, Irma Thomas
Produced by H.B. Barnum; written by Irma Thomas
Imperial 66013   1964   *Billboard: #17*

830 TAKE IT TO THE LIMIT, The Eagles
Produced by Bill Szymczyk; written by Don Henley and Randy Meisner
Asylum 45293   1975   *Billboard: #4*

Annals of Self-Pity.

A crucial theme in pop music generally, latter-day rock and R&B performers have raised feeling sorry for your poor self to the status of an (exceptionally minor) art form. If whining pleases your palate and millions of James Taylor fans suggest that it can, you've arrived at the right review.

Irma Thomas's plaint may perhaps be the most justifiable. She was, after all, ripped off not just once but twice, and by two of the best: Otis Redding took her "Ruler of My Heart" and converted it into "Pain In My Heart," an experience that must have been leavened very little by the fact that he distinctly improved upon the original. Then the Rolling Stones took "Time Is On My Side," changed nothing much at all (oh, yeah, the guitar lick—big deal) and cashed bigger checks than Irma would ever see in her life.

Of course, the Stones can take no blame or credit for the angst that motivates "Wish Someone Would Care," since they didn't lift "Time" until a few months after "Wish" hit the Top 20, but Irma could undoubtedly see it coming. Sitting lonely in her living room, muttering to herself about injustice, "wondering how I made it and how it's gonna last," grimacing as she recalls every phony smile she's had to deliver as part of her job (any job—she could be dishing out donuts), Irma seems most disturbed that nobody really appreciates her pain. A familiar feeling, and not only to pop stars.

It's hard to do much with an emotional cliché, but H.B. Barnum doesn't just let it lay there, he tats the story up with gushing strings and a female chorus and portentous bells at the close, so that the full weight of Irma's Sad Sack enervation becomes unmistakable. In this regard, the record lives up to its intentions perfectly, and if you have a taste for this kind of self-immolation (and what critic doesn't?), it's actually almost radiant.

The Eagles were to seventies rock stars what Uncle Scrooge was to comic book characters, the richest, most renowned, and nevertheless the most dissatisifed and greediest. Aspiring to be a Great and Artistic Rock Band, they continually foundered on the fact that God—or the Muses or the Asylum A&R department or whoever the fuck guides these things—intended them to be a better-than-passable vocal group, sort of the Hollies with mesquite. As a result they became studio perfectionists. Someone once told me that they used to suck lemons to make sure that their pitch stayed steady, a practice which I've never known anyone else to follow but which sure fits with the emotional tenor of their continual pleas to be taken more seriously.

Actually, the Eagles were often decent Top 40 fare (although if you ever dare tell anyone I admitted it, I'll deny it) and "Take It to the Limit" is a good example of how their music worked. Its harmonies are country but the orchestration is right out of the Elton John handbook, layered on with a trowel and then sluicing on a little more, just to make sure you get the picture.

Which is meant to be the Big Picture, the story of a generation's inability to get to grips with its own restless desires, with the cramped horizons of today (ca. 1975) in contrast to the raw, wide-open promises of yesteryear (ca. 1969). I think. It's actually pretty hard to tell, because if the Eagles' arrangements were out of the Elton John handbook, not a bad place to rummage around, as these things go, their lyrics were unfortunately picked up at a Bernie Taupin rummage sale. To be charitable, one would have to call the best of them fuzzily thought out and in the end, after repeated Top 40 immersion, "Take It to the Limit" came to be my favorite mainly because it's the most ludicrous. This song, which wants so desperately to be taken as the heartfelt saga of a wasted generation, winds up summarizing itself in four lines:

> You can spend all your time makin' money
> You can spend all your love makin' time
> If it all falls to pieces tomorrow
> Will you still be mine?

I mean, huh? That grab ya? Huh? Huh? How should I know what it means; that was their job and they blew it. But if you've gotta fuck up, do it right and you'll get credit from me. Oh my yes.

Meantime, John Fogerty (as always) has a story to tell. It's a tragic tale, set to a chugging rockabilly beat (surprise, surprise—nice guitar break before the last verse, though) about a guy who's been out playing a circuit of California dives trying to become a star and after a year—a whole year!—is ready to quit in disgust. Just because somebody gave him a Next Big Thing write up and it didn't pan out with a record deal.

What makes "Lodi" even more ridiculous is that John Fogerty and Creedence Clearwater played that lousy circuit for more like a *decade* and never gave up, never quit. John Fogerty got *drafted* and still came back to being a musician. Maybe he thought that this was his story, but it sure wasn't:

If I only had a dollar, for every song I've sung
Every time I've had to play, while people sat there drunk
You know I'd catch the next train, back to where I live
Oh Lord, stuck in Lodi again

Sure sounds a lot like the Eagles', though.

831 SEND ME SOME LOVIN', Little Richard
Produced by Bumps Blackwell; written by Leo Price and
John Marascalco
Specialty 598   1957   *Billboard:* #54

The flip side of "Lucille," and the closest Richard ever came to conventional, Fats Domino-style New Orleans R&B with classic walking
bass and piano ostinato, honking sax, and perhaps his most sensual
vocal ever, languid and legato and full of gospel gasps. No big deal,
and better than about 98 percent of everything else you've ever heard.

832 HUNGRY, Paul Revere and the Raiders
Produced by Terry Melcher; written by Barry Mann and
Cynthia Weill
Columbia 43678   1966   *Billboard:* #6

A song I never understood until I saw my friend John Cafferty sing it
with his band, Beaver Brown. They presented it as an answer to the
question, "Why'd you join a rock and roll band?" But what grabbed
me more was Gary Gramolini's guitar line.

    The Raiders do the song differently, but it's still pretty great: The
center of the performance becomes the lethal bass line, and the lyric's
assertions have a lot more to do with class rage. But then, class rage
is another way of answering that question.

833 JUST ONE LOOK, Doris Troy
Produced by Artie Ripp; written by Gregory Carroll and
Doris Payne [Troy]
Atlantic 2188   1963   *Billboard:* #10

Doris Payne sang in her father's church choir and a bunch of gospel
groups, then switched to jazz with a trio called the Halos, then became

a songwriter, contributing "How About That," a minor hit, to the repertoire of Dee Clark in 1959. Troy made so little from her own records, she decided she was better off with a job. So she went into background work in New York studios, where she also cut demos for Chuck Jackson and Solomon Burke. None of this paid off very well, either; when next spotted, she was working the wrong end of Harlem's Apollo Theatre, as an usherette.

Fortunately, the guy doing the spotting was James Brown and with his help, she started cutting records again, first as part of a duo called Jay and Dee, then on her own. At last she came to Atlantic with producer Artie Ripp, one of the classic Brill Building hustlers, where they quickly cut "Just One Look."

"Just One Look" acquires its energy from piano triplets and a soft shuffle rhythm. It gathers its charm from Troy's husky, taut singing, whose staccato accents work against the almost-New Orleans underpinnings. The result is about as close to the heyday of girl group pop as R&B-fixated Atlantic ever got.

Though "Just One Look" went Top Ten, Troy again received little reward. By the end of the sixties, she'd removed herself to England, where she had a modest, long-running career highlighted by cutting a couple of tracks for the Beatles' Apple label. By the mid eighties, she was back in New York, working in a gospel program.

834 BABY SCRATCH MY BACK, Slim Harpo
Produced by J.D. Miller; written by James Moore
[Slim Harpo]
Excello 2273   1966   *Billboard:* #16

Nobody, not even Jimmy Reed, came closer to bringing the pure country blues of the Mississippi Delta to the Top Ten than Slim Harpo. And while that alone would be a major achievement, Harpo's version of those blues is a form of slinky, lewd, and lascivious expression whose open popularity is shocking in a country as puritan as America. Slim called it "an attempt at rock and roll for me," but if that's true, then he understood rock and roll in its most primitive sense, as an analogy for sheer, sweaty sexual exertion. I mean, you're entitled to think that Slim's croaking about how good his back feels just the same way you're entitled to think that the earth is flat. But then you have to explain that gritty guitar just like the rising of the sun.

835 GOODBYE BABY, Jack Scott
Produced by Joe Carlton; written by Jack Scott
Carlton 493   1958   *Billboard:* #8

Back home in Detroit, whenever the conversation would get around
to rockabillies, Jack Scott's name wasn't far away. And somebody
would inevitably say, "What a great voice! Whatever *happened* to him?"
And somebody would just as inevitably reply, "He's workin' the line,"
meaning that he'd fallen from stardom to just making cars like everybody else.

Maybe it was even true. Certainly, it should have been, as you'd
know just from seeing a picture of Scott, with the jet black hair slicked
straight back with a spit curl coming down his forehead and the thick,
hairy, powerful arms (he *always* wore short sleeves) and that hard, not
quite angry look in his eyes, let alone from listening to records like
"Leroy," his first hit, about his friend who screwed up and ended up
in "Cell Number 2," or "What in the World's Come Over You," so
mournful that it comes as close to being a man singing to a corpse as
anything this side of Elvis Costello's "Psycho," or "The Way I Walk"
("is just the way I walk"). He might have been the nicest guy in the
world. You didn't want to find out.

Pop culture hard guys ended up badly. Everybody's known that
since *Oliver Twist*, if not before. But who knows how hard Jack Scott
really was? The lyrics to "The Way I Walk" are lethal, but the song's
far scarier when the Cramps sing them, because Scott sounds so damn
boyish, and "Leroy," after all, is the story of his high school pal, Leroy
Johnson, not an autobiography. For that matter, "What in the World's
Come Over You," baleful as its implications are, is finally just a world-
weary country cheating song, albeit here given a peculiarly Canadian
chill.

At his best, Jack Scott was undeniably the greatest Canadian rock
and roll singer of all time (even if he did live in Detroit after he was
ten years old). "Goodbye Baby" is the best he did, a jaunty "forget
you, honey" country-rocker, full of emotional contradiction (he's kissing her off, he doesn't want her to cry, he's leaving because she's
worthless, he still sorta loves her) that makes it all the more credible,
or at least accurate. A lot of the time, what you're mostly hearing is
the backing group, the Fabulous Chantones, a sort of Northern Jordanaires, against the clunky guitars. Scott enters in his bass register,
which is maybe his most attractive voice, then slips up a few notches
to repeat the softly hiccuped "Guhd-bye, baby, bye bye," a grimly

percussive phrase, a few dozen times. That's about all there is to it. Or needs to be.

836 I'VE BEEN LONELY TOO LONG, The Rascals
Produced by The Rascals, Arif Mardin, and Tom Dowd; written by Felix Cavaliere
Atlantic 2377   1967   *Billboard:* #16

Holland-Dozier-Holland deserve royalties for the intro, but after Felix's organ comes in, the Rascals are on their own with one of the most distinctive performances in blue-eyed soul. The highlight, though, is Dino Danelli's drumming, which merges Benny Benjamin funk with Keith Moon power.

837 I MISS YOU, Klymaxx
Produced by Klymaxx and Lynn Malsby; written by Lynn Malsby
Constellation 52606   1984   *Billboard:* #5

Perhaps the greatest weeper of the eighties—and as close to cloning the best of Michael Jackson's trembly lipped ballad persona as any woman, or man, is liable to come. Klymaxx tugs every heartstring, shamelessly and deliciously.

838 FOR WHAT IT'S WORTH, Buffalo Springfield
Produced by Charles Greene and Brian Stone; written by Stephen Stills
Atco 6459   1967   *Billboard:* #7

In 1966 and 1967, crowds of longhairs gathered on the Sunset Strip near two clubs, the Whisky A-Go-Go and Pandora's Box, blocking sidewalks, smoking dope, spilling into the streets. In Los Angeles, where hostility to pedestrians is codified to the point of issuing as many jaywalking as traffic tickets, this ranked as a serious police problem, especially when neighborhood businessmen complained of the disruptions. Eventually, the cops were called in.

Los Angeles cops in those days were mostly recruited in the deep South—Mississippi and Alabama—and they had specific ideas about law and order and the proper modes of decorum. Called upon to rid the street of "undesirables," they busted heads.

Stephen Stills came into this scene fresh from prerevolutionary Nicaragua. "I saw the Sunset Strip riots—all the kids on one side of the street, all the cops on the other side. In Latin America, that meant there'd be a new government in about a week." He wrote "For What It's Worth" and Atco rush-released it as a single, dropping it into Buffalo Springfield's previously released album when it became a hit.

Actually, it ain't all that radical or even necessarily accurate. Faced with "battle lines bein' drawn," future blowhard Stills tries to keep his neutrality ("Singin' songs and carryin' signs / Mostly say hoo-ray for our side") but then, he'd managed to center on one of the most directionless, apolitical events of the decade. In fact, by keeping his passions in reserve, Stills predicts the neoliberalism of the seventies and eighties, in which the mode of protest is condemned with vigor equal to or greater than that which is used to condemn the injustice.

What's this doing here, then? Why, because Stills redeems himself with unforgettable guitar, a haunted vocal, and, thanks to Randy Meisner, great harmonies.

839 FOLLOW YOUR HEART, The Manhattans
Produced by Joe Evans; written by Sonny Bivins
Carnival 512   1966   *Billboard:* #92

840 KISS AND SAY GOODBYE, The Manhattans
Produced by Bobby Martin; written by Blue Lovett
Columbia 10310   1976   *Billboard:* #1 (2 weeks)

"Progressive doo-wop" is the name lead singer Blue Lovett gave in the seventies to Manhattans hits like "Shining Star," "There's No Me Without You," and "Kiss and Say Goodbye." And if there were such a thing as progressive doo-wop, then the Manhattans were the champions of it for they continued to have harmony hits even at the height of the disco era, when just about every other black singing group was nearly thump-thumped out of existence.

It was especially ironic that the Manhattans should be the ones to sustain themselves because their longevity never seemed likely. Lovett and Kenneth Kelly first came together in Jersey City in the late fifties, but it wasn't until the early sixties that they met up with the rest of the group: Sonny Bivins and Richard Taylor, who'd recorded as the Dorsets, and the group's original lead vocalist, George "Smitty" Smith. Though they made a few minor singles including one for Bobby Robinson's Enjoy label, it wasn't until 1964 that they had anything like a bite at a hit.

That belated first success was directly the result of linking up with producer Joe Evans, who had been around the chitlin' circuit for a couple of decades, touring and recording with the Clouds of Joy, Hot Lips Page, Lionel Hampton, Jay McShann, Louis Armstrong, and as music director for Ivory Joe Hunter. Evans worked in the backup band for Dick Clark's Caravan of Stars and with Choker Campbell's band that supported the Motortown Revue.

But he always wanted more, founding Cee Jay Records with Clarence Johnson in 1959, then starting his own Carnival label in Newark in 1961. A year or so later, Evans and Paul Williams (who'd had a huge jump blues dance hit with "The Hucklebuck" in the early fifties) met the Manhattans at Harlem's Hotel Theresa. "I told Paul the group was a million-dollar act but he thought I was crazy cause they looked so raggedy, like they had just got off a coal truck," Evans remembered. He was especially impressed that, with Lovett and Smith, the group had two distinctive leads, giving item versatility and stamina and an obvious link to the popular dual-lead gospel quartet style.

It was 1964 before the Manhattans' Carnival debut, "For the Very First Time" was issued, and it flopped, as did a second song, this one written by Lovett. The group always went over well live, though, and when Al Jefferson of Baltimore's WWIN told Evans that the group's records could be just as big if they weren't so pop, Evans worked overtime to funk up "I Wanna Be (Your Everything)." Not only did it hit on the R&B chart, but when Otis Redding saw them at the Apollo, he loved the act and took them on several tours with him.

Carnival never got offered a national distribution deal, maybe because the Manhattans' sound was always a little anachronistic in its direct links to gospel and doo-wop, and it seemed unlikely that they could repeat any of their minor successes. Despite that, nowhere is the strength of their approach more evident than on "Follow Your Heart," which uses a light soul background but centers attention on a Smitty Smith lead and its interaction with the backing voices in a way that harkened back to fifties groups more than anything since the very first Temptations hits in 1963 and 1964. It's the very modest intricacy of the record that made and continues to make it so charming.

Smitty died in 1970 of spinal meningitis, but the Manhattans stayed together (as they did after Richard Taylor left in 1976 as well). In 1972, they finally got their major label break, signing with Columbia and recording a whole series of hits, beginning with the million-selling

"There's No Me Without You." All the time, they stayed up to their old tricks, recording in Philadelphia with producer Bobby Martin and acquiring the Sigma Sound rhythm bed without sacrificing any of their distinctive soulfulness. "Kiss and Say Goodbye" rose out of 1976's oppressively dance-dominated R&B radio like a beacon from the past, its arrangement just too modern for the harmonizing to be denied. The blend, centering on a dryly romantic lead by Lovett and a marvelously corny basso recitation that (unlike the Barry White hits it resembles) stays well within the bounds of credible egomania, has weathered the decade since then without losing any of its gorgeous balance.

841 COME GO WITH ME, The Del-Vikings
Produced by Joe Averbach; written by Clarence Quick
Dot 15538   1957   Billboard: #4

Another blow to the forces of rock as all rebellion, all the time. The Del-Vikings are usually identified as a Pittsburgh group, because they first recorded in 1956 for Steel City label pioneer Joe Averbach after winning a WDAS talent contest.

But this integrated doo-wop quartet (with the nasal white guy singing lead) happened to be in Pittsburgh only because they were all stationed at a nearby Air Force base, where they were soldiering without exhibiting any signs of insurrection other than the occasional development of such potentially-but-not-inherently subversive vocal noises as "Dom dom dom dom, dom dee-doobie, dom." Although if one of them had the nerve to work out that ultrasoulful stuttering sax break in the barracks, he's lucky he wasn't court-martialed on the spot for excessive cool.

842 LET'S WORK TOGETHER, Wilbert Harrison
Produced by Juggy Murray; written by Wilbert Harrison
Sue 11   1969   Billboard: #32

Swamp blues from the auteur of "Kansas City," making a chart comeback after a fifteen year absence. Harrison had lost nothing in the interim. If anything, he'd grown a little more wily, for crude as this music is, it's also wise in the way it works its chunky beat and one-man-band instrumental setup (Harrison played harmonica, guitar, and a tambourine/drum kit more-or-less simultaneously) into a highly personal (i.e., rhythmically irregular) blues, that wraps around the feigned innocence of the lyrics, which capitalize perfectly on waning, willful sixties innocence: "Together we will stand / Every boy, girl, woman and may-an." He's also sharp enough to holler an out-of-context "Kansas City!" (just a reminder) and periodically cry "C'mon Tina!"—as if to hint that Sue's crossover star Tina Turner might be with him on the disc. If so, she kept her mouth shut; the woman who finally replies to Wilbert shouts a good octave too high to be the real McCoy. But Harrison didn't need the subterfuge; he was just shrewd enough to throw it in 'cause he wanted a hit. He got one too and if it wasn't quite "Kansas City," it was still good enough to get him an album deal and raise his performance fees for a few years. Now *that's* working together.

843 NEVER CAN SAY GOODBYE, Gloria Gaynor
Produced by Tony Bongiovi, Meco Mondardo, and Jay Ellis; written by Clifton Davis
MGM 14748   1974   *Billboard:* #9

Gaynor may have been the first of the disco "divas," the big-voiced, not especially funky singers who had the power to be heard above the thumping percussion and swirling strings that dominated seventies dance discs. Working entirely outside the soul tradition as Aretha Franklin had redefined it, Gaynor (and her successors) also stood apart from show tune conventions as redefined by Barbra Streisand. Perhaps their most important role was as icons—in a way that Michael Jackson's original never could, Gaynor's "Never can say goodbye" becomes a dreamy expression of a purely sexual intoxication, an experience that's as central to disco as drinking and cheating are to country.

844 JUST TO BE WITH YOU, The Passions
Produced by Paul Swain; written by Mary Kalfin
Audicon 102   1959   *Billboard:* #69

This Brooklyn quartet scored only one hit, but they must have had some magic. Not only did they manage to pull off one of the gems of Italian-American doo-wop with a singer named Jimmy Gallagher, not only were they discovered by the Mystics ("Hushabye"), but they got "Just To Be with You" in the form of a demo cut by the Cousins, who happened to be a pair of aspiring singers named Paul Simon and Carole King. Recorded with heavy echo and a perfectly nasal, sub-bel canto lead, there's little here that isn't formulaic. Or charming.

845 RUMORS, Timex Social Club
Produced by Jay Logan; written by Michael Marshall, Marcus Thompson, and Alex Hill
Jay 7001   1986   *Billboard:* #8

Just as real estate is the true religion of late twentieth-century America, our national sport is gossip. Like all sports, gossip as practiced today—on a spectrum that ranges from *The National Enquirer* to *World News Tonight*, which is even narrower than it sounds—is regulated both formally, through fairly well articulated rules, and informally, through protocols about which it is impolite to speak. For *People*, Liz Smith, *Entertainment Tonight*, *USA Today*, Dan Rather, Malcolm Forbes, and *Rolling Stone* alike, the assumption that a human life is valuable precisely in proportion to its celebrity is no more questionable than the idea that it takes ten yards to make a first down. That aside from making the headlines, the achievements of Donald Trump, Vanna White, and Joan and Jackie Collins are negligible or nonexistent or malignant must remain unspoken, unless you're waxing ironic or semiotic. Just like you don't run up the score on a team you've got to play again next season.

"Rumors" skirts a couple such taboos. Within the bounds of libel, it names names on the nastiest subjects. Just because the Club never says Jackson or Turner or Anton, that doesn't mean we don't know which possessors of the first names Michael, Tina, and Susan "they" are suggesting must be gay or nymphomaniacal or a dominatrix. Or at least, knew in the summer of 1986 because three or four years later, with one exception, it's entirely likely that a great many of us wouldn't be so sure, having moved on to other temporary passions.

The Social Club plays by the rules in at least one respect, however. They avowedly come to complain about such gossip, to deride unfounded stories (spread by "wicked women," needless to say). And as good gossips, they also are *most* shocked when the chicken returns to its roost: "My best friend says there's one out now about me and the girl next door."

Meaning that ultimately, the singer gossips about himself and the reason isn't only to give him the moral reassurance needed to chant "Stop spreadin' those rumors around / Stop, stop spreadin' the lies." It's also to validate his own identity—to prove he and his love life are worthy of the gossip's attention. Despite his own rhetoric, without that gossip, he feels he might cease to exist. And in the terms laid out for him by contemporary journalists, he's probably right.

846 COME AND GET YOUR LOVE, Redbone
Produced by Pat and Lolly Vegas; written by Lolly Vegas
Epic 11035 1974 *Billboard:* #5

Pat and Lolly Vegas are best known as the two most prominent American Indians in rock history, and because they wrote "Nikki Hoeky," a fine swamp pop tune that hit for Elvisoid P.J. Proby in 1967.

What they deserve more recognition for is this perfectly winsome record, which places a whole different cast upon the concept of "blue-eyed soul." With its vaguely Native American chant—"Heeey / heeey"—and its melodic modernization of Brenton Wood's "Gimme Little Sign," "Come and Get Your Love" 's soul is undeniable as its nonblack but very American origins. But then, as the bass chugs into the gutty guitar part and some aptly arranged string touches buttress the beat, you lose your worries about antecedents and simply succumb to the pure groove of the thing. A prototype of nothing, and a pleasure every time you hear it.

847 BYE BYE JOHNNY, Chuck Berry
Produced by Leonard Chess; written by Chuck Berry
Chess 1754 1960 Did not make pop charts

The Johnny B. Goode Saga Continues: same tempo, similar riff, but a lot more mellow. Chuck's made it now, and it shows. But he's not just cashing in; finding this many telling details in the story, and having the audacity to write the song from the perspective of Johnny's mother, had to cost him something. Although he makes it all seem so effortless and inevitable, who could guess—or fathom—the real price?

848 BLACK MAGIC WOMAN, Santana
Produced by Fred Catero and Santana; written by Peter Green
Columbia 45270 1970 *Billboard:* #4

Probably the funkiest hit single ever to come out of the San Francisco rock scene (at least, if you don't count Sly and the Family Stone as part of that scene, which the Haight-Ashbury bunch definitely didn't). It's a complete racial/musical collision, too: a Mexican-American guitar player steeped in the salsa of the Eastern Caribbean playing a black blues song written by a British/Jewish guitarist turned fundamentalist

Christian. What's amazing is how well the smouldering power of Santana's guitar and the husky yearning of his vocal have held up—a lot better than anything the other members of San Francisco's psychedelic squadron can claim.

849 SIXTY MINUTE MAN, Billy Ward and the Dominoes
Produced by Ralph Bass; written by Billy Ward and Rose Marks
Federal 12022   1951   *Billboard:* #17

Pianist Billy Ward's band became famous, or at least notorious, for making some of the lewdest R&B numbers of the early fifties. But by today's standards, what sticks out from "Sixty Minute Man" isn't the lyrics (what's an hour among friends?) but the lilting guitar, the thrilling high harmonies, and Bill Brown's wisecracking bass lead vocal. So you can't just dismiss the damn thing as a novelty even if its infamy—and its *seventeen* weeks at Number One on the *Billboard* R&B chart!—did provide grounds for antivulgarians to attack and discredit all of black pop. Closer listening is required, especially when you remember that six years later, "Wake Up Little Susie" was attacked on the same basis, and thirty more years on down the line, Congressmen stood up to denounce Madonna's "Like a Virgin." Proving that, even though squares never get the good stuff, the good stuff often galvanizes the opposition.

850 APACHE, The Incredible Bongo Band
Produced by Michael Viner; written by Jorgen Ingmann
MGM   Did not make pop chart

You've probably never heard of this ultraobscure discoid remake of Jorgen Ingmann's 1961 original, one of the first European attempts at quasi-rock. But you may know the Bongo Band's sound anyway, since its long, gutty passages of guitar, strings, bongo, and conga are among the most frequently sampled sounds of the late eighties. In fact, about the last place you can locate a copy is on the bootleg *Breaks and Beats* LPs prized by club deejays and scratchers.

According to Joel Whitburn's comment on "Bongo Rock," the group's 1973 remake of Preston Epps's 1959 hit (which did make the Hot 100—at 57), the Incredible Bongos were a studio group assembled in Canada by producer Michael Viner, the guy who staged the entertainment for Richard Nixon's second inaugural and a longtime crony of MGM chief and right-wing politician Mike Curb. Further evidence that good music and good politics have only a nodding acquaintance, important information in case you missed Elvis. Get into the break that closes out "Apache" and you may be inspired to seek revenge with your feet and hips.

851 HERE COMES THE NIGHT, Them
Written and produced by Bert Berns
Parrot 9749   1965   *Billboard:* #24

Van Morrison probably hates this over-the-top piece of pop fodder, and if he doesn't, he should, because it violates his entire painfully developed aesthetic of emotional excess within minimal musical gesture. Which may be the very reason I love it—this music gets in your face from the first big, booming, echoed notes of the (Jimmy Page?) guitar. Probably the least black sounding record Van's ever made, there are nevertheless hints of blues, the kind of white blues in which Merle Haggard and George Jones specialize. The lyric and rhyme structure are silly enough to have been cooked up on Music Row, too.

852 I DIDN'T KNOW I LOVED YOU (TIL I SAW YOU ROCK AND ROLL), Planet Patrol
Produced by Arthur Baker and John Robie; written by Gary Glitter and Mike Leander
Tommy Boy 837   1983   Did not make pop chart

In which hip-hop's best production team expropriates a trash-rock gem by Gary Glitter, a fat 'n' forty British teen idol of the seventies, and by adding to its quintessential nothingness 57 varieties of electronic effects, mostly percussive, make something approaching Art with a modicum of real passion. Planet Patrol allegedly consisted of five singers, but you can bet that the real energy here comes from Arthur Baker and John Robie's "digital and analog beat box," which ensures that the most energizing sound effects from the best video games are given a context in which they actually mean something. There's also a nice, brief break that sounds like what happens when a CD sticks in one groove. And baby, *that* is rock and roll.

853 JAILHOUSE ROCK, Elvis Presley
Producer not credited; written by Jerry Leiber and Mike Stoller
RCA 47-7035   1957   *Billboard:* #1 (7 weeks)

An enduring smash for at least three reasons: the great walking bass, Scotty Moore's invention of power chording, and D.J. Fontana's drumming, which is halfway between strip joint rhumba and the perfect New Orleans shuffle.

Elvis, meanwhile, is so wrapped up in making his own noise that he approaches Leiber and Stoller's odd lyric without reservation. Odd because, given the strictures of the white rock market, they had to have a romantic theme, but prisons are not sexually integrated. So we get "Number 47 said to Number 3 / You're the cutest jailbird I ever did see."

That this is anomaly, not Freudian revelation, is evidenced by the wholeheartedness with which Presley sings the lyric. In this society, if those words reflected "real" homosexuality, they would assuredly require some distancing mechanism . . . and Elvis doesn't even try, just throws himself straight at the song, not in the spirit of camp but with all the childlike fascination he brought to his first movies.

What's most annoying is that if Elvis hadn't been viciously smeared in the press ever since his death, we could just make the joke and leave this rather obvious analysis alone. Or maybe get to a more central point, such as the idea that for Elvis (at least during the fifties), *every* situation was charged with enormous sexual/musical energy, with little need to discriminate between one and the other.

854 I WANT A LOVE I CAN SEE, The Temptations
Written and produced by Smokey Robinson
Gordy 7015   1963   Did not make pop chart

Their second single, but the first one that really clicked, partly because Smokey Robinson provided them with the greatest rhythm track he'd conceived up to that point, a slowed down variation of the dance beat that powered the Contours' "Shake Sherrie." It's distinctively Smokey because of the way the words wrap around the beat (or is the beat following the verbal groove?). It's unmistakably Temptations because the guys go through such snappy routines, your heart cries to see them dance it. And it's inarguably Motown because the bass and drums would punch you in the face if you tried to argue them out of it, and the horns and even the scraper that adds more sandpaper to Al Bryant's (pre-David Ruffin) lead would help them out, you damn betcha.

855 ISRAELITES, Desmond Dekker
Produced by Leslie Kong; written by Desmond Dacres [Dekker] and Leslie Kong
Uni 55129   1969   Billboard: #9

So far ahead of its time was this first-ever American reggae hit that I actually heard idle speculation that Dekker's then-unintelligible lyrics (now easily deciphered after some years experience with hearing Jamaican patois) concealed an anti-Semitic tract. Who in the U.S. knew then that Jamaican pop music was dominated by Rastafarians, a religion of liberal Biblical construction, in which blacks transported to the Western Hemisphere were considered Ethiopians, but only because the Ethiopians were considered one of the twelve lost tribes. That is, Israelites.

So, Dekker sings about himself. Brilliantly, against one of the strongest tracks Leslie Kong constructed in his heyday. "Israelites" serves as a template for reggae's pop side, the part that dominated for its first decade or so.

856 DEAD MAN'S CURVE, Jan and Dean
Produced by Lou Adler; written by Jan Berry, Brian Wilson, and Roger Christian
Liberty 55672   1964   Billboard: #8

KFWB disc jockey Roger Christian certainly ranks as the only songwriter in rock history who got his start by reviewing a record over the air. It was Christian's disparaging on-air assessment of the automotive details in the Beach Boys' "409" that led him to meet Brian Wilson and begin writing with him. Christian wound up sharing credit on a string of Beach Boys hits, including "Don't Worry Baby," "Little Deuce Coupe," and "Shut Down." He also began writing with Jan Berry, the creative force in Jan and Dean.

Berry and Christian, but not Wilson, had a real life interest in fast cars. Every Saturday night, they met at the corner of Sunset and Vine and raced through the Hollywood streets, a practice as dangerous as it was thrilling. There was one especially gut-clenching spot, a tricky downhill turn just before you got to Westwood Avenue, near UCLA.

Christian was inspired to write "Dead Man's Curve" when he learned that one of his heroes, Mel Blanc (the voice of Bugs Bunny and Porky Pig), had crashed there. Centrifugal force threw Blanc's car into the oncoming lane; he wound up in the hospital for six months.

Christian took his idea to Berry (as with the Beach Boys, collaborator Wilson worked on music almost exclusively) and they decided to make the song into the story of a drag race, using their own cars: Christian ran a Jaguar XKE, Berry a Corvette Stingray. The disc jockey's idea was for the race to end in a dead heat; Berry pushed for the cars to crash.

That's both fitting and ironic, because two years later, Berry was permanently crippled by a crash ghoulishly similar to the one described in his famous monologue at the conclusion of "Deadman's Curve": "Well, the last thing I remember, Doc, I started to swerve, and then I saw the Jag slide into the curve. I know I'll never forget that horrible sight. I guess I found out for myself that everyone was right."

Berry infuses these words with an undercurrent of mockery (not for nothing were Jan and Dean sometimes called the Laurel and Hardy of the surf set) and the music punctuates his sentences with comic drama. (To hear Jan and Dean's full contempt for their masterpiece, dig up side four of the Jan and Dean set in United Artists' *Legendary Masters Series* [UAS 9961], an almost operatic excursion through the blackest rock and roll humor ever waxed.)

In fact, "Dead Man's Curve" is more notable as a hot rod/surf studio pastiche than as an actual song. The arrangement is overendowed with brass, the singing is nothing special (neither Jan nor Dean is any flatter than usual), the mix is muddy; only Hal Blaine's drumming stands out. On the other hand, if they'd gotten the music to the same realistic intensity as the lyrics, you'd bleed when you heard it. And then nobody would've played it on the radio. Except maybe KFWB.

857 A GOOD YEAR FOR THE ROSES, George Jones
Produced by Pappy Daily; written by Jerry Chestnut
Musicor 1425　1970　　Did not make pop chart

There's a tradition of maudlin goodbye songs in country music from which stems much of its bad reputation, since it is just such goo as Bobby Goldsboro's "Honey" that often crossed over to the Top 40, back when country music was still allowed to inhabit the same universe as rock and R&B.

"A Good Year for the Roses" isn't quite that bad a sob story, but aside from the columns of Bob Greene, it's hard to think of such a late-appearing recitation of unselfconsciously chauvinist male self-pity. George is aggrieved, after all, not only because his wife's walked out, taking his baby, but because "after three full years of marriage / It's the first time that you haven't made the bed." He's jealous of her half-drunk cup of coffee because "at least you thought you wanted it / That's so much more than I can say for me." Meanwhile, the oaf stands there talking about the garden.

Yet I'm still listening, and with pleasure, and even though the arrangement features the kinds of countrypolitan accoutrements—strings, a big crooning male chorus—that generally give me fits. Why? Well, it's that catch in George's voice, his way of throwing himself at the song and rendering the greeting card poesy of the chorus as if he's doing some hoary old hymn. And from the standpoint of honky-tonk heaven, maybe he is.

858 WHY DO LOVERS BREAK EACH OTHER'S HEARTS, Bob B. Soxx and Blue Jeans

Produced by Phil Spector; written by Phil Spector, Ellie Greenwich, and Tony Powers
Philles 110   1963   *Billboard:* #38

Bob B. Soxx was meant to be a *nom de studio* for Bobby Sheen, a good-enough R&B singer in the Clyde McPhatter mold, discovered first by Johnny Otis, then by Lester Sill, who sent him to Phil Spector. During Spector's brief tenure as East Coast A&R chief for Liberty Records, he cut a couple of sides with Sheen then brought him along as one of the first Philles acts.

But by the time they got to the studio, Spector was already (and justifiably) in love with the Blossoms, the Los Angeles female session group that featured Darlene Love. So "Why Do Lovers," like the other Soxx hits, "Zip-a-dee-doo-dah" and "Not Too Young to Get Married," revolves around Love's amazing singing. If Sheen's around, he can barely be discerned, except perhaps on some doo-wop nonsense syllables in the background at the start.

Despite a piano solo more rinky-dink than honky-tonk, the playing here is fine, one of the most spacious of the Wall of Sound productions, capped by a couple of explosive Hal Blaine fills on the final choruses. But it's really Love's show, one of the best of all the records on which she's featured.

859 MORE LOVE, Smokey Robinson and the Miracles

Written and produced by Smokey Robinson
Tamla 54152   1967   *Billboard: #23*

Smokey lost in a wilderness battle. The warring forces are divided among his own romantic longings, his equal love for the interplay of words and singing, and music so lush it's practically the score for a soul soap opera. The tussle isn't just between Robinson and one woman but between the limits of language and the effort to express an idea of eternity.

860 YOU CAN'T JUDGE A BOOK BY ITS COVER, Bo Diddley

Produced by Leonard Chess; written by Willie Dixon
Checker 1019   1962   *Billboard: #48*

The only one of Bo's hits that he didn't write and one of Willie Dixon's major displays of his comico-magic voodoo blues. Bo's the perfect vehicle, because his music represents such a weird alignment of primitive and ultramodern. Like his square-bodied guitar that plays raggedy ass but purely electrified versions of Delta blues, or the raw rasping that conveys the animist allusions of Dixon's words, suddenly erupting into the complaint: "You got your radio turned down too low. Turn it up!"

In a way, then, "You Can't Judge a Book" is a three-minute journey through rock and roll history, from its cultural roots in primitive society straight through to its unplanned expropriation of the electronic media—media invented and initially controlled by men and women who considered the likes of Dixon and Diddley complete barbarians. Had he ridden across mountains on a herd of elephants, Bo couldn't have told a truer tale.

861 LOVE AND HAPPINESS, Al Green

Produced by Willie Mitchell; written by Al Green and Teenie Hodges
Hi 2324   1977   Did not make pop chart

If academic culture hater Allan Bloom shut up long enough to listen to the music whose very existence makes him fume, he might find in the records of a Pentecostal hedonist like the Reverend Mr. Green a philosophy very much akin to the Greeks he claims to venerate. Or at least, the two ideas of the good life don't seem very far apart to me when the Rev boils it down to "love and happiness" as the quintessential desirables.

But then, Bloom could never get past the backbeat, suggestive as it is of the idea that unschooled black Vietnam veterans from Grand Rapids may be as perceptive and sensitive as the prep school brats that "educators" of Bloom's ilk believe are the only young lives that deserve decent book learning.

862 BETTER BE GOOD TO ME, Tina Turner
Produced by Rupert Hine; written by Mike Chapman, Nicky Chinn, and Holly Knight
Capitol 5387   1984   *Billboard:* #5

863 A FOOL IN LOVE, Ike and Tina Turner
Written and produced by Ike Turner
Sue 730   1960   *Billboard:* #27

One of the more glaring absences from *The Heart of Rock & Soul* is "River Deep—Mountain High," which Phil Spector produced for Ike and Tina in 1967. It isn't here because it sounds to me like a muddle, an album's worth of sounds jammed onto one side of a 45, with a little girl lyric that completely contradicts Tina Turner's true persona as the Queen of R&B Sleaze.

Of course, there aren't many other Ike and Tina records here, either, but that's mainly for the opposite reason: Ike Turner's productions with Tina were as undercooked as Phil's was overstewed. And for similar reasons, since Spector's need to prove his artistry was matched, if at all, only by Ike's complete disregard of anything that didn't result in a quick reward. So Tina's man slapped together live arrangements of good material and rushed them to market, without worrying exactly how well they'd translate to vinyl and the airwaves. The results are mainly as slapdash as the process.

Ike might have gotten away with it in the fifties, when he learned the studio and its tricks. Back then, just about everybody in R&B went for the quick buck. But in the sixties and seventies, he competed against some of the most sophisticated people who ever made records. The results didn't compare then and they don't hold up all that well now either.

To give the devil his due, at least Ike never made Tina sing about rag dolls and puppies. No, at the beginning he made of her the ultimate Victim of Love and at the end, he turned her into one slavering advertisement for a hot fuck. Which you didn't need a rock critic or a scandal sheet exposé to tell you was the product of a seriously screwed-up relationship. That's why "A Fool in Love" ranks as one of Ike and Tina's best records. It tells the truth and you can feel Tina's conviction in the general tenor of what she's singing (if not the specifics, which give her fella far too much credit for credibility).

On the basis of her mid-eighties comeback, it wouldn't have taken much studio sympathy for Tina to have become one of the outstanding recording artists of the sixties and seventies, as well as one of her era's nonpareil stage performers. After "Proud Mary" hit, Tina always insisted that she was a rock and roll, not an R&B singer, and I'm inclined to agree. "Better Be Good to Me," produced by an undistinguished hack and accompanied with slashing guitars and pounding drums played by the undistinctive Britrockers, the Fixx, rocks hard enough to short-circuit whole cities, and its musical charge is amplified by the lyric, which for once places the threat in *Tina's* hands. She has made several more famous records but will most likely never cut another quite this exciting.

864 WHOLE LOTTA LOVE, Led Zeppelin
Produced by Jimmy Page; written by Jimmy Page, Robert Plant, John Paul Jones, and John Bonham [Led Zeppelin]
Atlantic 2690   1969   *Billboard:* #4

Very likely the most vulgar record in *The Heart of Rock & Soul*—and to tell you the truth, I'm not sure I should have italicized that. With its ape-call midsection excised to fit onto a 45, "Whole Lotta Love" becomes an essence of grunge, a ragged, nasty projection of male hormonal anguish, that's as dangerous if it's feigned as it is if it's real. Page's phased guitar and Bonham's clattering drums offer cheap thrills and a soundtrack heated enough for the sheer animalism of Plant's rock hard passion play. (I never said the ape calls were inappropriate, just excessive.)

865 WHOLE LOTTA LOVING, Fats Domino
Produced by Dave Bartholomew; written by Fats Domino and Dave Bartholomew
Imperial 5553   1958   *Billboard: #6*

Fats Domino put more records on the pop chart than any other rock or R&B star of the fifties (except Elvis, of course)—sixty-five singles in an almost uninterrupted stream from 1955 to 1964. And 1955 is just when the pop charts start making consistent sense. He started scoring on the R&B chart (which usually listed only the ten or fifteen national best-sellers) in 1950, and if the charts had been desegregated sooner, his statistics would be even more impressive.

His music could hardly be expected to impress more. It's difficult not to underrate Fats, because his records so often feel the same: rollicking New Orleans piano shuffle expositions of winking lust. But in his case, that's a hallmark of consistent style not formulaic drudgery. "Whole Lotta Loving" is typical, which makes it very fine indeed.

866 WHEN YOU WALK IN THE ROOM, Jackie DeShannon
Producer not credited; written by Jackie DeShannon
Liberty 55645   1964   *Billboard: #99*

If Jackie DeShannon had grown up a decade later, she'd have been acknowledged as one of the best singer/songwriters. If she'd grown up in New York, rather than Kentucky, she might have become a celebrated Brill Building craftsman like Carole King and Ellie Greenwich; if she'd stuck around Nashville after writing Brenda Lee's "Dum Dum," she'd probably have her own air-conditioned bus, a swimming pool shaped like a piano, and a problem with either weight or pills.

But DeShannon went to L.A. and worked with Sharon Seeley, Eddie Cochran's songwriting girlfriend, and Jack Nitzsche, Phil Spector's arranger, and even Randy Newman and got taken for granted even when the Searchers were scoring big with two of her best, "Needles and Pins" (which she first recorded but didn't write) and "When You Walk in the Room" (which she both wrote and recorded). In fact, maybe the covers even hurt, lending her an image as a trash monger, rather than one of the most distinctive pop voices around. Certainly, there's got to be some reason other than a lingering love for show tune conventions why DeShannon had the hit with "What the World Needs

Now is Love" and the song still wound up identified with Barbra Streisand.

Her biggest hit, "Put a Little Love in Your Heart," isn't her best record. Neither is "What the World Needs Now," which is just too mushy. And her "Needles and Pins" is a hair too ponderous; without the twin guitar attack, it never takes off and soars as the Searchers did. But Jackie's "When You Walk in the Room" cuts the Searchers. The lyric reverie ("I close my eyes for a second and pretend it's me you want") achieves much more poignancy choking out of a woman's throat, and her husky, quavering reading reaches a quiet peak of despair on the beautiful bridge. And it's got a guitar line from which not only the Searchers but the Byrds learned a lot.

867 SOUL MAKOSSA, Manu Dibango
No producer credited; written by Manu Dibango
Atlantic 2971   1973   *Billboard:* #35

After all these years, this French-speaking West African's sax-laden disco-funk remains the only African record by an African to top the Top 40. However, the development of an intensified international music market, Paul Simon's 1986 hit, *Graceland*, and the long-standing affinities between American and several varieties of African pop (Dibango is from Cameroon but folks play dead on the one everywhere from Tangiers to Johannesburg) probably ensures that it won't have that title for long. But the tangy little guitar figure and smoking tenor line were so far ahead of their time that it might be another couple decades before "Soul Makossa" sounds like an oldie, anyhow.

868 MY LITTLE RED BOOK, Love
Produced by Jac Holzman; written by Burt Bacharach and Hal David
Elektra 45603   1966   *Billboard:* #52

L.A.'s baddest sixties group—not necessarily good-bad-but-not-evil, either. Singer Arthur Lee had the glare and leer of Jimi Hendrix, and if that didn't give him equal brilliance, he was at least up to making some of the nastiest garage rock going. Before he became an acid visionary, that is.

Love's "My Little Red Book," a Dionne Warwick melody that had been a British hit for Manfred Mann, probably ranks as the sleaziest job anybody ever did on a Bacharach-David song. The static guitar riff, the rudimentary bass bomp, the tambourine and shakers all do their best to compensate for the lack of a really good drummer while Lee yowls on about losing his girlfriend and getting out his little red book (Hugh Hefner told me those things were supposed to be *black*, but apparently Burt and Hal never got the word—or maybe they were Maoists), and chasing around town like a dog in heat. Which is ridiculous but that's okay, because when Lee starts to gabble "All I did was tahlk, tahlk abo-out'cha," he's hooked you for life.

869 I'M CRYING, The Animals
Produced by Mickie Most; written by Eric Burdon and Alan Price
MGM 13274 1964 *Billboard:* #19

Living up to their names again—though those roars sound as much like horny young Geordies as hungry beasts.

870 BACK IN MY ARMS AGAIN, The Supremes
Produced by Brian Holland and Lamont Dozier; written by Brian Holland, Lamont Dozier, and Eddie Holland
Motown 1075 1965 *Billboard:* #1 (1 week)

The Ronettes once alleged that the best part of breakin' up is in the makin' up but you could never prove it with a jukebox. Second chances apparently aren't within the province of rock and soul. After all, you or I could name hundreds, if not thousands of songs about getting together and falling apart, but there are damn few classics about getting back together.

Holland-Dozier-Holland delivered such a song to the Supremes, the first of Motown's many in-jokes—you know, the kind of thing where they put out "Someday We'll Be Together" and then announced that the Supremes were splitting up, or gave David Ruffin "My Whole World Ended (The Moment You Left Me)" as his first single after leaving the Temptations. Here, Diana swears her love affair deserves a second chance because she was swindled out of him the first time through the advice of her (real life) friends and partners Mary and Flo, who it turns out are having their own romantic problems, so who are they to say that Diana's guy is a bum? (Since her real life guy at the time was Berry

Gordy, the answer should have been as obvious as their last royalty check.)

Anyway, HDH were so taken with their success here that they used fundamentally the same melody for the Supremes' next single, "Nothing But Heartaches," and paid the price: "Back in My Arms" had been the group's fifth Number One in a row, and "Heartaches" broke the string.

871 TEARS ON MY PILLOW, Little Anthony and the Imperials

Produced by George Goldner; written by Sylvester Bradford and Al Lewis
End 1027   1958   Billboard: #4

Little Anthony and the Imperials had the most stellar set of advisers in doo-wop. After Anthony Gourdine paid his dues in the DuPonts (who recorded one single, "Prove It Tonight," for the Royal Roost jazz label in 1955), he joined the Chesters. That group was discovered by the master doo-wop songwriter/arranger Richard Barrett, who sent them to George Goldner, the harmony disc genius who ran Gee, End, Gone, Rama et al. Goldner had also been tipped on the group by his good friend and sometime business associate, disc jockey Alan Freed, whose show would prove instrumental in Little Anthony's later success. In fact, it was Freed, talking about the group on his program, who dubbed the diminutive Gourdine "Little Anthony." Who knows how the Chesters became the Imperials?

The key to everything, though, was Goldner's insistence that Anthony sing falsetto. It paid off with the group's very first single. The A side, "Two People in the World," opened with straight group harmony topped by Anthony's falsetto wails in the background, then gave way to a powerful, if unsubtle, verse sung by Anthony.

It was the flip side that the deejays and fans really went for though. Though the harmonies are less scintillating, Anthony's vocal on "Tears on My Pillow" shivered the spine with a classic crying lead, given the most minimal vocal and instrumental accompaniment but swamped in echo that brought forth all his delicately quavering sensuality. Anthony's wordless vocalizing at the end made it one of Goldner's most soaring edifices.

872 SING A SIMPLE SONG, Sly and the Family Stone
Written and produced by Sly Stone
Epic 10407   1969   *Billboard: #89*

Sly tossed it off as the B side of "Everyday People," but in other hands "Sing A Simple Song" might have been the best record of a career. As it was, the tune reached such a lowly chart position because deejays didn't start airing it until "Everyday People" 's chart run was about over.

In the musical and vocal exchanges between Morse code guitar, scathing organ and honking sax, bomping drums and bouncing bass, the grave bass voice of Larry Graham and Cynthia Robinson's gospel yowls plus Sly's own raw-throated screams, each phased and panned and tinkered with at the studio board, is a plan that completely contradicts the "do-re-mi-fa-so-la-ti-do" message of the lyrics. There's a darkness beneath the surface that hints at truths that "A simple song might make it bet-ter for a lit-tle while" can't touch. Or touches only at the end of a rope much shorter than expected.

873 MERCY MERCY MERCY, Larry Williams and Johnny Watson
Produced by Larry Williams; written by Joe Zawinul, Larry Williams, and Johnny Watson
OKeh 7274   1967   *Billboard: #96*

"Larry Williams didn't know whether he wanted to be a singer or a pimp," Bumps Blackwell, the producer of his fifties hits once said. As it turned out, Williams had long-running careers in both fields. "Mercy Mercy Mercy," a leering lyrics-added revamping of Cannonball Adderley's 1967 instrumental hit, represents the closest he ever came to fusing the two.

Blackwell claimed that Williams already had embarked upon his career as a pimp when they did their first session, a 1957 attempt to cover Lloyd Price's "Just Because." Price had just left Specialty records, where Blackwell served as house producer and bandleader. Price split because neither owner Art Rupe nor Blackwell thought he had a chance in hell of getting a hit by adding lyrics to a rocked-up version of an operatic theme. They found out they were wrong when Price's record started to take off in the South and ABC-Paramount signed it up for national pop release, and following the ethic of the day, they decided to cover it by using Lloyd's old pianist/valet, Williams.

Williams, born in New Orleans and raised in Oakland, returned to Northern California when Price was drafted in 1954, and once home, he began running a string of women. When the chance of a singing career again beckoned, he quickly moved to Los Angeles but without giving up what Blackwell called "the sporting life," even when he scored back-to-back million sellers with "Short Fat Fannie" and "Dizzy Miss Lizzy." By 1959, Williams stopped having hits and got busted for possession of narcotics; he was more likely selling than using.

The Beatles' versions of his "Dizzy Miss Lizzy" and "Bad Boy" revived Williams' career in the U.K., and in 1965, he and sidekick/guitarist Johnny Watson formed a traveling revue that toured England and recorded a pair of live albums (neither came out in the States). Returning to the U.S., Williams became a staff producer for CBS Records' revived OKeh label in 1966; among his first projects was a series of discs with Little Richard, including some first-rate remakes of Richard's Specialty catalog. (Richard returned the favor by remarking in his autobiography that Williams was "the worst producer in the world. He wanted me to copy Motown and I was no Motown artist.")

OKeh also released a couple of albums featuring Williams and Watson as a duo, and from the second of those, *Two for the Price of One*, came "Mercy Mercy Mercy," which added salty lyrics to the tune that pianist Joe Zawinul had penned for his boss, Cannonball Adderley. Its sly lyrics are a pimp's-eye view of female flesh on parade, though the verbal jousting is so high-spirited that it never seems quite as cruel as what one shudderingly imagines inspired it. In any event, the lyrical dialogue between two guys on a street corner makes a useful platform for a more muscular rendition of Zawinul and Adderley's soul-jazz. Trading leers, Williams and Watson are no match for Sam and Dave, but they're genuinely funky. Too much so for the Top 40, where their record was killed by a bland cover by the Chicago pop group, the Buckinghams, released on OKeh's white parent label, Columbia.

Williams never had another hit; his last album was released in 1979. By then, he'd already been busted a couple more times for dealing drugs. He was never charged with pimping, but it was working girls and heroin and cocaine, not music, that gave him his half-million dollar Laurel Canyon house and the Rolls Royce, Porsche, Buick Riviera, and Cadillac in the garage where his mother found him with a .38 bullet through his brain on the day after New Year's 1980.

The cops said it was suicide: Williams had just broken up with his third wife, losing custody of his daughter in the process. His friends and family said it was either a hit by rival drug dealers or an execution by a renegade Los Angeles police squad. Either way, Larry Williams found no mercy.

874 YOU DROPPED A BOMB ON ME, The Gap Band

Produced by Lonnie Simmons; written by Charlie Wilson,
Lonnie Simmons, and Rudy Taylor
Total Experience 8203   1982   *Billboard:* #31

Charlie Wilson and his brothers Robert and Ronnie came charging out of Oklahoma, three sizable black dudes in cowboy outfits who laid down irrepressible pop-funk under the guidance of producer Lonnie Simmons, paying about as much attention to the niceties of pop music as Barry Switzer's defensive lineman do to the chiropractic requirements of Nebraska tailbacks. "You Dropped A Bomb on Me" features an absolutely atomic guitar riff, seriously soulful vocal chanting (you couldn't exactly say it was singing), and a rhythm bed that features disco thump-thump-thump at the highest density ever achieved by mere mortals, right down to the tympani flourishes. If the lyrics weren't so explicit in their drug 'n' sex metaphors, these cowboys might have stolen a march on the Prince of *Purple Rain*. As it was, they were undoubtedly the best thing to come out of one of the odder epiphenomena of the early Reagan era: black America's brief infatuation with cowboy chic.

875 BOOK OF LOVE, The Monotones

No producer credited; written by Warren Davis,
George Malone, and Charles Patrick
Argo 5290   1958   *Billboard:* #5

One of the most famous commercial jingles of the fifties was a toothpaste ad that went, "You'll wonder where the yellow went / When you brush your teeth with Pep-so-dent." Everybody knew it because it was set to an insipid melody that stuck to your brain as effectively and annoyingly as a Moody Blues dirge. But aside from the honchos at Procter and Gamble, the only one who ever got anything good out of it was Charles Patrick of the Monotones.

The story goes that Patrick was in a Newark, N.J., music store, thumbing through stacks of sheet music, when he found an obscure song called "Book of Love" just as the Pepsodent spot came on in the background. To the same tune, he began to hum, "I wonder, wonder who / Who wrote 'The Book of Love.' " (Al Stillman, who also wrote "Home for the Holiday" and "Juke Box Saturday Night," as it turned out.) Liking the effect, Patrick took it to practice with his friends George Malone and Warren Davis.

By the time the Monotones recorded their "Book of Love," they were a quintet and to the Pepsodent-flavored chorus had been added some straightforward verses. They weren't much more than an outline, an unfleshed table of contents, but the chorus grew as they rehearsed, incorporating some tricky interplay between the drummer (virtually the only audible instrumentalist on the record) and a gravelly bass voice: "Oh I wonder, wonder who-ba-do, who! [downbeat] / Who wrote the book of love."

The Monotones never answered the question (in fact, they resisted recording the song until it turned out that their Jersey-bred rivals, the Kodaks, were thinking of swiping it for themselves) but few listeners, busy adding backseat chapters from their own lives, cared.

Anyway, a more intriguing mystery was where that "who-ba-do" came from. Some said it was the sound of a ball rhythmically hitting the window of the Monotones' rehearsal room, but no answer so mundane could quite capture its mysterious essence, which promised that if you did learn the secret of love's authorship—or manage to join its editorial board—you'd earn the right to goof for the rest of your days.

876 THAT'S WHERE IT'S AT, Sam Cooke
Produced by Hugo Peretti and Luigi Creatore; written by Sam Cooke and J. W. Alexander
RCA 8426   1964   Billboard: #93

To me, this B side of the posthumously released (and markedly inferior) "Cousin of Mine" constitutes better evidence of how Sam Cooke would have fit into the soul music of the future than even "A Change is Gonna Come." A slow ballad with bluesy guitar and surging saxes, "That's Where It's At" smacks of nothing so much as the mid-sixties Stax hits. With his wry "Ha, ha" and repetitious "Oh yeah," and his hints of testifying, Cooke shows that he still remembers all the old gospel tricks and now knows how to deploy them more avidly than he has since leaving the Soul Stirrers. Which is exactly what Otis Redding, Wilson Pickett, and Sam and Dave wound up doing in his absence.

877 LAUGH LAUGH, The Beau Brummels

Produced by Sly Stone; written by Ron Elliott

Autumn 8 1965 *Billboard:* #15

Rock and roll came to San Francisco and found its home in strip joints and suburban lounges, places more bohemian and distinctively less teenage than those where it came to rest in the rest of middle America. Tied into the town's beatnik atmosphere, it developed at odd angles to the music produced in the rest of the country.

Or anyway, a lot of it did. Some of the rest—the best part—developed along almost exactly the same lines but better, the development that would have been mainline elsewhere perhaps forced to an extreme by its juxtaposition with incipient mass bohemia. I'm thinking of two men, of course: John Fogerty, who founded Creedence Clearwater Revival, and Sly Stone, who said fuck it and formed his own group after trying to make a decent record with Grace Slick and the Great Society.

San Francisco was blessed with a visionary disc jockey, 300 pound Tom Donahue, a typical hot lipped AM Big Daddy, but the only one who had the vision to link the movement of the music and the Top 40 concept to the up-and-coming FM band. Like a lot of influential deejays, Donahue (who'd left payola-ridden Philadelphia on the heels of scandal) maintained many marginal music industry interests. One of the most important was Autumn Records, where he and his partner had the perspicacity to hire Sylvester Stewart from tough Vallejo as the A&R director and house producer, thus giving the label several big hits, including Bobby Freeman's "S-W-I-M", and some good tracks by the Tikis and the Mojo Men (and Sylvester reason enough to change his name after his strikeout with Grace and her friends).

Of all Autumn's hits, the best was "Laugh Laugh," by the Beau Brummels. Aside from the Byrds' "Mr. Tambourine Man," no other California group came so close to pure Mersey beat, though the folkish harmonies and harmonica foretell the Bay Area acid rock to come. Sly edited the Brummels down to three-minute classicism, focused on the pop song rather than the soloing and made sure the lyrics remained coherent, thus establishing a local tradition which almost no one pursued.

878 DON'T GIVE UP, Peter Gabriel with Kate Bush

Produced by Daniel Lanois and Peter Gabriel; written by
Peter Gabriel
Geffen 28463   1987   *Billboard:* #72

A stunning duet, more emotionally compelling than the big hit "Sledgehammer," even if it isn't half so danceable—even if it isn't funny at all. In fact, it took nerve to put out "Don't Give Up" as a single at all in the midst of the most dance-crazed decade of the rock era.

In quiet despair, Gabriel sings of life as an unemployed Briton, ruling out all avenues of relief with an eloquence that's as remarkable for its lack of bitterness as for its matter-of-fact acceptance, a perfect portrayal of working-class British stoicism damn near worthy of Orwell. Where Hank Williams once found himself sent to the river and failing to jump in only because the river was dry; where Bruce Springsteen found in the roiling waters a key to his past and perhaps a glimmer of the future; Gabriel looks down at the stream and fears he won't be able to fight off his compulsion: "Gonna stand on that bridge, keep my eyes down below / Whatever may come and whatever may go, that river's flowin' / That river's flowin'."

The music flows like the river, a wash of synthesizer and percussion, occasional piano notes spiking up out of the waves like so much flotsam. Then, in floats Bush, with her angelic soprano, to speak the words that deny defeat, deny it with the only force that's possible, by speaking the truth to the man's isolation, by letting him know that he is not alone but trapped with others, some of whom are ready to share with him the one item that has not yet been reckoned and rationed: their love. "Don't give up," she sings, her throat full, the words measured not so she can spare breath but so that her voice won't crack. "Don't give up, you're not the only one / Don't give up, no reason to be ashamed / Don't give up, because I believe that there's a place, there's a place where we belong."

By record's end, they haven't found it, but they haven't stopped searching either.

879 SO YOU WANT TO BE A ROCK 'N' ROLL STAR, The Byrds

Produced by Gary Usher; written by Jim McGuinn and Chris Hillman
Columbia 43987   1967   *Billboard:* #29

Neat merger of "Mr. Tambourine Man" and "Eight Miles High" that it is, "So You Want to Be a Rock 'n' Roll Star" is also a lyrical crock. Coming from some people, "If your hair is right and your pants are tight" might merely be a sarcastic recipe for what it takes. But it sounds pretty sanctimonious coming from the two biggest folkies in the Byrds (McGuinn finally graduated to a sub-Dylan solo career, Hillman left to play in neo-bluegrass bands). That is, from the two guys in the group who most felt that they *had* sold their "soul to the company / That is waiting there to sell plastic wares."

On the other hand, the best thing about hypocritical moralism is that it can make whatever it's attacking seem so attractive. For all its cautionary admonitions, the music makes "Rock 'n' Roll Star" so enticing that it's surely spawned more bands than it's discouraged. And personally, I always liked tight pants better than psychedelic granny glasses, anyway. I'm sure David Crosby agrees.

880 THE BOILER, Rhoda with the Special A.K.A.

Produced by Jerry Dammers; written by Joyce, Leyton, J. and N. Summers, Dakar, Barker, and Owens
2 Tone (UK) TT18   1982   Did not make pop chart

To say that "The Boiler" is a ska record about date rape is about as useful as describing the invasion of Grenada as an act of liberation.

In English slang, a "boiler" is an old bag, an unattractive woman fit to be fondled and fucked but not loved. That's how Rhoda Dakar describes herself in the opening lines of the song, and she says the word without prejudice, as matter-of-factly as she'd describe having boiled potatoes for dinner.

Against a muted background that owes as much to *Bitches Brew* as anything that the Specials ever played before or after, Dakar goes on to tell the story of being picked up by a "hunk," a good-looking hard guy who offers to pay for the clothes she's buying. He asks her out; she's thrilled, especially since—as she notes every few lines—she still sees herself as an old boiler.

They have a nice time, eating, drinking, dancing. She wants to go home. He insists she come back to his place. She resists. He's angered.

"Listen 'ere, girl, I bought that gear you got on. I bought you in 'ere tonight." He storms off; she follows, and they go toward his place in the bitter cold. He's walking so furiously she can barely keep up.

They come to a railroad bridge and when they're beneath it, he grabs her by the arm and begins beating her in the face, tearing at her clothes, and then begins to rape her.

At this point, Rhoda Dakar begins screaming.

And the record does not end. The music intensifies against her wails. And the record does not end. Her screams weaken; the music builds. And the record does not end. She chokes and gasps and sobs. And the record does not end.

881 RUBBER BISCUIT, The Chips
Producer not credited; written by Charles "Kenrod" Johnson
Josie 803   1956   Did not make pop chart

Studied pataphysical. Probably in the Catskills. Later, taught Martin Scorsese and John Belushi a lesson or two about the relationship between funky and funny. What more do you want? A r-r-r-ubber biscuit?

882 SOUL TWIST, King Curtis and The Noble Knights
Produced by Bobby Robinson; written by Curtis Ousley [King Curtis]
Enjoy 1000   1962   *Billboard:* #17

Long before the guitar achieved godhead, the dominant instrumental voice in rock and roll belonged to the saxophone, a remnant of the music's lineal descent from jump blues bands. R&B sax showed the influence of a whole generation of mellow-to-raggedy toned honkers, from Illinois Jacquet and Arnett Cobb to the main man of New York's fifties recording scene, Sam "The Man" Taylor.

They called Curtis Ousley King for a reason, though. Even more than Sam the Man and his other predecessors, Curtis's tone defined the raunchy noise that complemented the new brand of boogie. Though his own heart may well have belonged to jazz, Curtis played his lungs and heart out on records by everybody from the Coasters to Aretha Franklin. From the first New York Coasters session in about 1956 until his murder in a 1971 street fight, King Curtis backed just about every significant horn session in New York.

He'd come out of Fort Worth to play with Lionel Hampton in 1950, when he was just sixteen, and started making records on his own in 1953, which was about the same time when he began to back others on studio dates. Curtis's own fifties records tended toward bebop, but in sessions, he handled everything from the McGuire Sisters on up. It was Atlantic's producers, particularly Leiber and Stoller, who began to feature him more and more strongly (on the Coasters' "Yakety Yak," he's practically a second lead voice).

By 1962, Curtis had figured out how to make pop of his own choice. "Soul Twist," which owes a lot more to Texas blues and Curtis's own sense of how to make soul swing than it does to anything Chubby Checker ever foisted on the world, ranks with the raunchiest numbers ever to crack the Top 20.

883 LOVE T.K.O., Teddy Pendergrass
Produced by Kenneth Gamble and Leon Huff; written by Cecil Womack, Linda Womack, and Eddie Noble
Philadelphia International 3116　1980　*Billboard*: #44

"Love T.K.O." became a critical cult favorite in the late eighties as an album track for the Womacks (a husband and wife team, he Bobby's brother, she Sam Cooke's daughter and therefore Cecil's step-niece) but the best performance of the song came from Teddy Pendergrass, knocked out into hoarse despair and still not *quite* able to fully cut it loose. The tension between Teddy's passions and his willingness to let them flood out measures the difference between sixties and seventies soul men. His style becomes more conversational without hitting the dramatic heights of predecessors like Marvin Junior—or even what he does himself on some Harold Melvin and the Blue Notes sides—but you'll want to listen very closely before judging it inferior because there are subtleties here, in his moans and asides and grunts and hasty falsetto runs, that mark the work of a great singer.

884 JAILHOUSE RAP, The Fat Boys
Produced by Kurtis Blow; written by Kurtis Blow, Larry Smith, Mark Morales, Damon Wimbley, Darren Robinson, and S. Abbatiello
Sutra 137　1984　Did not make pop chart

The Coasters of hip-hop—if the Coasters had replaced Bobby Nunn's spoofing bass with the purely outrageous Human Beat Box—wind up in the slammer, as the result of 1) a midnight lust for pizza, and 2) an arrogant King of the Slops refusal to pay for a Burger King gorge. (The Beat Box either just came along to keep them company or lip-farting in public was a felony in New York.)

The fat boy jokes are all well and good but there's a darker undercurrent here than Leiber and Stoller ever gave the Coasters. "In jail, in jail without no bail," they chant on the break, over deep bopping piano and ruthless syndrums, "In jail, we're in jail because we failed." Though they return in the last verse to speak moralistically about how it was all their own fault, the music on that break speaks a greater truth.

885 DARLING BABY, Jackie Moore
Produced by Dave Crawford and Brad Shapiro; written by Brian Holland, Lamont Dozier, and Eddie Holland
Atlantic 2861   1972   Billboard: #22

A gorgeous gospel-tinged blues rendition of the Elgins' 1966 R&B hit that proves the oft-doubted affinity between Southern soul and the Motown brand. The grunting horns, blues guitar, and Aretha-influenced singing here top the lighter atmosphere of the original, but it's a close call, since Moore was always among the frothier Southern soul hitmakers anyhow, as lovers of "Precious Precious" and "Sweet Charlie Babe" will recall.

886 NATURAL HIGH, Bloodstone
Produced by Mike Vernon; written by Charles McCormick
London 1046   1973   Billboard: #10

The series of hits churned out by this Kansas City-bred soul-turned-funk sextet provided some of the prime pleasures of the mid-seventies. Though they had to go to England (on the undercard of an Al Green tour) to get a record deal, and in fact recorded "Natural High" in the village of Chipping Norton, Bloodstone's fusion of falsetto soul harmony with light funk instrumentation—and here, gentle orchestration and lyrics that fit the melody like a musical caress—gave them a grip on contemporary black pop tastes as solid as any that Gamble and Huff could have provided.

887 I BELIEVE IN YOU (YOU BELIEVE IN ME), Johnnie Taylor

Written and produced by Don Davis
Stax 0161   1973   Billboard: #11

I once asked a friend who edited a music industry trade paper (not *Billboard*) why album charts were based on sales only while singles charts factored in airplay. "Because if we based them only on sales, there wouldn't be anything but black records in the Top Ten," he replied. Oh.

That double standard helps account for the fact that Stax couldn't push Taylor's million-seller into the Top Ten—there remain hidebound pockets of this land where an R&B-based sound just isn't going to get airplay. Among the records that made Number One around the same time were Maureen McGovern's "The Morning After," Helen Reddy's "Delta Dawn," and "Half-Breed" by Cher, all godawful examples of the lily-white music that such programmers prefer. (All three of those records also sold a million, but remember, they were hyped at every step by charts which disproportionately reflected their airplay successes.)

"I Believe in You" seems a good topic for this discourse because such sweet-tempered soul rarely receives the critical respect it deserves, and often for similar reasons. Taylor tells his tale over a melody reminiscent of the Staple Singers' pop hits, elaborately arranged light gospel with flutes and strings and funky guitar, pouring out his faith in his lover despite the harshness of a world in which not only the charts are rigged. "One thing I can say about the people in the world today," he croons, "They see you with a good thing, they gonna take it away." That's on the money. With a bullet.

888 ENDLESS SLEEP, Jody Reynolds

Producer not credited; written by Jody Reynolds and
Delores Nance
Demon 1507   1958   Billboard: #5

Nightmare with reverb guitar. Jody sings the song on his way home from the shore, where he'd gone to find his baby after they've quarreled. When he got there, he found only her footprints—she'd thrown herself in. Jody knew, because he heard her voice "crying in the deep / Come join me baby in my endless sleep."

He threw himself in and struggled out into the shallow breakers to find her. Rather than fulfilling her wish and taking the big plunge himself, he dragged her back to the sand, only to hear the voice again, calling to him. But it no longer sounded like his baby—it's the sea itself, undisguised and annoyed that he has robbed it.

"Endless Sleep" is exactly as mystical/melodramatic as that synopsis sounds, but Reynold's sub-Elvis vocal and the Duane Eddy undertow of the guitar make it fascinating.

A special Bulwer Lytton Award for the opening lines: "The night was black, rain fallin' down / Looked for my baby, she's nowhere around."

889 HI-HEEL SNEAKERS, Tommy Tucker
Produced by Herb Abramson; written by Robert Higgenbotham [Tommy Tucker]
Checker 1067   1964   *Billboard:* #11

R&B in the Bizarro World: Tommy's love not only wears those high-backed tennis shoes, and a wig-hat on her head, he suggests she complement her red dress with boxing gloves " 'case some fool might wanna fight."

Tucker's journeyman soul man career gave no previous evidence of interest in such exotica. Coming out of Springfield, Ohio, he quietly backed a number of greater talents, including jazzman Roland Kirk. By 1959, he first recorded on his own, for Hi Records in Memphis, but without any chart action. Bouncing around, he landed in Asbury Park, New Jersey, where he was found by Herb Abramson, Ahmet and Neshui Ertegun's original partner in Atlantic Records and the guy to whose acute R&B ear may be credited this record's choice and bluesy guitar licks, reminiscent as they are of Hubert Sumlin's playing on vintage Howlin' Wolf sides.

"Hi-Heel Sneakers" might be about damn near anything—I mean, that could be a drag queen he's describing, I suppose—and its very freakishness has attracted all sorts of cover versions, including four which charted (in order of quality, they were by Stevie Wonder [1965], Jerry Lee Lewis [1965], Ramsey Lewis [1966], and Jose Feliciano [1968]). For just about all of the above, though, the words seem to compel frenzy. Tucker's laid-back and bluesy languor seems preferable, if only because it's so matter-of-fact, as if he'd lived all his life in precincts where to see such a strangely garbed dame would have been no more unusual than, say, running into a gal with a leopard skin pillbox hat down by Bob Dylan's joint.

890 OVERNIGHT SENSATION (HIT RECORD), Raspberries

Produced by Jimmy Ienner; written by Eric Carmen
Capitol 3946   1974   *Billboard:* #18

Eric Carmen wanted fame as badly as any guy who ever blow-dried his hair into a perfect bouffant, squeezed himself into nut-numbing tight pants, strapped on a guitar, and stepped to the mike to fake some Beatles harmony. Carmen wanted to have it all, which as he conceived it meant a band that rocked as tough and wild as the Who and crooned as smooth and tight as the Beach Boys, the lustful adoration of teenage nubiles, the cogent respect of rock critics, massive radio airplay and the royalty checks that go with it.

The second Raspberries single, "Go All the Way," won over a substantial number of nubiles and programmers, and his Liverpudlian cum Beach Boys power-pop writing and singing earned the allegiance of a coterie of critics, but not the across-the-board credibility for which he lusted. And since Carmen's taste in pop ran to all the right things musically (big drums, splashy cymbals, intricate voice-guitar dynamics) and all the wrong ones lyrically (really drippy love song sentiment works only when you conceal how hard it was to create it), the Raspberries had reached a dead end musically. After "I Wanna Be with You," the "Go All the Way" follow-up, they didn't crack the Top 20 for the next two years, and nobody could take the likes of "Let's Pretend" seriously unless they were willing to come out in favor of self-consciously puerile self-pity (as some were, believe it or not).

It turned out that Eric Carmen wanted a hit record worse than he wanted teenage lust, so he decided to tie up all his desires in one epic song, a love ode to chart success laden with radio and record industry jargon: "And if the programmer don't pull it / It's bound to get back the bullet."

The record was arranged as a pastiche of Carmen's favorites—the Beach Boys, the Beatles, the Who, and especially Phil Spector, for whom Jimmy Ienner subbed with surprising adequacy. The result was a tour de force, albeit a completely derivative and opportunistic one. It was also five and a half minutes long at a time when no Top 40 stations played anything over three and a half except under duress, and determinedly mid-sixties pop in its influences, at a time when FM rock stations disdained such stuff in favor of album rock pretensions with heavier throw weight.

Carmen wanted to call it "Hit Record," but Capitol Records thought that title too assertive so they saddled him with "Overnight Sensation" and compromised on the subtitle. It almost worked: The record crawled into the Top 20 and if the song had been about half as long, or if more listeners had shared Carmen's obsession with the mechanics of fame or understood his promo-man nomenclature, it could have gone all the way. As it is, in its own weird way, "Overnight Sensation" remains a very fine record, the thing that still makes me forgive Carmen (at least a little bit) when he surfaces on the radio in the late eighties with one of the schlock ballads that have finally given him fame and wealth at the expense of any pretense of credibility, of course.

891 NIGHTSHIFT, The Commodores
Produced by Dennis Lambert; written by Walter Orange, Dennis Lambert, and Franne Golde
Motown 1773   1985   Billboard: #3

Since they'd been given up for dead themselves after the departure of Lionel Richie, it's only too appropriate that it was the Commodores who came up with rock's greatest tribute to dead heroes. The busy backing track's effort at a contemporary dance sound can't conceal what it really is: Not a tribute to the departed Marvin Gaye and Jackie Wilson so much as a pastiche of their styles. But then, why should "Nightshift" have to hide the facts? It sounds damn near as sweet as its models, and manages to make at least some part of our mourning pleasurable, which is all that really counts.

892 PATCHES, Clarence Carter
Produced by Rick Hall; written by Ronald Dunbar and Norman [General] Johnson
Atlantic 2748   1970   Billboard: #4

The ultimate soul soap opera, written by transplanted Carolinian General Johnson for Alabama's last great blind guitar player. (Not to be confused with Dickey Lee's morbid "Patches," about a crosstown love affair that turns into dual suicide; this is the sob story about the orphaned sharecropper.) If Michael Jackson ever covers it, he's guaranteed a mini-series deal.

893 I ONLY WANT TO BE WITH YOU, Dusty Springfield
Produced by Ivor Raymonde; written by Mike Hawker and
Ivor Raymonde
Philips 40162   1964   *Billboard:* #12

"I Only Want to Be with You" is romantic trash, but there's something about Springfield's wholeheartedness that rescues the song and the arrangement from their own worst intentions. *Maybe* it's conviction, but the setup is so corny that even such a reformed folkie couldn't have believed it. (Could she?) Call it craft, and good luck trying to resist it.

894 BREATHLESS, Jerry Lee Lewis
Produced by Sam Phillips; written by Otis Blackwell
Sun 288   1958   *Billboard:* #7

In February 1958, Jerry Lee Lewis sang "Breathless," one of his more spectacularly silly stomps, in the film, *High School Confidential.* With that promotion in mind, Sam Phillips released it as his third single, following up "Whole Lotta Shakin' " and "Great Balls of Fire." The record stiffed.

Phillips arranged for Jerry Lee to perform "Breathless" on Dick Clark's new prime-time edition of "American Bandstand." Lewis performed with his usual roadhouse flair, but it didn't help record sales and airplay remained flat even with Clark pushing it in Philadelphia.

Then Clark offered Phillips a deal: Beechnut, Clark's sponsor, wanted to run a promotion in which they'd give away a certain single for sending in chewing gum wrappers. With nothing to lose, Sam agreed to use Jerry Lee's current stiff. And "Breathless" rocked straight into the Top Ten.

Smirnoff should be so lucky.

895 ROCKING PNEUMONIA AND THE BOOGIE WOOGIE FLU, Huey Piano Smith and the Clowns
Produced by Johnny Vincent; written by Huey Smith
Ace 530   1957   *Billboard:* #52

The classic New Orleans shuffle is a deterioration of parade rhythms—and that makes "Rockin' Pneumonia" a true classic of the locale, because these guys could really strut their stuff. Famous New Orleans session pianist Smith assembled the Clowns as front men because he couldn't sing, but the group he put together became notorious for, among other things, its transvestism. The voice babbling those great lines about jumping, falling, hollering, loving, kissing, and the other symptoms of this incurable disease is Bobby Marchan, the Sylvester of the fifties, which offers a sense of cultural continuity few of "Rockin' Pneumonia" 's admirers would have suspected.

896 WALK THIS WAY, Run-D.M.C.
Produced by Russell Simmons and Rick Rubin; written by Steven Tyler and Joe Perry
Profile 5112   1986   *Billboard:* #4

Credibility is perhaps the rock artist's most precious commodity. Like all others, it has recently been seriously devalued through various forms of misappropriation. For instance, in 1966, everyone including their fans understood that the Monkees were a cheap televised substitute for the Beatles, and while there could be legitimate differences of opinion about how charming or entertaining they or any of their records might be, there was certainly no chance that the Monkees were going to be mistaken for musical artists in the same sense as a real band—by which I mean anything on the scale from the Rolling Stones to ? and the Mysterians. But in 1987, when their record label and MTV resumed marketing the Old Monkees TV program and their records and ultimately a group called the New Monkees, gullible press, critics, and fans went along as if a reunion or revival of the Monkees was the same thing as the resurrection of the original Yardbirds.

Something similar has happened to Aerosmith. Understood in the seventies as a second-rate imitation of the Stones, with a first-rate guitarist offsetting a third-rate front man, Aerosmith may have been somebody's legit high school faves but there was little danger of mistaking them for artists. Their ambitions didn't encompass any such thing; they were out for quick, disposable kicks and if you liked them, they delivered. That this is 90 percent less than what the Rolling Stones delivered (no matter what the Stones promised) was obvious to all and sundry.

But by the mid-eighties, cynicism had so completely infested rock's marketplace of ideas that Aerosmith was revived not as somebody's favorite high school band but as an epitome of high energy rock and roll—a source point for what it's all about. In public, at least, nobody even bothered to gag.

Among those who'd loved the band's records in their adolescence were the guys in Run-D.M.C. The Aerosmith revival really took off when they asked guitarist Joe Perry and singer Steven Tyler to participate in this remake of one of the band's sexist blues anthems. Perry acquitted himself well, as usual, and Tyler's snotty snarl prospered in the hip-hop context, where there's always a premium on feigned nastiness. And the result was a really good record, one hell of a lot better than anything Aerosmith ever did.

Because Run-D.M.C. were, for good reason, among the most respected rap groups, Tyler, Perry, and thus Aerosmith acquired cachet and soon one found critical encomiums to the band blossoming, its name dropped as a reference point throughout the hinterlands of rock criticism, sometimes even diminished to 'smith to show *really* hip intimacy. It is now taken for granted that Aerosmith was a great band. Gimme a break or bring on the nineties.

897 SILENT MORNING, Noel
Produced by Roman Ricardo and Paul Robb; written by Noel Pagan
4th & Broadway 439   1987   *Billboard:* #47

"Silent Morning" presents itself as the bleakest dance record ever made, a seven-minute Latin hip-hop dirge, soundtrack for a black, Latin, and gay late-night club scene scourged by AIDS and the fear of it. Not that the lyrics ever mention a disease; they don't even hint at it. Noel's bereft tenor instead simply makes a lover's lament: "Silent morning, I wake up and you're not by my side . . . / Silent morning, they say a man's not supposed to cry . . . Silent morning, how could our love have lied."

So maybe a hundred years from now, no listener will be able to detect what any New Yorker could feel behind the music as it pumped over the radio. Maybe, by then, the jangled edge of the electronic percussion won't vibrate against nerves rattled by watching the deaths of friends, neighbors, lovers—the death of a way of life, the imploded destruction of a community.

Or maybe, in the future, when students are assigned to read *And the Band Played On*, Randy Shilts's classic account of the epidemic, they'll also be assigned to listen to Noel's music, as they still seek to explain our denial of the facts, even as we watched so many die.

Maybe, listening today, you can hear the evidence accumulate, the lives deteriorate, hard up against the remorseless beats of Little Louie Vega's mix. If you can't, just listen to Noel sing those first few words— "I'm on fire"—and try to figure whether he's singing about having the hots or sleeping with somebody with a bad case of night sweats.

898 SAN ANTONIO STROLL, Tanya Tucker
Produced by Snuff Garrett; written by Peter Noah
MCA 40444   1975   Did not make pop chart

899 ON THE OTHER HAND, Randy Travis
Produced by Kyle Lehning and Keith Stegall; written by Paul Overstreet and Don Schlitz
Warner Bros.   1988   Did not make pop chart

In pop terms, country music defines itself as the music most likely to be wiped out in the face of any oncoming trend. Nearly dismantled by rockabilly in the fifties, it experienced a small resurgence in the early sixties (at least singers like Buck Owens, Merle Haggard, and George Jones occasionally got their records into the lower reaches of the Top 40), and suffered at least as much as any other American pop style in the wake of the British Invasion, produced a few, mainly novelty and "outlaw," successes in the early seventies (Loretta Lynn, Dolly Parton, Waylon Jennings, Willie Nelson), and then all but disappeared as a market factor through the late eighties, until the resurgence of so-called neo-traditionalists like Randy Travis, the Judds, Steve Earle, and Dwight Yoakam. Disappeared so completely, in fact, that a few hysterics (including me) predicted its demise.

Even when it prospers, country does so in a ghetto, the same ghetto it has more-or-less willfully inhabited for the better part of two decades. As resistant to musical synthesis as much of its working-class constituency has been to racial integration (and for many of the same reasons, since creating a musical synthesis in America almost inevitably requires intimate racial interaction), country is more stultifying than any other genre. Three albums into their careers, it's impossible to be sure of the continued growth of Travis or Earle or Yoakam—five albums into theirs, the Judds are audibly depleted. Not one of them seems nurtured by a challenging creative community in the way that a similar pop or rock or dance or hip-hop performer sometimes can be. And when you get less career nurture than a rap group, you're in a *lot* of trouble. (Showing a performer how to repeat past successes as formula is not nurture, no matter what Ricky Skaggs tries to act like he believes.)

The loss is not only country's. The genre's estrangement from Top 40 means that pop listeners never hear some of the most arresting voices of their generation. Tanya Tucker, for instance, has been having hits since she was in her early teens. "San Antonio Stroll," her best record and a country chart Number One, digs a rocking groove even though the lead instrument is a fiddle and the guitar plays trills like a mandolin. Tucker's account of a Southern girlhood in which the central rite of passage is going to the Saturday night dance (partly 'cause it's a liberation from staying home and listening to the Opry), portrays an America that enormous numbers of people bought wholesale when Ronald Reagan served up a less detailed, poignant and believable version of it. But in a culture that despises the trappings of Southerness, Tucker never had a chance.

Randy Travis ought to be an exception, simply because he's the finest, gentlest, mellowest country craftsman of his generation, a latter-day Willie Nelson with a far better voice. "On the Other Hand," its arrangement mostly just a guitar strum and quiet bass, a few sweet piano licks and Travis's booming baritone, might have succeeded as some kind of housewife pop if not for the steel guitar licks that crop up at the end of the verses. At the very least it's the best temptation song anybody's come up with in years. Travis's singing gives it a meditative cast, as if each turn of phrase really is working out his reasons for not cheating. "On the Other Hand" not only topped the country charts, it was the dominant hit there for the better part of a year, creating in Nashville an almost Beatles-like spasm around Travis's rather blank persona, without the rest of the nation knowing anything more about him than whatever focus the occasional thirty-second hint on *Entertainment Tonight* could bring to bear. It's the kind of travesty that can only happen in a subculture pushed into a sprucely maintained corner.

900 EARTH ANGEL, The Penguins
Produced by Dootsie Williams; written by Curtis Williams and/or Jesse Belvin
DooTone 348   1954   *Billboard:* #8

"Earth Angel" earned legendary status as the first independent label rhythm and blues record to hit the *Billboard* pop charts. But the Penguins are famous for more than just surviving the notorious cover record industry—though that was in itself a major accomplishment. (The odious Crew Cuts did take the song Top Three on the basis of greater radio airplay, but the Penguins got vastly more jukebox plays and sold far more records, an estimated total of four million.)

Backed only by Curtis Williams's homespun piano chords, muted drums and the group's open-throated "oooo" and "waaa," lead singer Cleve Duncan sings in a trembly tenor reminiscent of the great Los Angeles singer, Jesse Belvin. Various sources report that Belvin wrote or cowrote this song, although the Penguins were from Fremont, many miles north of Belvin's haunts in Hollywood and Watts.

The group was recorded by Dootsie Williams of DooTone Records, but its most helpful associate was songwriter/arranger/impresario Buck Ram, later the proprietor of the Platters. Ram, then in his late forties, came up through the big band scene, working with Duke Ellington, the Dorseys, and Count Basie. He'd begun working as an artist's representative only in 1954; the Penguins, whose record hit the charts in December 1954 but made its impact in 1955, were his first major act. But he soon added the Flairs (featuring "Louie Louie"'s Richard Berry), the Teen Queens, Joe Houston, and many others.

"Earth Angel" could succeed in part because it had firm links with the pop past. Though such R&B ballads often were attacked at the time as the worst sort of oversimplified treacle, in truth they were (as Big Al Pavlow shows in *The R&B Book*) firmly rooted in Tin Pan Alley successes no more deviant than the Ink Spots. The slightly intensified beat and Duncan's wobbly warble added new elements, but they were right on the surface of anything but a radical break with what had been happening in pop music for many years.

Nevertheless, the Penguins belong firmly in the pantheon of the rock and roll era. Though they never again hit the national pop or R&B charts, they made good records for many years, for DooTone, Mercury, and Atlantic, among other labels. During the early sixties doo-wop revival, Duncan Williams reformed them and they gave budding songwriter Frank Zappa his first important record, "Memories of

El Monte," a lovely tribute to the site of the most famous doo-wop shows in the West Coast southland.

901 500 MILES AWAY FROM HOME, Bobby Bare
Produced by Chet Atkins; written by Bobby Bare, Hedy West, and Charlie Williams
RCA 8238   1963   *Billboard:* #10

"500 Miles" is well-known to urban folkies, one of those songs almost everybody does. Country music historian Bill Malone calls it a "traditional mountain song," but in the versions by Peter, Paul and Mary, et al., it's always credited to Hedy West, a singer/songwriter of the early sixties campus-based folk song movement.

Bobby Bare's version is quite distinct from any of the folk singers', not only because it's given a relatively expansive countrypolitan arrangement featuring a prominent choral background and big shuffling drums, but because he uses the song as the fulcrum for a monologue like the one to "Detroit City." In fact, "500 Miles Away from Home" was released just four months after that hit, and Bare uses it in a way that presupposes an awareness of the storyline of the earlier record, in which the country boy heads home after trying and failing to find success in the factories.

It's Bare's monologue that makes the record a keeper, too. Speaking in a voice that suggests Elvis as much as the one he used on the satiric "All American Boy" (as Bill Parsons in 1958), he chronicles his return journey, his altered perspective, and wonders "what they'll say when they see their boy lookin' this way." And though he blames it all on bad luck, you know that it's a Sisyphean journey he's on—a quarter century later, he's no closer to arriving than he was back in 1963.

For a generation of displaced country boys (and girls), there was symbolic truth in that treadmill tale that could never have made the same kind of sense to the button-down folk song crowd. And you can hear the consequences in all sorts of records, from the Kendalls' "Pittsburgh Stealers" to Rosanne Cash's "Runaway Train," records barely known to most of those who worship Bob Dylan.

902 IF WE MAKE IT THROUGH DECEMBER, Merle Haggard

Produced by Ken Nelson and Fuzzy Owen; written by Merle Haggard
Capitol 3746   1973   Billboard: #28

Merle Haggard was born in 1937 in dusty Bakersfield, California, two years after his parents arrived there from Oklahoma in the great Dust Bowl migration. The Haggards were always poor, living much of the time in a converted railroad car, and things got worse when Merle's father, a fiddler, died in 1946, leaving Merle under the sole supervision of his mother, a member of the Church of Christ who completely disapproved of pop music.

By the time he reached his teens, Haggard had two skills: guitar playing and theft. And by the time he reached nineteen, he had plenty of time to practice the former because the latter had gotten him sent to San Quentin, where he did four years. In 1960, released and arguably reformed, Merle set out to imitate his hero, Lefty Frizzell, last of the great forties honky-tonkers. He soon hooked up with Wynn Stewart, first of the California country stars, who hired him as the bassist in his road band and introduced him to Tally Records. Haggard cut his first single in 1961; by 1963, he'd charted with "Sing a Sad Song," and the next year "(All My Friends Are Going to Be) Strangers" gave him his first big break.

The things he'd learned and observed growing up rough and living rougher gave Haggard a wealth of material and an outlook that hasn't changed in thirty years of record-making. He's an embittered right-wing populist, his sympathy always for the working man but subject to various sorts of jingoism. While his musical standards are far too sophisticated and eclectic to countenance racism, "Okie from Muskogee" wasn't an accident, either. Haggard's not a cosmopolitan ideologue like Charlton Heston, but his politics aren't far from those of Ronald Reagan, who (while governor of California) officially pardoned Haggard for the crime that sent him to San Quentin.

"If We Make It Through December," with its corny vocal chorale and lilting guitar riff, was the first record—perhaps the first meaningful piece of pop culture—to come to grips with the fears, frustrations, and hopes-against-hope of the workers thrown into disarray by the initial round of deprivation as the world economy cooled after three decades of post-World War II expansion. In other words, this is Bruce Springsteen country, but Haggard is speaking ten years sooner, and in the voice of someone for whom rebellion isn't an idea, let alone an option.

903 I'M TORE UP, Billy Gayles with Ike Turner's Rhythm Rockers

Written and produced by Ike Turner
Federal 12265   1956   Did not make pop chart

The greatest rock and roll record ever made about the pleasures of drinking to get drunk . . . and with an Ike Turner guitar riff that rips through your guts like a premonition of the morning after. The Rhythm Rockers were the band that Ike took on the road around the South and Midwest before he found Tina, and their riffing horns and shuffling drums hark back to late forties roadhouse R&B. This is the kind of music that only gets made when people play together night after night after night to the point of exhausted inspiration. Though that guitar part comes from nowhere but B.B. King.

904 BY THE TIME I GET TO PHOENIX (edit), Isaac Hayes

Produced by Isaac Hayes; written by Jim Webb
Enterprise 9003   1969   *Billboard: #30*

For those who knew Isaac Hayes as one of the great Stax writer/producers, his emergence as a performer was a surprise; his appearance in the guise of a deep-throated crooner was amazing; coming up with a hit version of a Glen Campbell country-pop tune was pretty startling, even if that song had been written by Jim Webb; but the ultimate shock was that the record clocked in at 6:45, nearly enough time for three of his Sam and Dave hits. Well, actually, not quite the ultimate shock; it was even more astonishing to learn that the single had been *edited down* from an album track that lasted eighteen minutes, longer than the Stones' "Coming Home," Dylan's "Desolation Row," or even Jimi's "Voodoo Chile," yet less psychedelic than "MacArthur Park." Hayes had ventured where *nobody* had gone before, including Hendrix and Sly Stone, neither of whom was capable of a pop ballad.

Hayes made his music slow, somber and as slinky as great sex. He turned Webb's little pop song inside out, using a hint of the melody played by a thrumming organ and embellished with a single brushed cymbal to back his windy preachments on the power of love. The single's great virtue is that it cuts out the blather and gets to the meat, which is Isaac's invention of a back story that explains why the guy is leaving his lover in the main lyric. He's a country boy, you see, and when he finds his woman cheating on him, he gives her another chance but the *eighth* time he finds her out, he leaves his note on the kitchen table and splits.

By the time Hayes gets to the song itself, the singer's journey has become a personalized epic in a way that Campbell (or Webb, probably) could never have dreamed. Declaiming the words like a latter-day Brook Benton, cut loose inside his reinvention of the song, Hayes comes on like a modern Aesop. Hard to believe he was laying the groundwork for Barry White.

905 BANG A GONG (GET IT ON), T. Rex
Produced by Tony Visconti; written by Marc Bolan
Reprise 1032   1972   *Billboard:* #10

Marc Bolan is often perceived as a sort of poor man's David Bowie: They shared producer Tony Visconti, flirtatious androgyny, and an affinity for the early seventies British style known as "power pop." Each began his career by making florid albums, although Bolan's flower power poesy had far more groove than Bowie's West End theatrics.

When they turned to making rock and roll in the early seventies, Bolan again had all the best of it—at least in singles terms. While Bowie sometimes scored with stuffy, spacey funk, Bolan ripped into ripe, simple riffs, exulting in open expressions of sexual passion: "Bang A Gong" uses "dirty sweet" as its ultimate term of endearment, and that's just the tip of the iceberg. Coupled with the honking guitar line (so biting it makes the Chuck Berry reference he whispers at the end seem earned), Bolan's overheated yowling and groaning makes the record a comic-erotic masterwork.

906 DIRTY WATER, The Standells
Written and produced by Ed Cobb
Tower 185   1966   *Billboard:* #11

An extended horny snarl from the real stars of *Riot on Sunset Strip*, which was their home turf. Why their biggest record targets Boston and the women on the banks of the River Charles nobody ever quite understood. Maybe all those college dorms up there inspired Ed Cobb to thoughts of coeds, although the line he wrote wouldn't have been half as powerful without the way they sing it: "Fruuuuuuu-strated women / Have to be in by twelve o'clock," phrased with as much dour passion as Bob Dylan recounting his buddy's ninety-nine year sentence in "Percy's Song." Coupled with a Bo Diddley beat, that's all they needed. Which is a good thing, because that's all they had.

907 TRAIN KEPT A-ROLLIN', The Rock & Roll Trio
Produced by Owen Bradley; written by Bradshaw, Mann and Kay
Coral 61719   1956   Did not make pop chart

The Rock & Roll Trio were the other good rockers from Humes High in Memphis, Elvis's alma mater. Johnny Burnette, the lead singer and image focal point, played on the football team Elvis was kicked off for failing to cut his hair. Burnette went on to become one of the less objectionable teen idols ("You're Sixteen"). His brother, Dorsey, became a middling country-pop singer ("Tall Oak Tree"). Both Burnettes died young. Neither ever made a record half as good as this Tiny Bradshaw again. Not that there's much evidence that they wanted to, though in fairness a couple of their other sides, most notably "Lonesome Train", suggest they could have.

The third member of the Trio was guitarist Paul Burlison, who went on to nothing special: He's now a record collector and dealer in rare wax. (Actually, by the time the group recorded, it was a quartet, having added drummer Tony Austin, a cousin of Carl Perkins, in the same unannounced fashion as Elvis, Scotty, and Bill added D.J. Fontana.) Burlison pops up in fewer trivia books than the Burnettes, but he's the Trio's real hero.

Burlison was put on the path to the rock and roll pantheon by accident. In the process of being lugged around from gig to gig, one of the tubes in his amp was knocked loose—not completely out of its socket, but jarred enough so that when sound went through the speaker, it rattled. Instant fuzztone. His rock-historic decision was to keep the effect, work on it, improve it. And the guitar part in "Train Kept A-Rollin' " buzzes, crackles, and quavers like no guitar until the British bands of the following decade went to work. (In the case of the Yardbirds, went to work on "Train Kept A-Rollin'.") It's so good, you barely notice how much Burnette's "We trucked on down that ol' fair lane" sounds like um, something else.

908 HANG ON SLOOPY, The McCoys
Produced by Bob Feldman, Jerry Goldstein, and Richard Gottehrer; written by Bert Russell [Berns] and Wes Farrell
Bang 506   1965   *Billboard*: #1 (1 week)

A piece of The Rock and Roll Dream:

Rick Zehringer and his brother Randy learned to play guitar while going to junior high in Ohio and Indiana. They performed as the McCoys (after a Ventures instrumental, "The McCoy"), then became the Rick Z Combo and finally Rick and the Raiders, who actually squeezed out a local single, "You Know That I Love You." Somewhere in there, they added bassist Randy Hobbs and keyboardist Ronnie Brandon and built enough of a following around Dayton to get a gig opening for the Strangeloves when those shaggy pseudo-Aussies hit town in midsummer '65.

The Strangeloves went on tour with a mission from Bang label owner (and expert writer/producer) Bert Berns. He told them to be on the lookout for a rock group that could cover one of his old R&B hits, the Vibrations' "My Girl Sloopy." When the fake sheep farmers heard the McCoys (happily, at the end of the tour) they invited the group back to New York to make that very record. And the Zehringers gladly accepted, a decision made easier by the fact that their mom and pop were set to leave on vacation the next day and needed only change destination to accompany their kids. Or so the story goes.

Their parents' presence also proved beneficial when Rick and the Raiders was adjudged an inadequate name. Going through an old photo album, one of the Strangeloves saw a picture of Rick's first band, the McCoys, and the old moniker immediately became the band's new one. Similarly, when Rick Zehringer loomed as a potential mouthful for deejays, one of the Strangeloves-turned-producer figured out that the pint-sized guitar whiz could be dubbed Derringer.

Fittingly, then, "Hang On Sloopy" (as the rearranged tune was titled) was a one-shot. Despite its potent lubricity, and a wild-ass scream from Rick just before the final chorus, the McCoys retained a basic anonymity, abetted by their failure to score a follow-up.

909 ROCKIT, Herbie Hancock
Produced by Material and Herbie Hancock; written by
Herbie Hancock, Bill Laswell, and Michael Beinhorn
Columbia 04054 1983 *Billboard:* #71

Jazz purists like to boast that their virtuosos could cut huge hits any
time they wanted to, but the spotty record of so-called "jazz-rock fusion" makes that a brag of doubtful validity. Here's the exception that
proves the rule: Herbie Hancock, as good a keyboardist as there is in
contemporary jazz, delivers a disc that not only hit (its dance club and
music video impact went way beyond its chart position) but stood on
the cutting edge of hip-hop—though that was thanks mainly to his
collaborators from the avant-garde rock band Material.

With such associates and without them, Hancock has charted more
than a dozen singles on the R&B charts since the mid-seventies, although only "Chameleon" and "Rockit" have crossed over. But that's
not what proves the rule—the decisive evidence is that, with the exception of "Rockit," none of those singles marks any kind of innovation,
only pleasant and witty variations on standard themes from the jazzy
end of the danceable spectrum. There's not a hair of shame in Hancock
having made them, but they are nowhere near being pop's fount of
creative inspiration, either. What you've got here is a creative collision
between a couple (or maybe a few) streams of American musical tradition. Only a fool would pretend the whole river fed itself from a single
source.

910 HEAVY MAKES YOU HAPPY (SHA-NA-BOOM-BOOM), The Staple Singers
Produced by Al Bell; written by Jeff Barry and Bobby Bloom
Stax 0083 1971 *Billboard:* #27

More than any Jackson 5 record (except maybe "ABC"), "Heavy
Makes You Happy" deserves the title "bubble gum soul." It has the
right writers (the team that came up with that mindless pinnacle, "Mon-
tego Bay," no less), the right blend of nonsense syllables and non
sequiturs (Heavy *what?*), the appropriate brainless spark, and Mavis
and Pop Staples blend their voices as frothily as anything ever cooked
up in a Big Apple studio.

On the other hand, the Memphis Horns and a lowering blend of
electric piano and funky drumming make this music legit as soul, too,

no matter how close to clumsy the rudimentary guitar solo is. Call it sheer airheaded fun and that's plenty enough.

911 HANKY PANKY, Tommy James and the Shondells

Produced by Jack Douglas; written by Jeff Barry and Ellie Greenwich
Roulette 4686   1966   *Billboard:* #1 (2 weeks)

In the greatest dance clubs, there's a long, estimable tradition of deejay "exclusive." In the Bronx during the late seventies, pioneering hip-hop deejays scraped the labels off the discs they'd tracked down so that competitors couldn't find out what old or new jams they were spinning. The same kind of competition went on in Pittsburgh in the early sixties. Thus was born "Hanky Panky," a great dumb riff, and the career of Tommy James, the only bubble gum singer with rock and roll power.

James never should have heard "Hanky Panky." It was written in twenty minutes in a hallway outside a record session, as filler, by New York songmillers Barry and Greenwich and recorded by them under their studio name, the Raindrops, who released it as the B side of a flop called "That Boy John." It came out in late November 1963, the same week that John F. Kennedy was assassinated, and that was that. Still, some copies must have been shipped out to the Midwest. And somebody bought one, flipped it over, liked what he heard.

It wasn't Tommy James. He grew up in Niles, Michigan, on the Indiana border, near South Bend and Notre Dame University. While he was still underage, James (known then by his real name, Tommy Jackson) used to steal across to South Bend bars to hear bands. One night in 1964, he happened upon a group called the Spinners who had somehow learned "Hanky Panky."

James had had a band, called the Shondells, since he was in seventh grade. He'd made one single, "Long Pony Tail," for Jack Douglas of local radio station WNIL. When Douglas asked for more, Tommy suggested "Hanky Panky." Since he'd only heard the song on the fly, Tommy had to make up most of the words. It didn't make much difference—what counted was that lubricious guitar riff. Released on Douglas's regional label, Snap, the disc got local airplay in Michigan, Illinois and Indiana. By mid-1965, though, its run was over. Tommy graduated from high school and the Shondells split up. By December, he was out of work and didn't know exactly what to do with himself.

Then James got a call from a guy who identified himself as Mad Mike Metro, a Pittsburgh disc jockey. Mad Mike said that "Hanky

Panky" was Number One out there. A deejay named Bob Livorio dug through a bargain bin, came up with a copy of the Shondells' "Hanky Panky" and began playing it on his show. It became so successful that some enterprising local bootlegged it and it sold 80,000 copies in Pittsburgh before James and Douglas could license it to Roulette and have it nationally rereleased.

The other Shondells had already entered the adult world and weren't interested in getting back together, so Tommy flew to Pittsburgh, lip-synched some promotional dates and asked the first decent bar band he came across, a local quartet called the Raconteurs, if they wanted to fill in as the Shondells. They went on from there to several more memorably stupid hits, then sank quietly into a much-deserved oblivion, their songs occcasionally revived, their persona never mourned.

912 BETTY AND DUPREE, Chuck Willis
Produced by Ahmet Ertegun and Jerry Wexler; written by Chuck Willis
Atlantic 1168   1958   Billboard: #33

The record that really made Chuck king of the Stroll is a folkie standard that reworks "Frankie and Johnny" to a happy ending. So what's the point? I'd say the sax riff and the marimba undercurrent, though I could understand somebody going for Chuck's bold vocal instead. And then there's the implied threat, which makes you kind of wonder how the story might have gone if Willis had lived long enough to make a sequel in which Dupree finds out that his ring has not bought Betty's undying loyalty.

913 HEART AND SOUL, The Cleftones
Produced by George Goldner; written by Hoagy Carmichael and Frank Loesser
Gee 1064   1961   Billboard: #18

Another of George Goldner's inspired doo-wop revampings of Tin Pan Alley classics. "Heart and Soul" was written in 1938 for the film short, *A Song is Born* and hit Number One the same year in a version by Larry Clinton, though Goldner probably modeled the Cleftones arrangement on the 1952 remake by the Four Aces. But even though Hoagy Carmichael undoubtedly wrote bluesier than any other showtune composer (including Gershwin), he and Frank Loesser could never have dreamed that any of their standards would get such a radical reworking. Though the Latin bass guitar work is near-traditional, and the Darin/Dion-type lead not far from it, the beat charges more powerfully than in any previous rendition, the horn lines are loopy to the point of intoxication, and the swooping bass voice is simply outrageous, each "Yeaaaaah" transforming the original corn into something positively thrilling.

914 MOTHER-IN-LAW, Ernie K-Doe
Written and produced by Allen Toussaint
Minit 623   1961   Billboard: #1 (1 week)

Even Allen Toussaint's New Orleans piano shuffle can't redeem all bad jokes, but here, he does more for one of the oldest and worst than anybody since Ralph Kramden. But don't completely credit Toussaint's behind-the-scenes genius; K-Doe (originally Kador when he recorded for Specialty as a sub-Little Richard in the fifties) literally found the song in the great man's trash can and, since Ernie was going through a situation at home not helped by the one "sent from down below," he demanded that Toussaint resuscitate it.

Don't give K-Doe all the credit either, though. Those glorious bass repetitions of "Mother-in-law" come from the golden throat of Benny Spellman. Ernie repaid him in 1962 by singing on "Lipstick Traces," Benny's big hit.

915 I PROMISE TO REMEMBER, Frankie Lymon and the Teenagers
Produced by George Goldner; written by Jimmy Castor and Jimmy Smith
Gee 1018   1956   Billboard: #57

Sometimes cover versions cut both ways. Gee was all set to release "ABC's of Love" as the Teenagers' third single, when George Goldner learned that Mercury's Wing subsidiary had put out a version of "I Promise to Remember" by Jimmy Castor and the Juniors. It was Castor's song (he and Frankie had gone to junior high and grade school together) but Goldner figured he had the better version, so he rushed it out. Lymon, already a star, killed his buddy's record but he got a massive R&B hit in return, and by record industry standards, that's a deal nobody would hesitate over.

But that's a side issue. The meat of the matter is one of Lymon's strongest leads supported by Sherman Garnes's brilliantly straight-faced rendition of the opening line: "Hooly bop a cow, bop a cow, bop a cow cow." Everything squares hate about doo-wop is in those syllables, and everything worth loving about it's there, too.

916 GOING BACK TO CALI, LL Cool J
Produced by Rick Rubin; written by Rick Rubin and J. T. Smith
[LL Cool J]
Def Jam 07563   1988

Created by a couple of black street kids (rapper Cool J and his deejay, Cut Creator) produced by a Jewish middle-class longhair Led Zeppelin freak (Rubin) for a mindless yuppie exploitation flick based on a second-rate novel (*Less Than Zero*), "Going Back to Cali" probably comes closer to jazz than any other record in this book. Certainly, it's intro is pure bop, as are the swelling horn riffs.

But "Cali" is several other things as well: the deepest fusion of heavy metal and rap ever achieved, the most overmodulated bass line I've ever heard (it rumbles at low volume and approximates a slow-speed dental drill when you crank it up, as you must to get the full effect), a great example of scratching as the essence of hip-hop percussion, the last word on the great California dream: "Goin' back to Cali / to Cali / to Cali," chants a group, who could be anybody at all, from the Beastie Boys to LL himself. "I don't *think* so," replies Cool J, although he proceeds to mutter his way through some modern day "Surfer Girl" fantasies, anyway.

If Randy Newman and Brian Wilson ever get a load of "Cali," they'll invest in a condo sandbox and retire in terror.

917 SWINGING DOORS, Merle Haggard
Produced by Ken Nelson; written by Merle Haggard
Capitol 2289   1968   Did not make pop chart

The best honky-tonk number Merle ever recorded—so good (and with such great guitar) that it's probably also the best Buck Owens record anybody but Buck ever recorded.

Like a lot of honky-tonk, the association of heartache and booze

("Thanks to you I'm always here 'til closing time") creates a context in which working-class alcoholism can be justified, which is probably why the perfect way to hear a record like this—or Buck's "A-11" for instance—is coming out of a jukebox in a shot-and-a-beer joint. Preferably somebody else puts the quarter in and you snap out of it in time to remind yourself that that's Merle's problem, not yours. Because his singing is enough to make the whole world go on a bender, just to commiserate. Or anyway, that's its ambition.

918 REELING IN THE YEARS, Steely Dan
Produced by Gary Katz; written by Walter Becker and Donald Fagen
ABC 11352   1973   *Billboard:* #11

Cascading sheets of jazzy guitar and a high school—or is that college?—revenge motif in the lyric make "Reeling in the Years" a classic of Becker and Fagen's pre-obscurantist period. The lyrics eviscerate the not-quite-hip-enough as acidicly as anything since *Blonde on Blonde*, though these jibes are anything but opaque: "You've been telling me you were a genius since you were 17 / In all the time I've known you, I still don't know what you mean." Since rock and roll record sales are heavily concentrated among the young, the trenchantly sophomoric will always have a relevant place in the pantheon, especially when it's supported by playing this hot. Not as much fun when the later verses wax misogynystic, though.

919 COWBOYS TO GIRLS, The Intruders
Written and produced by Kenneth Gamble and Leon Huff
Gamble 214   1968   *Billboard:* #6

The breakthrough hit for the Gamble and Huff team, and thus a landmark in the history of R&B-based empires. Although not quite as scintillating as the duo's contemporaneous work with Jerry Butler on Mercury or with the various artists they produced for Atlantic, the template of the Philly International sound is here, especially the TSOP rhythm 'n' string (or you might say, vibes 'n' violins) section and the slightly strident pop-gospel harmony. And if the Intruders' Little Sonny Brown stands a cut below Teddy Pendergrass and the O'Jays' Eddie Levert as a lead singer, he nonetheless acquits himself well on this infectious tale of sexual awakening, perhaps the most charming song that Gamble and Huff ever penned.

920 HEAVEN MUST BE MISSING AN ANGEL, Tavares

Produced by Freddie Perren; written by Kenny St. Lewis and Freddie Perren
Capitol 4270   1976   *Billboard:* #15

Motown-trained (he was part of the Corporation, the team that produced the early Jackson 5), Freddie Perren derived just as much of his highly successful mid-seventies dance-soul style from Philadelphia International. His way of fusing those two soul styles led to a series of highly polished, ultrarhythmic records that featured some of the most intricate vocal arrangements of the disco period (although there is "I Will Survive" to forgive him for).

Perren found his most malleable vehicle in Tavares, five brothers from New Bedford, Massachusetts, of all places to find a soul group. But perhaps Ralph, Pooch, Chubby, Butch, and Tiny found their Cape Verdean ancestry useful in the highly internationalized disco era. Certainly, even though they'd grown up in a fishing town far from bright lights, their style lacked none of the sophisticated sheen you'd expect from big city boys.

Though Tavares had hits beginning in 1973 with the Johnny Bristol-produced "Check It Out," it wasn't until Perren took the helm a couple of albums down the line that they really clicked, perhaps because he best understood how to make their essentially unison style effective in an epoch that centered on solo individualists, or maybe just because he did the best job of updating a style that was essentially a throwback to the fifties. Either way, "Heaven Must Be Missing An Angel" is the most exciting of all their dozen or so R&B hits, a dance 'n' harmony extravaganza that stuck out from the rather mechanistic material around it when it was on the charts and sustains those thrills today.

921 THE VOW, The Flamingos

Produced by Leonard Chess; written by Motola, Carey, and Webb
Checker 846   1956   Did not make pop chart

922 BLUE VELVET, The Clovers
Produced by Ahmet Ertegun and Jerry Wexler; written by
Bernie Wayne and Lee Morris
Atlantic 1052   1955   Did not make pop chart

When I got married in 1979, my wife gave me two tasks for the wedding
(in addition to showing up). Buy a decent suit, she said, and took me
to Bloomingdale's. Find some music, she said, and left me to my own
devices. As will surprise no one who has hefted this tome, the result
was overkill. Three C-90s later, we had a fine collection of great rock
and roll love songs, which has well served not only our nuptials but
over the years, several of our friends'. Almost all of the music was
singles; the few selections that don't hold up are all album tracks.

As befits a know-it-all, the program was entirely of my own choosing. Advice was offered, but none was heeded. Except that I did happen
to mention the project to Southside Johnny Lyon, who said: "There's
one record you've *got* to have on there: 'Blue Velvet' by the Clovers."
"I hate 'Blue Velvet,' " I said. "That's cause all you know is Bobby
Vinton's version," he said. "That's your first slow dance with your wife.
It's gotta be." I had my doubts that on this particular occasion there
would be that kind of dancing; I'm as left-footed as I am left-handed.
But Johnny brooked no disagreement. "Just do it," he said. "Put it on
there and you'll see why."

I was right about the dancing but Southside was on the money
about the music. Though I doubt I'd have liked Tony Bennett's 1951
original any better than Vinton's saccharine 1963 hit, the Clovers' splendidly languourous recitation makes it seem as if every romance has all
the time in the world. The mellow sax riff, Harold Winley's grave bass,
and the group's exquisite harmonies set up leader Buddy Bailey as the
greatest wedding singer in history.

Meantime, riffling through stacks of old records, I came upon the
Flamingos' "The Vow," a more spritely doo-wop ballad, with a perfectly measured lead offset by an amazing falsetto gurgle at the end of
each verse. As a finale, there's also a spate of call-and-response between
the lead and one of the tenors that brings out the pure corniness of the
lyrics—and, in the context of a wedding, the occasion—in a way that
gently (not necessarily deliberately) satirizes the whole mythos of romantic love.

Marriage is the penultimate step toward recognizing that rock-as-
rebellion needs to be tempered with rock-as-reconciliation. (The ultimate? Parenthood.) If you're thinking of taking the plunge, these records—old to me, new to you, one borrowed, both deeply blue—are

necessary accoutrements, if you want the spirit of the occasion to fit as well as your wedding suit. And you do.

Thanks, Southside.

923 PRETEND YOU'RE STILL MINE, The Sheppards
Produced by Bunky Sheppard; written by Westberry and Atkins
Okeh 7173   1963   Did not make pop chart

Another gorgeous late doo-wop/early soul production for under-acknowledged producer Sheppard, this one with a lead by top tenor Murrie Eskridge that's pure fifties and a great organ wash in the background that's pure sixties. Thus another nail in the coffin of the notion that America wasn't producing great rock and roll the year before the Beatles hit. Unless you know some *other* name for that fusion.

924 TRAPPED BY A THING CALLED LOVE, Denise LaSalle
Written and produced by Denise LaSalle
Westbound 182   1971   *Billboard:* #13

Perhaps the first big soul hit to be written and produced by the woman who sang it, "Trapped By A Thing Called Love" was perfectly timed to match the tail end of the pre-disco R&B era and the height of the singer/songwriter boom. Not that there was any chance of confusing "Anticipation" with LaSalle's gritty Chicago-to-Memphis excursion, even though the lyric is a kind of confessional, in which Denise deplores the weakness that leads her to continue with a guy who "makes her give what [she] don't wanna give."

No, if Denise LaSalle was to be confused with anyone, it would have been Al Green, which was only natural because her support came from the same Willie Mitchell-led band. And no male chauvinism kept those guys from cutting grooves just as deep for her as they did for him.

925 GEE, The Crows
Produced by George Goldner; written by Bill Davis
Rama 5   1954   *Billboard:* #14

Back when rock and roll historians sought "the first rock and roll record" as avidly as explorers once looked for a Northwest Passage, "Gee" earned many points in the ongoing debate. Although it was preceded on the pop charts by almost a year by Sonny Til and the Orioles' "Crying in the Chapel," and while the Chords' "Sh-Boom," which hit around the same time, was somewhat bigger on the charts, the futile debate often came down in the Crows' corner for stylistic and sentimental reasons.

"The song became the first recording of black street corner singing to transcend the realm of R&B into the white pop market," writes Philip Groia in *They All Sang On the Corner*, the best New York doo-wop history. However arguable, Groia's point is interesting, since it sees "black street corner singing" as a genre distinct from earlier black harmony styles like those of the Mills Brothers and Ink Spots, who'd of course had white followings and Top 40 airplay for a couple of decades.

"[George] Goldner's record by the Crows, 'Gee' (1954), was sometimes described as the record that began the rock 'n' roll era because, unlike the earlier hit 'Crying in the Chapel' by the Orioles, 'Gee' was an original composition and had a quick dance rhythm," writes Charlie Gillett in *The Sound of the City*. "But 'Gee' was not a hit until almost a year after Bill Haley's 'Crazy Man Crazy.' " Gillett wrote his book in 1970, when the evolutionary merger of popular and folk musics into the variety of styles conglomerated as "rock and roll" was not understood (his book played a crucial role in beginning to build such an understanding). In those years, the rise of rock and roll was thought to be the result of a few men's invention, rather than a complex cultural process.

Once that process was better understood and acknowledged, historians could afford to be more cavalier about such proprietary claims of invention. "The record featured a handful of doo-wop cliches," wrote Big Al Pavlow dismissively in 1983, "and was actually more representative of that style than 'Sh-Boom,' but it wasn't the catalyst for change that 'Sh-Boom' became." That judgment is probably correct, although Groia suggests that it would be wise to moderate it, since the Crows were at least famous in Harlem for driving a huge new Chrysler with "Crows" painted on the side and were among the first doo-wop groups to try to crack mainstream show biz in Las Vegas. (They failed.)

The more relevant question is not how influential or how original but how good. To my ears, "Gee" sounds fine, strong unison harmonies giving way to Sonny Norton's strong if nasal lead, with a jumping band track that features a jazzy guitar break supported by strong piano and solid drumming. After the break, Norton's voice pleads and cries in fine fashion. As the first important hit for George Goldner, "Gee" perhaps came to seem more cliched than it is, because it played such a crucial role in establishing his hits.

Its role in Goldner's career is one more reason why the record acquired its mythic stature as the "first." Another was the Crows' history. They got together in Harlem in 1951, singing other people's hits. They had enough style even at the start to win neighborhood battles of the groups, and in 1953, worked up the courage to take the stage on Amateur Night at the Apollo Theatre, where (in Horatio Alger fashion) they were spotted and discovered by talent agent Cliff Martinez.

Martinez got the Crows a one-shot record deal with Jubilee, then worked them as backup for singer/pianist Vola Watkins, who also played and arranged behind the group. Martinez took them all to George Goldner, who recorded the act both with Watkins out front and with just the guys.

Goldner released "Gee" in June 1953 as the second single from their first session. It was Rama's second single. The first Rama release, Watkins' "Seven Lonely Days," sank immediately. "Gee" also flopped, though Goldner heard enough to keep cutting the group and, apparently, somebody kept promoting the record. Ten months after its release, in the spring of 1954, "Gee" hit the charts and ran all the way up to Number Two. Pavlow rates it the sixteenth most popular R&B hit of that year, after three "Annie" singles by the Midnighters, "Hearts of Stone" (the Charms cover version), Big Joe Turner's "Shake, Rattle and Roll," a couple each by Ruth Brown and Faye Adams, and of course, "Sh-Boom" (12), but ahead of sides by B.B. King, Dinah Washington, Muddy Waters, and Johnny Ace as well as the Spaniels' "Goodnite Sweetheart Goodnite," another occasional "first" candidate.

926 LIFE'S BEEN GOOD, Joe Walsh
Produced by Bill Szymczyk; written by Joe Walsh
Asylum 45493   1978   *Billboard:* #12

Truest-ever bourgeois blues, from the one member of the Eagles who didn't check his sense of humor at the door (he joined late, is the only explanation I've ever come up with), possibly the only guy in the history of rock and roll who ever went on tour with a chainsaw in his suitcase. On "Life's Been Good," Walsh sounds so laid-back he can barely squeak out his series of not-quite-parodistic descriptions of the more flagrantly consumeristic aspects of superstar lifestyle: "I've got a Maserati, goes 185 / I lost my license, now I can't drive." He had to softpedal the sex and drugs angles for Top 40 consumption, but anybody who's ever seen a doughnut will be able to fill in the blanks. The targets are pretty obvious, then, and might be no more edifying than the broadside japes Frank Zappa had been making for a decade, except that Walsh loves the trashy rock and roll that's made him rich, as the slide and fuzztone guitar with which he fills out the song prove, and his own awareness of the hollowness of the life he's living isn't about to make him stop. That adds more than a frisson of anguish to the whole project; it brings it home as an off-center blues.

927 MAMA USED TO SAY (American Remix), Junior
Produced by Bob Carter; written by Junior Giscombe and Bob Carter
Mercury 76132   1982   Billboard: #30

A great example of the importance of recording subtleties in eighties black pop. Back in 1982, I found it impossible to resolve how great Junior's Stevie Wonder growls and homespun advice on not growing up any sooner than you have to sounded on the radio with how flat they sounded at home. Finally, it dawned on me that I was listening to the *British* version of the record. Tee Scott had remixed for the American release (which also eventually came out in the U.K.), brightening the top and fattening the bottom until a not bad piece of Britfunk became the equivalent of an outtake from *Songs in the Key of Life*. Without Scott's changes, Junior would never have had—or deserved—the only hit of his career.

928 ONE HAS MY NAME, Jerry Lee Lewis
Produced by Jerry Kennedy; written by Eddie Dean, Dearest Dean, and Hal Blair
Smash 2224   1969   Did not make pop chart

To my ear, the best of Jerry Lee's early country hits. He began a C&W-only chart comeback in 1968, with "Another Place, Another Time," followed by "What's Made Milwaukee Famous," "She Still Comes Around," and "To Make Love Sweeter for You", then "One Has My Name," all in just over a year, all hitting the country Top Ten and none marking the pop charts any higher than the mid 90s.

Pop radio has always been more resistant to country crossover than to R&B, which makes for one of contemporary culture's more interesting puzzles. Blacks are at all acceptable of course, because the black entertainer fulfills even the bigot's stereotype. But the white working-class music that makes up country remains a regional taste. Significantly, the unreconstructed blues-based R&B of the seventies and eighties also comes nowhere near the national Top 40, though it's often among the best-sellers in the South and Southwest.

Another factor is the utter absence of contemporary dance beats from the country charts. But even during the urban cowboy craze of the late seventies, Motown's Commodores, featuring Lionel Richie, fared better than Nashville's Alabama.

In Jerry Lee's particular case, it's hard not to suspect an additional element of moral retribution. In many conservative quarters (and Top 40 radio is by nature conservative), Jerry Lee's reputation never recovered from his misunderstood marriage to his thirteen-year-old near-relation, Myra. The fact that marriages between couples that young—Jerry Lee was only twenty-one and already taking his third bride—were both common and legal in Louisiana never counted for anything, especially when the score was being tallied against a wild rebel like Lewis, who incarnated everybody's bad dreams about loony rednecks.

Too bad, because "One Has My Name" stands not only as a fine country performance but the best example extant of what young Southern singers like Lewis and Elvis fancied in Dean Martin. Jerry Lee's seriocomic melodrama in the halfspoken bridge incarnates Martin's chatty booziness, and when Lewis swings back into the final verse, he momentarily occupies Deano's persona entire—as if he'd dropped his middle name and become an impressionist.

929 DON'T MAKE ME OVER, Dionne Warwick
Written and produced by Burt Bacharach and Hal David
Scepter 1239   1962   Billboard: #21

Dionne's first hit was the result of a self-assurance rare among women, let alone black women, in the sixties. Working long hours in the studio with Burt Bacharach and Hal David, experienced songwriters and journeyman record producers who were trying to find a handle on her talent,

Warwick had the nerve (and sense) to tell them acidly, "Don't make me over." Out of that demand, Bacharach and David were savvy enough to fashion a song and a record (and then a series of them) which took advantage of Warwick's training in gospel groups (the Drinkard Singers, the Gospelaires), at Hart College of Music in Connecticut, and as a demo singer (with her sister, Dee Dee) on the New York studio scene.

Though it lacks the orchestral majesty of later hits like "Anyone Who Had a Heart" and "Walk on By," "Don't Make Me Over" displays a protofeminist sense of control. She doesn't even sound defensive when the lyrics read "I'm beggin' you." Rock critics make much of Lesley Gore's "You Don't Own Me," but I'll take "Accept me for what I am / Accept me for the things that I do" as a surer prophesy of the Chrissie Hyndes to come.

930 GHOST TOWN, The Specials
Produced by John Collins; written by Jerry Dammers
Chrysalis / 2 Tone   1981   Did not make pop chart

A haunting, haunted exploration of ska as Jamaican funk, more-or-less War as it might have sounded if the band had emerged from the industrial destitution of the British Midlands rather than south L.A. Specials leader Dammers wrote and sang it as a protest against the dance floor violence that was shuttering his favorite Coventry haunts, and against the endemic unemployment that was fostering it, but the record acquired its mythic stature—in the U.K., at any rate—when it traveled south to London, where it served as the soundtrack for the midsummer insurrection of black youth in the Brixton ghetto. As such you could consider it the ultimate answer to "Street Fighting Man," and contemplate at your leisure the spectacle of Mick Jagger watching these hot trombone licks smoldering amidst the ruins of the poorest parts of no-longer-so-sleepy London town.

931 THAT'S WHAT LOVE IS MADE OF, The Miracles
Produced by Smokey Robinson; written by Smokey Robinson, Bobby Rogers, and Warren Moore
Tamla 54102   1964   Billboard: #3

Only Smokey Robinson could have made soul out of the hoary "Snips, snails, puppy dog tails, sugar, spice 'n' everything nice." Not that he didn't make use of the most modern conveniences: the pulsations provided by James Jamerson and Benny Benjamin, some of the snappiest handclaps ever recorded, Earl Van Dyke's bluesy piano, and the Miracles own smooth and ceaseless harmonies. This is a confection, though, so what counts most is what goes on top: Smokey's own solid, sometimes smooth, sometimes squealing singing.

932 DEAD SKUNK, Loudon Wainwright
Producer not credited; written by Loudon Wainwright
Columbia 45726   1973   *Billboard:* #16

In the early seventies, when there was very little to laugh about on the Top 40, latter-day M*A*S*H hero Wainwright's song about the "Dead Skunk" "in the middle of the road / stinkin' to high heaven" hit like a breath of fresh air. And when it takes a fake bluegrass ditty about rotting road kill to raise a smile, times are grim indeed. But hey, we're talking about the days beyond smiles, when the waves of Brit-rock brought us aspiring classicists who enjoyed the sniffs of their own nattily arranged album-length farts and crossdressing poseurs whose art was supposed to lie in their archness, and when our own shores coughed up more than its fair share of gaunt visaged, self-important "song poets." A time when black music was moving from its period of greatest social consciousness to the monomania of dance floor hedonism and the most cheery white pop celebrated rocky mountain highs and the joys of rural sunshine with an idiot's leering, uncomprehending grin at its own privileged, deadass lassitude.

So when Wainwright turned up in the midst of all that to command his band, "C'mon, stink!" you knew you'd found a novelty that would last. And actually, for those who live in the near reaches of exurbia, if you can stomach Loudon's encyclopedic recitation of the possible varieties of road kill ("Now you got your dead cat and you got your dead dog / On a moonlight night you got your dead toad frog"), you can make a game of how much of it you can spot tonight on the way home from work. If the traffic lets up enough, you can even participate.

933 BEG ME, Chuck Jackson
Produced by Luther Dixon; written by Rudy Clark
Wand 154   1964   Billboard: #45

Your turn to crawl. Chuck's been jilted, but now his lover's returned
and he's out for a taste of revenge. Though in some ways "Beg Me"
makes The Eagles' "Take It Easy" seem an outpost of feminism, in
others it's just a stereotyped demand for romantic fidelity (it'd be *amazing* to hear a woman sing this song, and someone should). If you can
adjust to that, you can take pleasure in a gospel-like arrangement in
which "Now get down on your knees" has a connotation more, er
. . . spiritual than usual. Plus the drumming's great, the horns are fine
pre-Memphis soul, and I always liked the guitar break.

934 PRECIOUS WORDS, The Wallace Brothers
Producer not credited; written by Claudia Robinson
Sims 174   1964   Did not make pop chart

Another of the great mystery singles, meaning I don't know anything
about it except that it sounds great. The arrangement is pure country
church: a crude organ and a pair of cracked boyish tenors, opening
with pretty two-part harmony, resolve to the leader shouting and
preachifying, then return (through a simple piano flourish) to the harmonies. All centered on a secular love theme whose every phrase comes
straight out of the pulpit. There's nothing histrionic going on, just the
quiet pouring out of soul. Plenty enough for ears with the wisdom to
appreciate it.

935 STAY WITH ME, Lorraine Ellison
Produced by Jerry Ragovoy; written by Ragovoy and Weiss
Warner Bros. 5850   1966   Billboard: #64

They say that copies of Ellison's hyperdramatic ballad went for fifty
bucks in Harlem in the late sixties, and even though that reflected
scarcity (the disc got so little airplay that very few copies were pressed),
that was also back when you could buy an album in stereo for less than
five, and in mono for under four. The combination of Lorraine's gospel
background and producer Jerry Ragovoy's penchant for overorches-
tration emerges as a disc that, for all its undeniably overwrought
schlockiness, is oddly prescient in forecasting the excessively enunciated

divs of the seventies and eighties. If you covet screaming and romantic angst (does that mean, if you're a normal soul ballad fan?), you'll love this, too.

936 DON'T YOU WORRY 'BOUT A THING, Stevie Wonder
Written and produced by Stevie Wonder
Tamla 54245   1974   *Billboard:* #16

Stevie's original foray into the wilds of world pop is both more high-spirited than Bobby McFerrin's wildest dreams and much clearer about just what the world's got to worry about. Indeed, it's not a call to complacency at all, but an enticement to go out and explore, with the assurance that Stevie will "be standing right here while you check it out."

All I've ever found bothering me, while "Don't You Worry" was playing, is exactly where he dug up this song's unconscionably deep groove: Africa, the Caribbean, or some place clear off the map? Because it sure as hell wasn't Detroit. I've *been* there.

937 SCHOOL'S OUT, Alice Cooper
Produced by Bob Ezrin; written by Alice Cooper and Michael Bruce
Warner Bros. 7596   1972   *Billboard:* #7

In 1972, at the height of the critical infatuation with the idea that making stoopid noizes can sometimes result in great rock and roll, Lester Bangs wrote a *Rolling Stone* review declaring that Alice Cooper would some-day be regarded as the American Rolling Stones. *RS* reviews editor Jon Landau cut the line, and when Bangs protested, told the irate critic, "Lester, someday you'll thank me for this."

In June 1974, Landau received a note from Bangs, who'd gone on to become the enfant terrible of noiz rock criticism at *Creem.* It read, "Dear Jon: Two years ago, when I wanted to call Alice Cooper the American Rolling Stones, you wouldn't let me and said that someday I'd thank you. Thank you."

On the other hand, "School's Out" holds up better than the high seriousness of Pink Floyd's "We don't need no education." Even in the realm of intelligent noise, after all, honesty counts for a lot. And

Alice's "We got no class / And we got no principles," is—for better or worse—a truism, not a pun.

938 GINO IS A COWARD, Gino Washington
Produced by Sonny Saunders; written by Ronald Davis
Ric Tic 100   1963   Did not make pop chart

Gino Washington made a string of local hits for Detroit's mini-Motown Ric Tic in the early sixties, of which the best were "Gino," a wild boast expropriated (and rewritten as "I'm A Coward When It Comes to Love") by Bruce Springsteen in 1988, and its B side, "Puppet on a String," a ballad so dolorous that at one point the singer declares that if he's unable to receive his baby's love "I'll end my life by slashin' my wrists," which puts a rather fine point on it.

But more than any of the others, it was "Gino Is a Coward" that made Washington (a black kid whose first high school band featured future Detroit Wheels Johnny Badanjek and Jim McCarty) a hometown hero. A comically gritty blues boast that breaks down the beat into handclap components, featuring stretched-thin falsetto wails and as tinny a guitar solo as ever lit up the night, the record told a story so wild it's a miracle Leiber and Stoller didn't think of it first: Gino is brave enough to capture a gorilla bare-handed and ride the back of a dinosaur "just for the thrill 'n' pleasure," but "A girl get near to me / And the fear in me / Rocks, rolls, shimmies and shakes." Perhaps it's the real sequel to LaVern Baker's "Jim Dandy" series.

Had Gino stuck around another year or two, to witness the scooping up of local labels and artist rosters by Berry Gordy, he might have found himself in the same moderately well-known position as Ric Tic stablemate Edwin Starr (though Washington was by no means such a good singer, he was a better writer). But Gino got drafted. And though the Army put him in Special Services as an entertainer, it also sent him to Vietnam. Gino sang when he came home on leave—Rob Tyner of the MC5 remembers the shock of seeing Gino onstage in full dress uniform—but he couldn't really do anything to advance his career.

When he got out, Gino discovered that he was big in England, where the R&B scene had meanwhile blossomed into an international gold rush. But when the Who and Rolling Stones and other denizens of London nightlife talked about "Geno" Washington, they meant another person, a guy who'd been stationed at an American air base in England and got his start by knocking off the real Gino's act.

Gino went back to Detroit, watched his singing career fall apart, never saw much money but took what he did have and built up a successful advertising agency. He's best known in the Motor City today as the host of a TV show that often features up-and-coming talent (Anita Baker was a guest early in her career). Washington drives a white Rolls Royce and talks about reissuing his old singles on CD. The other Geno made a few singles, which were pretty bad, and for all I know is selling pizza today.

939 I DON'T WANT TO GO HOME, Southside Johnny and the Asbury Jukes

Written and produced by Miami Steve Van Zandt
Epic 50238   1976   Did not make pop chart

Sometime around 1972, Steve Van Zandt left his home in New Jersey and went to Las Vegas as a guitar player in a traveling oldies show. One night he saw one of his boyhood heroes, Ben E. King, singing in a lounge—which meant working for peanuts against massive inattention. The sight made Van Zandt a little homesick for the old crowd back at the Jersey shore, and it convinced him that there was still life in the soul hits, still good music to be made in that style, still mileage left in those old love song metaphors that always reeked of philosophy no matter how passionately they insisted they were only celebrating or denouncing careless, faithless, reckless love. So he went back to his room and wrote "I Don't Want to Go Home," and gave it to his friend, Southside Johnny Lyon to sing on Johnny's first album (which Van Zandt produced).

In that song, a bleary-eyed lover sits on a late night barstool and tells his woeful story—not unlike the guy in "Louie Louie" or the one in "Set 'Em Up Joe," except this guy isn't speaking to the bartender so much as just mumbling into his shot glass. Meantime, he's watching some veteran singer out of one corner of his eye and the words coming out of his mouth seem to jibe exactly with what he's fumbling to explain. Only one thing is certain—the one to which he continually returns. "I know the words to the songs I hear but I don't want to go home," he moans. "I know he's talkin' 'bout the way I feel—'cause I don't wanna go home."

Southside Johnny sings those words in the guise of a man taking account and finding a massive deficit. He works against a backdrop that Van Zandt borrowed from Leiber and Stoller's work with the Drifters, an arrangement so replete with soulful orchestration, riffing horns, and ostinato piano that it flew in the face of the hollow conventions of its day almost as much as the punk that was being made in England at just the same time. And maybe you can measure the difference between England and the U.S. as cultures by noting that, when each reached the end of this particular rope, one responded in scabrous despair with a noise heard all over the world, while the other insisted on hope—it's there in every bar of this music, especially in the ringing guitar Van Zandt plays into the fade-out, and it's there in Johnny's emphatically slurred phrasing of the chorus, with its unyielding demand: "I wanna know why we had to try, reach up and touch the sky / Whatever happened to you and I? And I don't want to go home."

You think that's just a love song? Must have missed the seventies altogether.

940 OOH POO PAH DO (Part Two), Jessie Hill
Produced by Allen Toussaint; written by Jessie Hill
Minit 607   1960   *Billboard:* #28

One of payola's wilder products: "Ooh Poo Pah Doo" came out at Mardi Gras time and deejay Larry McKinley, co-owner of Minit, pumped it over the New Orleans airwaves as a carnival record, which its beat certainly justified. Which makes the record an interesting test case of the theory (and my conviction) that no record ever became a hit with payola that wouldn't have made it on its own merits. Certainly nobody's ever cut a more joyous version of the New Orleans parade beat, and it's hard to beat a lyric in which the singer vows to drive his lover nuts and backs it up with a series of genuinely demented yowls. There's nothing more to "Ooh Poo Pah Do" than that, but then, why would there need to be?

941 URGENT, Foreigner
Produced by Robert John "Mutt" Lange; written by Mick Jones
Atlantic 3831   1981   *Billboard:* #4

"Urgent" features as much guitar twang as vintage Who and the best use anyone had made of Junior Walker in better than a decade. Foreigner may have been the original Anglo-American hard rock hacks, playing riffs and rhythms as hard and predictable as any band this side of Bad Company, but a couple of seasons without hits had left them wide open for the ministrations of Mutt Lange, the most underrated producer of the eighties. Here, Walker's guttural expostulations and reedy trills perfectly counterpoint Lou Gramm's hot 'n' horny grunt 'n' groan, with the whole thing underpinned by a Jew's harp synthesizer riff that blats rock and roll's Morse code for sexual desire. If "I Want to Know What Love Is" is Foreigner's "Bernadette," "Urgent" ("I'm not lookin' for a love that lasts / I know what I need and I need it fast") is its "Satisfaction." That makes it just like real life: A cheap date but a hell of a lot better than none at all.

942 THE BITCH IS BACK, Elton John
Produced by Gus Dudgeon; written by Elton John and Bernie Taupin
Decca 40297   1975   *Billboard:* #4

There are those who'll tell you that Elton John was the greatest pop rocker of the seventies but this blend of power-pop guitar chords and funky horns is the only time he ever convinced me. Still "The Bitch is Back" is convincing as hell, a shivering rock and roll brag in which John sets himself off by vowing to spit in the eye of anybody who tries to hold him back and reaches an apex of arrogance in the chorus:

> I'm a bitch, I'm a bitch, if I'm better than you
> It's the way that I move, the fact that I do

943 BABY, DON'T DO IT, The "5" Royales
Producer not credited; written by Lowman Pauling
Apollo 443   1953   Did not make pop chart

Big Al Pavlow ranks "Baby, Don't Do It" as the tenth most popular R&B record of 1953, slightly below the Royales' two-sided smash, "Help Me Somebody" / "Crazy Crazy Crazy" (Apollo 446). Though the double-sided hit came out a couple of months later, it's "Baby, Don't Do It" which sounds more up-to-date, dispensing with the group's conventional gospel harmony for an arrangement that melds an impassioned lead, a droning tenor sax by Charlie "Little Jazz" Ferguson, and Lowman Pauling's always biting guitar, plus one of the strangest lyric hooks I've ever heard: "If you leave me pretty baby, I'll be bread without no meat."

1953 represented the Royales' peak of popularity—"Baby, Don't Do It" rode atop the *Billboard* R&B chart for fourteen consecutive weeks. And it's not just roots—this music holds up just fine as it nears its fortieth anniversary.

944 AIN'T NOBODY HOME, Howard Tate
Written and produced by Jerry Ragovoy
Verve 10420   1966   *Billboard*: #63

Would Al Green's ideas about gospel-based phrasing—when to make falsetto leaps, how to ride the groove, and when to push—have nearly as much appeal emerging from a less spectacular vocal instrument? Tate, a fine journeyman in whose records the basic Green vocal concept arrived about three years early, provides the (or at least, an) answer, which is essentially "Not quite." But then you have to factor in the difference between master producer Willie Mitchell and mere workhorse Jerry Ragovoy, between the great Hi rhythm section and the Memphis Horns and Tate's much more anonymous New York studio backup, and between Green's great songs and the merely pretty good ones Tate had. The comparisons are fascinating, and maybe not as far in Al's favor as a gloss might indicate, because Tate keeps on pushing no matter what. On the other hand, you can be damned sure that Green would never have let Janis Joplin beat him for sheer intensity on something like "Get It While You Can." And then again, no less than B.B. King took a shot at "Ain't Nobody Home" and it's still Tate's version that's definitive.

945 I KNOW, Barbara George
Produced by Harold Battiste; written by Barbara George
A.F.O. 302   1961   *Billboard*: #3

A.F.O. ("All For One") was a musicians' collective formed by arranger Harold Battiste, so that New Orleans session musicians could see some profits from their work, rather than just the union's paltry scale, which was all they'd been getting through the city's Fats Domino/Little Richard heyday. Unfortunately, New Orleans was fading as a recording mecca, the musicians (who included pianist Allen Toussaint, drummer John Boudreaux, saxophonist Alvin "Red" Tyler, bassist Chuck Badie, and guitarist Roy Montrell) weren't businessmen, and their personal tastes ran to jazz rather than pop. As a result, A.F.O. became not United Artists but just another Apple gone down the drain.

But not before coming up with a couple of fine singles, Prince La

La's "You Put the Hurt on Me," a decent Ray Charles soundalike, and Barbara George's singular "I Know." "I Know" was based on the melody of the hymn, "Just a Closer Walk with Thee," taken apart and put back together again by the all-star session men (with Marcel Richardson filling in for Toussaint), and Melvin Lastie turning in a brilliant little cornet solo, all to juice up George's squeaky little voice.

Unfortunately, Juggy Murray, whose Sue label distributed A.F.O. nationally, soon bought up George's contract and neither the label nor the singer ever had another hit. The Big Easy's once-thriving recording scene soon petered out, with such stalwarts as drummer Earl Palmer and Battiste himself joining the Hollywood contingent that made hits for Phil Spector and everybody else.

946 EVERY LITTLE BIT HURTS, Brenda Holloway
Produced by Hal Davis and Marc Gordon; written by Ed Cobb
Tamla 54094   1964   Billboard: #13

Holloway made her mark at Motown in a variety of ways, most noticeably by being the only non-Detroit artist of its early heyday. She came from California and this breathy, string-laden ballad has some of the grainy and husky qualities of Jackie DeShannon's pop hits of the same period. But "Every Little Bit Hurts" is more reminiscent of the pop-soul set pieces Burt Bacharach and Hal David were constructing for Dionne Warwick in those years. Which also marks Holloway as the first really adult Motown artist, an impression reinforced by her use of former Four Preps accompanist Lincoln Mayorga on piano. Composer Ed Cobb was also in the Preps, though he rejected maturity in favor of creating the Standells' "Dirty Water."

947 SEA CRUISE, Frankie Ford
Produced by Johnny Vincent; written by Huey Smith
Ace 554   1959   Billboard: #14

Of all the forces that created rock and roll, the most underrated is magnetic recording tape, which changed the face of popular music by making its creation the product of what happened in studios rather than on stages. The change was fundamental, affecting not only the balance between composition and performance but the concept of performance itself, since the range of aural options encompassed whatever appealed to the people at the mike and behind the control board. Lots of rules flew out the window.

Not all of those changes were benign. Classical devotees have bemoaned from the start the ability of tape editing to cover up errors in technique, hardly a relevant criterion when it comes to pop, where virtuosity is frequently measured quite differently, but one that at least begins to suggest the kinds of "falsification" made available by multichannel tape. Tape offers virtually limitless opportunity to mix 'n' match performances: A portion of a tape can be transferred to an entirely different piece of music, some aspects can be erased or buried (or even, Lord it is true, spliced in backwards), all kinds of elements can be juggled and exchanged, swapped around until the stew of a given recording can be as complex as the story of the rise of rock and roll itself. And all this was possible *before* the latest generations of computer samplers, which functionally allow any recording artist or technician easy, immediate, high quality access to any previously recorded song or sound.

"Sea Cruise" is a landmark in studio sleight of hand. Sometime around the end of 1958, Huey Smith and his Clowns, featuring vocalist Bobby Marchan, traveled from their base in New Orleans upriver to Jackson, Mississippi to cut with a local record distributor, Johnny Vincent, owner of Ace Records. Ace had already scored a national hit with Smith on his "Rockin' Pneumonia and The Boogie Woogie Flu," and Vincent hoped to find more gold amongst the pianist/songwriter's store of novelty-oriented R&B tunes.

Vincent liked two of the Clowns' tracks, "Loberta" and "Sea Cruise," but didn't think Marchan's vocals up to snuff. So he brought in Frankie Ford (nee Guzzo), a young journeyman from nearby Gretna, Mississippi. Ford wasn't a great singer but his Southern/Italian accent, so reminiscent of Brooklynese, lent him a potential teen appeal akin to Dion and Bobby Darin, something that could decidedly not be said of a band named after a wallflower pianist and fronted by a black transvestite. So, without consulting Smith or Marchan, Vincent put Ford's voice over the Clowns' tracks. Ford wound up with a national hit and a brief tenure on the road fronting Smith's band. Smith wound up with a couple of important copyrights ("Loberta" became the pounding "Roberta"). Vincent found out that the Mickey Mouse teen-idol crap he'd been purveying with Jimmy Clanton (compared to whom, the modestly gifted Ford's talents resembled Fats Domino's) could be even more lucrative with better backing tracks. And until R&B historians uncovered the tale many years later, nobody but the New Orleans' musical community was ever the wiser.

948 MY LITTLE TOWN, Paul Simon with Art Garfunkel

Produced by Paul Simon and Phil Ramone; written by Paul Simon
Columbia 10230   1975   *Billboard:* #9

"My Little Town" is Simon and Garfunkel's final studio duet and, with the exception of "The Boxer," the best rock track they ever created. Simon takes the lead, using Garfunkel's eerie wimp-tenor to add an edgy thrill; the arrangement is heavy with brass, percussion, and thunderous bass chords from a grand piano. As a statement of Self-Importance (Simon's perpetual theme), it's tops.

Simon may have waited his entire career to create "My Little Town," which is an equally perfect expression of self-importance's companion: the revenge motif. Though the milltown detail tries to hide it, "My Little Town" is really a portrait of the middle-class Forest Hills, New York neighborhood where Paul and Art grew up. The relish they take in the delivery of lines like "It's not that the colors aren't there / It's just imagination they lack" suggests comeuppance for every intended and unintentional slight experienced in a pair of dismal teenage lives. Which happens to be a terrific topic for a rock song, especially when those slights include those this famous duo visited upon each other, grievances which had so profusely accumulated that, by the time of this session, their friendship had dissolved into mutual contempt. They managed to squeeze out a farewell tour and album anyway.

949 MY CITY WAS GONE, The Pretenders

Produced by Chris Thomas; written by Chrissie Hynde
Sire 29840   1982   Did not make pop chart

Like the Stanley Brothers' "Rank Stranger," Chrissie Hynde returns home to find everything she has known and loved altered beyond restoration. But the Stanleys find their home town itself unchanged; it's the loss of people they regret. For Hynde, the disappearance of her family is merely incidental. It upsets her far more that "the farms of Ohio had been replaced by shopping malls / And Muzak filled the air from Seneca to Cuyahoga Falls."

Several ways of measuring the discrepancy of these reactions present themselves. Most obviously, the Stanley Brothers were Pentecostal Christians, for whom the human soul was all that mattered. Hynde is a rock star narcissist; even in the verse about the loss of her family, it's her own nostalgic recollection that preoccupies her. Then again, the Stanleys were Southerners; there's an inevitable Civil War implication in the ravages they describe. Hynde, on the other hand, is not only Northern but cosmopolitan; she didn't leave for another part of the country, she's traversed continents and she's returned for a visit, without any of the Stanleys' intentions of settling down. (Which also links "My City Was Gone" to Tom T. Hall's "The Homecoming.")

More than anything, though, the records measure the temper of their times. The Stanleys lived in a day when the events of the world caused immeasurable, almost incomprehensible changes in everyday life. Hynde responds to a world in which people are already inured to massive changes. She barely notices that her loved ones are absent because in some spiritual sense, it was their vacancy that drove her from her home in the first place and because, perhaps, the people left in Ohio barely notice how profound the ruin of their environment has been. And Chrissie herself doesn't really expect them to have the ability to respond; she left, in another sense, to preserve the outrage that possesses her voice here against the numbness guaranteed to overwhelm it if she'd hung around. As a result, her bewildered "Hey, ho, where'd you go, O-hi-o" makes a mockery of the question, though without degrading at all the love that makes her continue to ask it.

950 YOU LEFT THE WATER RUNNING, Otis Redding

No producer credited; written by Dan Penn, Rick Hall, and Oscar Franks
Stone 209   1976   Did not make pop chart

In late 1976, while I was *Rolling Stone*'s record reviews editor, a new Otis Redding single crossed my desk. Poorly pressed and recorded (Otis's voice distorts badly on the count-off) and on an ugly red and black label I'd never heard of, it was still a fantastic version of Maurice and Mac's classic "You Left the Water Running." The B side was an anonymous instrumental, "The Otis Jam" by the Memphis Studio Band, who were certainly not Booker T and the MG's. That side, but not the vocal, gave a production credit to John Fred, familiar to me as the leader of John Fred and the Playboy Band, who had scored a weird psychedelic-swamp-bubble-gum hit, "Judy in Disguise with Glasses," in 1967.

Finding a new Otis track, let alone one this good, constituted a major thrill, and I spent quite a bit of time on the phone trying to track down the story. I happened to mention the track to my lawyer at the time, Mike Mayer, who also represented Atlantic Records and, though I didn't know it, the Otis Redding estate. A day or so later, Mayer asked me to show him the record. Shortly thereafter, the damn thing was pulled out of circulation, since nobody had bothered to clear the release with Otis's widow, Zelma.

This was a drag but also an opportunity. I called the distributor, Big O Records in Memphis, and asked what they were doing with the stock they had on hand, which was only a couple of hundred copies. Nothing they could do but destroy them, they told me. So I called Mayer and asked if he'd mind if I bought them up and gave them away to friends. I wouldn't sell them, just hand them out to friends and record collectors I knew. So I spent fifty or a hundred bucks and mailed out most of the stock, keeping perhaps a half dozen or so copies for myself. Over the years, those have dwindled down to the single one that I still own. Proving, I guess, that I'm a lousy record collector.

But it doesn't matter so much now, because anybody can hear Otis sing "You Left the Water Running" by picking up Atlantic's *The Otis Redding Story*, which features not only the music but an explanation of how Redding came to record the track. Seems that while Redding was visiting Muscle Shoals in the fall of 1966, Rick Hall, owner of Fame Studios, asked him to cut "You Left the Water Running" as a demo for Wilson Pickett, who was due to record there soon. Hall drummed on a box, Walden shook a tambourine, Otis sang and overdubbed a couple of background parts. Everything else was added later, the liner notes say, though by whom they don't mention. And indeed, Pickett's version (on *The Wicked Pickett*) does resemble Otis's gentle, soothing way with the tune, rather than Wilson's more predictable leather-lunged style.

951 STRAWBERRY FIELDS FOREVER, The Beatles
Produced by George Martin; written by John Lennon and Paul McCartney
Capitol 5810   1967   *Billboard:* #8

Given my interest in rock and soul music as creative responses to the project of recording music in the studio, rather than making it before a live audience, it's perhaps surprising that I don't think more highly of the Beatles' greatest aural montage. But while I'd never deny its virtues, "Strawberry Fields" remains a record whose virtues are somewhat more conceptual than actual. After all, if montage per se is the issue, then R. Dean Taylor's "Indiana Wants Me" means more in the history of Motown than many a Holland-Dozier-Holland dance classic.

In fact, montage matters only after more basic issues—a strong song and a big beat foremost among them—are taken care of. And while "Strawberry Fields" is one of the most stupendous feats of recording anyone accomplished during the sixties, its virtues are not among my idea of the Verities. There's a beat here, all right, but amidst the cellos and calliopes and English horns, the tapes running backwards and out of phase, the aural gimmickry that astonished every teen with a tape deck, it doesn't seem lost so much as secondary. And while the lyric has enormous resonance if you're interested in Lennon's life (as who ain't?), there's no way it moves from the personal to the universal with anything like the grace of, say, "Help," or for that matter, "Don't Let Me Down." Unless you'd rather work a rebus than dance.

So why, exactly, does "Strawberry Fields" have to be here? Because Lennon puts over his pretenses with such powerful singing that, for all its psychedelic obscurantism, the record acquires a pulse of its own. That is, his singing represents a total triumph of content over form, an injection of real life into a scenario that stands on the verge of "MacArthur Park."

952 SCHLOCK ROD, PART 1, Jan & Dean
Produced by Jan Berry; written by Don Altfeld, Jan Berry, Roger Christian, and Dean Torrence
Liberty 55641   1963   Did not make pop chart

I include this "Drag City" B side not only as the perfect riposte to "Strawberry Fields Forever"—which it is—but because it's a marvelous montage in its own right, with the guts and good sense to mercilessly savage the very hot rod songs on which Jan and Dean were busily making a fortune. Nobody's ever made a funnier car song parody, not even Nervous Norvus. In other words, this is "Strawberry Fields" if Ringo Starr had made it with production by Keith Moon. Well, I guess they would've had to have grown up in California. . . .

953 TALK TALK, The Music Machine
Produced by Brian Ross [Exec. Producer, Maurie Bercor]; written by Sean Bonniwell
Original Sound 61 1966 *Billboard:* #15

"Born to Be Wild" may have provided heavy metal its name, but "Talk Talk" gave it its style, both musical—pure stomping blues deterioration from start to finish—and attitudinal—"My social life's a dud / My name is really mud". That's high praise in my book, but finding it's akin to insult in yours wouldn't surprise me—or them.

954 (FOR GOD'S SAKE) GIVE MORE POWER TO THE PEOPLE, The Chi-Lites
Written and produced by Eugene Record
Brunswick 55450 1971 *Billboard:* #26

Chicago soul's answer to "Give Peace a Chance." One of the first big synthesizer-fed dance numbers, a nice twist on post-Norman Whitfield harmonies and, though the rhetoric is dated (and surprisingly reactionary in spots—i.e., "So whatever you got, just be glad you got it"), the proposition stands as fundamentally correct. Plus there's no Yoko on the B side.

955 THE RIGHT TO LOVE, The Blue Jays
Produced by Lew Werly Fairburn; written by Melvin Broxton
Milestone 2012 1962 Did not make pop chart

As far from the idylls of "Lover's Island" as you could possibly imagine. Backed this time by a spectral flute and group harmony out of a demonic doo-wop cartoon, Leon Peels wrestles with a reality as brutal as his earlier fantasy was beautiful.

Peels sings the opening lines a cappella, his voice stark and shaky as a field holler, the other Blue Jays answering each line with a massed "wee-ooh": "Birds have a right to fly / Lovers have a right to cry / And my heart cries to the heavens above / Why haven't I—why haven't I the right to love." From there, the story grows more dismal until the final verse, when Peels leaps for a falsetto "Won't someone," as if he could control his passions no longer, then regains his composure, finishes the verse but, as the chorus winds down, begins to shout his demands, "Give me the right, give me the right, give me the right" and then, leaping into his head voice again for a thrilling, ascending "to looooove." It's the true cry of an abandoned heart.

956 IT TAKES TWO, Rob Base and D.J. E-Z Rock
Produced by William Hamilton and Rob Base; written by Rob Base
Profile 7186   1988   *Billboard:* #36

In 1988, *Rolling Stone* selected its hundred best singles in a special issue designed as a sequel to its earlier list of the hundred greatest albums. The list was a first-rate travesty, in particular because while it was presented as the result of a consensus of what then passed for the magazine's staff of music critics, it turned out that editor Jann S. Wenner had falsified the results to satisfy certain social obligations. My own thought was that it was a lousy list because it lacked personality and, more than anything, because it operated from such an album-rock sensibility. There was no particular problem with "Satisfaction" as the number one pick, but the list excluded everything before 1963, and it was forged by a bizarre temperament that ranked "Good Vibrations," "Pride (In the Name of Love)," "Somebody to Love," "Hotel California," and "Crimson and Clover" well above "Papa's Got A Brand New Bag." To be charitable, *Rolling Stone* seemed to have missed the point.

In early 1989, *Spin*, Bob Guccione, Jr.'s challenge to *RS* hegemony, riposted in its fourth anniversary issue with a more creative list of greatest singles. Its number one choice was Base and E-Z Rock's "It Takes Two," a move critic David Hinckley accurately described as the equivalent of a three-year-old shooting his mother with a squirt gun in order to get her attention.

But at the same time, the choice was more than intriguing, making an effective argument (that sounds suspiciously like *Spin*'s excellent critic, John Leland) in favor of one of the great virtues of singles: their absolute *immediacy*, their ability to inspire and sustain enthusiasms beyond the bounds of what's reasonable, if not rational. Given its commonplace cynicism, *Spin* probably thought it was just making a statement about ephemerality, but it had chosen too well for that. "It Takes Two" is genuinely hot hip-hop, with E-Z Rock's turntable slashing through to electrogroove bedrock, and its clearly conscious reference to Marvin Gaye and Kim Weston's old hit—reinforced by the hook, an uncredited female crying, "It takes two to make things go right / It takes two to make it outta sight"—lends it the very historicity that the magazine wants to deny.

And on a purely personal level, its selection served as a reminder that this is just the kind of hot'n'nasty pseudoephemera that lends this discussion some continuing meaning, too.

957 HONEY BEE, Gloria Gaynor
Produced by Paul Leka; written by M. Steals, M. Steals, and M. Ledbetter
MGM 14706   1974   Did not make pop chart

Diva disco with bluesy "Superfly" guitar and stinging, zingy strings—bright, powerful, and ripe as genre stuff can only be when captured just moments before it becomes formula. The track and the performance, I mean. The song is simply a construction of clichés, which the rest of the program proceeds to transcend with sheer infectious energy.

958 CELEBRATION, Kool and the Gang
Produced by Eumir Deodato and Kool and the Gang; written by Ronald [Kool] Bell and Kool and the Gang
De-Lite 807   1980   Billboard: #1 (2 weeks)

Admit it, if you could get the taste of its use in Walter Mondale's Presidential nomination, the orgiastic nationalism of the Iran embassy hostage release, and a thousand horrible wedding band cover versions out of your mouth, you'd find "Celebration" one of the most flavorful funk riffs ever concocted. And what other funk band ever had a singer as good as James Taylor? (Well, P-Funk for the couple of months they had Philippe Wynne, but they didn't get a record half this swell out of it.) And you might as well learn its virtues, because you're gonna hear "Celebration" at every wedding you go to from now until the end of the century. Just hope they play the record, not a version dreamed up by some guy with hair transplants and a hatchback to fit his keyboard.

959 COME BACK MY LOVE, The Wrens
Produced by George Goldner; written by Bobby Mansfield
Rama 65   1955   Did not make pop chart

One of the most raucous of all the bird group doo-wops, "Come Back My Love" is also one of the most pop sounding, without much hint of gospel in the singing and all the blues coming from its wild sax and guitar parts. Indeed, in many respects Bobby Mansfield's lead would have comfortably fit into the blandest pop groups. Which doesn't mean he "sounds white," just that the rigid lines of American musical segregation mean more to broadcasters and retailers than they ever have in the minds and ambitions of performers or audiences. If Mansfield displays too much melisma too emotionally to have been in the Four Preps, that doesn't mean that in his own mind (or anybody else's reality), they were all that far apart. It's the synthesis that makes the music exciting, and if you write the pop aspirations of Harlem kids like him out of the rock and soul story, you don't *have* a synthesis.

960 IF YOU COULD READ MY MIND, Bobby Bland
Produced by Joe Scott; written by Deadric Malone
Duke 393   1966   Did not make pop chart

Seekers of the Sinatra of the blues, you've reached your goal. The arrangement is a bathos of strings, flute, and airy female chorus, the lyric a preposterous confection that's wonderfully absurd from its very first line.

But it's the way that Bland sings that first line that makes him a great singer, not just another saloon crooner. "If you could just read my mind," he sings and then pauses, lingering over the implications of the phrase, as if what he was about to create was a form of science fiction. Then, "You'd know just what I'm going to do." It's a great non sequitur, not least for its assumption that Bland might have trouble, right about then, reading his own.

And so it goes, a tour de force performance in which Bland never pushes, never strains and nevertheless leaves you feeling engulfed with a misery unmistakably *his*, the product of woes distinctly personal yet inseparable from all others.

961 FAMILY AFFAIR, Sly and the Family Stone
Written and produced by Sly Stone
Epic 10805   1971   *Billboard:* #1 (3 weeks)

His manager told *Rolling Stone* that "Family Affair" was the story of Sly's own life, which was being cut up by the factions that surrounded him in his stardom. Chief among these factions, David Kapralik hinted, was Sly's own family.

Sly told the magazine this was bullshit. "Song's not about that. Song's about a family affair, whether it's a result of genetic processes or a situation in the environment." Rumor at the time held that Sly had written it in response to demands made on him by black nationalist groups, who looked askance at his integrationist sensibility.

With fifteen years perspective, it also seems likely that "Family Affair," with its draggy rhythm struggling to stay in the groove like a late-night driver fighting off sleep, has a lot to do with the annoyances of the drug trade. Sly's voice snaps in and out of focus, sometimes in the middle of a line, as if he can't quite summon full attention, or isn't sure if this story—any story—would be worth the effort it takes to tell it.

The beat screams "Junkie!" more clearly than any other song that ever hit Number One. The metaphor fits a man plagued by the unwanted attentions of radical opportunists like a thousand dollar suit. At least a couple of Sly's relatives play and sing on the track. But I wouldn't guarantee you that any of those is what it's "about." Might be just some hip dance music from a guy who was losing control due to a wide variety of factors. Which means that if it's "about" anything, "Family Affair" is about all of the above and a lot more only the man who created it will ever really fathom. If *he* ever does.

962 THE SLUMMER THE SLUM, The Five Royales
Producer not credited; written by Lowman Pauling and Obediah Carter
King 6153   1958   Did not make pop chart

More evidence toward a theory of the Royales as the first genuinely modern rock band. The song's a pure blues-rocker—if you didn't know better, you might think you were listening to a dance tune called "Stompa-de-stomp." Lowman Pauling plays a guitar solo that takes the blues up and over the edge, stinging single-string riffs blasting off into 12-bar distortion the like of which would not be heard until British kids "discovered" feedback. And in the midst of all this, a raspy voice intones a profound protest: "Don't try to figure out where I come from / I could be a smart guy from Wall Street / I could be the Purple People Eater's son / But I can do the slummer the slum." And there's not a hint of brag in it, just the pure power of fact. Baby, *that* is rock and soul.

963 HAPPY, The Rolling Stones
Produced by Jimmy Miller; written by Mick Jagger and Keith Richards
Rolling Stones 19104 1972   *Billboard:* #22

Keith's greatest hit. Like a lot of delicacies, you wouldn't want it as a steady diet but when it comes into season, it's always welcome. For a guy who can't sing (or decide how to spell his last name), this is awful powerful stuff.

964 HARLEM NOCTURNE, The Viscounts
Producer not credited; written by Earle Hagen
Madison 123   1959   *Billboard:* #52

Imagine: There was actually a time in America when thoughts of Harlem at night were desirable, even thrilling. The history of this song circumscribes the history of that idea. Written around 1940 when Harlem was also a popular night spot for whites, a place associated more with good times and semi-illicit thrills than squalor and danger, "Harlem Nocturne" was picked up as the theme song of the Randy Brooks orchestra. The song next became a hit for former Lionel Hampton saxophonist Herbie Fields in 1953, then was further popularized by the jump bands of Johnny Otis and Ray Nobel. The Viscounts, a Jersey-based quartet, touched it up with splashy electric guitar and echoing drums but kept the bold saxophone to promise wee hours delights. Their "Harlem Nocturne" appeared at the very last minute. By 1959, the social events that made an instrumental portrait of America's black capital seem less enticing than threatening had begun to make their appearance. So while the Viscounts music remains evocative, it's hard to say how closely what it evokes resembles the world it set out to describe. We live today in a different universe.

965 I PUT A SPELL ON YOU, Screamin' Jay Hawkins

Produced by Leroy Kirkland; written by Screamin' Jay Hawkins
OKeh 7072 1956 Did not make pop chart

As raw and wild as any rhythm and blues ever waxed, "I Put a Spell on You" might be the greatest record ever made if raucous and weird were all it took. For postmodern cultural nationalists, it might be even better than that, an R&B classic that explicitly defines itself in terms more African than American, dabbling in voodoo imagery straight from the ancient lands. Not only does Hawkins invoke those powerful old griot spirits, he was shut down for doing so: When first issued, "I Put a Spell On You" had to be withdrawn by OKeh because stations all over the country banned it, alleging that its final round of ghoulish screams and moans simulated cannibalism. Hawkins, meantime, had the wit to open his shows by rising up out of a coffin, a move that not only dazzled teens in 1956, but wowed them again twenty years later when George Clinton adapted the gimmick for his post-psychedelic soul extravaganza, the Parliament/Funkadelic Revue.

Unfortunately for the savants, Jalacy Hawkins (as he was born in Cleveland in 1929) offers more credentials as conman than artist. There are two "official" versions of the creation of "I Put a Spell On You." Hawkins told Gerri Hirshey, in *Nowhere to Run*, her history of soul music, that he concocted the song when a huge bellow of grief rose up out of the center of his psyche after his girl walked out on him in Atlantic City sometime in the early fifties. But according to R&B historians Marcia Vance and Marv Goldberg, Hawkins was performing the tune as a straight ballad until OKeh A&R man Arnold Maxim got him drunk at the session, when he began to scream and holler and generally cannibalize his own concept. Rising out of a coffin wasn't even Hawkins' own idea; Alan Freed had to talk him into it.

Yet even taking all of that into account, wild, raw, weird, and raucous are not minor virtues in the history of rock and soul, and "I Put a Spell On You"—a record so outrageous that Jay's version never made even the national R&B charts, although it became famous in latter-day versions by Creedence Clearwater Revival and Arthur Brown—definitely deserves its place in the pantheon.

966 HOUND DOG, Elvis Presley
Produced by Chet Atkins; written by Jerry Leiber and Mike Stoller
RCA 47-6604 1956 *Billboard: #1 (11 weeks)*

The final measure of Elvis Presley's Top 40 genius: He topped the charts for almost three months with a souvenir he brought back as a joke from his first trip to Las Vegas (otherwise the most disastrous junket of his career). And from that day to this, hardly anybody has known the difference.

"Hound Dog" was written by Jerry Leiber and Mike Stoller at the request of bandleader Johnny Otis, who gave it over to blues shouter Big Mama Thornton, then working as part of his revue.* Houston-based Don Robey's Peacock label issued it in March 1953, and Thornton's "Hound Dog" spent seven weeks atop the R&B chart.

"Hound Dog" is probably the greatest example ever of the unfairness of presuming that all black R&B originals are better than later reinterpretations by white artists. Elvis has for years been saddled with charges that he ripped off Thornton, even though: 1) his arrangement owes next to nothing to hers, as both the music and lyrics are utterly different; and 2) he sings the hell out of the song while Thornton lumbers through it. But mainly only blues purists, not inclined to cut Elvis or anyone like him a break, have actually heard Thornton's record, though not only purists have leveled the charge.

Student of R&B that he was, Elvis undoubtedly knew Thornton's record but he apparently never thought of singing "Hound Dog" himself until he happened upon Freddy Bell and the Bell Boys out in Vegas, where Elvis was also working in April of 1956. Bell and his group, one of the first lounge acts to successfully incorporate rock and roll, did "Hound Dog" as an R&B travesty, and Presley and his friends got the joke.

They could hardly have missed it since the very countrified ways at which Bell was poking fun were causing the greatest bomb of Elvis's career, when he was virtually hooted out of the Frontier main room and forced to cancel the final week of his booking.

Bell had totally rearranged "Hound Dog," livening the tempo and coming up with some new lyrics (including "You ain't never caught a rabbit"). Presley took his reading nationwide on June 5, during his national TV appearance on Milton Berle's show. Rapt in his rendition, he thrust his pelvis and wiggled his hips to almost catastrophic effect; it was this performance more than any other that caused the nationwide

*Recent research by R&B historian Steve Propes calls even this into question.

uproar over his "lewdness." But looking back on it now, what burns from Presley's face is humor—he can barely keep from cracking up at his own jive.

"Hound Dog" was obviously a dangerous song and Elvis was reluctant to record it, especially after the unpleasant experience of being forced to don a tuxedo and sing "You ain't never caught a rabbit" into the face of a basset hound by jackass talk show host Steve Allen. Whatever his qualms, though, Elvis generally followed orders and the very day after his humiliation by Allen, he cut "Hound Dog" along with "Don't Be Cruel" at RCA's New York studio.

The "Hound Dog" that resulted is a funny, appealing record and Scotty Moore's scything guitar is no joke at all. It's sad that such a good example of Presley's willingness to laugh at himself and the sounds he loved has been so often used as a bludgeon by know-nothings.

967 ROCK THE BOAT, The Hues Corporation
Produced by John Florez; written by Wally Holmes
RCA 0232   1974   Billboard: #1 (1 week)

Disco's original trash classic. The cargo includes an overload of lyric cliché and a heap of brief breaks that were about to be extended to the edge of annoyance on several thousand far less amusing records. But "Rock the Boat" gets over on its freshness and the pure sultriness of Fleming Williams's lead vocal.

968 KEEP ON TRUCKIN', PART ONE, Eddie Kendricks
Produced by Frank Wilson and Leonard Caston; written by
Anita Poree, Frank Wilson, and Leonard Caston
Tamla 54238   1973   Billboard: #1 (2 weeks)

Eddie Kendricks may have been overshadowed by David Ruffin in the Temptations, but he had by far the more substantial solo career, thanks to that bane of Motownophiles: Disco.

Kendricks was one of the few first-rate soul singers to easily and rapidly make the transition to the new dance music through records like "Truckin'," "Girl You Need A Change of Mind," and "Date with the Rain." In fact, in trying to trace the history of disco, *Billboard* columnist Brian Chin refers to the "Eddie Kendrick Rule: That the release of 'People . . . Hold On' in June 1972 was arguably the first landmark of disco.''

Seventeen months later, "Keep on Truckin' " was the first disco hit to top the pop charts. Although the title phrase is associated with hippie icons like the Grateful Dead and comics artist R. Crumb, Kendricks believed it was the title that ensured that it was a hit. "The old people used to truck when they were dancing. And I knew the trucking industry would embrace the record," he told Fred Bronson.

To reach Number One, any record has to reach the "Convoy" crowd, so Kendricks must have been at least partly right. But the elements that keep "Truckin' " alive are jittery horns and fatback drums, chugging bass and wah-wah guitar, and a rhythmic bed of organ, strings and horns that links disco and the blaxploitation soundtrack music of Curtis Mayfield and Marvin Gaye. Kendricks rides the mix with shrieks and imprecations, demanding that the dancers show him some endurance out there. They came through as well as he did.

969 WONDERFUL WORLD, Louis Armstrong

Produced by Bob Thiele; written by George Weiss and Bob Thiele
A&M AM-3010   1988   Billboard: #24

This slight pop song from 1958 found itself in the Top 40 thirty years later as the perfect embodiment of world harmony. It's about a hundred times more convincing than *Good Morning, Vietnam*, the movie from whose soundtrack it was drawn and, with Armstrong's pained gravel voice pitted against lush strings, it sounds at least as modern as anything on the charts in 1988.

Armstrong was almost unquestionably the greatest musical talent this country has produced, a brilliant instrumentalist and band leader, improviser and recording artist, and one of the half-dozen most inspired and influential vocalists of the century. His use of his voice as a medium for emotional effects, damn the niceties, helped set the stage for a rock and soul generation that sometimes seem to offer nothing but such displays. That is, eighteen years after his death, a record Armstrong tossed off as a minor artifact when he was fifty-eight years old could shoot 'cross the horizon as one of the warmest, wittiest specimens of musical humanity and seem not only as contemporary but quite a bit more compelling than anything that surrounded it.

970 CONTROVERSY, Prince
Written and produced by Prince
Warner Bros. 49808   1979   *Billboard:* #11

The title track of his fourth album is the one where Prince gives the game away. Whatever outrages he catalogs (mostly having to do with, you know, sex 'n' drugs 'n' rock 'n' roll, although he gets his licks in on religion, too) he's so shameless, that's all they are: controversies, momentary passions, meant to be exploited but neither resolved nor left unresolved—he genuinely doesn't give a fuck, just wants you to pay attention to *him*. And of course, the groove's so sharp and deep and the superficialities of the lyric (right down to the recitation of the Lord's Prayer) that you can't help yourself anyway, and of course, most people missed the point.

Or at least that's what I think is going on here. If Prince really endorsed ideas like "Some people want to die / Just so they can be free," his mystic totalitarianism would be too threatening to be dealt with as frivolously as it deserves.

971 MORE THAN A FEELING, Boston
Produced by John Boyland and Tom Scholz; written by
Tom Scholz
Epic 50266   1976   *Billboard:* #5

The irony here is squarely in the title, for Tom Scholz (who basically made this record solo, then grafted on Brad Delp's yelping vocal and enlisted Boyland's production gloss to persuade the record company bureaucrats they weren't just putting out a homemade demo) is the ultimate perfectionist technocrat, who takes years making music as simple as this grandiloquent power ballad, then years to follow it up with bombast whose differences are undetectable to the untrained ear. But if "less than a feeling" would be a better description of the Scholz formula, it hardly matters during the 3:25 the original's playing, because the howling guitars and vocals combine to make the unified noise that marks great rock and roll, even at its most marginal.

972 A THOUSAND STARS, Kathy Young with the Innocents
Producer not credited; written by Eugene Pearson
Indigo 108   1960   Billboard: #3

Granted that "A Thousand Stars" is exactly the kind of stuff that led to the theory that rock was squelched by wimp in the pre-Beatles sixties, granted even that Kathy and her cronies are ripping off the Rivileers, an R&B group, this remains a remarkable record simply because the pure callowness of the lead vocal has never been matched. It's entirely possible that Karen Carpenter based her entire style on what Young sings here.

973 LOVERS WHO WANDER, Dion
Produced by Gene Schwartz; written by Ernie Maresca and Dion DiMucci
Laurie 3123   1962   Billboard: #3

In the South, the schematic of rock and roll was the fusion of (black) rhythm and blues and (white) country and western. The result was rockabilly and the impure blues of Chuck Berry and his ilk.

In the North, the schematic fused R&B not so much with Tin Pan Alley pop as with the Italian-American variant of operatic bel canto. You can hear this fusion at work in doo-wop, both black and white, and especially in the work of such Bronx-born rock singers as Bobby Darin and, most of all, Dion. It's the essence of "Lovers Who Wander," where Dion's phrasing derives directly from the pop bel canto of Frank Sinatra and his acolytes, while the drums and sax play insistent supercharged R&B.

That's just the theory. In fact, Elvis Presley modeled himself in part on Dean Martin and Mario Lanza, two of those who popularized bel canto pop, while Dion's first musical hero was none other than country giant Hank Williams.

974 JACK AND JILL, Ray Parker Jr. and Raydio
Written and produced by Ray Parker Jr.
Arista 0283   1978   *Billboard:* #8

Not quite the simple Sly and the Family Stone update it seemed upon
first release, but close enough to sustain interest even as Parker's subsequent releases followed a more clearly formulaic path.

Parker's sensibility considerably updates the basic Family Stone
funk posture—the similarities are mainly in the interactive vocals, because disco necessities have locked up the bottom more firmly than
anything from the sixties and the soundscape is dominated by synthesizer effects that didn't exist during Sly's heyday.

On the other hand, Parker employs the Sly vocal style as effectively
as anyone's used it since the master. And if his version of vision is
entirely self-serving (Jack sneaked down the hill because "he needed
love / Love he couldn't get from Jill"), why do you think they called
it the Me Decade?

975 I FEEL FINE, The Beatles
Produced by George Martin; written by John Lennon and
Paul McCartney
Capitol 5327   1964   *Billboard:* #1 (3 weeks)

That burst of guitar feedback at the top may not be the first in deliberately recorded history, but it was for sure the first to top the charts.
And what follows is simply the Beatles playing their best basic rock
and roll, with a standout Lennon vocal and cymbals splashing as lively
as the guitars.

976 MIND OVER MATTER, Nolan Strong and the Diablos
Produced by Jack and Devora Brown; written by Devora Brown
Fortune 546   1958   Did not make pop chart

As raucous as "The Wind" is spooky, but this time the prophecy is not
of Michael Jackson so much as Keith Richards's guitar style, circa
December's Children. Charlie Watts would never have let the beat
wander around like this, but then, Mick Jagger could never sing as well
as Nolan, so they're about even.

977 SEVEN DAY WEEKEND, Gary "U.S." Bonds
Produced by Frank Guida; written by Doc Pomus and Mort Shuman
LeGrand 1019   1962   *Billboard:* #27

Like all Bonds records, the band continually sounds like it's about two bars from altogether falling apart but somehow, everybody maintains their energy all the way through. On the surface, "Seven Day Weekend" sounds like a teenage lament, with its references to "Friday after school" and teachers calling Gary's name while he daydreams, but in reality, the song speaks volumes about the bohemian desires of its authors, the horseplayer and card sharp Doc Pomus and his near-relation, Mort Shuman, soon to move to the Parisian Left Bank and form a collaborative partnership with Jacques Brel. That is, there's nothing here, in the end, that the Rolling Stones of the Brian Jones era didn't mean to say (or manage to live out). Consequently, even though its Twist and "picture show" references date it as much as Gene Barge's rudimentary, scratchy sax, "Seven Day Weekend," with its gabbling chorus seconding Gary's every indolent desire, lives on as the distilled essence of rock's links to creativity in its laziest modes.

978 COME SOFTLY TO ME, The Fleetwoods
Produced by Bob Reisdorff; written by Gary Troxel, Gretchen Christopher, and Barbara Ellis
Dolphin 1   1959   *Billboard:* #1 (4 weeks)

The most weightless harmonies ever recorded make the Fleetwoods the Carpenters of the fifties—except Gretchen Christopher liked a good meal and Gary Troxel had the sense to sing "Dum dum, dum do dum, dooby doo" instead of words intended for bank commercials. Exactly what Barbara Ellis did—especially on this record—is hard to figure out. Hummed a lot, I suppose.

The fact that somebody was making this music in Olympia, Washington while virtually next door Rockin' Robin Roberts was exploring the mysteries of his bargain bin copy of "Louie Louie" and bands like the Wailers and Sonics and Raiders and Kingsmen were revving their engines is as reassuring as knowing that the president of your senior class and his cheerleader girlfriend just went bankrupt, while the hot rodder down the block has now franchised his fifteenth body shop.

979 MISTY BLUE, Dorothy Moore
Produced by Tom Couch and James Stroud; written by
Bob Montgomery
Malaco 1029   1976   *Billboard:* #3

One of the last deep soul hits to percolate to the top of the charts was
this lush arrangement of a song written in 1967 for countrypolitan star
Eddy Arnold by Nashville vet Bob Montgomery, Buddy Holly's high
school singing partner. Joe Simon did the original soul version in 1972,
but like Arnold's, his rendition found few takers at Top 40.

Part of Moore's advantage was that the song's plushness seemed
more credible coming out of a woman's mouth. But her crying improvisation near the end lends a soaring sense of triumph that the more
lugubrious interpretations by Simon and Arnold never discovered. And
that little victory not only led her straight up the Hot 100, it's what
made this disc the one that has lasted.

980 I DON'T LOVE YOU ANYMORE, Teddy Pendergrass
Produced by Kenneth Gamble and Leon Huff; written by
Kenneth Gamble and Leon Huff
Philadelphia International 3622   1977   *Billboard:* #41

Teddy's first solo hit. And though he's kissing his lover off and claims
it's a shame the spark's gone out of their relationship, he sound anything
but sad about it. In fact, his chants of the title phrase feel more like a
taunt, while in the verses, he promises to pay his alimony on time but
insists that the world will be a much better place in the wake of the
divorce. Nice metaphor for his feelings toward former wagemaster,
Harold Melvin, no doubt.

981 FEEL A WHOLE LOT BETTER, The Byrds
Produced by Terry Melcher; written by Gene Clark
Columbia 43332   1965   Did not make pop chart

Swimming in echo and phasing, with a guitar sound (and solo) out of
Jackie DeShannon via Love, high Beach Boys harmonies, and some of
the hottest, trebliest percussion of its day, "Feel A Whole Lot Better"
is the one early Byrds record on which their L.A. roots showed more

clearly than their genuflections in the direction of Dylan and/or the Beatles. Meaning it belongs as much or more to producer Terry Melcher than to Gene Clark, even though Clark was maybe the most unregenerate rocker in the group. Either way, this great band never again got quite so down and dirty as it does here, on the flip side of its second single (a pedestrian rendition of Dylan's "All I Really Want to Do").

982 EVERY 1'S A WINNER, Hot Chocolate
Produced by Mickie Most; written by Errol Brown
Infinity 50002   1978   *Billboard:* #6

Despite writing "Brother Louie," Hot Chocolate's Errol Brown never exhibited much ambition beyond having his music heard and sold. But that proved goal enough to make his multiracial, reggae-influenced group Britian's best trash singles act.

Hot Chocolate cut its first single, a reggae-ish cover of John Lennon's "Give Peace A Chance," for Apple but it scored its first hit a year or later with an absolutely unique fusion of R&B, reggae, and power pop devices. The synthesis brought them a variety of U.K. hits, starting with "Brother Louie" and "Emma," and two big ones in the States, "You Sexy Thing" (1975) and "Every 1's A Winner." Working with primordial pop producer Mickie Most (who'd earlier done the early Animals, Jeff Beck, and Herman's Hermits) but mostly writing his own material, Brown came up with mildly gimmicky surfaces, topped with his own heady, melismatic vocals, and underpinned by deeply embedded funk bass and percussion lines. On "Every 1's A Winner," the highlight is the synthesizer playing, but every note of the record makes a steady charge toward its target—the top of the charts approached not as a hackwork assignment but as the fulfillment of someone's dream and destiny.

983 BRING IT UP, James Brown
Produced by James Brown; written by James Brown and Nat Jones
King 6071   1967   *Billboard:* #29

The Man, lost in a wonderland of rhythm and funk, horns, drums, and his own eviscerating screams. You'll be thrilled to follow him as he wanders, purposeful and mapless—or at least you will be if you have enough sense to understand the power of suspending your sense to delve into your senses. In this respect, "Bring It Up" becomes a Jungian injunction, though it's hardly clear whether that dour old Calvinist would have been able to get to grips with the charms of this full-blown apostate Pentecostalism.

984 LADY MARMALADE, Labelle
Produced by Allen Toussaint; written by Bob Crewe and Kenny Nolan
Epic 50048   1975   *Billboard:* #1 (1 week)

Disco's greatest French lesson—and a hell of a lot more credible love song than "I Sold My Heart to the Junkman."

985 I FORGOT TO BE YOUR LOVER, William Bell
Produced by Booker T. Jones; written by Booker T. Jones and William Bell
Stax 0015   1969   *Billboard:* #45

One of the most trenchant bouts of self-criticism in the history of rock and soul. It's not the apology (in which he vows to spend his life making up) but Bell's awareness of his failures: "Have I done those little simple things to show you just how much I care?" he sings, so gently, sweetly, and carefully that the healing begins before the question ends. But if you plan to try this tactic at home—not such a bad idea—don't forget to hire the violins.

986 BARBARA-ANN, The Regents
Produced by Lou Ciccheti and Morris Diamond; written by Fred Fassert
Gee 1065   1961   *Billboard:* #13

Long before Brian Wilson bleated it with his brothers, Fred Fassert wrote "Barbara-Ann" for his sister, then gave it to his younger brother, Charles, who sang second tenor for a group that began its Bronx mini-career as the Desires in 1956. Given its raucous silliness, Fred may have intended only a typical brother-sister taunt, a travesty of the real Barbara-Ann's high school social ambitions. But when the renamed Regents—Guy Villari on the breathless falsetto lead, along with Sal Cuomo, Don Jacobucci, Tony "Hot Rod" Gravagna, and Charles Fassert—got hold of it, the song took on new life as a gasping expression of total teen desire. "Barbara-Ann" becomes not a name but a noise ("ba ba ba ba babaran"), a sound synonymous with rapture. The sax-man clearly agrees.

987 THE BOYS ARE BACK IN TOWN, Thin Lizzy
Produced by John Alcock; written by Phil Lynnot
Mercury 73786   1976   Billboard: #12

Best non-Springsteen Springsteen ever. Its loping pace and wild boys on the loose narrative achieve actual anthemic status, thanks to the surging guitar riffs that set up the song with their chugging, then break out in a beautifully melodic chorus. Lynnot proves that this kind of mythic male camaraderie, in which summer is celebrated as a time when drink and blood flow in correlated measure, extends to transcontinental slaps in the mug. Which probably wasn't any surprise to an authentic Irishman like himself anyhow.

988 ROCK YOUR BABY, George McCrae
Written and produced by H.W. Casey and Rick Finch
T.K. 1004   1974   Billboard: #1 (2 weeks)

The kickoff for the Miami dance record scene came with this lengthy (6:20) prefab groove, concocted by the same guys who brought you K.C. and the Sunshine Band, but with McCrae's spooky tenor floating over the top. Cut in forty-five minutes as a backing track that Casey (i.e., K.C.) found way out of his range, then finished in two takes when McCrae happened to wander into the studio, "Rock Your Baby," together with the Hues Corporation's "Rock the Boat" and MFSB's "TSOP" made 1974 the year that the new dance music really took over the top of the charts. McCrae went on to make other records, some of them quite good but none half so compulsively listenable. In typical disco fashion, it was the writer/producer team that had a career shaping up.

989 SHOT BY BOTH SIDES, Magazine
Produced by Mick Glossop and Magazine; written by
Howard DeVoto and Peter Shelley
Virgin VS200 [UK]   1978   Did not make pop chart

"I can be lonely sometimes. I can be lonely right in the middle of a crowd," Elvis Presley once said. But it took this band of *enfants misérables* to find the song that fit the thought. They did it with primordial punk stomp overridden by a great guitar riff (same one Bruce Springsteen used for "Roulette") and fleshed out with the saddest of all sad schoolyard stories, the one about the guy who can't fit in even with the other misfits. "Better worm my way into the heart of the crowd . . . / Shot by both sides / On my way to the outside of everything," croaks Howard DeVoto, expressing more truths than he perhaps imagines: The reason the others won't let him fit in, the reasons he doesn't want to, the reasons he does anyway, why he thinks it's a secret, why everybody really knows the score.

990 THE ABCS OF LOVE, Frankie Lymon & the Teenagers
Produced by George Goldner; written by Richard Barrett
Gee 1022   1956   *Billboard:* #77

Rocking fifties group harmony doesn't get any more basic than this hot, sweet little puppy-love jump tune, in which Frankie Lymon finally makes it all the way to "W, X, Y, and Z" before lapsing into a series of wordless "uh-uh-oh-oh" 's that are immediately matched by a squawking sax break.

But that's just another tribute to rock and roll as the art of planned spontaneity. Nothing here happens by accident, as evidenced by the track's recording history. The Teenagers cut it first on May 15, 1956. The arrangement was almost identical but the spark was missing, so George Goldner chose to release as the group's third single "I Promise to Remember," the only other side recorded that day. (That first version never saw the light of day until 1986, when it was included in the five record Frankie Lymon and the Teenagers boxed set assembled by Bob Hyde [Murray Hill].)

The Teenagers returned to the studio in August and as soon as Sherman Garnes cuts loose with that great bass introduction—"Boom boom de boom boom"—you can tell they've figured out their "ABCs." By the time Lymon makes his appearance, the whole show's ready to explode and Frankie cranks the energy to the max. Nobody's ever made "J, K, L, M, N-O-P, Q" sound half so sexy or so fully of the moment.

991 EVERY BREATH I TAKE, Gene Pitney
Produced by Phil Spector; written by Gerry Goffin and Carole King
Musicor 1011   1961   *Billboard:* #42

When Gene Pitney's self-made first single, "(I Wanna) Love My Life Away" failed to set the world on fire, his mentor, song publisher Aaron Schroeder, called in chips all over Broadway, getting songs and production help not only from Phil Spector, Gerry Goffin, and Carole King but Burt Bacharach and Hal David—even the top dogs Jerry Leiber and Mike Stoller consulted on the project, though it was their one-time protege, Spector, who drew the assignment.

Spector, whose Philles Wall of Sound wouldn't debut until the end of the year, placed Pitney's extraordinary high tenor in the center of a musical maelstrom: huge booming drums, shuddering cascades of strings, a chorus big enough for *How the West Was Won*, and the dead-of-night studio psychodrama that went with it, so that by the time he actually stepped to the microphone, Pitney wasn't sure exactly what he was singing (which was nothing more complicated than any of Phil's other commissioned tributes to the holiness of teen romance), only that it was both Big and Important.

The result is too much music for the slight song, a premonition of "River Deep—Mountain High." Somehow, the whole mess coalesces into a sound compelling for its very excesses. Pitney's vibrato and falsetto have never been employed more spectacularly (if often more appropriately), and Spector's kitchen sink has never been crammed so close to the brim.

The record flopped, of course. "Love My Life Away" had edged into the Top Forty at Number 39. Spector's grandiosity saw the promised land from a perch at Number 42 and then sank quickly out of sight. But everybody lived happily ever after anyway. Pitney's career took off when he was teamed with Bacharach and David for his next two singles, a pair of movie themes, "Town Without Pity" (Number 13) and "Liberty Valance" (Number 4). Schroeder's Musicor label, which he'd founded as a vehicle for Pitney, also became a force in country, releasing some of George Jones's greatest hits. And Philles let Spector give full vent to his eccentricities and excesses with records that sold millions.

992 5 MINUTES (C-C-C-CLUB MIX), Bonzo Goes to Washington

Produced by Jerry Harrison and D. Lazerus; written by The Gipper,
Jerry Harrison, and Bootsy Collins
Sleeping Bag 666-13   1984   Did not make pop chart

993 THE SIGN OF THE TIMES, Donna Fargo

Produced by Stan Silver; written by Donna Fargo
Columbia 04097   1983   Did not make pop chart

994 NO SELL OUT, Malcolm X with Keith LeBlanc

Produced by Keith LeBlanc; written by Malcolm X and Keith LeBlanc
Tommy Boy 840   1983   Did not make pop chart

Of the innumerable responses to Reaganism that range from Madonna's
"Holiday" and Bobby McFerrin's "Don't Worry Be Happy" to Bruce
Springsteen's *Nebraska* and Grandmaster Flash's "The Message," none
were more direct or militant than these three, which vectored in from
all over the spectrum: Fargo, a female country star with a waning career;
LeBlanc, a white session percussionist who made his rep with the Sugar
Hill Gang; Bonzo, composed of two great bassists, Jerry Harrison, of
the chic album rockers, Talking Heads, and Bootsy Collins, the James
Brown/P-Funk hero.

In late 1983, Ronald Reagan warmed up for one of his Saturday
afternoon radio broadcasts by proclaiming into a mike he didn't know
was open: "My fellow Americans, I'm pleased to tell you today that
I've signed legislation that will outlaw Russia forever. We begin bomb-
ing in five minutes . . ." Reporters in the next room heard him and
there was a brief flap in the papers. But no one made much of the full
lip-smacking relish Reagan's reading revealed. He sounds out of breath,
stumbles over the last few words in the flush of his glee—this, he's
clearly announcing, would be a most desirable climax for his reign.

Since the nation's journalists weren't up to the task of looking such
senile psychosis in the eye, let alone giving it its true name, Harrison
and Collins took on the task. They got a tape of the speech and backed
it with deep beats from bass and drums and synth, then cut and fractured
those words so many ways that there was no way to deny that a) Reagan
really said them, and b) they meant that he looked forward with trembling and joy to the forthcoming nuclear holocaust. If Walter Mondale

had had either brains or balls, he'd have used Bonzo's disc as a radio commercial.

Keith LeBlanc, on the other hand, simply heard an old album of Malcolm X speeches and was struck by their continuing relevance: "White black brown red yellow, it doesn't make any difference what color you are . . . The only thing power respects, is power . . . They take one little word out of what you say, ignore all the rest, then begin to magnify it all over the world to make you look like what you actually aren't." Besides his own electronically intensified hip-hop beats, LeBlanc mixed Malcolm with Malcolm, tossing one phrase off another, blending his words in their own various rhythms to create a marvelous and potent piece of politicized pop. ("No Sell Out" actually made the R&B charts for a week, the only one of these records to do so.)

Donna Fargo didn't necessarily see the urban squalor that led LeBlanc to Malcolm X, but what she spotted in the eyes of the men and women in her audience led her to make a protestation rare in the annals of country music. Not so much because it's a recitation over strings—from "Deck of Cards" forward, this kind of record has been a C&W staple—as because of her insistence that the out of work weren't just blacks and bums and those who lacked will but guys whose wives used to believe they could move mountains, that the story of the eighties wasn't patriotic glory but national shame as "a nightmare replaced the American dream."

"The Sign of the Times" is rampantly sentimental; it doesn't dare suggest the relationship of poverty and racism, or connect the swelling riches of the few with the impoverishment of "the farmer, the trucker, the teacher, the steelworker." But Fargo does dare to call Reagan's America what it was—what it remains—and that's rare in any field.

995 CRITICIZE, Alexander O'Neal
Produced by Jimmy Jam and Terry Lewis; written by Jellybean Johnson and Alexander O'Neal
Tabu 07600   1987   Billboard: #70

The truth of the matter, from the finest voice produced by the late eighties Minneapolis soul mill. More than anyone except Terence Trent D'Arby, O'Neal harks back to Motown's sweet-voiced soul men, and producers Jam and Lewis (his bandmates in the Time before Prince bounced Alexander for insufficient pliability) give him outstandingly modern grooves to work with. Here, O'Neal, with an assist from another Time alum, Jellybean Johnson, gives himself a witty text, in which he tries to talk his girl out of her need to dish everything from his choice of clothes to his choice of companions. A situation with which this writer could identify even without the bull's-eye title.

996 AMERICA THE BEAUTIFUL, Ray Charles
Producer not credited; written by Katherine Lee Bates and Samuel Ward
Dunhill 45-002   1987   Did not make pop chart

All the while I was writing *The Heart of Rock and Soul*, the music industry trade papers were filled with stories about the death of the single. They meant, of course, the death of the 45 RPM vinyl disc, not the death of singles per se.

The question is what will replace 45s. Beyond the status quo (and despite the presence of millions of turntables, the lack of any corporate incentive to update and improve rapidly disintegrating record pressing facilities made the 45's death a certainty), there were three alternatives: the twelve-inch vinyl single, the cassette single, and the CD single.

The vinyl twelve-inch seemed certain to survive only so long as the rest of vinyl; the preferred format for dance deejays (you can't scratch any of the other kinds of single) it never captured much allegiance among the rest of the audience.

The cassette single remains beloved only of those who listen solely in their cars. For everyday use, it has all of tape's usual disadvantages: incredibly ponderous access from one song to another (rewinding is always the longest distance between two points), the tape itself is susceptible to all kinds of bends, twists, stretches, and breaks, and its fidelity is the lowest of the lot. Besides, the cassette single uses neither of tape's big advantages: Its ability to contain very long musical programs and its rerecordability. But tapes are also the cheapest format to produce and package and therefore they've been the most avidly marketed.

Then there's the CD single, offering digital clarity a song or two (maybe three) at a time, an elegant format with virtually instant access to not only any track but to any point in any track. The ideal sound carrying device. Until you decide that consumers can't distinguish between the new U2 album and its various singles simply by looking at the price, but that they must be given the visual aid of a smaller size, to boot. (With, of course, a consequent diminishment of raw materials and costs. Selling one or two songs for $5.98 is even better than selling eight or ten for $15.95; do the math.)

Problem was, the CD player was designed to accept only a five-inch disc so playing a three-inch CD required an adapter, a clumsy plastic prosthetic that snapped around the outside of the disc to bring its overall circumference back up to five inches, the opposite of the way you used to snap those ugly little yellow things into the center of your 45s. Naturally, the sensitive laser technology of CD players was likely to misread a disc not centered in its adapter with perfect stability.

God knows why we had to be saddled with this monstrosity, when there's a perfectly acceptable CD alternative—a regular five-inch disc containing less music at a lower price—awaiting only a consumer boycott to become the dominant singles medium.

But in the end, it doesn't matter which format prevails. Singles will always be around because people listen to and remember and love music one song and one performance at a time; they're the way that pop music is most deeply and intensely appreciated, whether on the radio in hourly rotation or at home, picking the needle up and putting it back down five times in a row. What it's about is what's in the grooves (or bits, if you're waxing digital). Music is music and if rock and roll lovers have put up with the inconvenience of fitting a one-inch hole onto a ⅛-inch spindle for three decades, we'll certainly adapt to the CD adapter, or even the clumsiness of cassettes, if we have to.

To that end, here is the one three-inch CD single I have come to know and love, Dunhill's reissue of one of the greatest Ray Charles ballads of all time, a 1976 performance. (Back then, "America" was issued as a 45—Crossover 985, which made the lowest rungs of the R&B charts as Ray's eighty-first entry there.) Gasping and chortling, singing it bluesy and singing it utterly straight, Brother Ray converts this hoary chauvinism into a gorgeous, ironic, sweet-tempered sermon on the land he loves and knows a lot more about than the composers. By the end, when he starts to chant "America! America!" it's as if he's trying to seduce the nation. And you pretty much have to believe that he could.

At that point, if they wanted to embed the music in your brain cells and charge you for the privilege, you'd let 'em do it.

997 DON'T FEAR THE REAPER, Blue Oyster Cult
Produced by Sandy Pearlman and Murray Krugman; written by Donald Roeser (Buck Dharma)
Columbia 10384   1976   *Billboard:* #12

In which the world's brainiest heavy metal band finally focuses its sound and winds up with (besides the greatest Byrds knockoff in history) a

Really Big Statement on a Really Big Issue (which found its perfect context in an early scene in John Carpenter's *Halloween*, though Stephen King also made better use of it than your average oldies programmer does these days). There's something more chilling about the group's echoing Byrds-like "La la la, la la / La la la, la la" than its declaration that 40,000 die every day, which is proto-Jehovah's Witness crap that doesn't scare (or convince) anybody.

Ultimately, "Don't Fear the Reaper" is rock and roll as naked lunch, when everybody sees what's at the end of every fork. That is to say, music that concentrates the mind every bit as effectively as the punch in the face its metalloid impact so much resembles.

998 THE CHEATER, Bob Kuban and the In-Men
Produced by Mel Friedman; written by John Mike Krenski
Musicland 20001   1966   *Billboard:* #12

Life Imitates Art:
In the early sixties, St. Louis high school teacher Bob Kuban ran a brass-based band that soon acquired a bit of a local reputation. But Kuban couldn't find a vocalist, until he heard a lounge act called the Pacemakers, featuring a singer named Walter Scott. Kuban offered a job on the spot and Scott took it. Within a year, they'd cut their first single, "Jerkin' Time," on the local Norman label, and found steady work playing at halftime of St. Louis Hawks basketball games. By late 1965, bassist Mike Krenski had come up with "The Cheater," written around soul chords but with a brassy arrangement and a bulldozing vocal by Scott.

Released in October 1965, by January 1966, "The Cheater" was the number one song in St. Louis and taking off nationally as well. The band figured that Scott's vocal was the key to their success, and began billing the act as Bob Kuban and the In-Men, featuring Walter Scott. Though they couldn't tour extensively, because most of the In-Men were in college and fearful of losing their draft exemptions if they dropped out, they did do regional dates and appeared on such national TV shows as *Where the Action Is* and *American Bandstand*. They even got a one-shot spot in an L.A. soap opera called *Never Too Young*.

But by July, it was all over. Scott, Krenski, and organist Greg Hoeltzel split to form the Guise, a more Anglo-oriented band. Kuban loved brass and didn't want to go that route. When nothing came of the Guise, Scott rejoined him. When Scott wanted to tour, though, Kuban decided he'd rather stay home and so over the next few years, he built up his local following, becoming co-owner of a string of night-clubs while his new band, the Bob Kuban Brass, became regulars at St. Louis football and baseball intermissions.

Scott stayed out on the road, working steadily, going nowhere. In truth, on the basis of "The Cheater," there was little reason to think that he would. His singing there is good enough but the strength of the record is a really good brass arrangement, some nice drumming and guitar work, and especially its cautionary lyric, a warning against a love 'em and leave 'em philanderer: "Look out for the Cheater / Make way for the fool hearted clown," coupled with a concluding promise that someday someone would do to the Cheater what he'd done to the singer.

In the early eighties, Kuban and Scott got back together socially and fixed a date for a reunion show at the Fox Theatre in early 1984. Throughout the summer of 1983, as Scott popped into town between gigs, they continued to plan and scheme. In October 1983, they had their first rehearsal, at the nightclub where Kuban performed on Mondays. In late November, Scott called again but missed Kuban. They never spoke again. On December 27, Scott's wife, Jo Ann, reported him missing, saying he'd gone out to buy a part for his car and not returned. The next day, his car was found abandoned at the St. Louis airport.

In August 1984, Jo Ann Notheis (Scott's real surname) filed for divorce, charging that Scott had abandoned her. In April 1986, she remarried, to Jim Williams, whose wife, Sharon, died of head injuries apparently received in a car crash in October 1983. Scott's parents, suspicious since his disappearance, now pressed the case and in March 1987, Sharon Williams's body was exhumed and a new autopsy showed that she'd died of "blunt force trauma," not the accident. The medical examiner ruled the death a homicide.

In early April 1987, St. Louis sheriff's officers discovered a male body floating in a deep cistern ten feet from the house owned by Jim Williams. The Sheriff estimated that the body had been in the cistern for about three years. It was soon positively identified as Walter Scott and Jim Williams was arrested and charged with two counts of murder: beating his wife to death and shooting Scott. Two days later, Jo Ann Notheis Williams was tracked down and arrested on the same charges.

The case had still not come to trial almost two years later, though Williams's son, James Jr., did step forward with the claim that he'd tipped off the cops about the secret of the cistern. He also said that Sharon Notheis had been cheating on Walter Scott with his father for a year before Scott's death.

999 IT'S OVER, Roy Orbison
Produced by Fred Foster; written by Roy Orbison and Bill Dees
Monument 837   1964   *Billboard: #9*

Who else could have pulled off such a florid rock-bolero? With percussive guitars and riffling drums (and castanets) suggesting previously unsuspected flamenco nuances in Orbison's all-encompassing style, with the melody awash in strings and goosed by a ghostly chorus, and with the final encumbrance of some of the most overwritten lyrics in Nashville history ("Golden nights before they end / Whisper secrets to the wind," and then it gets *really* flowery), "It's Over" is a record only one of the two greatest white voices in rock and soul history could have redeemed.

And redeem it Roy does, mainly by crashing through all the goop to a chorus whose recognition of what he fears—"It's over," repeated three tremulous times—amounts to a personal triumph, a move that extracts from those maudlin lines the threads of dream and self-recognition that empower all Orbison's greatest hits.

1000 I'M NOBODY'S BABY NOW, Reparata & the Delrons
Produced by World United; written by Jeff Barry
RCA 47-8820   1966   Did not make pop chart

You can talk metaphorically about the Bangles and Go-Gos and even the Three Degrees as the last of the girl groups. But "I'm Nobody's Baby Now," an obscure Ronettes/Shangri-Las pastiche, is the only record I've ever heard whose sound and substance actually deserve that designation. Spectorian atmospherics, Blaine-like percussion crescendi and Shangri-Las–style recitatives build a sentimental portrait of a teenage love affair that's met its end. Reparata and the Delrons, who hit a year earlier with the almost-redeemably sappy "Whenever A Teenager Cries," never sang better. The sexual innuendo flies thick and fast, a world of touches and lessons in love ("all the things we did together") in which the true meaning is even more thinly concealed than it has been in previous Barry tunes like "Then He Kissed Me."

But that's not all. It's the combination of how and *what* that marks the end of an era. "I'm nobody's baby now," Reparata sings and then, echoing her own words as an afterthought, "I'm on my own. Nobody's baby now—I've got to find my part alone."

And so we did, and so we have.

1001 NO WAY OUT, Joyce Harris
Producer not credited; written by Joyce Harris
Infinity 005   c. 1960   Did not make pop chart

Like a lot of kids who went off to college in 1959, Michael Goodwin loved folk music. Having grown up the son of radicals, he knew more about it than most. But like a lot of kids who loved folk music, he also developed a passion for rock and roll and rhythm and blues. So he went to work at WVBR, the radio station on Cornell's campus as a jazz and folk DJ. Years later, when Goodwin had become a writer about film and food and music, he still referred to his WVBR days as "the best thing I did in college."

Michael especially cherished finals week, the exam period during the last week of each semester, when each of the student DJs would bring their favorite records into the station for the Rock and Roll Marathon, during which 'VBR blasted rock and roll and R&B day and night, as both a study aid and relief from study. Before the week was over, singles covered every surface of the studio, famous ones and obscure ones, records you'd heard every week for the past five years, records you'd never hear again.

In 1963, when he was a senior, Michael decided it was time to keep track. The day after finals, he arrived early in the morning at the bedraggled studio, finding nothing but stacks of singles, half-eaten boxes of pizza and the morning deejay spinning classical sides. Goodwin grabbed some reels of blank tape and locked himself into a cubbyhole with a tape deck and a turntable, then spent an entire day taping singles, hastily listing title and artist on sheets he taped to the outside of the tape boxes.

Graduating that spring, Goodwin packed up his tapes and went back to lower Manhattan. Bouncing around the next couple of years, trying to get a career started, busy ingesting the sixties as they happened, he barely had time to look back. But one day, long about 1966, he decided to listen to those college tapes.

For a reel or two, all was well. Some nice surprises, some old favorites, just about the way he recalled it. Then, out of nowhere, came a noise. "I've gotcha!" shouted a man. Bump. "I've gotcha." (Perhaps the needle had slipped; maybe it was meant that way.) "And there's no way ooooout!" he shouted.

Abruptly, a woman came in, hollering over crude bass and drums doing some kind of uptempo New Orleans breakdown: "Welllll," she began, as if gargling grit, "I don't wanna go and I don't wanna stay . . ." and they were off, trading lines with a vociferousness that Shirley and Lee never suspected, a crudity that Marvin Gaye and Tammi Terrell never countenanced, a desperate, surging passion that elevated the music far beyond the bounds of raucous primitive noise (despite one of the cheesiest blues guitar solos ever committed to vinyl). "I'm gonna jump out the winda," declares the guy, just before the end. "No way out," taunts the girl.

Goodwin sat stunned for a moment, then—like any normal person—got up and ran the tape back to hear it again. Meantime, he picked up the tape box to see who'd made this noise; he had absolutely no recollection of ever hearing "this weird primal scream of a record that cut through everything."

"The song before it was written down, and the song after it, but there was nothing about *this* one," he remembered a couple decades later. "I'd just screwed up and failed to write it down. Or maybe it was like some Satanic hand had erased it."

Michael grew obsessed by the record. "It was dumb, incoherent, except that it was so . . . shapely. And hypnotic. It was across the universe from what the Beatles were doing." Over the next couple of years, he played this rare treasure for a few people. They always liked it. But nobody had any idea who it might be, where it could have come from. Goodwin guessed New Orleans; others said Chicago or Los Angeles.

When he moved to California near the end of the decade and became friends with *Rolling Stone* colleague Greil Marcus, he'd hooked another one. Marcus played a tape copy of "No Way Out"—nobody knew for sure if that was the title but it hardly seemed likely to be anything else—for friends, music critics, R&B scholars, record collectors. Nobody knew what it was. Goodwin, delving deeper into the mystery, began to drop references to the mystery record in things he wrote. Others grew curious. Nobody got many facts.

Sometime in the mid-seventies, somebody identified the voice on "No Way Out" as an R&B singer named Joyce Harris, though that person knew nothing of who Joyce Harris might be, or where the record might have come from. A little later, Goodwin tracked down one copy of the actual disc; Infinity was an L.A. label, but he still thought the beat was from the Crescent City. Later, on a trip to New Orleans, he played a hunch and looked through record shops for Joyce Harris sides. He found a couple on the Fun label.

I'd been mesmerized when I first heard the thing, sometime in 1972, on a tape sent to me by Goodwin and Marcus operating in their guerilla media critic role as The Midnight Raiders. Framed by John Lennon's "Power to the People" and the Chi-Lites' "(For God's Sake) Give More Power to the People," it summarized everything not even such great polemics could express. For a while, "No Way Out" hit my tape deck frequently. Even a decade or more later, whenever I wanted to impress somebody with how rare and wonderful R&B and rock and roll could really be, I'd drag out that old cassette. It's on its last legs now; creaks when it's rewound. The first I knew that Goodwin had solved any part of the riddle came while I thumbed through the discography of *Stranded*, a book of rock criticism Marcus edited in 1979. There it was, one line of stark type: "Joyce Harris, 'No Way Out' (Infinity). c. 1960." It tickled me to know that someone now knew who, but the record label was too perfect—it had to be Greil's idea of a joke. I'd have thought the same if it had been on Fun.

I'm not sorry we know what we know. We're men, not dogs, and when we find a mystery, our job is to solve it, not roll in it. Yet I can't say I'm entirely unhappy that Michael Goodwin was careless that day in 1963. Pursuit is half the joy of this line of work.

The other half, and the better one, is listening, hearing, maybe understanding a little bit more. "No way out / Can't think of nothin' but a-lovin' you" Joyce Harris cries as I type these lines and I smile to myself and think of the two thousand records that almost but didn't quite make these pages.

APPENDIX

Alphabetical Listing of Songs in The Heart of Rock & Soul

Numbers in parentheses refer to text page

Billie Jean, Michael Jackson (*60*)
Bird Dog, The Everly Bros. (*482*)
Bird's the Word, The, The Rivingtons (*85*)
Bitch Is Back, The, Elton John (*597*)
Black Magic Woman, Santana (*537*)
Black Pearl, Sonny Charles & the Checkmates Ltd. (*250*)
Blue Bayou, Roy Orbison (*274*)
Blueberry Hill, Fats Domino (*37*)
Blue Monday, Fats Domino (*87*)
Blue Moon, Marcels (*340*)
Blue Moon of Kentucky, Elvis Presley (*397*)
Blue Suede Shoes, Carl Perkins (*64*)
Blue Velvet, The Clovers (*584*)
Boiler, The, Rhoda with The Special AKA (*557*)
Boogie Wonderland, Earth Wind and Fire with the Emotions (*471*)
Book of Love, The Monotones (*553*)
Book of Rules, The Heptones (*332*)
Borderline, Madonna (*501*)
Born in the U.S.A., Bruce Springsteen (*92*)
Born to Be Wild, Steppenwolf (*357*)
Born to Run, Bruce Springsteen (*23*)
Born Under a Bad Sign, Albert King (*388*)
Boxer, The, Simon & Garfunkel (*509*)
Boys Are Back in Town, The, Thin Lizzy (*622*)
Boys of Summer, The, Don Henley (*84*)
Brand New Me, Aretha Franklin (*439*)
Break Up to Make Up, The Stylistics (*425*)
Breathless, Jerry Lee Lewis (*565*)
Bridge Over Troubled Water, Aretha Franklin (*364*)
Brilliant Disguise, Bruce Springsteen (*272*)
Bring It on Home to Me, Sam Cooke (*252*)
Bring It Up, James Brown (*620*)
Bring the Boys Home, Freda Payne (*191*)
Brother Louie, Stories (*214*)
Brown Eyed Girl, Van Morrison (*282*)
Brown Eyed Handsome Man, Chuck Berry (*308*)
By the Time I Get to Phoenix, Isaac Hayes (*573*)
Bye Bye Johnny, Chuck Berry (*537*)
Bye Bye Love, The Everly Bros. (*166*)

Call Me (Come Back Home), Al Green (*174*)
Can I Get a Witness, Marvin Gaye (*238*)
Can't Give Her Up, Skipworth & Turner (*519*)

Can't Help Falling in Love, Elvis Presley (*489*)
Carol, Chuck Berry (*195*)
Cathy's Clown, The Everly Bros. (*345*)
Celebration, Kool & the Gang (*607*)
Chain of Fools, Aretha Franklin (*39*)
Change Is Gonna Come, A, Sam Cooke (*28*)
Chapel of Love, The Dixie Cups (*194*)
Cheater, The, Bob Kuban (*629*)
Cherry Oh Baby, Eric Donaldson (*474*)
Choice of Colors, Impressions (*334*)
Christmas (Baby Please Come Home), Darlene Love (*21*)
Church of the Poison Mind, Culture Club (*516*)
C'mon Everybody, Eddie Cochran (*355*)
Cold Hard Facts of Life, The, Porter Wagoner (*502*)
Cold Love, Donna Summer (*115*)
Cold Sweat, James Brown (*61*)
Come and Get These Memories, Martha & the Vandellas (*524*)
Come and Get Your Love, Redbone (*537*)
Come Back My Love, The Wrens (*608*)
Come Go with Me, The Del-Vikings (*534*)
Come On, Let's Go, Ritchie Valens (*485*)
Come Softly to Me, Fleetwoods (*618*)
Controversy, Prince (*615*)
Could It Be I'm Falling in Love, The Spinners (*270*)
Cowboys to Girls, Intruders (*582*)
Crackin' Up, The Gants (*500*)
Crazy Arms, Ray Price (*284*)
Crazy for You, Madonna (*103*)
Criticize, Alexander O'Neal (*626*)
Cruisin', Smokey Robinson (*174*)
Cry Cry Cry, Bobby Bland (*402*)
Cry Like a Baby, The Box Tops (*402*)
Crying, Roy Orbison (*75*)
Crying in the Chapel, Orioles (*260*)
Crying Time, Ray Charles (*231*)

Daddy Rollin', Dion (*299*)
Daddy's Home, Shep & the Limelites (*431*)
Da Doo Ron Ron, The Crystals (*21*)
Dance Dance Dance (Yowsah Yowsah Yowsah), Chic (*409*)
Dance to the Music, Sly & the Family Stone (*41*)
Dancing in the Dark, Bruce Springsteen (*199*)
Dancing in the Street, Martha and the Vandellas (*83*)

Dark End of the Street, The, James Carr (*268*)
Darling Baby, Jackie Moore (*560*)
Dawn, The Four Seasons (*384*)
Day Tripper, The Beatles (*261*)
Dead Man's Curve, Jan & Dean (*541*)
Dead Skunk, Loudon Wainwright III (*591*)
Dearest Darling, Bo Diddley (*359*)
Dedicated to the One I Love, The Five Royales (*131*)
Dedicated to the One I Love, The Shirelles (*131*)
De Doo Doo Doo, De Da Da Da, The Police (*437*)
Delirious, Prince (*251*)
Detroit City, Bobby Bare (*234*)
Devil or Angel, The Clovers (*491*)
Devil with a Blue Dress On / Good Golly Miss Molly, Mitch Ryder &
 the Detroit Wheels (*168*)
Devil with the Blue Dress, Shorty Long (*508*)
Didn't I (Blow Your Mind This Time), The Delfonics (*417*)
Dirty Water, The Standells (*574*)
Disco Inferno, The Trammps (*59*)
Doggin' Around, Jackie Wilson (*288*)
Do I Love You?, The Ronettes (*241*)
Do It Again, Steely Dan (*469*)
Domino, Van Morrison (*138*)
Donna, Ritchie Valens (*121*)
Donna the Prima Donna, Dion (*515*)
Don't Be Cruel, Elvis Presley (*91*)
Don't Dream It's Over, Crowded House (*451*)
Don't Fear the Reaper, Blue Oyster Cult (*628*)
Don't Give Up, Peter Gabriel with Kate Bush (*556*)
Don't It Make You Want to Go Home, Joe South (*305*)
Don't Let Me Be Misunderstood, The Animals (*467*)
Don't Look Back, The Temptations (*120*)
Don't Make Me Over, Dionne Warwicke (*589*)
Don't Mess Up a Good Thing, Fontella Bass & Bobby McClure (*494*)
Don't Play That Song, Aretha Franklin (*513*)
Don't Play That Song, Ben E. King (*513*)
Don't Say Nothing Bad About My Baby, The Cookies (*504*)
Don't Stop, Fleetwood Mac (*383*)
Don't Stop 'Til You Get Enough, Michael Jackson (*317*)
Don't Worry Baby, The Beach Boys (*54*)
Don't You Worry 'Bout a Thing, Stevie Wonder (*593*)
Do Right Woman—Do Right Man, Aretha Franklin (*336*)
Double Shot (Of My Baby's Love), Swingin' Medallions (*119*)

Do Wah Diddy Diddy, Manfred Mann (*232*)
Do You Believe in Magic, The Lovin' Spoonful (*408*)
Do You Love Me, The Contours (*20*)
Dream Lover, Bobby Darin (*447*)
Drift Away, Dobie Gray (*100*)
Drown in My Own Tears, Ray Charles (*110*)
Duke of Earl, Gene Chandler (*151*)

Earth Angel, The Penguins (*570*)
Edge of Seventeen (live), Stevie Nicks (*287*)
Endless Sleep, Jody Reynolds (*561*)
Everybody Loves a Winner, William Bell (*344*)
Everybody Needs Somebody to Love, Solomon Burke (*297*)
Every Breath I Take, Gene Pitney (*624*)
Every Breath You Take, The Police (*50*)
Everyday People, Sly & the Family Stone (*18*)
Every Little Bit Hurts, Brenda Holloway (*599*)
Every 1's a Winner, Hot Chocolate (*620*)
Expressway to Your Heart, The Soul Survivors (*395*)

Fa-Fa-Fa-Fa-Fa (Sad Song), Otis Redding (*102*)
Family Affair, Sly & the Family Stone (*609*)
Farther Up the Road, Bobby Bland (*232*)
Fast Car, Tracy Chapman (*493*)
Feel a Whole Lot Better, The Byrds (*619*)
Fever, Little Willie John (*81*)
54 46, Toots & the Maytals (*55*)
Fine Fine Boy, A, Darlene Love (*68*)
Fingertips, Part 2, Little Stevie Wonder (*122*)
500 Miles Away from Home, Bobby Bare (*571*)
Five Minutes, Bonzo Goes to Washington (*625*)
Follow Your Heart, The Manhattans (*532*)
Fool in Love, Ike & Tina Turner (*545*)
Fools Fall in Love, The Drifters (*495*)
(For God's Sake Give) More Power to the People, The Chi-Lites (*605*)
For the Love of Money, The O'Jays (*383*)
Fortunate Son, Creedence Clearwater Revival (*171*)
For What It's Worth, Buffalo Springfield (*531*)
For Your Love, The Yardbirds (*522*)
For Your Precious Love, Jerry Butler with the Impressions (*155*)
Freddie's Dead, Curtis Mayfield (*202*)
Free Nelson Mandela, Special AKA (*499*)
Friday on My Mind, The Easybeats (*466*)

Fun Fun Fun, Beach Boys (*154*)
Funky Broadway, Wilson Pickett (*220*)
Funky Broadway, Dyke and the Blazers (*220*)
Funkytown, Lipps Inc. (*141*)

Games People Play, Joe South (*498*)
Garden Party, Rick Nelson (*127*)
Gee, The Crows (*586*)
Georgia on My Mind, Ray Charles (*225*)
Get a Job, The Silhouettes (*276*)
Get Back, The Beatles (*412*)
Get Off Of My Cloud, The Rolling Stones (*41*)
Get Out of My Dreams, Get Into My Car, Billy Ocean (*236*)
Get Up I Feel Like Being a Sex Machine, James Brown (*116*)
Ghost Town, The Specials (*590*)
Gimme Some Lovin', The Spencer Davis Group (*119*)
Gino Is a Coward, Gino Washington (*594*)
Girls Just Want to Have Fun, Cyndi Lauper (*68*)
Give Him a Great Big Kiss, The Shangri-Las (*139*)
Give Me Just a Little More Time, The Chairmen of the Board (*251*)
Gloria, Them (*49*)
God Save the Queen, The Sex Pistols (*93*)
Goin' Back, The Byrds (*247*)
Goin' Back to Cali, LL Cool J (*581*)
Goin' Out of My Head, Little Anthony & the Imperials (*253*)
Goodbye Baby, Jack Scott (*530*)
Good Golly Miss Molly, Little Richard (*50*)
Good Lovin', The Young Rascals (*80*)
Goodnight Sweetheart Goodnight, The Spaniels (*160*)
Goodnite My Love, Jesse Belvin (*430*)
Good Rockin' Tonight, Elvis Presley (*45*)
Good Thing, Paul Revere & the Raiders (*520*)
Good Times, Chic (*52*)
Good Times, Sam Cooke (*401*)
Good Year for the Roses, A, George Jones (*542*)
Go Your Own Way, Fleetwood Mac (*319*)
Grand Tour, The, George Jones (*514*)
Great Balls of Fire, Jerry Lee Lewis (*128*)
Great Pretender, The, The Platters (*108*)
Green Onions, Booker T. & the MGs (*81*)
Green River, Creedence Clearwater Revival (*373*)
Groovin', The Rascals (*316*)

Gypsy Cried, The, Lou Christie (*411*)
Gypsy Woman, The Impressions (*310*)

Hang On Sloopy, The McCoys (*576*)
Hang Up My Rock and Roll Shoes, Chuck Willis (*277*)
Hanky Panky, Tommy James & the Shondells (*578*)
Happy, The Rolling Stones (*610*)
Happy Xmas (War Is Over), John & Yoko (*500*)
Harlem Nocturne, The Viscounts (*610*)
Have You Seen Her, The Chi-Lites (*291*)
Having a Party, Sam Cooke (*193*)
Heartaches by the Number, Ray Price (*261*)
Heart and Soul, The Cleftones, (*579*)
Hearts of Stone, The Jewels (*128*)
Heat Wave, Martha and the Vandellas (*38*)
Heaven Help Us All, Stevie Wonder (*410*)
Heaven Must Be Missing an Angel, Tavares (*583*)
Heaven Must Have Sent You, The Elgins (*496*)
Heavy Makes You Happy, The Staple Singers (*577*)
Hello Mary Lou, Rick Nelson (*281*)
Hello Stranger, Barbara Lewis (*453*)
Help, The Beatles (*184*)
Help Me Rhonda, The Beach Boys (*205*)
Here Comes the Night, Them (*539*)
He's a Rebel, The Crystals (*176*)
He's So Fine, The Chiffons (*42*)
He's Sure the Boy I Love, The Crystals (*176*)
He Stopped Loving Her Today, George Jones (*291*)
He Will Break Your Heart, Jerry Butler (*251*)
Hey! Baby, Bruce Channel (*87*)
Hey Joe, Jimi Hendrix (*335*)
Hide Away, Freddy King (*321*)
Hi-Heel Sneakers, Tommy Tucker (*562*)
Hippy Hippy Shake, Chan Romero (*92*)
Hit the Road Jack, Ray Charles (*40*)
Hitch Hike, Marvin Gaye (*511*)
Hold Back the Night, The Trammps (*192*)
Hold On I'm Comin', Sam & Dave (*23*)
Hold What You've Got, Joe Tex (*187*)
Holiday, Madonna (*477*)
Holiday in the Sun, Sex Pistols (*307*)
Hollywood Swingin', Kool & the Gang (*415*)
The Homecoming, Tom T. Hall (*435*)

Honey Bee, Gloria Gaynor (*607*)
Honey Don't, Carl Perkins (*440*)
Honky Tonk, Bill Doggett (*76*)
Honkey Tonk Woman, The Rolling Stones (*322*)
Hopes on Hold, Ruben Blades (*480*)
Hot Fun in the Summertime, Sly and the Family Stone (*221*)
Hound Dog, Elvis Presley (*612*)
House of the Rising Sun, The, The Animals (*64*)
House That Jack Built, The, Aretha Franklin (*449*)
Hully Gully Callin' Time, The Jive Five (*330*)
Hungry, Paul Revere & the Raiders (*528*)
Hungry Eyes, Merle Haggard (*223*)
Hungry Heart, Bruce Springsteen (*405*)
Hurt, Elvis Presley (*430*)

I Ain't Gonna Eat Out My Heart Anymore, The Rascals (*358*)
I Believe in You (You Believe in Me), Johnnie Taylor (*561*)
I Believe to My Soul, Ray Charles (*209*)
I Can See for Miles, The Who (*33*)
I Can't Explain, The Who (*269*)
I Can't Get Next to You, Al Green (*522*)
(I Can't Get No) Satisfaction, The Rolling Stones (*8*)
I Can't Help Myself, The Four Tops (*455*)
I Can't Live Without My Radio, LL Cool J (*363*)
I Can't Stand the Rain, Ann Peebles (*281*)
I Can't Turn You Loose, Otis Redding (*301*)
I Cried a Tear, LaVern Baker (*386*)
I Didn't Know I Loved You ('Til I Saw You Rock & Roll),
    Planet Patrol (*539*)
I Do, Marvelows (*298*)
I Do Love You, Billy Stewart (*373*)
I Don't Know What You Got, But It's Got Me, Little Richard (*202*)
I Don't Love You Anymore, Teddy Pendergrass (*619*)
I Don't Want to Cry, Chuck Jackson (*425*)
I Don't Want to Go Home, Southside Johnny & the
    Asbury Jukes (*595*)
I'd Rather Go Blind, Etta James (*429*)
I Fall to Pieces, Patsy Cline (*265*)
I Feel Fine, The Beatles (*617*)
I Feel for You, Chaka Khan (*233*)
If I Could Build My Whole World Around You, Marvin Gaye &
    Tammi Terrell (*73*)
If It Ain't One Thing, It's Another, Richard "Dimples" Fields (*392*)

If I Were Your Woman, Gladys Knight & the Pips (*340*)
I Forgot to Be Your Lover, William Bell (*621*)
I Fought the Law, Bobby Fuller Four (*74*)
I Found a Love, The Falcons (*358*)
If We Make It Through December, Merle Haggard (*572*)
If You Could Read My Mind, Bobby Bland (*608*)
If You Don't Know Me By Now, Harold Melvin & the Bluenotes (*193*)
If You Need Me, Wilson Pickett (*472*)
I Get Around, The Beach Boys (*178*)
I Gotta Dance to Keep from Crying, The Miracles (*246*)
I Got You Babe, Sonny & Cher (*160*)
I Got You (I Feel Good), James Brown (*155*)
I Heard It Through the Grapevine, Marvin Gaye (*1*)
I Know, Barbara George (*598*)
(I Know) I'm Losing You, The Temptations (*243*)
I'll Be Around, The Spinners (*428*)
I'll Be Doggone, Marvin Gaye (*456*)
I'll Be There, The Jackson Five (*215*)
I'll Go Crazy, James Brown (*394*)
I'll Try Something New, The Miracles (*415*)
I Love Music, The O'Jays (*345*)
I Love Rock 'n' Roll, Joan Jett & the Blackhearts (*300*)
I Love You, The Volumes (*173*)
I'm a King Bee, Slim Harpo (*438*)
I'm All Alone, Shep and the Limelites (*432*)
I'm a Man, Bo Diddley (*258*)
I'm a Man, The Yardbirds (*275*)
(I'm a) Road Runner, Junior Walker & the All Stars (*310*)
I'm Crying, The Animals (*549*)
I'm Down, The Beatles (*392*)
I'm in Love Again, Fats Domino (*314*)
I Miss You, Klymaxx (*531*)
I'm Lookin' for Someone to Love, Buddy Holly & the Crickets (*308*)
I'm Nobody's Baby Now, Reparata & the Delrons (*631*)
I'm Not a Juvenile Delinquent, Frankie Lymon & the Teenagers (*204*)
I'm So Young, The Students (*180*)
I'm Stone in Love with You, The Stylistics (*490*)
I'm Tore Up, Ike Turner's Rhythm Rockers featuring Billy Gayles (*573*)
I'm Walkin', Fats Domino (*524*)
I'm Your Puppet, James & Bobby Purify (*219*)
In Dreams, Roy Orbison (*47*)
I Need Your Loving, Don Gardner & Dee Dee Ford (*381*)
I Never Loved a Man (The Way I Love You), Aretha Franklin (*141*)

Jailhouse Rock, Elvis Presley (*540*)
Jamie, Eddie Holland (*520*)
Jam on Revenge (Jam on It), Newcleus (*420*)
Jenny Jenny, Little Richard (*508*)
Jenny Take a Ride, Mitch Ryder & the Detroit Wheels (*370*)
Jet, Paul McCartney/Wings (*505*)
Jim Dandy Got Married, LaVern Baker (*237*)
Johnny B. Goode, Chuck Berry (*2*)
Juicy Fruit, Mtume (*389*)
Jump, Van Halen (*26*)
Jumpin' Jack Flash, The Rolling Stones (*225*)
Just Like Real People, The Kendalls (*378*)
Just Like Tom Thumb's Blues (live), Bob Dylan (*172*)
Just My Imagination, The Temptations (*368*)
Just Once in My Life, The Righteous Brothers (*488*)
Just One Look, Doris Troy (*528*)
Just Out of Reach (Of My Two Empty Arms), Solomon Burke (*501*)
Just to Be With You, The Passions (*535*)

Kansas City, Wilbert Harrison (*125*)
Keep A-Knockin', Little Richard (*337*)
Keep on Truckin', Part 1, Eddie Kendricks (*613*)
Keep Searchin', Del Shannon (*255*)
Keep Your Hands Off My Baby, Little Eva (*121*)
Kharma Chameleon, Culture Club (*413*)
Kick Out the Jams, The MC5 (*157*)
Killer Joe, The Rocky Fellers (*398*)
Kiss and Say Goodbye, The Manhattans (*532*)
Kiss Me Baby, The Beach Boys (*205*)
Knock on Wood, Eddie Floyd (*302*)

La Bamba, Ritchie Valens (*64*)
Lady Marmalade, Labelle (*621*)
La La Means I Love You, The Delfonics (*382*)
Land of 1000 Dances, Cannibal & the Headhunters (*105*)
Land of 1,000 Dances, Chris Kenner (*105*)
Land of 1,000 Dances, Wilson Pickett (*105*)
Last Time, The, The Rolling Stones (*396*)
Laugh Laugh, The Beau Brummels (*555*)
Lawdy Miss Clawdy, Lloyd Price (*306*)
Lawyers in Love, Jackson Browne (*318*)
Layla, Derek and the Dominoes (*109*)
Leader of the Pack, The Shangri-Las (*448*)

Lead Me On, Bobby Bland (*82*)
Leavin' Here, Eddie Holland (*520*)
Le Freak, Chic (*219*)
Less Than Zero, Elvis Costello (*142*)
Let Her Dance, Bobby Fuller Four (*152*)
Let It Rock, Chuck Berry (*365*)
Let's Get It On, Marvin Gaye (*98*)
Let's Go Crazy, Prince (*131*)
Let's Go Get Stoned, Ray Charles (*167*)
Let's Work Together, Wilbert Harrison (*534*)
Let the Four Winds Blow, Fats Domino (*391*)
Let Them Talk, Little Willie John (*211*)
Liar Liar, The Castaways (*523*)
Lies, The Knickerbockers (*192*)
Life's Been Good, Joe Walsh (*587*)
Life's Little Ups & Downs, Charlie Rich (*473*)
Like a Rolling Stone, Bob Dylan (*8*)
Lion Sleeps Tonight (Wimoweh), The, The Tokens (*217*)
Little Darlin', The Diamonds (*148*)
Little Latin Lupe Lu, The Righteous Brothers (*298*)
Little Latin Lupe Lu, Mitch Ryder & the Detroit Wheels (*297*)
Little Red Corvette, Prince (*35*)
Little Sister, Elvis Presley (*288*)
Little Star, The Elegants (*100*)
Live to Tell, Madonna (*37*)
Living for the City, Stevie Wonder (*207*)
Loco-Motion, The, Little Eva (*41*)
Lodi, Creedence Clearwater Revival (*525*)
London Calling, The Clash (*120*)
Lonely Avenue, Ray Charles (*117*)
Lonely Surfer, The, Jack Nitzsche (*261*)
Lonely Teardrops, Jackie Wilson (*33*)
Lonely Weekends, Charlie Rich (*466*)
Long Tall Sally, Little Richard (*195*)
Looking for the Perfect Beat, Afrika Bambaataa & Soul
   Sonic Force (*139*)
Louie Louie, The Kingsmen (*12*)
Love and Happiness, Al Green (*544*)
Love Can't Turn Around (Club Mix), Farley "Jackmaster" Funk (*393*)
Love Child, The Supremes (*257*)
Love I Lost, The, Harold Melvin & the Bluenotes (*487*)
Love Is Like an Itching in My Heart, The Supremes (*469*)
Love Is Strange, Mickey & Sylvia (*63*)

Love Man, Otis Redding (*345*)
Lover's Island, The Blue Jays (*290*)
Lover's Question, A, Clyde McPhatter (*479*)
Lovers Who Wander, Dion (*616*)
Love's Gonna Live Here, Buck Owens (*325*)
Love So Fine, A, The Chiffons (*491*)
Love T.K.O., Teddy Pendergrass (*559*)
Love Train, The O'Jays (*277*)
Love Will Tear Us Apart, Joy Division (*502*)
Lucille, Little Richard (*431*)

Maggie May, Rod Stewart (*182*)
Make Me Your Baby, Barbara Lewis (*453*)
Making Love (At the Dark End of the Street), Clarence Carter (*44*)
Mama, He Treats Your Daughter Mean, Ruth Brown (*390*)
Mama Used to Say (American remix), Junior (*588*)
Manic Monday, The Bangles (*466*)
Mannish Boy, Muddy Waters (*226*)
(The Man Who Shot) Liberty Valance, Gene Pitney (*443*)
Many Rivers to Cross, Jimmy Cliff (*285*)
Mary's Little Lamb, Otis Redding (*452*)
Maybe, The Chantels (*99*)
Maybe Baby, Buddy Holly & the Crickets (*264*)
Maybellene, Chuck Berry (*155*)
May I, Maurice Williams & the Zodiacs (*328*)
Mean Old World, Little Walter (*224*)
Memphis Soul Stew, King Curtis (*468*)
Mercy Mercy, Larry Williams and Johnny Watson (*551*)
Mercy Mercy Me (The Ecology), Marvin Gaye (*407*)
Message, The, Grandmaster Flash & the Furious Five (*61*)
Middle of the Road, Pretenders (*513*)
Midnight Train to Georgia, Gladys Knight & the Pips (*210*)
Mighty Quinn (Quinn the Eskimo), The, Manfred Mann (*463*)
Milkcow Blues Boogie, Elvis Presley (*379*)
Mind Over Matter, Nolan Strong & the Diablos (*617*)
Mr. Tambourine Man, The Byrds (*145*)
Misty Blue, Dorothy Moore (*619*)
Money, The Flying Lizards (*506*)
Money, Barrett Strong (*163*)
Money Changes Everything, Cyndi Lauper (*162*)
Money Honey, Drifters (*265*)
Monkey Time, The, Major Lance (*244*)

More Love, The Miracles (*544*)
More Than a Feeling, Boston (*615*)
Mother-in-Law, Ernie K-Doe (*580*)
Mountain's High, The, Dick & DeeDee (*287*)
Mountain of Love, Harold Dorman (*326*)
My City Was Gone, Pretenders (*601*)
(My Friends Are Gonna Be) Strangers, Merle Haggard (*440*)
My Generation, The Who (*92*)
My Girl, The Temptations (*25*)
My Little Red Book, Love (*548*)
My Little Town, Paul Simon with Art Garfunkel (*601*)
Mystery Train, Elvis Presley (*16*)
Mystic Eyes, Them (*364*)
My Town, The Michael Stanley Band (*189*)
My True Story, The Jive Five (*135*)

Nadine, Chuck Berry (*426*)
Natural High, Bloodstone (*560*)
Need Your Love So Bad, Little Willie John (*38*)
Needles & Pins, The Searchers (*169*)
Neither One of Us (Wants to Be the First to Say Goodbye),
    Gladys Knight & the Pips (*296*)
Never Can Say Goodbye, Gloria Gaynor (*535*)
Never Give You Up, Jerry Butler (*493*)
New York's a Lonely Town, The Trade Winds (*242*)
Night Moves, Bob Seger (*316*)
Nightshift, The Commodores (*564*)
Night Time, The Strangeloves (*323*)
(Night Time Is) The Right Time, Ray Charles (*214*)
Night Train, James Brown (*293*)
Night Train, Jimmy Forrest (*293*)
1999, Prince (*159*)
19th Nervous Breakdown, The Rolling Stones (*133*)
Ninety-Nine and a Half Won't Do, Wilson Pickett (*134*)
96 Tears, ? & the Mysterians (*67*)
Nobody But Me, The Human Beinz (*244*)
Nobody Knows What's Goin' On (In My Mind But Me),
    The Chiffons (*516*)
No Sell Out, Malcolm X (*625*)
No Way Out, Joyce Harris (*632*)
Nowhere to Run, Martha & the Vandellas (*12*)
No Woman, No Cry, Bob Marley & the Wailers (live) (*314*)

Oh, Boy!, Buddy Holly & the Crickets (*474*)
Oh Girl, Chi-Lits (*224*)
Oh Me Oh My, Aretha Franklin (*455*)
Oh Pretty Woman, Roy Orbison (*32*)
Oh What a Night, The Dells (*208*)
Oliver's Army, Elvis Costello (*479*)
On Broadway, The Drifters (*49*)
One Dyin' & A-Buryin', Roger Miller (*448*)
One Fine Day, The Chiffons (*34*)
One Has My Name, Jerry Lee Lewis (*588*)
One Mint Julep, The Clovers (*321*)
One Monkey Don't Stop No Show, Joe Tex (*504*)
One More Heartache, Marvin Gaye (*130*)
One of a Kind (Love Affair), The Spinners (*296*)
One's On the Way, Loretta Lynn (*476*)
One Summer Night, The Danleers (*257*)
Only the Lonely, Roy Orbison (*19*)
Only the Strong Survive, Jerry Butler (*62*)
Only You (And You Alone), The Platters (*152*)
On the Other Hand, Randy Travis (*568*)
On the Radio, Donna Summer (*315*)
Oogum Boogum Song, The, Brenton Wood (*379*)
Ooh Poo Pah Do, Part 2, Jessie Hill (*596*)
Ooo Baby Baby, Smokey Robinson and the Miracles (*230*)
Out of Limits, The Marketts (*361*)
Over You, Roxy Music (*338*)
Overnight Sensation (Hit Record), Raspberries (*563*)

Pain in My Heart, Otis Redding (*436*)
Papa Don't Preach, Madonna (*199*)
Papa-oom-mow-mow, The Rivingtons (*85*)
Papa's Got a Brand New Bag, James Brown (*4*)
Papa Was a Rollin' Stone, The Temptations (*212*)
Part Time Love, Little Johnny Taylor (*437*)
Part Time Love, Ann Peebles (*437*)
Party Lights, Claudine Clark (*51*)
Patches, Clarence Carter (*564*)
Payoff Mix (Mastermix of G.L.O.B.E. & Whiz Kid's "Play That
    Beat Mr. D.J."), The, Double Dee & Steinski (*149*)
Peanut Butter, The Marathons (*372*)
Peggy Sue, Buddy Holly (*82*)
People Get Ready, The Impressions (*122*)
People Got to Be Free, Rascals, (*168*)

Peppermint Twist, Joey Dee & Starlighters (*295*)
Pill, The, Loretta Lynn (*476*)
Pink Houses, John Cougar Mellencamp (*228*)
Pipeline, The Chantays (*58*)
Piss Factory, Patti Smith (*461*)
Pittsburgh Stealers, The, The Kendalls (*227*)
Planet Rock, Afrika Bambaataa & Soulsonic Force (*107*)
Please Mr. Postman, The Marvelettes (*434*)
Please Please Please, James Brown (*192*)
Please Say You Want Me, The Schoolboys (*84*)
Pledging My Love, Johnny Ace (*244*)
Positively Fourth Street, Bob Dylan (*229*)
Pouring Water on a Drowning Man, James Carr (*423*)
Precious Words, The Wallace Brothers (*592*)
Pressure Drop, Toots and the Maytals (*154*)
Pretend You're Still Mine, The Sheppards (*585*)
Pretty Flamingo, Manfred Mann (*380*)
Pretty Little Angel Eyes, Curtis Lee (*334*)
Prisoner of Love, James Brown (*96*)
Private Number, William Bell & Judy Clay (*373*)
Promised Land, Chuck Berry (*93*)
Proud Mary, Creedence Clearwater Revival (*89*)
Psycho, Elvis Costello (*416*)
Psychotic Reaction, Count Five (*209*)
Pump Up the Volume, M/A/R/R/S (*357*)
Purple Haze, Jimi Hendrix (*178*)
Pushin' Too Hard, The Seeds (*410*)

Quarter to Three, Gary "U.S." Bonds (*99*)

Rag Doll, The Four Seasons (*273*)
Ramblin' Gamblin' Man, Bob Seger (*472*)
Ramblin' Man, The Allman Bros. Band (*317*)
Rank Strangers, The Stanley Brothers (*70*)
Rapper's Delight, The Sugarhill Gang (*407*)
Rave On, Buddy Holly (*45*)
Reach Out I'll Be There, The Four Tops (*5*)
Rebel-'Rouser, Duane Eddy (*377*)
Red Red Wine, UB40 (*369*)
Reeling in the Years, Steely Dan (*582*)
Reet Petite, Jackie Wilson (*193*)
Refugee, Tom Petty & the Heartbreakers (*441*)
Rescue Me, Fontella Bass (*215*)

Respect, Aretha Franklin (*10*)
Respect, Otis Redding (*376*)
Respect Yourself, The Staple Singers (*366*)
Revolution, The Beatles (*424*)
Ride Your Pony, Lee Dorsey (*393*)
Right to Love, The, The Blue Jays (*605*)
Rikki Don't Lose That Number, Steely Dan (*469*)
Rip It Up, Little Richard (*170*)
Rip Van Winkle, The Devotions (*421*)
Rivers of Babylon, The Melodians (*486*)
Rock & Roll, Led Zeppelin (*286*)
Rock & Roll Lullaby, B.J. Thomas (*88*)
Rock Box, Run-D.M.C. (*350*)
Rocking Pneumonia & the Boogie Woogie Flu, Huey Piano
    Smith & the Clowns (*566*)
Rockin' Robin, Bobby Day (*429*)
Rockin' Roll Baby, The Stylistics (*151*)
Rockit, Herbie Hancock (*577*)
Rock Me Baby, B.B. King (*294*)
Rock Steady, Aretha Franklin (*156*)
Rock the Bells, LL Cool J (*487*)
Rock the Boat, The Hues Corporation (*613*)
Rock Your Baby, George McCrae (*622*)
Roll Me Away, Bob Seger (*262*)
Roll Over Beethoven, Chuck Berry (*43*)
Rubber Biscuit, The Chips (*558*)
Rumble, Link Wray & His Ray Men (*306*)
Rumors, Timex Social Club (*536*)
Runaround Sue, Dion (*81*)
Runaway, Del Shannon (*353*)
Runaway Trains, Roseanne Cash (*387*)
Running on Empty, Jackson Browne (*262*)
Running Scared, Roy Orbison (*227*)
Run Through the Jungle, Creedence Clearwater Revival (*361*)

Sally Go 'Round the Roses, The Jaynettes (*258*)
San Antonio Stroll, Tanya Tucker (*568*)
Save It for Later, The English Beat (*445*)
Save the Last Dance for Me, The Drifters (*300*)
Say Boss Man, Bo Diddley (*419*)
Say Man, Bo Diddley (*323*)
Schlock Rod, Part 1, Jan & Dean (*604*)
School Day, Chuck Berry (*277*)

School's Out, Alice Cooper (593)
Sea Cruise, Frankie Ford (599)
Sea of Love, Phil Phillips (468)
Searchin', The Coasters (113)
Searching for My Love, Bobby Moore & the Rhythm Aces (418)
Secret Agent Man, Johnny Rivers (283)
Send Me Some Lovin', Little Richard (528)
Serpentine Fire, Earth Wind and Fire (216)
Seven Day Weekend, Gary "U.S." Bonds (618)
Sexual Healing, Marvin Gaye (342)
Shake, Sam Cooke (244)
Shake a Hand, Faye Adams (310)
Shake Rattle & Roll, Big Joe Turner (16)
Shake Sherrie, The Contours (384)
Shake You Down, Gregory Abbott (399)
Shakin' All Over, The Guess Who (271)
Shame Shame Shame, Shirley (And Company) (295)
Sh-Boom, The Chords (374)
She Loves You, The Beatles (31)
Sherry, The Four Seasons (188)
She's About a Mover, The Sir Douglas Quintet (323)
She's Got You, Patsy Cline (286)
She Thinks I Still Care, Little Willie John (377)
She Thinks I Still Care, George Jones (234)
Shining Star, Earth Wind & Fire (289)
Shoop Shoop Song (It's in His Kiss), The, Betty Everett (398)
Shot By Both Sides, Magazine (623)
Shotgun, Junior Walker & the All Stars (382)
Shout, Part 1, The Isley Bros. (356)
Sign of the Times, A, Donna Fargo (625)
Sign Your Name, Terence Trent D'Arby (480)
Silence Is Golden, The Four Seasons (117)
Silent Morning, Noel (567)
Since I Don't Have You, Skyliners (30)
Since I Lost My Baby, The Temptations (40)
Since I Met You Baby, Ivory Joe Hunter (344)
Sincerely, Moonglows (208)
Sing a Simple Song, Sly & the Family Stone (551)
Sir Duke, Stevie Wonder (464)
(Sittin' On) The Dock of the Bay, Otis Redding (17)
Six Days on the Road, Dave Dudley (291)
Sixty Minute Man, Clarence Carter (243)
Sixty Minute Man, Billy Ward & the Dominoes (538)

Skinny Legs and All, Joe Tex (*465*)
Sledgehammer, Peter Gabriel (*269*)
Slip Away, Clarence Carter (*303*)
Slippin' and Slidin', Little Richard (*313*)
Slippin' Into Darkness, War (*185*)
Slummer the Slum, The, The Five Royales (*609*)
Small Town, John Cougar Mellencamp (*189*)
Smarty Pants, First Choice (*478*)
Smiling Faces Sometimes, The Undisputed Truth (*435*)
Smoke Gets in Your Eyes, The Platters (*152*)
Smokey Joe's Cafe, The Robins (*254*)
So Far Away, The Pastels (*447*)
Soldier Boy, The Shirelles (*103*)
Soldiers of Love, Arthur Alexander (*352*)
Solsbury Hill, Peter Gabriel (*111*)
Some Kind of Wonderful, The Soul Brothers Six (*389*)
Something About You, The Four Tops (*488*)
Something in the Air, Thunderclap Newman (*404*)
Something So Strong, Crowded House (*404*)
Sooner or Later (One of Us Must Know), Bob Dylan (*145*)
Soothe Me, Sam & Dave (*392*)
Sorry (I Ran All the Way Home), The Impalas (*341*)
Soul Deep, The Box Tops (*236*)
Soul Makossa, Manu Dibango (*548*)
Soul Man, Sam & Dave (*335*)
Soul on Fire, LaVern Baker (*357*)
Soul Twist, King Curtis & His Noble Knights (*558*)
So You Want to Be a Rock 'n' Roll Star, The Byrds (*557*)
Spanish Harlem, Ben E. King (*282*)
Stagger Lee, Lloyd Price (*161*)
Stand!, Sly & the Family Stone (*352*)
Stand By Me, Ben E. King (*51*)
Stand By Your Man, Tammy Wynette (*475*)
Standing in the Shadows of Love, The Four Tops (*89*)
Starting All Over Again, Mel and Tim (*190*)
Stay, Maurice Williams & the Zodiacs (*29*)
Stayin' Alive, The Bee Gees (*457*)
Stay in My Corner, The Dells (*240*)
Stay with Me, Lorraine Ellison (*592*)
Steppin' Out, Paul Revere & the Raiders (*320*)
Stop Her on Sight (S.O.S.), Edwin Starr (*147*)
Stop! In the Name of Love, The Supremes (*496*)
Story Untold, The Nutmegs (*446*)

Stranger in Town, Del Shannon (*229*)
Strawberry Fields Forever, The Beatles (*603*)
Street Fightin' Man, The Rolling Stones (*98*)
Streets in Africa, Big Youth (*454*)
Stroll, The, The Diamonds (*201*)
Substitute, The Who (*222*)
Summer of '69, Bryan Adams (*412*)
Summertime, Billy Stewart (*181*)
Summertime Blues, Eddie Cochran (*524*)
Sun City, Artists United Against Apartheid (*444*)
Sunday Kind of Love, A, The Harptones (*420*)
Superstition, Stevie Wonder (*165*)
Surfin' Bird, The Trashmen (*85*)
Surfin' U.S.A., The Beach Boys (*343*)
Suspicious Minds, Elvis Presley (*280*)
Sweet Child O'Mine, Guns 'n' Roses (*255*)
Sweet Dreams (Are Made of This), Eurythmics (*504*)
Sweet Home Alabama, Lynyrd Skynyrd (*130*)
Sweet Little Sixteen, Chuck Berry (*124*)
Sweet Soul Music, Arthur Conley (*417*)
(Sweet Sweet Baby) Since You've Been Gone, Aretha Franklin (*249*)
Swinging Doors, Merle Haggard (*581*)

Take It to the Limit, The Eagles (*526*)
Take Time to Know Her, Percy Sledge (*250*)
Talk Talk, The Music Machine (*605*)
Tears on My Pillow, Little Anthony & the Imperials (*550*)
Tear the Roof Off the Sucker, The Parliament (*347*)
Tell Me Something Good, Rufus featuring Chaka Khan (*466*)
Temptation 'Bout to Get Me, The Knight Bros. (*356*)
Tender Years, George Jones (*439*)
Thank You (Falettinme Be Mice Elf Agin), Sly & the
  Family Stone (*136*)
That Is Rock & Roll, The Coasters (*142*)
That Lady, Isley Brothers (*443*)
That'll Be the Day, Buddy Holly & the Crickets (*29*)
That's Alright Mama, Elvis Presley (*212*)
That's What Love Is Made Of, The Miracles (*590*)
That's Where It's At, Sam Cooke (*554*)
Then He Kissed Me, The Crystals (*42*)
There Goes My Baby, The Drifters (*27*)
There Is, The Dells (*356*)
There Is Someone in This World for Me, Little Willie John (*257*)

There's a Moon Out Tonight, Capris (*267*)
There's No Other (Like My Baby), The Crystals (*223*)
These Arms of Mine, Otis Redding (*275*)
Think, The Five Royales (*284*)
Think, Aretha Franklin (*120*)
Think It Over, Buddy Holly & the Crickets (*308*)
Thin Line Between Love and Hate, The Persuaders (*213*)
This Is England, The Clash (*77*)
This Is My Country, The Impressions (*334*)
This Magic Moment, The Drifters (*279*)
Thousand Miles Away, A, The Heartbeats (*431*)
Thousand Stars, A, Kathy Young with the Innocents (*616*)
Thrill Is Gone, The, B.B. King (*349*)
Ticket to Ride, The Beatles (*26*)
Tighten Up, Archie Bell & Drells (*197*)
('Til) I Kissed You, The Everly Bros. (*498*)
Time After Time, Cyndi Lauper (*338*)
Tired of Being Alone, Al Green (*309*)
Today I Met the Boy I'm Gonna Marry, Darlene Love (*136*)
Tonite Tonite, The Mello-Kings (*525*)
Too Busy Thinking About My Baby, Marvin Gaye (*427*)
To the Aisle, 5 Satins (*385*)
Tracks of My Tears, The, The Miracles (*36*)
Tragic, The Sheppards (*367*)
Train Kept A-Rollin', The Rock & Roll Trio (*575*)
Tramp, Otis Redding and Carla Thomas (*66*)
Trapped By a Thing Called Love, Denise LaSalle (*585*)
Trenchtown Rock, The Wailers (*395*)
True Blue, Madonna (*183*)
Try Me, James Brown (*230*)
Try a Little Tenderness, Otis Redding (*108*)
Trying to Live My Life Without You, Otis Clay (*331*)
TSOP, MFSB (*264*)
Tumbling Dice, The Rolling Stones (*173*)
Tutti-Frutti, Little Richard (*11*)
Twist and Shout, The Beatles (*122*)
$2+2=?$, Bob Seger (*421*)
2000 Miles, Pretenders (*409*)
Two Tribes, Frankie Goes to Hollywood (*450*)

U Got the Look, Prince (*111*)
Um Um Um Um Um Um Um, Major Lance (*379*)
Under the Boardwalk, The Drifters (*216*)

Under Your Spell Again, Buck Owens (*462*)
Up on the Roof, The Drifters (*83*)
Uptight (Everything's Alright), Little Stevie Wonder (*34*)
Urgent, Foreigner (*596*)
U.S. Male, Elvis Presley (*423*)

Village of Love, Nathaniel Mayer and the Fabulous Twilights (*188*)
Voice Your Choice, The Radiants (*239*)
Voodoo Chile (Slight Return), Jimi Hendrix (*380*)
Vow, The, The Flamingos (*583*)

Wake Up Everybody, Harold Melvin & the Bluetones (*378*)
Wake Up Little Susie, The Everly Bros. (*280*)
Walking to New Orleans, Fats Domino (*113*)
Walk Like a Man, The Four Seasons (*151*)
Walk on By, Dionne Warwick (*241*)
Walk This Way, Run-D.M.C. (*566*)
Wanderer, The, Dion (*81*)
Wang Dang Doodle, Koko Taylor (*427*)
War, Edwin Starr (*212*)
Wavelength, Van Morrison (*179*)
Way Back Home, Junior Walker & the All Stars (*144*)
Way Over There, The Miracles (*359*)
Way You Do the Things You Do, The, Temptations (*346*)
We Are the World, U.S.A. for Africa (*458*)
We Can Work It Out, The Beatles (*447*)
We Got More Soul, Dyke and the Blazers (*417*)
We Gotta Get Out of This Place, The Animals (*508*)
Weight, The, The Band (*400*)
Welcome to the Boomtown, David & David (*519*)
Well All Right, Buddy Holly (*434*)
Wendy, The Beach Boys (*511*)
We're an American Band, Grand Funk Railroad (*442*)
Western Movies, The Olympics (*267*)
What a Fool Believes, The Doobie Bros. (*329*)
What Am I Living For, Chuck Willis (*262*)
What Becomes of the Brokenhearted, Jimmy Ruffin (*171*)
What'd I Say, Ray Charles (*33*)
What Have You Done for Me Lately, Janet Jackson (*491*)
What Kind of Fool (Do You Think I Am), The Tams (*355*)
What's Going On, Marvin Gaye (*24*)
What's Love Got to Do With It, Tina Turner (*452*)

You and Your Folks, Me and My Folks, Funkadelic (*347*)
You Can't Always Get What You Want, The Rolling Stones (*156*)
You Can't Hurry Love, The Supremes (*375*)
You Can't Judge a Book By Its Cover, Bo Diddley (*544*)
You Don't Know Like I Know, Sam & Dave (*294*)
You Don't Miss Your Water, William Bell (*206*)
You Dropped a Bomb on Me, The Gap Band (*553*)
You Haven't Done Nothin', Stevie Wonder (*274*)
You Keep Me Hanging On, The Supremes (*514*)
You Left the Water Running, Maurice and Mac (*95*)
You Left the Water Running, Otis Redding (*602*)
You'll Lose a Good Thing, Barbara Lynn (*397*)
You Lost the Sweetest Boy, Mary Wells (*496*)
You Make Me Feel Brand New, The Stylistics (*420*)
(You Make Me Feel Like) A Natural Woman, Aretha Franklin (*20*)
You Never Can Tell, Chuck Berry (*238*)
You Really Got Me, The Kinks (*391*)
You're a Wonderful One, Marvin Gaye (*259*)
You're Gonna Miss Me, The 13th Floor Elevators (*354*)
You're So Fine, The Falcons (*240*)
(Your Love Keeps Lifting Me) Higher and Higher, Jackie Wilson (*118*)
Your Precious Love, Marvin Gaye & Tammi Terrell (*91*)
Your Promise to Be Mine, The Drifters (*287*)
You Turn Me On, I'm a Radio, Joni Mitchell (*110*)
You've Lost That Lovin' Feelin', The Righteous Brothers (*6*)
You've Really Got a Hold on Me, The Miracles (*333*)

Index

ABOUT THE AUTHOR

Dave Marsh is the author of the best-selling Bruce Springsteen biographies, *Born to Run* and *Glory Days*, and a dozen other books about popular music including *Before I Get Old: The Story of the Who*. He also edited *The Rolling Stone Record Guide*. A former editor of *Creem* and *Rolling Stone*, he contributes essays, reviews and journalism to a number of publications, including *Playboy* and *The Village Voice*. Marsh currently edits *Rock & Roll Confidential*, a monthly newsletter about pop music and social issues, available by writing to Box 15052, Long Beach, CA 90815.

Ⓟ Plume (0452)

THE INSIDE STORIES

☐ **HOLLYWOOD BABYLON II by Kenneth Anger.** You'll just devour this feast of revelations that features names like Audrey Hepburn, Truman Capote, Elizabeth Taylor, Doris Day, Judy Garland, Frank Sinatra, Clark Gable, John Wayne, and so many more names whose faces you know so well, but whose secrets are now revealed in a way that you never imagined outside your wildest and most wicked fantasies. . . . (257212—$12.95)

☐ **THE MASTER BANKERS by Paul Ferris.** Investment banks have always been shrouded in mystery—and the glamour of wealth. Here at last is a fascinating portrait of how over twenty-five of the biggest and best firms sell stocks and bonds, manage mergers and acquisitions, and do billion-dollar deals in financial capitals throughout the world. This book names the names, tracks the deals and interviews the bankers and their blue-chip clients. (258146—$8.95)

☐ **CONVERSATIONS WITH CAPOTE by Lawrence Grobel.** In these extraordinary conversations, recorded over the last two years of Capote's life, the genius who elevated talk to art and gossip to literature lives on. As startling, candid, and controversial as the man himself, this book takes its place as a key part of the Capote legacy. (258022—$7.95)

☐ **THE SAUDIS Inside the Desert Kingdom by Sandra Mackey.** The fascinating tale of Saudi Arabia's culture-shock transformation from a Bedouin kingdom in the desert to a very strange world power is told for the first time from the inside. Sandra Mackey lived in the country for four years smuggling out a series of articles that got to the heart of Saudi society. "A superb book about a complex country of vital importance."—*St. Louis Post Dispatch.* (009480—$8.95)

☐ **VOICES FROM THE HOLOCAUST edited by Sylvia Rothchild. Introduction by Eli Wiesel.** A vivid, moving, and totally honest re-creation of the lives of 30 ordinary people caught in the tragic cataclysm of the war against the Jews. The stories told here are taken from tapes held in the William E. Weiner Oral History Library of the American Jewish Committee. "Important as a lesson and reminder of history."—*Library Journal* (008603—$10.95)

Prices slightly higher in Canada

Buy them at your local bookstore or use this convenient
coupon for ordering

NEW AMERICAN LIBRARY
P.O. Box 999, Bergenfield, New Jersey 07621

Please send me the books I have checked above. I am enclosing
$_____ (please add $1.50 to this order to cover postage and
handling). Send check or money order—no cash or C.O.D.'s. Prices and
numbers are subject to change without notice.

Name_____

Address_____

City_____State_____Zip Code_____

Allow 4-6 weeks for delivery.
This offer is subject to withdrawal without notice.